CLASSICS
IN
MARKETING

CLASSICS
IN
MARKETING

EDITED BY

C. GLENN WALTERS

Chairman and Professor of Marketing
Southern Illinois University at Carbondale

DONALD P. ROBIN

Professor of Marketing
Mississippi State University

Goodyear Publishing Company, Inc.
Santa Monica, California

Library of Congress Cataloging in Publication Data

Main entry under title:

Classics in marketing.

   1. Marketing—Addresses, essays, lectures.
I. Walters, Charles Glenn. II. Robin, Donald P.
HF5415.C5413   658.8   77-27511
ISBN 0-87620-191-5

Y-1915-1
ISBN: 0-87620-191-5

Current Printing (last digit):
10 9 8 7 6 5 4 3 2 1

Printed in the United States of America

Cover and Text Design: Russ Good
Production Editor: Pam Tully
Composition: Hightower Typesetting Co.
Art: Terry West

DEDICATED TO

Phoebe Poss
Donald E. Robin
Anna Pier Robin

PREFACE

This book is designed to acquaint the marketing student with some of the more representative literature surrounding the development of marketing theory. The authors feel that every student of marketing should have a working knowledge of the great individuals and the great ideas that make marketing the dynamic and complex field of study that it is today.

Historically, there have been four major approaches to the study of marketing. They are the: (1) commodity, (2) institutional, (3) functional, and (4) marketing management approaches. Each of these perspectives has contributed, over time, to the development of major concepts associated with a basic variable (products, channels, activities, and strategy) that forms the cornerstone of our knowledge of marketing. Today, scholars are beginning to integrate these approaches and this integration must be predicated on sound historical knowledge. Therefore, the authors believe it is natural that a book of marketing classics be organized around the historical approaches to marketing.

The materials selected for inclusion are taken from no particular time period. Although each approach may have been popular only for a particular time, thoughtful scholars continue to write about and make contributions to all four approaches. Thus relevant concepts about products, channels, functions, and strategy can be found in the earliest and latest publications. The authors did attempt to include, where possible, that one article most identified with the discovery of each approach. Articles were chosen which, in the judgement of the authors, had some significant affect on the development of marketing theory. Where possible, material by marketing pioneers was given priority. The number of articles fitting these criteria is substantial and no doubt worthy contributions were omitted because of a lack of space. Nevertheless, our research and helpful comments from colleagues indicate that the selection is representative of student needs to grasp the antecedents of marketing concepts and introduce major contributors to marketing thought.

No other book known takes the perspective presented by the authors. It is broad in concept and relates directly to the historical development of marketing. The readings are grouped into six sections. First, articles are presented that deal with the development and scope of marketing. The next four sections contain articles on the commodity, institutional, functional, and marketing management approaches. The sixth section concerns marketing responsibility. It is felt that this arrangement provides the greatest flexibility to the teacher and the student using the book.

The articles selected come from twenty-seven different sources including most of the major marketing journals plus books and monographs. They represent twenty-four different years between 1912 and 1969. Because of the emphasis on classics, it was felt that some of the more recent articles must stand the test of time before they are considered for inclusion. A total of forty-six articles by over thirty pioneering scholars is presented.

C. Glenn Walters
Donald P. Robin
February, 1977

CONTENTS

Cross-Reference Table   xiv

I DEVELOPMENT AND SCOPE OF MARKETING   1
    MARKETING DEVELOPMENT   3

    1 *George W. Robbins*
       Notions About the Origins of Trading   3
    2 *Wroe Alderson*
       Factors Governing the Development of Marketing
       Channels   15
    3 *Paul D. Converse*
       Development of Marketing Theory: Fifty Years
       of Progress   30
    4 *Robert Bartels*
       Influences on Development of Marketing Thought,
       1900-1923   44
    5 *Kenneth D. Hutchinson*
       Marketing As a Science: An Appraisal   59

    THE SCOPE OF MARKETING   68

    6 *Peter F. Drucker*
       Marketing and Economic Development   68
    7 *Philip Kotler and Sidney J. Levy*
       Broadening the Concept of Marketing   77

8 *David J. Luck*
Broadening the Concept of Marketing—Too Far   88
9 *William Lazer and Eugene J. Kelley*
Interdisciplinary Horizons in Marketing   92

II CONTRIBUTIONS OF THE COMMODITY APPROACH   101
CLASSIFICATION OF GOODS   103

10 *Melvin T. Copeland*
Relation of Consumers' Buying Habits to Marketing
Methods   103
11 *Leo V. Aspinwall*
The Marketing Characteristics of Goods   112
12 *Leo V. Aspinwall*
Parallel Systems of Promotion and Distribution   122

PRODUCT DEVELOPMENT AND USE   130

13 *Taylor W. Meloan*
New Products—Keys to Corporate Growth   130
14 *William R. Mason*
A Theory of Packaging in the Marketing Mix   141
15 *R. S. Alexander*
The Death and Burial of Sick Products   149
16 *Theodore Levitt*
Exploit the Product Life Cycle   161

III CONTRIBUTIONS OF THE INSTITUTIONAL APPROACH   181
INSTITUTIONAL RELATIONSHIPS   183

17 *Phillip McVey*
Are Channels of Distribution What the Textbooks Say?   183
18 *Robert W. Little*
The Marketing Channel: Who Should Lead This Extracorporate Organization   190
19 *Bruce Mallen*
Conflict and Cooperation in Marketing Channels   204
20 *Richard M. Clewett*
Checking Your Marketing Channels   222

INSTITUTIONAL FLOW CONCEPTS   229

21 *Roland S. Vaile, E. T. Grether, and Reavis Cox*
Channels of Distribution   229

22 *Leo V. Aspinwall*
   The Depot Theory of Distribution   236
23 *Bud Reese*
   Physical Distribution: The Neglected Marketing
   Function   243
24 *Paul D. Converse*
   Methods and Uses of Retail Trade Area Analysis   252
25 *Stanley C. Hollander*
   The Wheel of Retailing   261

IV   CONTRIBUTIONS OF THE FUNCTIONAL APPROACH   269
   DEFINING MARKETING FUNCTIONS   271

26 *Arch W. Shaw*
   Some Problems in Market Distribution   271
27 *Earl S. Fullbrook*
   The Functional Concept in Marketing   276
28 *Edmund D. McGarry*
   Some Functions of Marketing Reconsidered   287

FUNCTIONS IN THE MARKETING SYSTEM   302

29 *Frederick E. Webster, Jr.*
   Modeling the Industrial Buying Process   302
30 *Bent Stidsen*
   Interpersonal Communication and Personal Selling   315
31 *Edmund D. McGarry*
   The Propaganda Function in Marketing   328
32 *Harold C. Cash and W. J. E. Crissy*
   Comparison of Advertising and Personal Selling   339
33 *Joel Dean*
   The Role of Price in the American Business System   350
34 *Alfred R. Oxenfeldt*
   Multi-stage Approach to Pricing   357
35 *Lyndon O. Brown*
   Marketing Research Foundations for Changing
   Marketing Strategy   373

V   CONTRIBUTIONS OF THE MARKETING MANAGEMENT APPROACH   383
   THE MARKETING MANAGEMENT CONCEPT   385

36 *F. J. Borch*
   The Marketing Philosophy as a Way of Business Life   385

37 *Theodore Levitt*
Marketing Myopia   397
38 *Robert J. Keith*
The Marketing Revolution·   417
39 *Neil H. Borden*
The Concept of the Marketing Mix   423

MARKETS AND SEGMENTATION

40 *Wendell R. Smith*
Product Differentiation and Marketing Segmentation
as Alternative Marketing Strategies   433
41 *Richard N. Cardozo*
Segmenting the Industrial Market   440
42 *Paul H. Nystrom*
Consumers' Choice   457

VI THE RESPONSIBILITY OF MARKETING   467

43 *John H. Westing*
Some Thoughts on the Nature of Ethics In Marketing   469
44 *Richard H. Buskirk and James T. Rothe*
Consumerism—An Interpretation   475
45 *Consumer Advisory Council*
Protection of Consumer Rights   484
46 *Theodore N. Beckman*
The Value Added Concept as a Measurement of Output   489
47 *Reavis Cox*
Is Distribution Inefficient?   498

CONTRIBUTORS

Wroe Alderson
R. S. Alexander
Leo V. Aspinwall
Robert Bartels
Theodore N. Beckman
F. J. Borch
Neil H. Borden
Lyndon O. Brown
Richard H. Buskirk
Richard N. Cardozo
Harold C. Cash
Richard M. Clewett
Paul D. Converse
Melvin T. Copeland
Consumer Advisory Council
Reavis Cox
W. J. E. Crissy
Joel Dean
Peter Drucker
Earl S. Fullbrook
E. T. Grether
Stanley Hollander
Kenneth D. Huchinson

Robert J. Keith
Eugene J. Kelley
Philip Kotler
William Lazer
Theodore Levitt
Sidney Levy
Robert W. Little
David J. Luck
Edmund D. McGarry
Phillip McVey
Bruce Mallen
Taylor W. Meloan
Paul H. Nystrom
Alfred R. Oxenfeldt
Bud Reese
George W. Robbins
James T. Rothe
Arch W. Shaw
Wendell R. Smith
Bent Stidsen
Roland S. Vaile
Frederick E. Webster, Jr.
John H. Westing

Article Numbers for

Chapters in Text	Boone & Kurtz[1]	Enis[2]	Hanson[3]	Kotler[4]
1	1-9, 25-26, 34-37	1-5	1-9, 25-26, 34-37, 44-45	1-9, 25-26, 34-36
2	—	6-9, 37	—	—
3	33	—	27, 40	37-38, 40
4	27, 38-40	—	33	—
5	—	25-26	10-14	27
6	—	27	15-24, 45	—
7	10, 11, 14	38-40	27, 28, 30	39
8	12, 13	33	28, 29-30	—
9	15-20, 24, 45	10-14	31-32	10-11
10		28-30	34-44, 38-40	12-13
11	22	15-24		14
12	21	31-32		31-32
13	30	—		15-20, 22-24, 45
14	29	34-36, 41-45		21
15	28			30
16	31-32			29
17	—			28
18	—			
19	—			33
20	41-44			—
21				—
22				41-44
23				
24				
25				
26				
27				
28				
29				
30				

1. Louis E. Boone and David L. Kurtz, *Foundations of Marketing,* (Hinsdale, Illinois: The Dryden Press, 1977)
2. Ben M. Enis, *Marketing Principles,* 2nd edition, (Santa Monica, California: Goodyear Publishing Co., 1977).
3. Harry L. Hanson, *Marketing: Text and Cases,* 4th edition, (Homewood, Illinois: Richard D. Irwin, Inc., 1977).
4. Philip Kotler, *Marketing Management,* 3rd edition, (Englewood Cliffs, New Jersey: Prentice-Hall, Inc., 1976).

Classics in Marketing

McCarthy[5]	Pride & Ferrell[6]	Robin[7]	Rosenberg[8]
1-5, 25-26	1-6, 9, 25-26, 37, 40	1-9, 25-26, 34-37	1-9, 25-26, 37
6-9, 34-37, 40	34, 36	—	34-36
41, 42, 43	27, 38-39	—	6, 44-45
33	—	—	41-43
—	33	—	—
38-39	10-11,14	27, 38-40	—
—	12-13	—	38-40
40	31-32	—	—
27, 28	15-21, 45	—	—
—	22-23	33	27
—	19	10-11, 14	12-14
12-14, 10-11	30	12-13	—
11	28-30	—	10-11
12-14	27, 28, 30	28-30	31
15, 16	—	—	32
23, 45	41-44	31-32	—
22-23	—	15, 19-20	—
20, 21	35, 38-39	16-18, 21-24	29-30
19, 21	7-8	—	28
29	—	41-45	15-20, 24
28			22-23
29-30			21
31			33
—			—
32			—
—			—
—			
33			
44			
44-45			

5. E. Jerome McCarthy, *Basic Marketing,* 5th edition, (Homewood, Illinois: Richard D. Irwin, Inc., 1975).
6. William M. Pride and O. C. Ferrell, *Marketing: Basic Concepts and Decisions,* (Boston: Houghton Mifflin Co., 1977).
7. Donald P. Robin, *Marketing: Basic Concepts for Decision Making,* (San Francisco: Canfield Press, 1978).
8. Larry J. Rosenberg, *Marketing,* (Englewood Cliffs, New Jersey: Prentice Hall, Inc., 1977).

I

DEVELOPMENT
AND SCOPE
OF MARKETING

Marketing is a young field compared to many. The formal study of marketing dates back to approximately the turn of the century, and what we understand our field to be is the result of careful study, testing, and revision of concepts since that time. Marketing has made tremendous strides since 1900 in identifying variables, and today we are moving in the direction of a comprehensive theory.

The first section of this book, "Marketing Development," emphasizes the progress that marketing has made over approximately eighty years. By understanding the development and scope of marketing one can: (1) gain an appreciation of its progress toward a science; (2) identify the important pioneers that contributed to that development; (3) pinpoint marketing's current status as a field; and (4) demonstrate marketing dynamics. The articles were selected with these goals in mind.

Five articles discuss the development of marketing thought, from how marketing arose to an appraisal of marketing today as a science. The Robbins article explains several theories about the origins of trade including warfare, gift-giving, and specialization. The Alderson article picks up where Robbins leaves off. It explains the basis for the development of specialized marketing institutions and demonstrates the justification for marketing by means of increased efficiency. Converse and Bartels study the flow of marketing concepts. Converse relates specific ideas to marketing pioneers, while Bartels explains the early diffusion of the teaching of marketing throughout our major universities. The section ends with Hutchinson's evaluation of marketing as a science. The consensus is that the field has a way to go as a science even though a good start has been made.

"The Scope of Marketing" section contains just four articles. This limitation was due to the editors' emphasis on historical classics rather than current important contributions. Drucker provides an excellent explanation of the place and importance of marketing and the profit motive in our society. The Drucker article serves as a bench mark for Kotler and Levy to demonstrate how our perspective of marketing has broadened in recent years. Drucker looks back on the relationship of marketing to economics. Kotler and Levy take a broader societal view of the field. They see marketing as involved with both business and non-business activity. Luck takes exception to this view. He prefers to keep marketing specifically related to business. The Lazer and Kelley article brings marketing together with other social sciences by explaining the contributions of psychology and sociology to marketing. Thus, a field that began as a division of economics has broadened beyond the business college to use all the social sciences and more.

1

Notions About the Origins of Trading

George W. Robbins

The origins of trade have been the concern of economists and anthropologists in the past in order to trace or to relate the present functions of trade to their primeval beginnings and to discover the basic character of this economic usage. While this preoccupation with origins is disappearing from the scientific literature, it is not uncommon to find its implications and assumptions in the more popular literature of business, and particularly on the subject of salesmanship.

References are often made to premises concerning the origin of trading as a means of explaining or analyzing the ethical position of modern selling, imputing to present practices in the market place the circumstances and virtues of an assumed primeval genesis. It is, for example, not uncommon to hear trading spoken of as universal and natural. On the other hand, anthropological evidence reveals primitive cultures with a complete lack of competitive trading and with insignificant exchange practices.

In the face of these opposing positions, it is desirable to examine the various notions concerning the origins of trading and to appraise them in the light of their usefulness in the analysis of trading in our own society. It is possible to do this without a true chronological history of trading, or without attempting to formulate an organic-evolutionary concept of trading which takes the form of extracting from succeeding cultures certain common characteristics, with the conclusion that these have been passed down the lingering trail of institutional patterns.

Indeed, it should be evident that the accurate establishment of the origins of any human activity must await sufficient evidence from archaeological diggings.[1] The dearth of this evidence precludes a chronology that starts at the beginning. It is more profitable to avoid a historical recital in favor of an attempt to penetrate the internal logic of trading.

Reprinted from "Notions About the Origins of Trade," Vol. XI, No. 3, pp. 228–36
Journal of Marketing, published by the American Marketing Association.

Our concern here is with the efficacy of employing, as either inarticulate or expressed premises, notions about the origins of trading in the evaluation of present-day trading practices from a functional or an ethical viewpoint. Is an understanding of the origins of trade an essential matter in the study of the ethics of selling and buying? Will it help to answer the problems of honesty and efficiency in selling? Does it throw light on the problems of the contests and conflicts of trading today in the economic institution?

It should be clearly understood that this inquiry differs from, and is not in conflict with, the study of trade history as it can be established through adequate records.[2] It relates to those histories only insofar as their authors employ reference to origins; and it is, of course, possible to treat a matter historically without assuming an organic evolution based on obscure beginnings.

It is well to keep in mind that we are concerned with trading—buying and selling—as a matter of social behavior rather than as a technical process in marketing. It is essential to assume that trading is not a fortuitous or whimsical phenomenon, but rather an observable datum governed by laws of behavior that are subject to discovery. Moreover, it is no part of assumption here that trading is good or bad, strong or weak, or favorable to any given environment. These matters must emerge only as conclusions based on adequate observation of group activity in a definable situation.

THE MEANING OF TRADING

The term "trading" may mean many things to many people—competition, salesmanship, exchange, barter, transfer of title, persuasion, or even deception. It is not an oversimplification to say that a trade is an act of effecting an exchange of goods or services between a seller and a buyer; indeed, such a statement involves complexities of subtle premises. What lies both before and after the trade is of interest to this inquiry. The mere fact of communication between two individuals is a relatively superficial datum.

It may be helpful to clarify the thing we are discussing by examining definitions. Confusion will be avoided if it is remembered that a trade is a two-sided shield—it is both a purchase and a sale. While it is a popular misconception that the initiative in trading is largely with the seller, it is irrelevant to our purposes which side we take for reference. For the sake of brevity, only the selling side will be defined; and even the uninitiated may fill in a parallel definition of buying.

There are at least three types of definitions of *sale* which serve to illustrate the usual approaches to selling:

1. The legal: "Sale is an agreement by which one of the two contracting parties, called the 'seller,' gives a thing and passes title to it, in exchange for a certain price in current money, to the other party,

who is called the 'buyer' or 'purchaser,' who, on his part, agrees to pay such a price.''[3]

2. The vocational: A sale is the exchange of goods or services resulting from the exercise of the art of salesmanship.
3. The professional: A sale is an exchange of goods or services resulting from rivalry in the productive effort of creating demand and of rendering service in the satisfaction thereof.

The legal definition leads to a concept of trading that is narrow and restricted mainly to the technical fact of title transfer in a society characterized by a highly refined property concept. It fails to provide for the student of the economic or sociological aspects of trading adequate attention to the circumstances precedent or subsequent to that transfer.[4]

The vocational approach to selling, on the other hand, emphasizes the importance of the arts of persuasion rather than their functional position. By contrast, what may be called the professional approach calls attention to the fundamental circumstance of human wants and of the existence of rivalry in the performance of the services that create and satisfy those wants.[5] It is not concerned with the contractual character of the sale; for contrast is a usage of convenience, and the vast majority of sales are completed without the parties being aware that a legal contract is involved. Likewise, it does not deny that there is an important body of arts practiced by both sellers and buyers, which are effective in lubricating the process; but these arts are chiefly vocational techniques (however difficult to master). The professional approach places emphasis on the fundamental creative functions of selling in a highly competitive society.

While varying in approach, these three familiar concepts of selling have in common the functional position of selling in a society whose economic institution is characterized by a high degree of competitive effort—in short, a society like our own. In juxtaposition to these definitions, another, more fundamental, approach may be more suggestive of the real character of trading. A trade must always be a human relationship involving the behavior patterns of at least two persons.[6]

Hence, it is basically a *communication* and should be viewed as a part of the sociological field of communication.[7] It is subject to all the status barriers which define and separate individuals and groups. Again, any trade must be *cooperative* in the sense that two or more persons are acting together to achieve a new relationship which manifestly could not be achieved by each acting alone. Furthermore, every trade is an *organization* because it is a system, formal or otherwise, of consciously coordinated activities of at least two persons.[8] And lastly, the term is confined to situations where the ends are economic in order to exclude the multitude of other human relations which, without this modification, would fall unwanted into the area of our present concern.

Thus, we may define trading as a cooperative organization in communication to achieve economic ends. This definition carries no connotations with respect to the characteristics which may surround trading as the result of differing practices, usages, instruments, and mores to be found in the economic institution either at different times or in different locations. Like all other organizations in communication, trading belongs to a social institutional pattern, and becomes a part of the usages of that pattern. Specifically, it is part and parcel of the system of regulating economic contest and conflict, and is itself subject to contests and conflicts with usages of the other social institutions, martial, familial, educational, recreational, religious, scientific, and governmental.[9]

From the historical viewpoint, any inquiry into the nature of trading, to be significant, must be one that takes cognizance of the particular institutional fabric of which it is a part. To say that trading in our society today has its roots in the behavior of our primeval ancestors, or to say that this notion is confirmed by the habits of our "contemporary ancestors,"[10] the nonliterate primitives now living, is to stretch the latitudes of scientific inquiry to the point of incredulity.

Yet it is true that many practitioners of selling base an important part of their philosophy on premises concerning the origins of trading that comprise the substance of these ideas. It is precisely this basic mistake of many writers on salesmanship that led them to attitudes which provoked the well-known, pointed, and inescapable criticism of salesmanship by Clarence Darrow.[11]

THE MAJOR HYPOTHESES

No one disputes the antiquity of trading; but the exact point and conditions of its origins provide the subject of consideration by many writers whose attempts may be classified in seven main hypotheses. Not a few students of anthropology and economics alike have supported one or more of these assumptions without even the benefit of tacit recognition of the implications.

1. Trading Is Instinctive

It is perhaps most widely held that "to trade, or 'swap' is an inborn trait in the human being."[12] A variation of this view was expressed by Sombart, who believed that some have an inherent capacity to become traders (undertakers) while others do not. "Either you are born a bourgeois or you are not. It must be in the blood, it is a natural inclination."[13]

This palpable view is undoubtedly a sufficient explanation to many salesmen; it is certainly a comfortable refuge from the penetrating criticism of some of the ancient and modern practices of the marketplace. If it is "natural" to sell, then the criticism of traders is comment out of hand. But the evidence of scientific anthropology gives little support to this notion.

Not a few evidences exist to show that primitive peoples have existed for long periods without competitive trading.[14] The industrial civilization of the Incas is a striking case in point.[15] Polish peasants for centuries did not know the meaning of buying and selling between members of the same community. Their knowledge of trading came entirely from contacts with outsiders; and their resistance to selling has survived, since "even today, peasants dislike to trade with neighbors."[16]

While it is a rare culture that does not produce some exchanges of commodities on occasion, it is rather common to find that among primitives trading, insofar as it possessed any formal existence, arises mainly to facilitate exchange between members of different groups rather than between individual members of the same group.[17] In a culture where the institutions support a strict control of production and allocation of wealth, trading between individuals in the society becomes unnecessary, as in the case of the Incas, or vastly restricted, as in the case of Soviet Russia in the early years at least, where other stimuli than private profit were dominant.[18]

One would expect few psychologists to rank so complex a phenomenon as trading with fundamental instincts of self-preservation and sex as a basic drive. Unlike these fundamental urges, trading is not universal, intensive, or repetitive. And while it is true that trading appeared early in many different places and independently under different circumstances, these facts serve no more to demonstrate instinctiveness of trading than does the simultaneous scattered growth of the family institution prove that marriage is instinctive. Not only is this hypothesis too simple and superficial, but adherence to it may even retard the ability of present-day sales management to cope with its functional responsibilities.

2. Trading Grew Out of Warfare

This "hostility" hypothesis has trading growing out of war between clans or tribes. It pictures primitive man as essentially warlike because of the pressure of population on the means of subsistence. It assumes that warfare has economic roots, and that it is inevitable when man searches for the satisfaction of elemental wants. The reasoning follows that whereas man could satisfy his wants by warring on his neighbor, he soon learned that trading was an alternative possibility that had merit from the standpoint of group survival.[19]

This hypothesis has many faults, not the least of which is that it leads us into the difficult path of analyzing the origins of war, a path that is as rugged and unmarked as any other that goes in the direction of primeval origins. It is sufficient here to record that the hostility notion runs afoul of evidence of trading where war is unknown, as well as testimony pointing to the conclusion that both war and trading appear to develop from the same circumstances, and independently of each other. War was unknown among some primitives who carried on a rudimentary form of trade, notably the Eskimo and the Semang of the Malay Peninsula.[20]

The Arapesh tribe of New Guinea, naturally easy-going and yet pitted against physical barrenness that might be expected to produce strong rivalry for survival, finds great adventure in producing for others and actually regards it a sin to eat one's own kill. Motivation is achieved without competitive rivalry or war by a custom of having an official "insulter" for each man to taunt him publicly for his failure to produce feasts. So dreadful is this torture in the face of his peaceful nature, that a man looks forward to his reward—release from his "insulter" and retirement when his son reaches puberty. Thus, at least one primitive culture has institutionalized its lack of aggressiveness and self-interest, both of which would seem to be of some importance in the origin of either competitive trading or war.[21]

Nor is it easy to relate war and trading in the face of the fact that in many primitive peoples the rewards for war are personal and psychological rather than economic, and take the form of prestige supported by the evidence of another feather in the cap or another enemy's scalp on the belt. And the persistence of war, not only among primitives but in our own society, is difficult to explain if it is to be argued that trading supplanted war because of its demonstrated superior contributions to group survival; for wars have almost always provided a serious interference with economic life. Indeed, it seems well to avoid any attempt to relate trade to war as a fruitless inquiry in which observable data are altogether too lacking to support reasonable conclusions.[22]

3. Trading Originated in Predation

The "predatory" hypothesis is closely allied with the hostility notion. Because there are a few primitive tribes, such as the Bushman and the Apache, whose economies were regularly dependent upon the capture of wealth from other tribes,[23] and because there are a few evidences that modern business "is a complex and well-integrated series of frauds,"[24] some observers may conclude that trading began with the extraction of tribute and has never succeeded in getting away from the original predatory pattern.

The difficulty here lies in the abundance of evidence, historical and anthropological, that trading flourished between peoples who were entirely friendly and to whom the idea of tribute never seemed to occur. Moreover, predatory activities are not confined to the economic institution, but pervade the other social institutions as well. Indeed, political leaders, whether they be the heads of primitive tribes or of literate nations, have been among the most notorious tribute-extracting racketeers of history, and their predacity on merchants has all too often throttled trade.[25]

4. Trade Grew Out of Friendly Gift-giving

This "friendship" hypothesis is an explanation in diametrically the opposite vein. Professor Hoyt cites many examples of friendly gift-giving in primitive society and suggests that this practice may have led to learning the utility of exchange.[26] In primitive societies where the ownership of things was strongly identified with personal or group spiritual entity, the giving of gifts to neighboring tribal chiefs must indeed have stemmed from a genuine gregarious feeling and friendly goodwill.[27] The cynical view that a wise chieftain would buy off the predatory nature and power of his neighbor with gifts is not sufficient to explain the facts of anthropological research.

It is perhaps sufficient here to note that both war-making and gift-giving were means of communication, either or both of which may have been helpful in the discovery of trading. Professor Hoyt's emphasis on gift-giving as an origin of trading is supported by logic; for the atmosphere of gift-giving is a congenial one in which man may learn to perceive the utility of exchange.

5. Trading Originated with the "Silent Trade"

Silent trade is well-known to anthropologists as an early means of economic communication, and it appears in many isolated places among primitives. In this crude form, trade is initiated when one group leaves its wares on a promontory and retires from sight to permit another group to come out of hiding to inspect the goods and deposit its offering in return.[28]

Silent trade seems to have prevailed (1) where contact was between peoples of widely different cultures, (2) where languages were different, and (3) where fear or distrust was even more highly felt than were the economic motives of the intercourse. While the silent trade is an important fact in early communication, it throws little light on the real origins of trading. Its existence proves, however, that trading did occur between peoples who were motivated by neither the desire to make friends nor the will to annihilate.

It should also be recognized that neither party to the silent trade would have acted had he failed to develop an evaluation of the exchanged wares entirely apart from his own spirit or soul. Some degree of objectivity was implicit. Moreover, it is not plausible that this form of trading was an expression of instinct; it was discovered, developed, and learned as a crude but effective usage in the framework of the existing social institutions.

6. Trading Arose from Surpluses

Some students have suggested that trading originated because of the pressure of surplus goods resulting from the early division of labor in the primitive family or tribe.[29] Presumably the relative scarcity of goods was apparent in the periodic surpluses made available either through the efforts of nature or man. The plethora of cattle against the dearth of fodder may have suggested a gain from the exchange of cattle for fodder that was plentiful in a neighboring area.

This explanation fails on a number of grounds. There is practically no evidence that surpluses were accumulated by primitive families or clans excepting for anticipated emergencies.[30] Indeed, it is probable that excesses of things to eat or wear or use were regarded as "free goods" with respect to which transferable control did not even suggest itself until after trading as an instrument of communication developed. Moreover, much of the early trade in all parts of the world was in rare and exotic items "for which the demand was largely an expression of arbitrary value."[31] The primitive trading in ornaments and trinkets which gave their owners social prestige can hardly be said to stem from surpluses.

Too, a rational and administrative division of labor in primitive tribes, assumed in this hypothesis, cannot conceivably have preceded the need for it; and this need certainly compels outside markets as a *sine qua non*. The superficial explanation posed by the surplus hypothesis is to be found in the contemporary and popular notion that foreign trade exists because of surpluses resulting from the division of labor when in fact it is quite the other way around.

7. Trading Grew Out of the Development of the Property Concept

Tracing the origin of trading to the growth of the concept of property is a preoccupation of those who see in the exaggerated manifestations of trading in our society an overemphasis on private ownership. It is not appropriate to our purposes here to enter the controversy over the inequalities of property ownership or over the ways by which the function of property may be molded in the interests of social progress and public welfare.

It is merely essential to point out that in the manner in which the function of property is conceived as an end in terms of private advantage, special privilege, and exploitation will have a profound bearing on the practices in the marketplace. That many of these practices are subject to question today is not gainsaid; but to attack trading as a major evil growing out of the property concept is to engage in ardent speculation.

If by property we refer to the claim which gives transferable control over things,[32] then the property concept is best explained by the relative scarcity of these things in terms of the contest for individual and group survival.[33] While it is true that the extensive and complex exchange in our society presupposes a well-developed concept of property, it is far from true that crude trading could never have existed without even a simple property concept. Indeed, the very definition of property as anything with exchange value implies clearly that it is the need and practice of trading which called the property concept into use and aided materially in shaping its character. To say that property value existed before the fact of exchange is to indulge in a hopeless confusion of ideas and terms.

Trading and property concepts are both man-made and have developed in close relationship. They have certain characteristics in common: (1) both are dependent on the recognition of scarcity values; (2) both presuppose a divorcement of possessions from the individual's spiritual identity—an objective valuation of things; (3) both emerge from the same set of factors and must be explained in terms of a larger institutional concept.

Hence, to say that trading originated in the property concept and is a usage of property is to misinterpret the origins of both while leaving the essential character of each shrouded in confusion. In short, it is another example of the futility of tracing origins without the supporting evidences of observable data.

A RATIONAL EXPLANATION OF TRADING

The one thing in common which all of these hypotheses of the origins of trading have is a high degree of speculation unsupported by the accumulation of empirical data. It should be clear that any logic based upon premises like these is not acceptable to the social scientist. Indeed, social science has long since abandoned the methodology suggested by such speculations as those we have been examining.

If an explanation of trading is needed, it is to be found in the nature of man and of his adaptation to his environment through the institutions he builds. The universal, abiding, and repetitive characteristics of man to learn, to explore, to satisfy his curiosity, and to live with groups of other men have led him into an ever-expanding circle of experiences from which he has developed his learning and his patterns of associated living.[34] These attributes undoubtedly stem from the character of man's genes as distinguished from those of other animals. The explanation of trading lies neither in man's instincts nor his intelligence alone, but must be seen in terms of the patterns of the accumulated deposits of his activities in associated living.[35]

The essential prerequisite to trading, original or otherwise, is the development of the ability to valuate things in terms of other things rather than in terms of spiritual or mystical beliefs—to objectify and emanicipate one's belongings from his spiritual self and soul.[36] But this ability is by no means a guarantee that trading will be carried on in a society unless the folkways and mores are receptive to the changes which it imposes in the patterns of living.

Trading may be said to have been a slow discovery, made at a relatively early stage by peoples the world over, that followed the intellectual advance of valuation and which, in turn, vastly stimulated that advance, that grew out of the practices of associated living and, in turn, greatly affected these practices.

As contrasted with the other means of acquiring things, trading is by all odds the most complex. It is unique in that it alone is a two-way transaction.[37] The fact that trading has grown to such prominence and complexity as one of the dominant means of acquiring things is attributable, in part at least, to its relative survival value and to the character of the prevailing institutional patterns of which it is a part.

CONCLUSION

The answers to our original questions may now be seen in better perspective. Although it would be the height of pedantic scepticism to deny validity to a hypothesis because of the absence of all conceivable verification, nevertheless, the main assumptions examined all fall in the same category of speculation without adequate empirical verification, and they involve an outmoded methodology in the social sciences.

Even by the most tolerant sense of proportion and broad feeling for the evidence, any conceivable proof of the kinship of modern competitive trading to the earliest forms of barter and exchange would fail to offer a basis for a discussion of either ethics or efficiency of trading unless it be considered in a particular institutional framework. Consequently, it is not to be argued that the ethics of selling in our own society can be related to that of the societies in which origin may have occurred.

As a basis for the evaluation of the ethics of selling and buying in our own society, the concept that trading is a cooperative organization in communication for the purpose of achieving economic ends is one that properly expresses the internal logic of trading. For it implies in trading a concept in the economic institution whose usages entail a continuing contest and conflict with other concepts and usages prevailing in all of the social institutions. This view of trading permits one to proceed with an examination of the ethics of trading in our own society without the hindrance of a cloak of prejudgment drawn about it by speculation with respect to the ultimate origins of trading usages.

NOTES

[1]See Melville J. Herskovits, *The Economic Life of Primitive Peoples* (New York:Alfred A. Knopf, 1940), Pt. I, for detailed comment on methodology in economics and anthropology.

[2]As for example: Clive Day, *A History of Commerce* (New York: Longmans, Green, and Co., 1938); George Burton Hotchkiss, *Milestones of Marketing* (New York: The Macmillan Co., 1938); N. S. B. Gras, *An Introduction to Economic History* (New York: Harper & Brothers, 1922).

[3]Walter A. Shumaker and George Foster Longsdorf, *The Cyclopedic Law Dictionary*, 3rd ed. (Chicago: Callahan and Co., 1940), p. 992.

[4]This is not to say that the law has little influence on selling, but rather to emphasize that a legal definition is necessarily a cautious one and is more likely to represent a careful attempt to classify a concept rather than to penetrate it. It should be recognized, of course, that the law does place the intention of the parties to a contract in an important position as distinct from the transfer to title. See Nathan Isaacs, "Sales," *Encyclopaedia of the Social Sciences* Vol. VIII (New York: The Macmillan Co., 1931), pp. 511-16.

[5]By calling this approach "professional," it is not necessarily implied that selling is a profession. However the social responsibility of the seller today certainly suggests a professional attitude, and it is clear that the acceptance of business as a profession will only

follow, not precede, the adoption of such an attitude on the part of sellers. Cf. Louis Dembritz Brandeis, *Business—a Profession* (Boston: Small, Maynard & Co., 1914), pp. 1–12.

[6]This is the case even where impersonal or mechanical implements are employed, e.g., corporations, agents, or vending machines.

[7]Communication is "the process of exchanging commonly understood ideas, facts, or usages by means of language, visual presentation, imitation, suggestion." Constantine Panunzio, *Major Social Institutions* (New York: The Macmillan Co., 1939), p. 529.

[8]This concept has been used effectively by Chester I. Barnard in his interesting analysis of business organization. See, "Comments on the Job of the Executive," *Harvard Business Review,* Vol. XVIII (Spring, 1940), pp. 295–308. See also his *The Functions of the Executive* (Cambridge: Harvard University Press, 1938).

[9]Constantine Panunzio, *Major Social Institutions,* p. 7.
[10]Melville J. Herskovits, *Primitive Peoples,* p. 35.

[11]Clarence Darrow, "Salesmanship," *The American Mercury,* Vol. V (August 1925), pp. 385–92.

[12]Charles H. Fernald, *Salesmanship* (New York: Prentice-Hall, Inc., 1937), p. 44 ff.

[13]Werner Sombart, *The Quintessence of Capitalism* (London: T. Fisher Unwin, Ltd., 1915), p. 205.

[14]Melville J. Herskovits, *Primitive Peoples,* pp. 17–19.

[15]Elizabeth Ellis Hoyt, *Primitive Trade, its Psychology and Economics* (London: Kegan Paul, Trench, Trubner & Co., Ltd., 1926), p. 141.

[16]W. I. Thomas and F. Znaniecki, *The Polish Peasant in Europe and America* (1927), as quoted by E. L. Thorndike, *Human Nature and the Social Order* (New York: The Macmillan Co., 1940), p. 633.

[17]Melville J. Herskovits, *Primitive Peoples,* p. 133 ff.

[18]William Henry Chamberlin, "The Planned Economy," *Red Economics* (Boston: Houghton Mifflin Co., 1932), p. 9 ff. See also M. Ilin, *New Russia's Primer,* Vols. II and XIII (Boston: Houghton Mifflin Co., 1931).

[19]It is interesting that the opposite view is widely held also; namely, that trading inevitably leads to warfare. Elizabeth Ellis Hoyt cites evidence to support both views. *Primitive Trade,* Part VII. The fact that war and trade often appeared together as effect and cause may have been attributable to the fact that the traders (foreigners) were usually more advanced culturally than those on whom they called and thus had a higher capacity to injure [cf. Max Radin, *Manners and Morals in Business* (New York: The Bobbs-Merrill Co., 1939), p. 89 ff]. But they also should have had a higher capacity to serve, which may well have prevented conflicts!

[20]Margaret Mead, "Primitive Society," *Planned Society* (New York: Prentice-Hall, Inc., 1937), p. 16.

[21]*Ibid.,* p. 23.

[22]A more fruitful approach to the question of war and trade will be found in Lionel Robbins, *The Economic Causes of War* (London: J. Cape, 1940).

[23]Margaret Mead, "Primitive Society," p. 17 ff.

[24]J. P. Matthews and R. E. Shallcross, *Partners in Plunder* (Washington, New Jersey: Consumers' Research, Inc., 1935), p. 400. See also Clarence Darrow, "Salesmanship."

[25]N. S. B. Gras, *Business and Capitalism* (New York: F. S. Crofts & Co., 1939), p. 307 ff. See also Miriam Beard, *A History of the Business Man* (New York: The Macmillan Co., 1938).

[26]Hoyt, *Primitive Trade,* p. 104 and Part IV.

[27]To say that gift-giving is entirely a matter of goodwill or altruism, however, is to over-state the matter; for no matter how freely a gift is given, its presentation in primitive societies appears nearly always to create an obligation which, if neglected by the recipient, leads to loss of prestige or social disapprobation, which is a strong factor in shaping action. Cf. Herskovits, *Primitive Peoples,* p. 134.

[28]N. S. B. Gras, "Barter." *The Encyclopaedia of the Social Sciences,* Vol. II (New York: The Macmillan Co., 1933), p. 468 ff. Elizabeth Ellis Hoyt, *Primitive Trade,* p. 133 ff. Max Radin, *Manners and Morals,* p. 81 ff.

[29]Edward D. Page, *Trade-Morals,* 2nd rev. ed. (New Haven: Yale University Press, 1918), p. 58.See also Charles H. Fernald, *Salesmanship,* p. 44 ff.

[30]Max Radin, *Manners and Morals,* p. 85 ff.

[31]*Ibid.*

[32]Frederic B. Garver and Alvin H. Hansen, *Principles of Economics,* rev. ed. (Boston: Ginn and Co., 1937), p. 29 ff.

[33]Constantine Panunzio, *Major Social Institutions,* p. 216.

[34]A highly imaginative, yet penetrating essay on. this fundamental character of man as opposed to other animals is to be found in Clarence Day, *This Simian World* (New York: A. A. Knopf, 1936).

[35]Constantine Panunzio, *Major Social Institutions,* p. 143 ff.

[36]Elizabeth Ellis Hoyt, *Primitive Trade,* Part IV. That this emanicipation is universally or wholly accomplished today (or, indeed, should be) is not suggested. Contemporaries have "priceless" trinkets and sometimes order them interred with their remains. Businessmen have been known to defy the logic of the case by insisting on the use of their own photo-graphs as trademarks.

[37]The other means are strictly one-way: appropriation from nature, seizure from others, cultivation and making with the hands, gifts and inheritance, and gambling. H. K. Nixon, *Principles of Selling* (New York: McGraw-Hill Book Co., Inc., 1942), p. 41 ff.

2

Factors Governing the Development of Marketing Channels

Wroe Alderson

Everyone is affected by marketing channels, but few have had the occasion to try to understand them. Even the marketing specialist is likely to be limited to his own product field in his detailed knowledge of channels. It is true that there have been public investigations of channels from time to time, often prompted by a wave of indignation against the "middleman." Legislators and public officials are called upon to make decisions affecting channels without an adequate background concerning their place in the economy. Channels in one field are declared to consist of too many stages, and the conclusion is drawn that they are necessarily inefficient. In another it is asserted that channels are too highly integrated, with obvious implications as to the growth of monopoly....

...The purpose of this ... chapter is to discuss some of the underlying factors which are manifested in the development of channels generally. The first section of the chapter will show how intermediaries arise in the process of exchange and will explain how the independent but coordinated agencies known as marketing channels contribute to economic efficiency. The second section will assess the forces which bring about change and adjustment in the structure of marketing channels.

THE ORIGIN OF MARKETING CHANNELS

Human culture is characterized by the existence of an assortment of goods available to the individual for his personal use or similarly available to a family or household. This assortment may include articles of clothing or adornment, stocks of foods or fuel, kitchen utensils, weapons, tools. In a sense every item in the assortment may be regarded as a tool or instrument designed for specific uses. The significance of the assortment of goods in

From Wroe Alderson, "Factors Governing the Development of Marketing Channels," in R. M. Clewett, ed., *Marketing Channels* (Homewood, Ill.: Richard D. Irwin, Inc., 1954), pp. 5-22. Reprinted by permission.

the possession of the individual is that it provides the means or capacity for the various kinds of activities in which he may expect to engage.

It is rational for the individual to be prepared for all of the activities which are normal for his culture or for his station in life. Thus if any item in his basic assortment should be about to be used up or worn out, he will be interested in replacing it. As his status or other factors in his situation change, he may need to add new items to his assortment. An example of a crucial change of status which may require additional items is that from bachelorhood to married life. The point is that in either primitive or advanced cultures the individual and the household maintain the power to act by replenishing or extending the assortment of goods in their possession.

In a primitive culture most of the goods used within a household are produced by the members of the household. The term "produce" should be interpreted broadly enough here to include not only fabrication but the collection of natural objects not already in the possession of someone else. At an early stage in the development of economic activities it is found that some of the needs of a household or a tribe can be met more efficiently by exchange than by production. One family might be more skillful than another in making pots, while the second might be more skillful in making baskets. The first might be able to make two pots and the second two baskets faster than either could make one of each. If both families produce a surplus of the article they can make best and then they engage in exchange, both may get better quality goods at lower cost.

Exchange through Intermediaries

This is a very elementary example of the advantages of specialization in production and of the way that specialization is promoted through exchange. The purpose here is to show why exchange takes place through intermediaries and to consider the additional advantages which are gained through the development of middlemen and their alignment into marketing channels. To that end we may picture a slightly more complex exchange economy consisting of five households. Each is producing a surplus of some article used by all five. These articles might be pots, baskets, knives, hoes, and hats. In each case a surplus of four units is produced, and these units are then exchanged with the other households to obtain needed articles. Ten separate exchanges would be required (see figure 2-1).

FIGURE 2-1

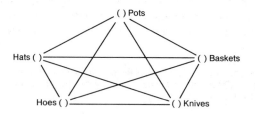

Now suppose that this pattern of decentralized exchange is replaced by a central market. All come together at an appointed place on the second Thursday in April, each bringing his surplus. This may be a time when they are coming together anyway to celebrate the spring festival of their rain god. The increased convenience with which the exchange is accomplished is indicated by figure 2-2.

FIGURE 2-2

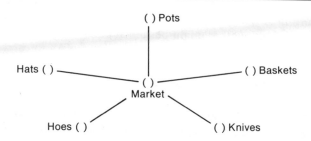

Only five trips are required instead of ten. Each participant has his surplus in readiness for exchange. This may not always be true in the case of decentralized exchange. When the potmaker visits the basketmaker to offer his wares, there may not be any finished baskets on hand and ready for exchange. In a primitive culture the goods and the parties to the transaction must be brought together at the same time and place in order for exchange to occur. The example given shows how much more easily this is accomplished through a central market. Here in its most elementary form is the creation of time and place utility, a concept which is generally associated with marketing. Time and place utility have held little interest for the general economist but deserve a more intensive analysis from the viewpoint of the marketing economist.

Centralized Exchange and Possession Utility

The next step in the evolution of exchange is for the market to be operated by an individual who may be called a dealer. Each of the five producers now engage in exchange with the dealer rather than with each other. The basketmaker, for example, trades his surplus to the dealer and receives back the items he requires to replenish his assortment. He may acquire a pot, a knife, a hoe, and a hat in a single transaction rather than through four separate transactions with the respective producers of these articles. In this way he saves time either to make more baskets or to devote to other pursuits. Possibly he will make five baskets instead of four, and the dealer will retain one basket in payment for his services.

Our simplified model of exchange now embraces what has been called "Possession utility" as well as "time and place utility." Effort is involved in the act of exchange itself. The dealer has created possession utility by bringing about the transfer of goods from producer to consumer with less effort than would be involved in direct trading. *Economic analysis of the factors in price equilibrium generally rests on the assumption that exchange transactions are costless. Marketing analysis directed toward an understanding of trade channels must begin with a recognition of the costs involved in the creation of time, place, and possession utility.*

The saving might not be very important in the example given of a primitive economy consisting of only five products. Cutting the number of transactions in half might not make a perceptible increase in productivity, and trading with each other might be valued in itself as a congenial form of social intercourse. The number of transactions necessary to carry out decentralized exchange is $\frac{n\,(n-1)}{2}$ where n is the number of producers and each makes only one article. Since the number of transactions required is only n if the central market is operated by a dealer, the ratio of advantage is $\frac{n-1}{2}$. Thus if the number of producers is raised from 5 to 25 the ratio of advantage in favor of an intermediary increases from 2 to 12. With 125 producers the ratio of advantage is 62. The figure 125 is a tiny fraction of the number of articles which must be produced to maintain satisfactory assortments in the hands of all of the consuming units in our complex modern culture. Even at this preliminary level of analysis, the ratio of advantage in favor of intermediary exchange is overwhelming. Exchange arises out of considerations of efficiency in production. Exchange through intermediaries arises out of considerations of efficiency in exchange itself.

Creation of Time and Place Utility

Intermediaries can increase the efficiency of exchange even when the producers and consumers under consideration are located in the same compact community. The advantages are greater when large distances intervene. Place utility takes on new aspects when the potmaker and the basketmaker are hundreds or even thousands of miles apart. When buyer and seller are so far apart, one or the other must take the initiative in closing the gap. One of them must call on the other if they are to negotiate face to face. One side or the other must assume the cost of moving the goods. Transportation and communication systems arise to bridge the distance. The railroads and trucking companies are in effect new types of specialized intermediaries serving buyer and seller more cheaply than they could serve themselves. It was no less an authority than Alfred Marshall who said that economic progress consists largely in finding better methods for marketing at a distance.[1] The number of intervening marketing agencies tends to go up as distance increases. Many eastern companies who sell directly to wholesalers in other parts of the country sell through manufacturers' agencies on the Pacific Coast. This type of arrangement was even more common in the past but has been dropped in some instances as communication with the Pacific region has improved. Distance, for the present purpose, is not to be measured in miles but in terms of the time and cost involved in communication and transportation. In this sense there are points 300 miles inland in China which are further away from Shanghai than is San Francisco. Tariffs and the formalities of customs clearance are also a form of distance. As a result, specialized import and export firms commonly enter into foreign trade in addition to other types of intermediaries.

Production and consumption may also be separated widely in time. The wheat crop which is harvested in June is destined to be consumed as bread or other foodstuffs over a period of a year or more thereafter. To bridge this gap in time is to create utility for both producer and consumer. One wishes to be paid as soon as the crop is harvested. The other wants bread as needed without having to maintain a stock of wheat in the meantime. Specialized intermediaries such as grain elevators and warehouses enter the picture and help create time utility through storage. Banks, insurance companies, and other specialized institutions help to minimize the costs and the risks of owning goods in the period between production and consumption. Retailers and wholesalers create time utility simply by holding stocks of goods available to be drawn upon by buyers. Without these facilities the only course open to the buyer would be to place an order with the producer and wait until the article could be produced and delivered. To be able to obtain the article at once instead of waiting is the essence of time utility. Another way of creating time utility is by selling on credit either to consumers or to other types of buyers. Through the installment purchase of an automobile, for example, the consumer is able to begin enjoying the use of the car long before it would be possible for him to pay for it in full. An automobile used partly for business, or other items entering into a further stage of production, may help to raise the money needed for purchasing the product.

Technological Distance and the Discrepancy of Assortments

Producer and consumer are often a long way apart not only in time and space but in other ways. A product has a very different meaning for its producer and for the ultimate consumer buyer. For the consumer it has the possibility of contributing to what might be called the potency of his assortment. That is the range of capacity for future action provided by all of the goods in his possession. The consumer judges the product in relation to anticipated patterns of behavior and considers how it will fit in with other products he expects to use. If it is a mechanical refrigerator it must fit into the space available for it in his kitchen or pantry, and be equipped to utilize the supply of electricity or domestic gas. If it is a tie, the wearer does not want the color to clash with the colors of his other clothing. The specifications of the ideal product from the consumer viewpoint are determined by use requirements, including the requirement of not detracting from the value in use of other items already in the assortment.

The goods that a producer has for sale are the expression of his skills and resources. Ideal specifications from his viewpoint would be those which made most effective use of his plant capacity and of the available labor and raw materials. If he makes more than one product his stock of finished goods may be regarded as an assortment in the sense that it constitutes a supply with diverse characteristics. In some cases the separate items will be quite unrelated from the viewpoint of the uses they serve. They may have nothing in common except that they were produced from the same materials or by similar processes. Two items may be linked even more closely, one being a primary product and the other a by-product. In any case it is a wholly different thing for goods to be found together because of convenience in production as compared to an assortment of goods that are all complementary in use.

The most convenient or constructive association of goods changes at each stage in the flow of merchandise from producer to consumer. This fact has been generalized as the "discrepancy of assortments."[2] Goods are associated for transportation because of physical handling characteristics and common origin and destination. Goods are associated for storage in terms of the length of time they are to be stored and the conditions needed to preserve them. Between the producer's stock of finished goods and the assortment in the hands of the consumer there may be other stocks or assortments maintained by retailers and wholesalers. The composition of these intermediate stocks is determined by the requirements of the functions performed.

The discrepancy of assortments places severe limitations on vertical integration of marketing agencies. A retail grocer typically relies on different wholesale sources for meat, produce, and packaged groceries. The requirements for storage, handling, and other aspects of the wholesale function are quire different in these three product fields. The retailer may provide the consumer who wants to buy peaches with a choice of fresh, canned, or frozen. Yet the routes by which the three items reached the grocery store would normally be quite different at both the wholesale and production levels. If it were not for the discrepancy of assortments, marketing channels might be more frequently integrated from top to bottom. Most fundamental of these discrepancies is that between producer stocks and consumer assortments. The product appears in a very different setting at these two levels and may be said to belong to the technology of production at one stage and the technology of use at the other. In addition to distance in time and space, marketing channels serve to bridge the technological gap (which may be regarded as a third form of distance between production and consumption).

Aspects of Sorting in Marketing

Fundamental to the adjustment effected through marketing channels are the four processes which may be bracketed under the name of "sorting." Most elementary of the forms of sorting is "sorting out." That means breaking down a heterogeneous supply into separate stocks which are relatively homogeneous. Sorting out is typified by the grading of agricultural products or by pulling out rejects in some manufacturing operations. A second form of sorting is accumulation, or bringing similar stocks together into a larger homogeneous supply. Accumulation of such stocks is essential to mass production and continuous manufacturing operations. Automatic machines are built with only a limited range of tolerance for variations in the materials processed.

The other two aspects of sorting are those which predominate in the distribution of finished manufactured goods. The first of these may be called "allocation." It consists in breaking a homogeneous supply down into smaller and smaller lots. This process in marketing is generally coincidental with geographical dispersal and successive changes in ownership. Allocation at the wholesale level has sometimes been called "breaking bulk." Goods received in carload lots are sold in case lots. A buyer in case lots in turn sells individual units.

The final aspect of sorting and the one which is most fundamental for this discussion may be called "assorting." That means building up assortments of items for use in association with each other. Both consumer buyers and industrial buyers enter the market for the purpose of building up assortments. Sellers undertake to facilitate assorting as carried on by buyers. Retail stores usually arrange goods in display according to categories of use rather than by producers or points of origin. Thus a consumer entering a department store can readily locate a department displaying all types of dresses. She does not have to go to a cotton department handling cotton sheets, rugs, awnings, and bandages in order to locate a cotton dress. Allocation and assorting go hand in hand in the channels of distribution. Purchase by the consumer is the common end point. It represents the completion of the process of allocation carried on by sellers and the culmination of economic activity in the replenishment or extension of the assortments in the hands of consumers.

Wholesaling is a manifestation of sorting as an essential marketing process. Goods are received from numerous suppliers and delivered to numerous customers. The essence of the operation is to transform the diversified supplies received into outgoing assortments on their way to customers. The justification for an independent wholesaling operation rests largely on the ratio of advantage growing out of this intermediate sorting. It has been pointed out elsewhere that this advantage goes up in relation to the product of the number of suppliers and the number of customers.[3]

The ultimate in intermediate sorting is seen in the freight classification yard. Trains of cars arrive over various routes. These trains are broken up and recombined according to the routes over which they will depart. Let us assume a simplified case in which five railroads come into the same terminal point. There are five production centers on each line or twenty-five in all. A train coming in over route A consists of 100 loaded cars. Twenty cars are picked up at each production center on route A, each destined for one of the centers on other lines. The same volume of freight originates on each of the other routes. Each of the production centers ships and receives twenty carloads of freight. Yet because of resorting at the central interchange the entire movement of 500 cars is completed by each of the five trains making a round trip over its own line. Note that there are no two cars for which both origin and destination coincide.

To summarize the case presented so far, intermediaries arise in the process of exchange because they can increase the efficiency of the process. The justification for the middleman rests on specialized skill in a variety of activities and particularly in various aspects of sorting. The principle of the discrepancy of assortments explains why the successive stages in marketing are so commonly operated as independent agencies. While economists assume for certain purposes that exchange is costless, transactions occupy time and utilize resources in the real world. Intermediary traders are said to create time, place, and possession utility because transactions can be carried out at lower cost through them than through direct exchange. In our modern economy the distribution network makes possible specialized mass production on the one hand and the satisfaction of the differentiated tastes of consumers on the other.

Routinization of Transactions

There is a final factor to be considered in explaining why a sequence of marketing agencies hangs together in such a way as to deserve the designation of channel. That is the fact that the cost of moving goods from one level to the next can be minimized if the transaction can be reduced to a routine. For a transaction to be routinized it must happen according to rules, and both sides must understand the rules. Even more fundamental is the need for confidence growing out of the established relationships of buyer and seller. Performance on each side rests on the belief that the other side will behave as expected. Out of long acquaintance each becomes a point of reference for habitual behavior by the other.

It is well to remember here certain linguistic coincidences. The word "customer" comes from the same root as the word "customary." Both derive from "custom," meaning habit or established practice. The word "routine" is readily traced to "route," which means a customary course or way. A related word is "channel," a variation on the word *canal* in Old French. Thus channel means a fixed and clearly marked route. In marketing practice there could be no channels without routines. Some advocates of the free market tend to regard all such institutional structures as restrictions on economic freedom....

One of the functions of advertising is to contribute to the routinization of repetitive transactions. A brand name comes to stand in the place of a set of product specifications. This avoids the need for specifying in detail what is wanted for every successive purchase of the same article. Routine handling of actual transactions is promoted when the majority of buyers come to prefer one brand or another. Thus discussion of product specifications is largely eliminated except from those transactions in which the buyer is considering a change. Channels of communication parallel and supplement the channels for the physical movement of goods.

Effective Search through Marketing Channels

The discussion of sorting heretofore assumes that the goods desired by buyers and the customers desired by sellers are readily available. Actually, a perfect market in that sense does not always exist. A buyer with a particular need starts looking for a product with the desired specifications with no assurance that a product of this precise character exists. The same is true for the producer who has increased his production but cannot be certain that customers are to be found to absorb his surplus. This aspect of market behavior may be called "searching." To the extent that buyers and sellers must cope with uncertainty they are engaged in a double search. If the search is successful it leads to the completion of the sorting processes of allocation and assorting which have already been considered.

What is called "shopping" is searching as carried on by consumers. The shopper starts out with some conception of what is wanted, more or less clearly defined. As a shopping trip proceeds the shopper gains knowledge as to what is available. At each stage the shopper has the option of taking something which is fairly satisfactory or continuing with the search. Usually the shopper does not search at random but goes to the most likely place first. The organization of retailing by separate lines of trade facilitates searching by consumers. The retailer, in buying new items for his store, may be regarded as representing the consumer in searching among sources of supply which are not readily available to the consumer. Thus channels facilitate searching as well as sorting. The same thing is true from the side of the producer who ordinarily searches for new customers through existing channels.

The search problem was analyzed from the military viewpoint during World War II. Principles of efficient search were developed governing such situations as airplanes searching for submarines. Searching in the market place absorbs effort, and this effort can be employed with varying degrees of productivity. The need for efficiency creates a need for specialists in searching as well as in sorting. Particularly is this true if the good to satisfy a need does not actually exist or the demand which can absorb a surplus has yet to be aroused. Special knowledge is required to locate the production facilities which can turn out a new product or the segment of the market which can most readily be induced to accept it. Such activities as product development and marketing research are expanding rapidly in the attempt to meet these problems.

The tendency to maximize productivity in economic activity leads to specialization in marketing as it does in production. A sequence of marketing agencies hangs together to constitute a channel for a given product. Cohesion is promoted by the advantages of the routine handling of transactions made possible by mutual confidence. The successive agencies tend at the same time to remain under separate ownership and control because of the discrepancy of assortments, the principle by which the natural association of products differs at each level. Both sorting and searching, the fundamental marketing functions, are facilitated by the existence of marketing channels. Exchange is inherently dynamic and tends to evolve a structure through which an increasing volume of transactions can be executed at the same or lower cost.

THE DYNAMICS OF MARKET ORGANIZATION

The system of marketing channels in an exchange economy is steadily undergoing change and adjustment. The exchange mechanism reacts to changes in production and consumption. The existence of an effective distribution system is in turn a potent factor affecting the behavior of producers and consumers. Finally, there is the principle of the proliferation of opportunity whereby the chance for success of a new business firm rests in part on the prior existence of other firms. This principle accounts for the steady growth in the number of firms at all levels but operates with special force with respect to firms engaged primarily in marketing. These dynamic aspects of market organization will be discussed in this section.

Expanding Markets

Market demand increases either because there are more people in the market or because of greater consumption per capita. Expansion of demand has been occurring for both reasons in the United States. Marketing channels have been undergoing modification both because of these increases and because of shifts in the distribution of population and in the patterns of consumption.

To predict the effect of increased population on consumption and hence on marketing channels it is necessary to consider the increase by age groups. Currently the increase has been greatest among infants and among elderly persons. A boom has resulted in certain classes of goods and in types of stores which handle them. Fewer young people are reaching marriageable age than a few years ago. This has caused a drop in the rate of family formation with repercussions affecting many intermediary agencies including plywood jobbers and furniture retailers. Increased consumption per capita is a result of increased productivity reflected in consumer income. The pattern of this increased demand is affected by such factors as the scarcity of domestic help. Housework is an activity subject to only slight increase in productivity with a consequent transfer of workers to other occupations. Workers are taking part of their increased productivity in the form of shorter hours. That helps to create demand for certain types of goods and services and to provide opportunities for the corresponding types of business firms.

Shifts of population have brought major changes in marketing channels in the postwar period. The marketing system has been largely reconstructed in some lines of trade, particularly in the Southwest and the Far West.

Changing Techniques of Production and Marketing

Technological change in production has a powerful impact on marketing, and the reverse is almost equally true. New products are introduced which in some cases cannot be handled by the older channels. A striking illustration is the recent development in the use of anhydrous ammonia as a fertilizer. This substance is forced into the soil in gaseous form, and special equipment is required. A new type of distributor has sprung up in the cotton growing area using pressure tanks for storage and delivery trucks equipped with specialized applicator nozzles.

In other cases, existing dealers and distributors have taken on the new technical products, but their selling and service activities have been greatly modified. Much time is spent on installations and on demonstrations to teach the consumer how to use the product effectively. To the extent that a marketing channel must transmit technical information, its efforts tend to become restricted to a limited number of items. Other factors on the production side which affect marketing channels include the relocation of basic industries such as steel. Another is the trend toward continuous process manufacturing resulting in new demands on the marketing system.

Changes in production methods and in market demand mean a constant shift in the task of marketing. The existence of independent intermediary agencies provides flexibility for effecting the necessary adjustments. New products can be introduced rapidly by securing the support of brokers or specialized distributors. The level of consumption can be maintained by causing goods of frequent purchase and established demand to be stocked in the maximum number of outlets. The general availability of service and repair parts encourages consumers to buy products whose sales would otherwise be more limited. Our productive plant and our marketing system is a single integrated mechanism with expansion on one side requiring expansion on the other.

Proliferation of Opportunity

The opportunity for a firm to specialize in marketing activities obviously depends on the existence of other firms. The development of one type of intermediary changes the marketing structure and may prepare the way for still another type. Instead of opportunity being exhausted by the entry of a new firm or type of firm, opportunity may be said to proliferate because of the several ways in which an existing firm may be the point of departure for a new one. First of all, the new firm may be the complement of the existing firm. The relation between complementary firms has been analyzed at some length by Boulding.[4]

Two firms are complementary when the existence of each increases the likelihood of the survival and success of the other. The relationship of complementary firms resembles the relation of symbiosis so frequently found among plant and animal species. The combination of firms or organisms is engaged in exploiting a joint opportunity. The exploition of joint opportunity by firms which are differentiated as to function is one of the most fundamental and characteristic features of marketing channels.

The combination of firms constituting a channel may consist simply of a manufacturer and a retailer. In other instances there may be two or more steps in between—as, for example, a wholesaler and a broker. If the channel is regarded as extending all the way from the producer of the raw material to the ultimate consumer, it may be still more complicated. Processing may take place at several points along the way with various kinds of marketing agencies in between. One illustration is the channel which brings a loaf of bread to the family table. The wheat grower sells to a local elevator which may ship to a terminal elevator or directly to the flour miller. The miller sells through a broker to bakers and wholesale grocers. The baker may provide home delivery through his own trucks or sell to a retail grocer who in turn sells to the consumer. Meanwhile, the wholesaler is selling flour to retail stores and small bakeshops, which in turn sell either flour or bread to the consumer.

The survival and prosperity of every firm in the channel is dependent upon the success of the others. If the baker is inefficient, the miller is penalized almost as directly as by his own inefficiency. If the earnings of both the miller and the baker would be increased by eliminating the flour broker, the latter would not be able to maintain his position. If some new type of intermediary could improve the input-output relationship of the channel as a whole, it would not take him long to gain a foothold.

Large manufacturing firms create opportunity for numerous smaller firms engaged in wholesaling and retailing. These smaller firms may complement the activities of the manufacturer in a highly specialized way, as in the case of most automobile dealers and appliance distributors. Large distributing organizations find their complements in a similar way among small producers. The large firm in either case often extends a variety of management services to the smaller firms. This practice is an indirect acknowledgment that the propserity of the large firm depends on the survival of the smaller. A notable example is found in tire marketing. The tire manufacturer stands ready to help his dealer in picking a location, planning store layout and fixtures, installing accounting controls, and in many other business problems.

Even though a complementary relationship is already well established, there may be an opportunity for a new firm to enter on one side or the other. The new firm is then competing for the opportunity to cooperate with existing firms. In some cases it may stimulate what is already being done as closely as possible. It may readily gain a foothold if it is competing with a firm which formerly held a monopoly in its limited field. Some of those who dealt with the pre-existent firm are disaffected and pleased to have a chance for a new connection. Others will give the newcomer a part of their business to help keep him alive as an alternative to their main connection. Sometimes the older firm is too cautious to expand, so that the newcomer provides the facilities needed for growth. In any case the new firm finds its opportunity in certain limitations of the older firm whose form of operations it is adopting.

More frequently the newcomer will deviate in one way or another from the established pattern. Its market position will be more secure if it performs a distinct function and one which the older firm is unable to assume. The deviation may consist of nothing more than setting up the same type of business in a different community. The deviant firm may attempt to appeal to consumers at a higher income level by offering additional services or to a lower income group by eliminating services and reducing prices.

Deviation may take the form of separating out a function to allow for more specialization, as in the case of the food broker who negotiates sales without assuming either ownership or possession of the goods. It may consist in combining functions for better coordination, as illustrated by the chain organization with both retail stores and a wholesale warehouse. A major deviant trend in recent times has been the wholesaler without stocks operating in fields where there is a need for intermediate financing and risk-taking but nothing to be gained through separate wholesale inventories.

The opportunity for a deviant firm frequently arises because of the self-imposed limitations in the policies of the established firm. The credit jeweler gets a chance because the old-line jeweler frowns on installment credit. Together they cover the market, but each occupies a niche that is closed to the other. Some manufacturers will sell only through wholesalers, leaving others to meet the desire for direct purchases by retailers. The stability of the first manufacturer's position rests largely on his distribution policy, but it does not enable him to control all of the business. An organization usually adopts a fixed policy to inspire confidence and thus to enable it to do an orderly and profitable business. There is no escape from the fact that the very announcement of a policy may give some other firm a chance to establish a foothold by deviating from this policy. To occupy a specified position is to leave other possible positions unoccupied.

It has been pointed out elsewhere that the drive for competitive advantage in position in any system keeps the system in ferment.[5] Not only does the competitive exploitation of opportunity lead to changes in the methods and structure of individual firms but it tends to bring about shifts in the number and character of firms in existence. In one sense there is a tendency toward an equilibrium number of firms by categories, but it is always an uneasy equilibrium within the channels of distribution. The number of firms tends to be equated to the number of available niches or footings in the market.

A niche may be defined as a place that is suited to the capacities of a person or an organized group. Such a footing in the market constitutes an effective opportunity for a firm if it represents a sufficient nexus of supply and demand to sustain the minimum operation necessary to survival. Both supply and demand are radically heterogeneous, so that there must be a continual sorting out of segments of supply and demand and a matching of these segments with each other. To discern the existence of such a nexus is to recognize opportunity.

The firms which make up marketing channels stand in a special relationship to economic opportunity. Since they require goods for resale rather than use, they are oriented to supply and demand of an intermediate character. Their opportunity is contingent on the willingness of others to use them as a channel. Yet many types of intermediate units find suppliers and customers ready to use them. The contingent nature of their opportunity does not operate so much to restrict their numbers as to create a constant potentiality for shifting channels. Some of the most fundamental channels of trade in the United States seem to have been in a constant state of revolution for decades.

The opportunity for all types of firms is inherently dynamic in a market economy since shifts in demand and in competition are always possible. The greater dynamism in marketing channels is only a matter of degree. Opportunity creates instability in the system because the exploitation of opportunity by one firm changes the outlook for other firms. In general it may be anticipated that the success of one firm or type of firm creates opportunity for others.

Only a free market economy gives full play to the principle of proliferation. A free market is not only a market in which existing enterprises are free to trade with each other. An even more fundamental freedom is freedom for all parties to try to organize the market from the standpoint of their best opportunity as they see it. In order for proliferation to take place promptly and constructively, the economy of a country must have the enterprise spirit and tradition as well as a favorable legal framework. In other words, the attempt of the individual to establish his own enterprise must be accepted as a normal aspect of the universal struggle for status. In an increasingly complex economy the aspirant seeking entry into the market must also have the training and experience which gives some chance of survival. The enterprise spirit might eventually be dulled or diverted if there was not a goodly number of entrants succeeding in such fields as retailing along with the many failures.

In summary, the analysis of factors affecting marketing channels rests on the conception of a system of action of which the individual firms are elements. Each firm struggles for survival and for improvement of its position within this system. This drive for position is not restrictive if the economic base of the system is stable or expanding. Instead, it manifests the proliferation of opportunity as the success of existing firms tends to open the way for others. This is particularly true of firms in intermediary distribution, since their opportunity resides in supplementing the activities of other firms. The network of firms in distribution can never come into a final stage of equilibrium, since any given state of the system provides opportunities for new firms, and the entry of these firms leads to a further change of state.

NOTES

[1]Alfred Marshall, *Principles of Economics,* 8th ed. (London: Macmillan & Co., Ltd., (1920), p. 397.

[2]David R. Craig and Werner K. Gabler, "The Competitive Struggle for Market Control," *Annals of the American Academy of Political and Social Science,* May, 1940.

[3]Wroe Alderson, "Scope and Function of Wholesaling in the United States," *Journal of Marketing,* September, 1949.

[4]K. E. Boulding, *A Reconstruction of Economics* (New York: John Wiley & Sons, 1950).

[5]Wroe Alderson, "Survival and Adjustment in Organized Behavior Systems," in Reavis Cox and Wroe Alderson, eds., *Theory in Marketing* (Chicago: Richard D. Irwin, Inc., 1950), p. 85.

3

Development of Marketing Theory: Fifty Years of Progress

Paul D. Converse

Before there was life on earth there were the phenomena of gravitation, chemistry, atomic energy, and the like. With the coming of life, there came principles of biology such as adaptation of environment, survival of the fittest, and reproduction. With the coming of man, there came human laws and methods of behavior—desire for food, protection, pleasure, awe of the divine, love of opposite sex, curiosity, constructiveness, desire for adventure. With the coming of private property and government there came the laws of economics—division of labor, exchange of goods, mediums of exchange, and laws of value as applied to goods, wages, rent. Economics has been defined as the science that considers or explains the wealth-getting and wealth-using activities of man. Economic theory may be thought of as logic to applied financial problems or problems of value. At least some schools of economic theory are little more than this. The limitation on this kind of theory is that many human actions are not logical. Perhaps man's emotions are more important than man's logic.

Commerce began in prehistoric times. With the advent of steam, however, commerce was given a great stimulus and territorial division of labor became important. When our railroad system was built in the 1870s and 1880s, factories grew in size and principles of management were developed. "Scientific management" came in. The output of these factories had to be sold. Advertising, salesmanship, and sales management increased in importance. It was realized that there was much waste in selling. So, the study of marketing! Some attention was paid to the study of advertising and selling in the closing years of the nineteenth century by businessmen, and by a few teachers. It was at the turn of the century that universities first began to offer courses in marketing. There were no

From Paul D. Converse, "Development of Marketing Theory: Fifty Years of Progress," in [Hugh Wales, ed.,] *Changing Perspectives in Marketing* (Urbana, Ill.: University of Illinois Press, 1951), pp. 1–31. Reprinted by permission.

textbooks for several years; in fact, satisfactory textbooks were not available at all until 1915, 1916, and 1917.

These early courses in marketing largely evolved from economics and management. They drew to a lesser extent on accounting, psychology, and history. Many of the early courses seem to have been largely descriptive. The teachers first had to find out how goods were marketed before they could offer constructive plans for improvements. Marketing having developed to a considerable extent from economics, much of our theory was derived from economics. As the marketing teachers studied business operations, some of the economic theories seemed rather abstract and impractical.

My own point of view was that economic theories gave us a starting point—or a series of hypotheses. It was my task to see if they worked. If they did not apply, I tried to find out how the theories had to be modified, or what new ones had to be formulated. Thus, many of the marketing theories we hold today are modifications of applications of older economic theories.

Some of the theories, laws, and techniques with which we have been most concerned are those of elasticity or flexibility of demand; of determining and forecasting consumer demand and purchases; of determining whether marketing is a decreasing, constant, or increasing cost industry; of measuring operating efficiency; of the relationship of costs to price and of other price determining factors; of marginal, supramarginal, and submarginal operators; of trade movements; of store location, and the law of rent; of sales forecasting, sales potentials, and territorial incomes; and of the total cost of marketing and its relationship to the cost of production, and to the welfare of the consumers.

Some of the specific fields in which students of marketing are especially interested are the following:

Demand.   This leads among other things to a study of population, number of persons and families, and their location; distribution of population by age; shifts in population; birth rates; marriage rates; death rates; and number of people employed and their earnings. Marketing students are particularly interested in consumer income, its amount, and distribution among families, among individuals outside family groups, and its geographical distribution. Marketing students are interested in human wants and desires, that is, how people spend their money and how they will spend it in the future. This leads to a study of fashion, fashion in homes, in household appliances and furnishings, in amusements and entertainment, in sports, in clothes, in foods, and in automobiles. Marketing students are interested in increasing or stimulating human wants, in general and for the goods of individual sellers. This leads to the study of advertising, salesmanship, and merchandising, marketing research, and packaging.

Prices.   Marketing involves a study of trade movement, both interregional and the specific places (towns) where consumers make their purchases. This leads to studies of locations of wholesale and retail stores, of transportation, packing, storing, and the physical handling of goods, of freight rates and storage costs, of regional resources and demands, of physical facilities such as railroads, highways, waterways, and warehouses.

Marketing is directly concerned with prices and price making forces such as supply and demand, as influenced by and their relationship to monopoly controls, customary prices, price setting by governments and associations of sellers, price competition, price controls, price policies, and price strategies.

Rent. Marketing is concerned with rent and its determination. This is related to location. The merchants often have the option of taking a high-rent location or of taking a low-rent location and spending more on advertising.

Operating Efficiency. Students of marketing are greatly interested in operating efficiency. They need to know how various goods are marketed, what trade channels are used, and what middlemen are involved. They should know how the various market institutions are organized and how they operate. This information is as essential to the student of marketing as the design of a machine is to the engineer, or human anatomy is to the surgeon. A study of operating efficiency may involve cost analysis, job analysis, employee supervision and training, work organization, and use of labor-saving devices. Marketing draws heavily on management and accounting. In passing, it may be remarked that cost accountants have done relatively little to develop distribution cost analysis and have left this field largely to students of marketing. Students and operators want to increase marketing efficiency—that is to increase the volume of goods or services marketed per man. Some units of comparison and evaluation are: sales per salesman, per employee, per square foot of space, per dollar invested in inventory; sales per dollar spent for rent; cost of a salesman's call; sales per advertising dollar; and cost of assembling an order, of delivery, of invoicing, of extending credit and making collections, of warehousing goods, of buying and receiving goods, and the like.

Fair Competition. Marketing students are interested in fair and unfair competition, in commercial law, in government regulations.

STUDY OF MARKETING

Goods have been marketed for thousands of years. The people engaged in marketing undoubtedly devoted much thought and gave much observation to their operations. Marketing operations must have been studied by the operators of caravans and ships in the ancient world. The results of their studies were used in their own operations and, if passed on to others, this was done largely by word of mouth. This situation existed very largely down to the beginning of the present century, although a small beginning was made on business literature in the last century. To give a few illustrations, Cyrus McCormick used field demonstrations and installment credit in the sale of his reapers; John Wanamaker was a great user of advertising and introduced truth in advertising when truth was the exception and not the rule. He used the one-price policy and introduced the absolute right of customers to return unsatisfactory merchandise. John Patterson used sales training and memorized sales talks. Little advance could be made in knowledge until what one man learned was written down for the use of others. Science grows step by step. Knowledge grows as recorded information is developed. One man can begin where another leaves off.

J. E. Hagerty began the study of marketing as a graduate student in the University of Pennsylvania by talking with businessmen to find how they operated. He said that businessmen were willing to talk with him and tell him about their operations but that they were surprised that a person from a university was interested; and they were curious to know why he wanted to know about marketing operations.[1]

It has been said that by 1880 our factories were capable of turning out more goods than current demand would absorb. This placed an emphasis on selling and on stimulating demand. With the recovery following the depression of the early 1890s there developed an increased interest in higher education. This became noticeable about 1900. Interest in business education at the college level began at this time. The first college courses in general marketing are said to have been offered at the Universities of Illinois and Michigan in the academic year 1901-02, although courses in transportation and foreign trade were offered earlier. These courses were undoubtedly quite different from present-day courses in marketing, but they showed the growing interest in the study of distribution.

The first students of marketing were interested in finding out how goods were marketed. Some of the early courses were probably more descriptive than many present courses. We must know how a machine operates before we can make improvements in it.

There have been three principal methods of teaching marketing. The first method used appears to have been the study of the middlemen or institutions engaged in marketing. It takes up a study of the operations of the various institutions and discovers how they market various products. It leads to a study of their services and their efficiency of operation and suggests improvements in their efficiency. This method is adapted to the needs of the students who are going into marketing—retailing, wholesaling, brokerage, advertising agencies, manufacturers' sales organizations, and the like.

The second method is to study the marketing of various commodities. This method has been used widely in the courses dealing in agricultural and industrial marketing. In these fields, such an approach is practical. The danger of the commodity method of studying marketing is that the courses become largely descriptive. Also, in general courses dealing with many products there is likely to be much repetition. If a course deals with one or a limited class of products, it is possible to make it analytical as well as descriptive.

To study the marketing of commodities, we must group or classify them according to some characteristics. They may be classified according to their physical characteristics, their methods of production, their methods of use, or by the buying habits of the consumers.[2] The buying habits of consumers is the most important method to students of marketing. Dean Hagerty, in teaching marketing before 1912, recognized two classes of goods: industrial and consumers' (the latter including fashion goods). C. C. Parlin, who became director of commercial research for the Curtis Publishing Company in 1911, classified goods as convenience, shopping, and emergency.[3] Copeland, in 1923 and 1924, added specialty goods, and subdivided industrial goods into five classes.[4] In my studies of retail trade movement, I have evolved a slightly different classification of consumer goods: fashion, service, convenience, and bulk.

The third method of studying marketing is the functional approach. In this method the various operations, services, or acts are studied. That is, the marketing of goods by middlemen is broken down into the various operations or functions and these are studied separately. This is analogous to a study of each process carried on in a factory. Thus transportation, buying, selling, storing, grading, transporting, packing, financing, risking are studied separately. These functions may be further subdivided. Thus transportation may be divided into rail, truck, water, terminal, and air transportation; or, it may be divided into rate-making operation, government regulation, traffic management, and financing. Selling may be divided into personal salesmanship, merchandise display, newspaper advertising, radio advertising, publicity, and the like.

Looked at in this way, the functional study of marketing may be older than some of the other methods of study, owing to the fact that transportation, packing, grading, and so forth, were studied by businessmen for years before marketing came to be taught in schools. Most of us think, however, of the functional approach as a method of analyzing overall marketing operations. We first list the functions performed in marketing certain commodities, or in certain trade channels. Some of these functions may be performed once, and others several times. For example, many products may be graded once and sold all the way through the trade channel by this grade; or a good may be inspected by each successive buyer and seller. By studying one function at a time, methods of increasing efficiency may be suggested. By looking at the overall marketing process, we may find ways of reducing the number of times that a function is performed. This suggests vertical integration as a method of reducing marketing costs.

As far as I know, the functional approach was first suggested by Arch W. Shaw. Mr. Shaw spent some years at Harvard helping to reorganize the Business School. He was particularly interested in marketing and wanted to find a scientific approach to its study. In attending a series of lectures by a German professor named Schmidt, he got the idea that every science must start with a concept. He got the idea of change from a lecture by a man named Cox on the "Religion of Pure Experience," which developed the idea of constant change. Thinking this over, he got the concept that marketing is matter in motion; that is, marketing must get goods from the producers to the consumers. Goods must be started in motion and kept in motion until they reach the ultimate consumer. There are two kinds of motion: physical, and that involving changes in ownership. Mr. Shaw tells me that he first worked out the concept of functions in a series of lectures he delivered in Dean Gay's course in English economic history. England, at the period under study, was becoming a great merchant nation. The idea of functions was developed in these lectures and was thought of in connection with the operation of middlemen. Thus we may say that the functional approach developed out of the middleman approach. Shaw first published his treatment of functions in 1912[5] and this marks a landmark in the development of science in marketing. Shaw's idea of functions was taken by Weld who worked it over, and stated it more logically and practically in 1917.[6] Weld's statement was generally used by students of marketing, especially by Cherington and Clark. Further subdivision and refinements were suggested by Theodore Macklin, Homer Vanderblue, and myself in 1921, and by myself in 1926. John Thurman Horner in 1925 suggested a valuable subdivision of the selling function. Maynard-Weidler-Beckman in 1927 added the gathering of market information to the list.[7] Franklin W. Ryan in 1935 further subdivided the functions and suggested a further subdivision and analysis of the buying and selling functions.[9] Professor E. D. McGarry in *Theory of Marketing* suggests placing more emphasis on the management function of policy formulation.

The functional method is the most analytical of the three methods, and is extremely valuable in both marketing research and in the teaching of marketing. A critical study of biology often involves a study of separate organs or limbs; a study of machine design and operation takes up the various parts before considering the machine as a whole.

Having briefly outlined the development and the principal methods of studying marketing, let us look at some of the hypotheses, theories, laws and techniques developed during the past fifty years....

IS MARKETING AN INDUSTRY OF INCREASING, DECREASING, OR CONSTANT COSTS?

Some, reasoning by analogy, surmised that retailing was like manufacturing, an industry of decreasing costs. Evidence gathered by the Federal Trade Commission and summarized in T.N.E.C. report No. 13 shows that the popular idea of decreasing costs in manufacturing industries is greatly exaggerated. Nystrom, writing in 1915,[10] said: "The total expenses of doing a retail business vary greatly. The causes for these variations may be inferred to be due to the kind of business, the location, the volume of business done, the class of business whether high or low grade, and the efficiency with which it is conducted. Expenses seem to vary with the size of the town—the larger the town the higher the expense." The Harvard Bureau said of retail grocery stores in 1917: "The lowest expense ratios were not found in the largest stores, nor the highest in the small stores. The greatest variations were commonly between stores of approximately the same size operating under similar conditions in a single locality."[11]

By 1922 enough expense figures on retailing were available to lead to the conclusion that retailing was either an industry of increasing or constant costs. This material was summarized at the December meeting of the American Economic Association by Weld.[12] The percentage cost of operating retail stores increases with their volume of sales but we know that expenses increase with the size of the town in which the stores are located. As many of the larger stores are in larger towns, the increase in expenses may result from the location of the store and not from the increased sales volume. In 1924, the writer said: "From these facts it seems safe to conclude that the law of decreasing costs operates within very narrow limits, if at all, in the case of merchandising concerns. The figures...indicate stores show increasing percentages of expenses with increasing sales, but this appears to be due to the factors other than the volume of business transacted."[13]

Few of the earlier studies had enough operating statements to allow satisfactory averages to be obtained when stores were grouped by town size and then tabulated by volume of sales. Dun & Bradstreet's retail surveys for the years 1936 and 1937 made such tabulations. Although results varied somewhat between types of retail stores, the evidence indicates that retailing is an industry of either constant or increasing costs, according to the definition followed.

We have fewer studies in the wholesale field. Some of these indicate that the law of decreasing costs operates to a limited degree among wholesalers. At least, the point of maximum efficiency, or lowest cost, is reached at a higher sales volume than with retailers. The lower expenses of middle sized or large wholesalers, however, is not enough to overcome other advantages of small or local wholesalers and we have very few large wholesale houses.

The fact that large retailers have no advantage in lower operating expenses is of great significance. The small retailer would appear to be in no danger of extinction and there would appear to be no need for his protection by law. We must not, however, be too quick to reach this conclusion for two reasons. First, large stores often have higher percentages of gross margin than small stores. Frequently this larger margin is sufficient to more than counterbalance their higher operating expenses and give them higher net profits. This higher gross margin must result either from higher selling prices or lower buying prices. The Robinson-

Patman amendment was enacted in part to prevent the large stores from securing unreasonably large buying advantages. Second, many large stores are integrated and perform both wholesaling and retailing; or engage manufacturing, wholesale, and retail operations. This type of organization may result in considerable savings in buying and selling and other functions between the wholesaler and retailer. To meet this advantage of the chains, the independent wholesalers and retailers have organized voluntary and cooperative chains and a well-known authority in the grocery field says that the volume of voluntary and retailer cooperatives is now larger than that of corporate chains and that their warehouses now supply many small chains.[14]

OPERATING EFFICIENCY

The fact that merchandising expenses by both wholesalers and retailers depend primarily upon individual efficiency cannot be overemphasized. All studies have shown extremely wide variations between the expenses of individual operators in the same trade. The same is true of manufacturing, mining, and farming costs. This variation was the basis of the marginal theory of price determination evolved and widely recognized by economists. It is the basis of bulk-line price fixing by our government. It was very widely used by government price-fixers in World War I. Needless to say, this method of price-fixing gives very high profits to some sellers. The graduated excess profits tax has been used to recover much of this profit. Under this tax, the Government allows the efficient businessman the fun of making a high profit and then takes most of it away from him. The wide variations in costs also explain many of the cost plus contracts used by government agencies.

VARIATION IN COSTS

Economists have much more generally recognized the wide variation in costs between different concerns than have businessmen. Time after time we hear businessmen say that their costs are approximately the same as those of competitors. Such statements usually are far from the truth. I have never seen nor heard of any dependable cost figures that show that most competitors have similar costs.

Some economists argue that under free competition competitors will "in the long run" have the same costs. The less competent producers will be eliminated. Many businessmen argue that this is not so. An incompetent or inefficient man is eliminated *but* by the time he fails he has learned something about the business and about his costs of operation so when he fails a new man takes over his place of business who is more ignorant than the former occupant was at the time of his exit. The economist retorts that he said in the "long run," and no one seems to know how long the "long run" is. There is, of course, a tendency for high cost operators to reduce their costs, especially if they know their costs are high. To illustrate, shortly after the business press published the fact that the Great Atlantic and Pacific Tea Company was operating its wholesale houses at three per cent, an executive of a large voluntary said: "We must get our wholesale expenses down to three per cent." Can you do it? "If the A. and P. can do it we can do it!"

Regardless of the truth of this argument, there is another reason why the costs of marketing concerns in the same trade will never become uniform. There are four factors of production—land, labor, capital, and management. The economist who says that costs will become uniform between competitors argues that labor tends to come to a common level of production, that capital costs tend to become equal, and that if one man has an advantage in land (raw material) that its value will increase so that when it is sold the buyer will have a cost so high that he will have no advantage. There may perhaps be some truth in this argument for the "long run" although we know that there is often a very great difference in the output of workers doing the same job with the same machines, and that one concern often has the benefit of new inventions or discoveries not available to his competitors.

However, management will never become of equal efficiency, and, in many marketing concerns, management is the most important factor in production. Management can never become of equal efficiency because of the element of time. Men owning and managing businesses are of various ages and a man's efficiency commonly varies with his age. A young man is inexperienced. If he inherits his business he may also be lazy. But his efficiency will increase for a number of years as he gains experience. The successful manager's efficiency commonly drops as he gets older. He loses a part of his energy and his doctor tells him to "ease up," or he reasons that he "can't take it with him" and should enjoy some of the fruits of his labor while still alive.

Thus, at any time, competing businesses are in the hands of managers of various ages and of widely different efficiency. Hence, if for no other reason, competitors have widely differing costs. This means that some have large profits, some have small profits, some just break even, and some lose money. The latter fail if their losses are continued. But a company may lose money for several years without using up its capital and quitting.

One other fact should be mentioned in this connection, that an operator often makes money one year and loses money in another year. In other words, the same concern is often a supramarginal operator in some years and a submarginal operator in other years. Profits in good years help to offset losses in poor years.[15]

This variation in costs between similar stores and other marketing institutions is important in the overall picture of marketing operations and especially to those interested in price theories and policies.

INTEGRATION

The study of operating efficiency leads to a study of vertical integration. The study of integration appears to be a very fruitful field of study and also a field of some popular interest as witnessed by the case of the U.S. Department of Justice against the A. and P. Tea Company.

We do not know just how much advantage integration between wholesaler and retailer or between manufacturer, wholesaler, and retailer has. In some cases it appears to be very great. In other cases it may be very little. This is one part of marketing that needs much more research.

PRICE DETERMINATION

Marketing students are much interested in price determination. One may almost say that price is the center and keystone of marketing. Marketing students have devoted much time to the study of price-fixing by monopolies, trade associations, and cartels. But the lead in stating the concept of monopolistic competition seems to have come from without the field. Marketing students have given much attention to price laws, especially resale price maintenance and anti-trust laws, and have studied their results. We have devoted much study to the relation of price to demand and have developed the concept of flexibility of demand. Perhaps this has been our main contribution to the theory of prices.

We have devoted much of our attention to the price policies and strategies of individual sellers. Shaw[16] used the policies of selling at the prevailing price, of selling at the market minus, and of selling at the market plus. This is quite different from the economist who assumed that all sellers sold at the same price. Theoretical economists have, however, now followed market economists in recognizing differentiation of products.

TRADE MOVEMENTS

Marketing includes studies of trade movements, interregional movements or movements between geographic areas, and the movement within geographical areas. Students of marketing have devoted much attention to movements of wholesale and retail trade within regions, to setting sales territories, to the location of wholesale and retail stores, and to the study of proper advertising areas, and the selection of media.

There have been several excellent studies of wholesale territories, but somewhat more progress appears to have been made in working out definite laws governing the movements of retail trade.

Retail as well as wholesale trade areas depend partly, if not largely, on the transportation facilities available. The early settlers along the Atlantic seaboard traveled by boat and horse. The advent of the steamboat led to a rapid development along our inland waterways. The coming of the railroad gave us a new geography. With railroad and horse transportation, trading villages were established every four to six miles with larger trading centers, usually the county seat towns, every twenty to thirty miles. The coming of the automobile and paved roads has modified this pattern. Some keen observers could see signs of coming changes as early as 1911. Changes in trade movements became marked in the years following World War I and marketing students became interested in the subject in the 1920s. My study of the subject began in 1925 and my first bulletin was published in April 1928.[17]

Dr. William J. Reilly, at the University of Texas, was studying the subject at the same time and issued two bulletins in 1928 and 1929 in which he formulated the Law of Retail Gravitation.[18] This law involves two factors, populations and distances: two trading center towns attract trade from the vicinity of the breaking points between their territories in direct proportion of their populations and inversely as the squares of the distance between them. The larger town has more stores and larger assortments of goods and is a more attractive shopping center than the smaller town and draws trade from greater distances. Distance takes time, and effort, and costs money. This limits the distance people will go to shop. Combining these two factors we have the law of retail gravitation. There are several limiting factors among them, such as conditions of the highways, traffic congestion, parking facilities, quality of stores, and the like. However, this law predicts the movement of retail trade in fashion goods with a high degree of accuracy.

In our studies at the University of Illinois we have measured the movement of trade from more than 100 towns and we have derived two additional formulas; one, from the law of retail gravitation, is used to set the boundaries of a town's trade area. The other, derived by deduction, indicates how much trade a town will lose to other towns and how much it will keep at home.[19] The distance factor measures primarily time consumed in reaching the trading center. When travel is by automobile, distance is more easily ascertained than time. In the Chicago metropolitan area it has been found that if time by public carrier is used instead of distance, the formula works well in predicting trade movement.

Several interesting uses have already been found for the laws of retail gravitation. A merchant can compute his trade area and thus know the territory in which to solicit business. For example, a department store was found to be spreading its advertising over a large territory. The trade area of the town was computed and it was advised to limit its advertising to this area. It did so. The same advertising expenditure increased its sales considerably. Evidently much of its previous advertising expenditure was wasted.

The merchants of a town can compute the town's trade area and then have consumer surveys made to find out how they "are doing." To illustrate, this was done in ten towns near the borders of the trade area of town A. In seven of these towns, A was securing less trade than predicted by the law. These seven towns were in competition with three other trading centers, B, C, and D. In three towns A was doing better than predicted by the formula. These were towns in which the competition was with trading center, E. Obviously the merchants of A were doing badly in competition with towns B, C, and D. The facts show the merchants where they are doing poorly and where they should improve their efforts. These facts should stimulate them to do so.

Newspapers can study the trade areas of their towns to ascertain the territories in which to build their circulations.

Merchants can determine their trade areas and then can plot their customers on maps and determine if they are securing trade from all parts of their trade areas to which their goods are adapted. If they find blank spots on the map, they know where to "dig in" to find the trouble and correct it.

These examples illustrate some of the uses that may be made of trade area analysis.

STORE LOCATION

Considerable knowledge has been obtained on the subject of store location during the past twenty years, particularly by chain store operators. We have found these men very willing to discuss the subject and pass on their information. Store location can as yet hardly be called a science, but the use of traffic counts of pedestrians and automobiles, and studies of transportation facilities and geographic factors influencing or limiting town growth can take much of the guess work out of locating stores. Facts on income, occupation, and industries together with highway mileages and populations of towns are of great help in selecting towns in which to place stores. Academic men have not done a great deal of research on the subject of store location. This appears to be a fruitful field for further study.

The classification of goods is of fundamental importance in the location of retail stores, in selection of the area to be covered by advertising, in selecting type of salesmen needed, and in the merchandising policies pursued. To illustrate, groceries are convenience goods, and a grocery store secures most of its trade from a relatively small area. Even a supermarket secures little trade, except that of farmers, from a radius of more than two or three miles. On the other hand, a store handling high quality fashion goods such as higher priced women's wear may attract trade from several counties, and some of the larger stores from parts of two or more states. The type or kind of goods handled is also important in choosing the specific location within a town.

RETAIL RENTS

We learned in economic theory that rent was price determined and not price determining. Yet when we obtained expense figures for large groups of retail stores we found that the percentage cost of rent increased as we went from poorer to better locations. It would have been very easy to conclude that the higher rents increased the total expenses of stores in downtown stores. Yet Nystrom, in his *Economics of Retailing* published in 1915, showed that this was not the case—that the better merchants were able to pay the higher rents because the better locations were more productive. They yield larger sales but the rents increase faster than the sales— that is, the percentage cost of rent increases. The better locations may yield sales at higher prices or the larger sales may enable the purchase of goods at lower prices because of a larger volume. Either lower buying prices or higher selling prices may increase the gross margin percentage.

The larger sales volume may allow a faster rate of stock turnover and this may reduce carrying charges. But more important, the better location yields larger sales and makes possible larger dollar profits. The better merchants bid for the better locations, and those with the greatest efficiency as measured by operating expenses other than rent get the best locations. Thus, the better locations yield more dollars, if not larger percentages, of profit.

We know that the percentage cost of rent increases from small rural villages and small towns as we go into larger and larger towns. The percentage cost of rent also appears to increase as we go from outlying districts into the downtown retail shopping districts near the 100 per cent locations. This fact is important to retailers and those advising retailers....

CONCLUSIONS

I have tried to indicate the very great progress during the past fifty years in the development of marketing knowledge and marketing literature. In 1900 most of the knowledge of marketing was in the minds of businessmen and scattered through census and other government reports, in books on general business or on selling, and in various business periodicals. There was no body of organized literature. Science has been defined as an organized body of knowledge, or a branch of knowledge dealing with a body of facts or truths systematically arranged. Marketing meets the conditions specified in these definitions and so can rightfully be called a science.

The first or pioneer stage has been passed. The next fifty years will be equally challenging and exciting and should produce greater knowledge than the past fifty years. New hypotheses will be evolved, tested, and developed into principles and laws. Research techniques will be refined and predictions can be made with greater assurance. Marketing is still a relatively new field. It is a field that will attract young scholars because it offers an opportunity to find out many new and interesting things.

NOTES

[1]*Journal of Marketing,* Vol. I, No. 1 (July, 1936).

[2]E. L. Rhodes, *Introductory Readings in Marketing* (1927), Chapter 2.

[3]Pamphlet, "Merchandising of Textiles," Curtis Publishing Company, 1912.

[4]"Relation of Consumer Buying Habits to Marketing Methods," *Harvard Business Review,* April, 1923; *Principles of Merchandising,* 1924.

[5]*Quarterly Journal of Economics,* August, 1912.

[6]*American Economic Review,* June, 1917.

[7]Theodore Macklin, *Efficient Marketing for Agriculture* (1921); Homer B. Vanderblue, "Functional Approach to Study of Marketing," *Journal of Political Economy,* October, 1921, pp. 377–83; Paul D. Converse, *Marketing Methods and Policies* (1921); John Horner, *Agricultural Marketing* (1925); H. H. Maynard, Walter Weidler, and Theodore Beckman, *Principles of Marketing* (1927), Chapters 3 and 27.

[8]*Harvard Business Review,* January, 1935.

[9]*Journal of Marketing,* January, 1943.

[10]Paul H. Nystrom, *Economics of Retailing, 1915,* p. 78.

[11]Harvard Bureau of Business Research, Bulletin No. 5.

[12]L. D. H. Weld, *American Economic Review,* Supplement, March, 1923.

[13]Paul D. Converse, *Marketing Methods and Policies,* rev. ed. (1924), p. 344.

[14]American Institute of Food Distribution, Inc., *Weekly Digest,* November 12, 1949.

[15]Professor Secrist pointed this out in his study of the operations of retail clothing stores; Horace Secrist, *Competition in the Retail Distribution of Clothing,* Northwestern University, Bureau of Business Research, Series II, No. 8, 1923; see also his *Triumph of Mediocracy.*

[16]A. W. Shaw, *An approach to Business Problems* (1916).

[17]*Automobile and the Village Merchant,* University of Illinois, Bureau of Business Research Bulletin No. 19, April, 1928.

[18]William J. Reilly, *Methods of Measurement of Retail Trade Territories,* Bureau of Business Research, University of Texas, 1928, multigraphed; *Methods for the Study of Retail Relationships,* Bureau of Business Research, University of Texas, Mon. No. 4, 1929. Also *The Law of Retail Gravitation* published by the author in 1931.

[19]Paul D. Converse, *A Study of Retail Trade Areas in East Central Illinois,* Bureau of Economic and Business Research. University of Illinois, October, 1943; *Retail Trade Areas in Illinois,* July, 1946; Paul D. Converse, "New Laws of Retail Gravitation," *Journal of Marketing,* October, 1949.

4

Influences on Development
of Marketing Thought,
1900-1923

Robert Bartels

CENTERS OF INFLUENCE UPON MARKETING THOUGHT

....The eminent marketing writers of the first two decades of this century.... found a natural attraction to universities renowned for their advanced economic thought, and the majority of the earliest marketing writers were sooner or later associated with such schools. Foremost among such institutions were the University of Wisconsin and Harvard University.

The Wisconsin Group

At the turn of the century the University of Wisconsin was a seat of progressive and liberal economic thinking, for on her campus were W.A. Scott, John R. Commons, Richard T. Ely, and H. C. Taylor. It was natural, therefore, that Wisconsin should play a leading role in the evolution of marketing thought. To her campus were attracted such pioneer students of marketing as Jones, Hagerty, Hibbard, Macklin, Nystrom, Butler, Converse, Comish, and Vaughan. Since the residence of some of these men at Madison overlapped, they were a stimulating influence upon one another.

Benjamin H. Hibbard. The impulse to study marketing came to Hibbard gradually, almost accidentally, growing for the most part out of conditions of his work. While living in northern Iowa, he had noticed for years that farmers sold their produce at a very low figure, whereas the same products were resold later at a much augmented price. In 1902, therefore, when he began teaching at Iowa State College in a small department of agricultural economics which aspired to do some research work but which

Excerpted from Robert Bartels, "Influences on Development of Marketing Thought, 1900-1923," in [Robert Bartels, ed.,] *Marketing Theory and Metatheory* (Homewood, Ill.: Richard D. Irwin, Inc., 1970), pp. 108–125. Reprinted by permission.

had no funds for such activity, he undertook a modest study of grain marketing, the novelty of which gained for him attention out of proportion to his findings.

A few years later, in 1913, Hibbard was invited to the University of Wisconsin to take charge of marketing studies and research. There he gave what was probably the first organized course in cooperative marketing of agricultural products, and he wrote a number of bulletins, particularly on the subject of marketing dairy products. In 1921, he published the book *Marketing Agricultural Products,* for which he is perhaps best known as a marketing writer.

Theodore Macklin. During the latter years of Hibbard's teaching at Iowa State College, Macklin, a student there, became interested in marketing. Immediately following his graduation in 1911, and while serving as a lecturer at the college, he assisted P. G. Holden, Director of Extension, in work which took him on observation trips throughout the state. Like Hibbard, Macklin was strongly impressed with the fact that while farmers did a fine job of producing, they did not perform the marketing task with equal effectiveness. His conviction that he should learn more about marketing led him in 1913 to the University of Wisconsin, where he studied the subject and received his Ph.D. in 1917. Macklin's selection of Wisconsin may have been influenced by Hibbard's transfer there in the same year.

Before completing his doctoral requirements, Macklin observed, studied, and taught agricultural marketing at Kansas State Agricultural College (1915-1916, 1918-1919). He became associated in 1919 with the University of Wisconsin in a professorship which continued until 1930, when he departed for California to become Chief of the State's Division of Markets. During the early years after his return to Wisconsin, he wrote his principal contribution to marketing literature, a book entitled *Efficient Marketing for Agriculture,* published in 1921.

Paul H. Nystrom. The Wisconsin terms of Nystrom, Hibbard, and Macklin overlapped by one year. Nystrom left Madison for Minnesota in 1914. During his stay in Wisconsin, he was instrumental in advancing marketing as a subject of economics; Hibbard was teaching the subject in the agricultural division of the University.

The marketing interests of Nystrom apparently were a by-product of other academic pursuits. His interest in the subject appeared relatively late in his scholastic development, arising out of his earlier experiences as a worker on farms and in retail stores until 1897, as a teacher and principal in Wisconsin schools until 1908, and as a special investigator for the Wisconsin Tax Commission during the summers of 1906, 1907, and 1908. Contrary to common procedure, it was after most of those varied activities that he proceeded to take his college training, receiving his Ph.B. in 1909, M.Ph. in 1910, and Ph.D. in 1914, all from Wisconsin. During that period of study he was also employed in the extension division of the University.

FIGURE 4-1 Lines of Personal Influence in the Development of Marketing Thought

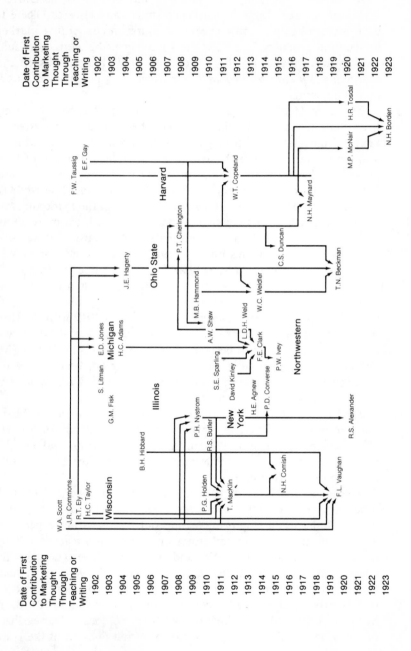

Nystrom's principal interest during those years was in economics, particularly in taxation. His interest in marketing reputedly grew partly from a study of taxation of retail establishments. In 1913, while yet an Assistant Professor of Political Economy at the University of Wisconsin, he published a book entitled *Retail Selling and Store Management.* The manuscript had been in circulation in mimeographed form as early as 1911, when it was used by extension classes of the University. He completed his graduate studies in 1914, and his doctoral dissertation was published the following year as his second book, *Economics of Retailing.*

After teaching for one year at the University of Minnesota, Nystrom interrupted his academic career with several years in business practice. From 1921-1927, he was director of the Retail Research Association and the Associated Merchandising Corporation. His writings were likewise interrupted, and not until after his return to teaching did he, in 1928, publish *The Economics of Fashion.* The contents of this book were drawn in large measure from his practical experience. Upon returning to teaching, he offered a course in the economics of consumption, and that too found ultimate expression in *The Economics of Consumption,* published in 1929.

Ralph Starr Butler.   Butler joined the staff of the University of Wisconsin in 1910 as an Assistant Professor of Business Administration, with responsibility for developing correspondence study courses in business for the University Extension Division. He went there fresh from a stimulating experience in Cincinnati as assistant to the Eastern Sales Manager of the Procter & Gamble Company, his first work in the field of marketing. He had been impressed with the fact that a manufacturer seeking to market a product had to consider and solve a large number of problems before he ever gave expression to the selling idea through salesmen or advertising. This recollection was vividly with him when he went to Wisconsin with responsibility for preparing the correspondence course.

When Butler arrived at Wisconsin, the curriculum included mostly courses which dealt with such specific business activities as bookkeeping, retail salesmanship, advertising, commercial law, courses which had prior to that time also been taught in other schools and colleges. Upon surveying the meager literature of business then available, he was astonished to find that none of it dealt with the broader considerations which lie behind the final expression of the sales idea. Since the subject had never been treated by any writer, he decided to prepare a correspondence course covering those marketing functions a manufacturer must perform before making actual use of salesmen and advertising.

After experiencing considerable difficulty in finding a name for this field of business activity, Butler finally decided upon "Marketing Methods." A course consisting of six printed pamphlets was published under that title by the University in the fall of 1910. The following year, Butler revised the same material for publication by the Alexander Hamilton Institute under the title *Selling and Buying,* as part of the fourteenth volume of its first series of textbooks. The title was changed to *Marketing* after a year or two, with further revision of the material. The only such book on the subject, it was widely used in schools and colleges for several years.

In 1911 also, Butler expanded the material and offered his course to resident students of commerce at the University. Although courses of similar content were then offered elsewhere, it is possible that Butler's was the first to use the title of "Marketing," even as his text was the first to appear with that term in the title. He later wrote some articles on marketing subjects, but his major contributions to the field have perhaps been made in his practice of marketing, during his many years as a distinguished business executive.

Newel H. Comish and *Floyd L. Vaughan.* Newel H. Comish was another marketing writer who also came under the Wisconsin influence. He took his Master's degree at Madison in 1915 and his Ph.D. in 1929. His work brought him into contact with Hibbard and Macklin, both of whom contributed to his training in the field. Very likely the influences of that environment, as well as of his own direct farm experience induced Comish later to write *The Cooperative Marketing of Agricultural Products,* published in 1929.

Floyd L. Vaughan was another early student of marketing at the University of Wisconsin, where he received his Ph.D. in 1923. Before that time he had had considerable teaching experience and had worked with the Federal Trade Commission. In 1920, with W. H. S. Stevens, he wrote on country grain marketing for *The Grain Trade,* Vol. 1. Following his work at Wisconsin, he published *Marketing and Advertising* in 1928.

Contribution of the Wisconsin Group

Thus, the men who studied, taught, and wrote of marketing at the University of Wisconsin were responsible for taking several of the initial steps in the establishment of marketing science. Attracted from different sections of the country and from both academic and practical pursuits, nurtured by the progressive atmosphere of the campus to which they gravitated, and mutually stimulated by their associations with one another, they are credited with several innovations. They crystallized the conception of this field of activity as *marketing* and were perhaps the first to use this term in the title of a course or book on the subject. They are credited with offering the first course in cooperative marketing through university extension correspondence and resident courses, and with the promotion of research in institutional as well as agricultural marketing. From that university, therefore, emanated during the early years of the century a strong influence upon the development of marketing thought and literature.

The Harvard Group

Another center of influence in the development of early marketing thought was at Cambridge, with Harvard University's Graduate School of Business Administration and its Department of Economics. The marketing contribution there has been distinguished and unique. In addition to producing much of its own marketing talent, Harvard has played a generous part in the intellectual development of other students whose residence there has been only temporary. Among the earlier contributors to marketing thought and literature who have either taught or studied at Harvard are the following: Cherington, Shaw, Copeland, Tosdal, Weidler, Maynard, McNair, Borden, and Vaile.

Paul T. Cherington. An example of the nature and importance of personal influence is found in the case of Cherington, whose interest in marketing was stimulated in part by his association with James E. Hagerty. The contact was made at the University of Pennsylvania, where Cherington was a student and Hagerty, while teaching, was assembling the material on marketing channels and institutions which constituted his Ph.D. dissertation in sociology. Cherington probably had commercial interests prior to his meeting with Hagerty, but it is understood that he acknowledged that personal contact and influence to be instrumental in molding his thought and interest in marketing.

Cherington received his B.S. in 1902 and, while carrying on graduate studies for which he received his A.M. in 1908, served also as Editor of Publications of The Philadelphia Commercial Museum. Upon leaving Philadelphia in that year, he went to Harvard University, where he taught marketing through 1935. For a number of years after that he devoted his efforts entirely to professional marketing research. As an early marketing writer, he is best known for *Advertising as a Business Force,* published in 1912, and for *The Elements of Marketing,* published in 1920.

A. W. Shaw. Shaw contributed to and partook of the Harvard influence when, about 1910, he went to Cambridge to help reorganize the new Graduate School of Business Administration. While there, he also lectured on busines policy. He wrote "Some Problems in Market Distribution" for the *Quarterly Journal of Economics* in 1912, the year of publication of the advertising book by Cherington, with whom he had close contact. His book, *An Approach to Business Problems,* was published in 1916.

Shaw's interest in marketing evidently developed after he had made notable contributions to general business practice. From the early 1900s, while in business with L. D. Walker, manufacturing office equipment, he widely observed business procedures as a means of devising improved systems and methods. Everywhere the uniformity of business needs and functions impressed him more forcibly than the diversity of circumstances in which the basic practices were found. He devoted himself, therefore, particularly through his magazine, called *System,* to advancing the interchange of ideas among businessmen, who, he felt, were retarding business progress by the narrow isolation of their individual interests and experiences. This effort to emphasize the order and uniformity of business also colored his later writings on marketing.

When he was at Harvard other factors contributed to his thinking, which resulted in the previously mentioned article entitled "Some Problems in Market Distribution." Having become more conscious of marketing activity, he was aware of the need for a name to identify the distributive activity, as Butler also had been. A German professor had made him aware of the fact that a science must have a concept. While seeking the concept for the unformulated and undescribed activity in which he was interested, his thinking was further influenced by an awareness of the constant change which pervades all things, an idea which he gained from a lecture on the religion of pure experience. Thus, he began to conceive marketing as the process of "matter in motion" and to discern therein the uniformity and order which he had found in other business practice.

At the same time he was influenced also by Dean Gay, whose lectures emphasizing the merchant in the economic history of England challenged Shaw to trace the activity of trade and its functions. At Gay's suggestion, Shaw later lectured to the former's class on what he had found out about the functions of the British merchant. The substance of the lecture became the content of the article published in the *Quarterly Journal of Economics.*

Melvin T. Copeland.   The weight of personal influence is clearly evident in the marketing career of Copeland, with respect to the factors which led him to become a specialist in knowledge of the cotton inudstry and those which stimulated his contribution to marketing literature in the form of a problems book.

His interest in the cotton industry was an outgrowth of a study made in 1906 as a graduate student in economics under the direction of Professor F. W. Taussig. The usual library research and field investigation familiarized him with the industry and its marketing activities. During the next six years, he taught economic history and economic resources of Europe at Harvard, spent a year abroad as a Traveling Fellow giving particular attention to cotton manufacturing, and returned to teach for two years at New York University. In 1912, the year of publication of his *Cotton Manufacturing Industry of The United States,* he returned to Harvard to the Graduate School of Business Administration with a specific assignment to start a course known as "Commercial Organization." Two years later the name of the course was changed to "Marketing."

Upon his return to Cambridge, his development was further influenced by his contact with Dean Gay, who, according to Copeland, had brought to the Graduate School the idea of teaching by "cases" and who required that instruction, insofar as possible, should be by discussion of problems rather than by lecturing. Copeland started to teach by this method in 1912. The following summer, as field agent of the newly established Bureau of Business Research, he gathered figures on the cost of doing business in retail shoe stores. The next year he was put in charge of a similar study of the retail grocery trade. In 1916 he was appointed Director of the Bureau of Business Research, in charge of the studies of operating expenses in various retail and wholesale trades. Thus, throughout the early years of his teaching career, Copeland was not only indoctrinated with the method of teaching from problems, but also by his experience prepared for the development and presentation of courses in that manner.

In 1919, when Wallace B. Donham became Dean of the Graduate School of Business Administration and when Copeland returned to teaching from his wartime service, one of Dean Donham's first requests was that he undertake the preparation of a problems book. This resulted in the publication of the first edition of Copeland's *Problems in Marketing*, published in 1920. In that same year, again at Dean Donham's request, the Bureau of Business Research undertook to organize a collection of problems for other courses. Copeland's continued research and contacts with business led ultimately to the publication in 1924 of his *Principles of Merchandising*.

Harry R. Tosdal.   Tosdal, like a number of other marketing writers, entered the field by way of the department of economics. Upon completion of his doctorate in 1915 at Harvard University, he taught economics at Massachusetts Institute of Technology (1915-1916), at Boston University (1916-1920), and at Harvard, as a lecturer on economics, from 1918-1920. In 1920, he became affiliated with the Graduate School of Business Administration on a full-time basis as an Associate Professor of Marketing and Director of Student Research. The following year, he published *Problems in Sales Management*.

Malcolm P. McNair.   McNair was one of the men whose training and experience were both gained at Harvard. He received two degrees there and has taught there since 1917. For the first three years, however, he instructed in government and English. In 1920, like Tosdal, he began to teach marketing. Five years later he published *Retail Method of Inventory* and, in 1926, *Problems in Retailing*.

Neil H. Borden.   The thinking of Borden concerning marketing as well as the character of some of his contributions to the field have been in some measure the product of his associations as a student and member of the staff at the Harvard Graduate School of Business Administration. Going there from the University of Colorado, where in 1919 he received his A.B. degree, he was exposed to the case method of teaching which Copeland and others had been developing for several years. Thus, not only the substance of his marketing thought but his convictions as to the method by which the subject should be taught were firmly molded by the guiding influence of his associates.

Following the completion of his M.B.A. work in 1922, he served as a case collector in the Harvard Bureau of Business Research. The following year he taught marketing under Professor Copeland, from the latter's newly published *Problems in Marketing.* He also assisted Daniel Starch in the latter's advertising course. Starch's interest in advertising came from his training as a psychologist, and, although he made some use of problems, his teaching method differed from that being developed at Harvard. When Starch left the school, Borden was put in charge of the advertising course and immediately put it on a problems basis. Out of that effort came his original edition of *Problems in Advertising,* published in 1927.

Contribution of the Harvard Group

In contrast to the University of Wisconsin, which early marketing writers left after their student days to teach elsewhere, the Harvard Graduate School retained on its teaching staff a large proportion of the early writers who studied there. Members of the Harvard staff were participants in the early development of principles of marketing, but their principal contribution throughout the years has been the compilation of marketing problems, both general and specialized.

The Middle Western Group

Notwithstanding the fact that the earliest marketing courses were offered mainly in the Middle West, the universities of that area, with the exception of Wisconsin, did not make major contributions to marketing thought and literature during the early years. That seeming paradox may have resulted not from the character of the marketing taught but from the nature of the offerings in economics. While these institutions had some notable economists on their faculties, none of them had such an aggregation of prominent economists as there were at Wisconsin and Harvard. Nevertheless, as interest in marketing grew, valuable contributions to the growing body of marketing thought were made by men working and teaching in Minnesota, Michigan, Illinois, and Ohio. Among the men of that group were Weld, Clark, Ivey, C.S. Duncan, Converse, Weidler, Maynard, and Beckman.

L. D. H. Weld. Weld was another early writer whose interest in marketing grew out of the demands of his working environment. Going to the University of Minnesota in 1912, he spent one year in the Economics Department before moving to the College of Agriculture, which was eager to develop knowledge of how Minnesota products were marketed. Farmers were particularly interested in the practice of cooperative marketing. Accordingly, Weld spent much of his time in finding out what became of products after they left the farms. He also taught one course in agricultural marketing. It is possible that the word "marketing" in the title was the first such use of the term in connection with a course on the marketing of farm products, notwithstanding the fact that Taylor and Hibbard were simultaneously covering similar ground in their course in farm management at Wisconsin.

Since there was practically no literature on the subject when Weld began to teach marketing in the fall of 1913, he had to develop his knowledge of it largely by his own resourcefulness. He studied at first hand the movement of grain through the Minneapolis Chamber of Commerce, and the use of future trading. His findings were reported to the Bureau of Markets of the U.S. Department of Agriculture, but were not published, reputedly because they put future trading and its economic functions in too favorable a light. Furthermore, he was called before a Minnesota legislative investigating committee, which tried to prove that he had been instructed by the trustees of the University to teach his dangerous doctrines about the efficiency of grain marketing through the Minneapolis Chamber of Commerce and about the beneficial functions of future trading.

In gathering information on marketing processes, Weld actually accompanied shipments of butter and eggs to the market in order to trace their course through the wholesalers, jobbers, and retailers in New York, Chicago, and other cities. He also studied pricing methods, commodity exchanges, auction markets, and the cooperative shipping associations of Minnesota.

The results of his investigations were twofold. First, he increased his knowledge of marketing for teaching purposes; second, he developed in his own mind some fundamental principles about marketing. After two years of this activity, he finished writing in 1915 *The Marketing of Farm Products,* which was published the following year, after Weld had gone to Yale. He remained at the Sheffield Scientific School for the two more years that he continued in the teaching profession. During his tenure there he continued in marketing research, with his interests mainly in the field of manufactured goods.

Another significant event of those years was perhaps the first associative effort among men interested in teaching marketing. In 1914, Weld had an opportunity to read before the American Economic Association a paper on "Market Distribution," thus making the first scientific presentation of the subject of marketing before that group. Four years later, at a meeting of the same Association in Richmond, Weld assembled five or six men who were interested in marketing for a discussion of their work. That small group, meeting annually and growing fairly rapidly, was the nucleus out of which later developed the National Association of Teachers of Marketing.

Fred E. Clark. A variety of factors contributed to the interest which Clark found in marketing. As a young man he sold house-to-house such commodities as Rand McNally Atlases, Wearever Aluminum Ware, and ironing boards. His first intellectual contact with marketing, however, was made during his graduate study, and the major influences upon his writing occurred after he had begun to teach.

Reared on a farm and schooled at Albion College, Clark went for graduate training in economics to the University of Illinois, where he was influenced by David Kinley, head of the Department of Economics and of the School of Commerce, to the end that his interests in practical economics and private business were enlarged. For his Master's thesis he chose a marketing subject, "The Cooperative Grain Elevator Movement in Illinois." Like all early students of marketing, he was much influenced by the works of such pioneers as Weld, Nystrom, Butler, Shaw, and Samuel E. Sparling of the University of Wisconsin.

From 1914 to 1919, following his academic training, Clark had a succession of one-year teaching appointments, the demands of which evidently caused him to shift his major interest from economics to marketing. By 1918 he had prepared in mimeographed form the first draft of his text, *Principles of Marketing,* which was used that year at the University of Michigan, where he was teaching. Henry C. Adams, head of the Economics Department there, gave him strong encouragement to write, as did Dean Heilman at Northwestern University, to which Clark moved in 1919. The book finally was published in 1922, after the first draft had been used as a text at Michigan, Minnesota, and Northwestern.

Paul W. Ivey.   Ivey's professional path closely paralleled that of Clark. Having taken his A.B. at Lawrence College, he did his Master's work concurrently with Clark at the University of Illinois. Each earned his degree there in 1913. Ivey, too, had a succession of teaching assignments which took him consecutively to Dakota Wesleyan, to the Universities of Michigan, Iowa, and Nebraska, and, in 1923, to Northwestern University, where by that time Clark had been for four years. After some years, he went to teach at the University of Southern California.

During his years of teaching, Ivey, like Clark, was evidently distilling from his experiences and business contacts the essence which he presented in his book, *Principles of Marketing,* published in 1921. The influences of his subsequent years evoked from him a series of publications specially related to the field of retail salesmanship.

Paul D. Converse.   The marketing interests and viewpoint of Converse were shaped significantly during his youth and college years by intellectual influences both parental and academic, which gave him a social consciousness as well as a high regard for practicality. In his father, a well-educated Presbyterian minister with interests in social reform, Converse saw, sometimes by contrast, the importance of practical applicability of theory. From his economic teachers, trained at Wisconsin, he gained a healthy respect for private property, profit, and individual initiative. From experience as an examiner for the Federal Trade Commission, he gained convictions of the soundness of "progressive" liberalism, the partiality of pressure groups, and the basic soundness of individual self-interests in the private enterprise system.

His first course in marketing was taken during a brief enrollment at the University of Wisconsin in 1915, where he studied under Ralph Starr Butler the material which appeared in the latter's book, *Marketing*. There he received the benefit of Butler's practical experience, a viewpoint which was valuable to him when, following three years of teaching at Washington and Lee, his Alma Mater, he began to teach marketing in 1915 at the University of Pittsburgh, a school characterized by a strong vocational emphasis. Because no general marketing textbooks were available, Converse had his students read Nystrom's *Economics of Retailing*. All of these influences led him to use mainly the middleman or institutional approach in his first book, *Marketing Methods and Policies,* published in 1921 while he was still teaching at Pittsburgh.

Moving to the University of Illinois in 1924, where the marketing work had been developed by Litman and Behrens, Converse came under two other influences of location. In that area he saw more clearly the importance of agricultural marketing. Away from a large metropolitan center, he de-emphasized vocational training and gave more attention to sound training in the fundamentals of marketing.

Walter C. Weidler.   One of the early students of James E. Hagerty who made a career in marketing, Weidler was enrolled during 1911-1912 in the course which Hagerty had started in 1905. As a graduate student at The Ohio State University, he briefly assisted both Hagerty and M. B. Hammond, labor economist, of whom he was also a protégé. He was faced with the decision as to whether he would specialize in marketing or in labor. On the one hand, he was better acquainted with marketing, having served an apprenticeship during earlier years in a wholesale dry goods company. He also had friends and relatives engaged in distribution. On the other hand, his intellectual interests seemed to lie in broader economic problems.

Continuing doctoral work at Harvard University, Weidler elected to take a course in marketing and applied for, but did not gain admission to, the section taught by Cherington. While taking the course with another professor, he also audited a labor course in the event that he should later wish to continue in that field. Upon his return to Ohio, however, the way opened for him to specialize in marketing rather than in labor, and ultimately he became coauthor of a text entitled *Principles of Marketing.*

C. S. Duncan.   The entrance of Duncan into the marketing field illustrates the influence of intellectual curiosity in encouraging, and the impotence of other occupational demands in preventing, the development of a genuine interest in a subject. His attention had first been drawn to marketing activity in the early 1890s while he was clerking in a general merchandise store in a small town. His many questions concerning marketing went mainly unanswered until, while teaching English at The Ohio State University and after reading a stimulating book by J. D. Whelpley entitled *Trade of the World,* he enrolled in a summer course in marketing being taught at the University of Chicago by a visiting professor, Paul Cherington. Duncan was on leave at the time to complete his doctoral requirements. That course, according to Duncan, had marked influence upon what he later thought and wrote on the subject, and showed him the possibilities of study in this field with which he had been so dimly acquainted and about which he had much curiosity. Following that course with Cherington, Duncan remained at Chicago for several years teaching marketing. His books, *Commercial Research* and *Marketing and Its Problems and Methods,* were published in 1919 and 1920, respectively.

Harold H. Maynard.   Like others whose predilection for marketing did not appear during their undergraduate years, Maynard became interested in marketing gradually, and evidently through fortuitous circumstances. As an undergraduate at Iowa State Teachers College, he was interested mainly in political science and collegiate debating. As a graduate student at the University of Iowa from 1914 to 1916, he became interested in economics and economic history. For his Master's thesis he studied credit unions, under the direction of Harvard-trained Eliot Jones. Marketing was not then taught at Iowa but, through his work in economic history, Maynard became familiar with the names and activities of prominent business leaders and developed receptivity to an interest in marketing.

Behind those intellectual influences, and in line with his interest in debating, were other experiences which contributed to this receptivity. At an early age he had done house-to-house and farm-to-farm selling. During the summers of his college years he had been business manager of a traveling Chautauqua unit and thus had not only excellent selling experience but also repeated opportunities to hear a lecture on the problems of small town merchants faced with growing chain store competition.

In 1916, Maynard enrolled in the marketing course offered at Harvard by M. T. Copeland and studied in mimeographed form some of the material which Copeland published in 1920 under the title *Problems in Marketing.* There, too, he came under the tutelage of Cherington, who replaced Copeland for the last sixty days of the term when the latter was called to Washington in connection with war work. The influence of contact with those two men was great enough to lead Maynard into the teaching of marketing after the war.

Following the war, he taught for one year at Vanderbilt University and for three years at Washington State College, before going to Ohio State in 1923 to initiate a course in Introduction to Business. Constantly he availed himself of opportunities to learn of marketing, writing a dissertation on "Marketing Northwestern Apples" while teaching retailing at Washington State College, and working in the established course in Marketing Problems at Ohio State. Having met Weidler at Harvard and having been brought to Columbus by his invitation, Maynard collaborated with him and T. N. Beckman in preparing *Principles of Marketing,* published in 1927.

Theodore N. Beckman. Beckman's discovery and pursuit of marketing interest was largely the result of an intellectual challenge. While awaiting acceptance of his application for admission to a diplomatic school with the idea of pursuing a career in the consular service, Beckman found interest in economics and business subjects at The Ohio University, where he was doing undergraduate work during the years prior to 1920. Hagerty's marketing course and the writings by Weld and Cherington helped him to see opportunities for expanding the knowledge of marketing and for correcting misconceptions therein. He renounced his diplomatic aspirations and began his career in marketing.

The inclination of his special marketing interests toward credit and wholesaling was the result of influences in his university environment. While teaching a general marketing course, and upon encouragement by Hagerty, who was also interested in the subject of credit, Beckman taught a short course in credit administration for the Columbus chapter of the Institute on Credit of the National Association of Credit Men. In preparing for this, he spent much time in credit offices of Columbus business concerns talking with credit managers. When the course was offered at the University in 1922, the inadequacy and incompleteness of the available literature and readings impelled the writing of his textbook, *Credits and Collections in Theory and Practice,* published in 1924. That book was accepted in fulfillment of the requirement for his doctoral dissertation, although for that purpose he had for considerable period been making a special study of wholesaling. Encouragement in the wholesaling study was given by C. S. Duncan, when others saw little or no profit in such an endeavor, and it too was ultimately published in book form.

Contribution of the Middle Western Group

The literary contributions of early Middle Western teachers of marketing appeared within the space of a few years around 1920 like the second of a succession of waves, the first of which had broken eight to ten years earlier in the writings of Butler, Cherington, Shaw, and Nystrom. During the decade from 1910 to 1920 early explorative concepts of marketing were refined, established, and augmented, and the study attained an integration which effectually terminated the pioneer stage of the development of marketing thought. Whereas at the beginning of the decade the field of study was delineated by the new concept and term "marketing," by the end of the decade the *principles* of marketing were being widely postulated. Students at the beginning of the century explored the marketing practices of businesses in general. Those who developed the subject ten years later, particularly at Wisconsin, specialized in the commodity analysis of marketing. Those whose contributions appeared following the First World War concentrated primarily on the functional aspects of marketing. Thus, the Middle Western group of writers contributed mainly an integration to the study of marketing, emphasizing functions and principles and treating the subject with a form and fullness which has since characterized the central body of marketing literature.

The New York Group

Although neither Columbia nor New York University made prominent contributions to marketing literature during the early years, they are deserving of mention in this review of influences. About 1920, toward the end of the period with which we are presently concerned, Hugh Agnew, whose teaching experience extended back a number of years and who was to become perhaps the first of the leading contributors to marketing thought in that area during the later years went to New York University. Nystrom and R. S. Alexander also began teaching in the New York area during the decade of the 1920s. They and others in that area who have been associated with marketing are distinguished primarily by their contributions to marketing thought developed from the institutional approach.

Hugh E. Agnew.   Employment factors were instrumental in shaping the thinking and writing of Agnew, giving emphasis to advertising and journalism. He had done typesetting on the campus paper at Hillsdale (Michigan) College, which he attended from 1893 to 1896. With this and other college publication experiences behind him, upon graduation from the University of Michigan in 1902 he bought a country newspaper. Successful direct mail advertising stimulated his interests in that means of selling and gave him a glimpse of what could be done with it.

In 1912, he took over the management of a newspaper business in Canton, Illinois. There he wrote several articles on advertising, and controversies incited by them led him to write more. In 1913, he joined the faculty of the University of Washington for a short period. He then went into advertising business until 1920, in which year he accepted simultaneously a professorship at New York University and an editorial position on *Printer's Ink*.

5

Marketing as a Science: An Appraisal

Kenneth D. Hutchinson

During the past few years one of the ways in which the increased interest in marketing subjects has expressed itself is in the rather intense exploration of the field with a view to determining the exact significance of its subject matter. More explicitly, several scholars have either attempted to demonstrate that marketing should be admitted into the category of a science, or have discussed the subject as though it already were included. Interest in the project first became apparent through the appearance of an exploratory survey made by P. D. Converse in *The Journal of Marketing.*[1] However, since this particular essay had the merit of not attempting any demonstration of the thesis that marketing is a science, one cannot be sure that the article really served as the foundation of future discussions on the problem.

At the time that Professor Converse wrote, regard for the application of scientific methodology to marketing problems was an increasing force, and the momentum of this interest carries on today. Three years later, Lyndon O. Brown discussed the need for the development of professional standards among marketing men in an essay which tended in the main not to regard the subject as a science, except possibly in one cloudy passage.[2] The question of the status of marketing appeared to be developing some urgency in the minds of numerous marketing scholars because in the next issue of the *Journal* there appeared a very thoughtful and searching article exploring the notion of developing a theory of marketing.[3] The authors were quite circumspect in writing this essay, omitting any direct reference to marketing as a science. Little doubt was left in the minds of the readers, however, that the authors considered marketing to be a unified body of thought; and from this one can infer that they suspect that it is a science.

Reprinted from Kenneth D. Hutchinson, "Marketing as a Science: An Appraisal," in *Journal of Marketing,* Vol. 16 (January 1952), pp. 286–93, published by the American Marketing Association.

At least one marketing scholar received this impression from that essay for, in the *Journal* the following spring, Roland S. Vaile wrote a communication[4] commenting on that point of view. If anyone held illusions as to the character of marketing, Professor Vaile's article should have removed them; but marketing men apparently have great tenacity and refuse to give up easily. Although the conclusion of this essay was that marketing did not have the earmarks of a science, the question of whether this was true was to be raised again on later occasions. In 1951 a new essay was presented on the question by Robert Bartels,[5] who concluded that marketing was indeed a science and entitled to respect as such.

It would be misleading to consider this latter essay as an isolated instance; the ferment which had been started in the minds of students of marketing was working steadily and other evidences of this conclusion (that marketing is a science) can be found. The Cox and Alderson article, to which reference has been made, led to a book of essays on marketing theory;[6] in some of these are further references to the science of marketing.[7] This compilation of essays affords a rather varied fare for the scholar seeking enlightenment on the true nature of marketing. Points of view differed and there were some who indicated their conviction that there was no such thing as a theory of marketing, and hence also, no science of marketing.[8]

REASONS FOR CONFUSION

This disagreement, or confusion, in the minds of marketing students over the nature of their field arises in no small part from the comprehensive character and variety of activities embraced by the term marketing. Three distinct types of activity are discernible. First, there is a group of activities which center around the day-to-day distribution of goods and services. Second, there are those activities which center around the interpretation of the subject in schools and colleges. Third, there is a group of activities which arises out of the explorations by market research men working on specific problems, some of which have rather broad implications. With these three different approaches to the field there would naturally arise some differences in viewpoints.

Of the first group, those whose job it is to distribute goods, almost no one would contend seriously that they are engaged in some form of scientific endeavor; wholesalers and retailers hardly fit the mold of scientists. Neither the second group, the teachers, nor the third group, the market research men, is so easily disposed of, particularly since some of them are concerned with systematizing the subject. All are interested in employing scientific methodology in the field. Members of these two groups have pressed the case most earnestly for the inclusion of marketing among the fields of science. We have seen, however, that there has been no unanimity of opinion among them. Their work with the scientific method has induced many of them to broaden their scopes, and it is to those who have attempted to demonstrate that marketing is a science that this essay is directed.

In appraising the progress that has been made in developing a science of marketing, one is tempted to make allowances for the relatively short period of time in which the issues have been under discussion. But after making whatever allowances are called for, one is likely to be somewhat disappointed over the lack of progress to date. One should expect far more in the way of results if the venture is to prove successful, and the dearth of progress to date lends the suspicion that the project is ill-advised. There seems to be little evidence to support the claim that all that is needed is time and patience until there will energe the new and shining science of marketing.

TWO APPROACHES TO DEMONSTRATING
THAT MARKETING IS A SCIENCE

In attempting to demonstrate that marketing is a science, two lines of approach to the problem are discernible. The first of these might pass under the name of the semantic approach according to which the various essayists wrestle with dictionary meanings, warping them and twisting them, until at last marketing is seen to have fulfilled many, though not all, of the requisite characteristics of a science. The pseudoprecision of this method may be highly admirable even though it lacks some perspective. A somewhat fairer interpretation of such semantic exercises might reasonably lead to the conclusion merely that marketing has now become a field for human study. Since there are many fields of study, and since not all of them are sciences, such a conclusion should not be looked upon as any great step forward.[9]

To be more explicit, a homely example might be drawn: the field of carpentry could conceivably turn out to be such a field of study. There are books written on the subject; it is taught in schools; and it concerns itself with human experience. Furthermore it has empirical laws of a sort (those of gravity and leverage, for example) and perhaps some theoretical ones (whether screws or nails are preferable in certain jobs). Now all this pedantry does not create a science out of the trade of carpentry; but it illustrates how pseudoscientific word jugglng might be used to convert many humble human activities into recognized sciences. Something of this sort is now appearing in marketing literature. The function of business, however, is the economic production and marketing of goods and services; if we insist, therefore, that marketing is a science, we must be prepared to admit manufacturing and finance. Unless one wants to broaden his conception of science so as to include nearly all human activity, he is not likely to achieve success in making marketing a science through this process of distorting the meaning of words.

The second approach to the task of demonstrating the scientific character of marketing might be called the economic. Students of marketing interested in "practical" as well as academic matters seem to find the time-worn theories of neoclassical economics to be unsatisfying or downright inapplicable. This has led to a wholesale onslaught on many of the time-honored concepts in which, curiously enough, they find many economists sympathetic. For some years economists themselves have been trying to free their subject from the fetters placed there by the static assumptions inherited from the classical school traditions. Some progress is being made in modernizing economic doctrines but there still remain numerous concepts which lack realism. It has been this factor which has encouraged students of marketing to pursue further the task of clarification; in fact—such work was essential.[10]

The result of such interest in economic theory is that considerable study by marketing theorists has been devoted to developing more refreshing viewpoints and more workable concepts. A review of progress to date indicates that much of it has stemmed from the practice of holding economic theories up to a critical light for reexamination. One might naturally wonder whether all this analysis is serving only to enrich current economic doctrines rather than to further the development of an independent set of marketing theories. From the standpoint of overall human understanding, such efforts of marketing men are probably not in vain. In the long run it may well turn out that theoretical economists have derived benefits from having their concepts held up to this different type of scrutiny. Marketing students will also benefit through the possession of a better tool of analysis which this criticism may produce.

In looking over the work of marketing theorists it appears that considerable effort has been expended in attacking the generally accepted, or "orthodox," if you will, doctrines which relate to price setting. It is apparently true that much of this body of thought has been erected upon a foundation which contains some rather unrealistic assumptions, and certainly some which appear foreign to a marketer. Thus far, however, the contributions of marketing theorists to economic theory of pricing remain restricted to the field of criticism. If one were to seek evidence of constructive scholarship along these lines he would discover that no notable body of new theory has been brought forth to replace the seemingly discredited notions. An even harsher observation could be made: the probing of marketers into economic theory has tended more to becloud than to clarify the issues. In casting the light of realism upon this field such a result may well have been unavoidable. It should be interesting to inspect a few of the concepts which have had their clarity dimmed.

To the neoclassical economist the concept of price was reasonably clear, whereas to the new marketing theorists there is no great certainty as to what is meant by the term. To them, price represents a wide composite of characteristics which are subject to notable variances which can conceivably differ with each transaction. Another concept which seemed to give the economist little trouble was that of a commodity. Under the new scrutiny, this also turns out to possess less clarity, varying to some extent from transaction to transaction, a fact which accounts for the varying prices. Although some attention has been directed by marketing theorists to such other concepts as competition, monopoly, market controls, and freedom of entry, it can be said with fair reliability that human comprehension of these subjects has been very little advanced. Whether one is inclined to agree with these immediate conclusions is of no great importance; what does seem to be important is the fact that marketing scholars can never expect to develop their own body of theory merely by critical appraisal of the shortcomings of another one. In time, some positive contributions must be forthcoming if the desired goal is to be achieved.

MARKETING NOT A SCIENCE

There is a real reason, however, why the field of marketing has been slow to develop a unique body of theory. It is a simple one: marketing is not a science. It is rather an art or a practice, and as such much more closely resembles engineering, medicine, and architecture than it does physics, chemistry, or biology. The medical profession sets us an excellent example, if we would but follow it; its members are called "practitioners" and not scientists. It is the work of physicians, as it is of any practitioner, to apply the findings of many sciences to the solution of problems. Among the sciences which the medical man employs are biology, physiology, chemistry, physics, psychology, and many more. Engineers and architects are also practitioners who make use of chemistry, physics, psychology and other sciences. It is a characteristic of a practice that the solution of each problem faced calls for a different and distinct combination of techniques and approaches. The fact that each problem is different, however, does not deter practitioners from approaching them in the scientific manner and spirit.[11]

What constitutes a science is a question which has been settled in general for centuries, but from time to time the issues arise again as new subjects are held up for scrutiny. Within modern times the areas of social study, the socio-economic fields, have caused considerable debate over the character of science itself. The trouble with attacking this problem from a semantic point of view is that words have multiple meanings and one is enabled to prove almost anything, and almost nothing, by careful selection of the definition which seems to fit his case. Since we are using words in this essay, we are in danger of falling into the same trap in trying to show that marketing is *not* a science that others have fallen into by trying to show that it *is* one, particularly when their demonstration has depended heavily upon the twist of word meanings. A much sounder approach to the problem would seem to be upon the ground of human experience, contrasting the place of science in human affairs with that of the arts.

Science is a word we apply to a multitude of varying activities carried on by man in his effort to understand his environment. For centuries man has attempted to comprehend the planetary processes which are all parts of the great universe of knowledge. It should be unnecessary in this age and with this group of readers to labor this particular concept; it might be more profitable to return to it after we have discussed the field of the arts.

The arts is also a comprehensive term covering human activities of a wide scope. To satisfy his wants, mankind has engaged in various practices over the centuries; as time has gone on, these practices have tended to become more complex. The various arts are those related to obtaining food, preparing clothing, and obtaining shelter, along with others which are related to aesthetic satisfactions. Man found early that he could thrive much better if he did not attempt to produce all of his commodities but instead would exchange some of his output with a neighbor who had a surplus of some other product. Early barter and later market transactions are the true predecessors of modern marketing. The forbears of modern marketing men were great merchants, not great scientists. It is the drollest travesty to relate the scientist's search for knowledge to the market research man's seeking after customers.

RELATIONSHIP BETWEEN MARKETING AND THE SCIENCES

What then is the relationship existing between the sciences and marketing if indeed there be one? The answer to this query has already been indicated but perhaps should be restated. Men of science have come to develop a systematic approach to their problems which is known as the scientific method. Hypotheses are developed, facts are gathered to support or confute the hypotheses, and then tests are conducted to see if hypotheses are sound. In actual research work, the techniques employed vary with the problem at hand but the spirit of careful analysis and testing is not relaxed. Engineers and physicians are trained to approach their problems in this spirit of scientific inquiry; marketing men are learning rapidly to follow their examples. What must be realized is that the method is open for all to use and that the employment of it does not necessarily make the user a scientist nor his subject a science. A physician who studies all of his patient's symptoms before prescribing, and who keeps checking up on the progress of his treatments, is still a practitioner and not a scientist.

Such a conclusion must be inevitable or else the gates will be opened to include almost all types of human activity under the heading of sciences. Dry cleaners often approach a problem in a scientific manner but dry cleaning is not a science, nor are road building, paint mixing, poultry raising and countless other human arts. The processes which culminate in getting goods from mines, fields, and factories into the hands of consumers with the least expenditure of time, effort and money are not those that will fit into the mold of a science. That many marketing problems call for extensive computations and calculations cannot be denied nor can the fact that the best approach to them is through some variant of the scientific method of investigation, trial and test. In actual practice, however, many, and probably most, of the decisions in the field resemble the scientific method no more closely than what is involved in reading a road map or a time table. If one remains unconvinced, he must be prepared to admit into the brotherhood of new sciences the fields of retailing, wholesaling and presumably salesmanship.

The arts and practices seem to differ from the sciences in still another respect. When problems present themselves to practitioners there is almost without exception rather serious urgency to have them solved. An engineering project must be put through immediately; a sick patient must be helped now; and a sales manager wants his analysis of the market from his research man as soon as (and usually sooner than) is possible. Any market research man who is working on a problem whose answer may not be found for another generation, or perhaps a century, would be an exception whereas such a circumstance is commonplace among the sciences where immediacy tends more to be the exception. At best this point of difference between the arts and the sciences is probably only a symptomatic effect rather than an underlying force separating the two.

Thinking along these lines has become confused in the minds of some individuals because of the tendency of scientists to desert their fields of research to attack some current practical problem. When a scientist leaves his field of scientific investigation to solve a difficult problem, he drops the role of a scientist seeking to expand man's grasp over the universe; he is no longer engaged in pushing out the frontiers of knowledge. At that point he becomes a practitioner in a role similar to the engineer, the physician and the architect. A physicist who leaves his pursuit of science to construct a machine (except one to further an experiment) becomes an engineer, even though one with a superior training in physics. The point being made here is not a new one, having been well settled in other fields of learning; but the truth of it seems to have been overlooked by numerous marketing men.

We do not intend to deny here that scientists should turn their attention to the solution of human problems, nor are we attempting to indicate that scientific endeavor should lack applicability. No claim is being presented here for the advantages of pure research, that form of activity which seems to do little more than satisfy the curiosity of some investigator. Science has a purpose; its function is to help mankind to understand his universe. Whether men will use the knowledge or will even misuse it is not the particular concern of the scientist. At present writing the problem of cancer is one of great concern to several fields of science and each one is developing an attack upon it. Some investigators are approaching the problem from the standpoint of the effect of behavior patterns upon its cause. Others study the structure of human cells, still others the effects of drugs, and still others the effects of radiation, and so on. This is a practical problem which science is trying to solve; but how any given patient suffering from the disease is to be treated is a problem for the practitioner.

The real dilemma of the marketing research man is that his own field of learning is inadequate to permit proper diagnoses and prescriptions, but that the other fields upon which he should be able to lean are themselves still in somewhat beginning stages. It may seem unfair to a 175-year-old science such as economics to classify it as "beginning," but one has only to examine the protests of marketing men over many economic concepts to learn the tenuous nature of economic principles. Sociology and psychology are also just beginning to build up a body of reliable doctrine and are far from complete tools for analysis. The market research man needs knowledge of population trends, consumer preferences, price trends, and purchasing power, merely to name a few of the concepts on which exact information is lacking. It is unfortunate that marketing research has to depend upon the numerous and inexact social sciences.[12]

While we are examining the place of marketing among the various fields of learning and activity, one further point should be made. Marketing men not infrequently contribute to one of the several sciences upon which they depend. In trying to find information to solve his immediate problem he may strike upon some principle which actually enlarges the science involved. Market problems vary widely in scope. Some are of almost no social consequence, being chiefly competitive in nature; others are broader in character and depend for solution upon a wide understanding of social forces and of human behavior. It is in the pursuit of these solutions that contributions to the fields of science result. Such additions to the universal body of knowledge must be looked upon as by-products of market research, and not its chief purpose.

Beyond such small contributions, however, there is an area in which marketing scholars can produce profound results in the sciences. There is evidence that already some of this work is being done. By focusing the attention of scientists upon those concepts which are inadequately developed, the inquiring minds of marketing men can do much to give useful direction to scientific investigation. Already, students of economics, sociology, and psychology are feeling the impact of this curiosity and are tending to advance knowledge along the lines demanded. Engineers and physicians have in their turn exerted powerful influences over the direction which scientific research should take. This aspect should not be overlooked in our quest for progress in the field.

CONCLUSION

An examination of the factors involved indicates that marketing is not a science, since it does not conform to the basic characteristics of a science. A much more realistic view shows it to be an art, in the practice of which reliance must be placed upon the findings of many sciences. Marketing research men, like engineers and physicians, have to adopt a scientific approach to their problems, but their relation to the fields of science are even closer than this. Although at times they may make a contribution to some field of science, their chief contribution should be that of directing the course of scientific investigation along the lines most needed.

NOTES

[1]P. D. Converse, "The Development of a Science of Marketing," *Journal of Marketing,* Vol. X, No. 1 (July 1945), p. 14.

[2]Lyndon O. Brown, "Toward a Profession of Marketing," *Journal of Marketing,* Vol. XIII, No. 1 (July 1948), p. 27. Brown states that there is a need for "precise raw materials which are the foundation of any science, and in turn the art of the practitioner in any field."

[3]W. Alderson and R. Cox, "Towards a Theory of Marketing," *Journal of Marketing,* Vol. XIII, No. 2 (October 1948), p. 137.

[4]Roland S. Vaile, "Toward a Theory of Marketing—A Comment," *Journal of Marketing,* Vol. XIII, No. 4 (April 1949), p. 520.

[5]Robert Bartels, "Can Marketing Be A Science?," *Journal of Marketing,* Vol. XV, No. 3 (January 1951), p. 319.

[6]R. Cox and W. Alderson, eds., *Theory in Marketing* (Chicago: Richard D. Irwin, Inc., 1950).

[7]In *Theory in Marketing,* C. West Churchman, in the essay "Basic Research in Marketing," discusses market research as though the field were a science. W. Alderson, in "Survival and Adjustment in Organized Behavior," refers to "the science of marketing." E. R. Hawkins, "Vertical Price Relationships," after making some penetrating analyses of economic theory, leaves the impression that marketing is a part of the science of economics.

[8]In the same work, G. L. Mehren, in the essay "The Theory of the Firm and Marketing," says that "there is no theory of marketing." E. T. Grether, in "A Theoretical Approach to the Analysis of Marketing," takes a cautious view of theorizing in the field, as does Oswald Knauth, in "Marketing and Managerial Enterprise."

[9]Dr. Bartels recognizes this widespread characteristic of marketing in the article referred to previously. After discussing the characteristics of an art, a discipline, and a science, he concludes that there is much in favor of accepting the subject of marketing as a science.

[10]Evidence of this concern for clarification and modification of economic theory can be found in Cox and Alderson, *Theory in Marketing.* Essays which are chiefly critiques of economic doctrines are: R. G. Gettell, "Pluralistic Competition;" E. T. Grether, "A Theoretical Approach to the Analysis of Marketing;" G. L. Mehren, "The Theory of the Firm and Marketing;" R. S. Vaile, "Economic Theory and Marketing;" E. R. Hawkins, "Vertical Price Relationships;" R. Cassady, Jr., "The Time Element and Demand Analysis;" A. G. Abramson, "Public Policy and the Theory of Competition;" R. Cox, "Quantity Limits and the Theory of Economic Opportunity;" and J. Dean, "Market Competition under Uniform F.O.B. Pricing."

[11]This point of view was expressed somewhat differently by R. S. Vaile in the *Journal of Marketing* article cited previously.

[12]We are accepting for present purposes the idea that economics and sociology are sciences, being fully aware that controversies exist over this point.

6

Marketing and Economic Development

Peter F. Drucker

MARKETING AS A BUSINESS DISCIPLINE

The distinguished pioneer of marketing, whose memory we honor today, was largely instrumental in developing marketing as a systematic business discipline—in teaching us how to go about, in an orderly, purposeful, and planned way to find and create customers; to identify and define markets; to create new ones and promote them; to integrate customers' needs, wants, and preferences, and the intellectual and creative capacity and skills of an industrial society, toward the design of new and better products and of new distributive concepts and processes.

On this contribution and similar ones of the founding fathers of marketing during the last half century rests the rapid emergence of marketing as perhaps the most advanced, certainly the most "scientific" of all functional business disciplines.

But Charles Coolidge Parlin also contributed as a founding father toward the development of marketing as a *social discipline.* He helped give us the awareness, the concepts, and the tools that make us understand marketing as a dynamic process of society through which business enterprise is integrated productively with society's purposes and human values. It is in marketing, as we now understand it, that we satisfy individual and social values, needs, and wants—be it through producing goods, supplying services, fostering innovation, or creating satisfaction. Marketing, as we have come to understand it, has its focus on the customer, that is, on the individual making decisions within a social structure and within a personal and social value system. Marketing is thus the process through which economy is integrated into society to serve human needs.

Reprinted from Peter F. Drucker, "Marketing and Economic Development" in the *Journal of Marketing* (January 1958), pp. 252–59, published by the American Marketing Association. The article was based on the Charles Coolidge Parlin Memorial Lecture sponsored by the Philadelphia Chapter of the American Marketing Association in 1957.

I am not competent to speak about marketing in the first sense, marketing as a functional discipline of business. I am indeed greatly concerned with marketing in this meaning. One could not be concerned, as I am, with the basic institutions of industrial society in general and with the management of business enterprise in particular, without a deep and direct concern with marketing. But in this field I am a consumer of marketing alone—albeit a heavy one. I am not capable of making a contribution. I would indeed be able to talk about the wants and needs I have which I, as a consumer of marketing, hope that you, the men of marketing, will soon supply—a theory of pricing, for instance, that can serve, as true theories should, as the foundation for actual pricing decisions and for an understanding of price behavior; or a consumer-focused concept and theory of competition. But I could not produce any of these "new products" of marketing which we want. I cannot contribute myself. To use marketing language, I am not even "effective demand," in these fields as yet.

THE ROLE OF MARKETING

I shall...confine myself to the second meaning in which marketing has become a discipline: The role of marketing in economy and society. And I shall single out as my focus the role of marketing in the economic development especially of underdeveloped "growth" countries.

My thesis is very briefly as follows. Marketing occupies a critical role in respect to the development of such "growth" areas. Indeed marketing is the most important "multiplier" of such development. It is in itself in every one of these areas the least developed, the most backward part of the economic system. Its development, above all others, makes possible economic integration and the fullest utilization of whatever assets and productive capacity an economy already possesses. It mobilizes latent economic energy. It contributes to the greatest needs: that for the rapid development of entrepreneurs and managers, and at the same time it may be the easiest area of managerial work to get going. The reason is that, thanks to men like Charles Coolidge Parlin, it is the most systematized and, therefore, the most learnable and the most teachable of all areas of business management and entrepreneurship.

INTERNATIONAL AND INTERRACIAL INEQUALITY

Looking at this world of ours, we see some essentially new facts. For the first time in man's history the whole world is united and unified. This may seem a strange statement in view of the conflicts and threats of suicidal wars that scream at us from every headline. But conflict has always been with us. What is new is that today all of mankind shares the same vision, the same objective, the same goal, the same hope, and believes in the same tools. This vision might, in gross oversimplification, be called "industrialization."

It is the belief that it is possible for man to improve his economic lot through systematic, purposeful, and directed effort—individually as well as for an entire society. It is the belief that we have the tools at our disposal—the technological, the conceptual, and the social tools—to enable man to raise himself, through his own efforts, at least to a level that we in this country would consider poverty, but which for most of our world would be almost unbelievable luxury.

And this is an irreversible new fact. It has been made so by these true agents of revolution in our times: the new tools of communication—the dirt road, the truck, and the radio, which have penetrated even the furthest, most isolated, and most primitive community.

This is new, and cannot be emphasized too much and too often. It is both a tremendous vision and a tremendous danger in that catastrophe must result if it cannot be satisfied, at least to a modest degree.

But at the same time we have a new, unprecedented danger, that of international and interracial inequality. We on the North American continent are a mere tenth of the world population, including our Canadian friends and neighbors. But we have at least seventy-five per cent of the world income. And the seventy-five per cent of the world population whose income is below $100 per capita a year receive together perhaps no more than ten per cent of the world's income. This is inequality of income, as great as anything the world has ever seen. It is accompanied by very high equality of income in the developed countries, especially in ours where we are in the process of proving that an industrial society does not have to live in extreme tension between the few very rich and the many very poor as lived all earlier societies of man. But what used to be national inequality and economic tension is now rapidly becoming international (and unfortunately also interracial) inequality and tension.

This is also brand new. In the past there were tremendous differences between societies and cultures: in their beliefs, their concepts, their ways of life, and their knowledge. The Frankish knight who went on Crusade was an ignorant and illiterate boor, according to the standards of the polished courtiers of Constantinople or of his Moslem enemies. But economically his society and theirs were exactly alike. They had the same sources of income, the same productivity of labor, the same forms and channels of investment, the same economic institutions, and the same distribution of income and wealth. Economically the Frankish knight, however much a barbarian he appeared, was at home in the societies of the East; and so was his serf. Both fitted in immediately and without any difficulty.

And this has been the case of all societies that went above the level of purely primitive tribe.

The inequality in our world today, however, between nations and races, is therefore a new—and a tremendously dangerous—phenomenon.

What we are engaged in today is essentially a race between the promise of economic development and the threat of international worldwide class war. The economic development is the opportunity of this age. The class war is the danger. Both are new. Both are indeed so new that most of us do not even see them as yet. But they are the essential economic realities of this industrial age of ours. And whether we shall realize the opportunity or succumb to danger will largely decide not only the economic future of this world—it may largely decide its spiritual, its intellectual, its political, and its social future.

SIGNIFICANCE OF MARKETING

Marketing is central in this new situation, for marketing is one of our most potent levers to convert the danger into the opportunity.

To understand this we must ask: What do we mean by "underdeveloped"?

The first answer is, of course, that we mean areas of very low income. But income is, after all, a result. It is a result first of extreme agricultural overpopulation in which the great bulk of the people have to find a living on the land which, as a result, cannot even produce enough food to feed them, let alone produce a surplus. It is certainly a result of low productivity. And both, in a vicious circle, mean that there is not enough capital for investment, and very low productivity of what is being invested—owing largely to misdirection of investment into unessential and unproductive channels.

All this we know today and understand. Indeed we have learned during the last few years a very great deal both about the structure of an underdeveloped economy and about the theory and dynamics of economic development.

What we tend to forget, however, is that the essential aspect of an "underdeveloped" economy and the factor the absence of which keeps it "underdeveloped," is the inability to organize economic efforts and energies, to bring together resources, wants, and capacities, and so to convert a self-limiting static system into creative, self-generating organic growth.

And this is where marketing comes in.

Lack of Development in "Underdeveloped" Countries

First, in every "underdeveloped" country I know of, marketing is the most underdeveloped—or the least developed—part of the economy, if only because of the strong, pervasive prejudice against the middleman.

As a result, these countries are stunted by inability to make effective use of the little they have. Marketing might by itself go far toward changing the entire economic tone of the existing system—without any change in methods of production, distribution of population, or of income.

It would make the producers capable of producing marketable products by providing them with standards, with quality demands, and with specifications for their product. It would make the product capable of being brought to markets instead of perishing on the way. And it would make the consumer capable of discrimination, that is, of obtaining the greatest value for his very limited purchasing power.

In every one of these countries, marketing profits are characteristically low. Indeed the people engaged in marketing barely eke out a subsistence living. And "markups" are minute by our standards. But marketing costs are outrageously high. The waste in distribution and marketing, if only from spoilage or from the accumulation of unsalable inventories that clog the shelves for years, has to be seen to be believed. And marketing service is by and large all but nonexistent.

What is needed in any "growth" country to make economic development realistic, and at the same time produce a vivid demonstration of what economic development can produce, is a marketing system: a system of physical distribution, a financial system to make possible the distribution of goods, and finally actual marketing, that is, an actual system of integrating wants, needs, and purchasing power of the consumer with capacity and resources of production.

This need is largely masked today because marketing is so often confused with the traditional "trader and merchant" of which every one of these countries has more than enough. It would be one of our most important contributions to the development of "underdeveloped" countries to get across the fact that marketing is something quite different.

It would be basic to get across the triple function of marketing—the function of crystallizing and directing demand for maximum productive effectiveness and efficiency; the function of guiding production purposefully toward maximum consumer satisfaction and consumer value; the function of creating discrimination that then gives rewards to those who really contribute excellence, and that then also penalizes the monopolist, the slothful, or those who only want to take but do not want to contribute or to risk.

Utilization by the Entrepreneur

Marketing is also the most easily accessible "multiplier" of managers and entrepreneurs in an "underdeveloped" growth area. And managers and entrepreneurs are the foremost need of these countries. In the first place, "economic development" is not a force of nature. It is the result of the action, the purposeful, responsible, risk-taking action, of men as entrepreneurs and managers.

Certainly it is the entrepreneur and manager who alone can convey to the people of these countries an understanding of what economic development means and how it can be achieved.

Marketing can convert latent demand into effective demand. It cannot, by itself, create purchasing power. But it can uncover and channel all purchasing power that exists. It can, therefore, create rapidly the conditions for a much higher level of economic activity than existed before, can create the opportunities for the entrepreneur.

It then can create the stimulus for the development of modern, responsible, professional management by creating opportunity for the producer who knows how to plan, how to organize, how to lead people, how to innovate.

In most of these countries markets are of necessity very small. They are too small to make it possible to organize distribution for a single-product line in any effective manner. As a result, without a marketing organization, many products for which there is an adequate demand at a reasonable price cannot be distributed; or worse, they can be produced and distributed only under monopoly conditions. A marketing system is needed which serves as the joint and common channel for many producers if any of them is to be able to come into existence and to stay in existence.

This means in effect that a marketing system in the "underdeveloped" countries is the *creator of small business,* is the only way in which a man of vision and daring can become a businessman and an entrepreneur himself. This is thereby also the only way in which a true middle class can develop in the countries in which the habit of investment in productive enterprise has still to be created.

Developer of Standards

Marketing in an "underdeveloped" country is the developer of standards—of standards for product and service as well as of standards of conduct, of integrity, of reliability, of foresight, and of concern for the basic long-range impact of decisions on the customer, the supplier, the economy, and the society.

Rather than go on making theoretical statements let me point to one illustration: The impact Sears Roebuck has had on several countries of Latin America. To be sure, the countries of Latin American in which Sears operates—Mexico, Brazil, Cuba, Venezuela, Colombia, and Peru—are not "underdeveloped" in the same sense in which Indonesia or the Congo are "underdeveloped." Their average income, although very low by our standards, is at least two times, perhaps as much as four or five times, that of the truly "underdeveloped" countries in which the bulk of mankind still live. Still in every respect except income level these Latin American countries are at best "developing." And they have all the problems of economic development—perhaps even in more acute form than the countries of Asia and Africa, precisely because their development has been so fast during the last ten years.

It is also true that Sears in these countries is not a "low-price" merchandiser. It caters to the middle class in the richer of these countries, and to the upper middle class in the poorest of these countries. Incidentally, the income level of these groups is still lower than that of the worker in the industrial sector of our economy.

Still Sears is a mass-marketer even in Colombia or Peru. What is perhaps even more important, it is applying in these "underdeveloped" countries exactly the same policies and principles it applies in this country, carries substantially the same merchandise (although most of it produced in the countries themselves), and applies the same concepts of marketing it uses in Indianapolis or Philadelphia. Its impact and experience are, therefore, a fair test of what marketing principles, marketing knowledge, and marketing techniques can achieve.

The impact of this one American business which does not have more than a mere handful of stores in these countries and handles no more than a small fraction of the total retail business of these countries is truly amazing. In the first place, Sears' latent purchasing power has fast become actual purchasing power. Or, to put it less theoretically, people have begun to organize their buying and to go out for value in what they do buy.

Secondly, by the very fact that it builds one store in one city, Sears forces a revolution in retailing through the whole surrounding area. It forces store modernization. It forces consumer credit. It forces a different attitude toward the customer, toward the store clerk, toward the supplier, and toward the merchandise itself. It forces other retailers to adopt modern methods of pricing, of inventory control, of training, of window display, and what have you.

The greatest impact Sears has had, however, is the multiplication of new industrial business for which Sears creates a marketing channel. Because it has had to sell goods manufactured in these countries rather than import them (if only because of foreign exchange restrictions), Sears has been instrumental in getting established literally hundreds of new manufacturers making goods which, a few years ago, could not be made in the country, let alone be sold in adequate quantity. Simply to satisfy its own marketing needs, Sears has had to insist on standards of workmanship, quality, and delivery—that is, on standards of production management, of technical management, and above all of the management of people—which, in a few short years, have advanced the art and science of management in these countries by at least a generation.

I hardly need to add that Sears is not in Latin America for reasons of philanthropy, but because it is good and profitable business with extraordinary growth potential. In other words, Sears is in Latin America because marketing is the major opportunity in a "growth economy"— precisely because its absence is a major economic gap and the greatest need.

The Discipline of Marketing

Finally, marketing is critical in economic development because marketing has become so largely systematized, so largely both learnable and teachable. It is the discipline among all our business disciplines that has advanced the furthest.

I do not forget for a moment how much we still have to learn in marketing. But we should also not forget that most of what we have learned so far we have learned in a form we can express in general concepts, in valid principles and, to a substantial degree, in quantifiable measurements. This, above all others, was the achievement of that generation to whom Charles Coolidge Parlin was leader and inspiration.

A critical factor in this world of ours is the learnability and teachability of what it means to be an entrepreneur and manager. For it is the entrepreneur and the manager who alone can cause economic development to happen. The world needs them, therefore, in very large number and it needs them fast.

Obviously this need cannot be supplied by our supplying entrepreneurs and managers, quite apart from the fact that we hardly have the surplus. Money we can supply. Technical assistance we can supply, and should supply more. But the supply of men we can offer to the people in the "underdeveloped" countries is of necessity a very small one.

The demand is also much too urgent for it to be supplied by slow evolution through experience, or through dependence on the emergence of "naturals." The danger that lies in the inequality today between the few countries that have and the great many countries that have not is much too great to permit a wait of centuries. Yet it takes centuries if we depend on experience and slow evolution for the supply of entrepreneurs and managers adequate to the needs of a modern society.

There is only one way in which man has ever been able to short-cut experience, to telescope development, in other words, to *learn something.* That way is to have available the distillate of experience and skill in the form of knowledge, of concepts, of generalization, of measurement—in the form of *discipline,* in other words.

THE DISCIPLINE OF ENTREPRENEURSHIP

Many of us today are working on the fashioning of such a discipline of entrepreneurship and management. Maybe we are further along than most of us realize.

Certainly in what has come to be called "Operation Research and Synthesis" we have the first beginnings of a systematic approach to the entrepreneurial task of purposeful risk-taking and innovation—so far only an approach, but a most promising one, unless indeed we become so enamored with the gadgets and techniques as to forget purpose and aim.

We are at the beginning perhaps also of an understanding of the basic problems of organizing people of diversified and highly advanced skill and judgment together in one effective organization, although again no one so far would, I am convinced, claim more for us that that we have begun at last to ask intelligent questions.

But marketing, although it only covers one functional area in the field, has something that can be called a discipline. It has developed general concepts, that is, theories that explain a multitude of phenomena in simple statements. It even has measurements that record "facts" rather than opinions. In marketing, therefore, we already possess a learnable and teachable approach to this basic and central problem not only of the "underdeveloped" countries but of all countries. All of us have today the same survival stake in economic development. The risk and danger of international and interracial inequality are simply too great.

Marketing is obviously not a cure-all, not a paradox. It is only one thing we need. But it answers a critical need. At the same time marketing is most highly developed.

Indeed, without marketing as the hinge on which to turn, economic development will almost have to take the totalitarian form. A totalitarian system can be defined economically as one in which economic development is being attempted without marketing, indeed as one in which marketing is suppressed. Precisely because it first looks at the values and wants of the individual, and because it then develops people to act purposefully and responsibly—that is, because of its effectiveness in developing a free economy—marketing is suppressed in a totalitarian system. If we want economic development in freedom and responsibility, we have to build it on the development of marketing.

In the new and unprecedented world we live in, a world that knows both a new unity of vision and growth and a new and most dangerous cleavage, marketing has a special and central role to play. This role goes beyond "getting the stuff out the back door," beyond "getting the most sales with the least cost," beyond "the optimal integration of our values and wants as customers, citizens, and persons, with our productive resources and intellectual achievements"—the role marketing plays in a developed society.

In a developing economy, marketing is, of course, all of this. But in addition, in an economy that is striving to break the age-old bondage of man to misery, want, and destitution, marketing is also the catalyst for the transmutation of latent resources into actual resources, of desires into accomplishments, and the development of responsible economic leaders and informed economic citizens.

7

Broadening the Concept
of Marketing

Philip Kotler and Sidney J. Levy

The term "marketing" connotes to most people a function peculiar to business firms. Marketing is seen as the task of finding and stimulating buyers for the firm's output. It involves product development, pricing, distribution, and communication; and in the more progressive firms, continuous attention to the changing needs of customers and the development of new products, with product modifications and services to meet these needs. But whether marketing is viewed in the old sense of "pushing" products or in the new sense of "customer satisfaction engineering," it is almost always viewed and discussed as a business activity.

It is the authors' contention that marketing is a pervasive societal activity that goes considerably beyond the selling of toothpaste, soap, and steel. Political contests remind us that candidates are marketed as well as soap; student recruitment by colleges reminds us that higher education is marketed; and fund raising reminds us that "causes" are marketed. Yet these areas of marketing are typically ignored by the student of marketing. Or they are treated cursorily as public relations or publicity activities. No attempt is made to incorporate these phenomena in the body proper of marketing thought and theory. No attempt is made to redefine the meaning of product development, pricing, distribution, and communication in these newer contexts to see if they have a useful meaning. No attempt is made to examine whether the principles of "good" marketing in traditional product areas are transferable to the marketing of services, persons, and ideas.

The authors see a great opportunity for marketing people to expand their thinking and to apply their skills to an increasingly interesting range of

Reprinted from Philip Kotler and Sidney J. Levy, "Broadening the Concept of Marketing," in the *Journal of Marketing,* Vol. 33 (January 1969), pp. 10–15, published by the American Marketing Association.

social activity. The challenge depends on the attention given to it; marketing will either take on a broader social meaning or remain a narrowly defined business activity.

THE RISE OF ORGANIZATIONAL MARKETING

One of the most striking trends in the United States is the increasing amount of society's work being performed by organizations other than business firms. As a society moves beyond the stage where shortages of food, clothing, and shelter are the major problems, it begins to organize to meet other social needs that formerly had been put aside. Business enterprises remain a dominant type of organization, but other types of organizations gain in conspicuousness and influence. Many of these organizations become enormous and require the same rarefied management skills as traditional business organizations. Managing the United Auto Workers, Defense Department, Ford Foundation, World Bank, Catholic Church, and University of California has become every bit as challenging as managing Procter and Gamble, General Motors, and General Electric. These nonbusiness organizations have an increasing range of influence, affect as many livelihoods, and occupy as much media prominence as major business firms.

All of these organizations perform the classic business functions. Every organization must perform a financial function insofar as money must be raised, managed, and budgeted according to sound business principles. Every organization must perform a production function in that it must conceive of the best way of arranging inputs to produce the outputs of the organization. Every organization must perform a personnel function in that people must be hired, trained, assigned, and promoted in the course of the organization's work. Every organization must perform a purchasing function in that it must acquire materials in an efficient way through comparing and selecting sources of supply.

When we come to the marketing function, it is also clear that every organization performs marketing-like activities whether or not they are recognized as such. Several examples can be given.

The police department of a major U.S. city, concerned with the poor image it has among an important segment of its population, developed a campaign to "win friends and influence people." One highlight of this campaign is a "visit your police station" day in which tours are conducted to show citizens the daily operations of the police department, including the crime laboratories, police lineups, and cells. The police department also sends officers to speak at public schools and carries out a number of other activities to improve its community relations.

Most museum directors interpret their primary responsibility as "the proper preservation of an artistic heritage for posterity."[1] As a result, for many people museums are cold marble mausoleums that house miles of relics that soon give way to yawns and tired feet. Although museum attendance in the United States advances each year, a large number of citizens are uninterested in museums. Is this indifference due to failure in the manner of presenting what museums have to offer? This nagging question led the new director of the Metropolitan Museum of Art to broaden the museum's appeal through sponsoring contemporary art shows and "happenings." His marketing philosophy of museum management led to substantial increases in the Met's attendance.

The public school system in Oklahoma City sorely needed more public support and funds to prevent a deterioration of facilities and exodus of teachers. It recently resorted to television programming to dramatize the work the public schools were doing to fight the high school dropout problem, to develop new teaching techniques, and to enrich the children. Although an expensive medium, television quickly reached large numbers of parents whose response and interest were tremendous.

Nations also resort to international marketing campaigns to get across important points about themselves to the citizens of other countries. The junta of Greek colonels who seized power in Greece in 1967 found the international publicity surrounding their cause to be extremely unfavorable and potentially disruptive of international recognition. They hired a major New York public relations firm and soon full-page newspaper ads appeared carrying the headline "Greece Was Saved From Communism," detailing in small print why the takeover was necessary for the stability of Greece and the world.[2]

An anticigarette group in Canada is trying to press the Canadian legislature to ban cigarettes on the grounds that they are harmful to health. There is widespread support for this cause but the organization's funds are limited, particularly measured against the huge advertising resources of the cigarette industry. The group's problem is to find effective ways to make a little money go a long way in persuading influential legislators of the need for discouraging cigarette consumption. This group has come up with several ideas for marketing antismoking to Canadians, including television spots, a paperback book featuring pictures of cancer and heart disease patients, and legal research on company liability for the smoker's loss of health.

What concepts are common to these and many other possible illustrations of organizational marketing? All of these organizations are concerned about their "product" in the eyes of certain "consumers" and are seeking to find "tools" for furthering their acceptance. Let us consider each of these concepts in general organizational terms.

Products

Every organization produces a "product" of at least one of the following types:

Physical products.   "Product" first brings to mind everyday items like soap, clothes, and food, and extends to cover millions of *tangible* items that have a market value and are available for purchase.

Services.   Services are *intangible* goods that are subject to market transaction, such as tours, insurance, consultation, hairdos, and banking.

Persons.   Personal marketing is an endemic *human* activity, from the employee trying to impress his boss to the statesman trying to win the support of the public. With the advent of mass communications, the marketing of persons has been turned over to professionals. Hollywood stars have their press agents, political candidates their advertising agencies, and so on.

Organizations.   Many organizations spend a great deal of time marketing themselves. The Republican Party has invested considerable thought and resources in trying to develop a modern look. The American Medical Association decided recently that it needed to launch a campaign to improve the image of the American doctor.[3] Many charitable organizations and universities see selling their *organization* as their primary responsibility.

Ideas.   Many organizations are mainly in the business of selling *ideas* to the larger society. Population organizations are trying to sell the idea of birth control, and the Women's Christian Temperance Union is still trying to sell the idea of prohibition.

Thus the "product" can take many forms, and this is the first crucial point in the case for broadening the concept of marketing.

Consumers

The second crucial point is that organizations must deal with many groups that are interested in their product and can make a difference in its success. It is vitally important to the organization's success that it be sensitive to, serve, and satisfy these groups. One set of groups can be called the *suppliers. Suppliers* are those who provide the management group with the inputs necessary to perform its work and develop its product effectively. Suppliers include employees, vendors of the materials, banks, advertising agencies, and consultants.

The other set of groups are the *consumers* of the organization's product, of which four subgroups can be distinguished. The *clients* are those who are the immediate consumers of the organization's product. The clients of a business firm are its buyers and potential buyers; of a service organization those receiving the services, such as the needy (from the Salvation Army) or the sick (from County Hospital); and of a protective or a primary organization, the members themselves. The second group is the *trustees* or *directors,* those who are vested with the legal authority and responsibility for the organization, oversee the management, and enjoy a variety of benefits from the "product." The third group is the active *publics* that take a specific interest in the organization. For a business firm, the active publics include consumer rating groups, governmental agencies, and pressure groups of various kinds. For a university, the active publics include alumni and friends of the university, foundations, and city fathers. Finally, the fourth consumer group is the *general public.* These are all the people who might develop attitudes toward the organization that might affect its conduct in some way. Organizational marketing concerns the programs designed by management to create satisfactions and favorable attitudes in the organization's four consuming groups: clients, trustees, active publics, and general public.

Marketing Tools

Students of business firms spend much time studying the various tools under the firm's control that affect product acceptance: product improvement, pricing, distribution, and communication. All of these tools have counterpart applications to nonbusiness organizational activity.

Nonbusiness organizations to various degrees engage in product improvement, especially when they recognize the competition they face from other organizations. Thus, over the years churches have added a host of nonreligious activities to their basic religious activities to satisfy members seeking other bases of human fellowship. Universities keep updating their curricula and adding new student services in an attempt to make the educational experience relevant to the students. Where they have failed to do this, students have sometimes organized their own courses and publications, or have expressed their dissatisfaction in organized protest. Government agencies such as license bureaus, police forces, and taxing bodies are often not responsibe to the public because of monopoly status; but even here citizens have shown an increasing readiness to protest mediocre services, and more alert bureaucracies have shown a growing interest in reading the user's needs and developing the required product services.

All organizations face the problem of pricing their products and services so that they cover costs. Churches charge dues, universities charge tuition, governmental agencies charge fees, fund-raising organizations send out bills. Very often specific product charges are not sufficient to meet the organization's budget, and it must rely on gifts and surcharges to make up the difference. Opinions vary as to how much the users should be charged for the individual services and how much should be made up through general collection. If the university increases its tuition, it will have to face losing some students and putting more students on scholarship. If the hospital raises its charges to cover rising costs and additional services, it may provoke a reaction from the community. All organizations face complex pricing issues although not all of them understand good pricing practice.

Distribution is a central concern to the manufacturer seeking to make his goods conveniently accessible to buyers. Distribution also can be an important marketing decision area for nonbusiness organizations. A city's public library has to consider the best means of making its books available to the public. Should it establish one large library with an extensive collection of books, or several neighborhood branch libraries with duplication of books? Should it use bookmobiles that bring the books to the customers instead of relying exclusively on the customers coming to the books? Should it distribute through school libraries? Similarly the police department of a city must think through the problem of distributing its protective services efficiently through the community. It has to determine how much protective service to allocate to different neighborhoods; the respective merits of squad cars, motorcycles, and foot patrolmen; and the positioning of emergency phones.

Customer communication is an essential activity of all organizations although many nonmarketing organizations often fail to accord it the importance it deserves. Managements of many organizations think they have fully met their communication responsibilities by setting up advertising and/or public relations departments. They fail to realize that *everything about an organization talks.* Customers form impressions of an organization from its physical facilities, employees, officers, stationery, and a hundred other company surrogates. Only when this is appreciated do the members of the organization recognize that they all are in marketing, whatever else they do. With this understanding they can assess realistically the impact of their activities on the consumers.

CONCEPTS FOR EFFECTIVE MARKETING MANAGEMENT IN NONBUSINESS ORGANIZATIONS

Although all organizations have products, markets, and marketing tools, the art and science of effective marketing management have reached their highest state of development in the business type of organization. Business organizations depend on customer goodwill for survival and have generally learned how to sense and cater to their needs effectively. As other types of organizations recognize their marketing roles, they will turn increasingly to the body of marketing principles worked out by business organizations and adapt them to their own situations.

What are the main principles of effective marketing management as they appear in most forward-looking business organizations? Nine concepts stand out as crucial in guiding the marketing effort of a business organization.

Generic Product Definition

Business organizations have increasingly recognized the value of placing a broad definition on their products, one that emphasizes the basic customer need(s) being served. A modern soap company recognizes that its basic product is cleaning, not soap; a cosmetics company sees its basic product as beauty or hope, not lipsticks and makeup; a publishing company sees it basic product as information, not books.

The same need for a broader definition of its business is incumbent upon nonbusiness organizations if they are to survive and grow. Churches at one time tended to define their product narrowly as that of producing religious services for members. Recently, most churchmen have decided that their basic product is human fellowship. There was a time when educators said that their product was the three R's. Now most of them define their product as education for the whole man. They try to serve the social, emotional, and political needs of young people in addition to intellectual needs.

Target Groups Definition

A generic product definition usually results in defining a very wide market, and it is then necessary for the organization, because of limited resources, to limit its product offering to certain clearly defined groups within the market. Although the generic product of an automobile company is transportation, the company typically sticks to cars, trucks, and buses, and stays away from bicycles, airplanes, and steamships. Furthermore, the manufacturer does not produce every size and shape of car but concentrates on producing a few major types to satisfy certain substantial and specific parts of the market.

In the same way, nonbusiness organizations have to define their target groups carefully. For example, in Chicago the YMCA defines its target groups as men, women, and children who want recreational opportunities and are willing to pay $20 or more a year for them. The Chicago Boys Club, on the other hand, defines its target group as poorer boys within the city boundaries who are in want of recreational facilities and can pay $1 a year.

Differentiated Marketing

When a business organization sets out to serve more than one target group, it will be maximally effective by differentiating its product offerings and communications. This is also true for nonbusiness organizations. Fund-raising organizations have recognized the advantage of treating clients, trustees, and various publics in different ways. These groups require differentiated appeals and frequency of solicitation. Labor unions find that they must address different messages to different parties rather than one message to all parties. To the company they may seem unyielding, to the conciliator they may appear willing to compromise, and to the public they seek to appear economically exploited.

Customer Behavior Analysis

Business organizations are increasingly recognizing that customer needs and behavior are not obvious without formal research and analysis; they cannot rely on impressionistic evidence. Soap companies spend hundreds of thousands of dollars each year researching how Mrs. Housewife feels about her laundry, how, when, and where she does her laundry, and what she desires of a detergent.

Fund raising illustrates how an industry has benefited by replacing stereotypes of donors with studies of why people contribute to causes. Fund raisers have learned that people give because they are getting something. Many give to community chests to relieve a sense of guilt because of their elevated state compared to the needy. Many give to medical charities to relieve a sense of fear that they may be struck by a disease whose cure has not yet been found. Some give to feel pride. Fund raisers have stressed the importance of identifying the motives operating in the market place of givers as a basis for planning drives.

Differential Advantages

In considering different ways of reaching target groups, an organization is advised to think in terms of seeking a differential advantage. It should consider what elements in its reputation or resources can be exploited to create a special value in the minds of its potential customers. In the same way Zenith has built a reputation for quality and International Harvester a reputation for service, a nonbusiness organization should base its case on some dramatic value that competitive organizations lack. The small island of Nassau can compete against Miami for the tourist trade by advertising the greater dependability of its weather; the Heart Association can compete for funds against the Cancer Society by advertising the amazing strides made in heart research.

Multiple Marketing Tools

The modern business firm relies on a multitude of tools to sell its product, including product improvement, consumer and dealer advertising, salesman incentive programs, sales promotions, contests, multiple-size offerings, and so forth. Likewise nonbusiness organizations also can reach their audiences in a variety of ways. A church can sustain the interest of its members through discussion groups, newsletters, news releases, campaign drives, annual reports, and retreats. Its "salesmen" include the religious head, the board members, and the present members in terms of attracting potential members. Its advertising includes announcements of weddings, births and deaths, religious pronouncements, and newsworthy developments.

Integrated Marketing Planning

The multiplicity of available marketing tools suggests the desirability of overall coordination so that these tools do not work at cross purposes. Over time, business firms have placed under a marketing vice-president activities that were previously managed in a semiautonomous fashion, such as sales, advertising, and marketing research. Nonbusiness organizations typically have not integrated their marketing activities. Thus, no single officer in the typical university is given total responsibility for studying the needs and attitudes of clients, trustees, and publics, and undertaking the necessary product development and communication programs to serve these groups. The university administration instead includes a variety of "marketing" positions such as dean of students, director of alumni affairs, director of public relations, and director of development; coordination is often poor.

Continuous Marketing Feedback

Business organizations gather continuous information about changes in the environment and about their own performance. They use their salesmen, research department, specialized research services, and other means to check on the movement of goods, actions of competitors, and feelings of customers to make sure they are progressing along satisfactory lines. Nonbusiness organizations typically are more casual about collecting vital information on how they are doing and what is happening in the market place. Universities have been caught off guard by underestimating the magnitude of student grievance and unrest, and so have major cities underestimated the degree to which they were failing to meet the needs of important minority constituencies.

Marketing Audit

Change is a fact of life, although it may proceed almost invisibly on a day-to-day basis. Over a long stretch of time it might be so fundamental as to threaten organizations that have not provided for periodic reexaminations of their purposes. Organizations can grow set in their ways and unresponsive to new opportunities or problems. Some great American companies are no longer with us because they did not change definitions of their businesses, and their products lost relevance in a changing world. Political parties become unresponsive after they enjoy power for a while and every so often experience a major upset. Many union leaders grow insensitive to new needs and problems until one day they find themselves out of office. For an organization to remain viable, its management must provide for periodic audits of its objectives, resources, and opportunities. It must reexamine its basic business, target groups, differential advantage, communication channels, and messages in the light of current trends and needs. It might recognize when change is needed and make it before it is too late.

IS ORGANIZATIONAL MARKETING A SOCIALLY USEFUL ACTIVITY?

Modern marketing has two different meanings in the minds of people who use the term. One meaning of marketing conjures up the terms selling, influencing, persuading. Marketing is seen as a huge and increasingly dangerous technology, making it possible to sell persons on buying things, propositions, and causes they either do not want or which are bad for them. This was the indictment in Vance Packard's *Hidden Persuaders* and numerous other social criticisms, with the net effect that a large number of persons think of marketing as immoral or entirely self-seeking in its fundamental premises. They can be counted on to resist the idea of organizational marketing as so much "Madison Avenue."

The other meaning of marketing unfortunately is weaker in the public mind; it is the concept of sensitively *serving and satisfying human needs*. This was the great contribution of the marketing concept that was promulgated in the 1950s, and that concept now counts many business firms as its practitioners. The marketing concept holds that the problem of all business firms in an age of abundance is to develop customer loyalties and satisfaction, and the key to this problem is to focus on the customer's needs.[4] Perhaps the short-run problem of business firms is to sell people on buying the existing products, but the long-run problem is clearly to create the products that people need. By this recognition that effective marketing requires a consumer orientation instead of a product orientation, marketing has taken a new lease on life and tied its economic activity to a higher social purpose.

It is this second side of marketing that provides a useful concept for all organizations. All organizations are formed to serve the interest of particular groups: hospitals serve the sick, schools serve the students, governments serve the citizens, and labor unions serve the members. In the course of evolving, many organizations lose sight of their original mandate, grow hard, and become self-serving. The bureaucratic mentality begins to dominate the original service mentality. Hospitals may become perfunctory in their handling of patients, schools treat their students as nuisances, city bureaucrats behave like petty tyrants toward the citizens, and labor unions try to run instead of serve their members. All of these actions tend to build frustration in the consuming groups. As a result some withdraw meekly from these organizations, accept frustration as part of their condition, and find their satisfactions elsewhere. This used to be the common reaction of ghetto Negroes and college students in the face of indifferent city and university bureaucracies. But new possibilities have arisen, and now the same consumers refuse to withdraw so readily. Organized dissent and protest are seen to be an answer, and many organizations thinking of themselves as responsible have been stunned into recognizing that they have lost touch with their constituencies. They have grown unresponsive.

Where does marketing fit into this picture? Marketing is that function of the organization that can keep in constant touch with the organization's consumers, read their needs, develop "products" that meet these needs, and build a program of communications to express the organization's purposes. Certainly selling and influencing will be large parts of organizational marketing; but, properly seen, selling follows rather than precedes the organization's drive to create products to satisfy its consumers.

CONCLUSION

It has been argued here that the modern marketing concept serves very naturally to describe an important facet of all organizational activity. All organizations must develop appropriate products to serve their sundry consuming groups and must use modern tools of communication to reach their consuming publics. The business heritage of marketing provides a useful set of concepts for guiding all organizations.

The choice facing those who manage nonbusiness organizations is not whether to market or not to market, for no organization can avoid marketing. The choice is whether to do it well or poorly, and on this necessity the case for organizational marketing is basically founded.

NOTES

[1]This is the view of Sherman Lee, Director of the Cleveland Museum, quoted in *Newsweek*, Vol. 71 (April 1, 1968), p. 55.

[2]"PR for the Colonels," *Newsweek*, Vol. 71 (March 18, 1968), p. 70.

[3]"Doctors Try an Image Transplant," *Business Week*, No. 2025 (June 22, 1968), pp. 64.

[4]Theodore Levitt, "Marketing Myopia," *Harvard Business Review*, Vol. 38 (July-August 1960), pp. 45-56.

8

Broadening the Concept of Marketing—Too Far

David J. Luck

The article by Philip Kotler and Sidney Levy in the January 1969 *Journal of Marketing* is intriguing and imaginative.[1] It also is based on premises which may lead to confusion regarding the essential nature of marketing. Further, it suggests a disparaging attitude toward the social benefits of our professional field. When such views are propounded by prominent authors, their uncritical acceptance seems likely. Therefore, one who vigorously (although respectfully) disagrees should voice his contrary opinions.

CONCEPT OR DEFINITION

Kotler and Levy's main thesis is that the "concept" of marketing is too limited because it excludes marketing in nonbusiness activities. They complain that marketing is "a narrowly defined business activity" whose nonbusiness usage has not been incorporated "in the body of marketing thought and theory." They seem to be asking that marketing be redefined, but they do not offer any explicit, new definition of marketing. The definition and demarcation of a field of knowledge is a basic matter that should be given searching concern.

How should marketing's definition be altered to satisfy their contentions? They contend that marketing affirms numerous "concepts" or "principles" [*sic*] which are applicable to a universal range of human activities or institutions, specifically including: political contests, police administration, employee recruitment, social welfare agencies, hospital services, education, labor unions, international relations, and organized religion. Thus, if the Heart Fund conducts a campaign to obtain

Reprinted from David J. Luck, "Broadening the Concept of Marketing—Too Far," in the *Journal of Marketing,* Vol. 33 (July 1969), pp. 53–63, published by the American Marketing Association.

contributions, it is engaging in marketing. If a clergyman is studying plans for his church's services to parishioners or the community, he, too, is engaging in marketing.

If a definition were framed to meet the authors' contentions, marketing no longer would be bounded in terms of either institutions or the ultimate purpose of its activities. If a task is performed, anywhere by anybody, that has some resemblance to a task performed in marketing, that would be marketing. Therefore, any institution that plans its services or future would be performing the marketing task of "product planning." The clergyman who was pondering his church's programs and had considered himself to be a theologian and spiritual leader turns out to be a marketer.

Before becoming so proprietary, it should be recognized that the marketing profession did not originate most of the concepts noted by the authors. For example, the authors indicate that the reexamination of "target groups, differential advantage, communication channels, and messages" constitutes a *marketing* audit—wherever this is performed. However, it should be noted that political leaders and parties were conducting these activities thousands of years before marketing existed as a field of serious study. Marketers' self-image may be pleasurably inflated by claiming that political campaigns are just another part of marketing, but what progress is to be gained by such reasoning? If one has tried to explain to someone the nature of marketing, with the present limited definition, he will have found it difficult. Attenuate marketing's definition to make it almost universal, and it will wholly lose its identity.

When seeking to annex the territory hitherto claimed by other disciplines, one is engaging in a game two can play. Marketers are much indebted to sociologists for concepts, data, and methods. How would sociologists be regarded if they were claiming for themselves most of the "consumer behavior" area of marketing? The field of management, with equal logic, might lay claim to all of marketing management.

PROPER BOUNDARIES OF MARKETING

A manageable, intelligible and logical definition of marketing can be fashioned when its scope is bounded with those processes of activities whose ultimate result is a *market transaction*. Marketing is concerned with markets, of course, and markets must be characterized by buying-and-selling. When one closely examines the nature and goal orientation of a persuasive campaign outside of marketing, such as a membership campaign of a labor union (one of the authors' examples), in contrast with the promotion of a marketed service (for example, life insurance), he is impressed with fundamental differences. By employing a firm, specific criterion in marketing's definition—that of the ultimate purchase-and-sale of a product or service—the vagueness and open-endedness of Kotler and Levy's "concept" is avoided.

This seems to rule most of the authors' examples out of bounds. A church does not sell its religious and redemptive services. Political parties do not sell specific services (unless corruptly committing illegal acts). The Heart Fund does not sell donations: there is no established price or terms of sale, and the donor is given no specific *quid pro quo*. Thus, a particular act must be related to an eventual or intended offer to buy and/or sell a specified good or service—with the terms of sale specified between the parties—or that act is not a *marketing* act, regardless of its nature.

This does not exclude marketing from nonbusiness institutions. The Government Printing Office, the New Jersey Turnpike, and the Women's Guild Bazaar at the church are all conducting marketing. Nor does this definition deter marketing specialists from rendering services to nonmarketing causes. Individual marketers may lend their talents to United Fund drives, political campaigns, or church program planning; however, marketers *qua* marketers do not perform these activities by definition.

THE BREADTH OF MARKETING

Let us return to the authors' contention that, in the currently accepted definition of marketing, it is a "narrowly defined business activity." How can one view the enormous scope of marketing and consider it to be "narrowly defined"?

It is pertinent to point out the obvious, that marketing is performed by some three million business firms, in addition to many nonbusiness enterprises in the United States alone. Marketing is concerned, too, with every consumer who buys or barters for goods and services. The utter fascination of marketing lies in its endless diversity, its ubiquitous performance, and its seemingly countless variables and unsolved problems —when defined *within* the bounds of activities ultimately concerned with buy-and-sell transactions. If marketers ever approach the solution of its myriad problems and are bored with any monotony that they find in it, it will be time to complain about its "narrow" definition.

WHY APOLOGIZE?

Kotler and Levy perhaps should be lauded since they are in company with other notables who have been declaring that marketing has not accomplished its societal goals. They are urging us to join those who are doing social good, and what could be more noble? They want us to justify ourselves by applying our "skills to an increasingly interesting range of *social* activity." (Italics added)

Perhaps the motives underlying such declarations are that marketers have guilt feelings because profit-making business activities may not be socially beneficial. If such logic were followed, it could be determined that the Post Office Department is a "societal activity" and United Airlines is not. The former is (notoriously) a nonprofit institution, while the latter earns substantial profit in providing its services. Those who patronize both the Post Office and United Airlines, however, might opine that the latter renders a more efficient or extensive service to society.

Social welfare largely depends much more on the private enterprise system and its marketing activities than on nonprofit institutions. Approximately 90 per cent of the United States gross national product is created and marketed by profit-seeking enterprise. Thus, such enterprise appears to be the mainstay of health, nutrition, and most other aspects of the affluent society. The marketing system works imperfectly at best, and there are pressing social needs which must be met with goods and services that are not bought and sold. All thinking men want to see the nonbusiness aspects of our society performed properly by other agencies when private or governmental businesses cannot or should not provide them. However, this is no reason to distort and attenuate the scope of "marketing" in order that we may see marketing participate where it does not.

The "we're not yet societal" syndrome is becoming fashionable to an unfortunate degree. It would divert marketers from the stern and difficult dedications to identifying marketing problems and their solutions and from energetically promoting the recognition and practice of efficient, responsive marketing. Those who give unselfish dedication to laboring effectively in nonprofit and nonmarketing institutions are applauded and everyone is urged to spare whatever efforts are possible in aiding and supporting them. However, let us not apologize for being marketers in the real sense. In the understanding and improvement of the marketing system lie all the challenges that one could desire.

NOTE

[1]Philip Kotler and Sidney J. Levy, "Broadening the Concept of Marketing," *Journal of Marketing,* Vol. 33 (January 1969), pp. 10-15.

9

Interdisciplinary
Horizons in Marketing

William Lazer and Eugene J. Kelley

The interdisciplinary approach to marketing includes utilization of contributions of the social and behavioral sciences, the physical sciences, and various areas of business administration and economics. The strength of the total approach lies in the addition of new dimensions and more meaningful perspectives to various marketing concepts, development of improved techniques for solving marketing problems, integration of findings and theories with marketing practice, and the development of a more widely applicable and generally useful body of marketing knowledge.

The potential promise of an interdisciplinary approach to the development of marketing theory was discussed by Wroe Alderson and Reavis Cox a decade ago. They wrote "that here and there in the literature of several intellectual disciplines are appearing the elements from which an adequate theory of marketing will be constructed."[1]

There has not yet been, however, any substantial acceptance of the development of a truly interdisciplinary approach to marketing knowledge. The use of other disciplines in marketing to date may be characterized as multidisciplinary.

Individual marketers have brought specific problems to psychologists, sociologists, anthropologists, social psychologists, and other behavioral scientists. In many instances these specialists were able to find solutions. The problems were studied, however, from the limited perspectives of particular subject-matter areas. As a result, the needed cross-fertilization of ideas and the integration necessary to obtain more widely applicable generalizations and marketing concepts have not occurred on any large scale.

The point of departure and the focus of study differ with each of the disciplines underlying marketing. But there are frequently great similarities in the methodology and content of marketing and that of other disciplines.

Reprinted from William Lazer and Eugene J. Kelley, "Interdisciplinary Horizons in Marketing," in the *Journal of Marketing,* Vol. 25 (October 1960), pp. 24–30, published by the American Marketing Association.

Marketing progress can be furthered by studying the similarities among disciplines rather than emphasizing the differences.

FIGURE 9-1 **Behavioral Science Contributions to Selected Marketing Management Problems**

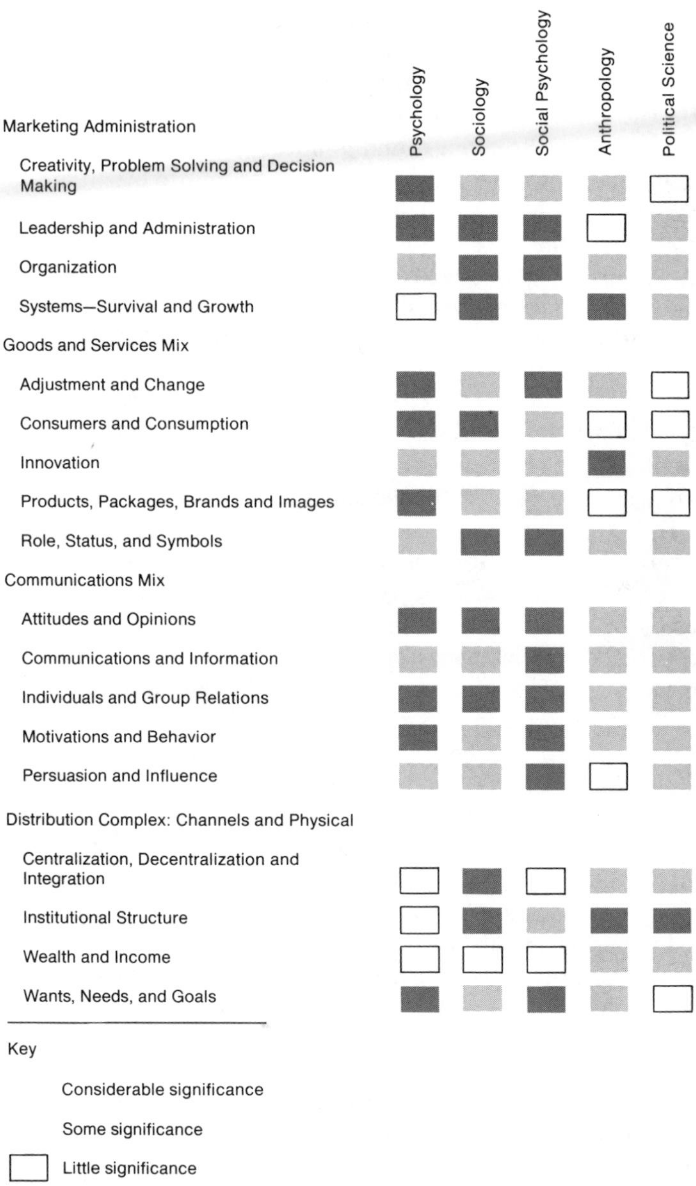

Marketing Administration	Psychology	Sociology	Social Psychology	Anthropology	Political Science
Creativity, Problem Solving and Decision Making	Considerable	Some	Some	Some	Little
Leadership and Administration	Considerable	Considerable	Considerable	Little	Some
Organization	Some	Considerable	Considerable	Some	Some
Systems—Survival and Growth	Little	Considerable	Some	Considerable	Some
Goods and Services Mix					
Adjustment and Change	Considerable	Some	Considerable	Some	Little
Consumers and Consumption	Considerable	Considerable	Some	Little	Little
Innovation	Some	Some	Some	Considerable	Some
Products, Packages, Brands and Images	Considerable	Some	Some	Little	Little
Role, Status, and Symbols	Some	Considerable	Considerable	Some	Some
Communications Mix					
Attitudes and Opinions	Considerable	Considerable	Considerable	Some	Some
Communications and Information	Some	Some	Considerable	Some	Some
Individuals and Group Relations	Considerable	Considerable	Considerable	Some	Some
Motivations and Behavior	Considerable	Some	Considerable	Some	Some
Persuasion and Influence	Some	Some	Considerable	Little	Some
Distribution Complex: Channels and Physical					
Centralization, Decentralization and Integration	Little	Considerable	Little	Some	Some
Institutional Structure	Little	Considerable	Some	Considerable	Considerable
Wealth and Income	Little	Little	Little	Some	Some
Wants, Needs, and Goals	Considerable	Some	Considerable	Some	Little

Key

Considerable significance

Some significance

Little significance

BEHAVIORAL SCIENCE CONTRIBUTIONS TO MARKETING

Figure 9-1 relates specific behavioral science concepts to particular problems being faced by marketing management. It illustrates the value of the interdisciplinary approach in extending the frontiers of marketing knowledge and in helping to solve marketing problems. For example, such concepts as communication and information, motivation and behavior, creativity, problem solving, and decision making have significant implications for effective marketing management. They are being investigated from different vantage points by such disciplines as psychology, sociology, social psychology, anthropology, and political science.

Topics of interest to marketing managers are grouped according to four major marketing problem areas in figure 9-1. These areas are marketing administration and the three major components of an integrated marketing program. A unified goal-directed marketing program and its resulting marketing mix is comprised of three submixes. These are the *goods-and-service mix,* which includes product and pricing elements; the *communications mix,* which includes the functional areas of advertising, sales promotion, and personal selling; and the *distribution mix,* which is comprised of channels of distribution and physical distribution activities. The figure illustrates the significance of the findings of several behavioral sciences to marketing management in solving specific problems within each of these areas.

These rankings are an attempt to relate in broad terms the degree of significance of the concepts. They were determined after an investigation of the literature of psychology, sociology, social psychology, anthropology, and several business administration areas. Specialists in these disciplines were consulted to substantiate the rankings. The rankings are necessarily subjective. Further research may result in modifications.

Many of the concepts cannot be conveniently classified as belonging to only one discipline. As intensive investigations are conducted into specific topics from an interdisciplinary perspective and as the multidimensional nature of concepts becomes more apparent, such tables will become more complex.

Psychologists, sociologists, anthropologists, and other social and behavioral scientists are not necessarily any more unified in the concepts they hold of their disciplines than are marketers. Complete agreement does not exist among these scientists as to the most promising lines of development for particular aspects of their subject-matter areas. The important marketing-subject area of motivation is an example. Motivation has been studied at considerable length by psychologists and other behavioral scientists. Rather than any one unified approach emerging, at least three major directions are being followed by psychologists studying motivation.[2]

First, there is the approach of laboratory psychologists who have tended to focus upon the physiological aspects of psychology. Then, there are clinical psychologists who have concentrated on the role of certain psychological factors in motivation. This group tends to minimize the biological drives as influencing human motivation and behavior. The third approach is represented by Gestalt psychologists, particularly Kurt Lewin and his followers. Of the three, this latter approach may have the greatest significance for marketing people in studying human motives and other related questions.

This Gestalt approach is essentially socio-psychological in nature. It stresses the thesis that people do react to environmental factors. From the Gestalt viewpoint, motivations and behavior are analyzed as a function of the particular person, his inherent drives, and of the immediate environment of which he is a part.

These three different psychological approaches are cited to indicate that in the disciplines underlying marketing a variety of theories and avenues to the understanding of human behavior may exist. The basic problems in utilizing behavioral science concepts in marketing management are to evaluate and reconcile the various theoretical explanations and research findings relating to a subject. The attempt to integrate numerous, and often conflicting, explanations of behavioral scientists into a practicable solution can become a highly perplexing experience.

Also, for many of the problems facing marketing management, the behavioral sciences do not as yet offer useful concepts or methods. Indeed, "the behavioral sciences as they now stand do not provide a large reservoir of immediately useful analytical concepts and models."[3] This is not a reason for ignoring the promise of these disciplines. It is a challenge to begin realizing the potential.

INTERDISCIPLINARY CONTRIBUTIONS TO MEASUREMENT IN MARKETING

Marketing practitioners and teachers are aware of the numerous measurement methods that have been developed by various subject-matter areas. The interdisciplinary approach has been used by many measurement tools such as scaling and ranking techniques, personnel tests, various projective techniques, interviewing and questionnaire methods, statistical sampling and measurements, and mathematical models and programming.

Figure 9-2 specifies some of the more promising contributions to measurement in marketing by five disciplines: sociology, psychology, social psychology, statistics, and operations research. It lists specific measurement techniques from each discipline which have been, or may be, profitably applied to marketing research. These techniques may be useful in solving problems in such marketing areas as: advertising, product and price analysis, sales forecasting, locational problems, competitive strategy, and estimating market potentials. They contribute to more precise cardinal and ordinal measurements in marketing and facilitate the planning and controlling of marketing operations.

FIGURE 9-2 **Measurement in Marketing**

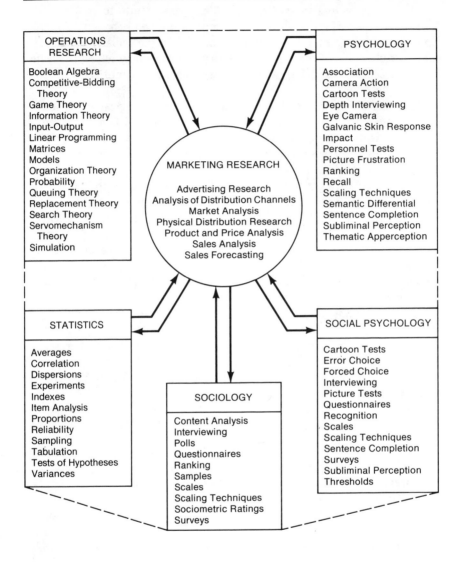

OPERATIONS RESEARCH	PSYCHOLOGY
Boolean Algebra	Association
Competitive-Bidding Theory	Camera Action
Game Theory	Cartoon Tests
Information Theory	Depth Interviewing
Input-Output	Eye Camera
Linear Programming	Galvanic Skin Response
Matrices	Impact
Models	Personnel Tests
Organization Theory	Picture Frustration
Probability	Ranking
Queuing Theory	Recall
Replacement Theory	Scaling Techniques
Search Theory	Semantic Differential
Servomechanism Theory	Sentence Completion
Simulation	Subliminal Perception
	Thematic Apperception

MARKETING RESEARCH

Advertising Research
Analysis of Distribution Channels
Market Analysis
Physical Distribution Research
Product and Price Analysis
Sales Analysis
Sales Forecasting

STATISTICS	SOCIAL PSYCHOLOGY
Averages	Cartoon Tests
Correlation	Error Choice
Dispersions	Forced Choice
Experiments	Interviewing
Indexes	Picture Tests
Item Analysis	Questionnaires
Proportions	Recognition
Reliability	Scales
Sampling	Scaling Techniques
Tabulation	Sentence Completion
Tests of Hypotheses	Surveys
Variances	Subliminal Perception
	Thresholds

SOCIOLOGY

Content Analysis
Interviewing
Polls
Questionnaires
Ranking
Samples
Scales
Scaling Techniques
Sociometric Ratings
Surveys

In many instances tools borrowed from behavioral sciences are adapted and modified by marketing researchers. Through refinements in application, the basic measurement techniques themselves are improved and marketing research thereby contributes to other disciplines.

This classification of measurement techniques merely suggests topics of interest. It is not comprehensive, and the categories are not necessarily comparable. There are a number of other important contributing subject-matter areas. Many of these techniques could be classified under several of the disciplines cited. In the figure this has been done only in a limited number of cases to avoid much duplication, but still to indicate the interdisciplinary overlapping of many of the methods of measuring specific aspects of human behavior.

THE INTERDISCIPLINARY CONCEPT
AND SYSTEMS ANALYSIS

The integration of the functional areas of business administration is an area where the interdisciplinary approach may be helpful. The problem is one of viewing a business enterprise as an operating system, as a whole. The impact of marketing, finance, production, or human-relations decisions on other aspects of company operations and on the business as a whole must be considered in a total cross-functional view of business enterprise.

Marketing administrators may be on the verge of a new level of sophistication in understanding marketing's role in the total system of business action. Managers are becoming increasingly interested in the interaction between the components of business enterprise. Forrester has pointed out that business achievement depends on the successful interaction among five subsystems—the flow of information, materials, money, manpower, and capital equipment within the firm.[4]

These five subsystems interlock to amplify one another within the total business complex. Conventional functional thinking may not be adequate for an understanding of the effects of these interactions. It does not allow for anticipated impacts on decisions, policies, organizational forms, and investment choices within the firm.

Figure 9-3 indicates the relationship of interdisciplinary activity to a marketing management system. The disciplines listed in the area bordering the external noncontrollable forces can be useful in providing information and insights about marketing.

Consumers are the focal point of the entire system of business action. They are separated from firms attempting to serve them in space, time, ownership, valuation, and knowledge. These separations tend to increase in complex socio-economic systems. Sellers attempt to overcome the barriers of space and time by communicating to the consumer the want-satisfying characteristics of the product offered through the marketing program.

The marketing program is but one significant element in the total business system. Marketing decisions should be made in terms of their impact on the company as a whole and their contributions to overall objectives. The human, financial, and physical resources of the firm should be factors in marketing decision making since the marketing program affects these factors. This corporate complex also includes the interrelation-

FIGURE 9-3 Schematic Illustration of a Marketing Management System

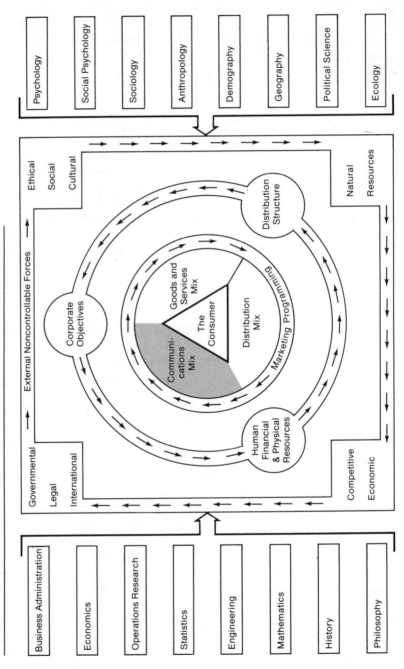

ships and coordination of the activities of the manufacturing firm with distributors and dealers as part of their joint effort to serve the consumer.

The interdisciplinary approach can be useful in understanding and even predicting the influence of these external forces on marketing decisions. Figure 9-3 emphasizes that marketing and corporate decisions are influenced, perhaps determined, by various forces which are largely beyond the control of the management of an individual enterprise. These include competitive, social, political, legal, ethical, and international forces. Change is represented in the figure by arrows. As business systems become more complex, the rate of change increases with corresponding increases in the complexity of business analysis and decision.

The systems approach to business action is particularly important to marketing executives and educators. They have a unique opportunity to integrate business-management functions into a meaningful whole and to take leadership in advancing systems thinking in business administration.

This opportunity stems from two related developments. First, businesses in the future will become more marketing oriented. Second, the total marketing concept will be adopted in which marketing is viewed as an integral subsystem within the total system of business action.

The greatest long-run contribution of the interdisciplinary approach to the study of marketing and business systems may be that of influencing the ways of thinking about marketing and business problems. Marketing students and practitioners using the interdisciplinary approach should gain added insights into the nature and scope of marketing management activities. This is because a person's concept of marketing, or any other subject, depends largely upon the knowledge of the area gained through his own or vicarious experiences.

Marketing problems may be viewed as problems arising from the gratification of human wants and needs. As such, particular marketing activities become a part of the more general problem of raising the standard of living through satisfying the needs of human beings. The discipline of marketing in this perspective is seen as a contributing component of a broader science which encompasses man and his culture.

Acceptance of the interdisciplinary approach does not mean that marketing men must become psychologists or sociologists, nor does it mean the men trained in the behavioral sciences should move over completely to marketing. The relationship between marketing and other disciplines is a reciprocal one. Marketing is concerned with the study of human action in the market place, the study of the process of exchange and economic transaction and of the interacting efforts and responses of buyers and sellers in the market. This sphere of human action is essential to our economic system and the study of it is growing in importance. The field of marketing provides a testing ground on which to verify, modify, and extend the hypotheses and relationships which have been described by various behavioral sciences.

The interdisciplinary approach can contribute greatly to a more penetrating and rigorous analysis of consumers in their socio-economic environment. As the body of knowledge about human behavior increases and is incorporated into marketing thought and practice, marketing management should be enabled to serve the needs of consumers more effectively.

The application of the interdisciplinary approach to marketing, however, is not a simple matter. Social scientists themselves experience great difficulty in communicating about and bridging disciplines. We are still a long way from a general science of human behavior which could be applied in marketing.

In the last analysis, it is likely to be the marketing men rather than pure behavioral scientists who will contribute most to the solution of difficult marketing problems and the development of marketing thought. In the future, as in the past, the major advances in marketing knowledge probably will come from people who have a marketing background and who possess an intense professional interest in advancing science in marketing.

NOTES

[1]Wroe Alderson and Reavis Cox, "Toward a Theory of Marketing," *Journal of Marketing,* Vol. 13 (October 1948), pp. 137–52, p. 142.

[2]Herta Herzog, "Behavioral Science Concepts for Analyzing the Consumer," paper given at the Conference of Marketing Teachers from Pacific Coast States, held at the University of California, Berkeley, September 9, 1958.

[3]G. L. Bach, "Some Observations on the Business School of Tomorrow," *Management Science,* Vol. 4 (July 1958), pp. 351–64, 354–55.

[4]J. W. Forrester, "Industrial Dynamics, A Major Breakthrough for Decision Makers," *Harvard Business Review,* Vol. 36 (July-August 1958), pp. 37–66.

II

CONTRIBUTIONS OF THE COMMODITY APPROACH

The commodity approach was perhaps the first unified perspective of marketing. It developed from many personal observations of how practitioners sold based on farm commodities. This approach became popular about the turn of the century, but was short-lived. The commodity approach had begun to decline by the period from 1910 to 1915. Unlike some of the later approaches, there was never any great debate among scholars concerning the content or concepts inherent in the commodity approach. This fact is perhaps due to the lack of any central unifying principle relative to a descriptive approach based on products. Lack of debate may have been instrumental in the decline of the approach as more exciting perspectives developed.

The greatest contributions of the commodity approach to marketing concern the classification of goods, and product development and use. Although the approach has declined, its effect lives on through our continually expanding understanding of product ideas. Knowledge of the commodity approach provides a feel for the complexity of our standard of living, and the need to fit the product to the buyers' requirements.

In the "Classification of Goods" section there are two articles with completely different concepts of the classification and use of products. The Copeland article is a classic because it was the first publication where products were classified. His breakdown into convenience, shopping, and specialty goods has become a standard in marketing literature. These goods were related to Copeland to the inclination of shoppers to travel and compare before buying. Copeland's classification was directed at final consumer goods. Aspinwall provides another alternative to the classification process. His method, which is based on specific characteristics inherent in all products, can be universally applied to all types of products in both the industrial and final consumer markets. Aspinwall demonstrates in his parallel systems theory how the classification works to develop marketing strategy.

The first article under "Product Development and Use" is by Meloan. He explains the importance of new products to the firm, sources of new products, and how to take advantage of the ideas in the organization. Mason discusses the importance of packaging the product. He explains the major functions of the package. Alexander suggests the product life cycle concept, although he doesn't develop it. He discusses the decline and death of products; a part of the discussion concerns a plan for selecting products to eliminate from the line. Articles on the commodity approach end with a classic by Levitt, an indepth treatment of the product life cycle. Perhaps no single concept has more potential for marketing. Levitt details the development, growth, maturity, and decline stages of the life cycle. He also shows the meaning of the concept for marketing management.

10

Relation of Consumers' Buying Habits to Marketing Methods

Melvin T. Copeland

From the standpoint of consumers' buying habits, merchandise sold in retail stores can be divided roughly into three classes:—(1) convenience goods, (2) shopping goods, and (3) specialty goods.[1] Using this classification, one of the initial steps in laying out a sales or advertising plan is to determine whether the article to be sold will be purchased by consumers ordinarily with shopping or without shopping, at points of immediate convenience or in central trading districts, with insistence on an individual brand, with merely brand preference, or with indifference to brand.

This preliminary analysis facilitates the determination of the kind of store through which the market for the specific product should be sought, the density of distribution required, the methods of wholesale distribution to be preferred, the relations to be established with dealers, and, in general, the sales burden which the advertising must carry.

CONVENIENCE GOODS

Convenience goods are those customarily purchased at easily accessible stores; examples are canned soup, tobacco products, electric light bulbs, safety razor blades, shoe polish, laundry soap, crackers, popular magazines, confectionery, and tooth paste. The consumer is familiar with these articles and as soon as he recognizes the want, the demand usually becomes clearly defined in his mind. Furthermore, he usually desires the prompt satisfaction of the want. The unit price for most articles in this class is too small to justify the consumer's going far out of his way or incurring the expense of a street-car fare in order to procure a special brand. It is for

From Melvin T. Copeland, "Relation of Consumers' Buying Habits to Marketing Methods," *Harvard Business Review,* Vol. 1 (April 1932), pp. 282–89, Copyright 1932 by the President and Fellows of Harvard College; all rights reserved.

such reasons as these that a product subject to this type of demand gains a large sales advantage when it is purveyed in numerous stores located at points easily accessible to consumers.

The consumer is in the habit of purchasing convenience goods at stores located conveniently near his residence, near his place of employment, at a point that can be visited easily on the road to and from his place of employment, or on a route traveled regularly for purposes other than buying trips. In sparsely settled districts, to be sure, the distance a consumer must travel to reach a store carrying convenience goods necessarily is greater than in densely populated districts, but fundamentally the buying habits are the same in all districts. Convenience goods, moreover, are purchased at frequent intervals by the average consumer, and these "repeat" purchases enable the stores handling such wares to secure adequate patronage with reasonably small investments in stocks of merchandise.

Typical retail establishments carrying convenience goods are grocery stores, drug stores, and hardware stores. A majority of these stores are unit stores,[2] but it is in the trade in convenience goods that chain store systems have shown the greatest development. One of the essential characteristics of chain store systems is the combination of the advantages of large-scale operation with those of small-scale selling by locating branches at points which can be reached easily by consumers for the purchase of convenience goods. The few chains of specialty stores, which for reasons to be indicated later operate on the principle of one store in a town, constitute an exception.

Because of the desire of consumers to purchase this type of merchandise at easily accessible stores, the manufacturer of a convenience article must aim to secure distribution of his product through a large number of stores in each territory. Many of the retail outlets commonly utilized for this purpose at the present time are small unit stores; consequently, to obtain this widespread distribution it is customary for most convenience goods to be sold through wholesalers. Whenever a manufacturer of a product in this category elects to sell directly to unit stores, he must develop a large sales organization and arrange for his salesmen to visit the retailers at frequent intervals.

SHOPPING GOODS

Shopping goods are those for which the consumer desires to compare prices, quality, and style at the time of purchase. Usually the consumer wishes to make this comparison in several stores. Typical shopping goods are gingham cloth, women's gloves, chinaware, and novelty articles. The typical shopping institution is the department store. Shopping goods are purchased largely by women. Ordinarily a special trip is made to the shopping center for buying such merchandise. As a rule, however, the specific store in which the purchase is to be made is not determined until after the offerings of at least two or three institutions have been inspected. The exact nature of the merchandise wanted may not be clearly defined in advance in the mind of the shopper; this is in contrast to the usual attitude in purchasing convenience goods. The purchase of shopping goods, furthermore, usually can be delayed for a time after the existence of the need has been recognized; the immediate satisfaction of the want is not so essential as in the case of most convenience goods. Because of the variety of merchandise which must be carried to satisfy the shopper and the relative infrequency of purchases of shopping articles by the average consumer, the store catering to the shopping trade must have a central location which attracts shoppers from a wide territory. In order to justify the expenses of operation in such a location, the volume of sales must be large. Conversely, it follows that the type of store which handles convenience goods ordinarily cannot carry a large enough variety and range of products to offer an attractive opportunity for shopping.

A store location suitable for trade in shopping goods usually is not adapted to the convenience goods trade; for the rental is high and the delivery interval inconvenient to consumers. It is seldom that a department store, for example, has found it possible to operate a grocery department at a profit. The factors of location, organization, and consumers' buying habits, which enable a department store to cater effectively to the shopping trade, handicap it in developing a business in convenience goods. When a manufacturer is laying out his marketing plans, therefore, he ordinarily finds it inconsistent to attempt to distribute his product through both department stores and scattered unit stores or through both department stores and chain stores. The type of store selected depends upon whether it is a shopping line, a convenience line, or a specialty line.

The number of stores selling shopping goods, furthermore, is much smaller than the number of convenience stores. The average size of the shopping store is large and its credit generally strong. This facilitates the marketing of shopping goods directly from manufacturer to retailer.

SPECIALTY GOODS

Specialty goods are those which have some particular attraction for the consumer, other than price, which induces him to put forth special effort to visit the store in which they are sold and to make the purchase without shopping. In purchasing specialty goods, the consumer determines in advance the nature of the goods to be bought and the store in which the purchase is to be made, provided a satisfactory selection of merchandise can be effected in that store. Whereas convenience goods are purchased at stores that are easily accessible, it ordinarily is necessary for the consumer to put forth special effort to reach the store selling specialty goods. As in the case of shopping goods, the actual purchase of a specialty article may be postponed for a time after the specific need has been felt by the consumer. Examples of specialty goods are men's clothing, men's shoes, high-grade furniture, vacuum cleaners, and phonographs. Specialty goods are purchased by both men and women, but men's purchases of specialty lines are a larger proportion of the total sales of such merchandise than in the case of shopping goods.

For specialty goods the manufacturer's brand, the retailer's brand, or the general reputation of the retail store for quality and service stands out prominently in the mind of the consumer. It is because of distinctive characteristics associated with the brand or the store that the consumer is prepared to rely upon the service, quality, and prices of merchandise without shopping. In numerous lines of specialty goods, such as men's shoes and clothing, the consumer prefers to deal with a store offering an attractive variety of styles and sizes from which to select. Purchases are made by each individual customer at infrequent intervals. Consequently, a specialty store generally is located at a point to which customers can be drawn from a wide area.

From the manufacturer's standpoint, a specialty line calls for selected distribution, in contrast to the general distribution essential for convenience goods. The dealers who are to handle the specialty line must be carefully selected on the basis of their ability to attract the class of customers to whom the product will appeal. Retailers must be chosen who can be relied upon to use aggressive selling methods in attracting customers to their stores. Frequently, exclusive agencies are granted to retailers for the distribution of specialty goods. An exclusive agency is seldom, if ever, justified for any line which is not a specialty line. It is only in the marketing of specialty goods, furthermore, that manufacturers have found it practical to operate retail branches.

Because of the part which each individual retail store handling the merchandise plays in the sale of the specialty goods; the care with which these stores must be selected; and the methods of cooperation which are essential between the manufacturer and the dealer, specialty goods are especially suited to distribution by direct sale from manufacturer to retailers. The manufacturer of specialty goods who works out his plan of distribution systematically on this basis also often finds it advisable, through his national or local advertising, to assume part of the burden of focusing the demand on individual stores.

In the case of several commodities, the articles tend to fall into more than one of these three categories. Staple groceries, for example, are clearly convenience goods; fancy groceries, on the other hand, are specialty goods. In each city there usually are from one to three stores which have a high reputation for specialties in groceries. Although these stores also sell staple groceries, their patronage is secured primarily on the basis of the specialties that they carry. Because of the limited market for such specialties and the volume of business necessary to justify carrying such a stock, ordinarily only one or perhaps two or three stores in a city can obtain enough business on these goods to warrant taking on a line of fancy groceries; in the same city, anywhere from one hundred to several hundred grocery stores are carrying convenience goods.

In the shoe trade, medium- and high-priced shoes for both men and women are specialty goods. Women's shoes which feature style novelties border on the shopping classification. The common grades of work shoes, on the other hand, border on the classification of convenience goods. The manufacturer of women's novelty shoes, for example, cannot advisedly leave the shopping institutions out of consideration in planning his sales program. The manufacturer of cheap work shoes, however, ordinarily must place his product in a larger number of stores than would be required were he selling medium-grade dress shoes for men.

Although women's ready-to-wear suits generally are shopping goods, a few manufacturers recently have been developing standard trade-marked lines, which tend to fall into the class of specialties. Several retail stores also have developed specialty reputations for women's ready-to-wear. In view of the conditions in the women's ready-to-wear field and also in several other fields, the average department store now seems to be faced definitely with the question of whether its merchandising should be primarily on a shopping basis or whether at least some of its departments should be developed on a specialty basis. The piece goods departments are likely to remain shopping departments. Shoes, men's clothing, women's ready-to-wear, furniture, silverware, and numerous other departments are being developed in several department stores as specialty departments, but generally without a conscious, well-coordinated policy for a store as a whole. In these specialty departments the emphasis is shifted from comparative prices and comparative styles to the special qualities and characteristics of the merchandise carried. In other department stores the merchandising is still almost entirely on a shopping basis, with the featuring of prices and bargains that are supposed to appeal to the shopper. In so far as department stores develop specialty departments, they will afford attractive outlets for manufacturers whose distribution otherwise would be through specialty stores.

RELATION OF BRANDS TO BUYING HABITS

Convenience, shopping, and specialty goods are sold both branded and unbranded. Because of the differences in the buying habits of consumers in purchasing these classes of goods, brands do not play the same part in the merchandising plans for all three classes, and the advertising problems of manufacturers are quite dissimilar for shopping, convenience, and specialty merchandise.

A brand is a means of identifying the product of an individual manufacturer or the merchandise purveyed by an individual wholesaler or retailer. The real demand for any commodity is the quantity which consumers will buy at a specific price. If a product is unbranded, the volume of the demand ordinarily depends upon the quantity that consumers elect to buy, either entirely upon their own initiative or as a result of the sales efforts of the retailers by whom it is sold. When sugar was sold in bulk, for example, the demand depended upon the amount consumers wished to purchase or were induced to purchase by retailers who featured the article; sales were not directly stimulated by the sugar refiner. For an unbranded product, the individual manufacturer seldom can afford to assume the burden of stimulating demand which cannot be specifically directed to the product of his own factory. For such an unbranded product the manufacturer must rely chiefly upon his ability to produce cheaply, in order to be able to offer low prices, and he must pursue merely passive selling methods or, at most, direct his sales efforts chiefly toward wholesale and retail merchants. If the product is branded, on the other hand, the manufacturer can undertake not only to direct the active demand to his particular product, but also to arouse latent demand by stimulating a larger number of consumers to want his product or by making previous consumers desire to use more of his product at a specific price. When the American Sugar Refining Company, in 1912, for example, began to put out sugar in packages bearing the company's trademark, the company not only was in a position where it could inform the consumer regarding the merits of that particular brand, but it also could practically undertake to induce consumers to use more sugar, as, for instance, in canning fruit.

With the development of the package trade, the tendency during recent years has been for an increasing proportion of convenience goods to be branded. The increase in the sale of crackers in packages, for example, in contrast to the former bulk sales, has given greater significance to brands of crackers and has facilitated the use of aggressive sales methods by cracker manufacturers. Among shopping goods there has been some increase in the number of brands, but large quantities of merchandise in this class still are sold unbranded. Specialty goods are all branded, except in a few cases where retail stores have reputations which practically render it unnecessary for them to have brands placed on the merchandise which they sell.

When a manufacturer undertakes to focus the potential demand upon his product with brand identification, he must consider the attitude in which the consumer ordinarily approaches the purchase of such an article. The attitude of the consumer may be that of: (1) recognition, (2) preference, or (3) insistence.

CONSUMER RECOGNITION

When a brand has any significance at all, it serves primarily as a cause for recognition. If the consumer's previous acquaintance with the brand has been favorable, or if the manufacturer's or dealer's advertising has made a favorable impression, other things being equal, the recognized brand will be selected from among other unrecognized brands or from among unbranded merchandise. For some products—such as silk goods, ginghams, and women's suits—pattern, style, and price are considered by the consumer, before brand. When the selection narrows down to a choice between articles of this sort approximately equal in pattern, style, and price, the recognition of a known brand sways the choice. The manufacturer of such goods, however, cannot hope ordinarily to secure many sales merely because of brand, if his product is higher in price or less popular in pattern and style than directly competing goods shown in other stores.

Consumer recognition—an acquaintance with the general standing of the brand—probably is the only attitude toward that brand which the manufacturer of a typical shopping line ordinarily can establish in the mind of the average purchaser by means of advertising and sales efforts. If the product has some special feature, as, for example, cotton fabrics dyed in fast colors or fast-colored silk goods loaded with a minimum of tetra-chloride of tin, it occasionally is possible to arouse the interest of the consumer to a point of preference.

A family brand, by which is meant a brand or trademark that is applied commonly to a group of different products turned out by a single manufacturer, serves primarily to establish consumer recognition for all products in the group as soon as the consumer becomes acquainted with one article bearing the common brand. The experience of retail dealers indicates that for shopping and convenience goods the common brand aids in promoting consumer recognition. If it is a specialty line, the experience of the consumer with one article bearing the brand is likely to establish in the minds of consumers at least an attitude of preference for other articles bearing the same brand. It is unsafe, however, for the manufacturer to count upon the family brand to develop more than consumer recognition without the presentation of sales arguments for each article bearing the brand.

CONSUMER PREFERENCE

Consumer recognition soon shades into consumer preference. When several brands of merchandise, which are similar in general qualities and in external appearance, are offered to the consumer by a retail salesman, the one for which previous experience, advertising, or perhaps the retailer's recommendation has created a preference, is chosen. The strength of the brand depends upon the degree of preference in the mind of the consumer. In purchasing convenience goods, for example, the consumer often approaches the retailer with the question, "Have you the X brand?" If the retailer does not have that brand in stock, another brand ordinarily is accepted by the consumer, or, if the retailer specifically urges another brand in the place of the one called for, a substitute may be taken by the consumer. This practice of asking for brands is common for many consumers in the purchase of convenience articles. The brand comes first in the consumer's mind and signifies to him the quality, style, or pattern of article, or the type of container that he wishes to obtain. In such cases the consumer has a preference for the brand asked for, but ordinarily it is not strong enough in this class of merchandise to make him insist on that brand to the point of visiting a less convenient store to make the purchase. It is because the consumer generally has merely the attitude of brand preference in purchasing convenience goods that it is essential for the manufacturer of such a product to place his wares on sale in a large number of stores in each territory.

CONSUMER INSISTENCE

The third stage in which the demand for branded articles manifests itself is consumer insistence. When the consumer approaches the purchase of an article in this attitude of mind, he accepts no substitute unless it is an emergency. This attitude of consumer insistence holds commonly in the purchase of specialty goods. To warrant undertaking to develop this attitude, the product must be so individualized in quality, in its special features, or in the service rendered by the manufacturer or retailer as to differentiate it distinctly from competing articles and to induce consumers to put forth special effort to secure that brand. The manufacturer of an electrical washing machine, for example, undertakes to present his sales arguments in such a way as to lead the consumer to insist upon the purchase of his particular make. Through advertising, the manufacturer of such a machine seeks to convince the consumer that his is the machine which should be purchased and that a store carrying this brand should be sought out.

The difference between no standing at all in the mind of the consumer, consumer recognition, consumer preference, and consumer insistence is one of the degrees to which the selling process has been carried with the consumer before he visits a retail store to make his purchase. If the consumer has no familiarity whatsoever with the brand of product to be purchased, the entire sales burden rests on the salesman in the store visited. If the consumer recognizes the brand, the manufacturer of that brand has taken the initial step in consummating the sale to the consumer. If the manufacturer has established consumer preference, the sale has proceeded one step further. If the consumer has the attitude of insistence, it remains merely for the retail salesman to close the sale.

Marketing costs generally are high. One of the first steps to be taken by a manufacturer, who is seeking to effect economies in selling his product, is to make an elementary analysis of the habits of consumers in buying articles of the sort he is producing. The formulation of an effective marketing plan must start with a consideration of the consumer; the next step is to adjust the plans of retail and wholesale distribution and the advertising program in accordance with the analysis of the buying habits of consumers among whom the market for the product is to be developed. This approach assures the maximum results from the sales efforts that are put forth.

NOTE

[1]The methods of marketing goods for retail distribution are essentially different from the methods of marketing goods for wholesale consumption. In the one case it is necessary to select marketing methods whereby the goods can be parceled out in small lots to individual consumers; in the other the sales are made in wholesale lots for large-scale use, as in manufacturing or in construction work.

[2]A unit store is a store, without an elaborate departmental organization, owned and managed as an independent unit for the sale of goods through local salesmanship.

11

The Marketing Characteristics of Goods

Leo V. Aspinwall

The characteristics of goods theory attempts to arrange all marketable goods in systematic and useful fashion. It has been tested both in the classroom and in application to business problems. It provides a perspective and frame of reference for organizing marketing facts and for weighing marketing decisions. Previous efforts included the three-way classification of products as convenience goods, shopping goods, and specialty goods. The characteristics of goods theory sets up a continuous scale rather than discrete classes and defines the criteria by which any product can be assigned to an appropriate place on the scale. All of these criteria lend themselves to objective measurement, at least potentially. By contrast, it would be rather difficult to distinguish a shopping good from a convenience good in positive, quantitative terms.

The marketing characteristics of a product determine the most appropriate and economical method for distributing it. To fix its position on the scale, representing the variation in these characteristics, is to take the first major step toward understanding its marketing requirements. To know these characteristics is to be able to predict with a high degree of reliability how a product will be distributed, since most products conform to the pattern. Serious departure from the theoretical expectations will almost certainly indicate the need for change and improvement in distribution methods. These considerations apply both to physical distribution and to the parallel problem of communications including the choice of promotional media and appeals. It follows also that goods having similar characteristics call for similar handling. Finally, if precise weights or values could be assigned to each characteristic, their combination would determine the unique position of a product on the marketing scale.

Reprinted from Leo V. Aspinwall, "The Characteristics of Goods and Parallel Systems Theories," in *Four Marketing Theories* (Business Research Division, University of Colorado, 1961).

CHARACTERISTICS OF GOODS THEORY

The problem-solving process often leads into totally unfamiliar areas which sometimes bring us to a dead end. Only occasionally do these probing excursions uncover new combinations of old ideas that have some relevance to the problem in hand. When such combinations prove to be useful the mind is quick to employ such combinations again for problems of the same general type, so that repeated use tends to formulate a framework of reference which can be readily used for problem solving. Into the framework thus formulated the problem can be fitted so that the relationship of the integral parts can be observed. This may well be a mental sorting operation which seeks to classify problems into similar groups for greater efficiency in the unending task of problem solving.

The characteristics of goods theory is the result of one of these mental excursions, and its repeated use has had the effect of crystallizing the combination of old ideas into a fairly stabilized form. The theory has been revised from time to time through the constructive criticism of my colleagues, but whether it will ever be in final form is doubtful, since the dynamic character of all marketing activity is such that changes are more likely than anything else. Somehow the thought of achieving a final state of equilibrium is rather frightening.

TABLE 11-1 **Characteristics of Goods Theory**

	COLOR CLASSIFICATION		
CHARACTERISTICS	**RED GOODS**	**ORANGE GOODS**	**YELLOW GOODS**
Replacement Rate	High	Medium	Low
Gross Margin	Low	Medium	High
Adjustment....................	Low	Medium	High
Time of Consumption...........	Low	Medium	High
Searching Time	Low	Medium	High

CHARACTERISTICS OF GOODS

The problem of weights or values being assigned to these individual characteristics has been one of the real difficulties in giving the theory a mathematical setting. So far that objective has not been fully achieved. We have been obliged to deal with relative values which might be considered as an intermediary stage in the theory's development. The analogy of an electric circuit may eventually prove useful in formulating a mathematical approach. Getting goods distributed is not unlike moving an electric current through resistance factors, each of which takes a part of the gross margin. When the good finally reaches the consumer's hands, ready for consumption, all of the gross margin has been used. Looking at this idea from the consumer end, the amount of the gross margin the consumer has given up in order to enjoy the utilities the good provides is, in fact, the voltage that the electric current must have in order to pass through the resistance factors and finally reach the consumer.

The decision as to the number and kinds of characteristics to be used was approached by setting up tests which these characteristics should meet. These criteria are:

1. Every characteristic selected must be applicable to every good.
2. Every characteristic selected must be relatively measurable in terms of its relationship to every good.
3. Every characteristic must be logically related to all the other characteristics.

This brings us to the point of defining a characteristic. A characteristic is a distinguishing quality of a good relative to its stable performance in a market and its relationship to the consumers for whom it has want-satisfying capacity. Under this definition five characteristics have been selected, each of which must in turn be defined. These are:

1. *Replacement rate.*   This characteristic is defined as *the rate at which a good is purchased and consumed by users in order to provide the satisfaction a consumer expects from the product.* The replacement rate is associated with the concept of a flow or movement of units of a good from producer to ultimate consumer. The idea is somewhat akin to a turnover rate, except that our understanding of turnover is related to the number of times per year that an average stock of goods is bought and sold. Replacement rate as used here is consumer oriented. It asks how often the consumer buys shoes: once each month, once each six months, or once each year? It does not ask whether or not the shoes have been consumed, but only how often the market must be ready to make shoes available for consumers. This characteristic differentiates the rate or flow of different goods and attempts to envision the market mechanism that will meet the aggregate needs of consumers. This is marketing in motion as dictated by consumer purchasing power.

It may be helpful to introduce a few illustrative cases and at the same time show how the idea of relative measurement is used. Loaves of bread, cigarettes, and packets of matches all have high replacement rates in terms of relative measurement. Some people consume bread more often than others, yet the average frequency of all bread eaters in a consumption area determines the replacement rate for bread. In comparison with grand pianos, bread has a high replacement rate and grand pianos have a low replacement rate. Men's shirts and ready-to-wear have medium replacement rates when compared to bread and grand pianos. Here we can visualize fast moving streams, slow moving streams and moderately moving streams of different kinds of goods, each with its characteristically different rate of replacement.

2. *Gross margin.* The definition of gross margin as used here is not different from its use in marketing generally. *The money sum which is the difference between the laid in cost and the final realized sales price is* the gross margin. It is brought to mind at once that there are several gross margins involved in moving goods from factory gates to final consumer. What is meant here is the summation of all the gross margins involved. It is that total money sum necessary to move a good from point of origin to final consumer. It might be thought of as channel costs or as the fare a good must pay to reach its destination. In the amount of gross margin is less than the fare needed, the good will not reach destination. The calculation of the gross margin is a market-oriented function which is based, in the final analysis, on the amount of money a consumer will exchange for a particular good. If the consumer elects to pay a money fund which is less than the production cost and the necessary marketing costs, the good will not be marketed because the gross margin is too low in relation with the other characteristics. The availability of gross margin is the force that operates our marketing system. Suppose a consumer wishes to procure a pack of cigarettes from a vending machine and the machine is set to operate when a twenty-five cent piece is inserted in the slot. Nothing would happen if a ten-cent piece were dropped into the slot, except that the ten-cent piece would be returned to the customer. The gross margin contained in the twenty-five-cent piece was large enough to bring the consumer the cigarettes he needed.

This may be the appropriate place to call attention to the fact that whenever the flow of goods is arrested for whatever reason, costs begin to take a larger share of the planned gross margin and may actually prevent a good from reaching the final market. Such losses as may have been incurred in the stoppage must be borne by someone, and the calculations made by marketing men are such that loss situations cannot be tolerated, and the flow of goods will be stopped. The secondary action in such a case is that a money flow back to the producer also stops, which in turn closes down production. While this may be oversimplified, it does emphasize the importance of gross margin to the whole economic process.

Certain types of goods are necessarily involved in storage by reason of their seasonal production. Storage assumes the availability of the needed amount of gross margin to pay these costs, otherwise such goods would not be stored. Whatever takes place during the movement of goods from producer to consumer affects gross margin.

This is the first opportunity to test these characteristics against the criteria set up for their selection. It has been shown that the replacement rate is applicable to all goods and that the replacement rate is relatively measurable. Lastly the question must be asked: Is the replacement rate related to gross margin? This is without doubt the most important relationship of all those needing demonstration in this theory. The relationship

FIGURE 11-1 Schematic Array of a Few Selected Goods
(Plotted in terms of yellow goods)

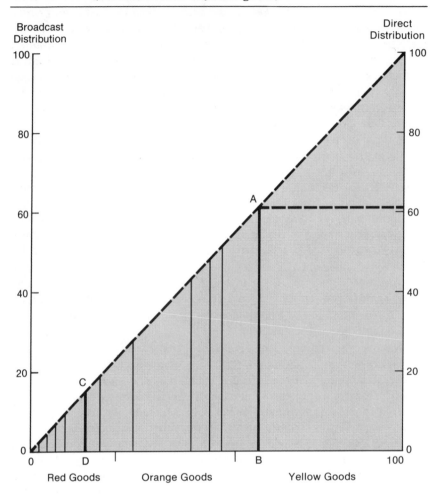

is inverse. Whenever replacement rate is high gross margin is low and, conversely, when replacement rate is low then gross margin is high. Thus, when goods move along at a lively clip the costs of moving them are decreased. This relationship brings to mind some economic laws which bear on the situation. The theory of decreasing costs seems to apply here to show that marketing is a decreasing-cost industry. This might be stated as follows: As the number of units distributed increases, the cost per unit distributed tends to decrease up to the optimum point. Mass distribution insofar as marketing is concerned has important possibilities. This is amply demonstrated in modern marketing operations. Goods handling in modern warehouses has been studied in this light and warehousing costs have been decreased, which in turn has expedited the flow of goods into consumers' hands. Here again, economic laws operate to induce the seller to pass on savings in marketing costs. Small decreases in gross margin tend to bring forth a disproportionately larger market response.

The relationship of replacement rate and gross margin has thus far been concerned with the increasing side of the relationship. When replacement rate is low and gross margin is relatively higher, it is not difficult to envision higher marketing costs. Almost at once it can be seen that selling costs will be relatively higher per unit. The gross margin on the individual sale of a grand piano or major appliance must bear the cost of direct sales, including salaries and commissions for salesmen who negotiate with prospective buyers and very often make home demonstrations. The fact that shipping costs are higher in moving pianos is well known. If carlot shipments are used there are likely to be some storage costs involved, and this additional cost must come out of gross margin. It can be shown that high-value goods such as jewelry and silverware reflect this relationship in much the same way. This inverse relationship between replacement rate and gross margin strikes a balance when goods with a medium rate of replacement are involved.

3. *Adjustment.*   An important characteristic which pertains to all goods and which has been named "adjustment" is defined as *services applied to goods in order to meet the exact needs of the consumer.* These services may be performed as the goods are being produced or at any intermediate point in the channel of distribution or at the point of sale. Adjustment as a characteristic of all goods reflects the meticulous demands of consumers that must be met in the market. Even in such goods as quarts of milk there is evidence of adjustment. Some consumers demand milk with low fat content, others require milk with high fat content, to name but one of the items of adjustment which pertains to milk. The matter of size of package, homogenized or regular, and even the matter of added vitamins come under adjustment. The services applied to milk are performed in the processing plant in anticipation of the adjustments the consumer may require. Here slight changes in the form or in size of package are adjustments performed in advance of the sale of the product. This type of adjustment imposes additional costs involving somewhat larger inventories and the use of a greater amount of space, with all that this implies. It can be easily understood that costs are involved whenever adjustments are performed, so that additional amounts of gross margin are necessary. Adjustments made at the point of production become manufacturing costs which only mildly affect the marketing operation, so that the measured amount of adjustment in the marketing channel is relatively low.

Goods with a high replacement rate have low adjustment, but the reverse is true when goods have low replacement rates. Goods with a medium replacement rate have a medium amount of adjustment. Here the inverse relationship between replacement rate and adjustment has been demonstrated, as well as the direct relationship between gross margin and adjustment.

4. *Time of consumption.*   Time of consumption as a characteristic of goods can be defined as *the measured time of consumption during which the good gives up the utility desired.* This characteristic is related to the replacement rate to a considerable degree, since goods with a low time of consumption are likely to have a high rate of replacement. The inverse relationship is true, but a low time of consumption does not mean that a repetitive purchasing program is maintained by the same consumer. Aspirin gives up its utility in the short period of time during which it is being consumed, but a purchase replacement may not occur until another headache needs attention. The idea of consumption time is more closely related to nondurable and durable goods both in the consumer and industrial classes.

The time of consumption characteristic pertains to all goods, and the amount of this time is relatively measurable, which satisfies the criterion of relationship to all goods and the criterion of relative measurability. The final criterion of relationship to all other characteristics is also met in that low time of consumption is directly related to adjustment and gross margin and inversely related to the rate of replacement.

5. *Searching time.*   The characteristic of searching time can be defined as *the measure of average time and distance from the retail store* and hence convenience the consumer is afforded by market facilities. Suppose the need to purchase a package of cigarettes comes up for immediate attention for a consumer. The amount of effort exerted on his part to procure the needed cigarettes is correlated with the amount of searching time. In this case the amount of inconvenience suffered is usually very low since the market has reacted to the fact that there is a wide and insistent demand for cigarettes. To meet this demand, points of purchase are established wherever large numbers of potential customers are to be found. The result of such market action is that cigarettes can be purchased at many different places and in many different institutions, and the searching time is low. The old idea is expressed in another way: consumers are motivated by a drive for convenience. Out of these relationships we have come to recognize "the span of convenience" for each product. Consumers cannot easily be forced to expend an amount of time and energy that is disproportionate to the satisfaction they expect to receive from the goods in question.

It can easily be seen that for certain goods the searching time will be low, while for certain other goods the searching time will be much larger. The amount of time and energy expended by a customer in the process of furnishing a new home would be very great and therefore, searching time would be correspondingly high. There is the need for examining the offerings of many stores, and even though these stores may be located fairly close to each other, in all probability they will be located at some distance from the consumer's home. The reality of this situation is expressed in the characteristics of the goods. Searching time can be readily envisioned by the fact that we have many more market outlets for cigarettes than we do for grand pianos or furniture and, therefore, market availability for cigarettes is low and for pianos it is high.

Searching time is directly related to gross margin, adjustment, and time of consumption, and is inversely related to replacement rate. Searching time as a characteristic of goods pertains to all goods and for each and every good it is relatively measurable.

This information can now be fitted into a chart which will keep the relationships of the characteristics of goods in position as they pertain to all goods. This chart will show that goods with the same relative amounts of these five characteristics fall into the same broad classifications. Arbitrary names can be fitted to these broad classifications for greater convenience in conveying ideas about goods and the various ways in which they are distributed.

COLOR CONCEPT

This chart introduces an additional element into the characteristics of goods theory: the color classification. The idea that goods with similar characteristics are similar to each other lends itself to the establishment of three large classes of goods that can be named in such a manner as to convey the idea of an array of goods. The choice of color names may be inept in some respects, but the idea of an array of goods, based upon the sum of the relative values of characteristics of goods, is important. The length of light rays for red, orange, and yellow, in that order, is an array of light rays representing a portion of the spectrum. For our present purpose it is more convenient to use the three colors only, rather than the seven of the full spectrum. The idea of an infinite graduation of values can be envisioned by blending these colors from red to yellow with orange in between. This is the idea we wish to convey as concerning all goods.

The sum of the characteristics for each and every good is different, and the sum of characteristics for red goods is lower than the sum of the characteristics for yellow goods. The chart shows red goods to have four low values and one of a high value, while yellow goods have four high values and one low.

It is useful to stress this tension between replacement rate and the other four marketing characteristics, since they all tend to decrease as replacement rate increases. That is equivlent to saying that as demand for a product increases, marketing methods tend to develop which reflect economies in the various aspects of marketing costs. It is easily possible, of course, to transform replacement rate into its inverse for use in arriving at a weighted index of the five characteristics. If replacement rate were expressed as the average number of purchases in a year, the inverse measure would be the average number of days between purchases. This measure would be low for red goods and high for yellow, like all of the other characteristics.

A schematic diagram can now be set up which represents all possible graduations in goods from red through orange to yellow. As shown in figure 11-1, a simple percentage scale from 0 to 100 is laid out on both coordinates. It is true that the weighted value for any product could be laid out on a single line. Yet there is an advantage in the two-dimensional chart for the purpose of visualizing an array of goods. The scale of values thus really consists of all the points on the diagonal line in the accompanying chart. Since there is an infinite number of points on any line segment, the scale provides for an infinite array of goods. If the chart were large enough, vertical lines could be drawn with each line representing a product now on the market. Even after these lines were drawn there would still remain an infinite number of positions in between. Many of these positions might serve to identify goods which have been withdrawn from the market or others which might be introduced in the future.

Line AB represents a good having an ordinate value of 63, indicating the sum of the characteristics of this good. In the general classification it has 63 per cent yellow characteristics and 37 per cent red characteristics. Translated into marketing terms, this good might be ladies' ready-to-wear dresses sold through department stores and shipped directly from the factory to these stores in the larger cities. The smaller cities are served by wholesalers who carry small stocks of these goods along with other dry goods items. Thus the marketing channels utilized for distributing this good would be direct to large department store accounts and semibroadcast through specialty wholesalers serving smaller city accounts.

Line CD in its position near the red end of the scale has a yellow characteristics value of 15 and a red value of 85, which puts this good in the large classification as a red good. The sum of the characteristics value in the scale 0 to 100 is 85 per cent red. This might well be a soap product which is sold mainly by broadcast distribution using a broker, wholesaler, retailer channel. The 15 per cent yellow characteristic might indicate specialty salesmen's activity involving factory drop shipments. The latter type of distribution is more direct and might account for the 15 per cent of direct distribution from the factory to the retailer.

The position of a good on the color scale is not static. Most products fall in the yellow classification when they are first introduced. As they become better known and come to satisfy a wider segment of consumer demand, the replacement rate increases and the good shifts toward the red end of the scale. Thus there is a red shift in marketing which offers a rather far-fetched analogy to the red shift in astronomy which is associated with the increasing speed of movement of heavenly bodies. There is also an opposing tendency in marketing, however, resulting from the constant shrinking of gross margin as a good moves toward the red end of the scale. Marketing organizations, in the effort to maintain their gross margin, may improve or differentiate a good which has moved into the red category, so that some of these new varieties swing all the way back into yellow. Thereafter the competitive drive for volume serves to accelerate the movement toward the red end of the scale again.

CONCLUSION

This characteristics of goods theory provides a basis for making marketing policy decisions concerning goods of all kinds and gives an insight into the way in which marketing channels can be used. The use of the broad color classification provides a basis for more exact communication in dealing with marketing problems.

12

Parallel Systems of
Promotion and Distribution

Leo V. Aspinwall

The sponsor of a product must decide how it is to be promoted and what channels to use for its physical distribution. He is confronted with a variety of possibilities both for stimulating demand and for moving his product to the consumer. It turns out that there is a parallel relationship between these two aspects of the marketing problem with a distribution system and its appropriate counterpart in promotion usually occurring together. This pairing of systems occurs because the promotion and distribution requirements of a product are both dependent on the marketing characteristics of the goods. The preceding [chapter] explained how goods might be arrayed according to their marketing characteristics into groups designated as red, orange, and yellow. It was further shown that this array could be translated into a numerical scale and presented in simple graphic form. The purpose of the present [chapter] is to indicate how the position of a product on this scale can be used to identify the parallel systems of promotion and distribution which should be used in marketing the product.

THE PARALLEL SYSTEMS THEORY

This set of ideas has come to be designated as the parallel systems theory. It is the kind of theory which is intended to be helpful in resolving fundamental practical issues in marketing. Theory alone cannot settle all the details of a marketing plan. It may save much time and effort by indicating the starting point for planning and the appropriate matching of systems of promotion and distribution. The gross margin earned on a product provides the fund which must cover the costs of marketing distribution and marketing promotion. The management of this fund involves many of the most critical decisions with which marketing executives

Reprinted from Leo V. Aspinwall, "Parallel Systems of Promotion and Distribution," in *Four Marketing Theories* (Business Research Division, University of Colorado, 1961).

have to deal. Even slight errors of judgment in this regard may spell the difference between profit and loss.

The parallel systems theory begins with a simple thesis which may be stated as follows: The characteristics of goods indicate the manner of their physical distribution, and the manner of promotion must parallel that physical distribution. Thus, we have parallel systems, one for physical distribution and one for promotion. The movement of goods and the movement of information are obviously quite different processes. It was to be expected that specialized facilities would be developed for each function. The fact that these developments take place along parallel lines is fundamental to an understanding of marketing. A few special terms must be introduced at this point for use in discussing parallel systems.

A channel for the physical distribution of goods may be either a short channel or a long channel. The shortest channel, of course, is represented by the transaction in which the producer delivers the product directly to its ultimate user. A long channel is one in which the product moves through several stages of location and ownership as from the factory to a regional warehouse, to the wholesaler's warehouse, to a retail store, and finally to the consumer. The parallel concepts in promotion may be compared to contrasting situations in electronic communication. On the one hand there is the closed circuit through which two people can carry on a direct and exclusive conversation with each other. On the other hand there is broadcast communication such as radio and television whereby the same message can be communicated to many people simultaneously.

In general, long channels and broadcast promotion are found together in marketing while short channels and closed circuit or direct promotion are found together. The parallel systems theory attempts to show how these relationships arise naturally out of the marketing characteristics of the goods.

CHARACTERISTICS OF GOODS AND MARKETING SYSTEMS

It will be remembered from the preceding [chapter] that goods were arrayed according to their marketing characteristics as red, orange, and yellow. Marketing systems can be arrayed in similar and parallel fashion. Red goods call for long channels and broadcast promotion. Yellow goods call for short channels and closed circuit promotion. Orange goods are intermediates as to their marketing characteristics and, hence, are intermediate as to the kind of distribution and promotion systems which they require. There is a continuous gradation from red to yellow and from broadcast to direct methods of marketing.

One of the fundamental marketing characteristics of goods is replacement rate. That is the frequency with which the average consumer in the market buys the product or replenishes the supply of it carried in his household inventory. Red goods are goods with a high replacement rate. A market transaction which occurs with high frequency lends itself to standardization and specialization of function. The movement of goods and the movement of information each becomes clearly marked and separate. Opportunity arises for a number of specialized marketing agencies to participate in distribution, and the result is what has been called the "long channel." Messages to the ultimate user become as standardized as the product itself. This type of information and persuasion does not need to follow the long distribution channel from step to step in its transmission from producer to consumer. Such messages are broadcast to consumers through both electronic and printed advertising media which provide a more appropriate channel.

Yellow goods are low in replacement rate and high in other marketing characteristics such as adjustment. Requirements for this class of goods tend to vary from one user to another. Adjustment embraces a variety of means by which goods are fitted to individual requirements. The marketing process remains relatively costly and a large percentage of gross margin necessarily goes along with high adjustment. The opportunity for standardization and specialization is slight compared to that of red goods. Physical movement and promotion remain more closely associated, with a two-way communication concerning what is available and what is needed finally resulting in the delivery of the custom-made product. A transaction between a man and his tailor would illustrate this type of marketing. Many kinds of industrial equipment are specially designed for the given user and would also be at the extreme yellow end of the scale. The short channel is prevalent in such situations, and all promotion or related communication moves through a closed circuit.

Many products lie in the middle range which has been designated as orange goods. They have been produced to standard specifications but with the knowledge that they will have to be adapted in greater or less degree in each individual installation. The replacement rate is high enough to offer moderate opportunity for standardization and specialization. At least one intermediary is likely to enter the picture, such as an automobile dealer buying from the manufacturer and selling to the consumer or an industrial distributor serving as a channel between two manufacturers. The car sold to customers may be of the same model and yet be substantially differentiated to meet individual preferences as to color and accessories. Broadcast media are used in promotion but not on the same scale relatively as for soaps or cigarettes. The industrial distributor is often supported in his efforts by specialty salesmen or sales engineers employed by the manufacturer. Advertising of a semibroadcast character is likely to be used. That is to say that messages are specially prepared for various segments of the market for which the appeal of the product is expected to be somewhat different. This approach lies between the standardized message to all users on the one hand and the individualized closed circuit negotiation on the other.

One qualification which may properly be suggested at this point is that marketing systems are not quite so flexible as this discussion suggests, but must conform to one type or another. Thus a channel for physical distribution could have two steps or three steps but not two and a half. Nevertheless the picture of continuous variation along a scale is generally valid because of the combinations which are possible. A producer may sell part of his output through wholesalers who service retailers and sell the remainder direct to retailers. The proportions may vary over time so that one channel presently becomes dominant rather than the other. Similarly broadcast promotion may gradually assume greater importance in the marketing mix even though a large but declining amount of adjustment is involved in some individual sales.

MOVEMENT OF GOODS AND MOVEMENT OF INFORMATION

The schematic relationship between goods and marketing systems is shown in figure 12-1. This simple diagram depicts the parallels which have been discussed. It will be noted that the segment of the line allowed is greater for orange goods than for red goods and greater for yellow than for orange. It is a readily observable fact that the number of separate and distinct items in any stock of goods increases as replacement rate decreases. A drug store, for example, has to sell more separate items to achieve the same volume of sales as a grocery store. An exclusive dress shop will need more variation in styles and models than a store operating in the popular price range. Paint brushes, files, or grinding wheels will be made up in a great multiplicity of specifications to serve the industrial market as compared to the few numbers which suffice for the household user. Red goods by their very nature are those in which a single item is bought frequently because it meets the requirements of many occasions for use while in the yellow goods more numerous items with less frequent sales are required for a more accurate matching of diverse and differentiated use situations.

Figure 12-2 is intended to demonstrate the relationship between goods and the methods of distribution and promotion. It is not intended to show an accurate mathematical relationship since the data from which it is constructed are not mathematically accurate, but it does implement understanding of the problems with which marketing executives must deal. The reasoning is deductive, moving from the general to the specific and provides a quick basis for reaching an answer which can readily be adjusted to a specific case. The readings from the diagram are in complementary percentages that must be accepted as rough measurements of the kinds and amounts of distribution and promotion. Long channel distribution and broadcast promotion are grouped together as related elements of the marketing mix and designated as "broadcast" for the sake of simplicity. The line representing these two elements in combination slopes downward to the right since this type of expenditure can be expected to be relatively high for red goods and relatively low for yellow goods. Similarly, short channel distribution and closed circuit communication are thrown together under the designation of "direct." The line representing direct promotion and distribution slopes upward from left to right.

APPLICATION TO A MANAGEMENT PROBLEM

A short time ago a project was undertaken for a well-known manufacturer whose operation is such that the range of products his company manufactures covers the scale from red good to yellow goods. In following the reasoning of the characteristics of goods theory and the parallel systems theory he was able to locate a certain product in its position on the base line. He drew the ordinate representing this product and found from the diagram that the distribution indicated was a modified direct distribution and that accordingly a considerable amount of direct promotion should be used. In reviewing what actually was being done with this product he knew that promotion was mostly broadcast while the distribution was a modified direct. Thus, promotion and distribution were not running parallel and such a finding for this product provided a substantial explanation of the poor performance this product was making. Research had confirmed that it was an excellent product and that it was priced correctly so that a reasonable volume of sales should have been expected. The planned sales for the product were not realized and to correct this situation a more extensive broadcast promotion program was launched, but from this program little or no increase in sales was realized. At this the manufacturer decided that it would be worth a try to follow out the indicated promotional and distributional plan shown in the parallel systems theory analysis. A program of direct promotion was initiated and results were immediately forthcoming. The full sales expectations were realized and the manufacturer decided

FIGURE 12-1 **Relationship Between Goods and Marketing Systems**

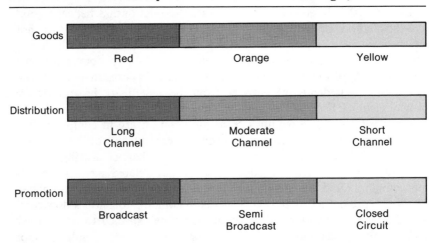

to establish a special division to handle the product which since that time has produced even more sales at considerably below the estimated costs.

A somewhat closer look at this case revealed that broadcast promotion was reaching thousands of people who were in no way qualified users of the product and that the type of advertising message was such that qualified users were unable to specify the product even if they wished to do so. A careful study of the problem showed that the direct promotion had produced all of the sales results. Thus the cost of the broadcast promotion had to be borne by qualified users and the result was a higher price than would have been needed if direct promotional means had been employed. The final result of this operation was that prices were lowered and the profit position for the manufacturer and all institutions in the distribution channel was improved.

Product B_2 in figure 12-2 represents the product discussed in its correct position. Reading the ordinate value in the vertical scale shows that the product it represents should be distributed 69 per cent direct and that promotion should also be 69 per cent direct. The complementary 31 per cent reading shown indicates that 31 per cent of the distribution should be broadcast and 31 per cent of the promotion should be of the broadcast type. Product B_1 (figure 12-2) is product B_2 as it was incorrectly located on the base line array of goods. The incorrect location was based on a measurement of the method of promotion that was being used. Actually this product was being distributed correctly by a modified direct method, and consequently consumers who might have been influenced to use the product had no means by which to exercise their wishes; the product was not available in retail stores in such a way as to make it readily available to qualified customers.

By making analyses of products and their distribution and promotional programs, it will be found that many products are not in conformity with the parallel systems theory, and yet seem to be successful products. This would not of itself disprove the theory. Such results might indicate that better results might be had if the programs were modified in the direction indicated by the theory. This can often be done at a comparatively small cost by using test sales areas in which the adjustment can be made without affecting the national system in which the product may be operating. The results from such experimentation should confirm the analysis made under the parallel systems theory. A large amount of case material has been collected on the parallel systems theory but there seems to be an almost endless variety of cases, and there is a need for constant study of the problem in light of the improvements in communications and distribution.

CONCLUSION

A further definition for broadcast promotion seems to be needed as well as for direct promotion. Whenever promotional means are used, without knowledge in advance of the identity of prospective users, the promotional

FIGURE 12-2 **Parallel Systems Theory**

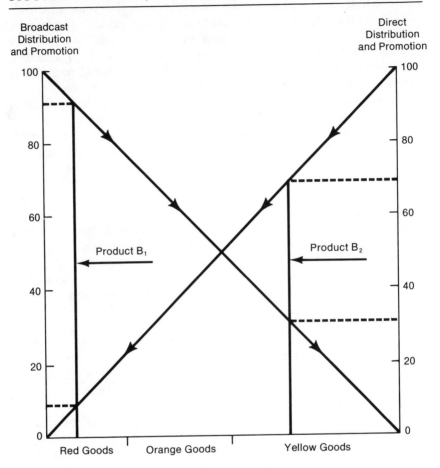

means is considered to be broadcast. The firm employing broadcast promotional means relies upon the chance contact with potential customers for the product or service. The broadcast distributional means for such a product are so arranged that the customer for the product who has been reached by this type of promotion can exercise his choice conveniently and quickly. Retail stores are available within a short radius of the consumer who may wish to purchase the product. Thus, the sales gap is shortened both as to time and distance and the effectiveness of the broadcast means of promotion is enhanced. The key fact that makes this type of marketing economical is that while the prospective users are unidentified, they represent a large proportion of the general public which will be exposed to the broadcast message. The opposite of broadcast promotion is direct promotion. The definition of direct promotion turns on the fact that the recipient of the direct communication is known in advance, so that the message reaches the intended purchaser by name and address or by advance qualification of the prospect as to his need and ability to purchase the product. The most direct means would be a salesman who calls upon a selected prospect whose address and name are known in advance, and where judgment had been passed upon his need for the product, and whose ability to pay for the product has been ascertained. The next in order might be a direct first-class letter or telegram sent to a prospect. Then perhaps door-to-door selling or mailing to persons found on selected mailing lists. These selected means of direct promotion used show a widening sales gap between the customer and the product. It is readily seen that broadcast promotion creates the widest sales gap. At the same time it can readily be seen that the marketing radius over which the customer may have to search for the product is increased. Compensating for this increased radius are the more intensive means of promotion that result from direct promotion, which will induce the customer willingly to undertake greater inconveniences of time and distance in order to procure the product.

These definitions relate directly back to the characteristics of goods theory. Whenever a high replacement is involved it becomes physically impossible to effect distribution by direct means. Such a situation calls for mass selling and mass movement of goods wherein all economies of volume selling and goods handling are brought into play. The low gross margin on the individual transaction requires that the aggregate gross margin resulting from mass selling be ample to get the job done. It seems ludicrous to think of fashioning cigarettes to the consumers' needs at the point of sale, putting on filters and adjusting lengths to king size. The gross margin required to do such a job would put cigarettes in the price class of silverware and the number of people who could purchase on that basis would be very small. But mounting a diamond in a special setting is not at all ludicrous, because the gross margin available is large enough to undertake such adjustment. It would be redundant to go through the whole list of characteristics since it is perfectly clear what the relationships would be.

These two theories are excellent marketing tools and aid materially in understanding the marketing processes and their interactions. At the same time they may become dangerous tools in the hands of those who are not skilled in marketing. Even the experienced practitioners need to be fully cognizant of the technological advances as they occur and how these advances affect marketing processes. Skill in use of these tools should increase with experience in applying them to actual marketing situations.

13

New Products—Keys to Corporate Growth

Taylor W. Meloan

IMPORTANCE OF NEW PRODUCTS

No phase of marketing management has received greater attention in industry during recent years than has new product planning, research, and development. The reasons for this stress are obvious. In most industries competitive pressures require a constant flow of technologically new goods, or improvements in existing ones if corporate sales and profits are to be sustained or enhanced. In chemicals, metal working machinery, industrial installations, and transportation equipment, as examples, new products have accounted for 40 to 80 per cent of sales increases during the past five years. The same is true in many consumer goods markets. The drug, cosmetic, photographic, toy, and household goods fields have been especially prolific of new product introductions in the immediate past. Some relatively small firms have blossomed overnight on the basis of a single new development that has caught on.

The recent softening of our economy has not resulted in less emphasis on new products. Indeed, it has doubtless led to an increase in overall research and development, and more new technology as firms have continued to scramble for the consumer and/or the industrial dollar....

NEW PRODUCT BATTING AVERAGES

For years we have read that four out of five new products fail. This cliché stems from an early postwar study of 200 leading packaged goods manufacturers. Since respondents were asked about their success with products actually introduced, it is contended that the failure rate would have been even greater if those which never reached the commercialization stage, on

Reprinted from a paper by Taylor W. Meloan, "New Products—Keys to Corporate Growth," presented at the Winter Conference of the American Marketing Association, December 28-30, 1960, St. Louis, published by the American Marketing Association.

which management spent considerable time and talent in laboratory, field, and office, had also been included in the calculations.[1] And since the sample was restricted to *large* firms, it is often argued that the success ratio would have been much less had *smaller*, and presumably less sophisticated firms, been included in the survey. However, these are unproven hypotheses that are partially refuted by later data. In a survey completed in New England in 1954 of eighty-two firms making industrial goods, 357 of 515 new products introduced during the previous five-year period were considered to be successful. Of this group, 45 per cent enjoyed sales equal to expectations, while 19.5 per cent exceeded projected volume.[2] Study of new product success ratios in the electronics field during the same period produced similar conclusions. A survey of sixty-five prominent concerns completed in 1960 revealed a fifty-fifty new product success-failure average.[3]

Success Criteria

In part, these differing ratios stem from lack of common norms for defining product success. While sales volume and profits are traditional ones, ancillary success criteria cited by marketing managers include the following: tapping new markets, making other orders possible, absorbing excess capacity, providing potential for expansion, reinforcing a firm's reputation as a leader, and reducing returns or complaints about performance. A high score on one or more of the foregoing criteria could result in a new product with a mediocre sales record being considered a satisfactory addition to a line.

Failure Rates in Consumer versus Industrial Fields

There is reason to believe that consumer goods producers often experience a higher new product failure rate than do those making industrial goods. Generally there are more distribution variables to consider in successfully launching new consumer products than is the case with industrial ones. And the extensive promotional budget required for many nationally distributed consumer goods in highly competitive lines create difficult-to-achieve break-even points which are not common in job-order industrial fields where limited markets and small volume do not necessarily spell failure. Admittedly, however, large research investments in technologically new industrial products can lengthen pay-out periods unduly, thereby creating situations comparable to those faced by new consumer goods in intensely competitive markets.

NEW PRODUCT POLICY GUIDES

Although many firms now have written statements covering their new product emphasis or objectives, there is considerable evidence indicating that these policy guides are frequently so broad that they are of limited value in channeling effort. Product scope, desirable mix, and profitability criteria are too often inadequately covered. The marketing managers of other concerns indicate that written product policy statements are unnecessary because of the close rapport among members of the top management team. But when they give differing replies to questions about new product plans there is obvious reason to question their agreement.

Clear-cut Goals Needed

The first and most elementary step in achieving new product planning, research, and development maturity is to formulate logical accomplishment goals. This implies a complete audit of company strengths and weaknesses. An objective analysis of production capacity, availability of materials, adequacy of labor, management talent, and distribution facilities provides the basis for future planning. What one firm may reasonably expect to accomplish may be a pie-in-the-sky dream for another.

Production and Marketing Concentricity

In many successful companies, the key factor influencing the selection of new products for development and commercialization is the degree to which they fit or mesh with the present line. A high degree of production accord exists when present plant, labor, equipment, and manufacturing processes can be used in making new products. Acceptable adjustment requires minimum additions or alterations in one or more of these production categories. Such firms also consider it desirable when a contemplated addition to the line can be manufactured with materials and components identical or similar to those used in current production. This is the rationale of the Ekco Products Company, which is probably best known to most of us for its housewares and cutlery. Because of this firm's production know-how with metals, its primary areas of product interest are other houseware items and builders' hardware.

From a marketing standpoint, new product harmony exists when established distribution outlets and sales organizations can be used to move a new good or line through the pipelines. Helene Curtis Industries, Inc., for example, is interested chiefly in new products that may be sold through drug, grocery, department, and variety stores—its traditional channels. The possibility of using the same service or repair facilities and personnel enhances the fit between current products and new ones as does blanket brand identification. The recent introduction of the Hoover Company's new floor polisher was facilitated by the firm's half century image as a leader in home cleaning equipment.

Decisions Depend Upon Objectives

Lack of a high degree of production or marketing adjacency between established products and contemplated new ones does not necessarily mean that new product ideas should be discarded. This decision depends upon a firm's objectives. As the Cheshire Cat commented to Alice in Wonderland, where one goes depends a great deal on where he wants to get to. Smoothing out seasonal fluctuations in sales was reported to be a prime consideration behind the purchase of the assets of the Inserting and Mailing Machine Company by Bell and Howell. Textron, Inc. has sought to overcome low profits in the textile field by moving into defense, industrial, and consumer goods industries where at least 20 per cent after taxes on net worth may be earned. Textiles account for only 17 per cent of Textron's current sales volume. Most West Coast aircraft companies have established commercial products divisions largely because of short run insecurity over cold war temperature changes, and the longer run phasing out of military air frame construction. In short, there are many pertinent and often interrelated reasons why firms move into new lines or industries.[4]

Propagation and Acceptance of Criteria

In most companies, including those previously cited, product scope and mix are usually determined on the basis of multiple criteria. Regardless of what they are, such considerations should be *recorded, disseminated, understood, promoted,* and *accepted* by all appropriate personnel through the intermediate management levels of the enterprise. The establishment of product line parameters should not stifle management imagination, but rather guide it in directions designed to maximize the achievement of company objectives. And consideration of ideas which clearly fall outside of the boundaries that have been set up should require exceptional justification.

Annual review of product policy statements is desirable to make sure that they continue to reflect corporate objectives. If they have been carefully drafted initially, only minor changes should be needed from time to time in the absence of an abrupt shift in management thinking.

NEW PRODUCT IDEA SOURCES

Study of a large number of new product case histories fails to show any single source of ideas as the most fruitful one. Generally, however, internal sources are cited more often than external ones as creative seedbeds. Some companies seem to have a dearth of suggestions while others are deluged with them. The key factor stimulating the internal flow of ideas appears to be an innovationist philosophy which pervades the entire organization. A highly motivated management team in a permissive organization that is known to be willing to accept the risks of new product evolution is almost sure to be more productive of ideas than equally competent men in an authoritarian, or "fat and tired" firm that is primarily interested in maintaining the status quo.

In part, however, the number of product ideas available for consideration is a function of a firm's definition of "newness." Concerns that limit product change to minor variations in operation, design, color, or packaging are likely to have more ideas to consider than those that seek true technological newness. And companies with well structured R&D facilities and engineering laboratories typically get more worthwhile ideas internally than do smaller companies that perforce often turn to external sources such as customers, raw material suppliers, competitors, firms in allied fields, government agencies, consulting organizations, research institutes, or free-lance product analysts.

Independent Idea Screeners

Organizations that specialize primarily in generating new product ideas and/or analyzing those submitted by outsiders for clients are a relatively new breed of business service. Because of the cost and complexity of finding worthwhile product ideas, 140 Los Angeles metal products manufacturers of everything from wheelbarrows to missile components belong to Associated Specialists, Inc.—a former trade association that actively solicits new products for its members.[5] In Boston, the Product Development Corporation screens for its twelve clients between 300 and 400 suggestions submitted weekly by outsiders. According to PDC, one idea of practical merit can be winnowed from every 1,000 submitted.[6] About 2 per cent of those received by Associated Specialists are worthy of development. In spite of the modest percentage of worthwhile ideas turned up by organizations like PDC and Associated Specialists, there is every reason to believe that other similar services will be started in the near future.

Legal Hazards

Use of such outside agencies can mitigate to some degree the legal hazard of having a confidential relationship thrust upon a company for alleged or actual use of an unsolicited idea. Cautious firms that decline to consider unpatented suggestions from outsiders often return such letters with covering notes stating that mail clerks stopped reading when the nature of the correspondence became apparent. Other companies return suggestions with release forms for the signature of those submitting ideas. Generally these waivers disclaim liability if the company examines the proposal. They specify further that payment shall be at the firm's sole discretion and shall not exceed a stipulated amount. The obvious purpose of these steps is to preclude a confidential relationship developing unless and until agreement is reached regarding compensation, if any, for the idea.

Rather than enter into royalty arrangements with outsiders, many companies prefer to buy outright ideas or information which interests them, or they may escrow the proposition with a third party who is technically qualified to evaluate its merits. In any event, most attorneys consider it highly unwise to submit unsolicited ideas to a panel or a committee of technical or management personnel for evaluation prior to limiting corporate obligations to the outsider.[7] On the other hand, some marketing managers argue that so few ideas from outsiders have any real merit that a critical review of all confidential disclosures can hardly put a firm in serious legal danger. This is more likely to be true in smaller firms, and especially those making industrial goods, than it is with large, well-known manufacturers of consumer products. Many prominent companies receive hundreds of suggestions weekly from outsiders. Without the use of legal safeguards in handling them, it is almost a foregone conclusion that certain of them would result in lawsuits.

Advertising for Ideas

A few companies combine their research for new products with institutional advertising. A recent American Machine and Foundry Company display advertisement in the *Los Angeles Times* identified the firm as creators of leisure time products for the consumer, and manufacturers of chemical and electromechanical equipment for industry and defense. Readers were invited to telephone for an appointment to discuss ideas for new products that might fit within the marketing and manufacturing capabilities of an AM&F division, or that could form the basis for an entirely new product line. About 300 replies were received of which fifty merited further consideration. Several of the suggestions were found to be worthy of detailed study. AM&F contemplates repeating this experiment in other cities.[8]

New Products by Merger

Companies that seek new products or lines via merger sometimes make known their interest in acquisitions by print advertising too, especially in business and trade publications. Generally, however, they rely on brokers, consultants, bankers, business friends, and aggressive "scouting" for leads. For example, the L. A. Young Spring and Wire Company, a diversified producer of seats and mattresses, power tail gates, dump truck bodies, and electronic equipment, has compiled a mailing list of 1,500 influential businessmen and community leaders around the country who are reminded occasionally of Young's interest in other enterprises.[9]

Securing acquisition leads is no less difficult than generating ideas for internal development. However, well financed, respected companies that are considered to be merger conscious apparently do not lack for candidates from whom to choose. The Glidden Company and Purex Corporation are reported to be contacted regularly by firms that wish to affiliate with them. And, while it may be presumed that there are many "cats and dogs" among the list, well managed, desirable firms are also available for consideration. Sometimes they favor merger with a larger and stronger company in order to secure new capital for continued growth. In many other instances, the management of a closely held corporation may want to sell out in order to realize a capital gain, or to make possible an exchange of stock that has tax advantages.

ORGANIZATION FOR ACTION

Regardless of whether a firm expands its line by development of products within the firm, through purchase of existing businesses or products, or by pursuing an ambidextrous policy, organization for action is necessary. Without *motivation, direction,* and *coordination* of staff specifically charged with new product responsibility, it is unlikely that anything will happen. In many firms, initial discussions about the desirability of new products have not led to the creation of appropriate plans and procedures for internal development because executives were too absorbed in day-to-day operations.

New Product Departments

In recognition of the importance of new product evolution as a full time activity, more and more firms are setting up new product or product planning departments. As yet, they rarely exceed four or five managerial members. In fact, many of them initially consist of only a director. The key purposes of these managers and departments are to mesh the gears of the new product creation process, and to insure continuity of effort. Liaison between technical and marketing research and development must be maintained, as well as multidirectional communication between staff and line production, finance, and sales personnel. Frequently, too, the work of independent design, marketing, or management consultants must be coordinated with that of the company. Usually product planning managers report directly to top management; common alternatives provide for reporting to the president or executive vice-president, to the vice-president of research and development, or to the vice-president of marketing or sales.[10]

Use of Committees

Because of the interfunctional nature of successful new product evolution, many companies use one or more kinds of committees to facilitate action in addition to or in lieu of product planning personnel. In some firms, product idea teams plus product screening or evaluation committees have been set up. Creative, divergent thinkers are sought for the former groups, while the latter committees are usually composed of those with analytical, convergent minds who review critically the output of the idea teams. In other firms, these functions are performed by one committee. It generates ideas of its own, passes judgment on those submitted by others within the firm, and reviews suggestions from outsiders that have been cleared by the legal department. If the company has a product planning department, one or more members are usually assigned to each committee. Often the product planning manager is either chairman or secretary of idea and/or screening committees. He seeks to establish a creative climate and a sense of momentum in their deliberations. This is important because committee members usually have day-to-day responsibilities that often seem more pressing. Another common responsibility of product planning department members who are assigned to committees is the maintenance of records about group decisions. Such committees may also be chaired by a member of general management, marketing management, or by an R&D officer. In any event, all of the foregoing areas plus marketing research, finance, production, and sales are likely to be represented.

While the use of committees and/or new product departments are the prevailing ways of expediting new product evolution, this responsibility is borne in some companies solely by the research and development department, by the sales department, or by a member of top management, even the president. The Stauffer Chemical Company is a successful case in point. The president directs all new product activities personally.

Initial Appraisal

Preliminary screening is an obvious initial step in winnowing new product wheat from chaff. Regardless of whether it is done by a committee, a department, or an individual, experience and judgment are used at this stage far more than formal research. If a firm has established its overall objectives and scope of product interest, the delineation of preliminary screening criteria should not be too difficult. Ideas are considered in the light of these factors. Reference tools largely consist of the telephone, knowledgeable people in the firm, and the reference library.[11] In many companies, from one hour to two days is a common range per idea. Of course, obviously inappropriate ones are rejected immediately.

Feasibility Analyses

Ideas that survive preliminary screening are generally subjected next to more detailed technical and marketing analyses. To facilitate research and interdepartmental communications, product proposals are usually prepared at this stage describing the idea and its purposes in concrete terms. Some companies have forms for this purpose that are quite detailed. That of Beckman Instruments is eight pages. Like many others, it provides space to record the results of research and the estimates of functional specialists about project feasibility. A majority of companies use checklists of some sort for this purpose. Those that conduct analyses-in-depth commonly include sections covering the project cost and time schedule, the target date for completion, estimated average return on investment, patent possibilities and restrictions, projected sales in dollars and units for x years, pricing, product life, the effect, if any, on the current line, the competitive situation, manufacturing fit, channels of distribution, promotional investment, and a project P & L statement or break-even chart.

Evaluation Formulas

A few companies have experimented with numerical formulas or equations to secure a quantitative indication of an idea's worth. They include the Quaker Oats Company, Monsanto Chemical Company, Olin Industries, Inc., and American Alcolac. In most of these schemes, the rater assigns a point score from a specified range to each of a series of product criteria. In some of them, plus and minus values are used. Others require simple mathematical calculations. But they all provide a total point score or an index number. Their purpose is to establish priorities for developmental consideration. A few firms using new product rating systems have scored past projects, successful and unsuccessful as bench marks for comparison. These schemes have been controversial. Opponents argue that they are arbitrary and lack flexibility. Supporters rebut with the contention that they force consideration on an organized basis of all of the key variables influencing product success. And their users point out that the factors and weights can be modified to meet changing conditions. They also point out that the ratings can be supported or refuted by other data.

The foregoing implies that all companies conduct a detailed study of projects that have survived preliminary screening. This is not always the case. Some firms seek only a broad spectrum of executive opinion about ideas under consideration. They reserve more detailed analysis until the project has been authorized. In other companies, the depth of analysis depends largely upon the investment in the contemplated product.

Coordination of the Analysis Phase

Like preliminary screening, the analysis phase of new product investigation is coordinated in most firms either by a committee, by the new products department, or cooperatively by both. In companies favoring committees, the preliminary screening group may also coordinate the feasibility investigation. In other firms, these activities are kept separated. In large concerns with many projects under consideration, several teams or sponsor groups may be coordinating feasibility studies simultaneously. Team membership depends upon the research requirements. If the firm has a new products department, it is usually represented on each group, and part of the data gathering is done by that department. Naturally, other areas and functional specialists must be called upon for help too. In firms that do not rely upon committees and/or new products departments to coordinate idea analyses, this phase of product evolution will likely be directed by a designated member of general management, marketing management, sales, or R&D.[12]

When the feasibility investigation is complete, the data must be summarized with a recommendation—usually by the executive in charge of the research. Often segmental approvals by area heads are secured. Then proposals are examined *in toto* by the executive committee of the firm and/or by the officials in charge of new products. They may approve the project, table it, or reject it. Or they may authorize additional research before a final decision is made.

Acquisition Screening

Organization for action is equally necessary if a company embarks upon an acquisition program. However, the screening arrangements for mergers are usually less complex than those required for internal evolution of products. The former is often done under the direction of the president, chairman, member of the board of directors, or a designated top management representative.[13] Firms like the Rockwell Manufacturing Company use extensive evaluation check lists, and functional specialists within the firm are called upon as needed in the analysis process. Consultants are often used too, especially to conduct management audits. Generally, attention is given to the candidate's production facilities, inventories, finances, market position, and product lines.

SUMMING UP

Most concerns are still experimenting with organizational procedures and techniques for new product evolution. There is no one best way that will fit every firm. The foregoing approaches must be adapted creatively to meet specific company needs. Intelligent planning, an intense pioneering spirit, and continuity of effort are key attributes in achieving success. New product planning, research, and development is still in its youth, but it is on the threshold of maturity.

NOTES

[1]Ross Federal Research Corporation, "A Survey of 200 Leading Package Goods Manufacturers on Experiences and Problems Prevalent in the Introduction of a New Product" (New York: Ross Federal Research Corporation, 1945), p. 4.

[2]William B. Martz, "A Survey of Reasons Behind the Introduction of New Industrial Products" (Cambridge, Massachusetts: School of Industrial Management, Massachusetts Institute of Technology, unpublished manuscript, 1954), p. 37.

[3]Booz, Allen & Hamilton, "Management of New Product" (Chicago: Booz, Allen & Hamilton, 1960), pp. 14–15.

[4]See Thomas A. Staudt, "Product Diversification," *Harvard Business Review* (November-December 1954), pp. 122-23, for a list of forty-three reasons for diversification.

[5]Interview with C. W. Farrar, Executive Secretary, Associated Specialists, Inc., Los Angeles, California on December 10, 1960.

[6]Interview with William Donohue, Vice President, Product Development Corporation. Boston, Massachusetts on December 18, 1960.

[7]See Bessie A. Lepper, "Ideas From Outsiders Can Be Dangerous," *Chemical Week* (August 17, 1957), pp. 107-112, and John W. Bohlen, "Legal Considerations in Product Development and Introduction," in *Establishing a New Product Program* (New York: American Management Association, 1958), pp. 30-36.

[8]Interview with Hamilton Herman, Vice President, Research and Development, American Machine & Foundry Company, New York, New York on December 22, 1960.

[9]Russell B. Robins, "New Products by Proxy," *Marketing's Role in Scientific Management* (Chicago: American Marketing Association, 1957), pp. 74-78.

[10]See E. Jerome McCarthy, "Organization for New Product Development," *The Journal of Business* (April, 1959), pp. 128-32 for a review of organizational structures for new product development.

[11]"Survey Report: How to Plan New Products," *The Iron Age* (October 17, 1957), p. 88.

[12]See James H. Wolter, "An Evaluation of the Process of New Product Idea Evaluation for Consumer Goods" (Bloomington, Indiana: School of Business, Indiana University, unpublished manuscript, 1960), pp. 67-107, for a detailed review of the preliminary screening and feasibility analysis phases of new product evolution.

[13]See George D. McCarthy, "Premeditated Merger," *Harvard Business Review* (January-February, 1961), pp. 74-82 for an excellent discussion of the organizational structure and personnel used in screening mergers.

14

A Theory of Packaging
in the Marketing Mix

William R. Mason

It is axiomatic that the job of packaging is to sell. But after that banality has been voiced, what guides to management judgment—what theories, if you will—influence the choice of a package?

This article is not a check list of features that should be built into a package, but a rough guide to basic judgments management must bring to bear in its choice of packaging before the particulars of type face, combination of colors, package count, or printing method are up for decision.

The critical judgments that must be made on the packaging choice concern the "mix" of packaging attributes best able to perform, in different degrees, the particular functions of the package that are believed to be important to sales. The basic judgment in choice of packaging is "What jobs should the package do, and how completely should it do each?" The answers to the lesser decisions can fall into place once the "mix" of desirable packaging attributes has been determined, once the assignment of basic functions desired of the package has been made. Frequently, too much effort and time are devoted to making lesser decisions, usually on questions of graphic art, rather than this basic judgment.

The packager may accept as a guide, when making basic decisions on product "mix," that: *"The major purpose of any package is to influence or control the location of product storage within the marketing channel."* "Storage," as I am using the term, means the holding of goods for future use at any level along the marketing channel, *including the level of the ultimate consumer.* Even at the ultimate consumer level, the product may be stored in several places: sugar, for example, may be stored on a shelf or on

From William R. Mason, "A Theory of Packaging in the Marketing Mix," *Business Horizons,* Vol. 1 (Summer 1958), pp. 91–95, © 1958, by the Foundation for the School of Business at Indiana University. Reprinted by permission.

the table. The packager is interested in getting the bulk of his product's storage as near as possible to the point of ultimate use.

The functions of the product's package are:

- protecting the product
- adapting to production line speeds
- promoting the product
- increasing product density[1]
- facilitating the use of the product
- having re-use value for the consumer.

The performance of a package in the first two of these basic functions is relatively easy to measure through physical testing procedures. And, because it is comparatively easy to evaluate the degrees to which these functions are fulfilled by any package under consideration, such measurement is very common. Today, it must be a rare package that reaches its market without being rated objectively on its degrees of protection and production line adaptability. However, these ratings seem to be applied too often without consideration of the package's ability to fulfill its other possible functions.

There are four other major jobs that the package can do at least partially; these should be assigned priority by company management, but often they seem to be neglected.

All packages have the opportunity to perform, at least partially, each of these functions. But it is an unusual package that performs each to the same degree. That the package gives a superior performance of one function does not necessarily mean that it will give a superior performance of another. Because he needs to choose a package, the packager, whether he recognizes it or not, must assign priorities to the value of each of these functions to further his product's sale and use.

To illustrate, it is usually easy to create a package that has uniquely promotable features quite aside from graphic arts; that is, a package that could eminently perform the promotional function. But something else has to give. Using such a package may require sacrificing a good job in one of the other areas, for example in adaptability to production line speeds, or in failure to increase package density. In like fashion, it is frequently possible to build a feature facilitating product use into a package—but not always without sacrificing some measure of product protection.

After all, when a package is criticized as a poor sales or use builder, it can be criticized fairly only when its performance of *each* of the basic functions is evaluated. A product may seem "overpackaged" simply because the packager's assignment of priorities differs from the critic's.

INTERRELATIONSHIPS

Let's examine in a little more detail the way each function impinges on the others.

Protecting the Product.   Beyond the requirements imposed by various governmental, carrier, and trade practice rulings, there usually are a substantial number of alternatives open to management with regard to product protection, even during the period when the product is in its distribution channel. To illustrate, even though a carrier ruling may require the product's twenty-four-count carton to have a minimum corrugated fiber-board strength of, say, a 100-pound test, a company's management may choose board that meets more severe tests in order to permit higher stacking or use of mechanized materials-handling equipment by certain important handlers at various levels in the product's distribution channel. Accordingly, in such a situation, an opportunity to tailor the product's package to its product-protection job alone is relinquished because of a desire to better the package's performance of its density-increasing and promotional jobs.

But perhaps a more important range of product-protection considerations occurs at the time of product use, especially when the product is partially used. How much protection should the bread wrapper give a partially used loaf of bread? Will incorporating the use-facilitating features of a pouring spout or a tear tape opening require yielding too much product protection?

Adapting to Production Line Speeds.   Sometimes the operating speeds of packaging equipment do not match the speeds of other equipment in the production line. Until recently, for instance, the normal operating speeds of wrapping machinery that would handle polyethylene film did not match the normal production line speeds for many products. Two or more wrapping machines were often required in a production line, and the results were poor space utilization, greater capital investment, and sometimes greater labor costs. As an alternative to these wastes, the packager "made do" with other types of film that could be handled by high-speed wrapping equipment but lacked some of polyethylene's protective attributes. New types of wrapping machines have largely corrected this situation. But the point is that the freedom of the packagers to better their packages' protective attributes was limited.

The question of a package's adaptability to production line speeds, however, usually crops up before the package is actually used. The packager's advertising agency or his sales department suggests a new package with striking promise of being able to fulfill the promotional or use-facilitating function better than current packaging; but, upon analysis, the suggested new package is found to require either slow-downs in production line speeds or investment in new packaging equipment. The company's management is then obliged to judge whether or not the suggested package's better performance of the promotional or use-facilitating functions justifies the slower line speed or the different packaging equipment.

Promoting the Product.   Features may be built into a package which are promotable to consumers, to customers, and to intermediaries in its product's distribution channel. But sometimes a feature desirable for promotion to one of the three is not desirable for one of the others. Features that minimize a retailer's loss or pilferage are, presumably, important to him; but they are not necessarily of any interest to consumers. Features that minimize a consumer's embarrassment at purchase can increase a retailer's stacking or display difficulties and make inventory control more trying.

Even granting a package feature that is promotable regardless of level in its product's distribution or use, incorporation of the feature into the package frequently requires sacrificing some good package performance of one of the other basic package functions. For example, a gift-wrapped set-up box complete with nosegay of artificial flowers is a highly promotable candy package, as is a rigid plastic, reusable package for razors that is large enough to hold a fishing lure. But both packages sacrifice density for better promotion.

Increasing Product Density.   This seems to be the area where the packager's sales department on the one hand, and his purchasing and production departments on the other, are most often in disagreement about the choice of packaging. Except on those occasions when the sales department recommends yielding a package's higher density in order to improve its promotional value, the sales department is usually advocating increased package density. It improves relations with carriers; it permits better utilization of space throughout the distribution channel, thus encouraging fuller inventory stocks in the pipeline; and it permits more units to be displayed per assigned running foot of self-service display space. But it frequently slows production line speeds and increases per-unit packaging cost.

Usually this issue turns on package shape. The cylinder, for instance, is an efficient package shape for liquids; a given measure of liquid can be packaged cylindrically with less material than is necessary for any rectangular container holding the same amount of liquid. But the normal twelve-count (3 x 4 put-up) layer of a twenty-four-count carton will occupy significantly less shelf space if it holds rectangular packages rather than the same number of cylindrical packages with the same amount of liquid.

But bettering a package's performance of its density-increasing function can inhibit good performance in other areas too. The density of many candy packages, for instance, could be improved significantly, but not without loss of their value as items specifically tailored for re-use as sewing baskets or cookie tins. Increasing density could also lessen the package's value as a promotional vehicle or as a promotable item in itself. Package designers seem better able to build points of brand differentiation into a twelve-ounce beer bottle than into the higher-density twelve-ounce beer can.

Facilitating the Use of the Product.   Excluding changes in the graphic art of packages, most package changes in recent years have been in facilitating the product's use. All the changes to tear tapes, pouring spouts, squeeze bottles, aerosol cans, and so forth would have to be included here. And, as is obvious to anyone exposed to the mass advertising media, bettering the package's fulfillment of this function has proved to be a means of bettering the package's performance in promotion.

In many cases, however, where the use-facilitating function of a package has been improved, a case can be built that some degree of product protection has been sacrificed. And, bettering the package's use-facilitating job sometimes means relinquishing some package value as a re-use container for the consumer. The flow of a viscous liquid perhaps can be directed a little more accurately or easily from the mouth of a narrow-necked glass jar than from a tin can, but packaging the liquid in the glass jar means sacrificing the protection against impact provided by the tin can. The tear tape makes a corrugated carton easier to open but, for many purposes, lessens its value as a reusable container. Some shaker openings make cleanser or spice packages easy to use but, once used, leave the product exposed.

Having Re-Use Value for the Consumer.   Perhaps the competition of the various functions of the package for recognition by company managements is most apparent in this area. In recent years, according much recognition to this function of the package seems not to have been in vogue. Typically, designing a package to do its other jobs well has meant slighting its re-use value—the previous illustrations of candy and razors notwithstanding. A package's re-use value generally has suffered with successive changes unless its reusability has been very promotable.

THE PRINCIPLE, THE COROLLARY, AND RECENT TRENDS

Assuming that two "mixes" are in conflict or partial conflict, management may find the answer by deciding which will be more likely to push product storage as far from the packager as possible. This is, of course, another way of saying that the basic purpose of a product's package should be as much as possible to maximize product inventory near the point of use or possible use. If neither "mix" holds promise of increasing product inventory at the point of use, does either hold promise of increasing product storage at the next level back from the point of use? If neither "mix" aids in getting the product stored on the dining room table, does either help in getting more of the product inventories on the kitchen shelves? If neither helps there, which encourages the greater amount of well-placed open display at retail? If it is a tie between the two package "mixes" at this level which of the two has promise of encouraging the greater retailer inventory, regardless whether in open display or not?

It follows, then, that the most successful package changes are those whose impact is greatest at a level in the product's marketing one step forward from the level currently storing the channel's largest share of the product.

Most recent packaging changes can be understood a little better if viewed against the backdrop of these generalizations. Interestingly, they explain current trends in package design that, on the surface, seem to be running in opposite directions. For instance, recently some company managements have been increasing package size or package count. Other managements have unit-packaged, lessened package size, or reduced package count. But both apparently contradictory approaches have the same purpose—*to maximize product inventory as close to a point of use as possible.* Let's examine a few recent package changes in light of these generalizations (I am referring to those changes that typically affect more than just the package's graphic art):

Changes Involving Package Size or Count.   Proprietary medicine, soap powder or detergent, beverages, and toilet tissue are among those widely distributed consumer products whose recent package changes have included addition of "king" or "giant economy" size packages to their lines. Table salt, facial tissue, crackers, and cereal are among the items, distributed in large part through the same marketing channel, which have added smaller-size packages or "unitized" packages to their lines. In each case, promotion turning on "convenience" to the user frequently has accompanied the introduction of the new package size. Where the move has been to increase the package size, packagers are trying to encourage the consumer to maintain inventories of their particular brands far in excess of the consumer's normal needs for the product during any reasonable time span between shopping trips. In effect, the packagers are trying to move a greater share of their channel's total storage function closer to the point of use—from retailer to consumer in this particular illustration. Where the move has been to lessen package size, it is apparent that the packagers are trying to move storage location further forward: to get facial tissues into purses as well as on the vanity; to get brand-identified salt on the dining room, breakfast, TV, or barbecue table as well as on the pantry shelf; to get a half-dozen varieties of cereal in the home rather than in the store in anticipation of a family's vacillating demands. Again, the packagers are trying to move a greater share of the channel's total storage closer to the point of use.

Changes Involving Package Shape.   Ice cream and milk, in both powdered and liquid forms, are examples of items that have been undergoing changes from cylindrical to space-saving rectangular packages. In part, at least, the change has been precipitated by increased recognition of the marketing channel's limited capacity to store items under refrigeration and of its eagerness to husband its shelf space. In effect, the change permits a greater share of the inventory to be moved forward.

Changes Involving Packaging Materials. This is the area where packagers' desires to push storage forward probably have been most apparent. And, incidentally, it is in this area that the lie is put to the belief that a package's prime job is protection of the product. If product protection were the prevailing consideration, few if any of certain kinds of change in packaging materials would ever have taken place. For example:

1. Changes from opaque to transparent materials usually have been represented as irrefutable evidence of the packager's good faith in allowing his customers to see his product. Understandably, the suppliers of transparent packaging materials have done what they could to further this impression. But conversion from opaque to transparent packaging typically has meant something else as well: *It has been a means of obtaining favorable open display shelf space at retail,* where the product could be seen by the consumers. In effect, it has meant moving part of the storage function forward in the channel from concealed storage or low-traffic locations to prominent, high-traffic locations. Small wonder that such a premium has come to be placed on transparency, even for products not especially attractive to the eye.

2. Changes from rigid to flexible materials have almost always meant relinquishing some measure of product protection, and the recent changes from rigid to semirigid or flexible packaging are legion. The changes, while requiring some loss of product-protection value, typically have given the product an especially promotable package, one with conspicuous promise of moving product storage closer to a point of use.

Changes Involving Addition of "Ease-of-Opening" or "Ease-of-Use" Attributes. I believe that, where they have been successful, package changes incorporating this kind of feature have tended to move product storage increasingly closer—however slightly—to the point of use. Typically, the movement of storage effected by such "ease-of-opening" package changes has not been at the consumer level in the product's marketing channel; it has been at the retail level. Perhaps it could be argued that the extremely successful rigid flip-top cigarette package has helped move the smoker's storage of his cigarettes a little closer to the point of their use, but the main value of the package with regard to its movement of product storage has been at the retail level. The package, again, was a means of obtaining a good, high-traffic position in open display for the particular brands of cigarette that pioneered this packaging change. It was something distinctly new that could be promoted to the marketing channel itself—quite aside from its being amenable to use in effective promotion to smokers—for brands not having so extensive or complete retail inventories as those enjoyed by more popular brands.

In summary, the choice of a product's package, no less than the choice of the total selling effort brought to bear on the product, has to represent a reconciliation of a variety of functions, each of which has potential merit in furthering the sale of the product, but all of which are, in part at least, mutually exclusive.

The most successful reconciliation will be the one that, to return to our original axiom, produces the most sales. It will emphasize that function which pushes the bulk of product storage one step farther along the marketing channel and one step closer to the ultimate consumer.

NOTE

[1]That is, increasing the ratio of product volume to package volume.

15

The Death and Burial
of "Sick" Products

R. S. Alexander

Euthanasia applied to human beings is criminal; but aging products enjoy or suffer no such legal protection. This is a sad fact of business life.

The word "product" is used here not in its broad economic sense of anything produced—such as wheat, coal, a car, or a chair—but in its narrower meaning of an article made to distinct specifications and intended for sale under a separate brand or catalogue number. In the broader sense of the word, certain products may last as long as industrial civilization endures; in the narrow sense, most of them are playthings of change.

Much has been written about managing the development and marketing of new products, but business literature is largely devoid of material on product deletion.

This is not surprising. New products have glamor. Their management is fraught with great risks. Their successful introduction promises growth in sales and profits that may be fantastic.

But putting products to death—or letting them die—is a drab business, and often engenders much of the sadness of a final parting with old and tried friends. "The portable six-sided, pretzel polisher was the first product The Company ever made. Our line will no longer be our line without it."

But while deletion is an uninspiring and depressing process, in a changing market it is almost as vital as the addition of new products. The old product that is a "football" of competition or has lost much of its market appeal is likely to generate more than its share of small unprofitable orders; to make necessary short, costly production runs; to demand an exorbitant amount of executive attention; and to tie up capital that could be used more profitably in other ventures.

Reprinted from R. S. Alexander, "The Death and Burial of 'Sick' Products," in the *Journal of Marketing*, Vol. 28 (April 1964), pp. 1–7, published by the American Marketing Association.

Just as a crust of barnacles on the hold of a ship retards the vessel's movement, so do a number of worn-out items in a company's product mix affect the company's progress.

Most of the costs that result from the lack of an effective deletion system are hidden and become apparent only after careful analysis. As a result, management often overlooks them. The need for examining the product line to discover outworn members, and for analysis to arrive at intelligent decisions to discard or to keep them, very rarely assumes the urgency of a crisis. Too often, management thinks of this as something that should be done but that can wait until tomorrow.

This is why a definite procedure for deletion of products should be set up, and why the authority and responsibility for the various activities involved should be clearly and definitely assigned. This is especially important because this work usually requires the cooperation of several functional groups within the business firm, including at least marketing, production, finance, and sometimes personnel.

Definite responsibility should be assigned for at least the following activities involved in the process: (1) selecting products which are candidates for elimination; (2) gathering information about them and analyzing the information; (3) making decisions about elimination; and (4) if necessary, removing the doomed products from the line.

SELECTION OF PRODUCTS FOR POSSIBLE ELIMINATION

As a first step, we are not seeking the factors which influence the final decision to delete or to retain, but merely those which indicate that the product's continuation in the production mix should be considered carefully with elimination as a possibility. Although removal from the product line may seem to be the prime aim, the result is not inevitably deletion from the line; instead, careful analysis may lead to changes in the product itself or in the methods of making or marketing it.

Sales Trend.   If the trend of a product's sales is downward over a time period that is significant in relation to the normal life of others like it, its continuation in the mix deserves careful examination. There may be many reasons for such a decline that in no way point toward deletion; but when decline continues over a period of time the situation needs to be studied.

Price Trend.   A downward trend in the price of a new product may be expected if the firm introducing it pursues a skimming-price policy, or if all firms making it realize substantial cost savings as a result of volume production and increased processing know-how. But when the price of an established product whose competitive pattern has been relatively stabilized shows a downward trend over a significant period of time, the future of that product should receive attention.

Profit Trend.   A declining profit either in dollars or as a per cent of sales or investment should raise questions about a product's continued place in the product line. Such a trend usually is the result of a price-factory cost squeeze, although it may be the outcome of a loss in market appeal or a change in the method of customer purchase which forces higher marketing expenditures.

Substitute Products.   When a substitute article appears on the market, especially if it represents an improvement over an old product, management must face the question of whether to retain or discard the old product. This is true regardless of who introduces the substitute. The problem is especially difficult when the new product serves the same general purpose as the old one but is not an exact substitute for it.

Product Effectiveness.   Certain products may lose some of their effectiveness for the purpose they serve. For example, disease germs may develop strains that are resistant to a certain antibiotic. When this happens, the question of whether to keep or delete the drug involves issues not only of the interests of the firm but of the public welfare.

Executive Time.   A possible tipoff as to the location of "illness" in a product mix lies in a study of the amount of executive time and attention devoted to each of the items in the product line. Sick products, like sick people, demand a lot of care; but one must be careful to distinguish the "growing pains" of a new product from the more serious disorders of one that has matured and is now declining.

The six indicators mentioned do not of themselves provide evidence justifying deletion. But they can help management to single out from a line of products those upon which it can profitably spend time and money in analyzing them, with elimination from the line as a *possibility*.

ANALYSIS AND DECISION MAKING ABOUT "SICK" PRODUCTS

Although the work of analyzing a sick or decrepit product is usually done by people other than the management executives who decide what to do about it, the two processes are interdependent. Unless the right factors are chosen for analysis and unless the work is properly done, the decision is not likely to be an intelligent one. Accordingly, these two factors will be discussed together.

What information does a decision maker need about a product, and what sort of analysis of it should he have in order to render a sound verdict as to its future? The deletion decision should not turn on the sole issue of profitability. Profit is the most important objective of a business; but individual firms often seek to achieve both long-run and short-run objectives other than profit.

So, in any individual case the critical factors and the weights assigned them in making a decision must be chosen in the light of the situation of the firm and the management objectives.

Profits

Profit management in a firm with a multi-product line (the usual situation in our economy) is not the simple operation generally contemplated in economic theory. Such a firm usually has in its product mix (1) items in various stages of introduction and development, some of which may be fantastically profitable and others deep "in the red"; (2) items which are mature but not "superannuated," whose profit rate is likely to be satisfactory; and (3) declining items which may yield a net profit somewhat less than adequate or may show heavy losses.

The task is to manage the whole line or mix so that it will show a satisfactory profit for the company. In this process, two questions are vital; What is a profit? How much profit is satisfactory?

Operating-statement accounting makes it possible to determine with reasonable accuracy the total amount of net profit a company earns on an overall basis. But when the management of a multi-product firm seeks to determine how much of this total is generated by its activities in making and marketing each product in its mix, the process is almost incredibly complex; and the results are almost certain to be conditioned on a tissue of assumptions which are so debatable that no management can feel entirely comfortable in basing decisions on them.

This is because such a large portion of the costs of the average multi-product firm are or behave like overhead or joint expense. Almost inevitably several of the items in the product mix are made of common materials, with the same equipment, and by manpower which is interchangeable. Most of the company's marketing efforts and expenses are devoted to selling and distributing the mix or a line within the mix, rather than individual items.

In general, the more varied the product mix of a firm, the greater is the portion of its total expense that must be classified as joint or overhead. In such a company, many types of cost which ordinarily can be considered direct tend to behave like overhead or joint expenses. This is particularly true of marketing costs such as advertising that does not feature specific items; personal selling; order handling; and delivery.

This means that a large part of a company's costs must be assigned to products on some arbitrary basis and that however logical this basis may be, it is subject to considerable reasonable doubt in specific cases. It also means that if one product is removed from the mix, many of these costs remain to be reassigned to the items that stay in the line. As a result, any attempt to "prune" the product mix entirely on the basis of the profit contribution, or lack of it, of specific items is almost certain to be disappointing and in some cases disastrous.

But if a multi-product firm could allocate costs to individual items in the mix on some basis recognized as sound and thus compute product-profit accurately, what standard of profit should be set up, the failure to meet which would justify deletion?

Probably most managements either formally or unconsciously set overall company profit targets. Such targets may be expressed in terms of dollars, although to be most useful in product management they usually must be translated into percentages on investment, or money used. As an example, a company may have as its profit target fifteen per cent on investment before taxes.

Certainly *every* product in the mix should not be required to achieve the target, which really amounts to an average. To do so would be to deny the inevitable variations in profit potential among products.

Probably a practical minimum standard can be worked out, below which a product should be eliminated unless other considerations demand its retention. Such a standard can be derived from a balancing out of the profit rates among products in the mix, so as to arrive at the overall company target as an average. The minimum standard then represents a figure that would tip the balance enough to endanger the overall target.

What role, then, should considerations of product profit play in managerial decisions as to deletion or retention?

1. Management probably will be wise to recognize an overall company target profit in dollars or rate on investment, and to set in relation to it a minimum below which the profit on an individual product should not fall without marking that item for deletion (unless other special considerations demand its retention).

2. Management should cast a "bilious eye" on all arguments that a questionable product be kept in the mix because it helps to defray overhead and joint costs. Down that road, at the end of a series of decisions to retain such products, lies a mix entirely or largely composed of items each busily "sopping up" overhead, but few or none contributing anything to net profit.

3. This does not mean that management should ignore the effect of a product deletion on overhead or joint costs. Decision makers must be keenly aware of the fact that the total of such costs borne by a sick product must, after it is deleted, be reallocated to other products, and with the result that they may become of doubtful profitability. A detailed examination of the joint or overhead costs charged against an ailing product may indicate that some of them can be eliminated in whole or in part if it is eliminated. Such costs are notoriously "sticky" and difficult to get rid of; but every pretext should be used to try to find ways to reduce them.

4. If a deletion decision involves a product or a group of products responsible for a significant portion of a firm's total sales volume, decision makers can assess the effects of overhead and joint costs on the problem by compiling an estimated company operating statement after the deletion, and comparing it with the current one. Such a forecasted statement should include expected net income from the use of the capital and facilities released by deletion if an opportunity for their use is ready at hand. Surviving joint and overhead expenses can even be reallocated to the

remaining products, in order to arrive at an estimate of the effect that deletion might have not only on the total company net income but on the profitability of each of the remaining products as well. Obviously such a cost analysis is likely to be expensive, and so is not justified unless the sales volume stakes are high.

Financial Considerations

Deletion is likely not only to affect the profit performance of a firm but to modify its financial structure as well.

To make and sell a product, a company must invest some of its capital. In considering its deletion, the decision makers must estimate what will happen to the capital funds presently used in making and marketing it.

When a product is dropped from the mix, most or all of the circulating capital invested in it—such as inventories of materials, goods in process, and finished goods and accounts receivable—should drain back into the cash account; and if carried out in an orderly fashion, deletion will not disturb this part of the capital structure except to increase the ratio of cash to other assets.

This will be true, unless the deletion decision is deferred until product deterioration has gone so far that the decision assumes the aspect of a crisis and its execution that of a catastrophe.

The funds invested in the equipment and other facilities needed to make and market the "sick" product are a different matter. If the equipment is versatile and standard, it may be diverted to other uses. If the firm has no need of it and if the equipment has been properly depreciated, management may find a market for it at a price approaching or even exceeding its book value.

In either case, the capital structure of the company is not disturbed except by a shift from equipment to cash in the case of sale. In such a case management would be wise, before making a deletion decision, to determine how much cash this action promises to release as well as the chances for its reinvestment.

If the equipment is suited for only one purpose, it is highly unlikely that management can either find another use for it or sell it on favorable terms. If it is old and almost completely depreciated, it can probably be scrapped and its remaining value "written off" without serious impairment of the firm's capital structure.

But if it is only partly depreciated, the decision makers must weigh the relative desirability of two possible courses of action: (1) to delete immediately, hoping that the ensuing improvement in the firm's operating results will more than offset the impairment in capital structure that deletion will cause; or (2) to seek to recapture as much as possible of its value, by continuing to make and market the product as long as its price is enough to cover out-of-pocket costs and leave something over to apply to depreciation.

This choice depends largely on two things: the relation between the amount of fixed and circulating capital that is involved; and the opportunities available to use the funds, executive abilities, manpower, and transferable facilities released by deletion for making profits in other ventures.

This matter of opportunity costs is a factor in every deletion decision. The dropping of a product is almost certain to release some capital, facilities, manpower skills, and executive abilities. If opportunities can be found in which these assets can be invested without undue risk and with promise of attractive profits, it may be good management to absorb considerable immediate loss in deleting a sick product.

If no such opportunities can be found, it is probably wise to retain the product so long as the cash inflow from its sales covers out-of-pocket costs and contributes something to depreciation and other overhead expenses. In such a case, however, it is the part of good management to seek actively for new ventures which promise satisfactory profits, and to be ready to delete promptly when such an opportunity is found.

Employee Relations

The effect which product elimination may have on the employees of a firm is often an important factor in decisions either to drop or to retain products.

This is not likely to be a deciding factor if new product projects are under development to which the people employed in making and marketing the doubtful product can be transferred, unless such transfer would deprive them of the earning power of special skills. But when deletion of a product means discharging or transferring unionized employees, the decision makers must give careful thought to the effect their action is likely to have on company-union relations.

Even in the absence of union pressure, management usually feels a strong sense of responsibility for the people in its employ. Just how far management can go in conserving specific jobs at the expense of deferring or foregoing necessary deletions before it endangers the livelihood of all the employees of the firm is a nice question of balance.

Marketing Factors

Many multi-product firms retain in their marketing mixes one or more items which, on the basis of profits and the company financial structure, should be deleted. To continue to make and market a losing product is no managerial crime. It is reprehensible only when management does not know the product is a losing one or, knowing the facts, does not have sound reasons for retaining it. Such reasons are very likely to lie in the marketing area.

Deletions of products are often deferred or neglected because of management's desire to carry a "full line," whatever that means. This desire may be grounded on sound reasons of consumer patronage or on a dubious yearning for the "prestige" that a full line is supposed to engender. But there is no magic about a full line or the prestige that is supposed to flow from it. Both should be evaluated on the basis of their effects on the firm's sales volume, profits, and capacity to survive and grow.

Products are often associated in the marketing process. The sale of one is helped by the presence of another in the product mix.

When elimination of a product forces a customer who buys all or a large part of his requirements of a group of profitable items from the firm to turn to another supplier for his needs of the dropped product, he might shift some or all of his other patronage as well. Accordingly, it is sometimes wise for management to retain in its mix a no-profit item, in order to hold sales volume of highly profitable products. But this should not be done blindly, without analysis.

Rarely can management tell ahead of time exactly how much other business will be lost by deleting a product, or in what proportions the losses will fall among the remaining items. But in many cases the amount of sales volume can be computed that will be *hazarded* by such action; what other products will be subject to that hazard; and what portion of their volume will be involved. When this marketing interdependence exists in a deletion problem, the decision makers should seek to discover the customers who buy the sick product; what other items in the mix they buy; in what quantities; and how much profit they contribute.

The firm using direct marketing channels can do this with precision and at relatively little cost. The firm marketing through indirect channels will find it more difficult, and the information will be less exact; but it still may be worthwhile. If the stakes are high enough, marketing research may be conducted to discover the extent to which the customer purchases of profitable items actually are associated with that of the sick product. Although the results may not be precise, they may supply an order-of-magnitude idea of the interlocking patronage situation.

Product interrelationships in marketing constitute a significant factor in making deletion decisions, but should never be accepted as the deciding factor without careful study to disclose at least the extent of the hazards they involve.

Other Possibilities

The fact that a product's market is declining or that its profit performance is substandard does not mean that deletion is the *only* remedy.

Profits can be made in a shrinking market. There are things other than elimination of a product that can be done about deteriorating profit performance. They tend to fall into four categories.

1. *Costs.*   A careful study may uncover ways of reducing factory costs. This may result from improved processes that either eliminate manpower or

equipment time or else increase yield; or from the elimination of forms or features that once were necessary or worthwhile but are no longer needed. The natural first recourse of allocating joint and overhead costs on a basis that is "kinder" to the doubtful product is not to be viewed with enthusiasm. After reallocation, these costs still remain in the business; and the general profit picture has not been improved in the least.

2. *Marketing.*   Before deleting a product, management will be wise to examine the methods of marketing it, to see if they can be changed to improve its profit picture.

Can advertising and sales effort be reduced without serious loss of volume? A holding operation requires much less effort and money than a promotional one.

Are services being given that the product no longer needs?

Can savings be made in order handling and delivery, even at some loss of customer satisfaction? For example, customers may be buying the product in small orders that are expensive to handle.

On the other hand, by spending more marketing effort, can volume be increased so as to bring about a reduction in factory cost greater than the added marketing expense? In this attempt, an unexpected "assist" may come from competitors who delete the product and leave more of the field to the firm.

By remodeling the product, "dressing it up," and using a new marketing approach, can it be brought back to a state of health and profit? Here the decision makers must be careful not to use funds and facilities that could be more profitably invested in developing and marketing new products.

3. *Price.*   It is natural to assume that the price of a failing product cannot be raised. At least in part, its plight is probably due to the fact that it is "kicked around" by competition, and thus that competition will not allow any increases.

But competitors may be tired of the game, too. One company that tried increasing prices found that wholesalers and retailers did not resent a larger cost-of-goods-sold base on which to apply their customary gross profit rates, and that consumers continued to buy and competitors soon followed suit.

Although a price rise will not usually add to the sum total of user happiness, it may not subtract materially from total purchases. The decision makers should not ignore the possibility of using a price reduction to gain enough physical volume to bring about a more-than-offseting decline in unit costs, although at this stage the success of such a gambit is not likely.

4. *Cross Production.*   In the materials field, when small production runs make costs prohibitive, arrangements may sometimes be made for Firm A to make the *entire* supply of Product X for itself and Competitor B. Then B reciprocates with another similar product. Such "trades," for instance, are to be found in the chemical business.

Summation for Decision

In solving deletion problems, the decision makers must draw together into a single pattern the results of the analysis of all the factors bearing on the matter. Although this is probably most often done on an intangible, subjective basis, some firms have experimented with the formula method.

For example, a manufacturer of electric motors included in its formula the following factors:

- Profitability
- Position on growth curve
- Product leadership
- Market position
- Marketing dependence of other products

Each factor was assigned a weight in terms of possible "counts" against the product. For instance, if the doubtful item promised no profits for the next three years, it had a count of fifty points against it, while more promising prospects were assigned lesser counts. A critical total for all factors was set in advance which would automatically doom a product. Such a system can include other factors—such as recapturing invested capital, alternate available uses of facilities, effects on labor force, or other variables peculiar to the individual case.

The use of a formula lends an aura of precision to the act of decision making and assures a degree of uniformity in it. But obviously the weights assigned to different factors cannot be the same in all cases. For example, if the deletion of a doubtful product endangers a large volume of sales of other highly profitable items, that alone should probably decide the matter.

The same thing is true if deletion will force so heavy a writeoff of invested funds as to impair the firm's capital structure. Certainly this will be true if all or most of the investment can be recaptured by the depreciation route if the product stays in the mix.

This kind of decision requires that the factors be weighted differently in each case. But when managers are given a formula, they may tend to quit thinking and do too much "weighing."

THE DELETION OF A PRODUCT

Once the decision is made to eliminate a product, plans must be drawn for its death and burial with the least disturbance of customer relations and of the other operations of the firm.

Such plans must deal with a variety of detailed problems. Probably the most important fall into four categories: timing; parts and replacements; stocks; and holdover demand.

Timing.   It is desirable that deletion be timed so as to dovetail with the financial, manpower, and facilities needs for new products. As manpower and facilities are released from the dying product and as the capital devoted to it flows back into the cash account, it is ideal if these can be immediately used in a new venture. Although this can never be completely achieved, it may be approximated.

The death of a product should be timed so as to cause the least disturbance to customers. They should be informed about the elimination of the product far enough in advance so they can make arrangements for replacement, if any are available, but not so far in advance that they will switch to new suppliers before the deleting firm's inventories of the product are sold. Deletion at the beginning of a selling season or in the middle of it probably will create maximum customer inconvenience, whereas at the end of the season it will be the least disturbing.

Parts and Replacements.   If the product to be killed off is a durable one, probably the deleting firm will find it necessary to maintain stocks of repair parts for about the expected life of the units most recently sold. The firm that leaves a trail of uncared-for "orphan" products cannot expect to engender much good will from dealers or users. Provision for the care and maintenance of the orphan is a necessary cost of deletion.

This problem is much more widespread than is commonly understood. The woman who buys a set of china or silverware and finds that she cannot replace broken or lost pieces does not entertain an affectionate regard for the maker. The same sort of thing is true if she installs draperies and later, when one of them is damaged, finds that the pattern is no longer available.

Stocks.   The deletion plan should provide for clearing out the stocks of the dying product and materials used in its production, so as to recover the maximum amount of the working capital invested in it. This is very largely a matter of timing—the tapering off of purchase, production, and selling activities. However, this objective may conflict with those of minimizing inconvenience to customers and servicing the orphan units in use after deletion.

Holdover Demand.   However much the demand for a product may decline, it probably will retain some following of devoted users. They are bound to be disturbed by its deletion and are likely to be vocal about it; and usually there is little that management can do to mitigate this situation.

Sometimes a firm can avoid all these difficulties by finding another firm to purchase the product. This should usually be tried before any other deletion steps are taken. A product with a volume too small for a big firm to handle profitably may be a money-maker for a smaller one with less overhead and more flexibility.

NEGLECT OR ACTION?

The process of product deletion is important. The more dynamic the business, the more important it is.

But it is something that most company executives prefer not to do; and therefore it will not get done unless management establishes definite, clearcut policies to guide it, sets up carefully articulated procedures for doing it, and makes a positive and unmistakable assignment of authority and responsibility for it.

Exactly what these policies should be, what form these procedures should take, and to whom the job should be assigned are matters that must vary with the structure and operating methods of the firm and with its position in the industry and the market.

In any case, though, the need for managerial attention, planning, and supervision of the deletion function cannot be overemphasized. Many business firms are paying dearly for their neglect of this problem, but unfortunately do not realize how much this is costing them.

16

Exploit the Product
Life Cycle

Theodore Levitt

Most alert and thoughtful senior marketing executives are by now familiar with the concept of the product life cycle. Even a handful of uniquely cosmopolitan and up-to-date corporate presidents have familiarized themselves with this tantalizing concept. Yet a recent survey I took of such executives found none who used the concept in any strategic way whatever and pitifully few who used it in any kind of tactical way. It has remained—as have so many fascinating theories in economics, physics, and sex—a remarkably durable but almost totally unemployed and seemingly unemployable piece of professional baggage whose presence in the rhetoric of professional discussions adds a much coveted but apparently unattainable legitimacy to the idea that marketing management is somehow a profession. There is, furthermore, a persistent feeling that the life cycle concept adds luster and believability to the insistent claim in certain circles that marketing is close to being some sort of science.[1]

The concept of the product life cycle is today at about the stage that the Copernican view of the universe was 300 years ago: a lot of people knew about it, but hardly anybody seemed to use it in any effective or productive way.

Now that so many people know and in some fashion understand the product life cycle, it seems time to put it to work. The object of this article is to suggest some ways of using the concept effectively and of turning the knowledge of its existence into a managerial instrument of competitive power.

Since the concept has been presented somewhat differently by different authors and for different audiences, it is useful to review it briefly here so that every reader has the same background for the discussion which follows later in this article.

From Theodore Levitt, "Exploit the Product Life Cycle," in *Harvard Business Review,* Vol. 43 (November-December 1965), pp. 81–94. © 1965 by the President and Fellows of Harvard College; all rights reserved.

HISTORICAL PATTERN

The life story of most successful products is a history of their passing through certain recognizable stages. These are shown in Figure 16-1 and occur in the following order:

- *Stage 1. Marketing Development*—This is when a new product is first brought to market, before there is a proved demand for it, and often before it has been fully proved out technically in all respects. Sales are low and creep along slowly.
- *Stage 2. Market Growth*—Demand begins to accelerate and the size of the total market expands rapidly. It might also be called the "Take-off Stage."
- *Stage 3. Market Maturity*—Demand levels off and grows, for the most part, only at the replacement and new family-formation rate.
- *Stage 4. Market Decline*—The product begins to lose consumer appeal and sales drift downward, such as when buggy whips lost out with the advent of automobiles and when silk lost out to nylon.

FIGURE 16-1 **Product Life Cycle—Entire Industry**

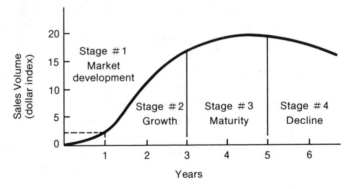

Three operating questions will quickly occur to the alert executive:

- Given a proposed new product or service, how and to what extent can the shape and duration of each stage be predicted?
- Given an existing product, how can one determine what stage it is in?
- Given all this knowledge, how can it be effectively used?

A brief further elaboration of each stage will be useful before dealing with these questions in detail.

Development Stage

Bringing a new product to market is fraught with unknowns, uncertainties, and frequently unknowable risks. Generally, demand has to be "created" during the product's initial *market development stage.* How long this takes depends on the product's complexity, its degree of newness, its fit into consumer needs, and the presence of competitive substitutes of one form or another. A proved cancer cure would require virtually no market development; it would get immediate massive support. An alleged superior substitute for the lost-wax process of sculpture casting would take lots longer.

While it has been demonstrated time after time that properly customer-oriented new product development is one of the primary conditions of sales and profit growth, what have been demonstrated even more conclusively are the ravaging costs and frequent fatalities associated with launching new products. Nothing seems to take more time, cost more money, involve more pitfalls, cause more anguish, or break more careers than do sincere and well-conceived new product programs. The fact is, most new products don't have any sort of classical life cycle curve at all. They have instead from the very outset an infinitely descending curve. The product not only doesn't get off the ground; it goes quickly under ground—six feet under.

It is little wonder, therefore, that some disillusioned and badly burned companies have recently adopted a more conservative policy, what I call the "used apple policy." Instead of aspiring to be the first company to see and seize an opportunity, they systematically avoid being first. They let others take the first bite of the supposedly juicy apple that tantalizes them. They let others do the pioneering. If the idea works, they quickly follow suit. They say, in effect, "The trouble with being a pioneer is that the pioneers get killed by the Indians." Hence, they say (thoroughly mixing their metaphors), "We don't have to get the first bite of the apple. The second one is good enough." They are willing to eat off a used apple, but they try to be alert enough to make sure it is only slightly used—that they at least get the second big bite, not the tenth skimpy one.

Growth Stage

The usual characteristic of a successful new product is a gradual rise in its sales curve during the market development stage. At some point in this rise a marked increase in consumer demand occurs and sales take off. The boom is on. This is the beginning of Stage 2—the *market growth stage.* At this point potential competitors who have been watching developments during Stage 1 jump into the fray. The first ones to get in are generally those with an exceptionally effective "used apple policy." Some enter the market with carbon-copies of the originator's product. Others make functional and design improvements. And at this point product and brand differentiation begin to develop.

The ensuing fight for the consumer's patronage poses to the originating producer an entirely new set of problems. Instead of seeking ways of getting consumers to *try the product,* the originator now faces the more compelling problem of getting them to *prefer his brand.* This generally requires important changes in marketing strategies and methods. But the policies and tactics now adopted will be neither freely the sole choice of the originating producer nor as experimental as they might have been during Stage 1. The presence of competitors both dictates and limits what can easily be tried—such as, for example, testing what is the best price level or the best channel of distribution.

As the rate of consumer acceptance accelerates, it generally becomes increasingly easy to open new distribution channels and retail outlets. The consequent filling of distribution pipelines generally causes the entire industry's factory sales to rise more rapidly than store sales. This creates an exaggerated impression of profit opportunity which, in turn, attracts more competitors. Some of these will begin to charge lower prices because of later advances in technology, production shortcuts, the need to take lower margins in order to get distribution, and the like. All this in time inescapably moves the industry to the threshold of a new stage of competition.

Maturity Stage

This new stage is the *market maturity stage.* The first sign of its advent is evidence of market saturation. This means that most consumer companies or households that are sales prospects will be owning or using the product. Sales now grow about on a par with population. No more distribution pipelines need be filled. Price competition now becomes intense. Competitive attempts to achieve and hold brand preference now involve making finer and finer differentiations in the product, in customer services, and in the promotional practices and claims made for the product.

Typically, the market maturity stage forces the producer to concentrate on holding his distribution outlets, retaining his shelf-space, and, in the end, trying to secure even more intensive distribution. Whereas during the market development stage the originator depended heavily on the positive efforts of his retailers and distributors to help sell his product, retailers and distributors will now frequently have been reduced largely to being merchandise-displayers and order-takers. In the case of branded products in particular, the originator must now, more than ever, communicate directly with the consumer.

The market maturity stage typically calls for a new kind of emphasis on competing more effectively. The originator is increasingly forced to appeal to the consumer on the basis of price, marginal product differences, or both. Depending on the product, services and deals offered in connection with it are often the clearest and most effective forms of differentiation. Beyond these, there will be attempts to create and promote fine product distinctions through packaging and advertising, and to appeal to special market segments. The market maturity stage can be passed through rapidly, as in the case of most women's fashion fads, or it can persist for generations with per capita consumption neither rising nor falling, as in the case of such staples as men's shoes and industrial fasteners. Or maturity can persist, but in a state of gradual but steady per capita decline, as in the case of beer and steel.

Decline Stage

When market maturity tapers off and consequently comes to an end, the product enters Stage 4—*market decline.* In all cases of maturity and decline the industry is transformed. Few companies are able to weather the competitive storm. As demand declines, the overcapacity that was already apparent during the period of maturity now becomes endemic. Some producers see the handwriting implacably on the wall but feel that with proper management and cunning they will be one of the survivors after the industrywide deluge they so clearly foresee. To hasten their competitors' eclipse directly, or to frighten them into early voluntary withdrawal from the industry, they initiate a variety of aggressively depressive tactics, propose mergers or buy-outs, and generally engage in activities that make life thanklessly burdensome for all firms, and make death the inevitable consequence for most of them. A few companies do indeed weather the storm, sustaining life through the constant descent that now clearly characterizes the industry. Production gets concentrated into fewer hands. Prices and margins get depressed. Consumers get bored. The only cases where there is any relief from this boredom and gradual euthanasia are where styling and fashion play some constantly revivifying role.

PREPLANNING IMPORTANCE

Knowing that the lives of successful products and services are generally characterized by something like the pattern illustrated in figure 16-1 can become the basis for important life-giving policies and practices. One of the greatest values of the life cycle concept is for managers about to launch a new product. The first step for them is to try to foresee the profile of the proposed product's cycle.

As with so many things in business, and perhaps uniquely in marketing, it is almost impossible to make universally useful suggestions regarding how to manage one's affairs. It is certainly particularly difficult to provide widely useful advice on how to foresee or predict the slope and duration of a product's life. Indeed, it is precisely because so little specific day-to-day guidance is possible in anything, and because no check list has ever by itself been very useful to anybody for very long, that business management will probably never be a science—always an art—and will pay exceptional rewards to managers with rare talent, enormous energy, iron nerve, great capacity for assuming responsibility and bearing accountability.

But this does not mean that useful efforts cannot or should not be made to try to foresee the slope and duration of a new product's life. Time spent in attempting this kind of foresight not only helps assure that a more rational approach is brought to product planning and merchandising; also, as will be shown later, it can help create valuable lead time for important strategic and tactical moves after the product is brought to market. Specifically, it can be a great help in developing an orderly series of competitive moves, in expanding or stretching out the life of a product, in maintaining a clean product line, and in purposely phasing out dying and costly old products.[2]

Failure Possibilities...

As pointed out above, the length and slope of the market development stage depend on the product's complexity, its degree of newness, its fit into customer needs, and the presence of competitive substitutes.

The more unique or distinctive the newness of the product, the longer it generally takes to get it successfully off the ground. The world does not automatically beat a path to the man with the better mousetrap.[3] The world has to be told, coddled, enticed, romanced, and even bribed (as with, for example, coupons, samples, free application aids, and the like). When the product's newness is distinctive and the job it is designed to do is unique, the public will generally be less quick to perceive it as something it clearly needs or wants.

This makes life particularly difficult for the innovator. He will have more than the usual difficulties of identifying those characteristics of his product and those supporting communications themes or devices which imply value to the consumer. As a consequence, the more distinctive the newness, the greater the risk of failure resulting either from insufficient working capital to sustain a long and frustrating period of creating enough solvent customers to make the proposition pay, or from the inability to convince investors and bankers that they should put up more money.

In any particular situation the more people who will be involved in making a single purchasing decision for a new product, the more drawn out Stage 1 will be. Thus in the highly fragmented construction materials industry, for example, success takes an exceptionally long time to catch hold; and having once caught hold, it tends to hold tenaciously for a long time—often too long. On the other hand, fashion items clearly catch on fastest and last shortest. But because fashion is so powerful, recently some companies in what often seem the least fashion-influenced of industries (machine tools, for example) have shortened the market development stage by introducing elements of design and packaging fashion to their products.

What factors tend to prolong the market development stage and therefore raise the risk of failure? The more complex the product, the more distinctive its newness, the less influenced by fashion, the greater the number of persons influencing a single buying decision, the more costly, and the greater the required shift in the customer's usual way of doing things—these are the conditions most likely to slow things up and create problems.

vs. Success Chances

But problems also create opportunities to control the forces arrayed against new product success. For example, the newer the product, the more important it becomes for the customers to have a favorable first experience with it. Newness creates a certain special visibility for the product, with a certain number of people standing on the sidelines to see how the first customers get on with it. If their first experience is unfavorable in some crucial way, this may have repercussions far out of proportion to the actual extent of the underfulfillment of the customers' expectations. But a favorable first experience or application will, for the same reason, get a lot of disproportionately favorable publicity.

The possibility of exaggerated disillusionment with a poor first experience can raise vital questions regarding the appropriate channels of distribution for a new product. On the one hand, getting the product successfully launched may require having—as in the case of, say, the early days of home washing machines—many retailers who can give consumers considerable help in the product's correct utilization and thus help assure a favorable first experience for those buyers. On the other hand, channels that provide this kind of help (such as small neighborhood appliance stores in the case of washing machines) during the market development stage may not be the ones best able to merchandise the product most successfully later when help in creating and personally reassuring customers is less important than wide product distribution. To the extent that channel decisions during this first stage sacrifice some of the requirements of the market development stage to some of the requirements of later stages, the rate of the product's acceptance by consumers at the outset may be delayed.

In entering the market development stage, pricing decisions are often particularly hard for the producer to make. Should he set an initially high price to recoup his investment quickly—i.e., "skim the cream"—or should he set a low price to discourage potential competition—i.e., "exclusion"? The answer depends on the innovator's estimate of the probable length of the product's life cycle, the degree of patent protection the product is likely to enjoy, the amount of capital needed to get the product off the ground, the elasticity of demand during the early life of the product, and many other factors. The decision that is finally made may affect not just the rate at which the product catches on at the beginning, but even the duration of its total life. Thus some products that are priced too low at the outset (particularly fashion goods, such as the chemise, or sack, a few years ago) may catch on so quickly that they become short-lived fads. A slower rate of consumer acceptance might often extend their life cycles and raise the total profits they yield.

The actual slope, or rate of the growth stage, depends on some of the same things as does success or failure in Stage 1. But the extent to which patent exclusiveness can play a critical role is sometimes inexplicably forgotten. More frequently than one might offhand expect, holders of strong patent positions fail to recognize either the market-development virtue of making their patents available to competitors or the market-destroying possibilities of failing to control more effectively their competitors' use of such products.

Generally speaking, the more producers there are of a new product, the more effort goes into developing a market for it. The net result is very likely to be more rapid and steeper growth of the total market. The originator's market share may fall, but his total sales and profits may rise more rapidly. Certainly this has been the case in recent years of color television: RCA's eagerness to make its tubes available to competitors reflects its recognition of the power of numbers over the power of monopoly.

On the other hand, the failure to set and enforce appropriate quality standards in the early days of polystyrene and polyethylene drinking glasses and cups produced such sloppy, inferior goods that it took years to recover the consumer's confidence and revive the growth pattern.

But to try to see in advance what a product's growth pattern might be is not very useful if one fails to distinguish between the industry pattern and the pattern of the single firm—for its particular brand. The industry's cycle will almost certainly be different from the cycle of individual firms. Moreover, the life cycle of a given product may be different for different companies in the same industry at the same point in time, and it certainly affects different companies in the same industry differently.

ORIGINATOR'S BURDENS

The company with most at stake is the original producer—the company that launches an entirely new product. This company generally bears most of the costs, the tribulations, and certainly the risks of developing both the product and the market.

Competitive Pressure

Once the innovator demonstrates during the market development stage that a solid demand exists, armies of imitators rush in to capitalize on and help create the boom that becomes the market growth, or takeoff, stage. As a result, while exceedingly rapid growth will now characterize the product's total demand, for the originating company its growth stage paradoxically now becomes truncated. It has to share the boom with new competitors. Hence the potential rate of acceleration of its own takeoff is diminished and, indeed, may actually fail to last as long as the industry's. This occurs not only because there are so many competitors, but, as we

noted earlier, also because competitors often come in with product improvements and lower prices. While these developments generally help keep the
market expanding, they greatly restrict the originating company's rate of
growth and the length of its takeoff stage.

All this can be illustrated by comparing the curve in figure 16-2 with
that in figure 16-1, which shows the life cycle for a product. During Stage 1
in figure 16-1 there is generally only one company—the originator—even
though the whole figure represents the entire industry. In Stage 1 the
originator is the entire industry. But by Stage 2 he shares the industry
with many competitors. Hence, while figure 16-1 is an industry curve, its
Stage 1 represents only a single company's sales.

Figure 16-2 shows the life cycle of the originator's brand—his own sales
curve, not that of the industry. It can be seen that between Year 1 and
Year 2 his sales are rising about as rapidly as the industry's. But after
Year 2, while industry sales in figure 16-1 are still in vigorous expansion,
the originator's sales curve in figure 16-2 has begun to slow its ascent.
He is now sharing the boom with a great many competitors, some of whom
are much better positioned now than he is.

Profit Squeeze

In the process the originator may begin to encounter a serious squeeze on
his profit margins. Figure 16-3, which traces the profits per unit of the
originator's sales, illustrates this point. During the market development
stage his per-unit profits are negative. Sales volume is too low at existing
prices. However, during the market growth stage unit profits boom as
output rises and unit production costs fall. Total profits rise enormously.
It is the presence of such lush profits that both attracts and ultimately
destroys competitors.

FIGURE 16-2 **Product Life Cycle—Originating Company**

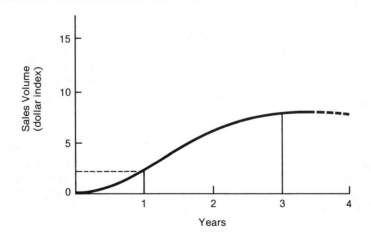

Consequently, while (1) industry sales may still be rising nicely (as at the Year 3 point in figure 16-1), and (2) while the originating company's sales may at the same point of time have begun to slow down noticeably (as in figure 16-2), and (3) while at this point the originator's total profits may still be rising because his volume of sales is huge and on a slight upward trend, his profits per unit will often have taken a drastic downward course. Indeed, they will often have done so long before the sales curve flattened. They will have topped out and begun to decline perhaps around the Year 2 point (as in figure 16-3). By the time the originator's sales begin to flatten out (as at the Year 3 point in figure 16-2), unit profits may actually be approaching zero (as in figure 16-3).

FIGURE 16-3 Unit Profit Contribution Life Cycle—Originating Company

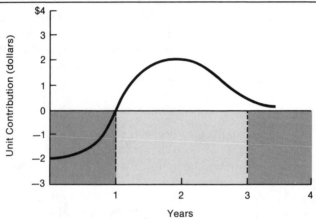

At this point more competitors are in the industry, the rate of industry demand growth has slowed somewhat, and competitors are cutting prices. Some of them do this in order to get business, and others do it because their costs are lower owing to the fact that their equipment is more modern and productive.

The industry's Stage 3—maturity—generally lasts as long as there are no important competitive substitutes (such as, for example, aluminum for steel in "tin" cans), no drastic shifts in influential value systems (such as the end of female modesty in the 1920s and the consequent destruction of the market for veils), no major changes in dominant fashions (such as the hour-glass female form and the end of waist cinchers), no changes in the demand for primary products which use the product in question (such as the effect of the decline of new railroad expansion on the demand for railroad ties), and no changes either in the rate of obsolescence of the product or in the character or introductory rate of product modifications.

Maturity can last for a long time, or it can actually never be attained. Fashions goods and fad items sometimes surge to sudden heights, hesitate momentarily at an uneasy peak, and then quickly drop off into total obscurity.

Stage Recognition

The various characteristics of the stages described above will help one to recognize the stage a particular product occupies at any given time. But hindsight will always be more accurate than current sight. Perhaps the best way of seeing one's current stage is to try to foresee the next stage and work backwards. This approach has several virtues:

- It forces one to look ahead constantly, to try to reforesee his future and competitive environment. This will have its own rewards. As Charles F. Kettering, perhaps the last of Detroit's primitive inventors and probably the greatest of all its inventors, was fond of saying, "We should all be concerned about the future because that's where we'll have to spend the rest of our lives." By looking at the future one can better assess the state of the present.
- Looking ahead gives more perspective to the present than looking at the present alone. Most people know more about the present than is good for them. It is neither healthy nor helpful to know the present too well, for our perception of the present is too often too heavily distorted by the urgent pressures of day-to-day events. To know where the present is in the continuum of competitive time and events, it often makes more sense to try to know what the future will bring, and when it will bring it, than to try to know what the present itself actually contains.
- Finally, the value of knowing what stage a product occupies at any given time resides only in the way that fact is used. But its use is always in the future. Hence a prediction of the future environment in which the information will be used is often more functional for the effective capitalization on knowledge about the present than knowledge about the present itself.

SEQUENTIAL ACTIONS

The life cycle concept can be effectively employed in the strategy of both existing and new products. For purposes of continuity and clarity, the remainder of this article will describe some of the uses of the concept from the early stages of new product planning through the later stages of keeping the product profitably alive. The chief discussion will focus on what I call a policy of "life extension" or "market stretching."[4]

To the extent that figures 16-2 and 16-3 outline the classical patterns of successful new products, one of the constant aims of the originating producer should be to avoid the severe discipline imposed by an early profit squeeze in the market growth stage, and to avoid the wear and waste so typical of the market maturity stage. Hence the following proposition would seem reasonable: when a company develops a new product or service, it should try to plan at the very outset a series of actions to be employed at various subsequent stages in the product's existence so that its sales and profit curves are constantly sustained rather than following their usual declining slope.

In other words, advance planning should be directed at extending, or stretching out, the life of the product. It is this idea of *planning in advance* of the actual launching of a new product to take specific actions later in its life cycle—actions designed to sustain its growth and profitability—which appears to have great potential as an instrument of long-term product strategy.

Nylon's Life

How this might work for a product can be illustrated by looking at the history of nylon. The way in which nylon's booming sales life has been repeatedly and systematically extended and stretched can serve as a model for other products. What has happened in nylon may not have been purposely planned that way at the outset, but the results are quite as if they had been planned.

The first nylon end-uses were primarily military—parachutes, thread, rope. This was followed by nylon's entry into the circular knit market and its consequent domination of the women's hosiery business. Here it developed the kind of steadily rising growth and profit curves that every executive dreams about. After some years these curves began to flatten out. But before they flattened very noticeably, Du Pont had already developed measures designed to revitalize sales and profits. It did several things, each of which is demonstrated graphically in figure 16-4. This figure and the explanation which follows take some liberties with the actual facts of the nylon situation in order to highlight the points I wish to make. But they take no liberties with the essential requisites of product strategy.

FIGURE 16-4 **Hypothetical Life Cycle—Nylon**

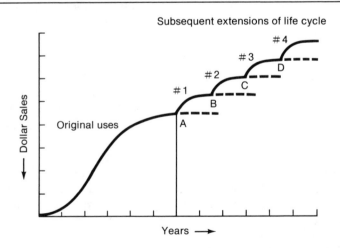

Point A of figure 16-4 shows the hypothetical point at which the nylon curve (dominated at this point by hosiery) flattened out. If nothing further had been done, the sales curve would have continued along the flattened pace indicated by the dotted line at Point A. This is also the hypothetical point at which the first systematic effort was made to extend the product's life. Du Pont, in effect, took certain "actions" which pushed hosiery sales upward rather than continuing the path implied by the dotted line extension of the curve at Point A. At Point A action #1 pushed an otherwise flat curve upward.

At Points B, C, and D still other new sales and profit expansion "actions" (#2, #3, #4, and so forth) were taken. What were these actions? Or, more usefully, what was their strategic content? What did they try to do? They involved strategies that tried to expand sales via four different routes:

1. Promoting more frequent usage of the product among current users.
2. Developing more varied usage of the product among current users.
3. Creating new users for the product by expanding the market.
4. Finding new uses for the basic material.

Frequent Usage.   Du Pont studies had shown an increasing trend toward "bareleggedness" among women. This was coincident with the trend toward casual living and a declining perception among teenagers of what might be called the "social necessity" of wearing stockings. In the light of those findings, one approach to propping up the flattening sales curves might have been to reiterate the social necessity of wearing stockings at all times. That would have been a sales-building action, though obviously difficult and exceedingly costly. But it could clearly have fulfilled the strategy of promoting more frequent usage among current users as a means of extending the product's life.

Varied Usage.   For Du Pont, this strategy took the form of an attempt to promote the "fashion smartness" of tinted hose and later of patterned and highly textured hosiery. The idea was to raise each woman's inventory of hosiery by obsolescing the perception of hosiery as a fashion staple that came only in a narrow range of browns and pinks. Hosiery was to be converted from a "neutral" accessory to a central ingredient of fashion, with a "suitable" tint and pattern for each outer garment in the lady's wardrobe.

This not only would raise sales by expanding women's hosiery wardrobes and stores' inventories but would open the door for annual tint and pattern obsolescence much the same as there is an annual color obsolescence in outer garments. Beyond that, the use of color and pattern to focus attention on the leg would help arrest the decline of the leg as an element of sex appeal—a trend which some researchers had discerned and which, they claimed, damaged hosiery sales.

New Users.   Creating new users for nylon hosiery might conceivably have taken the form of attempting to legitimize the necessity of wearing hosiery among early teenagers and subteenagers. Advertising, public relations, and merchandising of youthful social and style leaders would have been called for.

New Uses. For nylon, this tactic has had many triumphs—from varied types of hosiery, such as stretch stockings and stretch socks, to new uses, such as rugs, tires, bearings, and so forth. Indeed, if there had been no further product innovations designed to create new uses for nylon after the original military, miscellaneous, and circular knit uses, nylon consumption in 1962 would have reached a saturation level at approximately fifty million pounds annually.

Instead, in 1962 consumption exceeded 500 million pounds. Figure 16-5 demonstrates how the continuous development of new uses for the basic material constantly produced new waves of sales. The exhibit shows that in spite of the growth of the women's stocking market, the cumulative result of the military, circular knit, and miscellaneous grouping would have been a flattened sales curve by 1958. (Nylon's entry into the broadwoven market in 1944 substantially raised sales above what they would have been. Even so, the sales of broadwoven, circular knit, and military and miscellaneous groupings peaked in 1957.)

Had it not been for the addition of new uses for the same basic material —such as warp knits in 1945, tire cord in 1948, textured yarns in 1955, carpet yarns in 1959, and so forth—nylon would not have had the spectacularly rising consumption curve it has so clearly had. At various stages it would have exhausted its existing markets or been forced into decline by competing materials. The systematic search for new uses for the basic (and improved) material extended and stretched the product's life.

Other Examples

Few companies seem to employ in any systematic or planned way the four product life-stretching steps described previously. Yet the successful application of this kind of stretching strategy has characterized the history of such well-known products as General Foods Corporation's "Jell-O" and Minnesota Mining & Manufacturing Co.'s "Scotch" tape.[5]

Jell-O was a pioneer in the easy-to-prepare gelatin dessert field. The soundness of the product concept and the excellence of its early marketing activities gave it beautifully ascending sales and profit curves almost from the start. But after some years these curves predictably began to flatten out. Scotch tape was also a pioneer product in its field. Once perfected, the product gained rapid market acceptance because of a sound product concept and an aggressive sales organizaion. But, again, in time the sales and profit curves began to flatten out. Before they flattened out very much, however, 3M, like General Foods, had already developed measures to sustain the early pace of sales and profits.

Both of these companies extended their products' lives by, in effect, doing all four of the things Du Pont did with nylon—creating more

FIGURE 16-5 **Innovation of New Products Postpones the Time of Total Maturity—Nylon Industry**

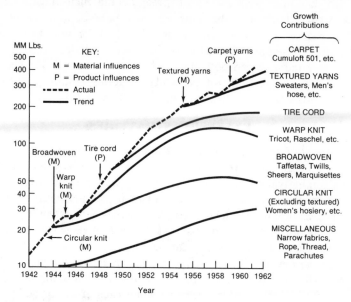

Source: *Modern Textile Magazine* (February 1964), p. 33. © 1962 by Jordan P. Yale.

frequent usage among current users, more varied usage among current users, new users, and new uses for the basic "materials":

1. The General Foods approach to increasing the frequency of serving Jell-O among current users was, essentially, to increase the number of flavors. From Don Wilson's famous "six delicious flavors," Jell-O moved up to over a dozen. On the other hand, 3M helped raise sales among its current users by developing a variety of handy Scotch tape dispensers which made the product easier to use.

2. Creation of more varied usage of Jell-O among current dessert users involved its promotion as a base for salads and the facilitation of this usage by the development of a variety of vegetable flavored Jell-O's. Similarly, 3M developed a line of colored, patterned, waterproof, invisible, and write-on Scotch tapes which have enjoyed considerable success as sealing and decorating items for holiday and gift wrapping.

3. Jell-O sought to create new users by pinpointing people who could not accept Jell-O as a popular dessert or salad product. Hence during the Metrecal boom Jell-O employed an advertising theme that successfully affixed to the product a fashion-oriented weight control appeal. Similarly, 3M introduced "Rocket" tape, a product much like Scotch tape but lower in price, and also developed a line of commercial cellophane tapes of various widths, lengths, and strengths. These actions broadened product use in commercial and industrial markets.

4. Both Jell-O and 3M have sought out new uses for the basic material. It is known, for example, that women consumers use powdered gelatin dissolved in liquids as a means of strengthening their fingernails. Both men and women use it in the same way as a bone-building agent. Hence Jell-O introduced a "completely flavorless" Jell-O for just these purposes. 3M has also developed new uses for the basic material—from "double-coated" tape (adhesive on both sides) which competes with ordinary liquid adhesives, to the reflecting tape which festoons countless automobile bumpers, to marker strips which compete with paint.

EXTENSION STRATEGIES

The existence of the kinds of product life cycles illustrated in figures 16-1 and 16-2 and the unit profit cycle in figure 16-3 suggest that there may be considerable value for people involved in new product work to begin planning for the extension of the lives of their products even before these products are formally launched. To plan for new life-extending infusions of effort (as in figure 16-4) at this pre-introduction stage can be extremely useful in three profoundly important ways.

1. *It generates an active rather than a reactive product policy.* It systematically structures a company's long-term marketing and product development efforts in advance, rather than each effort or activity being merely a stop-gap response to the urgent pressures of repeated competitive thrusts and declining profits. The life-extension view of product policy enforces thinking and planning ahead—thinking in some systematic way about the moves likely to be made by potential competitors, about possible changes in consumer reactions to the product, and the required selling activities which best take advantage of these conditional events.

2. *It lays out a long-term plan designed to infuse new life into the product at the right time, with the right degree of care, and with the right amount of effort.* Many activities designed to raise the sales and profits of existing products or materials are often undertaken without regard to their relationship to each other or to timing—the optimum point of consumer readiness for such activities or the point of optimum competitive effectiveness. Careful advance planning, long before the need for such activity arises, can help assure that the timing, the care, and the efforts are appropriate to the situation.

For example, it appears extremely doubtful that the boom in women's hair coloring and hair tinting products would have been as spectacular if vigorous efforts to sell these products had preceded the boom in hair sprays and chemical hair fixers. The latter helped create a powerful consumer consciousness of hair fashions because they made it relatively easy to create and wear fashionable hair styles. Once it became easy for women to have fashionable hair styles, the resulting fashion consciousness helped open the door for hair colors and tints. It could not have happened the other way around, with colors and tints first creating fashion consciousness and thus raising the sales of sprays and fixers. Because understanding the reason for this precise order of events is essential for appreciating the importance of early pre-introduction life-extension planning, it is useful to go into a bit of detail. Consider:

For women, setting their hair has been a perennial problem for centuries. First, the length and treatment of their hair is one of the most obvious ways in which they distinguish themselves from men. Hence to be attractive in that distinction becomes crucial. Second, hair frames and highlights the face, much like an attractive wooden border frames and highlights a beautiful painting. Thus hair styling is an important element in accentuating the appearance of a woman's facial features. Third, since the hair is long and soft, it is hard to hold in an attractive arrangement. It gets mussed in sleep, wind, damp weather, sporting activities, and so forth.

Therefore, the effective *arrangement* of a woman's hair is understandably her first priority in hair care. An unkempt brunette would gain nothing from making herself into a blond. Indeed, in a country where blonds are in the minority, the switch from being an unkempt brunette to being an unkempt blond would simply draw attention to her sloppiness. But once the problem of arrangement became easily "solved" by sprays and fixers, colors and tints could become big business, especially among women whose hair was beginning to turn gray.

The same order of priorities applies in industrial products. For example, it seems quite inconceivable that many manufacturing plants would easily have accepted the replacement of the old single-spindle, constantly mantended screw machine by a computerized tape-tended, multiple-spindle machine. The mechanical tending of the multiple-spindle machine was a necessary intermediate step, if for no other reason than that it required a lesser work-flow change, and certainly a lesser conceptual leap for the companies and the machine-tending workers involved.

For Jell-O, it is unlikely that vegetable flavors would have been very successful before the idea of gelatin as a salad base had been pretty well accepted. Similarly, the promotion of colored and patterned Scotch tape as a gift and decorative seal might not have been as successful if department stores had not, as the result of their drive to compete more effectively with mass merchandisers by offering more customer services, previously demonstrated to the consumer what could be done to wrap and decorate gifts.

3. *Perhaps the most important benefit of engaging in advance, pre-introduction planning for sales-extending, market-stretching activities later in the product's life is that this practice forces a company to adopt a wider view of the nature of the product it is dealing with.* Indeed, it may even force the adoption of a wider view of the company's business. Take the case of Jell-O. What is its product? Over the years Jell-O has become the brand umbrella for a wide range of dessert products, including cornstarch-base puddings, pie fillings, and the new "Whip'n Chill," a

light dessert product similar to a Bavarian Creme or French Mousse. On the basis of these products, it might be said that the Jell-O Division of General Foods is in the "dessert technology" business.

In the case of tape, perhaps 3M has gone even further in this technological approach to its business. It has a particular expertise (technology) on which it has built a constantly expanding business. This expertise can be said to be that of bonding things (adhesives in the case of Scotch tape) to other things, particularly to thin materials. Hence we see 3M developing scores of profitable items, including electronic recording tape (bonding electron-sensitive materials to tape) and "Thermo-Fax" duplicating equipment and supplies (bonding heat-reactive materials to paper).

CONCLUSION

For companies interested in continued growth and profits, successful new product strategy should be viewed as a planned totality that looks ahead over some years. For its own good, new product strategy should try to predict in some measure the likelihood, character, and timing of competitive and market events. While prediction is always hazardous and seldom very accurate, it is undoubtedly far better than not trying to predict at all. In fact, every product strategy and every business decision inescapably involves making a prediction about the future, about the market, and about competitors. To be more systematically aware of the predictions one is making so that one acts on them in an offensive rather than a defensive or reactive fashion—this is the real virtue of preplanning for market stretching and product life extension. The result will be a product strategy that includes some sort of *plan for a timed sequence of conditional moves.*

Even before entering the market development stage, the originator should make a judgment regarding the probable length of the product's normal life, taking into account the possibilities of expanding its uses and users. This judgment will also help determine many things—for example, whether to price the product on a skimming or a penetration basis, or what kind of relationship the company should develop with its resellers.

These considerations are important because at each stage in a product's life cycle each management decision must consider the competitive requirements of the next stage. Thus a decision to establish a strong branding policy during the market growth stage might help to insulate the brand against strong price competition later; a decision to establish a policy of "protected" dealers in the market development stage might facilitate point-of-sale promotions during the market growth stage, and so on. In short, having a clear idea of future product development possibilities and market development opportunities should reduce the likelihood of becoming locked into forms of merchandising that might possibly prove undesirable.

This kind of advance thinking about new product strategy helps management avoid other pitfalls. For instance, advertising campaigns that look successful from a short-term view may hurt in the next stage of the life cycle. Thus at the outset Metrecal advertising used a strong medical theme. Sales boomed until imitative competitors successfully emphasized fashionable slimness. Metrecal had projected itself as the dietary for the overweight consumer, an image that proved far less appealing than that of being the dietary for people who were fashion-smart. But Metrecal's original appeal had been so strong and so well made that it was a formidable task later on to change people's impressions about the product. Obviously, with more careful long-range planning at the outset, a product's image can be more carefully positioned and advertising can have more clearly defined objectives.

Recognizing the importance of an orderly series of steps in the introduction of sales-building "actions" for new products should be a central ingredient of long-term product planning. A carefully preplanned program for market expansion, even before a new product is introduced, can have powerful virtues. The establishment of a rational plan for the future can also help to guide the direction and pace of the ongoing technical research in support of the product. Although departures from such a plan will surely have to be made to accommodate unexpected events and revised judgments, the plan puts the company in a better position to *make* things happen rather than constantly having to react to things that *are* happening.

It is important that the originator does *not* delay this long-term planning until after the product's introduction. How the product should be introduced and the many uses for which it might be promoted at the outset should be a function of a careful consideration of the optimum sequence of suggested product appeals and product uses. Consideration must focus not just on optimum things to do, but as importantly on their optimum *sequence*—for instance, what the order of use of various appeals should be and what the order of suggested product uses should be. If Jell-O's first suggested use had been as a diet food, its chances of later making a big and easy impact in the gelatin dessert market undoubtedly would have been greatly diminished. Similarly, if nylon hosiery had been promoted at the outset as a functional daytime-wear hosiery, its ability to replace silk as the acceptable high-fashion hosiery would have been greatly diminished.

To illustrate the virtue of pre-introduction planning for a product's later life, suppose a company has developed a nonpatentable new product— say, an ordinary kitchen salt shaker. Suppose that nobody now has any kind of shaker. One might say, before launching it, that (1) it has a potential market of "x" million household, institutional, and commercial consumers, (2) in two years market maturity will set in, and (3) in one year profit margins will fall because of the entry of competition. Hence one might lay out the following plan:

1. *End of first year: expand market among current users*
   Ideas—new designs, such as sterling shaker for formal use, "mascu-

line'' shaker for barbecue use, antique shaker for "Early American" households, miniature shaker for each table place setting, moisture-proof design for beach picnics.

2. *End of second year: expand market to new users*
Ideas—designs for children, quaffer design for beer drinkers in bars, design for sadists to rub salt into open wounds.

3. *End of third year: find new uses*
Ideas—make identical product for use as a pepper shaker, as decorative garlic salt shaker, shaker for household scouring powder, shaker to sprinkle silicon dust on parts being machined in machine shops, and so forth.

This effort to prethink methods of reactivating a flattening sales curve far in advance of its becoming flat enables product planners to assign priorities to each task, and to plan future production expansion and capital and marketing requirements in a systematic fashion. It prevents one's trying to do too many things at once, results in priorities being determined rationally instead of as accidental consequences of the timing of new ideas, and disciplines both the product development effort that is launched in support of a product's growth and the marketing effort that is required for its continued success.

NOTES

[1] For discussions of the scientific claims or potentials of marketing, see George Schwartz, *Development of Marketing Theory* (Cincinnati: South-Western Publishing Co., 1963); and Reavis Cox, Wroe Alderson, and Stanley J. Shapiro, eds., *Theory in Marketing* (Homewood, Ill.: Richard D. Irwin, Inc., Second Series, 1964).

[2] See Philip Kotler, "Phasing Out Weak Products," *Harvard Business Review* (March-April 1965), p. 107.

[3] For perhaps the ultimate example of how the world does *not* beat such a path, see the example of the man who actually, and to his painful regret, made a "better" mousetrap, in John B. Matthews, Jr., R. D. Buzzell, Theodore Levitt, and Ronald E. Frank, *Marketing: An Introductory Analysis* (New York: McGraw-Hill Book Company, Inc., 1964), p. 4.

[4] For related ideas on discerning opportunities for product revivification, see Lee Adler, "A New Orientation for Plotting a Marketing Strategy," *Business Horizons* (Winter 1964), p. 37.

[5] *I am indebted to my colleague, Dr. Derek A. Newton, for these examples and other helpful suggestions.*

III

CONTRIBUTIONS OF THE INSTITUTIONAL APPROACH

The institutional approach to marketing was popular from about 1910 to 1940. In its original form, it dealt primarily with the operation of specific types of business, such as retailers, wholesalers, and manufacturers. It was the first perspective to engender debate over the content of marketing. The institutional approach has broadened with the passing years. Marketers are now more concerned with institutional relationships and marketing systems than with the explanation of how a specific type of business operates. As a result, some of the more important and lasting marketing concepts have developed out of the institutional approach.

The institutional approach can contribute in several ways to our understanding of marketing. It has provided for the identification and classification of business. It provides insight not only into internal business operations but also competition between firms. The channel concept has led to a greater appreciation for the interdependence of firms, and it has led to the emergence of physical distribution as an important business function. The concept of channel flows has improved our knowledge of marketing change, and specified types of firm-to-firm and firm-to-market relationships.

The five readings in the section "Institutional Relationships" demonstrate important channel concepts. McVey maintains that the role of middlemen has been misrepresented by an oversimplified treatment in the literature. Little gives an excellent discussion of the relative merits of manufacturer, wholesaler, and retailer middlemen leading the marketing channel. Mallen explains the meaning of conflict and cooperation in a channel and how to deal with it. Clewett explains why channels are important and discusses the process of change in the marketing channel.

There are five readings in "Institutional Flow Concepts," dealing with different types of market flows in the channel. Vaile, Grether, and Cox develop the flow concept as it applies to marketing. They explain the types and direction of marketing flows. Aspinwall demonstrates how marketing institutions act as depots for the physical flow of goods, and he shows how the flow is controlled by consumers. Reese explores the neglected function of physical distribution and suggests answers to the problem. Converse develops Reilly's idea of market flows. He provides his own formula for determining the direction of consumer trade flows between competing cities. The section ends with Hollander's "wheel of retailing." Hollander explains the nature of institutional change and adjustment in marketing.

17

Are Channels of Distribution
What the Textbooks Say?

Phillip McVey

Perhaps Wroe Alderson said as much as is safe to say when he described a marketing channel as a group of firms which "constitute a loose coalition engaged in exploiting joint opportunity in the market."[1]

THEORY AND ACTUALITY

Certainly too much is said about channel relationships in many published textbooks for businessmen and students, if one is to look for proof in current marketing practice. The picture usually given is one of long lists of various types of middlemen and facilitating agencies, which differ minutely but precisely in functions performed. Alignments of particular types are presented as "right" or "customary" for a given commodity or type of producer. Furthermore, it is often implied that it is the producer who selects all the links in the channel and establishes the working arrangements with them, down to and including the outlet which sells his goods to the final user.

Several popular college textbooks in marketing illustrate this manu-facturer-oriented approach to channel planning.[2] One reason for fairly standard treatment of channel building is that the growth of marketing knowledge has proceeded from a description of the activities of existing business firms, leaning heavily on data provided by the U.S. Censuses of Wholesale and Retail Trade. The framework appears orderly and well planned. But little recognition is given to the probability that some channel sequences "just grew" like Topsy, without direction or intent of known parents.

Reprinted from Phillip McVey, "Are Channels of Distribution What the Textbooks Say?" in the *Journal of Marketing,* Vol. 25 (January 1960), pp. 61-65, published by the American Marketing Association.

The Census method of counting, whereby each separate establishment is assigned to a single traditional category on the basis of a *major-portion-of-dollar-volume* rule, tends to produce more orderliness in the picture than probably exists. It tends to obscure a great deal of "promiscuous distribution" and channel jumping. The Census rule, like the Procrustean bed of Greek mythology, effectively reduces the number of categories into which firms are sorted, and avoids hybrid, nondescript classifications.

Yet hybridity is too common among marketing firms to be ignored. For example, almost any wholesaler will do some business at retail; similarly, it is not uncommon for a broker to find himself holding title to a given lot of goods, thus becoming temporarily a merchant middleman. A realistic classification may require the use of relative terms to identify types of operation, according to a range of variables—for example, the *degree* to which a firm caters to a given customer group, or the *frequency* with which a function is performed.

Further study of marketing textbooks may lead a reader to conclude that: (a) middlemen of many types are available to any manufacturer in any market to which he wishes to sell, and within each type there is an ample selection of individual firms; (b) the manufacturer habitually controls the selection and operation of individual firms in his channel; and (c) middlemen respond willingly as *selling agents* for the manufacturer rather than as *purchasing agents* for a coveted group of customers to whom the middlemen sell.

Yet none of these conclusions is entirely valid.

In a product line such as fashion apparel, a garment maker may have an extremely limited choice of types of middlemen: the selling agent, the broker, the direct-buying retailer, or the chain store buying office. The general absence of service wholesalers from this line of trade is not correctable by manufacturers' *fiat*.

In a particular market area, the choice may be even more limited. Of individual firms of a given type, there may be no choice at all. These limitations arise, of course, because of the free choices made by the middlemen as to locations, customer groups, and product assortments they elect to sell.

IS THE "CHANNEL" AN ACADEMIC CONCEPT?

Integrated action up and down a channel is a rare luxury in marketing. Why? It may be that the "channel of distribution" is a concept that is principally academic in usage and unfamiliar to many firms selling to and through these channels.

Instead of a channel, a businessman is likely to concern himself merely with suppliers and customers. His dealings are not with all of the links in the channel but only with those immediately adjacent to him, from which he buys and to which he sells. He may little know nor care what becomes of his products after they leave the hands of some merchant middleman who has paid him for them and released him to return to problems involving his special functions. A manufacturer may not even consider himself as standing at the head of a channel, but only as occupying a link in a channel that begins with his suppliers.

Policies

Choice of a channel is not open to any firm unless it has considerable freedom of action in matters of marketing policy. Other areas of policy seem to be treated with more respect. For example, it is well recognized that a *price* policy is an authoritarian privilege open only to those sellers who possess power to withhold goods from the market in considerable quantities, or who have the choice of alternative markets and the means to solicit them. Usually a differentiated product is necessary. Therefore, a wheat farmer can seldom have anything resembling a price policy.

Likewise, a *design* policy is meaningful only when variations in product characteristics have been understood and accepted by customers to be of significance. Manufacturers of semi-finished or component parts, or of textile "gray goods" cannot enjoy this luxury in most cases.

Similarly, the selection of a multi-stage channel is not the prerogative of a manufacturer unless his franchise is coveted by the middlemen he seeks, as being more valuable to them than their franchise would be to him.

Names such as Sears Roebuck and Company, Macy's, or Kroger mean a great deal more to the customers of these retailers than do the brand names of most of the items sold in their stores. These firms control the channels for many products, even to the point of bringing into existence some manufacturing firms needed to fill gaps in their assortment. In the same manner some national wholesalers, holding the reins of a huge distributive system, are more powerful than either their suppliers or their customers. In such extreme cases the power position is obvious. The big company, regardless of its position in the channel, tries to make its plans and policies effective by taking the initiative for coordinated action.

UNCERTAINTY AMONG SMALLER FIRMS

As to the many thousands of middle-size and small companies that truly characterize American marketing, the power position is speculative, vacillating, and ephemeral. Strength in certain market areas, the temporary success of a product, ability to perform a certain needed type of financing or promotional effort—these and similar factors enable companies to assume power.

On the other hand, financial reverses, an unfortunate sales campaign, or even the lack of accurate market news—these factors can shift power elsewhere, possibly to another link in the channel or to another firm in the same link. In any case, the opportunity of any firm is contingent upon the willingness of others to use it as a link in the channel.

Comparison with Advertising Media

Selection of middlemen has been likened to the selection of advertising media. In both instances the task is to find a vehicle which has an existing coverage (or circulation) which coincides with the market desired. A region blanketed with a neat mosaic of distributors' territories will appear on a map much like the same region covered by television stations.

However, there is an important difference. Seldom does an advertising medium restrict its availability. The advertiser's product need not be sold first to the medium on the grounds of self-interest. Only occasionally will a middleman accept any product he is offered. The requirement that he invest his own money and effort forces him to be selective in terms of probable outcome or profit. No seller can afford to neglect the task of selling *to* the middlemen he seeks, as well as *through* them. Nearly every comprehensive campaign of consumer advertising allots substantial effort to dealer promotion and distributor promotion. Indeed, much consumer advertising is undertaken primarily for the stimulating effect it will have upon middlemen.

Middlemen's Reactions

Middlemen's reactions to new-product offerings probably deserve more attention from manufacturers than usual. Wholesalers and retailers, as well as agent middlemen, enjoy an excellent position from which to make keen judgments of a product's probable successes within local markets. Free from the manufacturer's proclivity to "fall in love with the product," but not primarily concerned with its ultimate usage characteristics, middlemen who are alert merchandisers can look at the product with an eye to salability alone.

Yet it is common practice for manufacturers to force acceptance with a heavy barrage of consumer advertising, introductory high-markup offers, free merchandise, combination deals, cooperative advertising schemes, and the like. These may have the effect of "mesmerizing" middlemen, and of clouding the issue of the product's own rate of initial acceptance.

Lack of effective vertical communication in most channels is a serious deterrent. Possibly no other proof of the weakness of manufacturers' control over channels is so convincing as their inability to obtain facts from their own ultimate and intermediate markets. Information that could be used in product development, pricing, packaging, or promotion-planning is buried in nonstandard records of middlemen, and sometimes purposely secreted from suppliers.

Channels research is one of the most frustrating areas of marketing investigation, since it requires access to data collected by firms which are independent, remotely situated, and suspicious. Unless given incentive to do so, middlemen will not maintain separate sales records by brands sold. Extracting the needed figures by preferred units of measure is often a hopeless task. To get such data, one producer of pipe tools adopted a device commonly used with electric appliances: a "warranty registration" questionnaire attached to the tools. Ostensibly designed to validate users' damage claims, its true purpose was to discover where, when, how, and by whom the tools had been sold.

Communication downward from the manufacturer is also faulty, placing in doubt the claim that all links in the channel are bound together by common objectives. For example, it is seldom practical to disclose a forthcoming promotional plan in all its details and to ask the middlemen whether the plan will be timely, acceptable, and supportable by their efforts. To do so would jeopardize the advantage of surprise, usually a significant competitive stratagem. Yet the value of synchronized, coordinated action on any new plan by all firms in the channel is obvious.

MIDDLEMEN'S VIEWS

Channel Building

To the extent that any middleman can do so, he should think of himself primarily as a purchasing agent for his customers, and only secondarily as a selling agent for his suppliers. The planning of his product line will proceed from an analysis of a finite customer group in which he is interested . . . to the selection of goods capable of satisfying those needs . . . and then to the choice of available suppliers who can provide those goods. Of course, he may actually begin his assortment with one or more basic products, chosen by him as a way of defining the area of customer needs in which he elects to deal.

From that point on, however, his chief stock in trade becomes not the franchises of important suppliers, but rather his customer group. He is interested in selling any product which these customers desire to buy from him. The attractiveness of any new offering by a supplier is not to be judged by the size of the markup or commission, nor the unusual nature of the product, nor details of its manufacture, nor the promises of manufacturer's advertising support.

The key question is: Does it fit the line? That is, does it complement the other products that he sells, in terms of salability to precisely the same group of buyers? His list of customers is probably less subject to intentional revision than are many other aspects of his business. Is it not at this point, then, that channel building starts?

Some unusual product combinations may result from this approach. A manufacturer's agent selling baby garments in the Southwest took on a line of printed business forms, which the small retailers on whom he called were seeking. An Omaha wholesaler successfully added grocery products to his liquor business. A Cleveland distributor of welding equipment rejected a portable farm welder offered by his principal supplier, since he had no contact with farmers, but was interested in carrying a line of warehouse tractors and lift trucks.

Approach to New Prospects

In some cases a middleman may deem it worthwhile to shift from his current customer group to a new list of prospects, in order to find a market for a particularly promising new product. In the main, however, he will not do so. His approach to new prospects is based on their close similarity to those now on his customer list. To all these persons he attempts to become known as a helpful specialist in a well-defined set of recurring needs. The scope of his line, and the interrelation of products in it, must be known to the bulk of his customers. Scrambled merchandising, or stocking of unrelated items, will tend to split his market into many small groups.

Assortment Sales

Furthermore, the middleman attempts to weld all of his offerings into a family of items which he can sell in combination, as a packaged assortment, to individual customers. His selling efforts are directed primarily at obtaining orders for the assortment, rather than for individual items. Naturally the greatest *numbers* of his transactions will seldom be made in this way; but often his greatest volume and more profitable sales to "blue-chip" accounts will be assortment sales.

Catering to assortment sales has considerable significance to channel operation, because the kind of sales service which a middleman can offer a single-product supplier is affected thereby. Since he is relatively disinterested in pushing individual items, the middleman is criticized for failure to stress a given brand, or for the poor quality of his salesmen's product knowledge, his disuse of suppliers' advertising materials, his neglect of certain customers (who may be good prospects for individual items but not for the assortment), and even for his unrefined systems of record keeping, in which brand designations may be lost.

THE MIDDLEMAN AS AN INDEPENDENT MARKET

The middleman is not a hired link in a chain forged by a manufacturer, but rather an independent market, the focus of a large group of customers for whom he buys. Subsequent to some market analysis of his own, he selects products and suppliers, thereby setting at least one link in the channel.

After some experimentation, he settles upon a method of operation, performing those functions he deems inescapable in the light of his own objectives, forming policies for himself wherever he has freedom to do so. Perhaps these methods and policies conform closely to those of a Census category of middleman, but perhaps they do not.

It is true that his choices are in many instances tentative proposals. He is subject to much influence from competitors, from aggressive suppliers, from inadequate finances and faulty information, as well as from habit. Nonetheless, many of his choices are independent.

As he grows and builds a following, he may find that his prestige in his market is greater than that of the suppliers whose goods he sells. In some instances his local strength is so great that a manufacturer is virtually unable to tap that market, except through him. In such a case the manufacturer can have no channel policy with respect to that market.

NOTES

[1]Wroe Alderson, "The Development of Marketing Channels," in Richard M. Clewett, ed., *Marketing Channels for Manufactured Products* (Homewood, Ill.: Richard D. Irwin, Inc., 1954), p. 30.

[2]Examples are found in: T. N. Beckman, H. H. Maynard, and W. R. Davdison, *Principles of Marketing,* sixth edition (New York: The Ronald Press Company, 1957), pp. 44–45. C. F. Phillips and D. J. Duncan, *Marketing Principles and Methods,* third edition (Homewood, Ill.: Richard D. Irwin, Inc., 1956), p. 562. M. P. McNair, M. P. Brown, D. S. R. Leighton, and W. B. England, *Problems in Marketing,* second edition (New York: McGraw-Hill Book Company, Inc., 1957), p. 66.

18

The Marketing Channel: Who Should Lead this Extra-corporate Organization?

Robert W. Little

This inquiry is directed toward the potential for leadership and control of marketing channels. Various types of firms, in the narrow sense, comprise a marketing channel, and any one theoretically could serve as its leader. An attempt is made to answer the implicit question: Who should be the "Channel Captain"? First, the relevance of the question and then the case for central direction will be briefly discussed. The bases for control of an interorganizational network follow. The analysis is primarily devoted to the identification of the principals who might direct the channel, and to the answer of the following questions: Who is in the best position to lead the channel? Who has the power to do so? Who should lead?

THE QUESTION OF LEADERSHIP

"Leadership" and "control" are abstract terms and are often used interchangeably. Here control is interpreted as the ability to predict events or to achieve a desired outcome. This can be realized by the capacity to direct or command the activity or behavior of others. Leadership is a somewhat broader term which suggests the *exercise* of control. This can come about in channel terms, primarily through the use of economic sanctions or incentives. It can also be realized by persuasiveness—the capacity to communicate and negotiate with different parties to achieve a better understanding of common goals and therefore more effective cooperation. A change in the behavior or perception of any channel member toward a position or goal desired by the leader is evidence of effective control through leadership.

Reprinted from Robert W. Little, "The Marketing Channel: Who Should Lead this Extracorporate Organization?" in the *Journal of Marketing,* Vol. 34 (January 1970), pp. 31–38, published by the American Marketing Association.

The questions raised in this article provide an approach to understanding the need for leadership in marketing channels. Knowledge of the bases for control, initial judgments regarding what institution(s) can lead the channel, and some limited suggestions about who should lead can evolve. These judgements and understandings are necessary for firms that want to control *their* marketing channels. Important strategy considerations for potential channel leaders may also be suggested. Other channel members will also benefit because they should understand more fully their role in channel operations as well as their relationships with others in the system. They can capitalize on this knowledge to enhance their own positions when bargaining with the channel leader and others in the system. Scholars with public policy interests will find this inquiry relevant, too. If channel direction is likely to be pursued at any rate, and achieved in many cases, those concerned with the role of channel activities in the economy can begin to judge who should be the channel leader, and under what conditions. They can proceed to decisions regarding what limitations, if any, are necessary outside the channel itself.

THE CASE FOR CHANNEL LEADERSHIP

In an advanced, high mass consumption economy, marketing channels should be directed by some member firm. At least two logical bases support this assertion. The first rests on simple observation and deduction. Many firms have sought and achieved control of significant portions of their channel(s). In the absence of strong goals superordinate to a profit motive, they seek control because profits are perceived to be enhanced. The widespread existence of integrated firms constitutes presumptive evidence that economies are realized by formal organization of all or part of the channel. Examples are voluntary and cooperative chains, corporate chains, franchise alignments, manufacturers' dealer organizations, and sales branches and offices. To argue that partial integration is accomplished merely to secure greater profits through market control in an oligopolistic or monopolistic sense, is simply too easy a response: Heflebower supports this view at least partially in his conjectures on mass distribution.[1]

A second and more persuasive logical base rests on the simple recognition of the marketing channel as an interorganizational system. It has the disadvantages of large-scale organizations. Because firms are loosely arranged, the advantages of central direction are in large measure missing. The absence of single ownership, or close contractual agreements, means that the benefits of a formal power (superior, subordinate) base are not realized. The reward and penalty system is not as precise and is less easily effected. Similarly, overall planning for the entire system is uncoordinated and the perspective necessary to maximize total system effort is diffused. Less recognition of common goals by various member firms in the channel, as compared to a formally structured organization, is also probable.

Argument Against Central Direction of the Channel

Some would argue that the best ordering of firms and their relationships one with another is determined by the free play of market forces, the assignment of functions, and activities being the result of continuing "make or buy" decisions by different firms. Middlemen and other specialized agencies offer external economies to manufacturers or to others by absorbing one or more activities for several firms and, by aggregating these, achieve an optimum scale operation not available to individual client firms. These arguments, however, are based on the constraints of the traditional competitive models. Entrepreneurs *do* seek to gain control over the activities of others, and they realize it in varying degrees. They do so because their operations are affected, often quite significantly, by the activities of others in the channel.

BASES FOR CHANNELS CONTROL AND LEADERSHIP

The bases for control in channels arise most logically from the sources of inefficiency inherent in any organization. These are summed up in the three broad classes of conflict—structure, communications, and joint decision making.[2] In order to reduce these, some form of power must be exercised. A restrictive and simplified perspective is proposed which is especially relevant for economic institutions. Only two forms of power are generalized—economic and position power. Although innumerable sources of economic power exist, it is ultimately manifest in concentration of capital resources. Position power evolves from the placement of a firm, function, or activity in a given structure. The locus of a particular establishment in a channel (geographically or in terms of a functional or activity flow, for example, negotiation or ownership transfer) may confer power—a capacity to direct or to change—on the person or firm who holds that place or position. Juxtaposition between two firms or activities may also prove to be a significant nodal point to which a power element accrues. At a more specific level of analysis, differences between physical distribution flows and others might lead to shift or simply different arrangements of power.

POTENTIAL CHANNEL LEADERS

In a complex, high mass consumption economy, small retailers and wholesalers have neither the position to lead nor the necessary economic power to do so. The key consideration in terms of position power is access to markets. Small retailers and whosesalers offer only a few customers to the channel system, and thus their bargaining position vis-à-vis large firms at any level in the channel is insignificant. However, they are in a position to provide market information. They should be intimately familiar with customers' preferences and habits. But often they neither acquire these data nor, if they do, share them with others. There are several reasons to explain such reticence. For example, their goals are different from large firms.

Often they do not recognize the importance of formal collection and analysis of these data, and lack sufficient funds and time to do so. Small retailers and wholesalers have little economic power either; by definition they are *small* and therefore have few capital resources.

If not small middlemen, who can lead? Large manufacturers can lead, and sometimes small ones too. But first, large wholesalers and retailers must be considered. A new context is suggested for their study.

The Multilevel Merchandiser

An analysis of "pure" wholesalers and retailers excludes too much channel activity when the greater part of consumer and industrial-commercial exchanges are considered. Most trade flows through integrated marketing institutions. In the United States, and probably in any high mass consomption economy, there is no such thing as just a "large retailer." There are only large, or huge, retail-wholesale integrated organizations. Whether corporate chain, voluntary chain, or retailer-cooperative, the distinctions between them are less significant than their points of commonality. In any of these categories, many retail outlets are tied directly to some form of wholesale organization. Small "independent," retailer members attached to a voluntary or cooperative organization have, in reality, quite limited sources of supply outside their own retail-wholesale channel. In practice they are nearly as limited in their choices as are retail unit managers in many corporate chains. Outside the system, additional contactual and transactional costs are most often exorbitant. McVey suggests that some wholesalers command access to their local markets,[3] but almost no small retailer has such power. He chooses from the key wholesale establishment with which he is aligned, and perhaps from two or three others. In customary terms, then, to consider retailers or wholesalers as potential channel captains is misleading. The relevant institution is the combined wholesale-retail organization. The term W-R or R-W, the lead symbol denoting the force of leadership, indicates this marketing agency.

In addition, many conventionally identified manufacturers are excluded since ownership of their own sales branches and offices removes them from any reasonable concept of a "pure" unaligned entity. Also, many vertical relationships between manufacturers and distributors are of a rigid contractual nature. When these involve relatively permanent commitments over a wide range of functional requirements by both parties, they resemble more closely an ownership arrangement than the concept of independent operations. These organizations are identified as M-W and W-M.

Finally, there are the fully integrated organizations. The huge, general merchandise retail organizations include not only Sears and Penney types of operation, but also national department store chains such as Allied Stores and Marshall Field (R-W-M). These are not simply combined retail-wholesale organizations, but represent direct ownership (sometimes extensive) or control (often extensive) of manufacturing and service facilities. In addition, major automobile, appliance, and petroleum refiners, and perhaps a few others, own retail outlets or have tight, contractual, semi-permanent relationships with retailers (M-W-R). There is,

finally, the W $\stackrel{R}{\cdot_M}$ integrated organization—McKesson, for example—

where the wholesaler makes central decisions for some manufacturer and retailer components of the channel. For the moment, this is treated as an aberration which will drift ultimately to M-W-R or R-W-M.

There are seven potential channel leaders to consider, and each should be classified into two types. One encompasses all organizations integrated by direct ownership; the other includes those maintained by long-standing, contractual relationships. They cover a wide range of required activities and go well beyond the simple buy-sell relationships established by independent firms.

In order to keep the number of institutional types manageable a new institution, the multilevel merchandiser (MLM), is introduced. The MLM includes all retail- and wholesale-directed organizations: the R-W, the W-R,

the W $\stackrel{R}{\cdot_M}$, the R-W-M, and the W-M. This is not an unreasonable

grouping; the distinction between corporate chains, retailer-cooperatives, and wholesale voluntaries is much less than their similarity. The R-W-M also has many points in common with the previous two although more differences exist; approximately the same analysis can be used for all of

these. Although rare, the W-M and the W $\stackrel{R}{\cdot_M}$ are by definition,

merchandising oriented and, to the extent they exist, are considered MLM. The analysis of manufacturer-integrated organizations, M-W-R and M-W, parallels the discussion of the manufacturer, and is considered later. In spite of the problems involved, this generalization eliminates much of the confusion and obscurity inherent in the present definitional literature. The introduction of these new terms does not solve the existing taxonomy problems; indeed, it is compounded by adding new terms. However, the different perspective is believed to provide a useful point of departure for channel study.[4]

Craig and Gabler provided the landmark study of partial integration. They observed that integration organized backward from the retailer (R-W) went with the market situation and integration organized forward from the wholesaler (W-R) went against the market situation. Their ultimate conclusion was that from "...the strictly business interest of the consumer...the retailer-guided system of distribution is to be preferred."[5] But operational differences today between wholesaler-sponsored voluntary chains and retailer-cooperative chains (and even retail-corporate chains) are insubstantial. In fact, it is difficult to distinguish one from another. To the extent that they apply today, Craig and Gabler's conclusions can be safely extended to all MLM organizations. Most MLM organizations are large enough to have considerable economic power and, in addition, their position affords them access to large markets. They are also in a position to provide market information. Certainly, they can be considered as potential channel leaders.

The Manufacturer

Large manufacturers are potential leaders of channels, by definition, since they have economic power. But small manufacturers may also serve as potential sources of control and direction of a vertical, interorganizational structure. As Borden has emphasized, limited economic power hampers their opportunity, but a good product offers control possibilities.[6] This is a manifestation of position strength. Those in the position of controlling a new product—desired by many consumers—can elect to offer or withhold their product from various middlemen and therefore exercise control. Craig and Gabler observed this long ago.

> As long as the existing demand or newly awakened demands exceed the supply, selling was easy and its costs were low. Whoever could make the wanted merchandise was in a strategic position to guide and direct its distribution.[7]

Clearly, large manufacturers enjoy similar position strength.

Although they observed a shift to sellers' markets later on, and followed this with the judgment that retailer-guided channel systems were best, Craig and Gabler failed to consider the enormous diversity and dynamism in an advanced, technologically diverse, economy. Many different products are in different states of development at the same time. There is no such thing as a *general* buyers' or sellers' market. Consequently, manufacturers—large and small—and MLM organizations are potential leaders of marketing channels.

THE LEADER—MLM OR MANUFACTURER?

Economic Power

Either an MLM organization or a large manufacturer can lead because ability rests on economic power. They can control resources, "buy" time by utilizing staff specialists, and employ their resources in a manner to help the channel reduce conflict arising from any of the basic sources of organizational conflict. For example, either organization can employ research personnel to learn more about customers and markets and therefore reduce uncertainty and improve communications throughout the channel. They have the economic power to communicate and enforce a greater recognition of the system's common goals which are congruent with some goals in each member firm. They have the ability to enforce, through economic sanction, a reward and penalty system within the interorganizational structure. They are thus able to design and administer joint-decision efforts and responsibilities in a manner that can lead to less conflict than would likely be the case without their intervention.

Position Power

The MLM.   Position in the channel offers unique advantages to each party. The MLM has access to large markets manufacturers seek to reach. The larger the MLM and the greater the market its establishments serve, the more important is its adoption decision to most manufacturers; therefore, the MLM holds a strong potential for leadership. The strength of the MLM is much more than just a simple bargaining coalition which, Kuhn observes, "...differs from an organization in that it does not jointly produce anything, but only raises bargaining power by limiting the opponent's alternatives—i.e. by reducing competition."[8]

The MLM creates additional values for the system. In terms of decision making, its assembled resources, technology, skill, and experience place it in a unique position to reduce system inefficiencies. And it can realize substantial economies from the routinization of transactions. When considering structural changes, the MLM's power is often enormous. Because of its size and position in the market, the MLM can absorb directly a large measure of uncertainty for manufacturers regarding the acceptance of products by assuring them access to widespread markets. Indirectly, uncertainty may also be reduced for other manufacturers when the MLM markets its own brand.

These organizations are estimated to make merchandising decisions for two-thirds or more of all retail markets, since even many "convenience store" merchandising decisions, as well as decisions by corporate and contractual chains, are determined by the MLMs. The MLM chooses from many manufacturers' offerings which it may add, exclude, or drop almost at will. It has extraordinary influence over the degree of success realized by even the largest manufacturers. For example, in six markets studied by Borden, five corporate chains and two voluntary organizations controlled sixty-five per cent of the grocery market in the least concentrated market. In the most concentrated market, six corporate chains and two voluntary organizations controlled ninety-three per cent of the market.[9] Market concentration in most nongrocery fields is undoubtedly lower but still strong enough to support similar conclusions.

Limitations on the MLM.   Leadership and direction appear heavily weighted toward the MLM, but there are important offsetting factors to consider. When product development and demand-creation functions are considered, the MLM's position strength is substantially diminished. Only rarely are product modifications different enough to suggest that the MLM has provided any real sense of direction when offering its own reseller brands. Strength is minimal because the MLM's principal function is selecting and maintaining wanted stocks. The MLM is in no position to pursue demand creation or product-development functions. Many have the financial strength to accomplish this, but it is not their role. In theory, retail units are closest to the consumer and therefore the MLM is in a good position to lead by identifying user preferences. In reality, its specialists are much too concerned with selecting and maintaining stocks, and providing and merchandising the services that accompany them, to be able to meet this role. Retailers' brands are economically feasible only after widespread market acceptance has been established. Only with fully accepted generic products can the MLM assume the risk of introducing its own brands. This is summarized in the following generalizations: "The greater the acceptance by final users of a generic class of goods, the more likely control over channels through which these products flow will be held by the MLM."

The Manufacturer.   Manufacturers have significant position strength although it varies with changing market conditions. With a new product and substantial financial resources, the manufacturer can establish strong consumer demand, and control of channels is relatively easily established. Middlemen tend to accept complete, multifaceted, well-planned programs of new product introductions.[10] However, only large manufacturers are able to develop total programs for new product introduction and promotion and can, therefore, be clearly identified as channel leaders for new products.

With a good product but little financial strength, the manufacturer must offer high gross margins and other incentives to encourage middleman support. (The *Colgate Doctrine,* supporting refusal to deal, is still the small manufacturer's most fundamental protection.[11]) Position strength and control is exercised by the small manufacturer, but it is less easily realized and maintained.

Once a strong consumer franchise is established, however, even the small manufacturer enjoys fairly easy control which is often maintained into market maturity.

Limitations on Manufacturers.   But there are also offsetting influences regarding manufacturers' position strength. The MLM controls all the products branded for its organization. Also, MLMs, where territories overlap, are in competition with one another. Some handle the same manufacturer's products and others handle close substitutes. This complicates the analysis in a sense and adds some confusion because the MLM prefers exclusive territorial rights. Greater position strength for the manufacturer is, therfore, suggested. In general, however, the desire for full market coverage by manufacturers tends to weaken their position, and as a result probably more than offsets the apparent strength noted above.

In addition, even a strong manufacturer brand is weakened by the nature of the MLM's operation. As Sevin has aptly remarked: "All merchandising decision making...is necessarily done at the level of the individual item—e.g., what to buy, display, promote; how to price, etc."[12] Beyond the initial choice of a generalized assortment, any middleman must base his product selection on the basis of gross-margin dollars. Loyalty to selected channel members and/or antagonism to others should not interfere with his individual item decisions; he operates within a fixed space and returns per cubic foot concern him most.

Furthermore, even the largest manufacturer seldom can afford the luxury of his own distribution system. While a few may be able to achieve broad enough coverage through their own sales branches and offices, most manufacturers will be forced to use independent wholesalers and MLMs to reach a variety of customer types in addition to those who can be reached through their own system. Those controlling their own retail outlets almost always will be forced to secure additional representation in other retail stores. Most items stocked by the MLM have close substitutes. Usually, the reverse is not the case—the supplier needs many different MLMs.

Finally, market maturity is usually reached when there are substantial increases in industry capacity, through the entry of close substitutes from other manufacturers' and resellers' brands. This more or less defines market acceptance of the generic product class; economic power is then the ultimate determinant of channel control. At this final stage, effective control tends to lean toward the MLM, especially for the small manufacturer.

Summary

Strength of position and economic power is indeterminate. Throughout a product's life cycle, the manufacturer's income and consumer franchise will increase while his exclusiveness, unless he has a very uncopiable product, will tend to depreciate. As this takes place, the manufacturer's *position* strength will tend to decline because less uncertainty surrounds the product and more substitutes are available, but his *ability* to direct will increase because his economic power is enhanced. Similarly, movement through the cycle alters the MLM's strength. With products of long standing acceptance where demand creation is less necessary, the MLM can enter the market with its own generic product, and thus create and direct a new channel. At the same time, however, the increasing strength of the manufacturer's brand makes the MLM less able to reject the product than before. Too many of its customers demand it.

In general, the MLM and the manufacturer must share leadership of the channel. In a period of generic product acceptance, however, the MLM tends to hold the greater measure of power. The MLM not only can decide to enter the market with its own brand, but it can decide *which* of the leading brands it will stock. The producer's power is substantially weakened under these conditions. The wider distribution requirements of most manufacturers, then, suggest a distinct imbalance in favor of MLM organization.

Three generalizations help to summarize the channel leadership role.

- MLM organizations are in the best position to lead channels because the value to the manufacturer of market access provided by each MLM far exceeds the value of one more product to the MLM merchandising mix.
- The more product sources are available to the MLM within a channel system, the more the locus of power will tend to shift toward the MLM.
- Reciprocally, the wider the manufacturer's product line, the greater his economic significance to MLM organizations and the greater his potential power.

RELEVANCE FOR MARKETING MANAGEMENT

The value and uses of economic power to seek leadership of the channel should be clear to the manufacturer and the MLM. The manufacturer can use economic power to establish a stronger consumer franchise for his product(s) and to gain its acceptance by desired middlemen. The MLM can employ its resources to provide more and better market access for its suppliers. Both can utilize their capital resources to "encourage" greater recognition of common goals that, by definition, all channel members share in part. Their economic and position strength can also be used to coordinate more effectively the joint decision responsibilities of various member firms, and to facilitate communication and understanding between and among all members. Both can also use economic resources to support more careful studies of market structures and functions which should lead to the searching out of new alignment alternatives...the discovery of "better" channels.

For the MLM, knowledge of its role in the channel network can support a more effective bargaining stance with suppliers, and buyers, and can lead to a fuller realization of its own goals. How many consumers' foods manufacturers do not want space in A&P or Super-Valu stores? The manufactuer, on the other hand, can use the knowledge of his unique position with greater force. He should know more about his final users than other channel members. In addition, he knows more about his own product(s) than does anyone else. He can and should exploit this knowledge in convincing the desired middlemen to accept and/or continue his products. In addition, a manufacturer's strong product franchise, accompanied by a realistic gross margin, severely limits the MLM's ability to bargain. Are there many appropriate retail outlets that do not carry Crest or Gillette?

Small wholesalers, retailers, and manufacturers who are not leaders can also benefit from the knowledge of who holds a strategic position and economic power. The recognition of the source of leadership gives them the opportunity to seek out channels guided by those who appear to be best able to contribute to their own individual goals. Understanding the relationships between all members in the channel should also lead to acceptance of one's role within the channel(s) involved. Also, nonleader members should recognize the *reality* of competing channel systems. This is simply an extension of the valuable concept of Smith and Kelley's competing retail systems.[13] A retailer, for example, must realize that much of his competition comes not only from similar establishments close by but also from retail outlets linked with other vertical market structures.

Knowledge of the economic and position strength of various channel members is also valuable to those outside the channel. It is important to those who wish to study the overall institutional structure of the economy and specifically the role of marketing channels in contributing to growth and welfare. This is part of the final question considered in this article.

WHO SHOULD LEAD?

The preceding questions about position and ability are at least conducive to empirical measures. Although the discussion is theoretical, limited historical data lend some support to the conclusions. Now a move further away from the empirical measures is necessary. Who should lead? The question is important, although there are no definitive answers and subjective standards must be employed.

Choice and Efficiency

Two measures, choice and efficiency, guide the following analysis. They are necessarily conflicting goals in a narrow sense, but compatible in the broader perspective. The United States has supported the ideal, and in large measure, the reality of widespread individual choice which is most succinctly expressed in Lord Acton's paraphrased words: "The degree of civilization is directly proportional to the degree of choice." This requires an important qualification. Choice means "real" choice, choice from knowledge. When a buyer selects "A" rather than "B" on the basis of presumed differences that are in fact mere distortions, the choice process is perverted. A second difference is manifest in product complexity. Given reasonable knowledge and effort, if a buyer is unable to learn the relevant factors involved in an exchange, he chooses from ignorance rather than from knowledge. Channel agencies, and more specifically their employees in dealing with others, can help to confound or to clarify "real" choice.

The second criterion is efficiency—matching goods and consumption at the least cost consistent with widespread choice. The efficiency criterion implies that nonmaterial goals are enhanced or made more attainable, by material progress.

Generalizations on Who Should Lead

Who should lead? Not nearly enough is known; however, some logical bases exist, relative to analyzing this question and several hypotheses can be developed.

That part of the marketing mix which is most difficult to match is the essence of competition. Wasson identifies product as the most important competitive tool because "...what one man can do another can find a way to copy, sooner or later. Thus, all differential advantages are temporary, and the successful can remain so only through continual innovation."[14] His view is a good one, but needs qualification. The most important competitive tool is the one most difficult to copy. For a local producer of liquid detergent, the competitive issue is the advertising budget. The factor most difficult for him to match, in his struggle with Procter and Gamble, Lever Brothers, and others, is the size of the advertising budget. In competition with Magnavox or Bell and Howell, another manufacturer might find the discovery and control of the channel as the competitive issue. For many the research capacity of DuPont is most difficult to match. From any perspective, size is most difficult to match if the small firm is compared vis-à-vis the large.

Competitive advantage must be identified for each prospective channel leader in order to determine which will encourage the greatest choice at the highest efficiency. The manufacturer's best opportunity for differential advantage is the development of new products and services. The resulting consumer franchise is his principal means to economic power and other goals. If new products and services are matched, the manufacturer's advantage is lost.

Merchandising organizations, MLM, seek differential advantage primarily through locations. While customer and merchandising services are important, location of retail outlets is *the* competitive variable because it is the most difficult to match. The merchandiser's own brands also provide differential advantage but are more easily duplicated. In terms of choice, the MLM offers little to the consumer that is especially different when it selects various generic products for its own brand. These comprise a small part of its stock anyway, and it cannot accept the risk of new product introduction.

Both the manufacturer's and the MLM's ploys extend consumer choice. But in a high mass consumption society, wedded to the automobile and characterized by excess transport capacity, consumer choice is advanced more by new product introductions, than it is by new brand introductions and additional retail locations. This is true unless brand proliferation, to which both the manufacturer and MLM contribute, leads to such an array of substitute products that the consumer cannot learn important differences.

If new products provide more choice than new locations, then the manufacturer should lead marketing channels. But the efficiency question must be answered too. Manufacturers' new product costs must be compared with MLMs' costs absorbed in selecting and developing additional locations. They must also be compared with MLMs' costs in diverse locations, many of which operate at less than optimum scale. To measure which of these is greater is difficult if not impossible. But the efficiency criterion is stated as requiring system performance at the least cost consistent with widespread choice, and choice is always costly. Narrowly observed, distribution of one electric razor through one channel is more efficient that distribution of ten razors through fifteen channels. Choice is expanded in the latter case, however, and society has decided that choice is safer and worth the additional cost. Thus, unless the cost of developing new products rises beyond socially acceptable limits, manufacturer-directed channel systems are best suited to achieve consumer goals; therefore, manufacturers should lead.

REPRISE

Speculation, theory, and model building have far outstripped the quest for empirical verification. We must have more reports in the classic mold of Cox and Goodman, and Craig and Gabler.[15] In marketing, we use a few scientific tools, but the facts are mostly literary.[16] This is not really surprising in view of the enormously complicated relationships involved. The questions, answers, and perspectives set out in this paper have been shaped by some of the things we know, and by some of the things we should know. But they are unfulfilled. More empiricism is needed. For example, data indicating the relative strength of MLM organizations in various industries would establish more clearly a need for further study. Determining the nature and extent of diseconomies in large corporate and highly contractually integrated channels, as opposed to less formally organized ones, could add important insights. Analysis of the relative efficiency of formal and informal channels for each basic marketing flow or function—physical distribution, promotion, information, and communication for example—is needed. Finally, the conclusion suggested here regarding who should lead is highly subjective. Attempts to establish appropriate empirical measures should be pursued.

NOTES

[1]Richard B. Heflebower, "Mass Distribution: A Phase of Bilateral Oligopoly or of Competition?" *American Economic Review,* Vol. XLVII (May 1957), pp. 274–85; published concurrently in *Adaptive Behavior in Marketing,* Robert D. Buzzell, ed. (Chicago, Ill.: American Marketing Association, 1957), pp. 139–52.

[2]Russell L. Ackoff, "Structural Conflict Within Organizations," pp. 427–38, and Richard E. Walton, "Theory of Conflict in Lateral Organizational Relationships," pp. 409–26, both in *Operational Research and the Social Sciences* (London, England: Tavistock Publications, 1966). The close parallel between these conflicts and Alderson's characteristics of the organized behavior system will not be lost on marketing scholars.

[3]Phillip McVey, "Are Channels of Distribution What the Textbooks Say?" *Journal of Marketing,* Vol. 25 (January 1960), pp. 61–65.

[4]See Louis P. Bucklin, "The Economic Structure of Channels of Distribution," in *Marketing: A Maturing Discipline*, Martin T. Bell, ed. (Chicago, Ill.: American Marketing Association, 1960), pp. 379–385, for an excellent basis for diagramming internal channel functions to supplement this MLM genus. See also Louis P. Bucklin and Stanley F. Stasch, "Basic Problems in the Study of Channels," Working Paper No. 35 (Berkeley, Calif.: University of California, Institute of Business and Economic Research, November 1967). The authors offer a persuasive argument for adoption of polythetic marketing taxonomies.

[5]David R. Craig and Werner K. Gabler, "The Competitive Struggle for Market Control," *The Annals of the American Academy of Political and Social Science,* Vol. 209 (May 1940), pp. 84–107.

[6]Neil H. Borden, *Acceptance of New Products by Supermarkets* (Boston, Mass.: Harvard University, Division of Research, Graduate School of Business Administration, 1968), p. 13.

[7]Craig and Gabler, "Competitive Struggle," pp. 84–107.

[8]Alfred Kuhn, *The Study of Society: A Multidisciplinary Approach* (London, England: Tavistock Publications, 1960), p. 385.

[9]Borden, *Acceptance of New Products,* p. 13.

[10]Borden, *Acceptance of New Products,* pp. 180–84.

[11]*United States* vs. *Colgate,* 250 U. S. 300 (1919).

[12]Charles H. Sevin, *Marketing Productivity Analysis* (New York: McGraw-Hill Book Company, Inc., 1965), p. 34

[13]Paul E. Smith and Eugene J. Kelley, "Competing Retail Systems: The Shopping Center and the Central Business District," *Journal of Retailing,* Vol. XXXVI (Spring 1960), pp. 11–18.

[14]Chester R. Wasson, *The Economics of Managerial Decision* (New York: Appleton-Century-Crofts, 1965), p. 3.

[15]Reavis Cox and C. S. Goodman, "Marketing of Housebuilding Materials," *Journal of Marketing,* Vol. 21 (July 1956), pp. 36-61; and Craig and Gabler, "Competitive Struggle," pp. 84–107.

[16]Kenneth E. Boulding, *The Impact of the Social Sciences* (New Brunswick, N.J.: The Rutgers University Press, 1966), pp. 3–23.

19

Conflict and Cooperation
in Marketing Channels

Bruce Mallen

The purpose of this paper is to advance the hypotheses that between member firms of a marketing channel there exists a dynamic field of conflicting and cooperating objectives; that if the conflicting objectives outweigh the cooperating ones, the effectiveness of the channel will be reduced and efficient distribution impeded; and that implementation of certain methods of cooperation will lead to increased channel efficiency.

DEFINITION OF CHANNEL

The concept of marketing channel is slightly more involved than expected on initial study. One author in a recent paper[1] has identified "trading" channels, "nontrading" channels, "type" channels, "enterprise" channels, and "business-unit" channels. Another source[2] refers to channels as all the flows extending from the producer to the user. These include the flows of physical possession, ownership, promotion, negotiation, financing, risking, ordering, and payment.

The concept of channels to be used here involves only two of the above-mentioned flows: ownership and negotiation. The first draws merchants, both wholesalers and retailers, into the channel definition, and the second draws in agent middlemen. Both, of course, include producers and consumers. This definition roughly corresponds to Professor Breyer's "trading channel," though the latter does not restrict (nor will this paper) the definition to actual flows, but to "flow-capacity." "A trading channel is formed when trading relations, making possible the passage of title

Reprinted from Bruce Mallen, "Conflict and Cooperation in Marketing Channels," in *Reflections on Progress in Marketing*, L. George Smith, ed., 1964, pp. 65–85, published by the American Marketing Association.

and/or possession (usually both) of goods from the producer to the ultimate consumer, is consummated by the component trading concerns of the system."[3] In addition, this paper will deal with trading channels in the broadest manner and so will be concentrating on "type-trading" channels rather than "enterprise" or "business-unit" channels. This means that there will be little discussion of problems peculiar to integrated or semi-integrated channels, or peculiar to specific channels and firms.

CONFLICT

Palamountain isolated three forms of distributive conflict.[4]
1. Horizontal competition—this is competition between middlemen of the same type; for example, discount store *versus* discount store.
2. Intertype competition—this is competition between middlemen of different types in the same channel sector; for example, discount store vs. department store.
3. Vertical conflict—this is conflict between channel members of different levels; for example, discount store vs. manufacturer.

The first form, horizontal competition, is well covered in traditional economic analysis and is usually referred to simply as "competition." However, both intertype competition and vertical conflict, particularly the latter, are neglected in the usual micro-economic discussion.

The concepts of "intertype competition" and "distributive innovation" are closely related and require some discussion. Intertype competition will be divided into two categories: (a) "traditional intertype competition" and (b) "innovative intertype competition." The first category includes the usual price and promotional competition between two or more different types of channel members at the same channel level. The second category involves the action on the part of traditional channel members to prevent channel innovators from establishing themselves. For example, in Canada there is a strong campaign, on the part of traditional department stores, to prevent the discount operation from taking a firm hold on the Canadian market.[5]

Distributive innovation will also be divided into two categories: (a) "intrafirm innovative conflict" and (b) "innovative intertype competition." The first category involves the action of channel member firms to prevent sweeping changes within their own companies. The second category, "innovative intertype competition," is identical to the second category of intertype competition.

Thus the concepts of intertype competition and distributive innovation give rise to three forms of conflict, the second of which is a combination of both: (1) traditional intertype competition, (2) innovative intertype competition, and (3) intrafirm innovative conflict.

It is to this second form that this paper now turns before going on to vertical conflict.

Innovative Intertype Competition

Professor McCammon has identified several sources, both intrafirm and intertype, of innovative conflict in distribution, i.e., where there are barriers to change within the marketing structure.[6]

Traditional members of a channel have several motives for maintaining the channel status quo against outside innovators. The traditional members are particularly strong in this conflict when they can band together in some formal or informal manner—when there is strong reseller solidarity.

Both entrepreneurs and professional managers may resist outside innovators, not only for economic reasons, but because change "violates group norms, creates uncertainty, and results in a loss of status." The traditional channel members (the insiders) and their affiliated members (the strivers and complementors) are emotionally and financially committed to the dominant channel and are interested in perpetuating it against the minor irritations of the "transient" channel members and the major attacks of the "outside innovators."

Thus, against a background of horizontal and intertype channel conflict, this paper now moves to its area of major concern: vertical conflict and cooperation.

Vertical Conflict—Price

The Exchange Act.   The act of exchange is composed of two elements: a sale and a purchase. It is to the advantage of the seller to obtain the highest return possible from such an exchange and the exact opposite is the desire of the buyer. This exchange act takes place between any kind of buyer and seller. It the consumer is the buyer, then that side of the act is termed shopping; if the manufacturer, purchasing; if the government, procurement; and if a retailer, buying. Thus, between each level in the channel an exchange will take place (except if a channel member is an agent rather than a merchant).

One must look to the process of the exchange act for the basic source of conflict between channel members. This is not to say the exchange itself is a conflict. Indeed, the act or transaction is a sign that the element of price conflict has been resolved to the mutual satisfaction of both principals. Only along the road to this mutual satisfaction point or exchange price do the principals have opposing interests. This is no less true even if they work out the exchange price together, as in mass retailers' specification-buying programs.

It is quite natural for the selling member in an exchange to want a higher price than the buying member. The conflict is subdued through persuasion or force by one member over the other, or it is subdued by the fact that the exchange act or transaction does not take place, or finally, as mentioned above, it is eliminated if the act does take place.

Suppliers may emphasize the customer aspect of a reseller rather than the channel member aspect. As a customer the reseller is somebody to persuade, manipulate, or even fool. Conversely, under the marketing concept, the view of the reseller as a customer or channel member is identical. Under this philosophy he is somebody to aid, help, and serve. However, it is by no means certain that even a large minority of suppliers have accepted the marketing concept.

To view the reseller as simply the opposing principal in the act of exchange may be channel myopia, but this view exists. On the other hand, failure to recognize this basic opposing interest is also a conceptual fault.

When the opposite principals in an exchange act are of unequal strength, the stronger is very likely to force or persuade the weaker to adhere to the former's desires. However, when they are of equal strength, the basic conflict cannot so easily be resolved. Hence, the growth of big retailers who can match the power of big producers has possibly led to greater open conflict between channel members, not only with regard to exchange, but also to other conflict sources.

There are other sources of conflict within the pricing area outside of the basic one just discussed.

A supplier may force a product onto its resellers, who dare not oppose, but who retaliate in other ways, such as using it as a loss leader. Large manufacturers may try to dictate the resale price of their merchandise; this may be less or more than the price at which resellers wish to sell it. Occasionally, a local market may be more competitive for a reseller than is true nationally. The manufacturer may not recognize the difference in competition and refuse to help this channel member.

Resellers complain of manufacturers' special price concessions to competitors and rebel at the attempt of manufacturers to control resale prices. Manufacturers complain of resellers' deceptive and misleading price advertising, nonadherence to resale price suggestions, bootlegging to unauthorized outlets, seeking special price concessions by unfair methods, and misrepresenting offers by competitive suppliers.

Other points of price conflict are the paperwork aspects of pricing. Resellers complain of delays in price change notices and complicated price sheets.

Price Theory.   If one looks upon a channel as a series of markets or as the vertical exchange mechanism between buyers and sellers, one can adapt several theories and concepts to the channel situation which can aid marketing theory in this important area of channel conflict.[7]

Vertical Conflict—Non-Price

Channel conflict not only finds its source in the exchange act and pricing, but it permeates all areas of marketing. Thus, a manufacturer may wish to promote a product in one manner or to a certain degree while his resellers oppose this. Another manufacturer may wish to get information from his resellers on a certain aspect relating to his product, but his resellers may refuse to provide this information. A producer may want to distribute his product extensively, but his resellers may demand exclusives.

There is also conflict because of the tendency for both manufacturers and retailers to want the elimination of the wholesaler.

One very basic source of channel conflict is the possible difference in the primary business philosophy of channel members. Writing in the *Harvard Business Review,* Wittreich says:

> In essence, then, the key to understanding management's problem of crossed purpose is the recognition that the fundamental (philosophy) in life of the high-level corporate manager and the typically (small) retail dealer in the distribution system are quite different. The former's (philosophy) can be characterized as being essentially dynamic in nature, continuously evolving and emerging; the latter, which are in sharp contrast, can be characterized as being essentially static in nature, reaching a point and leveling off into a continuously satisfying plateau.[8]

While the big members of the channel may want growth, the small retail members may be satisfied with stability and a "good living."

ANARCHY[9]

The channel can adjust to its conflicting-cooperating environment in three distinct ways. First, it can have a leader (one of the channel members) who "forces" members to cooperate; this is an autocratic relationship. Second, it can have a leader who "helps" members to cooperate, creating a democratic relationship. Finally, it can do nothing, and so have an anarchistic relationship. Lewis B. Sappington and C. G. Browne, writing on the problems of internal company organizations, state:

> The first classification may be called "autocracy." In this approach to the group the leader determines the policy and dictates or assigns the work tasks. There are no group deliberations, no group decisions....
> The second classification may be called "democracy." In this approach the leader allows all policies to be decided by the group with his participation. The group members work with each other as they wish. The group determines the division and assignment of tasks....
> The third classification may be called "anarchy." In anarchy there is complete freedom of the group or the individual regarding policies or task assignments, without leader participation.[10]

Advanced in this paper is the hypothesis that if anarchy exists, there is a great chance of the conflicting dynamics destroying the channel. If autocracy exists, there is less chance of this happening. However, the latter method creates a state of cooperation based on power and control. This controlled cooperation is really subdued conflict and makes for a more unstable equilibrium than does voluntary democratic cooperation.

CONTROLLED COOPERATION

The usual pattern in the establishment of channel relationships is that there is a leader, an initiator who puts structure into this relationship and who holds it together. This leader controls, whether through command or cooperation, i.e., through an autocratic or a democratic system.

Too often it is automatically assumed that the manufacturer or producer will be the channel leader and that the middlemen will be the channel followers. This has not always been so, nor will it necessarily be so in the future. The growth of mass retailers is increasingly challenging the manufacturer for channel leadership, as the manufacturer challenged the wholesaler in the early part of this century.

The following historical discussion will concentrate on the three-ring struggle between manufacturer, wholesaler, and retailer rather than on the changing patterns of distribution within a channel section, i.e., between service wholesaler and agent middleman or discount and department store. This will lay the necessary background for a discussion of the present-day manufacturer-dominated vs. retailer-dominated struggle.

Early History

The simple distribution system of Colonial days gave way to a more complex one. Among the forces of change were the growth of population, the long distances involved, the increasing complexity of new products, the increase of wealth, and the increase of consumption.

The United States was ready for specialists to provide a growing and widely dispersed populace with the many new goods and services required. The more primitive methods of public markets and barter could not efficiently handle the situation. This type of system required short distances, few products, and a small population, to operate properly.

Nineteenth Century History

In the same period that this older system was dissolving, the retailer was still a very small merchant who, especially in the West, lived in relative isolation from his supply sources. Aside from being small, he further diminished his power position by spreading himself thin over many merchandise lines. The retailer certainly was no specialist but was as general as a general store can be. His opposite channel member, the manufacturer, was also a small businessman, too concerned with production and financial problems to fuss with marketing.

Obviously, both these channel members were in no position to assume leadership. However, somebody had to perform all the various marketing functions between production and retailing if the economy was to function.

The wholesaler filled this vacuum and became the channel leader of the nineteenth century.

The wholesaler became the selling force of the manufacturer and the latter's link to the widely scattered retailers over the nation. He became the retailer's life line to these distant domestic and even more important foreign sources of supply.

These wholesalers carried any type of product from any manufacturer and sold any type of product to the general retailers. They can be described as general merchandise wholesalers. They were concentrated at those transportation points in the country which gave them access to both the interior and its retailers, and the exterior and its foreign suppliers.

Early Twentieth Century

The end of the century saw the wholesaler's power on the decline. The manufacturer had grown larger and more financially secure with the shift from a foreign-oriented economy to a domestic-oriented one. He could now finance his marketing in a manner impossible to him in early times. His thoughts shifted to some extent from production problems to marketing problems.

Prodding the manufacturer on was the increased rivalry of his other domestic competitors. The increased investment in capital and inventory made it necessary that he maintain volume. He tended to locate himself in the larger market areas, and thus did not have great distances to travel to see his retail customers. In addition, he started to produce various products; and because of his new multiproduct production, he could reach—even more efficiently—these already more accessible markets.

The advent of the automobile and highways almost clinched the manufacturer's bid for power. For now he could reach a much vaster market (and they could reach him) and reap the benefits of economics of scale.

The branding of his products projected him to the channel leadership. No longer did he have as great a need for a specialist in reaching widely dispersed customers, nor did he need them to the same extent for their contacts. The market knew where the product came from. The age of wholesaler dominance declined. That of manufacturer dominance emerged.

Is it still here? What is its future? How strong is the challenge by retailers? Is one "better" than the other?

Disagreement Among Scholars

No topic seems to generate so much heat and bias in marketing as the question of who should be the channel leader, and more strangely, who is the channel leader. Depending on where the author sits, he can give numerous reasons why his particular choice should take the channel initiative.

Authors of sales management and general marketing books say the manufacturer is and should be the chief institution in the channel. Retailing authors feel the same way about retailers, and wholesaling authors (as few as there are), though not blinded to the fact that wholesaling is not "captain," still imply that they should be, and talk about the coming resurrection of wholesalers. Yet a final and compromising view is put forth by those who believe that a balance of power, rather than a general and prolonged dominance of any channel member, is best.

The truth is that an immediate reaction would set in against any temporary dominance by a channel member. In that sense, there is a constant tendency toward the equilibrium of market forces. The present view is that public interest is served by a balance of power rather than by a general and prolonged predominance of any one level in marketing channels.[11]

John Kenneth Galbraith's concept of countervailing power also holds to this last view.

For the retailer:

> In the opinion of the writer, "retailer-dominated marketing" has yielded, and will continue to yield in the future greater net benefits to consumers than "manufacturer-dominated marketing," as the central-buying mass distributor continues to play a role of ever-increasing importance in the marketing of goods in our economy....
>
> ...In the years to come, as more and more large-scale multiple-unit retailers follow the central buying patterns set by Sears and Penneys, as leaders in their respective fields (hard and soft goods), ever-greater benefits should flow to consumers in the way of more goods better adjusted to their demands, at lower prices.[12]

> ...In a long-run buyer's market, such as we probably face in this country, the retailers have the inherent advantage of economy in distribution and will, therefore, become increasingly important.[13]

> The retailer cannot be the selling agent of the manufacturer because he holds a higher commission; he is the purchasing agent for the public.[14]

For the wholesaler:

> The wholesaling sector is, first of all, the most significant part of the entire marketing organization.[15]

...The orthodox wholesaler and affiliated types have had a resurgence to previous 1929 levels of sales importance.[16]

...Wholesalers have since made a comeback.[17] This revival of wholesaling has resulted from infusion of new management blood and the adoption of new techniques.[18]

For the manufacturer:

...the final decision in channel selection rests with the seller manufacturer and will continue to rest with him as long as he has the legal right to choose to sell to some potential customers and refuse to sell to others.[19]

These channel decisions are primarily problems for the manufacturer. They rarely arise for general wholesalers....[20]

Of all the historical tendencies in the field of marketing, no other is so distinctly apparent as the tendency for the manufacturer to assume greater control over the distribution of his product....[21]

...Marketing policies at other levels can be viewed as extensions of policies established by marketing managers in manufacturing firms; and, furthermore, ...the nature and function can adequately be surveyed by looking at the relationship to manufacturers.[22]

Pro-Manufacturer

The argument for manufacturer leadership is production oriented. It claims that they must assure themselves of increasing volume. This is needed to derive the benefits of production scale economies, to spread their overhead over many units, to meet increasingly stiff competition, and to justify the investment risk they, not the retailers, are taking. Since retailers will not do this job for them properly, the manufacturer must control the channel.

Another major argumentative point for manufacturer dominance is that neither the public nor retailers can create new products even under a market-oriented system. The most the public can do is to select and choose among those that manufacturers have developed. They cannot select products that they cannot conceive. This argument would say that it is of no use to ask consumers and retailers what they want because they cannot articulate abstract needs into tangible goods; indeed, the need can be created by the goods rather than vice-versa.

This argument may hold well when applied to consumers, but a study of the specification-buying programs of the mass retailers will show that the latter can indeed create new products, and need not be relegated to simply selecting among alternatives.

Pro-Retailer

This writer sees the mass retailer as the natural leader of the channel for consumer goods under the marketing concept. The retailer stands closest to the consumer; he feels the pulse of consumer wants and needs day in and day out. The retailer can easily undertake consumer research right on his own premises and can best interpret what is wanted, how much is wanted, and when it is wanted.

An equilibrium in the channel conflict may come about when small retailers join forces with big manufacturers in a manufacturer leadership channel to compete with a small manufacturer-big retailer leadership channel.

Pro-Wholesaler

It would seem that the wholesaler has a choice in this domination problem as well. Unlike the manufacturer and retailer though, his method is not mainly through a power struggle. This problem is almost settled for him once he chooses the type of wholesaling business he wishes to enter. A manufacturers' agent and purchasing agent are manufacturer-dominated, a sales agent dominates the manufacturer. A resident buyer and voluntary group wholesaler are retail-dominated.

Methods of Manufacturer Domination

How does a channel leader dominate his fellow members? What are his tools in this channel power struggle? A manufacturer has many domination weapons at his disposal. His arsenal can be divided into promotional, legal, negative, suggestive, and, ironically, voluntary cooperative compartments.

Promotional. Probably the major method that the manufacturer has used is the building of a consumer franchise through advertising, sales promotion, and packaging of his branded products. When he has developed some degree of consumer loyalty, the other channel members must bow to his leadershp. The more successful this identification through the promotion process, the more assured is the manufacturer of his leadership.

Legal. The legal weapon has also been a poignant force for the manufacturer. It can take many forms, such as, where permissible, resale price maintenance. Other contractual methods are franchises, where the channel members may become mere shells of legal entities. Through this weapon the automobile manufacturers have achieved an almost absolute dominance over their dealers.

Even more absolute is resort to legal ownership of channel members, called forward vertical integration. Vertical integration is the ultimate in manufacturer dominance of the channel. Another legal weapon is the use of consignment sales. Under this method the channel members must by law sell the goods as designated by the owner (manufacturer). Consignment selling is in a sense vertical integration; it is keeping legal ownership of the goods until they reach the consumer, rather than keeping legal ownership of the institutions which are involved in the process.

Negative Methods.   Among the "negative" methods of dominance are refusal to sell to possibly uncooperative retailers or refusal to concentrate a large percentage of one's volume with any one customer.

A spreading of sales makes for a concentrating of manufacturer power, while a concentrating of sales may make for a thinning of manufacturer power. Of course, if a manufacturer is one of the few resources available and if there are many available retailers, then a concentrating of sales will also make for a concentrating of power.

The avoidance and refusal tactics, of course, eliminate the possibility of opposing dominating institutions.

Suggestives.   A rather weak group of dominating weapons are the "suggestives." Thus, a manufacturer can issue price sheets and discounts, preticket and premark resale prices on goods, recommend, suggest, and advertise resale prices.

These methods are not powerful unless supplemented by promotional, legal, and/or negative weapons. It is common for these methods to boomerang. Thus a manufacturer pretickets or advertises resale prices, and a retailer cuts this price, pointing with pride to the manufacturer's suggested retail price.

Voluntary Cooperative Devices.   There is one more group of dominating weapons, and these are really all the voluntary cooperating weapons to be mentioned later. The promise to provide these, or to withdraw them, can have a "whip and carrot" effect on the channel members.

Retailers' Dominating Weapons

Retailers also have numerous dominating weapons at their disposal. As with manufacturers, their strongest weapon is the building of a consumer franchise through advertising, sales promotion, and branding. The growth of private brands is the growth of retail dominance.

Attempts at concentrating a retailer's purchasing power are a further group of weapons and are analogous to a manufacturer's attempts to disperse his volume. The more a retailer can concentrate his purchasing, the more dominating he can become; the more he spreads his purchasing, the more dominated he becomes. Again, if the resource is one of only a few, this generalization reverses itself.

Such legal contracts as specification buying, vertical integration (or the threat), and entry into manufacturing can also be effective. Even semiproduction, such as the packaging of goods received in bulk by the supermarket can be a weapon of dominance.

Retailers can dilute the dominance of manufacturers by patronizing those with excess capacity and those who are "hungry" for the extra volume. There is also the subtlety, which retailers may recognize, that a strong manufacturer may concede to their wishes just to avoid an open conflict with a customer.

VOLUNTARY COOPERATION

But despite some of the conflict dynamics and forced cooperation, channel members usually have more harmonious and common interests than conflicting ones. A team effort to market a producer's product will probably help all involved. All members have a common interest in selling the product; only in the division of total channel profits are they in conflict. They have a singular goal to reach, and here they are allies. If any one of them fails in the team effort, this weak link in the chain can destroy them all. As such, all members are concerned with one another's welfare (unless a member can be easily replaced).

Organizational Extension Concept

This emphasis on the cooperating, rather than the conflicting objectives of channel members, has led to the concept of the channel as simply an extension of one's own internal organization. Conflict in such a system is to be expected even as it is to be expected within an organization. However, it is the common or "macro-objective" that is the center of concentration. Members are to sacrifice their selfish "micro-objectives" to this cause. By increasing the profit pie they will all be better off than squabbling over pieces of a smaller one. The goal is to minimize conflict and maximize cooperation. This view has been expounded in various articles by Peter Drucker, Ralph Alexander, and Valentine Ridgeway.

> Together, the manufacturer with his suppliers and/or dealers comprise a system in which the manufacturer may be designated the primary organization and the dealers and suppliers designated as secondary organizations. This system is in competition with similar systems in the economy; and in order for the system to operate effectively as an integrated whole, there must be some administration of the separate organizations within that system.[23]

Peter Drucker[24] has pleaded against the conceptual blindness that the idea of the legal entity generates. A legal entity is not a marketing entity. Since often half of the cost to the consumer is added on after the product leaves the producer, the latter should think of his channel members as part of his firm. General Motors is an example of an organization which does this.

> Both businessmen and students of marketing often define too narrowly the problem of marketing channels. Many of them tend to define the term channels of distribution as a complex of relationships between the firm on the one hand, and marketing establishments exterior to the firm by which the

products of the firm are moved to market, on the other. . . . A much broader more constructive concept embraces the relationships with external agents or units as part of the marketing organization of the company. From this viewpoint, the complex of external relationships may be regarded as merely an extension of the marketing organization of the firm. When we look at the problem in this way, we are much less likely to lose sight of the inter-dependence of the two structures and more likely to be constantly aware that they are closely related parts of the marketing machine. The fact that the internal organization structure is linked together by a system of employ-ment contracts, while the external one is set up and maintained by a series of transactions, contracts of purchase and sale, tends to obscure their common purpose and close relationship.[25]

Cooperation Methods

But how does a supplier project its organization into the channel? How does it make organization and channel into one? It accomplishes this by doing many things for its resellers that it does for its own organization. It sells, advertises, trains, plans, and promotes for these firms. A brief elaboration of these methods follows.

Missionary salesmen aid the sales of channel members, as well as bolster the whole system's level of activity and selling effort. Training of resellers' salesmen and executives is an effective weapon of cooperation. The channels operate more efficiently when all are educated in the promotional techniques and uses of the products involved.

Involvement in the planning functions of its channel members could be another poignant weapon of the supplier. Helping resellers to set quotas for their customers, studying the market potential for them, forecasting a member's sales volume, inventory planning and protection, etc., are all aspects of this latter method.

Aid in promotion through the provision of advertising materials (mats, displays, commercials, literature, direct-mail pieces) ideas, funds (coopera-tive advertising), sales contest, store layout designs, push money (PM's or spiffs), is another form of cooperation.

The big supplier can act as management consultant to the members, dispensing advice in all areas of their business, including accounting, personnel planning, control, finance, buying, paper systems or office procedure, and site selection. Aid in financing may include extended credit terms, consignment selling, and loans.

By no means do these methods of coordination take a one-way route. All members of the channel, including supplier and reseller, see their own organizations meshing with the others, and so provide coordinating weapons in accordance with their ability. Thus, the manufacturer would undertake a marketing research project for his channel, and also expect his resellers to keep records and vital information for the manufacturer's use. A supplier may also expect his channel members to service the product after the sale.

A useful device for fostering cooperation is a channel advisory council composed of the supplier and his resellers.

Finally, a manufacturer or reseller can avoid associations with potentially uncooperative channel members. Thus, a price-conservative manufacturer may avoid linking to a price-cutting retailer.

E. B. Weiss has developed an impressive, though admittedly incomplete list of cooperation methods (table 19-1). Paradoxically, many of these instruments of cooperation are also weapons of control (forced cooperation to be used by both middlemen and manufacturers. However, this is not so strange if one keeps in mind that control is subdued conflict and a form of cooperation—even though perhaps involuntary cooperation.

Extension Concept Is the Marketing Concept

The philosophy of cooperation is described in the following quote:

> The essence of the marketing concept is of course customer orientation at all levels of distribution. It is particularly important that customer orientation motivate all relations between a manufacturer and his customer— both immediate and ultimate. It must permeate his entire channels-of-distribution policy.[26]

This quote synthesizes the extension-of-the-organization system concept of channels with the marketing concept. Indeed, it shows that the former is, in essence, "the" marketing concept applied to the channel area in marketing. To continue:

> The characteristics of the highly competitive markets of today naturally put a distinct premium on harmonious manufacturer-distributor relationships. Their very mutuality of interest demands that the manufacturer base his distribution program not only on what he would like from distributors, but perhaps more importantly, on what they would like from him. In order to get the cooperation of the best distributors, and thus maximum exposure for his line among the various market segments, he must adjust his policies to serve their best interest and, thereby, his own. In other words, he must put the principles of the marketing concept to work for him. By so doing, he will inspire in his customers a feeling of mutual interest and trust and will help convince them that they are essential members of his marketing team.[28]

SUMMARY

Figure 19-1 summarizes this paper. Each person within each department will cooperate, control, and conflict with each other (notice arrows). Together they form a department (notice department box contains person boxes) which will be best off when cooperating (or cooperation through control) forces weigh heavier than conflicting forces. Now each department cooperates, controls, and conflicts with each other. Departments together also form a higher level organization—the firm (manufacturer, wholesaler, and retailer). Again, the firm will be better off if department cooperation is maximized and conflict minimized. Finally, firms standing vertically to each other cooperate, control, and conflict. Together they form a

TABLE 19-1 **Methods of Cooperation as Listed**[27]

1. Cooperative advertising allowances
2. Payments for interior displays including shelf-extenders, dump displays, "A" locations, aisle displays, etc.
3. P.M.'s for salespeople
4. Contests for buyers, salespeople, etc.
5. Allowances for a variety of warehousing functions
6. Payments for window display space, plus installation costs
7. Detail men who check inventory, put up stock, set up complete promotions, etc.
8. Demonstrators
9. On certain canned food, a "swell" allowance
10. Label allowance
11. Coupon handling allowance
12. Free goods
13. Guaranteed sales
14. In-store and window display material
15. Local research work
16. Mail-in premium offers to consumer
17. Preticketing
18. Automatic reorder systems
19. Delivery costs to individual stores of large retailers
20. Studies of innumerable types, such as studies of merchandise management accounting
21. Payments for mailings to store lists
22. Liberal return privileges
23. Contributions to favorite charities of store personnel
24. Contributions to special store anniversaries
25. Prizes, etc., to store buyers when visiting showrooms—plus entertainment, of course
26. Training retail salespeople
27. Payments for store fixtures
28. Payments for new store costs, for more improvements, including painting
29. An infinite variety of promotion allowances
30. Special payments for exclusive franchises
31. Payments of part of salary of retail salespeople
32. Deals of innumerable types
33. Time spent in actual selling floor by manufacturer, salesmen
34. Inventory price adjustments
35. Store name mention in manufacturer's advertising

distribution channel that will be best off under conditions of optimum cooperation leading to consumer and profit satisfaction.

CONCLUSIONS AND HYPOTHESES

1. Channel relationships are set against a background of cooperation and conflict; horizontal, intertype, and vertical.

2. An autocratic relationship exists when one channel member controls conflict and forces the others to cooperate. A democratic relationship exists when all members agree to cooperate without a power plan. An anarchistic relationship exists when there is open conflict, with no member able to

FIGURE 19-1

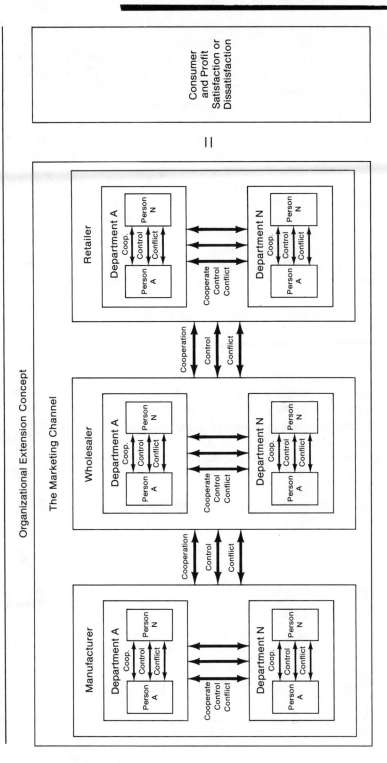

impose his will on the others. This last form could destroy or seriously reduce the effectiveness of the channel.

3. The process of the exchange act where one member is a seller and the other is a buyer is the basic source of channel conflict. Economic theory can aid in comprehending this phenomenon. There are, however, many other areas of conflict, such as differences in business philosophy or primary objectives.

4. Reasons for cooperation, however, usually outweigh reasons for conflict. This has led to the concept of the channel as an extension of a firm's organization.

5. This concept drops the facade or "legal entity" and treats channel members as one great organization with the leader providing each with various forms of assistance. These are called cooperating weapons.

6. It is argued that this concept is actually the marketing concept adapted to a channel situation.

7. In an autocratic or democratic channel relationship, there must be a leader. This leadership has shifted and is shifting between the various channel levels.

8. The wholesaler was the leader in the last century, the manufacturer now, and it appears that the mass retailer is next in line.

9. There is much disagreement on the above point, however, especially on who should be the leader. Various authors have differing arguments to advance for their choice.

10. In the opinion of this writer, the mass retailer appears to be best adapted for leadership under the marketing concept.

11. As there are weapons of cooperation, so are there weapons of domination. Indeed the former paradoxically are one group of the latter. The other groups are promotional, legal, negative, and suggestive methods. Both manufacturers and retailers have at their disposal these dominating weapons.

12. *For maximization of channel profits and consumer satisfaction, the channel must act as a unit.*

NOTES

[1]Ralph F. Breyer, "Some Observations on Structural Formation and the Growth of Marketing Channels," in *Theory in Marketing,* Reavis Cox, Wroe Alderson, Stanley J. Shapiro, eds., (Homewood, Ill.: Richard D. Irwin, Inc., 1964), pp. 163–75.

[2]Ronald S. Vaile, E. T. Grether, and Reavis Cox, *Marketing in the American Economy* (New York: The Ronald Press Co., 1952), pp. 121 and 124.

[3]Breyer, "Observations," p. 165.

[4]Joseph C. Palamountain, *The Politics of Distribution* (Cambridge: Harvard University Press, 1956).

[5]Isaiah A. Litvak and Bruce E. Mallen, *Marketing: Canada* (Toronto: McGraw-Hill of Canada, Limited, 1964), pp. 196–97.

[6]This section is based on Bert C. McCammon, Jr., "Alternative Explanations of Institutional Change and Channel Evolution," in *Toward Scientific Marketing,* Stephen A. Greyser, ed. (Chicago: American Marketing Association, 1963), pp. 477–90.

[7]Bruce Mallen, "Introducing the Marketing Channel to Price Theory," *Journal of Marketing* (July 1964), pp. 29–33.

[8]Warren J. Wittreich, "Misunderstanding the Retailer," *Harvard Business Review* (May-June 1962), p. 149.

[9]The term "anarchy" as used in this paper connotes "no leadership" and nothing more.

[10]Lewis B. Sappington and C. G. Browne, "The Skills of Creative Leadership," in *Managerial Marketing,* rev. ed., William Lazar and Eugene J. Kelley, eds. (Homewood, Ill.: Richard D. Irwin, Inc., 1962), p. 350.

[11]Wroe Alderson, "Factors Governing the Development of Marketing Channels," in *Marketing Channels for Manufactured Products,* Richard M. Clewett, ed. (Homewood, Ill.: Richard D. Irwin, Inc., 1954), p. 30.

[12]Arnold Corbin, *Central Buying in Relation to the Merchandising of Multiple Retail Units* (New York: unpublished doctoral dissertation at New York University, 1954), pp. 708–9.

[13]David Craig and Werner Gabler, "The Competitive Struggle for Market Control," in *Readings in Marketing,* Howard J. Westing, ed. (New York: Prentice-Hall, 1953), p. 46.

[14]Lew Hahn, *Stores, Merchants and Customers* (New York: Fairchild Publications, 1952), p. 12.

[15]David A. Revzan, *Wholesaling in Marketing Organization* (New York: John Wiley & Sons, 1961), p. 606.

[16]*Ibid.,* p. 202.

[17]E. Jerome McCarthy, *Basic Marketing* (Homewood, Ill.: Richard D. Irwin, Inc., 1960), p. 419.

[18]*Ibid.,* p. 420.

[19]Eli P. Cox, *Federal Quantity Discount Limitations and Its Possible Effects on Distribution Channel Dynamics* (unpublished doctoral dissertation, University of Texas, 1956), p. 12.

[20]Milton Brown, Wilbur B. England, John B. Matthews, Jr., *Problems in Marketing,* 3rd ed. (New York: McGraw-Hill, 1961), p. 239.

[21]Maynard D. Phelps and Howard J. Westing, *Marketing Management,* rev. ed. (Homewood, Ill.: Richard D. Irwin, Inc., 1960), p. 11.

[22]Kenneth Davis, *Marketing Management* (New York: The Ronald Press Co., 1961), p. 131.

[23]Valentine F. Ridgeway, "Administration of Manufacturer-Dealer Systems," in *Managerial Marketing,* rev. ed., William Lazer and Eugene J. Kelley, eds. (Homewood, Ill.: Richard D. Irwin, Inc., 1962), p. 480.

[24]Peter Drucker, "The Economy's Dark Continent," *Fortune* (April 1962), pp. 103 ff.

[25]Ralph S. Alexander, James S. Cross, Ross M. Cunningham, *Industrial Marketing,* rev. ed. (Homewood, Ill.: Richard D. Irwin, Inc., 1961), p. 266.

[26]Hector Lazo and Arnold Corbin, *Management in Marketing* (New York: McGraw-Hill, 1961), p. 379.

[27]Edward B. Weiss, "How Much of a Retailer Is the Manufacturer," in *Advertising Age,* July 21, 1958, p. 68.

[28]Lazo and Corbin, *Management in Marketing,* p. 379.

20

Checking Your Marketing Channels

Richard M. Clewett

WHY CHANNELS ARE IMPORTANT

Need for Speed

The Daily Salad Company manufactured perishable salads which it sold direct to retail food stores. The salads required frequent delivery and close control to insure freshness. Daily Salad's owner-manager, Fred Mall, was so familiar with this channel that he assumed it was the one for his two new lines—pickles and jelly.

As sales of these new products increased in the stores, Fred felt that territories should be revised. Closer analysis revealed it to be a channels problem. Pickles and jelly had a longer shelf life than the old line and could be put into a separate and less expensive channel. They did not need speed. Fred then began distributing them through wholesalers and chain warehouses.

Buyer Attitudes

Changes in consumer attitude may drastically affect the channels for existing products. For instance, the tremendous growth of baking mixes switched large quantities of lard and shortening from retail store or consumer channels to baking mix manufacturers or industrial channels. This situation changed the relative importance of the two markets and the two channels. A periodic analysis of trends will help you detect such changes before your product feels their full force.

One manufacturer added an infant cereal to his line, and sold it through drug channels. As infant cereals became more common, consumers

From "Management Aids for Small Manufacturers," *Small Business Administration,* Washington, D.C. (January 1961). Reprinted by permission.

regarded them as a food item and bought them at food stores. The manufacturer's sales kept declining until he started using food brokers.

New Approaches for New Products

In the early stage new products commonly require different distribution from that needed after they are well established and widely accepted. For instance, the XYZ Company started distributing its new high priced germicidal toilet soap through drug stores and prestige department stores. When consumer acceptance had made the soap more of a staple, the company moved it to food stores. In time this became the main type of retail outlet for this soap.

A manufacturer of low cost special tools for working laminated plastic sheets added to his line a forming press selling for several thousand dollars. He soon learned that his distributors were not in touch with a large part of the potential press market. Also, they were not able to instruct operators in using the press and could not service it. Here, again, the marketing channel was wrong.

Another case is a paper company which added to its line a patented mulch paper for agricultural use. It initially sold the new product direct to users. Attempting to get widespread distribution the company decided to sell the product through selected coarse-paper wholesalers who were already selling the company's other products. At first, the plan seemed successful because the wholesaler bought carload lots. Later the company realized he was only building up his inventory. Also, the wholesaler could not sell the mulch paper to final users because his contacts with the market were limited. The new product did not fit the old channel, and the company withdrew it from the wholesale outlets.

New markets may require new channels. A pneumatic drill manufacturer found that the channel used and services provided in selling direct to the mining industry were not adequate. He learned that a different channel, distributors, was needed to meet the construction market's special requirements.

A paint manufacturer distributed a new household floor wax through his existing outlets, hardware and paint stores. Sales increased for a while but leveled off at a small percentage of the total sales for this type of product. His investigation showed that the old channel exposed the new product to only a small part of the market. Actually, most consumers bought their floor wax in food stores.

Conflicts Can Cause Trouble

Multiple channels sometimes contain conflicts. If they are not resolved beforehand, these conflicts can wreck your distribution.

One manufacturer learned this the hard way when he tried to use scrap materials by introducing a ladder attachment through one of the large mail-order houses. He ran up against two unforeseen problems: (1) Instead of receiving a few orders for large shipments, the company was asked to ship small quantities to many points. This small order problem and added inventory increased costs beyond those anticipated. (2) Later the manufacturer tried to increase sales by selling through the hardware trade. Here he found the discounts required by wholesalers and retailers were greater than he had planned on. This meant a much higher retail price in hardware stores than the price in the mail-order catalog. The hardware trade objected to the mail-order price and competition. Hardware stores refused to sell the product, so the manufacturer could not expand into this channel. Hindsight indicates that more information and a clearer idea of possible channels might have allowed him to operate in both channels.

In contrast, a manufacturer of "do-it-yourself" woodworking equipment introduced his product through a large mail-order house. He let it be the sole seller for a definite period as a reward for introducing the product. He planned to sell through customary channels in the second phase of marketing his new product. He minimized possible conflicts between the two channels before he made arrangements with the mail-order house.

REASONS FOR NEGLECT

Channels represent one of the keystones of marketing success, yet *they* are frequently neglected. Why? Here are some of the more important reasons.

No "Flags"

Channels are not "flagged" (identified by name) on your operating records. No item on the profit and loss statement makes you focus attention on distribution channels, as is the case of advertising, personal selling, and other expenses. The problems caused by channel weaknesses are usually first diagnosed as problems of advertising, sales, or pricing. Only after checking out these more obvious activities is the possibility of weakness in marketing channels considered.

Long-Run Aspects Create Confusion

Marketing channels are generally considered a long-run problem. This results in such assumptions and attitudes as:
1. Channels are fixed and that other marketing activities must be planned around them.
2. The need for channel changes will be considered in the future. Of course, the future never comes unless (a) some definite time is set for a periodic review or (b) serious trouble makes immediate attention imperative. Under emergency conditions short-run measures generally prevail.

3. The channel problem consists of getting the most desirable outlets of a *specific type,* such as hardware wholesalers or electrical distributors. Viewed this way, significant trends may be ignored. Shifts in buying habits of final purchasers and increasing importance of new outlet types may be overlooked.

INFORMATION YOU NEED

To solve distribution channel problems you need information about who buys the product as well as where, when, and how it is bought. You may get this information from market studies made by your company, or from other sources such as trade associations, trade publications, and government agencies. In addition, you should know something of the characteristics of the selling methods your outlets use and their selling costs. This knowledge helps you to determine what you can expect from them in return for a given margin.

You should also know the relative importance of different channels in terms of sales volume and profit. It helps you also to know the importance of different classes of buyers especially if direct sale is involved.

You will want to do some sales analysis as well as distribution cost analysis based upon your records. You can get the methods used for these analyses from books ...

Council Can Help

As a manufacturer you may find it useful to form an advisory council of some of the middlemen handling your product so you can obtain detailed information about opportunities for improving your marketing. This committee could help in your search for information about:

1. Changes in buyer preference.
2. Changes in location of buyers. For instance, a manufacturer of pumps for domestic water systems was losing sales because his channels served the farm market instead of the suburban market. The growth market was in suburban areas not yet connected to water mains. He added outlets serving these areas and increased his sales.
3. Changes in concentration of buyers. Many manufacturers have found that the rapid growth of the Far West and Southwest has made it profitable to shift channels. They stopped using agents and started selling directly to wholesalers or distributors.
4. Changes in consumer income.

Be Aware of Problems

If you are thinking about selling a new product in your existing channels, you will want to be sure that those channels meet the new product's requirements. If the channels do not suit the product, you may be creating serious problems by using them. Those problems can be:

1. Introduction of new selling problems which your sales force is not able to handle
2. Overloading your sales force and causing it to neglect either the new or old product
3. Inadequate market coverage because the markets for the old and new products are not the same
4. Excessive costs because the channel provides more services and skills than the new product needs
5. An unrealistically low cost because the channel provides less services and skills than the new product needs

Sometimes a company's sales growth may be restricted by its distribution plan. This situation may exist because of:

1. Incomplete information about the consumer's buying desires
2. Eagerness to get a product on the market without thinking about future opportunities
3. Eagerness to get a product on the market without thinking about possible conflicts created by a given channel
4. Failure to provide for the addition of new channels that may be needed to reach new types of customers

MAKING NEEDED CHANGES

Changing Distributors

You may be forced to add new types of outlets or make other changes in distribution because of changing conditions. You may have to do this even at the risk of creating some ill will among your existing dealers or distributors. Appliance manufacturers, for instance, could not ignore the discount houses. Health and beauty aid manufacturers had to decide whether to sell through food outlets in spite of drug store opposition.

In the industrial field you cannot overlook the highly specialized middlemen. Neither can you forget that you may have to help service your product. This is especially true when your products and services become more complex, and your competitors are offering service. Here you will be bypassing your existing distributors and dealers, and your main problem will be to minimize their dissatisfaction.

When you examine the buying habits and attitudes of consumers or industrial users, you may find that you need to eliminate gradually exclusive distributors. Your sales volume may be restricted if you continue to sell through them where they are no longer needed.

Or your case may be like that of a materials handling equipment manufacturer with limited finances. He initially sold through distributors because this allowed him to tie up a minimum of capital. As he improved his financial position, he removed the original limitation and added manufacturers' agents. In this way he achieved better market coverage, greater control of his product, and reduced his costs.

Shifting Channels

What are some of the indicators that may reveal the need for channel changes? Your checklist of them should include:

Consumers or Users

1. Shifting trends in buying habits
   a) Types of sources from which they buy
   b) How they buy—amounts, frequency, terms, and other products bought along with yours
2. Development of new needs in relation to service, parts, or technical help

Middlemen

1. Change in relative importance of outlet types applicable to your product
2. Changes in the amount of profit distributors and dealers can make with your product
3. Changes in policies and activities of each type of outlet in relation to your product on the following points
   a) Priority of customer types and areas to which type of outlet sells
   b) Inventory—what and how much will be stocked
   c) Promotional effort devoted to product

Manufacturer's Own Organization

1. Change in financial strength
2. Higher or lower sales volume of existing products
3. Changes in marketing personnel or organization
4. Revised marketing activities:
   a) New objectives in terms of the relative importance of different customer groups and areas to be sold
   b) Addition of new products
   c) More personal selling and advertising effort
   d) Different order-filling procedures, physical distribution arrangements, and inventory policies

Competitors

If your competitors have changed their distribution plans you may need to adjust your own plan. You may not want to copy their arrangements. What is effective for your competitors may not be effective for you because of different policies, personnel, management experience, distribution points, and other differences. You should be alert to the possibility that your competitor may have started on a new course at the most opportune time. Poor timing may doom an otherwise useful plan.

PUTTING PLANS ON PAPER

Importance

In checking your marketing channels, you need to write out your distribution plan. A short, clear-cut statement will help you to determine if your plan is sound. Upon reading it you may discover loopholes that will demand drastic revision of the plan.

Your written plan should show how each marketing person in the channel from your plant to the consumer will benefit by pushing your product through the pipeline. In other words, put yourself in their shoes when writing down how they and the consumer will benefit from your product. If you can show these benefits on paper, chances are the agent, wholesaler, retailer, and the consumer will have little trouble recognizing them when they are considering your proposition.

Elements to Include

A satisfactory distribution plan will include the following:
1. A clear statement of geographic markets and customer-types to be sold, arranged in order of importance
2. The types of resellers to be used on all levels of distribution
3. The coverage plan; that is, whether distribution will be through as many outlets as possible, through a selected number in each area, or through exclusive distributors and dealers
4. The kind and amount of marketing effort expected of each type of outlet
5. The kind and amount of marketing effort you, the manufacturer, will contribute.
6. Policy statements regarding any areas of conflict, such as special or "house" accounts.
8. Adequate incentives to cause resellers to do the job you expect of them.

21

Channels of Distribution

Roland S. Vaile, E. T. Grether,
and Reavis Cox

WHO DOES THE WORK OF MARKETING

The Importance of Intermediary Agencies

....In much of the [following] discussion it will prove convenient to eliminate producers and consumers from the description and to concentrate our attention upon intermediary agencies that specialize in some one or another aspect of marketing. From time to time the producers and consumers must come back into the discussion but, since most of the work of marketing is done by intermediaries, much of our analysis can properly be devoted to them.

Attention also will be concentrated upon those who participate primarily in domestic marketing. A number of specialized agencies work chiefly in the international markets. They help import or export goods. Wherever it seems appropriate their presence will be noted and their work will be described....

Flows in Marketing

....The work of the institutions and agencies of marketing and their relationships to each other are difficult to describe in generalized terms. A helpful procedure is to fall back upon one of the most basic concepts of marketing—the channel of distribution. We can best understand the channel of distribution by thinking of marketing as a combination of flows of the sorts charted in figure 21-1.

Excerpted from Roland S. Vaile, E. T. Grether, and Reavis Cox, "Channels of Distribution," *Marketing in the American Economy* (New York: The Ronald Press Co., 1952), pp. 107, 113, 121, 124–28. Reprinted by permission.

FIGURE 21-1 **Flows in Marking**

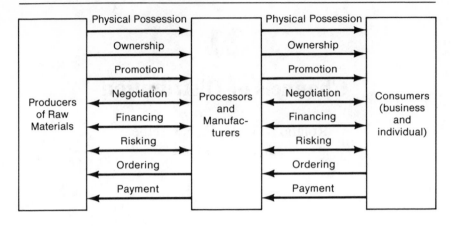

.... That is, we may think of goods as originating with producers of raw materials, then moving through a sequence of processers and manufacturers into the hands of the business organizations or ultimate consumers who use them up. The term "moving" must be taken to cover much more than the physical movement of the goods themselves. It also covers passage of the rights and responsibilities of ownership and the burdens of financing and risking to successive agencies; transmittal of impulses to buy or sell; the arrangement of successive transactions; the accumulation and distribution of market information; transfers of instructions as to what shall be made; and payment for the goods and services provided.

Direction of Flow

Flows of physical possession, ownership, and negotiation are typically forward in the sense that each change normally takes the goods farther away from the producers of raw materials and closer to the consumers. Flows of ordering and payment are typically backward in the sense that an order usually is transmitted or a payment usually is made to someone at an earlier stage in the sequence of processing and handling. Flows of information, financing, and risking, typically go in either direction.

The Channel of Distribution

A channel of distribution may be thought of as the combination and sequence of agencies through which one or more of the marketing flows moves. Each flow is a series of movements from one agency to another. When we try to differentiate two channels used for a particular good or the channels for two different goods, we do so by describing the different kinds of agencies used or the different sequences in which particular agencies may appear. Agencies are differentiated from each other partly by classification on such bases as those described earlier in this chapter, but also according to the combination of flows in which they participate, the points along each flow at which they come into the picture, and the parts of the flows for which they take responsibility.

In its simplest form, a channel is limited to the movement of one unit of goods in one flow. Thus we may think of a small quantity of cotton moving physically from the field where it is grown to a wagon and then, successively to a gin, a storage platform, a freight car, a warehouse, another freight car, another warehouse, a truck, a carding room, a spinning room, a weaving room, another truck, a finishing plant, another truck, a cutter's plant, another freight car, a wholesaler's warehouse, another freight car, another truck, a retailer's marking room, a retailer's warehouse, a store counter, a shipping room, another truck, and the consumer's home, where it appears as a shirt ready to be worn. Again, we may think of the flow of ownership for the same cotton from farmer to cotton merchant, to weaving mill, to converter, to cutter, to wholesaler, to retailer, to consumer.

In its more complicated forms, the channel includes all combinations and sequences of all the agencies used in all the flows, possibly with an indication of the quantitative importance of each. It may apply to a whole class or type of goods and to a company, a trade, or an industry. In its most complex form, it describes typical or actual flows of broad classes of goods (say consumers' goods or industrial goods) or charts the marketing structure as a whole.

Channels with Typically Forward Flows

Figures 21-2 to 21-5 show how a channel combines agencies to market a commodity. Figures 21-2 and 21-3 chart three forward flows in the marketing of nonmetallic cable (a product used in home building) from the point of manufacture to the building site. These flows are the flow of physical possession, the flow of ownership, and the flow of negotiation. No attempt has been made in these charts to trace raw materials from the copper mines, rubber plantations, and other sources to the cable manufacturing plant, or to carry the cable forward through the sale of the house to the consumer. Neither do these charts try to indicate the relative importance of each alternative flow or to show all possible variants.

Figure 21-2 shows that any particular unit of this product moves physically from manufacturing plant to building site either directly or through some selection out of three other points—an electrical distributor's warehouse, a retail store, and the contractor's stockroom. The particular unit of cable may touch none of the intermediate points, or one or two of them, or all three. The work of transportation is done by three sorts of facilities—railroad cars, trucks operated by independent haulers, and trucks belonging to the contractor.

FIGURE 21-2 Physical Flow of Nonmetallic Cable

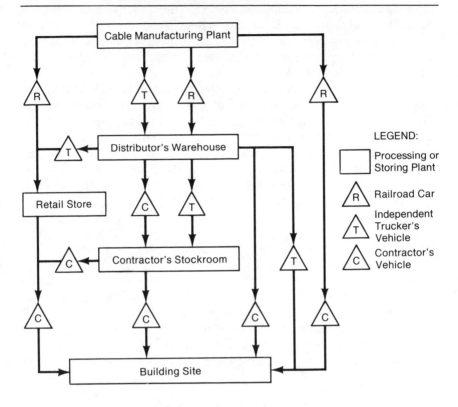

Figure 21-3 shows that ownership of the cable flows (1) from manufacturer to distributor to contractor, or (2) from manufacturer to retailer to contractor, or (3) from manufacturer to distributor to retailer to contractor. Some of these agencies that appear in the physical flow charted by figure 21-3 do not appear here at all.

The flow of promotion (also in figure 21-3) introduces several additional agencies, notably an advertising agency and two trade journals. It shows that aggressive efforts to develop business through personal selling are confined to distributors, and that nonpersonal selling is directed toward both distributors and contractors.

Channels with Typically Backward Flows

Figure 21-4 shows how orders and payments for furniture might flow from consumer to manufacturer. The order typically flows directly from consumer to retailer. Between the retailer and the manufacturer there is a trade show at which the retailer looks over the exhibits of the manufacturers and places his orders. If his sales exceed what he bought in this way, he usually will send "fill-in" orders directly to the manufacturer.

FIGURE 21-3 **Flows of Ownership and Promotion for Nonmetallic Cable**

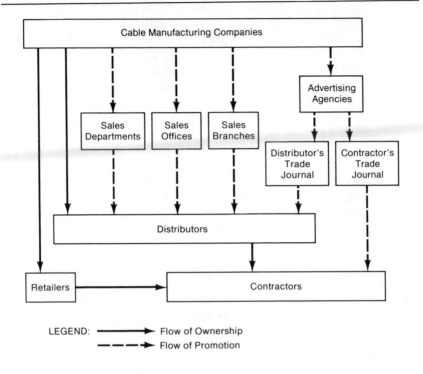

LEGEND: ──────▶ Flow of Ownership
        ── ── ──▶ Flow of Promotion

FIGURE 21-4 **Flows of Ordering and Payment for Furniture**

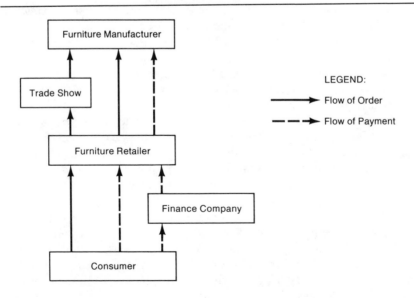

LEGEND:

──────▶ Flow of Order

── ── ──▶ Flow of Payment

A weakness of a flow chart such as figure 21-4 is that it does not always show the correct time sequence. Ordinarily a retailer places his orders with manufacturers before he has received orders for the goods from consumers, and he makes his own deliveries from stock. Sometimes, however, business is done on a custom basis. That is, the consumer orders, then the retailer orders, and finally the manufacturer makes goods to fit the orders in hand.

The first flow of payment in figure 21-4 is straightforward: the consumer pays the retailer, who pays the manufacturer. The timing may be reversed in that the retailer pays the manufacturer before he receives payment from his own customer. If so, he faces a financing problem. This can be solved in several ways, most of which would appear in a flow of financing and might change the flow of payment. For example, if the retailer sells his receivables to a finance company, the consumer may pay the finance company rather than him. Here again the sequence may vary. In many cases the finance company will advance funds to the retailer, who promptly pays the manufacturer. Payment of the finance company by the consumer comes last.

Channels with Typically Two-Way Flows

Figure 21-5 illustrates a common arrangement of the flows of negotiation, financing, and risking. It is used by a canner who distributes through wholesale grocers to retailers. Transactions ordinarily are negotiated directly between the consumer and the retailer, and between the retailer and the wholesaler. The flow may be in either direction, since either party may take the initiative. Negotiations may also be direct between the wholesaler and the canner, but quite commonly arrangements are made through brokers. Here also the flow may be in either direction, the choice depending chiefly upon how plentiful the goods are. Brokers ordinarily represent canners but may act for the buyer when goods are scarce. If "negotiation" is defined to include the transfer of information back and forth, the commercial research agency is a unit in this channel. It can be a very important unit transmitting information about consumers' needs and preferences back to the canner.

Since the production of canned foods is highly seasonal, whereas consumption is spread throughout the year, the industry has a heavy financing problem. Figure 21-5 shows that the necessary funds can flow into the system from some combination of two possible sources—commercial banks that make loans to one or more enterprises in the channel, and individual investors who buy ownership interests in or make loans to these enterprises. Individual investors may invest their funds by buying into or lending to an enterprise at any of the three levels in the channels—canning, wholesaling, or retailing. The financing can then flow forward, as when the canner sells to a wholesaler or to a retailer on long terms or when the retailer sells to the consumer on charge accounts. It can also flow backward, as when the wholesaler pays for goods which he then puts into storage, or

FIGURE 21-5 **Flows of Negotiation, Financing, and Risking
for Canned Food**

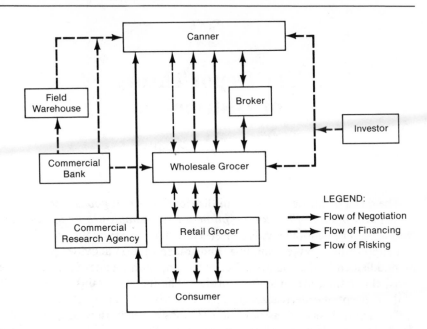

when he advances funds to the canner during processing. Bank loans for these purposes may be made either to the wholesaler or to the canner, the loan to the canner being made either directly or through a field warehouse.

The placing and flow of risk depend chiefly upon the kinds of arrangement made when title passes and the sorts of guarantee given by buyer and seller. Normally the risk flows forward, each successive agency assuming its share as it takes title. Wholesalers can reach backward to relieve canners of some risk by agreeing to pay a firmly stated price for future shipments. Alternatively and more commonly canners may reach forward to relieve wholesalers of some risk by giving them a guarantee against price declines on goods taken into storage.

NOTES

[1]The investments of individuals take many different forms and may be "involuntary" in the sense that they consist of earnings retained in a business by its managers without explicit authorization by its stockholders. In practice, a business goes to individuals for financing very infrequently. In the intervals, it borrows from banks, obtains credit from its suppliers, or uses what it calls its own funds but what are really the assets of its owners. A third possible source of funds—the federal government—is not included in figure 21-5.

22

The Depot Theory
of Distribution

Leo V. Aspinwall

The thesis of the depot theory of distribution is that *goods tend to move towards the point of final consumption at a rate established by the ultimate consumer.* The depot theory is concerned with the performance of all direct and supporting storage, handling, and transportation activities performed by middlemen in the channel of distribution, on an actual cost of service basis, eliminating merchandising profits. The thesis contains the essentials of the concept of orderly marketing, an objective of all marketing activities.

The depot theory of distribution envisions a steady flow of goods from the point of production to final consumption. The intermediary institutions facilitating this flow are in fact the depots. Depot is a military term and refers to the storage of supplies purely as a service function. The depot theory of distribution considers the performance of the depot function on the basis of costs of services performed.

The import of the depot theory of distribution is the identification of a trend in marketing toward the elimination of merchandising profits. The old idea of a merchant was that he "bought low and sold high." The merchant was an independent enterpriser who bought his goods and then sold them so as to take the difference between the sales price and his cost; this difference, or gross margin, contains all handling costs plus an extra merchandising profit. When transportation facilities and communications were less advanced than they are today, a merchant anticipated the needs of his customers and bought goods in advance of their needs and for this charged a merchandising profit in addition to the cost he had incurred in handling and storing. The merchant's strategy was to attempt to achieve a monopoly position in a limited market. Merchandising profits, under any conditions, are justifiable if the goods or services provide utilities to the

From L. V. Aspinwall, "The Depot Theory of Marketing," in *Managerial Marketing: Perspectives and Viewpoints,* W. Lazer and E. Kelley, eds. (Homewood, Ill.: Richard D. Irwin, Inc., 1962) pp. 652-59. Reprinted by permission.

consumer. Under less advanced and developed states of communication and transportation real utilities are provided by merchandisers performing these functions. Competition under modern conditions is so intense that merchandising profits are very difficult to obtain.

This current competitive situation points up the depot concept and forecasts the trend in the distribution of products. The depot identifies a function of marketing which performs all storage and handling costs on a cost basis so as to put goods in retailers' hands at lowest possible costs. The competitive retail market demands this policy of management to keep goods flowing into consumption at the rate dictated by consumers, eliminating any stoppage of the flow. Stoppage of the flow causes costs to increase and losses are almost certain to be encountered.

Managing the physical distribution of goods requires utilization of total resources in the most effective manner. Thus, it is necessary to use mass shipments at times in order to take advantage of the rate differential between less than car and full car lots.

The depot function involves warehousing activities; large lots are broken into smaller lot shipments. Under the depot theory, goods are stored for the minimum time. The steady flow of goods is maintained between the manufacturer and the consumer. In this theory the amount of gross margin added to the goods is a channel cost representing the cost of services performed by the depot.

It is apparent that in order to provide economic and orderly distribution, goods which are at opposite ends of a scale, such as pianos and cigarettes, require different distribution patterns. The depot theory is related to the characteristics of goods theory. The latter theory explains that goods, based on the characteristics, are distributed either by a broadcast system or a direct system. Such goods as grand pianos or electronics computers move directly from the manufacturer to the final consumer, with little or no depot function being performed. Goods such as cigarettes or cereals have at least one stop where the depot function is performed in moving from manufacturer to retailer and then to the consumer.

ADVANCING TECHNOLOGY AND MARKETING ADJUSTMENTS

Since the end of World War II, many of the advances in distribution are traceable to materials handling improvements and to new developments in communication. The full impact of recent technological advances has not yet been realized in marketing. The development of the modern data processing, for example, has provided almost instantaneous feed-back information, from the active final sales areas to production centers. As a result, production schedules can be geared more closely to actual sales. This means that inventory risks are minimized at each point in the channel. The quantities and types of goods are adjusted to meet consumer needs more precisely.

The physical transportation of all goods inevitably involves time and costs which means that the physical characteristics of the goods must be taken into account. Valuable high density goods, such as diamonds, are better able to bear higher transportation costs than low-value, bulky type of goods, such as coal, which must be moved at lower transportation costs, and which involve more time in transit. Inventory costs occur whenever physical goods are transported. These inventory costs must be added to the factory costs of the goods, along with transportation costs. Even in current marketing practices these costs are added and are not the basis for calculating a merchandising profit by mid-channel operators.

For example, a Chicago packer receives hourly and daily information on the sales of beef in Los Angeles areas. The beef is shipped by air freight overnight, so the amount and quality needed for that day's sale arrives early in the morning. Planes fly at high altitude and the need for refrigeration is eliminated. The hanging beef is landed in Los Angeles at the lowest net cost of inventory and transport. Chicago-processed beef is competitive with beef processed in the Los Angeles area. This seems to violate the bulky low-value rule on transportation. However, by eliminating refrigeration costs and landing the beef in Los Angeles without the damage due to bruising which occurs in truck or rail shipments, a firm acceptance for the branded meats of the Chicago packer was earned in the West Coast market. This contract fed, Mid-West beef is taken mainly by hotels and restaurants which cater to upper income customers in Los Angeles. In this instance, cultivation of this profitable segment of the fresh meat market is made possible through the advances in communication and transportation.

The backward integration of retail food is illustrative of the strong tendency to emphasize the depot function and to obtain lowest total physical distribution costs. Large warehouses are built at strategic distribution points. They perform a complete depot function for the stores they support. Even the large delivery trucks are managed on a fleet basis including the provision for all repair services. Trucks are loaded in late afternoon and are dispatched to their destinations during the night hours to avoid daytime traffic. Goods are unloaded at the stores during the night and are processed during the early morning hours, before heavy shopping begins. Trucks frequently maintain radio contact with the main warehouse so that in breakdowns goods can be transferred quickly to empty trucks returning to the central warehouse.

The mechanized equipment used minimized manual handling in depot operations. Goods flow to stocking areas on conveyer belts and roller devices. The stocking areas are located so as to require the least movement of goods. For example, heavy, low-value, bulky goods, such as packaged sugar in 100-pound bags, have a high replacement rate. The stocking area for these goods is closed to the final order assembly. If low-value, bulky items are directed into remote stocking areas, costs would be excessive. Mathematical formulas have been developed to calculate precisely the most economical stocking location.

These activities illustrate the efforts to reduce depot function costs to the lowest possible level. Goods are distributed to retail outlets at the delivered warehouse cost, plus the actual depot function costs. The retail outlet receives these goods F.O.B. warehouse at delivered costs, plus the transportation costs to the retail location. Transportation costs are computed on a ton-mile basis. They are credited to the warehouse as income, supporting truck operations.

The operation of the warehouse is conducted on service cost basis. It is completely devoid of any merchandising profits. Depot activities, therefore, are strictly service operations. The costs of these activities consist of physical handling costs of land, buildings, and equipment. Additional means are employed in wholesale cooperative organizations designed to minimize taxes, hence reduce depot costs.

The essence of the depot theory of distribution is that goods tend to move towards the point of final consumption at a rate dictated by the final consumer. The consumption rate is governed by costs. Whenever the factory gate price of a product, plus the depot function costs, plus the retailing costs are greater than the estimated utilities received from the product by consumers, the entire flow of an item stops. Such goods in the channel not yet in the hands of retailers are in fact distress merchandise. Losses are involved and information is fed back to the producer who immediately stops production.

The withholding of purchasing power by consumers for reasons other than price results in inventory losses. Design, quality, color, and style of goods are also bases for market rejection. The increasingly rapid feedback of information limits some of the risks of inventory ownership. The use of computers to process information from geographically separated markets provides immediate market information. This facilitates improved production control. The ideal model of linked information systems (which can never be achieved) would be one where all producers would be served with a unified market information service so that distressed merchandise would be marketed in the most orderly way.

Production complexities are such that it is frequently not possible to respond promptly to changes indicated by market information. Such delays can erase many of the advantages gained by the feedback system.

MERCHANDISING PROFITS ARE CONFINED LARGELY TO RETAILERS AND PRODUCERS

Retail inventories should be maintained at a level sufficient to afford consumers a range of merchandise to meet wants and needs. The maintenance of inventories involves risks for which the retailer must be compensated. If adequate profit margins are not available, retailers will attempt to limit their risks by maintaining inadequate inventories. When wanted goods are not available at convenient retail outlets, the consumer must perform a more extensive search function. The process of seeking out sources may become so inconvenient and burdensome that consumers will either go without, or substitute other goods with approximately the same utilities. The searching process involves the expenditures of time, energy, and money. The limit of the span of convenience is reached whenever the sum of convenience costs is greater than the net satisfactions in utilities of the commodities sought. Areas of profitable retail opportunity may exist in areas lacking these convenience services for consumers. Merchants attempt to locate retail establishments within the span of convenience of as many consumers as possible.

Services performed at the depot enhance the chances of retail survival by affording lower cost goods. Depot operations eliminate payment of profits to wholesalers and warehousemen, and lower the costs of retail operations. Lower merchandise costs seem to indicate increased profit opportunities and tend to encourage more enterprisers to enter retailing. This, in turn, increases retail competition.

THE PRODUCERS' MERCHANDISING PROFIT

Competition between manufacturers is such that a pure merchandising profit is seldom available. Manufacturers' profits come for the most part from the position of being a reliable supplier. Steel mills, for instance, are operated on the backlog of firm orders upon which a normal manufacturing profit is taken. A merchandising profit becomes available when prospects for orders are such that production rates can be increased beyond the break-even point. The profit position of large integrated industries is, in general, somewhat better than that of retailers, since there are fewer competing units.

One example of a recent operation of a merchandising profit at the producers' level was the case of the success of the first manufacturer to penetrate the weight-reducing food market. The increase in market value of the manufacturer of Metrecal's stock over a comparatively short period of time, indicates the merchandising profit afforded this timely operation.

Product differentiation is a widely used strategy of manufacturers. Brands provide consumers a means of identifying a product which has earned acceptance. Branding is a competitive tactic which attempts to place a manufacturer's product in a special class. The hope is that consumers will seek out the branded product on the basis of satisfactory experience in using the product. The branded product is thus partially removed from the competition of unbranded products as well as from other branded products. Even so, competition and innovation of other brands bid for a share of the market. Such pressures force the branded item away from a merchandising profit and into a position of normal profit.

Market segmentation is also used in connection with the strategy of product differentiation. This means that by design a product is fashioned for a special segment or group of consumers. The high income group who can afford to buy expensive automobiles is an example. The market for cameras is segmented into the professional group and the amateur group. A branded camera designed for professionals does not have to compete with branded cameras intended for the less skilled segment of the camera market. Here too, the forces of competition and innovation move the manufacturer into a normal profit position much akin to the depot concept.

RETAIL COMPETITION GENERATED BY
THE DISCOUNT HOUSE

Marketing men had begun to think that the problem of the discount house had been disposed of as a passing innovation in retailing. For a time it was believed the discount house came into being through the availability of distress merchandise in the market. Sharp operators constantly searched the market for opportunities to bid for goods that had stopped moving in the distribution channel and, by reason of their accumulation, were causing charges of interest on the investment, storage, and insurance costs. Owners had to dispose of such goods at whatever price the market would afford. Lines of merchandise accumulated on this basis were not complete and offerings to the public were made from low-rent facilities on a cash basis. Price was the main consideration; often well-known brands could be found at very low prices. But the discount house now flourishes in an organized way, offering standard nondistress merchandise, so that well-established retailers are undertaking this type of operation on their own.

At an opening of a large discount house branch in a rapidly growing suburb of Los Angeles, California, over 40,000 (police estimate) people struggled to get into the store. The Los Angeles papers carried a sixteen-page insert of offerings including furniture, appliances, groceries, ready-to-wear, shoes, and auto accessories, in fact almost everything in the department store range. A $300 mink cape was offered for $10 to people who had registered and whose name was drawn in a lottery. Well-known brands of appliances were offered at prices about half of their established value. The building is in a prime location within a shopping center which is one of the largest in southwest Los Angeles. All of this is unorthodox in terms of discount house operations, indicates the vitality of the discount house, and is another illustration of the strong trend towards the depot concept of distribution. A merchandising profit under discount house operations arises only through fortuitous circumstance and normal profits are likely to rule, made up of the delivered cost of goods plus handling costs.

Reputable manufacturers now sell directly to discount houses. One case involves a nationally known manufacturer of a complete line of consumer products. The goods, all from the same production line, are branded with four different line brands. Unbranded goods from the production line are sold to discount houses. The discount houses are obliged to buy in case lots and they are not allowed fill-ins from open stock. Here again the depot concept obtains, with goods moving directly to the final retail outlet at the lowest possible prices and sold with the handling costs added.

RECAPITULATION

The thesis of the depot theory of marketing distribution is: Goods tend to move towards the point of final consumption at a rate dictated by the ultimate consumer. The theory points to a strong trend in marketing towards the management of marketing activities on a cost-of-service basis and the consequent diminution of merchandising profits. A merchandising profit is a charge added to the cost of goods for the assumption of inventory risks; it is mainly based upon the anticipations of consumers' needs in advance of the time of consumption. There is a strong element of fortuity in a merchandising profit. Speculation and risk assumption attendant upon inventory ownership are involved in a merchandising profit. It is an increment added beyond the actual service costs incurred in handling the goods.

The operations of the chain supermarkets in food distribution, with their backward integration into warehouses and manufacturing, have been cited as an illustration of the depot theory. The operations of the discount house with manufacturers selling directly to these outlets, further emphasizes this trend. The mail-order houses operate on a near discount house basis, and the former 5-and-10 chains give evidence of greater attention to merchandising lines outside their former operations, with cut-rate practices employed. Careful observers of the current marketing scene have commented on the strong tendency towards low-cost handling of goods. The rapid advances in transportation and communication open up new methods of conducting marketing operations, so that the "propensity to consume" is in fact being heightened.

23

Physical Distribution: The Neglected Marketing Function

Bud Reese

He read the company's ads and talked to its salesman. He liked what he read and heard, and placed a trial order to be delivered in six weeks.

That was seven weeks ago—and still no sign of the shipment. He has decided to wait another three days before canceling; *and he has decided to stick with his regular supplier.*

A lot of promotion and sales effort has gone down the drain, whether the shipment arrives in the three days or not. The cause of the waste is faulty physical distribution—not having the product at the place at the right time.

This situation is hypothetical, but similar situations are by no means unusual in industry today, say the nation's physical distribution specialists. These experts on the movement of finished goods to customers and distributors all seem to agree that: *Sales are being lost and advertising claims are falling on deaf ears because of faulty physical distribution; and marketing men are primarily to blame for permitting this situation to exist.*

They say that marketing men have sadly neglected this important facet of their job—despite the fact that in the area of physical distribution there exists industry's finest opportunity to improve customer service *and reduce costs.*

They say that the movement of goods is overmanaged, undermanaged and mismanaged—at one and the same time. The purpose of this article is to examine the reasoning behind this rather unanimous belief, and to answer these basic questions:

1. Should marketing men concern themselves with the physical distribution of their company's products?
2. If physical distribution is a function of marketing, are industrial marketing men neglecting it?

From Bud Reese, "Physical Distribution: The Neglected Marketing Function," in *Industrial Marketing,* Vol. 46 (October 1961), pp. 102–106. Reprinted by permission.

3. What needs to be done to improve physical distribution? And what part do marketers have to play in this movement?

"For the average firm, physical distribution consumes between twenty-five and thirty-three per cent of each sales dollar [that is, the cost of warehousing, transportation, etc., make up from twenty-five to thirty-three per cent of the total cost of products delivered at the customer's location]. A firm's longevity may well depend upon reducing this third highest cost of doing business [after labor and materials]."

That statement was made by Dr. Donald J. Bowersox, assistant director of business development for REA Express, New York, at a June meeting of the American Marketing Association.

And at an American Management Association conference, Paul A. Wassmansdorf, marketing administration consultant for General Electric Co., New York, said:

> There is a growing belief that the costs of physical distribution which are not readily apparent are perhaps as great as the obvious ones. These are the costs that result from not having the right goods at the right place at the right time.
>
> The first, and possibly the largest of these costs is the cost of lost sales. Unfortunately, a great deat of work remains to be done in computing the cost of sales as a result of an unbalanced flow of goods. The preliminary work that has been done, however, indicates that the cost of lost sales is substantially larger than anyone has suspected . . . many sales are lost without the seller's knowing it.

A check with physical distribution executives and consultants brought out two more immediate reasons for marketing men to take a new, long look at the way their companies move their goods to customers and distributors. The two are closely related.

1. *The cost-service struggle.* Marketing and sales management are caught in the middle, between the field sales force asking for faster delivery and top management demanding cost reductions.

Field sales wants inventories maintained in each customer's back yard; but, maintaining many localized field inventories is an expensive habit.

2. *Less stocking by distributors.* And yet, the majority of the experts contacted by *Industrial Marketing* admit that industrial companies are being forced into adding more warehouses because an increasing number of industrial distributors are shirking their stocking function.

The manager of a newly established branch warehouse in Chicago said, "My company hated to create my job, but they had no choice. Distributors are becoming brokers, refusing to carry adequate stock. Our competitors face the same problem, and are establishing more branch warehouses; we have to go along."

THE 'BOTTOMLESS CUP'

Speaking at an American Management Association meeting, Jerome P. Shuchter, market research director of Federal Pacific Electric Co., Newark, N.J., told why his company's marketing and sales management decided to devote more attention to the problem of physical distribution:

> We backed into our general warehousing policy some ten years ago. With sales expanding rapidly and freight costs mounting, we had to reach an understanding about the function of warehouses. Two different concepts were under consideration: (1) The "emergency stock" theory—were warehouses to be used only to provide local emergency stocks to our distributors? Under this theory, bulk shipments would normally be made directly from our central warehouse in Newark. (2) The "bottomless cup" theory—were warehouses to be a full-dress distribution channel, with large stocks available locally? Under this theory, our distributors could stock lightly and be assured of an unlimited secondary source of supply.
>
> On the table were surveys backing the emergency-stock viewpoint. They showed the tremendous inventory saving that could be achieved through this approach. They showed conclusively that direct LCL [less than car load] shipments to customers were more economical than through use of the warehouse as a dog-leg station.
>
> We reached an easy decision that day—and had to toss it out the next month! The pace of industrial and corporate growth almost passed us by. There was no way in the world we could hold to the emergency-stock concept if even one of our major competitors took the road to all-out customer service through large local backup stocks. And many of our competitors did take that road. The bottomless-cup theory carried the day.

Judging from what has been said and written on the subject, Federal Pacific Electric is just one of many industrial companies to be forced into bottomless-cup physical distribution. The function of having the product at the right place at the right time, of meeting customer service demands, has become an important determinant of sales effectiveness.

'MOST NEGLECTED'

In his AMA speech Dr. Bowersox said, "Among the many problems consuming the time and talents of marketing executives, those most neglected relate to physical distribution."

At the same meeting, Philip F. Cannon, vice-president of Barrington Associates, New York, stated, "I don't want to be so trite as to say—as other speakers over the years have said—that there is no more promising field for improvement than physical distribution; but that is really the way I feel. Allow me, if you will, to say at least this much: I think that in physical distribution there is a great potential for improving customer service and

reducing costs. And, this potential stands relatively unexploited. This is
virgin territory.''

Why do these men feel that physical distribution is being "neglected"
by marketing men?

Mr. Cannon explained it this way:

> The fact that physical distribution, as something other than a cost factor, has
> received very little attention suggests that perhaps there is something peculiar
> or particularly difficult about this function.
>
> The fact is, however, that the technical, procedural, and operational
> aspects of physical distribution do not pose any more difficult problems than
> are found in manufacturing or selling. The real reason for the neglect of
> physical distribution, I believe, is that it is usually not organized very well.
> Too many physical distribution functions are left to fall between the chairs,
> creating many "grey areas" where objectives, policies, and organizational
> lines are at best fragmentary, if they exist at all. Most commonly, the
> functions of distribution are split haphazardly between manufacturing and
> sales...
>
> Not infrequently, in discussing job responsibilities with senior marketing
> executives, we have had them wryly add, "Oh yes, another part of my job
> includes liaison with the plant shipping department."

WHO DOES WHAT?

In his book, *Modern Marketing Management*, Ferdinand F. Mauser,
marketing professor at Wayne State University, wrote, "All too often...
inter and intraplant flow of goods are under traffic, and the control of
regional warehouses and inventories are under the jurisdiction of the sales
department.''

The manager of a warehouse on the outskirts of Chicago said that in his
company, traffic, finished goods inventory control, and order processing
are directed by the controller; planning of warehouse space is done by the
planning manager; order status inquiry is headed by the sales manager; and
the factory manager controls finished goods materials handling and
warehouse management.

Mr. Shuchter of Federal Pacific Electric said that before his company
woke up to the importance of physical distribution:

> We had no...really consistent concept of the distribution function. True, we
> did have a traffic manager; someone did schedule shipments; someone did
> back the process with production schedules; someone did modernize and lay
> out new warehouses; and someone from the marketing department did
> bird-dog the activity, policing warehouse expenses and counting inventories.
> But, all these activities were carried on in different departments, with
> insufficient common direction and policy.

The phsyical distributions specialists say that because of this hodge-podge of authority, customers receive incorrect answers to their order status inquiries; orders are not processed with dispatch; and, in general, customer service suffers severely.

WHAT'S THE ANSWER?

What is the answer to the Hydra-headed distribution problem. Centraliza-tion of physical distribution planning, obviously—but under whom? And just what would this person administer?

Here, again, the experts seem to agree. They say that the man for the job is the marketing manager. But, they are quick to qualify their suggestion. They realize that the man with the marketing manager title in many companies is really the sales manager, given the title to pay lip service to the "marketing concept."

In such cases, the experts suggest that a new marketing title be established, as is being done by an increasing number of companies; the title being that of physical distribution manager.

Why couldn't the job simply be given to the sales manager, or the production manager, or the controller?

Mr. Shuchter answered this question bluntly: "There has never been a sales manager who thought he had too much inventory—or a finance manager who thought he had too little. There has never been a production manager who thought production runs were long enough—or a sales manager who didn't prefer smaller, more frequent runs."

Mr. Cannon was more specific as to what happens to physical distribution when it is sales-directed:

1. "Sales is naturally inclined to provide customer service at any cost, i.e., it might well overinvest in branch warehouse inventories [Mr. Bowersox said that for a typical warehouse it takes about seventy-five per cent more inventory to satisfy ninety-five per cent of customer sales from stock than it does to satisfy eighty per cent], incur excessive LCL or LTL shipping costs, and so forth.

2. "The traffic department is called upon to serve other divisions or functions of the business, such as manufacturing and purchasing; its position under sales may limit its ability to render corporate service.

3. "Branch warehouses tend to be located automatically with branch sales offices, even though the organization and location of selling functions in a territory bear no relationship to the economics of warehouse location.

[John T. Thompson, general manager of distributor products, Raytheon Co., Westwood, Mass., has stated that field warehouses frequently create availability problems rather than solve them, and sometimes they inject a communications delay point.]

4. "Sales executives get saddled with an operating function for which

they may have little training, and less understanding—physical distribution economics.''

Mr. Mauser wrote that:

Out of habit, sales departments often promise deliveries on the first and fifteenth. The distribution executive who creates an awareness of the importance of staggering promised delivery dates induces a smoother and less costly outgoing flow of merchandise. The sales department should be checked to determine what the lag time is between the customer's placing the order and its actually arriving in the shipping department. Such a check may reveal delays which often mean the difference between high and low transportation costs and between prompt deliveries and less satisfactory ones. It is often surprising to discover the extent of internal delay to which an order is subjected.

Mr. Cannon said the following might happen when distribution is directed by manufacturing:

1. "Operations are restricted under the dominance of the manufacturing point of view, which generally tends to be introverted and which cannot evaluate objectively the needs of marketing for physical distribution support.

2.   "Distribution is treated as a subordinate and secondary function that does not merit first-rate, top-drawer attention from manufacturing executives.''

QUALIFICATIONS

What would be the qualifications of this physical distribution manager? Would he be a traffic manager with planning authority?

Most physical distribution specialists say "no" to the idea of a glorified traffic manager. They say that the traffic manager's preoccupation with detail and activity that is massively routine usually disqualifies him for the job of physical distribution manager. The right man for the job would be:

• Appreciative of the fundamental nature and importance of physical distribution in corporate planning.
• Familiar with distribution costing. "On a national average," says Dr. Bowersox, "transportation services account for less than twenty-five per cent of the total cost incurred in marketing logistics [physical distribution]. A total cost perspective provides the analytical framework necessary for a penetrating evaluation of alternative distribution systems. It is interesting to note that astute distribution planning will often lead to higher transportation cost...total cost is the fundamental concept."
• Appreciative of the need for exacting research to support distribution planning. In place of crude approximations, fictitious averages and intuitive

guesses, distribution planning must be the result of effectively utilizing electronic data processing and quantitative techniques.

Dr. Bowersox explained that many advancements in this area of quantitative techniques have mushroomed under the catch-all label of operations research, including a technique commonly called linear programming. He said:

> While much criticism can be voiced on the relative sterility of OR in providing significant payoffs to date, if quantitative techniques do hold the promise of significant payoffs, it is reasonably certain they will be realized first among logistics problems.
>
> The foundations for this prediction are simple: many elements of total cost distribution are quantifiable and can be approximated by near linear relationships...It is safe to generalize that better than ninety per cent of historical distribution planning lacked the benefits of system logic, mathematical structure, and, in many cases, even advanced statistical analysis. The history of distribution planning represents an era of stagnant checklists and static formulas.

So much for the man; now for his job. Here's what the majority of the experts contacted by *Industrial Marketing* say should be administered by the physical distribution manager:

1. *Transportation and traffic*—The movement of inbound materials to the factory, and the movement of finished goods from the factory to final customers, branch warehouses and regional distribution centers, another factory, freight forwarding or classifying points.

2. *Finished goods inventory control*—The method of a company's data processing system may dictate the assignment of the responsibility for actual maintenance of the inventory records elsewhere; but where circumstances warrant, it may be logical for distribution to maintain these records, particularly where branch warehouse inventories are concerned.

Sales and finance would, of course, have the major voices in determining levels of inventory; but, finished goods are the immediate physical responsibility of distribution, which serves as the connecting link between sales and manufacturing.

3. *Location of branch warehouses*—First, sales would define service, in terms of number of days between the date of an order from the customer and the date of its delivery to the customer. Then it would be the distribution manager's responsibility to maintain at least this level of service. As was pointed out earlier, the organization and location of selling functions in a territory bear no relationship to the economics of warehouse location.

4. *Operation of branch warehouses*—Sales management skills and energies are best devoted to selling, not in handling the routines of warehouse operation.

5. *Order processing and administration*—This would include: (1) acknowledgment, done under policies issued by sales; (2) credit review, done under policies, procedures, and current credit ratings issued by the treasurer's office; (3) pricing, done under strict formulas and price lists issued by sales; (4) order editing, done as specified by the controller and by sales; (5) invoice preparation and mailing, as prescribed by the controller; (6) reorder from production—inventory replenishment according to formulas emanating from manufacturing, as well as from distribution.

Many physical distribution specialists claim that order processing time can be cut from a third to a half through organization of the various facets under one man.

6. *Customer service*—Distribution should also be concerned with answering inquiries on order status from salesmen and customers. Distribution would not, of course, be responsible for technical service.

7. *Materials handling*—Manufacturing has historically been responsible for this function, say the experts. They point out, however, that in-process materials handling methods are not readily applicable to finished goods handling.

8. *Package design*—Merchandising and sales aspects of package design are not the concern of physical distribution. However, package design as it affects the handling and transporting of merchandise is his concern.

IMPROVEMENT

Are the physical distribution specialists correct in suggesting that planning of the movement of finished goods to customers and distributors be centralized? Compare the improvements in customer service and the reduction of marketing costs possible through proper physical distribution management with the distribution system of the early growth days of Federal Pacific Electric, as described by Mr. Shuchter:

Sam O'Toole was the 1949 version of Ramac. He guided the destiny of our stock from its source for many years. With orders and memos tucked in every pocket, he charged through each day as though it were the decisive moment in human history.

Emergency! The ABC Distributing Co. placed an order for twelve 400-amp, three-pole, solid neutral switch devices three months ago. The order, it seems, has been misplaced and now the salesman, Sam's buddy, is on the phone crying his heart out: He faces cancellation of the $600 order and other reprisals too terrible to mention. The card inventory shows zero.

Enter Sam O'Toole. From the dark recesses of the stockroom he drags out three of the precious devices. His friend, Jake the foreman, will convert two from similar units. Up in the factory Sam has spotted five almost-complete assemblies coming down the line. He drags the plant manager (no lesser mortal will do) to the spot and stands panting as the foreman is ordered to stop all work until the devices are complete.

That's ten down and two to go. In a flash Sam has wired the people at the St. Louis warehouse that the switch they will receive today is to be airfreighted back to Newark. And finally Sam calls a Paterson distributor who is sure to help him out by returning a switch he has in stock. His task complete, Sam calls the salesman to promise shipment of eight switches today and four tomorrow, and knows in his heart that this was a job well done. (Sam, by the way, was also the best pitcher our softball team ever had.)

As for the future, in an American Management Association report on physical distribution, A. W. Greene, editor of *Distribution Age,* Philadelphia, wrote:

In 1965 there will be many physical distribution managers. They will come from traffic and transportation, from warehousing, from industrial engineering, from production, marketing, and sales. Each will have greater scope and greater breadth of vision than the present pioneers of distribution management.

I see such a man at his desk. It's a clean desk, except for rows of push-buttons, intercoms, and other executive gadgets. Behind him, and on all sides, there are live charts and graphs, pulsating with electronic recordings of up-to-the-moment inventories at all distribution points. There are direct wire communications lines to all points.

As the distribution manager of 1965 sits in his white tower of control, his telephone rings. An angry voice is heard: "Nine weeks ago I sent you an order for three sizes of your model X-5 components. You promised seven-week delivery. As of now, I haven't received a single unit. If I don't get this shipment by the end of the week, cancel the order."

Well, . . . maybe in 1966 . . .

24

Methods and Uses of Retail Trade Area Analysis

P. D. Converse

Analyses of retail trade areas are useful in helping retailers to select locations for stores, to determine their probable trading territories, to measure the purchasing power of those territories, to ascertain whether they are drawing trade from all parts of their territories, and to decide whether they are covering their territories with adequate advertising. They should know why they are attracting trade from other trading areas or why they themselves are losing trade to competing towns. The merchants of a town, whether independent retailers or chain-store managers, should know what the consumers in the area think of their stores, the assortments of goods carried, the quality of their goods, their prices, their advertising, and their services. Furthermore, the general reputation of the town, its amusements, and its various professional and personal services have their effect upon trade movements. If the merchants of a town are handicapped by the fact that their town has a reputation which keeps some trade away, they may take steps to remedy the situation by publicity, advertising, and personal salesmanship.

Manufacturers also may find retail trade analyses very useful in setting sales quotas, in establishing agencies intelligently, and in selecting the most effective advertising media. From the point of view of the manufacturer, the population of a town may be less significant than the population and income of its trading area.

By ascertaining the facts in regard to retail trade movement in the districts which they serve, newspapers can determine in what communities

Paul D. Converse, *A Study of Retail Trade Areas in East Central Illinois* (Urbana, Ill.: University of Illinois Press, 1943), pp. 7–15. Reprinted by permission.

they should attempt to promote their circulation. Adequate coverage of a trading area with newspaper circulation will benefit both publishers and merchants.

Two specific cases may be described which indicate the usefulness of a retail trade area analysis to an individual merchant. In the first case, a merchant whose store handled a good quality of shopping goods and was located in an Illinois city with a population of more than 25,000 decided to make an analysis of his trading area. Although his store was well established and had a good reputation for the quality of its goods, sales volume had been relatively stable for some years and profit margins low. To maintain volume and move overstocks, he often resorted to special sales. He felt that the quality of his merchandise, his reputation, his location, and his advertising should secure larger sales and a higher percentage of profit. Since he handled high-quality shopping goods, it seemed logical that he should secure trade from the better residential districts in the entire trade area of the town. An analysis of the area, he believed, would show whether he was actually getting this trade.

By using methods for determining the boundaries of retail trading areas...he found the logical area from which he could be expected to attract customers. He then compared his actual coverage of this area, as shown by the address of credit and cash customers, with that suggested by the theoretical boundaries. The results showed that he had a fairly satisfactory coverage, with the exception of one high-income section of his own city—a section which he had been especially proud to regard as giving him a large share of its business.

Now that he knew the facts, he could use one of two methods for filling the gap in his coverage. He had been advertising in only one of the two newspapers published in the town. He could place his advertising in both papers, or he could supplement his newspaper advertising by sending extensive direct-mail matter to families not reached by the paper in which he was advertising. A consumer survey of the section would help him find out why he was not receiving trade from its residents. It might be that the goods he handled did not meet their demands, or they might not be satisfied with the services of his salespeople. Such a survey can be best made by an outside research organization.

A somewhat different type of survey was made by a department store in a large primary trading center. This town is large enough to attract considerable trade for a radius of 100 miles or more, and has a newspaper whose Sunday edition covers the entire area rather thoroughly. The store advertised liberally and drew trade from places more than 100 miles away. It decided to make an attempt to discover what these out-of-town customers wanted—to find out why they came to the store and what kind of goods they bought. The assumption had been that people from the smaller towns and rural districts came to the larger town to shop chiefly because of lower prices. Goods offered in the bargain basement had therefore been strongly featured in the Sunday paper, which was circulated widely in the rural territory.

However, a test proved that this assumption was incorrect. During selected periods, the names and addresses of cash customers were secured; information as to the addresses of credit customers was available in the files. The addresses of both cash and credit customers were then punched in cards, together with data as to departments patronized and goods bought. When the results were tabulated, it was found that very few families who lived more than thirty miles away patronized the bargain basement. Instead, the people from the smaller places usually bought the better grades of goods—in many cases, better than those purchased by residents of the trading center. The conclusion was that better quality, or larger assortments, rather than lower prices, led people to shop in larger trading centers instead of in their home towns. As a result, the store in question changed its advertising outside a twenty-five-mile zone to feature high-grade goods and new fashions.

METHODS OF DETERMINING TRADING AREAS

There are a number of methods for determining the boundaries of retail trade areas: listing the license numbers of all automobiles parked in the retail section of the trading center on selected days, and obtaining the addresses of their owners from the state motor vehicle license records; plotting the circulation of the newspapers published in the trading center and of those in competing towns (in larger cities, the afternoon papers); plotting the addresses of credit and cash customers of stores in the trading center and in competing towns which sell shopping goods; tracing through bank transit sheets checks on out-of-town banks given to retailers;[1] interviewing consumers and retailers near the supposed boundaries of the area and questioning them as to local buying habits; and the application of the law of retail gravitation developed by William J. Reilly.[2]

Reilly developed the law of retail gravitation by plotting the retail trade areas of various cities from the charge accounts on the books of their better department stores and specialty shops. He then checked the operation of the law by using newspaper circulation figures and interviews with consumers and merchants.[3]

The listing of license numbers of parked automobiles in order to obtain the addresses of the owners has been found reasonably accurate. For best results, lists of license numbers in competing trading centers should be made in order to determine their relative strength in districts near the boundaries between the areas. However, even a listing of automobiles parked in only one town may help the merchants in directing their advertising to the areas in which prospective customers may be found.[4]

The circulation of the daily papers published in a trading center usually agrees fairly well with the trading area from which the town attracts customers. There are, however, many exceptions to be found. Some ambitious circulation managers push their circulation well beyond the logical trading area, hence circulation areas alone do not provide a satisfactory measure of the drawing power of competing trading centers. In a later section of this [chapter], the relation of trade movement and newspaper circulation for eleven towns in East Central Illinois will be discussed.

ANALYSIS OF TRADING AREAS

Once the boundaries of an area have been determined by one or more of the methods suggested, there are various means by which the trading habits of its residents may be examined.

Statistical Analysis

Much valuable information is accessible in published sources. The Bureau of the Census publishes figures showing values of owned homes and rentals paid in towns. Estimates of the income of residents in towns and cities can be derived from these figures and compared with retail sales in the area to trace the flow of trade.[5] For mixed urban and rural areas, estimates of income may be derived from Census figures for value added in manufacturing industries; cash farm income; incomes produced by wholesalers, retailers, and service industries; and wages received in mineral, forest, and fishery industries.[6] The total amounts may then be compared with retail sales in the trading center and in its tributary territory. It is difficult, however, if not impossible to build up a figure for the total income of an area in this way. If the boundaries of a trade area can be determined accurately, it may be possible to derive a figure for total income from the dollar amount of its retail sales, by using a figure showing the percentage of income spent in retail stores.[7]

The shifts in trade within a metropolitan area over period time may be estimated by computing the percentages of the total retail trade obtained by various towns or sections of towns in the period. Figures for such parts of towns are not published, but the Bureau of the Census will furnish such breakdowns for the cost of the work.[8] In case a metropolitan area is made up of many municipalities, published Census data are available and may prove valuable.[9]

The income of counties may be estimated by allocating the income of the state to the counties on the basis of agricultural production of marketings, payrolls, and number of income tax returns.[10] Figures showing automobile registrations, number of wired homes, number of radios, circulation of leading magazines, bank clearings, savings bank deposits, growth or decline of population, composition of population, and occupations of residents may be very helpful in examining the area and interpreting its statistical data.

A serious limitation on the use of Census data which should be kept in mind is that the figures given are for political divisions, such as counties and cities, whereas retail trade crosses political boundaries freely. The allocation of county figures to different trade areas when the area includes parts of several counties is very difficult.

Traffic Counts

Pedestrian and automobile traffic counts are most useful in planning the best locations for stores and for advertising signs. Such counts are relatively easy to make, and may be helpful not only to individual concerns but also to city planners, highway engineers, and others.

Consumer Surveys

Consumer surveys are made by asking a representative sample of consumers where they buy various commodities and why. This is one of the most useful and satisfactory methods, but its cost limits its application. For an accurate survey the sample must be carefully selected, the questionnaires must be so worded as to secure the desired information, and the interviewers must be tactful, well trained, and adequately supervised. The technique of questionnaire surveys has been developed to such an extent that a high degree of accuracy can be attained.

The consumers may be asked in what towns or in what stores they purchase various commodities. They may be asked how often they shop in certain towns, what method of travel they use, what newspapers they read, what radio stations they listen to, and what changes in buying habits they have made, or expect to make. Most of the data for the present study were secured by this method.

Dealer Surveys

Retailers in towns near the boundaries of trade areas may be asked what towns attract the most trade from their areas. In the author's opinion, such information is valuable when one of the competing towns definitely outdraws the other; but information obtained in this way is not sufficiently accurate when the competing towns secure approximately equal amounts of trade from the area.

Checking Merchandise and Services

Both individual merchants and the town as a whole may profit by a careful investigation of the types of merchandise available in local stores and the service facilities of the community. Customers may be attracted to a town primarily because of its banks, medical services, or amusements. People prefer to shop in towns with enough retail outlets to provide a wide selection of goods. It is therefore to the advantage of a merchant to be located in a town which has good stores in other lines. It has been said that it takes at least three stores which handle a given type of shopping goods to make an attractive shopping center. A careful check of merchandise, prices, and service agencies in the town and a comparison of these with those offered in competing trading centers may prove of great value.

The Law of Retail Gravitation

The movement of retail trade is from the smaller to the larger towns.[11] The larger the town, other things being equal, the larger the assortments of goods found in its stores, and the more services and amusements offered there. Hence, the larger the town, the more attractive it is as a shopping center, especially for the more expensive shopping goods. However, in many cases it is necessary to travel farther to reach a larger town than to reach a small town, and the greater the distance, the more the time and expense required. Consumers are thus *attracted* to larger towns by the greater assortments of merchandise, services, and amusements, and *repelled* by the longer trips necessary to reach them.

Reilly's Law, which measures the resultant effect of these two factors, is stated as follows: "Two cities attract retail trade from any intermediate city or town in the vicinity of the breaking point approximately in direct proportion to the populations of the two cities and in inverse proportion to the square of the distances from these two cities to the intermediate town." The breaking point is defined as "a point up to which one city exercises the dominating retail trade influence, and beyond which the other city dominates." The distances are measured along the most direct improved highways.[12]

The law of retail gravitation considers only two factors—population and distance. Reilly mentions eleven other factors which influence the amount of retail trade secured by a city:

1. Transportation facilities—railroad, bus, air lines, highway, express, and parcel post rates, etc.
2. Lines of communication—newspaper circulation, radio station coverage, telephone rates
3. Classes of consumer territory surrounding the city
4. Density of population around the city
5. Proximity of larger cities
6. Business attractions of the city, such as selection of goods, delivery and credit services, banking facilities, and general reputation of the town as a place to shop
7. Social and amusement attractions of the city, such as theaters, athletic contests, churches, fairs, etc.
8. Parking facilities
9. Competition offered by smaller cities
10. Topographical and climatic conditions of the city
11. Leadership of businesses in the city

A few of the modifying factors deserve comment. Traffic congestion on inadequate highways near a large city or on its streets may cause some people to travel away from the city and to shop in suburban or satellite towns. This factor is said to have led to a definite decentralization of the retail stores of our larger cities in the past fifteen years. The presence of a smaller town through which trade must flow to reach a larger town may limit the amount which reaches the larger town. Some towns have more concentrated or convenient shopping districts than others. For example, a town built around a public building or park is said to be a less convenient town for shoppers than a town without such an obstruction.

Two other facts should be mentioned: consumers travel farther to buy high-priced than low-priced goods; and upper-income families travel farther to shop than low-income families. Hence a town in which can be found higher-priced goods that appeal to the upper-income families may expect to attract trade from greater distances than a town whose stores carry lower-priced goods.

According to the law of retail gravitation, a change in the relative population of competing trading centers will change their drawing power and the boundary between their trade areas. New highways may be built from time to time; these may change the distances between competing trading centers and intermediate towns, and consequently change the proportions of trade going from the intermediate towns to the trading centers. One purpose of this study is an attempt to determine whether consumers in intermediate towns do change their shopping habits in accordance with the law of retail gravitation when such changes occur; and, if so, how long it takes them to do this. Illinois started building its system of paved highways in the early 1920s. These highways apparently changed existing trade patterns which had grown up when travel was by railroad and later by automobile over dirt roads. Some additional roads were paved in the 1930s and these may have further modified trade patterns.

Two formulas are used in applying the law of retail gravitation. The first is used to determine what proportions of the trade which goes from an intermediate town to two competing towns each of these towns should attract. It is stated as follows:[13]

If B_a is the proportion of trade attracted by city A

B_b is the proportion of trade attracted by city B

P_a is the population of city A

P_b is the population of city B

D_a is the distance from intermediate town to city A

D_b is the distance from intermediate town to city B

then

$$\frac{B_a}{B_b} = \left(\frac{P_a}{P_b}\right)\left(\frac{D_b}{D_b}\right)^2$$

The second, derived from the first by assuming that B_a is equal to B_b, is used to determine the breaking point between the trade areas of two towns. The breaking point, or boundary, is the point at which the trade moving in opposite directions is equal—half of it going to city A and half to city B. Of course, a town may draw considerable trade for a short distance beyond the breaking point, and merchants who sell higher-priced shopping goods may profitably extend their advertising beyond the mathematically computed boundary. The second formula is expressed as follows:

If A is the first city and B is the second city, the distance from B to the breaking point between the trade areas of the two cities will be equal to

$$\frac{\text{Distance from A to B}}{1 + \sqrt{\dfrac{\text{Population of A}}{\text{Population of B}}}}$$

The use of these two formulas may be illustrated by using the example of Gibson City, an intermediate town between Champaign-Urbana and Bloomington. The population of Champaign-Urbana is 37,366 and that of Bloomington, 39,851; Gibson City is thirty-one miles from Champaign-Urbana and thirty-four miles from Bloomington.

Substituting in the first formula, we have

$$\frac{B_a}{B_b} = \frac{37,366}{39,851} \times \left(\frac{34}{31}\right)^2 = 1.128$$

If Champaign-Urbana attracts 1.128 times as much trade from Gibson City as Bloomington does, the comparative percentages attracted are: Champaign-Urbana $\dfrac{1.128}{2.128}$, or fifty-three percent; Bloomington $\dfrac{1.000}{2.128}$, or forty-seven per cent.

The second formula is used to determine the breaking point between Champaign-Urbana and Bloomington along the highways used by Gibson City consumers in visiting these two primary trading centers.

The distance from Bloomington to this breaking point is equal to

$$\frac{31 + 34}{1 + \sqrt{\dfrac{37,366}{39,851}}} = \frac{65}{1 + \sqrt{.938}} = \frac{65}{1.97} = 33.0 \text{ miles.}$$

NOTES

[1]For an explanation of this method see Austin S. Bratcher, *A Method of Delineating Retail Trade Zones* (School of Business and Public Administration, University of Arizona, 1939), or an article by the same author in the *Journal of Marketing* (January 1939).

[2]William J. Reilly, *The Law of Retail Gravitation* (New York: published by the author, 1931).

[3]*Methods for the Measurement of Retail Trade Territories* (Bureau of Business Research, University of Texas, 1928, multigraphed); and *Methods for the Study of Retail Relationships* (Bureau of Business Research, Research Monograph No. 4, University of Texas, 1929).

[4]For an application of this method, see Bulletin No. 44 of the University of Illinois Bureau of Business Research, *A Survey of a Retail Trading Area,* 1932.

[5]For a suggested method see Paul D. Converse and R. V. Mitchell, "Movement of Retail Trade Within a Metropolitan Area," *Journal of Marketing* (July 1937).

[6]For a suggested method see Paul D. Converse, "Analyses of Retail Trading Areas," *National Marketing Review* (Spring 1936).

[7]*Ibid.*

[8]This method was applied to Metropolitan Los Angeles. See W. K. Bowden and Ralph Cassady, Jr., "Decentralization of Retail Trade in the Metropolitan Market Area," *Journal of Marketing* (January 1941).

[9]This is true, for example, of Boston. See Richard P. Doherty, *Trends in Retail Trade and Consumer Buying Habits in the Metropolitan Boston Retail Area* (Bureau of Business Research, Boston University, September 1941). This study traced the changes in the movement of retail trade by computing the per capita retail sales for zones consisting of groups of towns. It also included a consumer survey.

[10]See, for example, W. M. Adamson, *Income in Counties in Alabama, 1929-1935* (Bureau of Business Research, University of Alabama, 1939); and *Sales Management:* Survey of Buying Power (published annually).

[11]There is some backflow from the larger to the smaller towns, partly because of lower prices in the latter. A recent Bureau study, however, found that this backflow to small towns in central and southern Illinois was relatively insignificant, except for sales by roadside retailers, such as filling stations, restaurants, and refreshment stands. See Bulletin No. 59, *Trends in Rural Retailing in Illinois 1926-1938,* published in 1939.

[12]Reilly, *The Law of Retail Gravitation,* p. 9.

[13]*Ibid.,* pp. 70ff.

25

The Wheel of Retailing

Stanley C. Hollander

"The wheel of retailing" is the name Professor Malcolm P. McNair has suggested for a major hypothesis concerning patterns of retail development. This hypothesis holds that new types of retailers usually enter the market as low-status, low-margin, low-price operators. Gradually they acquire more elaborate establishments and facilities, with both increased investments and higher operating costs. Finally they mature as high-cost, high-price merchants, vulnerable to newer types who, in turn, go through the same pattern. Department store merchants, who originally appeared as vigorous competitors to the smaller retailers and who have now become vulnerable to discount house and supermarket competition, are often cited as prime examples of the wheel pattern.[1]

Many examples of conformity to this pattern can be found. Nevertheless, we may ask: (1) Is this hypothesis valid for all retailing under all conditions? (2) How accurately does it describe total American retail development? (3) What factors cause wheel pattern changes in retail institutions?

The following discussion assembles some of the slender empirical evidence available that might shed some light on these three questions. In attempting to answer the third question, a number of hypotheses should be considered that marketing students have advanced concerning the forces that have shaped retail development.

TENTATIVE EXPLANATIONS OF THE WHEEL

1. *Retail Personalities.* New types of retail institutions are often established by highly aggressive, cost-conscious entrepreneurs who make every penny count and who have no interest in unprofitable frills. But, as

Reprinted from Stanley C. Hollander, "The Wheel of Retailing," in the *Journal of Marketing,* Vol. 25 (July 1960), pp. 37–42, published by the American Marketing Association.

P. D. Converse has suggested, these men may relax their vigilance and control over costs as they acquire age and wealth. Their successors may be less competent. Either the innovators or their successors may be unwilling, or unable, to adjust to changing conditions. Consequently, according to this view, deterioration in management causes movement along the wheel.[2]

2. *Misguidance.* Hermann Levy has advanced the ingenious, if implausible, explanation that retail trade journals, seduced by profitable advertising from the store equipment and supply industry, coax merchants into superfluous "modernization" and into the installation of overly elaborate facilities.[3]

3. *Imperfect Competition.* Although retail trade is often cited as the one type of business that approaches the Adam Smith concept of perfect competition, some economists have argued that retailing actually is a good example of imperfect competition. These economists believe that most retailers avoid direct price competition because of several forces, including resale price maintenance, trade association rules in some countries, and, most important, the fear of immediate retaliation. Contrariwise, the same retailers feel that service improvements, including improvements in location, are not susceptible to direct retaliation by competitors. Hence, through a ratchet process, merchants in any established branch of trade tend to provide increasingly elaborate services at increasingly higher margins.[4]

4. *Excess Capacity.* McNair attributes much of the wheel effect to the development of excess capacity, as more and more dealers enter any branch of retail trade.[5] This hypothesis rests upon an imperfect competition assumption, since, under perfect competition, excess capacity would simply reduce margins until the excess vendors were eliminated.

5. *Secular Trend.* J. B. Jefferys has pointed out that a general, but uneven, long-run increase in the British standard of living provided established merchants with profitable opportunities for trading up. Jefferys thus credits adjustments to changing and wealthier market segments as causing some movement along the wheel. At the same time, pockets of opportunity have remained for new, low-margin operations because of the uneven distribution of living-standard increases.[6]

6. *Illusion.* Professor B. Holdren has suggested in a recent letter that present tendencies toward scrambled merchandising may create totally illusory impressions of the wheel phenomenon. Storewide average margins may increase as new, high-markup lines are added to the product mix, even though the margins charged on the original components of that mix remain unchanged.

DIFFICULTIES OF ANALYSIS

An examination of the actual development of retail institutions here and abroad does shed some light on both the wheel hypothesis and its various explanations. However, a number of significant difficulties hinder the process.

1. Statements concerning changes in retail margins and expenses are the central core of the wheel hypothesis. Yet valid information on historical retail expense rates is very scarce. Long-run changes in percentage margins probably do furnish fairly reliable clues to expense changes, but this is not true over short or intermediate periods. For example, 1957 furniture store expense rates were about five percentage points higher than their 1949-1951 average, yet gross margins actually declined slightly over the same period.[7]

2. Historical margin data are somewhat more plentiful, but these also have to be dredged up from fragmentary sources.[8]

3. Available series on both expenses and margins merely note changes in retailers' outlays and receipts. They do not indicate what caused those changes and they do not report changes in the costs borne by suppliers, consumers, or the community at large.

4. Margin data are usually published as averages that may, and frequently do, mask highly divergent tendencies.

5. A conceptual difficulty presents an even more serious problem than the paucity of statistics. When we talk about "types" of retailers, we think of classifications based upon ways of doing business and upon differences in price policy. Yet census categories and other systems for reporting retail statistics are usually based upon major differences in commodity lines. For example, the "pineboard" druggists who appeared in the 1930s are a "type" of retailing for our purposes. Those dealers had cruder fixtures, charged lower prices, carried smaller assortments, gave more attention to turnover, and had less interest in prescriptions than did conventional druggists. Yet census reports for drugstores necessarily included all of the pineboards that maintained any sort of prescription department.

Discount houses provide another example of an important, but amorphous, category not reflected in census classifications. The label "discount house" covers a variety of retailers. Some carry stocks, others do not. Some carry stocks, others do not. Some have conventional store facilities, whereas others operate in office buildings, lofts, and warehouses. Some feature electrical appliances and hard goods, while others emphasize soft goods. Some pose as wholesalers, and others are practically indistinguishable from all other popular priced retailers in their fields. Consequently discount dealers' operating figures are likely to be merged into the statistics reported for other appliance, hardware, or apparel merchants.

EXAMPLES OF CONFORMITY

British

British retailing provides several examples of conformity to the wheel pattern. The grocery trade has gone through several wheel-like evolutions, according to a detailed analysis made by F. G. Pennance and B. S. Yamey.[9]

Established firms did initiate some changes and some margin reductions, so that the pattern is obscured by many cross currents. But the major changes seem to have been due to the appearance and then the maturation, first, of department store food counters; then, of chain stores; and finally, of cut-price cash-and-carry stores. Now supermarkets seem to be carrying the pattern through another evolution.[10]

Jefferys also has noted a general long-run upgrading in both British department stores and chains.[11] Vague complaints in the cooperative press and a decline in consumer dividend rates suggest that wheel-like changes may have occurred in the British cooperative movement.[12]

American

Very little is known about retail margins in this country before the Civil War. Our early retail history seems to have involved the appearance, first, of hawkers, walkers, and peddlers; then, of general stores; next, of specialty stores; and finally, of department stores. Each of these types apparently came in as a lower-margin, lower-price competitor to the established outlets, and thus was consistent with the wheel pattern. We do not know, however, whether there was simply a long-run decline in retail margins through successive improvements in retail efficiency from one type to another (contrary to the wheel pattern), or whether each of the early types was started on a low-margin basis, gradually "up-graded," and so provided room for the next entrant (in accordance with the pattern).

The trends toward increasing margins can be more easily discerned in many branches of retailing after the Civil War. Barger has described increases over the years 1869-1947 among important retail segments, including department stores, mail-order firms, variety stores, and jewelry dealers. He attributes much of the pre-World War I rise in department store margins to the absorption of wholesaling functions. Changes in merchandise mix, such as the addition of soda fountains and cafeterias to variety stores and the upgrading of mail-order merchandise, seem to have caused some of the other increases. Finally, he believes changes in customer services have been a major force in raising margins.[13] Fabian Linden has extended Barger's observations to note similar 1949-1957 margin increases for department stores, variety chains, and appliance dealers.[14]

Some other examples of at least partial conformity to the wheel pattern may be cited. Many observers feel that both discount-house services and margins have increased substantially in recent years.[15] One major discount-house operator has stated that he has been able to keep his average markup below twelve per cent, in spite of considerable expansion in his facilities and commodity mix.[16] However, the consensus seems to be that this probably is an exception to the general rule.

A study of gasoline pricing has pointed out how many of the so-called "off-brand" outlets have changed from the "trackside" stations of prewar days. The trackside dealers typically maintained unattractive and poorly equipped installations, at out-of-the-way locations where unbranded gasoline was sold on a price basis. Today many of them sell well-promoted regional and local brands, maintain attractive, efficient stations, and provide prompt and courteous service. Some still offer cut prices, but may have raised their prices and margins up to or above national brand levels.[17] Over time, many of the pineboard druggists also seem to have become converted to fairly conventional operations.[18]

NONCONFORMING EXAMPLES

Foreign

In underdeveloped countries, the relatively small middle- and upper-income groups have formed the major markets for "modern" types of retailing. Supermarkets and other modern stores have been introduced in those countries largely at the top of the social and price scales, contrary to the wheel pattern.[19] Some nonconforming examples may also be found in somewhat more industrialized environments. The vigorous price competition that developed among Japanese department stores during the first three decades of this century seems directly contrary to the wheel hypothesis.[20] B. S. Yamey's history of resale price maintenance also reports some price cutting by traditional, well-established British merchants who departed from the wheel pattern in the 1880s and 1890s.[21] Unfortunately, our ignorance of foreign retail history hinders any judgment of the representativeness of these examples.

American

Automatic merchandising, perhaps the most "modern" of all American retail institutions, departed from the wheel pattern by starting as a high-cost, high-margin, high-convenience type of retailing.[22] The department store branch movement and the concomitant rise of planned shopping centers also has progressed directly contrary to the wheel pattern. The early department store branches consisted of a few stores in exclusive suburbs and some equally high-fashion college and resort shops.

Only in relatively recent years have the branches been adjusted to the changing and more democratic characteristics of the contemporary dormitory suburbs. Suburban shopping centers, too, seem to have appeared first as "Manhasset Miracle Miles" and "Ardmores" before reaching out to the popular price customers. In fact, complaints are still heard that the regional shopping centers have displayed excessive resistance to the entry of really aggressive, low-margin outlets.[23] E. R. A. Seligman and R. A. Love's study of retail pricing in the 1930s suggests that pressures on prices and margins were generated by all types of retailers. The mass retailing institutions, such as the department and chain stores, that had existed as types for many decades were responsible for a goodly portion of the price cutting.[24] As McNair has pointed out, the wheel operated very slowly in the case of department stores.

Finally, Harold Barger has described the remarkable stability of overall distributive margins during the years 1919-1947.[25] Some shifting of distributive work from wholesalers to retailers apparently affected their relative shares of the total margins during this period, but this is not the type of change contemplated by the wheel pattern. Of course, the stability Barger notes conceivably could have been the result of a perfectly smooth functioning of the pattern, with the entrance of low-margin innovators providing exactly the right balance for the upcreep of margins in the longer established types. But economic changes do not come in smooth and synchronized fashion, and Barger's data probably should indicate considerably wider oscillations if the wheel really set the mold for all retailing in the postwar period.

CONCLUSIONS

The number of nonconforming examples suggests that the wheel hypothesis is not valid for all retailing. The hypothesis, however, does seem to describe a fairly common pattern in industrialized, expanding economies. Moreover, the wheel is not simply an illusion created by scrambled merchandising, as Holdren suggests. Undoubtedly some of the recent "upcreep" in supermarket average margins is due to the addition of nonfood and other high margin lines. But in recent years the wheel pattern has also been characteristic of department store retailing, a field that has been relatively unreceptive to new commodity groups.[26]

In some ways, Jefferys' secular trend explanation appears most reasonable. The tendency of many established retailers to reduce prices and margins during depressions suggests also that increases may be a result of generally prospering environments. This explanation helps to resolve an apparent paradox inherent in the wheel concept. Why should reasonably skilled businessmen make decisions that consistently lead their firms along seemingly profitable routes to positions of vulnerability? Jefferys sees movement along the wheel as the result of sensible, businesslike decisions to change with prospering market segments and to leave the poorer customers to low-margin innovators. His explanation is supported by the fact that the vulnerability contemplated by the wheel hypothesis usually means only a loss of market share, not a loss of absolute volume. At least in the United States, though, this explanation is partially contradicted by studies showing that prosperous consumers are especially prone to patronize discount houses. Also they are equally as likely to shop in supermarkets as are poorer consumers.[27]

The imperfect competition and excess capacity hypotheses also appear highly plausible. Considerably more investigation is needed before their validity can be appraised properly. The wheel pattern developed very slowly, and very recently in the department store field. Yet market imperfections in that field probably were greater before the automobile gave the consumer shopping mobility. Major portions of the supermarket growth in appliance distribution occurred during periods of vastly expanding consumption, when excess capacity probably was at relatively low levels. At the moment there is little evidence to suggest any clear-cut correlation between the degree of market imperfection and the appearance of the wheel pattern. However, this lack may well be the result of the scarcity of empirical studies of retail competition.

Managerial deterioration certainly must explain some manifestations of the wheel, but not all. Empires rise and fall with changes in the quality of their leadership, and the same thing seems true in business. But the wheel hypothesis is a hypothesis concerning types of retailing and not merely individual firms. Consequently, the managerial-deterioration explanation holds true only if it is assumed that new people entering any established type of retailing as the heads of both old and new companies are consistently less competent than the first generation. Again, the fact that the wheel has operated very slowly in some fields suggests that several successive managerial generations can avoid wheel-like maturation and decay.

NOTES

[1]M. P. McNair, "Significant Trends and Developments in the Postwar Period," in A. B. Smith, ed., *Competitive Distribution in a Free, High-Level Economy and Its Implications for the University* (Pittsburgh: University of Pittsburgh Press, 1958), pp. 1–25.

[2]P. D. Converse, "Mediocrity in Retailing," *Journal of Marketing,* Vol. 23 (April 1959), pp. 419–420.

[3]Hermann Levy, *The Shops of Britain* (London: Kegan Paul, Trench, Trubner & Co., 1947), pp. 210–211.

[4]D. L. Shawver, *The Development of Theories of Retail Price Determination* (Urbana: University of Illinois Press, 1956), p. 92.

[5]McNair, "Significant Trends," pp. 1–25.

[6]J. B. Jefferys, *Retail Trading in Great Britain, 1850-1950* (Cambridge: Cambridge University Press, 1954), various pages, especially p. 96.

[7]Cited in Fabian Linden, "Department Store Operations," *Conference Board Business Record,* Vol. 14 (October 1958), pp. 410–414.

[8]See Harold Barger, *Distribution's Place in the American Economy Since 1869* (Princeton: Princeton University Press, 1955).

[9]F. G. Pennance and B. S. Yamey, "Competition in the Retail Grocery Trade, 1850-1939," *Economica,* Vol. 22 (March 1955), pp. 303–317.

[10]"La Methode Americaine," *Time,* Vol. 74 (November 16, 1959), pp. 105–106.

[11] Jefferys, "Trading in Great Britain."

[12] "Battle of the Dividend," *Co-operative Review,* Vol. 36 (August 1956), p. 183; "Independent Commission's Report," *Co-operative Review,* Vol. 38 (April 1958), pp. 84–89; "£52 Million Dividend in 1957," *Co-operative Review* (August 1958), pp. 171–172.

[13] Barger, "Distribution's Place," p. 82.

[14] Linden, "Department Store Operations," pp. 410–414.

[15] D. A. Leohwing, "Resourceful Merchants," *Barron's,* Vol. 38 (November 17, 1958), p. 3.

[16] S. Masters, quoted in "Three Concepts of Retail Service," *Stores,* Vol. 41 (July-August 1959), pp. 18–21.

[17] S. M. Livingston and T. Levitt, "Competition and Retail Gasoline Prices," *The Review of Economics and Statistics,* Vol. 41 (May 1959), pp. 119–132.

[18] Paul C. Olsen, *The Marketing of Drug Products* (New Brunswick: Rutgers University Press, 1948), pp. 130–132.

[19] H. S. Hettinger, "Marketing in Persia," *Journal of Marketing,* Vol. 15 (January 1951), pp. 289–297; H. W. Boyd, Jr., R. M. Clewett, & R. L. Westfall, "The Marketing Structure of Venezuela," *Journal of Marketing,* Vol. 22 (April 1958), pp. 391–397; D. A. Taylor, "Retailing in Brazil," *Journal of Marketing,* Vol. 24 (July 1959), pp. 54–58; J. K. Galbraith and R. Holton, *Marketing Efficiency in Puerto Rico* (Cambridge: Harvard University Press, 1955), p. 35.

[20] G. Fukami, "Japanese Department Stores," *Journal of Marketing,* Vol. 18 (July 1953), pp. 41–49.

[21] "The Origins of Resale Price Maintenance," *The Economic Journal,* Vol. 62 (September 1952), pp. 522–545.

[22] W. S. Fishman, "Sense Makes Dollars," *1959 Directory of Automatic Merchandising* (Chicago: National Automatic Merchandising Association, 1959), p. 52; M. V. Marshall, *Automatic Merchandising* (Boston: Graduate School of Business Administration, Harvard University, 1954), pp. 108–109, 122.

[23] P. E. Smith, *Shopping Centers* (New York: National Retail Merchants' Association, 1956), pp. 11–12; M. L. Sweet, "Tenant-Selection Policies of Regional Shopping Centers," *Journal of Marketing,* Vol. 23 (April 1959), pp. 399–404.

[24] E. R. A. Seligman and R. A. Love, *Price Cutting and Price Maintenance* (New York: Harper & Brothers, 1932).

[25] Barger, *Distribution's Place,* pp. ix, x.

[26] R. D. Entenberg, *The Changing Competitive Position of Department Stores in the United States by Merchandise Lines* (Pittsburgh: University of Pittsburgh Press, 1957), p. 52.

[27] R. Holton, *The Supply and Demand Structure of Food Retailing Services, A Case Study* (Cambridge: Harvard University Press, 1954).

IV

CONTRIBUTIONS OF THE FUNCTIONAL APPROACH

Significant contributions to marketing thought have come from proponents of the functional approach. The functional approach was popular between 1940 and 1960. It overlapped the institutional approach on the early side and the marketing management approach on the later side. However, no perspective of marketing—not even marketing management—has had a greater impact than functions. Most marketing curriculums today are still organized around the functional approach with such courses as advertising, personal selling, sales management, marketing research, pricing, purchasing, and logistics.

The study of marketing functions makes several contributions to the marketer's knowledge. First, it provides insight into the activities that are universally applied in marketing operations. Second, it clearly demonstrates the breadth and depth of the marketing manager's task. Third, it provides one of the best foundations for analyzing marketing problems. Fourth, it emphasizes the interrelationship of marketing activities.

Our presentation of representative classics from the functional approach is divided into two parts: "Defining Marketing Functions" and "Functions in the Marketing System." There are ten articles in this section. The defining of marketing functions concerns the debate over what constitutes the functional approach. Shaw is given credit for conceptualizing the approach, and his classic article leads off the section. Fullbrook provides a historical development of the functional approach and develops its popular interpretation. McGarry indicates weaknesses in the approach and provides a new way of interpreting marketing functions.

The presentation of "Functions in the Marketing System" provides a broad look at the place and importance of the more important functions of marketing in our economic system. Webster provides a good overview of buying, including the major steps in the buying process which have been adopted for use in both industrial and consumer markets. Stidsen explains personal selling as a communications process, and he analyzes the meaning of selling ability. McGarry discusses advertising. He explains the difference between propaganda and education, compares advertising to personal selling, and develops the more common motives used in advertising. Cash and Crissy provide a straight-forward comparison of the similarities and differences between the use of advertising and personal selling. Dean makes a plea for adapting price to changing conditions and and points to some important changes taking place in this area. Oxenfeldt outlines the stages for developing price strategy in what some feel was a cornerstone article for the development of marketing management. Brown shows how marketing research can be used in the development of marketing strategy.

26

Some Problems in Market Distribution

Arch W. Shaw

THE ACTIVITIES OF BUSINESS

When a workman in a factory directs the cut of a planer in a malleable steel casting, he applies motion to matter with the purpose and result of changing its form.

When a retail clerk passes a package of factory-cooked food over the counter to a consumer, he applies motion to matter with the purpose and result of changing its place.

Isolate any phase of business, strike into it anywhere, and invariably the essential element will be found to be the application of motion to matter. This may be stated, if you will, as the simplest ultimate concept to which all the activities of manufacturing, selling, finance, and management can be reduced.

Starting with the simplest concept, it is at once evident that we have an obvious and easy basis for the classification of business activities—a simplifying, unifying principle from which to proceed rather than some mere arrangement by kind or characteristic of the materials, men, operations, and processes in the various departments of a business enterprise.

The nature of the motion does not of itself supply the key to this basic classification. For while the action may be characteristic of one part of a business and not duplicated elsewhere, like the pouring of molten metal in a foundry or the making up of a payroll, it may, in contrast, be common to all the departments into which the organization is divided, such as the requisition of a dozen pencils or a box of paper clips. It is not until we single

Excerpted from Arch W. Shaw, "Some Problems in Market Distribution," in Hugh G. Wales, ed., *Changing Perspectives in Marketing* (Urbana: University of Illinois Press, 1951), pp. 32–38, 42–43. Reprinted by permission.

out the common fundamental element and inquire, "What is the purpose of this motion?" that we find the key.

I do not wish to exaggerate the importance of this simple and apparently obvious concept; but for me it has opened a way to locate the activities of business and disclose their relations to one another and to their common object, and so has proved a device of daily use. For the final function of the classification, as it is the practical problem of all business, is to identify those motions which are purposeless, so that they may be eliminated, and to discover those motions, old or new, which are of sound purpose, so that they may be expedited.

When, upon studying an individual motion or operation in itself and in relation to the other associated activities, no satisfactory answer can be found to the question, "What is its purpose?", you have strong grounds for assuming that it is a nonessential and useless motion. It may have the sanction of house tradition or trade custom, but its superfluous character persists and the wisdom of eliminating it becomes plain. Conversely, a new motion proposed for adoption, though never before tried in the trade, may still have value. Purpose again is the decisive test. From the social standpoint, any motion which has no valid purpose or result is economically useless and wrong. The effect of employing such a motion in business, like the effect of omitting a useful motion, is to limit profits that otherwise might rise.

So the purpose of the analysis, from the manager's point of view, is not alone to position the activities of business and develop their relationship, but also to order his thinking so that he can more readily see what activities he should discontinue and what others he should encourage, perfect, or add.

This does not always mean a reduction in the total number of motions. In our roundabout system of production,[1] with its minute subdivision of labor, it is possible to make a greater number and variety of motions and distribute them over a longer period of time, yet increase the eventual output or decrease the cost through the group effectiveness of all the motions.

In the three operations already mentioned—those of the factory workman, the retail clerk, and the office typist—each application of motion was for an economically valid purpose, and each instance was typical of one of the three great groups of business activities:

1. The activities of production, which change the form of materials.
2. The activities of distribution, which change the place and ownership of the commodities thus produced
3. The facilitating activities, which aid and supplement the operations of production and distribution[2]

Whatever the nature or kind of any business activity, its final effect is one of these three.

PROBLEMS OF THE DISTRIBUTOR

The progress that has been made in organizing production is the result of systematic study. Methods of study that have proved fruitful in other fields have been applied to the problems of manufacture and a body of organized knowledge is being built up.

Why has not similar systematic study been given to the problems of distribution? The explanation is found in a glance back over our economic history. Chief among the causes for the industrial changes leading to the establishment of the factory system in England in the eighteenth century was the constant widening of the market. For a century thereafter the necessity of supplying a continually expanding market, as the population increased with unprecedented rapidity and means of transportation steadily improved, made production the predominant problem.

The development of producing capacity has been tremendous. New processes have been and are being introduced. New forces have been called into play. If our producing possibilities are to be fully utilized, the problems of distribution must be solved. A market must be found for the goods potentially made available.

Our whole civilization has been characterized by increasing standards of living due to the demand of the individual for more goods and more highly differentiated goods. The most pressing problem of the businessman today, therefore, is systematically to study distribution, as production is being studied. In this great task the businessman must enlist the trained minds of the economist and the psychologist. He must apply to his problems the methods of investigation that have proven of use in the more highly developed fields of knowledge. He must introduce the laboratory point of view.

The problem presented by the United States as a consuming market is a complex one. Here are a hundred million people distributed over an area of more than three million square miles (excluding Alaska). Some are gathered in the large cities, where millions jostle elbows. Some are scattered over great areas with considerable distances between them and their neighbors. Some daily pass hundreds of retail stores; some must ride miles to reach the nearest store. Extremes in purchasing power exist. Many have scarcely sufficient buying power to pay for the necessities of life. A few can satisfy the most extravagant whims of the human imagination. In between lie varying degrees of purchasing power.

Their wants are as widely varied as their purchasing power. Environment, education, social custom, individual habits, and all the variations in body and mind tend to render their wants diverse. In each individual certain conscious needs are constantly being gratified by the purchase of goods produced for such gratification. There are also the conscious needs which go ungratified because of the individual's limitations in purchasing power and the existence of other needs that seem of greater importance. Finally there are the unformulated, subconscious desires which fail of expression because the individual is perhaps even ignorant of the existence of goods which would gratify them.

Our accepted system of distribution was originally built upon the satisfying of staple needs. With production still lagging, the pressure of the market made it unnecessary for the businessman to search out unformulated human needs. Only in more recent years, when the development of production (potentially outstripping the available market) has shifted the emphasis to distribution, has the businessman become a pioneer on the frontier of human wants. Today the more progressive businessman is searching out the unconscious needs of the consumer, is producing the goods to gratify them, is bringing to the attention of the consumer the existence of such goods, and in response to the demand so aroused, is transporting the goods to the consumer.

The economists tell us of the "consumer's surplus." Briefly, this is the difference between the objective market value of a commodity and the subjective value of the commodity to the individual consumer. Each individual sets up for himself a ratio among commodities which finds expression in the prices he is willing to pay for one or another commodity rather than go without it. These subjective valuations constitute the demand side of the market. The interplay of supply and demand in a competitive market determines a price at which the consumer can obtain the article.

If this market price is above the level that is fixed by the subjective ratio of exchange of the consumer, he drops out of the market, utilizing his purchasing power to secure other commodities. But if the market price is below that which the consumer would be willing to pay to obtain the commodity, he makes his purchase. Then the difference between his subjective ratio of exchange and the objective market ratio of exchange constitutes his "consumer's surplus."

The activity of the more advanced distributors in differentiating commodities has tended to break down the orthodox methods and policies of distribution. This development necessitates an analysis of the possible price policies of the present day merchant-producer....

METHODS OF DISTRIBUTION

In the early stages in distribution, the purchasers saw the actual goods before sale was made.

Later, sale by sample appeared. The purchaser bought goods represented to be identical with the sample he was shown. The introduction of this method of sale was necessitated by the widening of the market and was made possible by improvement in commercial ethics and increasing standardization of product. The purchaser had to have confidence not only in the producer's honest intention to furnish goods identical to the sample, but also in his ability to produce identical goods. Hence, increasing uniformity in product through machine methods of applying standard materials in its manufacture was a factor in the increase of sale by sample.

Sale by description is the most modern development in distribution. Here an even higher ethical standard is required than for sale by sample. Moreover, sale by description requires a higher level of general intelligence than sale in bulk or sale by sample. Sale by description in its modern development is, in a sense, a by-product of the printing press.

All three methods of sale are in use in modern commercial life. The consumer still makes a large part of his purchases under a system of sale in bulk. He sees the goods before he buys them. The middleman, buying in larger quantities, generally purchases from the sample. But sale by description becomes each year more important in every stage of the distribution system.

The root idea in sale by description is the communication of ideas about the goods to the prospective purchaser by spoken, written or printed symbols and facsimiles. This method takes the place of the sight of the goods themselves or a sample of them. It is obvious that this requires that the purchaser shall have sufficient intelligence to grasp ideas either through spoken, written or printed symbols.

The ideas to be conveyed to the prospective purchaser in sale by description are such as will awaken an effective demand for the commodity in question. The awakening of demand is the essential element in selling. It must be remembered, however, that the distributor has the further task of making it possible to gratify that demand by making the goods physically available to the buyer.

With sale in bulk, this problem merges with the selling, since the goods are physically present when the sale is made; while in sale by description the physical distribution of the goods is a problem distinct from the awakening of demand. And it is a problem that requires equal attention, for it is obviously useless to awaken the demand unless the goods to satisfy it are available.

NOTES

[1]See E. V. Bohm-Bawerk, *Positive Theory of Capital,* pp. 17–20.

[2]Businessmen and economists, though dealing with the same forces and the same phenomena, do not always agree on terminology. The economist speaks of the agencies of production as land (or natural agents), labor, capital, and organizing ability; and he includes in production the activities which the businessman groups separately under the heads of distribution and various facilitating functions. To the businessman the term production covers the activities which are concerned directly with the manufacture of articles. He uses concrete terms: plant and equipment instead of capital, materials instead of land or the products drawn directly from the land. He uses the economist's term in describing the active agency as labor, but speaks of organization rather than the organizing ability. In the following pages the language of the businessman is used, though new phrases are occasionally used to characterize the regrouping of activities.

27

The Functional Concept
in Marketing

Earl S. Fullbrook

The functional approach in studying marketing is almost as old as marketing literature. Following its early introduction it received wide acceptance by writers in the field and it has continued to hold a very important place in marketing literature and teaching. Today it is the exception when any general work on marketing does not give some attention to marketing functions. Not only has the functional approach come to be common in marketing books but it is found frequently in texts used for courses in principles of economics and for introductory courses in the field of business organization and management.

In spite of the length of time the functional concept has been in use and in spite of its wide currency at the present time, it appears that little has been accomplished since the early years toward any significant refining of the concept. It is apparent from any careful survey of the material in the field that there is no very clear-cut and generally accepted interpretation of, or method of handling, marketing functions. The writer believes the functional approach can be a very useful device but contends that a great deal must be done in further developing it before all its possibilities can be realized. The following pages aim to emphasize this need and to suggest the lines along which further development should proceed.

ORIGIN

Credit for originally introducing the functional concept to marketing belongs to A. W. Shaw, one of the pioneers in the field of marketing literature, whose writings "mark the real beginning of the scientific analysis of marketing problems."[1] He dealt with marketing functions in

Reprinted from Earl S. Fullbrook, "The Functional Concept in Marketing," in the *Journal of Marketing,* Vol. IV (January 1940), pp. 229–237, published by the American Marketing Association.

his paper on "Some Problems in Marketing Distribution" which was published in 1912.[2] This was three years before the period from 1915 to 1917 which Converse has designated as the "first or pioneer period" in marketing literature.[3] The functional concept, therefore, extends back to the very beginning of marketing literature.

Not long after Shaw introduced the functional approach into marketing, others began to use and to develop it. Important among those using and contributing to the development of the idea in the early years were Weld, Cherington, Vanderblue, and Macklin.

INTERPRETATIONS OF EARLY WRITERS

In introducing the subject into marketing, Shaw spoke not of functions of marketing but of functions of middlemen. Although he offered no formal definition of the term, his treatment makes it clear that he thought of functions as steps or tasks to be performed by someone in the process of marketing goods. He explained that they might be divided between middlemen on an area basis or on a functional basis or that they might be distributed on one basis at one time and on another basis at another time.[4] If functions can be allocated to distributive agencies in a variety of ways, it must follow that they are tasks which can be divorced from, and treated separate from, the agencies which perform them.

Weld wrote at some length on marketing functions in 1917.[5] He defined them as: "The services that must be performed in getting commodities from producer to consumer."[6] This definition indicates that Weld regarded functions as tasks and his discussion leaves no doubt about the interpretation. He described marketing functions as essential steps involving various difficulties, which are more difficult to perform for some commodities than for others, and which require that in each case the methods of performance be adapted to the needs.

Cherington gave considerable attention to marketing functions in *The Elements of Marketing* which appeared in 1920. More definitely than any of his predecessors he stressed the need for analyzing the functions separate from their actual performance—the need "to get back of the forms of distribution to the actual functions."[7] He believed that if the functional approach was to be of much value in dealing with marketing problems, it was essential that the problems involved, not the agencies used, be given prime consideration—that attention be fixed "not upon the forms of devices which have been developed and which must be regarded as temporary and external features, but rather, upon the functions of marketing as the permanent element of the problem."[8] Functionaries, he pointed out, are constantly changing while functions cannot undergo corresponding change.[9]

The same distinction between functions and agencies was implied, at least, by Vanderblue in 1921. He believed the functional approach was the logical one "because the specialists exist to perform certain functions" and "because the problems involved in the marketing machinery and marketing process can be developed and isolated by an exposition in terms of the functions performed."[10]

Also in 1921 there was published Macklin's *Efficient Marketing for Agriculture,* which contained a discussion of marketing functions, although they were designated as marketing services. The study of marketing, he states, in order to be practical "must examine the methods of rendering these services and the agencies which provide them" and "must examine the various marketing services and determine why they are performed." The confusion of services with methods or agencies, he adds, "blurs the whole subject of marketing" and "has rendered futile much of the marketing criticism up to the present time."[11]

Thus the writers who first dealt with marketing functions treated them as necessary steps or tasks to be performed in the process of getting goods from producers to consumers. They generally regarded the functional treatment as a means of analyzing what had to be done to get goods from producers to consumers and as providing a basis for determining how the job could be done best. They maintained definite distinctions between the work to be done (functions) and the means of doing it (functionaries).

CURRENT TREATMENT OF FUNCTIONS

Three general methods of handling marketing functions are in current use. The least effective of these, and hardly meriting recognition as a method of treatment, is to list the functions and, in a few brief statements, attempt to indicate the nature of each. Little is done to show their significance or to relate them to the rest of the material.

A second method is to list the functions and then describe them primarily by describing the ways in which they are performed. This tends to result in a description of the agencies and methods used to perform the functions —a description of marketing machinery and processes. From such a treatment there is great danger the reader will conclude that a function is an activity to be considered only in terms of how it is performed. It is the result which Macklin warned against—a confusion of services with methods or with agencies which blurs the whole subject of marketing.

The third procedure, which follows closely the lead of those who introduced and developed the concept, is to list the functions and to explain, more or less adequately, the problems encountered in the performance of each. In this approach a function is considered as a service or task to be performed and an analysis is made to determine exactly what must be done to secure an efficient performance of each. Such an analysis tends to maintain a separation between the problems involved in the functions and the machinery used in performing them.

The above methods may easily be combined and this is what many writers tend to do. The results, however, tend to be inconsistent, in that some functions are analyzed in terms of the problems to which they give rise while the treatment of others consists of little more than a description of how they are performed in current marketing practice. Such a combination is hardly logical.

Something of the situation which exists today, at least among teachers of marketing, is indicated in the *Report of the Committee on Definitions* of the National Association of Marketing Teachers in 1935, where it is stated that:

> During the past year the Committee has attempted to deal with two marketing terms which seem to represent the ultra ultimate in confusing and diversity of usage. These two terms are "Marketing Function" and "Wholesaling." There is pretty general agreement as to what constitutes a satisfactory formal definition of the former of these terms. No great degree of agreement exists among those interested in marketing, however, as to the specific activities which should be classified as *marketing functions.*[12]

The wide differences of opinion existing among those interested in marketing, as to what the significant functions are, suggest that the acceptance of a formal definition does not mean a great deal, and the variations in the way the term is used in marketing discussions further suggest that the ability to agree on a formal definition does not insure a common interpretation of the term when put to use. Not only do we find significant differences in ideas as to what should be included in the list of marketing functions but there are also fundamental variations in ideas as to just what marketing functions involve. It would appear, therefore, that further study of the functional concept is needed.

USES OF THE FUNCTIONAL APPROACH

The introduction, development, and continued use of the functional approach in marketing must be due to a belief that it offers certain significant advantages. As a basis for further discussion, consideration needs to be given to these advantages, since the definition and interpretation of marketing functions should be developed with due consideration of the uses or purposes to which the concept is to be put.

To Weld, the functional approach offered a method of outlining the field of marketing and emphasizing the various and numerous activities involved in it. Because many people, even though realizing that there are functions to be performed, have no appreciation of their complexity or the difficulties of performing them, he says "a classification of marketing functions is absolutely fundamental to a study of and an understanding of the marketing machinery."[13]

To Vanderblue, the functional approach supplied a basis for analyzing marketing problems. According to his view the analysis of marketing problems along functional lines conforms with both the market structure and commercial practice and "is the logical approach in dividing the larger problem into its constituent problems, which can be considered singly, and then brought together in a consideration of the problem as a whole."[14]

In many current treatments these same advantages of the functional approach are stressed. Clark says:

> So important are these functions to the marketing process that the best approach to many of the problems involved in marketing—whether the object is to understand general marketing processes or the processes used in marketing particular products—is an understanding of these essential services. Such knowledge enables one to understand why middlemen exist, why marketing is costly, why certain marketing institutions and devices have developed, and often furnishes the best approach to the solution of specific marketing problems.[15]

According to Converse the:

> ...reader who is to understand the discussion of middlemen and commodities fully, should first have some knowledge of the various marketing functions .... The reader can then have them in mind while studying middlemen and commodities, and thus be in a better position to understand and criticize the activities of the middlemen and the methods by which goods are marketed.[16]

The functional approach, Killough states:

> ...attempts to apply to marketing, methods of analysis that have been employed with gratifying results in the scientific study of factory management. This approach breaks the subject up into processes that must be performed in the movement of goods from farm or mine to factory and from factory or farm to ultimate consumers.... Analysis of the marketing functions, one by one, contributes to a clearer understanding of the different elements of marketing cost and facilitates selection or creation of agencies which perform the functions most economically.[17]

These and many similar comments are evidence that the functional approach is thought to serve important uses. Briefly summarized, the possibilities of the functional method in studying marketing are:

1. It is a method of defining the field. Marketing is defined as including "those business activities involved in the flow of goods and services from production to consumption."[18] What are these activities? How can the number and variety of them best be distinguished and emphasized? It is very easy to overlook some of them and to underestimate the importance of others but the chance of doing so is materially reduced by the functional method. It affords an advantageous way of describing the ramifications and complexities of the field of distribution and of explaining the high costs of marketing.

2. Study along functional lines provides a good basis for understanding marketing agencies and processes. By analyzing them in terms of the functions they perform it is easier to determine why certain agencies exist, why certain methods are followed, and why certain costs are encountered. A full knowledge of the nature and significance of the several functions leads to a more complete understanding of all agencies and processes.

3. The functional method provides a sound basis for analyzing marketing problems. The great majority of problems in distribution cannot be solved satisfactorily without breaking them up into their elements. Functions provide a basis for doing so, whether the problem involves general marketing processes, methods of marketing individual commodities, or individual marketing agencies and devices. Differences in the marketing of different types of commodities can be explained in terms of functions; the marketing of a single product can be planned in terms of the functions that must be performed; and the need for, and efficiency of, individual institutions may be evaluated by ascertaining if they are performing essential functions more efficiently than could be done by some other institution or combination of institutions.

These possibilities of the functional approach, however, are seldom realized and it is the writer's contention that if they are to be realized to any marked degree, it is essential that we have a more adequate interpretation and treatment of the functional concept.

PROPOSED INTERPRETATION

The interpretation of marketing functions proposed here is not a new one. It is merely a proposal that an idea found in the discussions of marketing functions from the beginning be developed to its logical conclusion.

A function of marketing should be regarded strictly as a step, task, or service to be performed in getting goods from producers to consumers. This is in accord with the usual definition.[19] That the performance of a function requires activity is granted. That it is logical to regard a function as an activity to be performed is also granted. To so regard it, however, increases the probability that attention will center upon the activities performed instead of upon the nature and extent of the job which has to be done and which gives rise to the activities. If it is not in accord with the usual meaning of the word to define a function in terms of what has to be done, some other term had better be substituted. Breyer speaks of the "elements of the marketing task"[20] and there is much in favor of some such designation.

By regarding a function solely as a task or service that requires performance, it can be analyzed entirely distinct from its actual performance and if the functional treatment is to yield significant results, such procedure is essential. The authors previously quoted have indicated the desirability of analyzing institutions and processes on a functional basis, but this is a productive method of attack only when, on one hand, the functions are treated as tasks to be done and, on the other, institutions and processes are recognized merely as the agencies or methods for getting the tasks done. Only after gaining a clear understanding of the nature of a task and of what its performance requires, can one evaluate agencies or methods that are used, or might be used, in doing the job.

The functions of marketing are readily adapted to such a treatment. They can be completely analyzed in terms of what the performance of each requires with little or no reference to the ways they are performed in practice. To do so results in a description of the problems encountered in getting goods from producers to consumers and affords a really sound basis for considering how these problems or tasks can be handled best.

All marketing institutions and processes have come into existence to perform marketing functions. The justification for these agencies must be that they perform essential functions. It is necessary, then, that the tasks involved be outlined separately from their actual performance. The function is what is done. The agency used to do it should be selected and shaped according to the task it has to do. In other words, first determine the problem—what has to be done—and then determine the best way of doing it. After the functions involved in a given marketing problem have been analyzed adequately attention can be turned to the best methods of performing them.

To merely indicate some of the possibilities of the method, it will be applied to two representative marketing functions.

EXAMPLES OF PROPOSED TREATMENT

The transportation function involves the movement of goods from places of production to places of consumption. It is an absolutely essential step in marketing because so few goods are consumed at the place where they are produced.

What does the performance of the transportation function involve? Is it a simple or difficult task? Will its performance add much or little to the cost of getting products to consumers? Obviously the answer varies with different commodities and even for similar commodities under different conditions. But why? What are the factors that cause these differences? Is it not possible to discover a group of factors which can be used to analyze the transportation function in relation to any commodity?

While not offered as inclusive of all significant factors, the following suggests where the proposed type of analysis leads. The ease or difficulty of performing the transportation function for any commodity is determined by such elements as the distance it must be moved, its value or bulk, the degree of its perishability, the speed with which it must be moved, and the ease with which it can be handled in loading and unloading.

These factors can be applied to any commodity or group of commodities. As they are applied to different commodities in an effort to ascertain what the transportation function involves, totally different results may be secured. For some items—bulky, perishable ones that must be moved long distance—it develops that the function is an expensive one: for other items—valuable, durable ones—the transportation function is far less troublesome and costly.

It should be observed that such an analysis of the transportation function steers clear of methods of performance. Applied to eggs, for instance, the analysis runs along these lines. Eggs are very perishable and must be protected from both breakage and deterioration. This requires very careful packing, protection from too cold and too warm weather, and careful handling in loading and unloading. Eggs, being somewhat bulky, require considerable shipping space. On the average they must be moved long distances. Where producers and consumers happen to be very close together the function is immensely simplified.

Other products, like coal, are very bulky and must also be moved considerable distances, but are very durable and lend themselves to easy methods of loading and unloading. In the case of still another type of good, such as jewelry, there is very small bulk and great value and, although it must be carefully packed and protected and often carried great distances, the transportation function is relatively simple and inexpensive.

From such an analysis, in which no consideration is given to methods of performance, even the beginner can easily see what the transportation function amounts to, can realize that entirely different types of transportation facilities are needed for different products, and can understand why the cost of transportation is a big factor in the prices of some products and of little importance in others.

As a second example consider buying, one of the so-called "typical marketing functions." The function of buying involves having available for consumers what they want, when they want it. It includes having the right goods at the right place, at the right time, in the right quantities, and at the right prices. Since the average consumer uses so many different commodities, produced in so many and widely scattered places, the task of arranging to have each and every one available is a very important and a very complicated assignment.

What are the special phases of the buying function? As described by Converse, buying includes: (a) determining needs, (b) finding a seller, (c) negotiating price and other terms, and (d) payment, or arranging for credit.[21] This breakdown provides a satisfactory basis for starting the analysis but is only a beginning. It is desirable that each of these aspects be studied to determine what is required for its efficient performance.

If the right goods are to be at the right place, someone must do a lot of planning. In order to determine needs, markets must be carefully studied. Such factors as income, age, sex, nationality, occupations, business conditions, style movements, and price changes which affect the type and amount of goods purchased must be examined and evaluated. Some individual or institution must do it, but the job of doing it can be described advantageously without describing the agencies that do it and the methods they use. In attempting to analyze the task, why complicate it by mixing in agencies that are, or might be, engaged in performing the task? To do so tends to color the thinking and the real nature of the problem involved is not properly determined.

That striking differences are encountered in trying to determine the needs for different commodities is obvious. For a staple commodity, like salt, few difficulties are met in determining needs, whether being done for the country as a whole, for a sectional market, or for the customers of a given retailer. People continue to consume about the same kind of salt in about the same quantities. On the other hand, to anticipate the demand for a product like women's ready-to-wear gives rise to no end of difficulties. Women can be depended upon to buy something different than they purchased last time. Just what styles, colors, prices, and sizes will they want? And how much? Here the correct answers are not so easy to find. Methods of analyzing demand have to be developed.

Seeking sources of supply is the next phase of buying. An efficient performance of this step requires more than merely finding some place where the desired goods can be purchased. A careful consideration of all potential sources is called for in order that the best ones can be selected. Hence the number, nature, and location of sources will determine how difficult is the performance of this step for any particular commodity. For an item like fresh tomatoes the selection of sources is complicated because the sources may shift from week to week and month to month. First they must be obtained from one place, a little later in the season from another, and so on through the year. Furthermore the sources are not certain from year to year. A source that yields an abundant supply of fine tomatoes one year may offer only an inferior supply, or none at all, the next. Also there are so many widely scattered, small-scale producers that it is very difficult to know the possibilities of all of them. It is not surprising that many different agencies are involved in concentrating such produce in wholesale markets.

Automobiles present a contrast in respect to sources. There are only a limited number of producers. These are large, well-known, and relatively stable from year to year. Furthermore, trade names are very important and there is but a single source from which a given kind of car can be had. Here is one of the reasons why few types of middlemen are used in marketing automobiles.

The remaining phases of the buying function lend themselves to similar treatment, but it is unnecessary to go further to show that it is feasible to analyze marketing functions with little or no reference to how they are performed in practice and that doing so opens up much greater possibilities for making functions mean something and for making the functional approach serve constructive purposes.

CONCLUSION

A thorough and consistent analysis of marketing functions in terms of *what has to be done* to perform them efficiently, instead of in terms of *how they are done* in practice, would increase greatly the value to marketing of the functional concept. Such an analysis was suggested by those who originally introduced the idea, but too generally those who have followed in the field have not applied it. As a result the functional method has not accomplished what was expected of it and what it might accomplish if functions were adequately interpreted and analyzed.

NOTES

[1]Homer B. Vanderblue, "The Functional Approach to the Study of Marketing," *Journal of Political Economy,* Vol. XXIX (October 1921), p. 676.

[2]A. W. Shaw, "Some Problems in Market Distribution," *Quarterly Journal of Economics,* Vol. XXVI (August 1912), pp. 703–765.

[3]Paul D. Converse, "The First Decade of Marketing Literature," *Natma Bulletin Supplement* (November 1933), p. 1.

[4]A. W. Shaw, *Some Problems in Market Distribution* (Cambridge: Harvard University Press, 1915), pp. 76–77.

[5]L. D. H. Weld, "Marketing Functions and Mercantile Organization," *American Economic Review,* Vol. VII (June 1917), pp. 306–318.

[6]*Ibid.,* pp. 317–318.

[7]Paul T. Cherington, *Elements of Marketing* (New York: The Macmillan Company, 1920), p. 44

[8]*Ibid.,* p. 56.

[9]*Ibid.,* p. 50.

[10]Homer B. Vanderblue, "The Functional Approach to the Study of Marketing," *Journal of Political Economy,* Vol. XXIX (October 1921), p. 682.

[11]Theodore Macklin, *Efficient Marketing for Agriculture* (New York: The Macmillan Company, 1922), pp. 29, 280–281.

[12]*Report of the Committee on Definitions,* published by the National Association of Marketing Teachers (May 1935), p. 13.

[13]Weld, "Marketing Functions," p. 306.

[14]Vanderblue, "The Functional Approach," p. 682.

[15]Fred E. Clark, *Principles of Marketing* (New York: The Macmillan Company, 1932), p. 11.

[16]Paul D. Converse, *The Elements of Marketing* (New York: Prentice-Hall, Inc., 1938), p. 24.

[17]Hugh B. Killough, *The Economics of Marketing* (New York: Harper and Brothers, 1933), p. 101.

[18]"Definitions of Marketing Terms," Consolidated Report of the Committee on Definitions, *National Marketing Review,* Vol. I (Fall 1935), p. 156.

[19]The definition of a marketing function recommended by the Committee on Definitions of the National Association of Marketing Teachers is: "A major specialized activity performed in marketing." *National Marketing Review,* Vol. I (Fall 1935), p. 156.

[20]Ralph F. Breyer, *The Marketing Institution* (New York: McGraw-Hill Book Company, 1934), p. 5.

[21]Converse, "The First Decade," p. 57.

28

Some Functions of Marketing Reconsidered

Edmund D. McGarry

WEAKNESS OF THE FUNCTIONAL ANALYSIS

From the beginning of the systematic study of marketing, a great deal of attention has been given to the analysis of marketing functions. A large number of articles has been published on the subject in various professional journals, and practically every textbook on marketing attempts to make some use of such an analysis in its presentation.[1] Yet, despite all these writings, there is little general agreement as to what the functions are or as to the purpose of defining them. Nevertheless, the importance of discovering the functions and of using them to analyze marketing problems is generally recognized. Agnew, Jenkins, and Drury state that "one of the most urgent needs of the present time is the accurate analysis and evaluation of different functions."[2] Alexander says: "Writers on the subject are by no means agreed as to the precise activities which belong to this category [marketing functions]. The lists that have been suggested contain from as few as eight to as many as twenty or thirty such functions. There is no standard group of them."[3]

Dissatisfaction with the present status of functional analysis is evidenced by the following statement recently distributed by the Committee on Definitions of the American Marketing Association:

> It is probably unfortunate that this term [marketing function] was ever developed. Under it students of marketing have sought to squeeze a heterogeneous and nonconsistent group of activities. For example, the functions of assembling, and dividing, if such functions exist, are performed through buying, selling, and transporting. Grading, standardization, and packaging

From Edmund D. McGarry, "Some Functions of Marketing Reconsidered," in *Theory in Marketing,* Reavis Cox and Wroe Alderson, eds., (Homewood, Ill.: Richard D. Irwin, Inc., 1950) pp. 263–79. Reprinted with permission.

are adjuncts of selling. Merchandising, when performed by the manufacturer, is partly a production and partly a manufacturing activity. Such functions as assembling, storage, transporting, are broad general economic functions, while selling, and buying are essentially individual in character. All these discrete groups we attempt to crowd into one class and label marketing functions.[4]

It is the purpose of this essay (a) to point out some of the discrepancies and inconsistencies in the use of the term "function," (b) to clarify some of the concepts regarding marketing, and (c) to set forth tentatively a list of functions that—for the purpose of making more understandable the part that marketing plays in modern society—appears to be more comprehensive and more useful than those now used. In order to accomplish this purpose, it is necessary to redefine marketing and to reorient the approach to the subject on a broad scale. Fortunately, marketing is one of the youngest of the disciplines that have grown out of economics, and there should be no encrusted reasoning or vested interests to inhibit the student from making such changes as the analysis requires. The very fact that there is wide disagreement lays the basis for experimental thinking.

It should not be necessary to point out that, in suggesting a new and different basis for functional analysis, the writer of this essay anticipates neither general acceptance of his ideas nor general agreement as to their value. Disagreement is healthful in so far as it stimulates thought. The purpose of this article is exploratory, and it is hoped that its conclusions will be sufficiently controversial to stimulate discussion of the fundamentals of the science of marketing. With this end in view, the writer himself reserves the privilege of changing his mind should his position prove untenable.

DEVELOPMENT OF THE FUNCTIONAL CONCEPT

The first application of the term "function" in connection with marketing is commonly attributed to Shaw, who, in 1912 enumerated the functions of middlemen as follows: sharing the risk; transporting the goods; financing the operations; selling (communication of ideas about the goods); and assembling, assorting, and reshipping.[5] L. D. H. Weld applied the functions of middlemen—as developed by Shaw, with some changes of his own—to the process of marketing as a whole, because, as he explained, "they are not always performed by middlemen, but often to a greater extent by producers themselves," and "it should be noted that the final consumer performs part of the marketing functions."[6]

With the coming of textbooks, functional analysis became popular. Most writers, following Weld, took over bodily the functions of middlemen and applied them with certain changes in terminology to the process of marketing in general. It was not until Breyer called attention to the need for a different approach in the treatment of marketing as an institution from that used in studying marketing agencies that students came to realize that some reorientation was necessary.[7]

Actually, there is no more reason to consider the functions of middlemen to be necessarily the same as the functions of the marketing process than there is to consider the functions of a carburetor to be the functions of a car. The use of the functional terminology interchangeably for different parts of the system and for the system as a whole points to two errors in definition. One involves the definition of the term "marketing," and the other the definition of the term "function."

"Marketing," according to the Committee on Definitions of the American Marketing Association, "is a series of activities which are involved in the flow of goods from production to consumption";[8] or, to use the definition presently proposed by the same Committee, marketing is "the performance of business activities that direct the flow of goods and services from producer to consumer or user."[9] In both these definitions, there is a vague implication that marketing begins at the factory door (or the farm gate or the mine head) and ends at the turnstile of the supermarket. In other words, marketing is the work that middlemen usually do. Neither of the definitions embraces the idea that marketing is often a major directive factor in production and that it extends its influence into consumption; nor does either comprehend that conceivably the consumer might also be the producer, as would theoretically be possible in a fully integrated cooperative institution. In short, there is no recognition of the part that marketing plays in the economic system or in social behavior generally.

"A marketing function," according to the Committee on Definitions, "is a major specialized activity performed in marketing."[10] Thus, it appears that marketing is simply a bundle of activities in the flow of goods, and a marketing function is any one of the bigger activities in the bundle.[11] One might readily draw the analogy of a wheel in a machine. The activity of the wheel consists, of course, in turning around and around. This, then, is its function; and the machine itself may be defined as a lot of wheels going around and around. Clearly, this describes the machine in a primitive sort of way, and it may conceivably be of aid in some types of analysis; but it is questionable that it leads to any profound understanding of the machine. Is it any wonder that the most persistent criticism of marketing is that it is purely descriptive?

One must not, however, minimize the difficulty of developing a sound definition of "marketing," particularly when it has to run the gauntlet of the numerous and individualistic members of a large committee. It is generally conceded that, in our present economy, the essential element in marketing has to do with the passing of title, since ownership is required for use. But how can a definition be formulated that will be equally applicable to an economy of free enterprise; to an economy based on purely communistic principles, where ownership is theoretically held by the state; and to a purely cooperative economy, where ownership and operation of production facilities are in the hands of consumers? To meet these problems, as well as the problem of broadening the concept to include the overall purpose of marketing, the following definition is proposed:

Marketing is that phase or aspect of an economy that has to do with and results in the changes in custody of, responsibility for, and authority over goods, to the end that goods produced by many agencies are made available for the convenience and satisfaction of different users.

It will be noted that "marketing," as just defined, is not limited to two points—production and consumption; instead, it is a phase or aspect of the entire economy, the implication being that it is a pervasive element that penetrates every part of the economy.[12] The term "responsibility for" is meant to include not only changes in private ownership in a capitalistic economy, but also changes of custody from person to person, even where ownership is maintained in a single organization. The definition also includes the main purposes of marketing, the essential reasons for the process.

THE MEANING OF "FUNCTION"

With the above definition of "marketing" in mind, it is possible to turn to the problem of defining the functions of marketing. To secure a sound definition for the term, it is well to ask, first: What should be the purpose of functional analysis? The answer is that, by breaking the process down into its functions, it is possible to separate the essential from the nonessential elements. Functional analysis should enable the analyst to evaluate the activities that are performed in terms of ultimate objectives and thus to emphasize those that are necessary and subordinate or eliminate those that are not. Such an analysis should give perspective to the study of marketing and make clear the place of the process in the conceptual scheme of the economy. Through the study of functions, changes in the structure of marketing caused by shifting, combining, or eliminating activities from one agency to another should be made understandable.

Obviously, such purposes as these cannot be attained as long as functions are defined merely as certain activities, even when an attempt is made to separate the good from the bad or the major from the minor activities. When this is done, all that is accomplished is a description of the process involved; and activities such as looking into the future, guessing as to what is in the consumer's mind, and so on ad infinitum, might just as well be called "functions" as the activities usually selected. No one will deny that these are important activities of marketers and that description is a necessary first step in analysis, but it is difficult to see how any particular purpose is served by enumerating them as separate functions.

The term "function" should be so defined as to meet the purpose for which it is used. The function of the heart is not simply to beat, which is its activity, but rather to supply the body with a continuous flow of blood. The term "functional architecture" implies that a building is designed for a purpose. In like manner, "functions of marketing" should denote a purposefulness in the marketing process; and the term should be used only in connection with activities which must be performed in order to accomplish the general purpose. Thus, accounting is not a function of marketing, although no one would think of carrying on business without it. The term "function" should be restricted to the *sine qua non* of marketing, those things without which marketing would not exist.[13]

The ideal to which marketing aspires is to distribute to consumers all the goods that full employment of all resources makes possible in such a way that each can secure what he wants within his income, with a minimum of delay and inconvenience. Under these circumstances, in a capitalistic economy, each would be able to buy what he could afford, and the money received from his buying would result in the financing of further production without waste. The continuous flow of goods to consumers and the continuous flow of money back into production are implied.

A careful study of the so-called "functions of marketing," as stated by the various writers on the subject, reveals that the most difficult problem is to be found in those activities having to do with changing of title, which practically all authorities agree is the central core of the marketing process. Most writers have denominated these activities "the buying function" and "the selling function." Some have brought the two together under the head of "exchange functions" or "bargaining functions." Others have tried to get away from the buying and selling concepts by calling them, respectively, "assembly" and "dispersion."

In 1934, Breyer broke sharply with the recognized authorities and proposed a fundamentally new approach to the whole problem. He insisted "that the searching work and the negotiation work rather than who performs them (seller or buyer) are the fundamental, distinctive characteristics of the marketing task involved, and that selling and buying are merely two different aspects of these two primal types of activity.... When viewing the marketing institution as an integral unit.... our functional conceptions, contactual and negotiatory, are more useful for purposes of analysis and synthesis than are the customary selling function and buying function concept."[14]

It is apparent that Breyer's analysis, excellent as it is, is essentially a subdivision of "the bargaining transaction," as developed by Commons.[15] Its conclusions are based heavily on legal considerations, and it does not comprehend what would happen to the marketing process under a purely authoritarian or collectivist regime. Further, it fails to come to grips with one of the most subtle and pervasive elements in modern marketing, viz., the use of persuasion in influencing the bargaining transaction. Using Breyer's concepts as a starting point, however, it is possible to set up a list of functions that will satisfy these objections, as well as those mentioned previously.

A NEW LIST OF MARKETING FUNCTIONS

Before taking up the functions here developed individually, it is desirable to outline the list in the order of the progression in which they are usually undertaken, as follows:

1. Contactual (Breyer)—the searching out of buyers and sellers
2. Merchandising (Alexander)—the fitting of the goods to market requirements
3. Pricing—the selection of a price high enough to make production possible and low enough to induce users to accept the goods
4. Propaganda—the conditioning of the buyers or of the sellers to a favorable attitude toward the product or its sponsor
5. Physical distribution—the transporting and storing of the goods
6. Termination—the consummation of the marketing process

The Contactual Function. The contactual function, according to Breyer, is the process of searching out the market. In the American economy, it consists of finding out either who the potential buyers are or who the potential sellers are, where they are located, and how they can be reached. It also includes media analysis that aims to discover which type of medium is likely to be most effective in reaching that segment of the market that affords potential customers for a particular item. Likewise, it includes the analysis of distribution channels to discover which outlets are most likely to be patronized for a particular good. Thus, the contactual function comprehends not only the staking-out of the segment of the market that it is desirable to exploit but also the making and maintaining of such contact with potential customers as is necessary to discover their desires. In cases where the buyer takes the initiative, the function consists in finding the most acceptable sources for the goods. In the case of consumer cooperative integration, the contactual function may represent both a searching-out of sources and a searching-out of potential members of the cooperative.

The Merchandising Function. The Committee on Definitions, in its earlier statement, gave as a definition of "merchandising" the following: "The adjustment of merchandise produced or offered for sale to customer demand. It involves the coordination of selling with production or buying for resale. . . . It involves the selecting of the product to be produced or stocked and deciding such details as the size, appearance, form, dressing of the product (packaging, etc.), quantities to be bought or made, time of purchase or production, price lines to be carried or made, etc."[16]

Copeland and Learned have defined "merchandising" as follows: "Merchandising is product planning. The job of merchandising is to ascertain the characteristics of the merchandise for which there is a potentially profitable demand, to prepare instructions for the manufacturing plant in order that it may be able to produce goods for which a demand exists, to aid in developing plans for promoting the sales, and to supervise the various routine operations in connection with these activities. It includes the determination of what to make, how much, at what time, and at what price."[17]

The writer of this essay prefers to omit pricing from the merchandising function and to consider it as a function in itself. Thus, the merchandising function includes all the adjustments made in the goods and in their presentation to meet the needs and desires of potential consumers or users. It includes quality determination as well as measurement, packaging, branding, and display at strategic points to stimulate consumer interest.

There is an implication in the definitions quoted that merchandising is wholly carried on by the seller. However, the activities enumerated can, with equal validity, be carried on by the buyer, as is done when he sets up specifications to guide his source in processing the items. And they may be performed in an integrated totalitarian system in which the state or some other organization determines just what will be produced and how it will be presented.

The Pricing Function. Even though both of the definitions quoted above include pricing as a part of merchandising, it seems that pricing is far too important to be relegated to such a minor role. A considerable part of the time and thought of the marketer is given to the problem of what price to pay or what price to accept. The suggestion of Breyer that "the forces which shape the amount of [that] price are the supply and demand forces of the market" and that pricing is therefore not a function of the marketing institution, can be given little weight, since these factors do not operate in a vacuum, but actually consist of evaluations made and expressed by buyers and sellers.[18] It is the making of these evaluations that constitutes the function of pricing in marketing.

It should be made clear that the pricing function has to do with the determination of reservation prices, offering prices, or acceptance prices, and that these are not necessarily the same as the prices at which the goods actually move. The decisions on prices here contemplated depend on the purposes the various parties have in mind. In the case of free trading on organized exchanges, the decisions depend largely upon the individual estimates of future price changes. On the other hand, where the prices are administered by management, a large number of factors is involved— for example, the expected demand, the cost of production and selling, the price of competing articles, and the pricing policies of other concerns in the trade. "A change in price," says Knauth, "is a nervous affair. The perfect price cannot be reasoned out. The only guide is public reaction which is discovered by trial and error."[19]

The Propaganda Function. The term "propaganda," originally had to do with the propagation of "the faith." It has come to mean, however, any scheme or plan for the propagation of a belief or an opinion in which the propagandist has an interest. Objections may be offered to the term because it now carries a connotation that is somewhat invidious. However, since the invidiousness itself appears to be derived from the fact that the propagandist has "an ax to grind," and since this is in no place more evident than in the business world, the word seems to be all the more appropriate for describing the marketing function.[20]

Under the propaganda function would fall all the methods used by the seller to influence people to buy from him and all the methods used by the buyer to induce sellers to sell to him. Thus, it would include all advertising, whether product or institutional; publicity of various kinds; and personal selling. In short, propaganda includes all the efforts put forth in business for the purpose of persuading and inducing a person in the market to act in a way that is favorable to the interest of the propagandist. It is a conditioning process organized to focus on the recipient all those environmental factors favorable to the interest of the propagandist. It aims not only to secure the attention and the favorable attitude of the recipient but also to persuade and induce him to act in a favorable way.

The Physical Distribution Function. Under the merchandising function, one may include time and space elements implied in the words "right time" and "right place." This use of the term would imply that the physical distribution function, which includes transportation and storage, is a part of the merchandising function. However, since this function is almost universally recognized, either as a single function or as "transportation" and "storage," and is adequately defined in practically all textbooks, there is little need to discuss it at length here.

The Termination Function. Breyer says that "after the contact between the producer and consumer has been made it becomes necessary to arrive at an agreement....on at least three essentials: the quality, the quantity, and the price of the services to be exchanged." Since these three elements are subject to negotiation, he terms the process "the negotiation function."[21] As stated above, Breyer's concept is fitted into the framework of the purchase-sale transaction in a free economy and thus lacks the breadth necessary to encompass marketing under a fully controlled economy. If the functions are to be made all-inclusive, it is necessary to find a term much broader than "negotiation." Such a term should embrace not only those factors that culminate in a contract, but also the carrying-out of the terms of the contract to the point at which marketing ends. To fulfill these requirements, the term "termination function" has been chosen. This term has an advantage in that it has come into rather extensive usage, particularly with reference to government contracts.

If one assumes, as is done here, that the adjustment of the goods to the consumers and the adjustment of the consumers to the goods takes place largely through the functions of merchandising and propaganda, then the area of negotiation is considerably reduced. However, the negotiation of the actual sale—the meeting of the minds of the parties—still remains. And, in our economy, after the terms of sale are agreed upon, there is usually the overt legal act of transferring title. The termination function, then, is the consummative act for which all of the other functions have been preparatory. Under it falls the determination of the terms of sale for each specific transaction, including delivery dates, credit arrangements, guarantees, and service policies that have been agreed upon. However, it must be remembered that marketing does not end with the payment for and the acceptance of the goods, because, in practice, there often remains a contingent moral and (sometimes) a legal obligation on the part of the seller that the goods be satisfactory. In cases of a fully controlled economy, the termination function would include all the processes necessary to place the goods under the responsibility of those who are to use them, to bring to an end the responsibility of those who have brought the goods this far, and such other contingent actions as the economy may require.

THE COORDINATION OF MERCHANDISING AND PROPAGANDA FUNCTIONS

The merchandising and propaganda functions are conceived in this analysis as coordinate in adjusting products to their prospective users, on the one hand, and in adjusting potential users to the products made for them, on the other. The necessity for these adjustments grows out of the general thesis (a) that products—whether made by man or produced by nature— seldom, and perhaps never, completely meet the preconceived notions of what those who are to use them want,[22] and (b) that wants for specific goods with definite characteristics are determined largely by environmental factors that are to some extent controllable. Since this conception departs most widely from the accepted doctrine, it is necessary that its basis be carefully examined.

In classical economic theory, there was an assumption (implied or expressed) that for every economic good a demand existed; for, by definition, an economic good was something that was wanted and that was scarce.[23] Wants were usually explained as stemming from biological or physiological needs—for example, the needs for food, clothing, and shelter. Essentially, then, wants for goods existed; they could not be created; and they ripened into demand as the wanter secured purchasing power. This concept of demand as something existing had a much more realistic basis in the market at the time of the early economists, when it was formulated, than it has today.[24] Under conditions of low-level consumption and a sellers' market, there was little need for and little possibility of discrimination on the part of consumers among products with small differences; consequently, product differentiation had but little appeal.[25] However, it is another story when we consider an economy in which most of the basic wants of practically all the people are continuously satisfied. As the level of consumption rises, more attention is paid to small differences—differences often imperceptible in so far as the inherent physical properties of the goods are concerned.[26]

From the standpoint of marketing under modern conditions, the demand for products is largely created. Man chooses one item rather than another because of a more favorable attitude toward the chosen item than toward the item that is not selected. This attitude is not something that is native and in existence; rather, it is created by a multitude of environmental factors. Among the most potent of these factors are those derived from what the individual himself has experienced or observed about the item and what has been communicated to him by others. Whether he knows it or not, a person's mind is largely made up from a complex of rational and irrational, tangible and intangible factors, many of which are imponderable and impossible to define. Furthermore, these factors, taken together, often have an importance greater than price in the making of choice.[27] For this reason, the two-dimensional logic of those economists who use price and quantity as the sole analytical measures for their problems is wholly inadequate for the understanding of the multidimensional demand factors that face the marketer under conditions of high-level consumption.

Marketing writers, however, have tended to follow the lead of the older economists without much qualification and with practically no criticism. They have failed to emphasize the difference between what is wanted or desired in a generalized way and what is wanted as to a specific product. It is, of course, the particular product that is sold in the market—a fact that should constitute one of the main differences of approach between marketing and economic theory. The marketer deals with individualized items, usually standardized within low tolerances, and each transaction is undertaken under a more or less different set of circumstances. He attempts to fit his particular product to the desires of a large number of different individual personalities, each of which is beset with different necessities, whims, and attitudes.

Under mass production, a high degree of product standardization is necessary, and little attention can be paid to the narrow differences in the desires of individual consumers except as they form a pattern for a group. If a producer cannot find or influence a sufficiently large segment of the population to accept his product, he cannot afford to underwrite the facilities that will enable him to sell at prices consumers will be willing to pay.[28] He is therefore under compulsion to build into the product characteristics that a sufficient number of customers will want, or to use the influences at his disposal to persuade them to want what he has made, or to do both. What the consumer wants or may be induced to want is often impossible to define in terms of physical characteristics, not only because there are no adequate measures of the characteristics that different consumers consider important, but also because the many alternatives the consumer may consider in his particular case are unknown and practically unknowable in advance of production. For this reason, the producer must constantly rely upon a process of trial and error in the market to discover what is wanted, and upon a process of indoctrination and propaganda to persuade consumers to accept what it is practicable to produce.[29]

MARKETING AND ECONOMIC REFORM

Under communism, socialism, and most other reform movements, marketing is in the hands of the state. Usually, this means that a central bureaucracy of so-called "experts" is set up for the purpose of determining what the public is to have in the form of goods and services that are distributed according to some preconceived plan. Theoretically, free choice of goods by the public is possible and could be implemented by directives from the board.[30] Innovations in goods are initiated by the board on the basis of objective tests, and "the wastes of competition" are thus eliminated. Advertising, except for simple statements concerning new products available, is generally prohibited; and propaganda, usually under the guise of education, takes the form of indoctrinating the public with the idea that only by these means can the maximum satisfactions be secured.

Inherent in the reasoning of these reforms is the theory that definite and objective wants exist that must be satisfied, and that it is possible for properly trained experts to determine what these wants are and to manage the economy in such a way that they can be supplied. The problem of adjusting goods to the consumer so that nice differences, which only the consumer himself can evaluate, can be secured, is largely ignored except in so far as the people can reject or accept what is offered them. Goods presumably are to be so standardized as to fit the needs of the people. People, rational beings as they are presumed to be, will attain the highest standard of living by accepting the goods that are designed for them by the experts. And, since much of the differentiation among products in capitalistic countries represents conspicuous consumption, it is considered unnecessary and undesirable.

Assuming the validity of all the arguments that the proponents of these reforms put forth as to the workability of their plans, it is conceivable that systems of this type might provide the basic needs of consumers; and, if free choice is permitted, it is possible that a certain amount of flexibility could be attained. However, the absence of any strong incentive on the part of the committee of experts to discover new types of wants, even though they act under directives to do so, seems to preclude the development of want-making as distinguished from want-satisfying machinery. Unless some such machinery is set up to perform the functions of merchandising and commercial propaganda, it is difficult to conceive how the system could lead to high-level consumption, the very essence of which is the close adjustment of particular goods to the individual's personality—the indulgence of whims and idiosyncrasies that, from our point of view, make life worth living. This is not to say that the population might not be propagandized into a sense of satisfiedness and even smugness; but, under these conditions, the individual could never develop the self-expression in terms of goods that is so necessary to one's personal adjustment to his environment.

SUMMARY AND CONCLUSION

The so-called "functions" of marketing, as enumerated and explained in most marketing textbooks, are really certain activities performed by different agencies in marketing. They describe somewhat mechanistically the processes through which goods pass from the producer to the consumer, with emphasis upon the relationships among the different marketing agencies. Such an analysis is inadequate for the purpose of explaining marketing in its broader aspects and defining its place in the social structure. To accomplish this latter objective, it is necessary to define functions in terms of purposefulness for society and to focus attention on the relationship of the marketing system to the environmental field in which it operates.

If it is assumed that people's wants, in so far as they apply to specific items of goods, are created by environmental factors and that goods cannot be made under conditions of mass production to meet all the varying specifications of individual consumers or users, then it becomes a major task of marketing to reconcile the notions of potential users as to what they desire with the products that businessmen find it practical to provide. This means, on the one hand, that goods must be found or devised that will, as nearly as possible, meet the preconceived notions of users as to nature, quality, and price, and that these goods must be presented at the proper time and under the most congenial conditions to appeal to users; and it means, on the other hand, that potential users must be conditioned to accept the goods as the best possible compromise between what they think they want and what they can get.

When considered from this point of view, the marketing task can be broken down into six different necessary functions, each of which contributes to the overall purpose expressed above, as follows:
1. The contactual function, which has to do with the searching-out of potential customers or suppliers and the making of contact with them
2. The merchandising function, which comprises the various activities undertaken to adapt the product to the users' ideas of what is wanted
3. The pricing function, which has to do with the prices at which goods are offered or at which they will be accepted
4. The propaganda function, which includes all the methods used to persuade the potential users to select the particular product and to make them like the product once they have it
5. The physical distribution function, which comprises the transportation and storage of the goods

6. The termination function, which has to do with the actual change in custody of and responsibility for the goods and is the culmination of the process

These six functions cut vertically through the channels of distribution. They are performed in part by the various agencies of distribution and in part by producers and consumers. The development and refinement of these functions have been major factors in the attainment of high-level consumption in free-enterprise countries, and it is difficult to conceive that any system of economy can reach such high levels without developing machinery to perform these functions.

In the light of this approach, marketing is something more than mere buying and selling at a profit; it is something more than a machine for matching supply with demand for the purpose of determining price; it is something more than a system of institutions for the distribution of goods. In a comprehensive sense, marketing is all of these; but in addition, and more fundamentally, it is the phase of the economy through which, in large part, man in the modern world makes his adjustment to his environment in terms of psychic desires and physical goods.

NOTES

[1] For an excellent summary of different points of view concerning marketing functions, see E. S. Fullbrook, "The Functional Concept in Marketing," *Journal of Marketing,* Vol. IV (January 1940), 229-37.

[2] H. E. Agnew, R. B. Jenkins, and J. C. Drury, *Outlines of Marketing* (New York: McGraw Hill Book Co., Inc., 1942), p. 47.

[3] R. S. Alexander, F. M. Surface, R. F. Elder, and W. Alderson, *Marketing* (Boston: Ginn & Co., 1940), p. 89. Actually, Ryan, in attempting to give a complete and detailed picture of the distribution process, lists 120 functional elements grouped into 16 functional categories, as "one of the many possible ways of presenting the elements of marketing" (F. W. Ryan, "Functional Concepts in Market Distribution," *Harvard Business Review,* XIII [January 1935], 205-24).

[4] From a tentative mimeographed statement distributed by the Committee in 1947.

[5] A. W. Shaw, "Some Problems in Market Distribution," *Quarterly Journal of Economics,* XXVI (August 1912), 703-65.

[6] L. D. H. Weld, "Marketing Functions and Mercantile Organization," *American Economic Review,* VII (June 1917), 306-18.

[7] R. F. Breyer, *The Marketing Institution* (New York: McGraw-Hill Book Co., Inc., 1934), p. 8.

[8] "Definitions of Marketing Terms," consolidated report of the Committee on Definitions, *National Marketing Review,* I (Fall 1935), p. 156.

[9] "Report of the Definitions Committee," *Journal of Marketing,* XIII (October 1948), 202-17.

[10] *Report of the Definitions Committee, 1948,* p. 210.

[11]Ryan, in his "pragmatic" approach to the problem, explains that he uses the word "function" in its ordinary meaning as the name of each of the recognizable items or elements of marketing activity because it is the most widely used and the most acceptable English word available. It means the normal activity of the thing, its actual performance (Ryan, "Functional Concepts," p. 213).

[12]"Exchange of goods occurs in the most primitive of societies and trade between nations has flourished throughout history, but under modern capitalism marketing has become not only all pervasive but central to the whole economic system" (Leverett S. Lyon, "Marketing," *Encyclopaedia of the Social Sciences*, X, 133).

[13]It is recognized, of course, that different sets of functions may be formulated for different levels of analysis and for different purposes.

[14]Breyer, *The Marketing Institution.*

[15]J. R. Commons, *Institutional Economics* (New York: Macmillan Co., 1934).

[16]"Report of the Committee on Definitions" (1935), 156. As its latest definition of "merchandising," the Committee on Definitions recommends the following: "The planning involved in marketing the right merchandise, at the right place, at the right time, in the right quantities and at the right price" (*Report of the Definitions Committee, 1948*, p. 211).

[17]M. T. Copeland and E. P. Learned, *Merchandising of Cotton Textiles* (Cambridge: Harvard Bureau of Business Research, 1933).

[18]Breyer, *The Marketing Institution*, p. 11.

[19]O. W. Knauth, *Managerial Enterprise* (New York: W. W. Norton & Co., Inc., 1948), p. 118. See also his article "Considerations in the Setting of Retail Prices," *Journal of Marketing*, XIV (July 1949), 1–12.

[20]Borden uses the term "merchandising function," i.e., "the function of determining product form," and the term "promotional function," i.e., "the function of stimulating and fashioning consumers' desires for his product" (N. H. Borden, *The Economic Effects of Advertising* [Chicago: Richard D. Irwin, Inc., 1942], p. 36).

[21]Breyer, *The Marketing Institution*, p. 6.

[22]"The fact that consumers buy certain things does not necessarily mean that they are satisfied with them, or that there was a plan in buying them. Psychologists who realize that wants are irrational feel that it is their task to explain, and perhaps to predict, consumer behavior; but their explanations cannot very well run in terms of specific goods and services. In their analysis, what is wanted may be something that will satisfy a half-dozen different cravings, and the number of alternatives is almost infinite—if the consumer has enough money" (W. E. Atkins *et al.*, *Economic Behavior*, rev. ed., [Boston; Houghton Mifflin Co., 1939], p. 761).

[23]For a clear statement of the inadequacy of the older point of view and the development of a comprehensive theory applied to modern conditions, see E. H. Chamberlin, *The Theory of Monopolistic Competition* (Cambridge: Harvard University Press, 1933). Chamberlin's analysis includes changes in product and in selling costs, as well as in prices and quantities. His product and selling costs correspond, respectively, to merchandising and propaganda as used in the present analysis.

[24]"As a people we have become steadily less concerned about the primary needs–food, clothing and shelter. . . . Our wants have ranged more widely and we now demand a broad list of goods and services which come under the category of 'optional purchases' " (Committee on Recent Economic Changes of the President's Conference on Unemployment, *Recent Economic Changes* [New York: McGraw-Hill Book Co., Inc., 1929], I, xv).

[25]The term "low-level consumption" characterizes an economy in which consumption rises but little above "the level of bare subsistence for the many plus some gewgaws for

the wealthy few.'' It represented the "simple process of grasping for whatever food, clothing, and shelter could be produced and making them last as long as possible." The term "high-level consumption" denotes "an economy in which the output of goods is considerably more than enough to provide for the prime needs of the population." For a full discussion of high-level consumption see W. H. Lough, *High Level Consumption* (New York: McGraw-Hill Book Co., Inc., 1935).

[26] "The satisfactions, in an economic sense, which the consumer seeks in merchandise are only partly concerned with intrinsic properties" (P. H. Cherington, *People's Wants and How to Satisfy Them* [New York: Harper & Bros., 1935], p. 166).

[27] "It is arguable that under modern conditions a firm enlarges its market more frequently and more effectively by increasing expenditure on marketing devices to capture consumers than by that price cutting to woo customers, which was assumed by the classical theory of competition to be the normal procedure" (Maurice Dobb, "Middleman," *Encyclopaedia of the Social Sciences*, X, 417).

[28] "Advertising and selling effort in so far as they influence demand may create uniformities of desires so that mass production of specialized articles may be disposed of..... Unless sufficient uniformities exist or are created, his (the businessman's) product cannot be sold at a profitable price" (H. R. Tosdal, "The Advertising and Selling Process," *Annals of the American Academy of Political and Social Science*, CCIX [May 1940], 66-67.

[29] "Significant differentiations to the consumer are those things which give him satisfaction, and he expresses his judgment of them by buying or refusing to buy. Hence in a free economy whether or not differentiations are meaningless or inconsequential must be determined in the end by consumers' behavior" (Borden, *Effects of Advertising*, p. 660).

[30] Lange, a leading authority on the economics of socialism, claims that a system "with neither free choice in consumption not in occupation" would be undemocratic in character and incompatible with the ideals of the socialist movement. "Such a system would scarcely be tolerated by any civilized people. A distribution of consumers' goods by rationing was possible in the Soviet Union at a time when the standard of living was at a physiological minimum and an increase in the ration of any food, clothing, or housing accommodation was welcome, no matter what it was. But as soon as the national income increased sufficiently, rationing was given up, to be replaced to a large extent by a market for consumers' goods. And, outside of certain exceptions, there has always been freedom of choice of occupation in the Soviet Union. A distribution of consumers' goods by rationing is quite unimaginable in the countries of Western Europe or in the United States" (O. Lange, *On the Economics of Socialism*, Benjamin Lippencott, ed. [Minneapolis: University of Minnesota Press, 1938], p. 95).

29

Modeling the Industrial Buying Process

Frederick E. Webster, Jr.

The aim of the industrial marketer is to influence the industrial buying process to his advantage. To accomplish this objective, he tries to create an awareness of his product offering, and to develop favorable attitudes toward his offering at certain key points within the buying organization. For a favored competitive position, the marketer must offer a combination of product quality, service, and price which provides the most effective solution to customer company problems. The success of the marketer's efforts depends upon his understanding of how the buying decision is made, including the location of responsibility and authority for buying, the processes by which alternatives are identified and decision criteria are established, and how alternatives are evaluated and selected.

Industrial buying decisions are made by individuals functioning as part of an organization. To understand the industrial buying process, therefore, one must study both individual and organizational decision making. Virtually all studies of industrial buying patterns and processes have been of the descriptive case study variety. With a few notable exceptions (see References 3, 4, 5, and 8) there has been no attempt to analyze the industrial buying process, i.e., to identify and assign priorities to the variables which are important in the buying decision and to find causal relationships among them. This article presents an analytical description of the industrial buying process, an identification of the critical variables, and some statements about their interrelationships. By advancing a four-part descriptive mode, a way of viewing the industrial buying process is suggested which has been found useful as a guide to research in industrial marketing.

While this model of the industrial buying process has not been tested empirically for its descriptive validity or predictive ability, it is based upon

Reprinted from Frederick E. Webster, Jr., "Modeling the Industrial Buying Process," in the *Journal of Marketing Research,* Vol. 2 (November 1965), pp. 370–76, published by the American Marketing Association.

interviews with approximately 135 individuals in 75 companies, representing a cross-section of organizational responsibilities and SIC classifications. The model has not been developed as a vehicle for presenting research findings, but as an expository device which attempts to structure the buying process in a manner which suggests specific research needs and opportunities. As a general model, it may also be productive of insights into the buying process which have significance for the marketer by highlighting the need for particular kinds of information as the basis for strategy decisions.

PROBLEMS IN DESCRIPTION, ANALYSIS, AND GENERALIZATION

To be effective, an industrial marketing program must mesh closely with the buying process of the customer organization. It would be convenient if similar buying processes were used by all customers or even by those customers in a particular segment. Such is not the case. Available research evidence strongly suggests that prevailing generalizations about buying patterns characterizing particular industry segments or types of companies are likely to be misleading. For example, during participation in a recent study of the markets for a particular group of chemical products, not only were eight distinct market segments (classified on the basis of products bought and industry affiliation) found, but within each segment there were from two to five subsegments each of which followed markedly different purchasing patterns. These subsegments were identified on the basis of the organizational responsibilities of the people who actively participated in the buying process. In one subsegment, the purchasing agent exercised the major influence, but relied heavily upon laboratory personnel for analysis and recommendations. In another subsegment, major influence was exercised by the foreman of the production process who relied upon production engineering for advice and recommendations.

Unfortunately, no consistent and predictable relationship has been found to exist between particular subsegments in terms of who influences the decision process and more tangible descriptive variables, such as size of company or the customer company's industry affiliation. The strongest research findings are still incomplete. For example, one of the studies revealed that as reciprocity becomes more important, top management becomes more actively involved, technical people become less involved and a bias is created against technological innovation in purchased products. The direction of causation is uncertain. Does reciprocity cause bias against innovation, or is the lack of an innovative attitude conducive to reciprocity? Or, is there a common underlying element in both, such as a low tolerance of risk? What factors in an organization contribute to low tolerance of risk? In short, available research is more productive of questions than answers.

The problem may be that *too much* is "known" about industrial buying. There is probably little information of a descriptive and factual nature about the details and nuances of the industrial buying process that has not been reported in one form or another. Industrial advertising media provide a continual stream of studies describing the buying process of those industry segments which are their audiences. A conceptual structure is lacking to provide direction to research and analysis, and much of the research is, therefore, duplicative. Without an analytical structure it is difficult to identify the critical factors and relationships which need explanation.

The first step in building an analytical structure, or model, is to simplify the problem so that it is manageable. Any model is nothing more than a simplified representation of a more complex situation, and is an attempt to state the variables which will affect the situation being studied (see Ref. 1). Preliminary research results suggest a dissection of the industrial buying process into four elements: (1) problem recognition; (2) organizational assignment of buying responsibility and authority; (3) search procedures for identifyng product offerings and for establishing selection criteria; and (4) choice procedures for evaluating and selecting among alternatives.

The following section attempts to describe some dimensions of the four elements of the buying process. There is no attempt to describe all of the details and ramifications which characterize each stage. Several generalizations are advanced, but these may not be valid for all industrial buying situations. Nonetheless, it is possible to make some statements about the nature of the buying process in terms broader than those applying to a particular company. While these statements provide shaky ground upon which to build a marketing strategy, they may be productive of insights into the nature of the buying process for both the researcher and the practitioner.

PROBLEM RECOGNITION

Industrial organizations purchase goods and services to solve a particular problem. While there is little that could be called impulse buying in industrial organization, there appears to be more subjective evaluation and persuasion in the industrial buying process than some writers have indicated. To view the industrial buying process as completely objective and rational is to ignore the essential fact that industrial buyer-seller relationships involve interaction among people. Likewise, some companies may buy goods and services because of something like pride of possession, just as an individual may buy a new car when he does not really need one. The company-owned computer, the modern glass and steel office building, the services of a consultant, and the "institutional" advertisement in a prestigious business publication all may be purchased for reasons not related to strict economic considerations.

However, most purchases are made in response to a particular need or problem which can be solved by the purchase of products or services, a buying situation. Industrial customers are concerned with profits and budgets. A company cannot spend a large sum of money, regardless of the benefits which might be derived, if it does not have (or cannot obtain) the money. Furthermore, if the industrial marketer cannot persuade his potential customers that the purchase of his offering can result in greater profits, either through reducing costs or providing the opportunity for greater revenues, he stands little chance of making the sale.

Industrial organizations develop an awareness of the need to buy products from outside vendors in a wide variety of ways. While much additional research is needed on the problem-recognition process, the following factors have been found to create buying situations:

1. Regularly scheduled review of vendor performance
2. The initiative of product development and design departments
3. The marketing initiative of potential suppliers
4. Difficulty in maintaining the production process due to slow delivery, inadequate quality control, or unavailability of desired quantities from present suppliers
5. Value analysis programs
6. New construction, or renovation of existing facilities
7. Reaching reorder points for items purchased routinely

Problem recognition can be rephrased as dissatisfaction with the present level of goal attainment. Like consumer marketing, industrial marketing presents opportunities for persuasion and for creating dissatisfaction with the ability of presently used products to perform a given function. That is, industrial marketers can cause potential customers to raise their goals, to expect a higher level of satisfaction. In this case, buying motivation is the result of the seller increasing the buyer's aspiration level.

In other cases, goals are raised by the buyer as a result of his own initiative. The buyer is under constant pressure to do better, to deliver more value, generally defined as the ratio of quality to price. Engineering personnel frequently improve products and methods of production, to improve salability, productive efficiency, or to reduce costs. This desire to do better is stimulated by such factors as new competitors, price cutting, pressures created by managers, and personal ambitions of the individuals involved. Despite the apparent rationality of the industrial buying process, any thorough model must explicitly recognize the host of personal, organizational, and environmental factors which influence the level of aspiration of individual buying influences and bring about reappraisal and redefinition of goals. There is no doubt that marketing efforts provide a major input to the goal-setting stage of the industrial-buying, decision-making process (see Reference 3).

These goals do not reflect the maximum level attainable, but rather an acceptable level. The postulate of acceptable level goals is a major building block of the behavioral theory of the firm developed by Cyert, March, Simon, and others (see References 2 and 6). One of the basic hypotheses of the behavioral theory of the firm is that satisfactory profits, not maximum profits, provide the criterion against which decision makers evaluate alternatives. Individuals within the firm do not try to find *the best* alternative, but rather any alternative that meets these acceptable level goals which provide criteria for evaluation of alternatives.

Thus, the first part of a model of the industrial buying process must be a model of the problem-recognition or need-definition stage. A problem or need presents a potential buying situation when a purchased item can help solve the problem. A problem is generally defined as the perception of a difference between the desired and actual level of goal attainment; a problem can result either from a change in goals or a change in performance. Because of the large number of vendors and products available in most market segments, and the low probability of finding all of them, the use of acceptable level goals seem to be particularly necessary for the industrial buyer.

ASSIGNMENT OF BUYING AUTHORITY

As noted, industrial purchasing decisions are made by individuals functioning within formal organizations (whose functioning is facilitated by informal organizations) which define the individual's responsibility for the purchasing decision on a specific product or products. Preliminary research results indicate that an individual's responsibility in a given buying situation will be a function of the technical complexity of the product, its importance to the firm either in dollar terms or in terms of its relationship with the firm's production process, the product-specific technical knowledge which the individual has, and the individual's centrality in the production process.[1] An individual's influence on the purchase decision is directly determined by his organizationally defined responsibility.

The assignment of responsibility for the purchase decision to a central purchasing department reflects a basic change in purchasing philosophy. Centralization of purchasing responsibility is based upon an assumption that knowledge of the market, *not* knowledge of the physical product, is of major importance in the buying decision. Purchasing agents tend to concentrate on price, vendor performance, delivery, and similar variables which are determined by market and competitive pressures, rather than upon the technical and physical aspects of the product.

These distinctions between product and market variables, and the importance attached to them by purchasing decision makers, are very hard to make in practice. The purchasing agent may be acutely sensitive to product quality as a variable. Or, the assignment of responsibility for a group of products to a buyer may reflect that individual's strong technical competence and knowledge as it applies to those products. Conflicts between the purchasing department and the using department are often the result of disagreement about the relative importance of product variables vs. market variables.[2] Both types of variables must be taken into account in a model of industrial buying behavior. Therefore, our model of the assignment of responsibility for the industrial buying process consists of the following propositions derived from our preliminary studies of the buying situation:

1. The relative importance of product variables vs. market variables in the buying decision increases as
    a) The technical complexity of the product increases
    b) The importance of the product to the firm's production process increases
    c) The number and size of firms on the supply side of the market decreases
2. The relative importance of the influence of the central purchasing department on the buying decision increases as
    a) Market variables become more important relative to product variables
    b) The size of the firm and the spatial separation of its activities increases
    c) The organization assigns specific responsibility to the purchasing department, in a formal sense
3. Conversely, the relative importance of the using or operating department in the buying decision increases as
    a) Product variables become more important relative to market variables
    b) The experience of the firm in buying and using the product decreases
4. Top management personnel influence the buying decision
    a) More, as the dollar value of the purchase increases
    b) Less, as the size of the firm increases

Further research is needed to identify the variables which determine the assignment of responsibility, and to measure their influence.

THE SEARCH PROCESS

Industrial buyers have two tasks which require the collection and analysis of information. First, the criteria against which to evaluate potential vendors must be established, based on a judgment as to what is needed and what is available. Second, alternative product offerings must be identified in the market.

The search process starts with an evaluation of goals. If the present state of goal attainment is satisfactory, there is no need for search. However, even if the present goals are being attained, evaluation of the goals may suggest the possibility of raising the goals and the level of attainment. If the goals are raised, the level of attainment may thereby become unsatisfactory and the search for new alternatives must be initiated. Furthermore, the search process itself may also indicate the need to raise or lower the goals which initially were set in the buying situation. Goal evaluation in actual buying practices is most clearly seen in such activities as value analysis programs within companies, in periodic requests for competitive bids on regularly purchased items ("to keep our present suppliers honest"), and in purchasing agents' seminars. Vendors' marketing efforts, as previously stated, can also provide the stimulus for goal evaluation.

Because most industrial buyers have imperfect knowledge of the market, it is impossible for the buyer to continue his search until he is sure he has found *the* best alternative. This is so simply because he could never be certain that he had identified *all* available alternatives, and therefore could identify that which was best. As suggested by Marschak (see Reference 7), it might be possible for the buyer to estimate the *expected* value of additional information, and to stop the search when this value was less than the cost of gathering that information. While some kind of intuitive judgment may be exercised which resembles this quasi-marginal calculus, it is unlikely that most buyers consciously apply this process. Here again, present data and understanding are incomplete.

The established criteria may not (and probably will not) be the optimal levels available in the market, because the buyer does not have complete information. Rather, the criteria represent the acceptable level goals for the purchase decision to achieve. During the search for available alternatives, the buyer may find that: (1) one or more of the goals is unattainable; (2) two or more of the goals are in conflict; or (3) the goals have been set too low. As a result of this new information, the buyer will revise the goals, thus setting new criteria against which to evaluate alternatives.

Even if search were costless (which it is not) and if the buyer had access to information about all markets (which he does not), the time factor places a limitation upon the amount of search and hence, upon the number of alternatives identified and considered. Most purchase decisions have time constraints, dates when orders must be placed, deliveries received, and when the material will actually be used. Likewise, the buyer has a time constraint in the number of hours in the day which must be allocated over several buying actions and responsibilities. Time is a major constraint upon the amount of market information which can be obtained.

Once the goals have been defined, and preliminary screening criteria established, the buyer searches for product offerings (product-vendor combinations, or brands) available in the market. The first step in the search process is the identification of information sources, focal points for information about one or more alternatives which might be available. These information sources would include vendors' salesmen (both manufacturers and distributors), catalogs, trade journal advertising, company personnel, purchasing personnel in other companies, industrial trade shows, and so on. The procedures followed in this search of information sources are not well understood, and little is known about how these information sources are sought out and used. It is likely, however, that the search process is largely routinized (or programmed) for the individual buyer and that he follows more or less fixed and habitual patterns in his search of the market. These routines or search rules involve selective *perception,* simply stated as a tendency to rely upon certain sources of information and to ignore others. For example, a given buyer may tend to rely more or less exclusively on catalogs for a major portion of his search, to request visits from salesmen after he had identified their product offering through catalogs, and to ignore trade journal advertising altogether.

It also seems likely that these search rules change over time and are modified as the result of success or failure of the rules in helping the buyer to achieve his goals. This can be called *organizational learning.* More specifically, we would expect that unsuccessful search would result in a change of search rules, mainly the consideration of new sources of information.

It is hypothesized that search continues until a sufficiently large number of alternatives have been identified. What constitutes a sufficiently large number of alternatives is determined by the particular buying situation and the search rules involved. (This is an obvious opportunity for further research.) One dimension of the search rule is the number of alternatives which must be identified before the search is stopped. This parameter frequently expresses itself in the size of the vendor list. There is evidence to suggest that one alternative offers enough in many procurement situations. Charles G. Moore, Jr., has conducted some research investigations which suggest that buyers have rigorous definitions of the acceptable size of the vendor list, which usually contains no fewer than three and no more than five alternatives (see Reference 8).

The rules of search may further specify the order in which particular information sources are to be used. From the work of Cyert, Simon, March, and others, it would be hypothesized that the search process would move from the consideration of familiar alternatives, especially present vendors, toward the consideration of new and unfamiliar alternatives. Cyert and March have characterized this as "constrained" or "simple-minded search," which is defined by a tendency to search in the neighborhood of known alternatives and, when search is not successful, to use increasingly complex search and to consider increasingly radical alternatives (see Reference 2). In the case of the industrial buyer, this is seen (from the research evidence) in a tendency to consider present vendors first in meeting new requirements, then to consider familiar information sources such as trade publications and acquaintances to identify new alternatives, and finally to search for new information sources which might suggest new alternatives. One reason for this sequence is that as search becomes more complex, it also becomes more costly.

It would be expected that a large amount of adaptive behavior would be exhibited in the industrial buying process. Both goals and search rules (as well as decision rules) are likely to be modified to reflect the extent of the organization's success in achieving its goals.

While there is ample evidence that buyers do use routine search procedures, a need exists for information and conceptualization on *how* the search is conducted. This need is suggested by the following questions, for which available evidence can provide only partial answers:

1. How do buyers establish or learn routines for searching the market?
2. What is the value of various information sources to buyers?
3. How efficiently do buyers use available information and information sources?
4. What organizational and market pressures influence the rate of search?
5. What is the relative frequency of buyer-initiated vs. seller-initiated contact?
6. How and when are search producers modified as the result of "learning" during the search?
7. What are the specific factors that trigger the search procedures?
8. How are the results of search communicated back to decision centers within the organizations?

There are literally hundreds of similar questions about buyer search which need answers. These answers would not only be of interest to students of marketing and purchasing, but would also have direct applicability for the marketing executive in making a better response to market opportunities. They also would undoubtedly show how the industrial marketing process could be more efficient, with direct benefits for both buyers and sellers.

The industrial marketer's promotional decisions should be based on the process by which buyers identify available product-vendor combinations. Just as buyers are seeking sellers in the market, so are sellers seeking buyers. They will find one another more easily if they are aware of each other's activities. Industrial marketing efficiency can be measured, in part, by the precision with which the two search procedures overlap.

THE RELATIONSHIP BETWEEN SEARCH AND CHOICE

Having identified some alternative product offerings, the buyer must choose among alternatives. The choice process is guided by the use of decision rules provided by objectives, policies, and procedures established for buying actions by management and specific criteria for evaluating the variables of the product offering. *Parameters* are those factors which are assumed to be given, or uncontrollable by the decision maker; *variables* are those factors which can be influenced or controlled by the decision maker. The buyer may assume, for example, that he will have to accept the going price in the market, in which case price would be a *parameter* in his decision making. On the other hand, he might try to change the price through negotiation, thus treating it as a *variable* in his decision process, as a factor which can be influenced (or controlled) by his action. Whether price is a parameter or a variable depends on the buyer's perception of the market.

Decision rules must be applied to real alternatives, however, and it is relatively meaningless to make abstract generalizations about decision rules in the absence of specific alternatives. This position is taken for two reasons. First, it is quite likely that the search process itself will reveal which factors must be taken as parameters and which can be treated as variables. For example, the buyer may find that he cannot change the fact that only one quality level is available (a parameter), but he can influence the price he will pay (a variable). Second, the sequential nature of the search process provides the alternatives with which the choice process must be performed. Consequently, the way search is conducted and the specific alternatives which are identified determine the final choice as much as the decision rules employed.

This is not to deny that choice procedures are firmly established and followed. Decision rules *do* exist; but, because goal setting, the search process, and the decision process are so closely related, it is dangerous to discuss the decision process in the absence of the search process. For example, a decision rule may be embodied in a search rule: Continue searching until a feasible alternative is identified, then stop.

The above points have been summarized by Cyert and March:

> It is awkward to assume perfect knowledge in the theory of the firm, and introducing expected value calculations in the case of risk solves only some of the problems. In particular, Simon and others have argued that information is not given to the firm but must be obtained, that alternatives are searched for and discovered sequentially, and that the order in which the environment is searched determines to a substantial extent the decisions that will be made. In this way, the theory of choice and the theory of search become closely intertwined and take on prime importance in a general theory of decision making.[3]

THE CHOICE PROCESS

The last element of the proposed descriptive model of the industrial buying process is choosing among those identified alternative product-vendor combinations. The following description of the choice process consists of three stages: vendor qualification, comparing offerings with specifications, and comparing offerings with each other. While this formulation lacks completeness, it is not intended as a complete description of how buyers select sellers in actual practice. Rather, it summarizes the important classes of variables which may be considered by the buyer, and which the analyst will want to consider in describing or analyzing the buyer's behavior.

The first step in selecting a vendor to fulfill a given requirement is to determine whether the vendor is qualified as an approved source. A qualified vendor is one approved as a source of supply, based upon evaluation of such factors as credit rating, financial strength, management ability, years in business, size and quality of production facilities, and (frequently) the ability of the product to pass certain laboratory, quality control, and performance test standards. For some kinds of purchases, some companies will not consider new, unproven suppliers, because it is too risky. Others will allow any potential supplier to submit to qualification procedures and, if these criteria are met, add him to the vendors' list.

The next step in the choice process is to compare the vendor's product with the criteria, or specifications that have been established. These criteria would include constraints such as: specific product features and quality levels; highest acceptable price, satisfactory availability—quantities and delivery time; and minimum acceptable service offerings, e.g., installation, application, maintenance, and repair. The third and final step is to compare those alternatives which meet all of the stated specifications and to select one (or more) which provides the greatest value to the buyer.

As a framework for research and analysis, this model is sufficiently general and simple to include most procurement decisions. It suggests the importance of the analyst's understanding the influence of the relative importance which the buyer assigns to three classes of variables—price, quality, and service. Obviously, it tells nothing about the process by which these priorities are determined; that must be a matter of empirical investigation. How does a buyer determine the trade-offs between quality, price, and service? Under what conditions does he simply try to optimize on *one* variable—for example, get the lowest possible price as opposed to trying to optimize the value of the *combination* of all three classes of variables? How does he relate differences in quality level to differences in price?

SUMMARY

With all the descriptive detail available about the industrial buying process, a way must be found for structuring this information to identify the important variables and causal relationships. The model proposed here presents an analytical structure that divides the buying process into four segments:

1. *Problem Recognition.* A buying situation is created by the recognition of a problem which can be solved by making a purchase. A problem exists when there is a perceived difference between goals and actual performance, and can be caused by a change in either goals or performance. Goal-setting and problem-recognition are influenced by personal and impersonal factors, both internal and external to the buying organization. Research is needed to identify the major factors and their influence on the buying decision.

2. *Buying Responsibility.* Buying decisions are made by individuals working as part of an organization. The assignment of buying responsibility is influenced by industry, company, market, product, and individual factors. Some propositions about the influence of these factors have been drawn from exploratory field studies.

3. *The Search Process.* Individuals have more or less routine methods for gathering information for the purposes of identifying alternative problem solutions and establishing criteria for evaluating buying alternatives. Search can result in change in goals, and goals serve as selection criteria. As search becomes more complex and considers new information sources, it also becomes more costly. Cost and time factors constrain the amount of search.

4. *The Choice Process.* The final stage in the industrial buying decision is the selection of one or more suppliers. The choice process is closely related to the search process—the order in which alternatives are identified influences the final decision. The relationship between three classes of variables (price, quality, and service) and the influence of priorities assigned to each, are important areas for empirical investigation.

This model is only the start toward rationalization of the industrial buying process. There is a need for greater specificity and measurement of variables and causal relationships. Improved efficiency in industrial marketing can result from a more effective response to the buying process. For the researcher in marketing, the industrial buying process is full of opportunities. Communication, organization, and decision theorists all have a major role to play in furthering an understanding of the industrial buying process.

REFERENCES

[1]Seymour Banks, *Experimentation in Marketing* (New York: McGraw-Hill Book Co., Inc., 1965).

[2]Richard M. Cyert and James G. March, *A Behavioral Theory of the Firm* (Englewood Cliffs, N.J.: Prentice-Hall, Inc., 1963).

[3]————, H. A. Simon and D. B. Trow, "Observation of a Business Decision," *Journal of Business,* 29, No. 4 (October 1956), 237–248.

[4]John A. Howard and Charles G. Moore, Jr., *A Descriptive Model of the Purchasing Function,* unpublished monograph (Graduate School of Business, University of Pittsburgh, 1963).

[5]Theodore Levitt, *Industrial Purchasing Behavior: A Study of Communications Effects,* (Division of Research, Graduate School of Business Administration, Harvard University, 1965).

[6]James G. March and Herbert A. Simon, *Organizations* (New York: John Wiley & Sons, Inc., 1958).

[7]Jacob Marschak, "Remarks on the Economics of Information," in *Contributions to Scientific Research in Management* (Los Angeles: Division of Research, Graduate School of Business Administration, University of California at Los Angeles, 1959), pp. 79–97.

[8]Charles G. Moore, Jr., "A Model of the Industrial Purchasing Process," unpublished and undated working paper, Administrative Science Center, University of Pittsburgh.

NOTES

[1]The term *production process* is defined in broadest terms to include such functions as office procedures and maintenance; in short, any process or system which uses a procured product.

[2]For conflict to exist, the following conditions must exist: (1) a perceived need for joint decision making, (2) divergent goals, or (3) divergent perception of outcomes. The first is a necessary condition, the second and third are sufficient conditions.

[3]See Reference 2, p. 10.

30

Interpersonal Communication and Personal Selling

Bent Stidsen

In view of the important and exciting developments presently occurring in the fields of mass communication and so-called information technology, the problems of interpersonal communication and personal selling undoubtedly appear somewhat prosaic. Not everyone can program and operate a computer but there are few who would admit to a lack of expertise when it comes to interpersonal communication. Advertising campaigns are usually planned and developed with the assistance of agency experts and subsequently subjected to carefully controlled pre- and post-testing procedures. Personal selling is another matter. Few will admit to ignorance in administering and interpreting psychological tests or in formulating methods for motivating salesmen.

Indeed, personal selling is one of the rare activities for which there appear to be more solutions than problems and more answers than questions. While most of us flounder miserably in the face of the simplest communication encounters, we are perfectly willing to make sweeping statements about, or engage in wholesale manipulations (at least on paper) of the psychological and motivational structure of salesmen. Not even a trained psychologist would feel secure in applying some of the methods of motivating salesmen which are reported in the popular literature.

The purpose of this paper is to discuss some aspects of personal selling from the point of view of communication. The aim is to show that an individual salesman's performance effectiveness is closely interrelated with the organizationally or managerially determined definition of what constitutes a good performance. If, in the course of pursuing this objective,

Reprinted from Bent Stidsen, "Interpersonal Communication and Personal Selling," in M. S. Mayer and R. E. Vosburgh, eds., *Marketing for Tomorrow. . . Today,* Proceedings of the 1967 June Conference of the American Marketing Association, pp. 111–116, published by the American Marketing Association.

a few myths are exploded, then the purpose of this paper has been fully achieved.

1. The role of personal selling in the marketing mix.
2. A general concept of communication and inter-communication.
3. The meaning of selling ability.
4. The role of organizational control in personal selling.

All of these topics are closely interrelated and questions concerning the role and function of personal selling, selling ability, and control requirements cannot be resolved separately or even subjected to intelligent debate separately without incurring the risk of developing suboptimal solutions or simply engaging in useless polemics. The potential role of personal selling in the marketing mix can no more be discussed and established apart form some concept of selling ability than the control requirements can be established apart from some concept of the purpose or function of personal selling. As pre-McLuhanites, however, we must necessarily proceed from beginning to end in a certain sequence even if this entails some overlap among the various sections.

THE ROLE OF PERSONAL SELLING

There seems to be general agreement that personal selling is here to stay as an element of the marketing mix. But occasionally furious debate arises as to the future role of personal selling. On the whole, these debates have generated more heat than light despite the fact that massive opinion surveys have been enlisted to "prove" that personal selling will be more (or less) important in the future than it has been in the past. The truth of the matter, of course, is that no one really knows. But if some of the controversies surrounding the role of personal selling are to be subjected to useful and intelligent debate, let alone resolved, it is necesary first to agree upon a common set of premises. The low prestige of personal selling[1] cannot be argued away by citing evidence of its economic usefulness. If social prestige is a relevant factor in personal selling (and it seems to be, at least from the point of view of recruiting), then deliberate attempts must be made to improve its image in social terms.

This confusion of premises, or basic assumptions, extends to areas other than personal selling and it boils down to a question of whether an activity should be examined in moral terms (e.g., is it right or wrong), social terms (e.g., is it useful or prestigious), economic terms (e.g., is it profitable or not), psychological terms (e.g., is it more effective than other means of communication), physical terms (e.g., can salesmen distribute messages more, or less, efficiently than other media). The fact that a marketing activity such as personal selling can be both effective and inefficient—or economically profitable and socially harmful—at one and the same time, is often ignored in the debates about the nature of the role of personal selling.

The emphasis here will be on the psychological or individual-to-individual effectiveness of personal selling. But, as already mentioned, to resolve the question of what makes a good salesman it is necessary to develop some idea of the fundamental role, that is, the strengths and weaknesses, of personal selling. A simplifying example will be useful here to illustrate the interrelationships of the significant variables involved.[2]

One of the basic aims of all communicative interaction is influence or control. Picture a team of eleven football players all dressed in red sweaters occupying one-half of a normal playing field. These football players will in effect serve as customers whose behavior is to be influenced. The object of the game about to take place is thus to develop a way of controlling this group of players.

One approach to this problem would be to use a form of mass communication. The advertising-oriented manager might ask permission to observe the eleven players in action for a while. He soon discovers that despite the tremendous variety of alternative patterns available, these eleven players tend to use only a limited set of patterns. A few of the players seem to dominate the play which invariably ends with one of the players grounding the ball, say between the goal posts. It may not be the same player who makes the touchdown every time, but the advertising-oriented manager need not be overly concerned. By placing an obstacle at the point where the ball carrier crosses the line he can hope to prevent touchdowns at that point. It turns out, of course, that the opposing team is preparing to ground the ball outside of the goal posts. So other obstacles are placed along the line until some pattern has been achieved which enables the manager to control the situation at least some of the time.

Any expert—an operations researcher, for example—who observes the process just outlined will quickly realize that the problem of influencing the outcome of the game cannot really be solved by trial and error. Far too many games will be lost in the process. So he proposes the development of a formal information system. He launches a major research effort and discovers that the behavior of the players is governed by processes located in their brains. He therefore proceeds to link each player, via electrodes inserted in their heads, to a computer placed on the goal line. He will, of course, have to pause a few years to invent the necessary transduction equipment and other technical gadgets. The computer can now, by means of a set of successive predictions, direct a robot to the exact spot where a player is going to cross the goal line. Perfect predictability has been achieved.

While all this has been going on a sales manager (who also happens to be an amateur cybernetician) is observing with badly concealed disdain. He has quickly recognized that an even better solution to the problem of influencing the outcome of the game is to put eleven players in white sweaters on the field.

The mass communicative approach attains effectiveness largely in terms of the numbers involved. So long as enough resources are available (and the rules of the game are known by the advertising manager) it is bound to have some influence upon the outcome of at least some games. The operations research solution is similarly dependent upon the researcher's knowledge of the rules of the game besides being quite infeasible in other respects. The principle illustrated in the third solution is the "law of requisite variety" developed in cybernetics.[3] This law, simply stated, suggests that to control any behavioral system the variety of complexity of that system must be matched by the controlling system.

With respect to marketing strategy the law of requisite variety indicates that the more unpredictable the behavior of customers with respect to the intentions of sellers, the less effective it is to attempt to reach them by means of mass communication, that is, by placing generalized messages in their paths.

Is it ever possible to predict the behavior of the customer? The answer is a conditional yes. Insofar as the generalized cultural and social rules of the "game" can be known and insofar as the image and utility of some product or service can be related to the process of acting out these rules, mass communication is not only possible but undoubtedly very effective. That is, some products or services can often be related to values, utility concepts, and standards held in common by many individuals. It is, of course, here that marketing research can play its strongest and most valuable role by seeking to discover and explain the rules of the "games" involving the purchase and use of products with generalized appeal.

There are many situations, however, where it is nearly impossible to predict: (a) how a given product or service can be related to concepts and uses familiar to prospective buyers; (b) where prospective buyers would search for the product; (c) who the prospective buyers are; (d) how the prospective buyers will use the product; and (e) how these buyers will evaluate the product. If one or more of these qualities cannot be predicted in general, and if their prediction is crucial for the continued marketing of some specified product, *then* there is a requirement for personal selling.

Perhaps a tentative law of requisite variety in marketing can be formulated as follows: The more varied the values and uses people attribute to a product (or the more complex functioning of that product), and the more important it is that the product be used and evaluated as intended by the seller, the greater the requirement for competent interpersonal communication in the selling approach.

The role of personal selling may, therefore, be described as one of facilitating the matching of product offerings and buyer requirements where this matching cannot be achieved by any other means such as advertising or sales promotion. It follows that one important dimension of selling ability is the individual salesman's competence in matching and influencing the variety or behavioral complexity of prospective buyers.

COMMUNICATION AND INTERCOMMUNICATION

The purpose of personal selling is often defined as that of selling. But this definition is obviously a tautology—a mere truism. What is selling to mean in operational terms? What are the significant variables which influence an individual or an organization to become (or to avoid becoming) a customer?

It appears that the significant variables which differentiate sellers and buyers—and which differentiate buyers from nonbuyers—can be adequately expressed in terms of the concepts of data, information, and knowledge.[4] Data are the words, pictures, and sounds that form the messages which marketers seek to place in the environments of prospective and actual customers. Information denotes the data to which customers can and do attribute meaning and usefulness as guidelines for behavior. Knowledge denotes the concepts and values in terms of which an individual converts data into information.

Data become information to an individual through the process known as communication. An individual's ability to communicate may therefore be taken to involve his ability to take into account and relate to data in his environment. This ability is, of course, both dependent upon and limited by his knowledge about what is and what is not important, true, useful, advantageous, and suitable for him.

Sellers and buyers can influence each other only via their respective abilities to take into account their data environments, that is, through their respective communication processes. There are essentially two means by which such influences can be effected. One is mass communication in which the sender relies upon his ability to predict or anticipate the things people in general will consider relevant and advantageous with respect to the sender's intentions. The other is interpersonal communication, or intercommunication. Intercommunication implies a continually evolving relationship between sender and receiver, two-way communication, and a process of mutual influence over time. Intercommunication is specific rather than general in orientation—particularistic rather then universalistic.

The fundamental characteristic and function of personal selling is intercommunication. Sales can be achieved in many ways, both planned and accidental, but only personal selling can achieve the close and evolving mutuality of means and goals which is crucial to the continued marketing of many products. And the essential strengths to be sought for and encouraged in individual salesmen is their ability to take into account and communicate to the individualized and specific aspects of a buying situation and to evolve with that situation over time.

THE MEANING OF SELLING ABILITY

A unique characteristic of personal selling is that it can facilitate the adaptation of promotion messages delivered to individual buyers or buying organizations who differ in their knowledge, information processing capacity, and use requirements with respect to specific products and services. How then might the significant abilities required of the individual salesman be characterized?

This is, of course, a highly controversial area. Countless theories and plain myths have been propagated as the ultimate solution to the vexing question of what makes a good salesman. Three basic viewpoints compete for attention:

—the viewpoint suggesting that the necessary and sufficient conditions for a good sales performance inhere in the salesman's psychological structure;
—the viewpoint that the necessary and sufficient conditions for a good sales performance inhere in the noises and gestures that salesmen make, and
—the viewpoint suggesting that the necessary and sufficient conditions for a good sales performance inhere in the things sales managers do to salesmen.

The first viewpoint leads to concern with and search for the so-called psychological traits of a good salesman. Is it possible to choose from the general population a certain segment which by definition make good salesmen? The answer to this question is not as clear-cut as it might appear from the literature concerning itself with selection. The key variable in human behavior with which no selection technique has yet been able to deal satisfactorily, is *change*. Human beings are resourceful in adapting to their environments. A salesman who perceives that rewards are based on his ability to keep his supervisor happy will quickly adapt and do just that. Obviously, supervisors can be kept happy in many ways not all of which involve customer relations.

The second viewpoint leads to concern with the development of rules for "how to sell," that is, what things to do and say where and at what time. The third viewpoint leads to concern with such questions as how to select, motivate, evaluate, and compensate salesmen.

In all three cases, each of which represents a distinguishable segment of the available literature, the salesman appears to take on the quality of a robot-like individual—a Pavlovian dog—who exhibits amazingly simple desires, aspirations, and abilities. It is perhaps encouraging in some respects that no one seems yet to have found quite the right bell with which to activate salesmen.

To be sure, these approaches to the study of salesmanship are entirely defensible if the salesman is in fact required to perform in a robot-like manner. If some selling situations can be adequately dealt with by a sort of wandering loudspeaker (and they do work), then it is indeed important that these loudspeakers be carefully programmed and that they have clean fingernails.

But these requirements do not even begin to tax the potential capacities of salesmen. In fact, any rule of constraint imposed upon a salesman with respect to his performance in front of buyers, while possibly serving a useful control purpose, is as likely to limit as it is to enhance his effectiveness. The salesman who works with a prepared pitch may well succeed in obtaining some orders. But the fact that he does so has little or nothing to do with *his* behavioral competence, and it probably has a great deal to do with chance.

To give at least a semblance of operationality to the concept of selling ability two major dimensions have been identified (table 30-1). One of these dimensions comprises a set of categories of orientation and activities involved in the selling task. The other dimension comprises a set of levels of motivational concepts and standards one or more of which may serve as sufficient conditions for an acceptable sales performance depending upon organizationally defined requirements.

TABLE 30-1 **An Outline of the Compact Model**

◄————————— **Direction of Control**

Direction of Limitations ————————►

	Physical	*Behavior*	*Performance*	*System*	*Values*
Awareness					
Adaptability					
Ability to Influence					
Integrative Ability					
Commitment					

Direction

of

Action

Awareness

A basic requirement for the performance of a successful selling job is that salesmen be aware of the function they are to serve. Awareness denotes the concepts or knowledge a salesman possesses pertaining to his own role with respect to both buyers and his own organization. In general a salesman cannot take into account those aspects of a buying system of which he is not aware or to which he does not attribute importance. This point may at first glance seem obvious, but it has certain important implications which are often overlooked in the design of methods for motivating salesmen. It is important to keep in mind that salesmen cannot be "motivated" to do that which they do not know how to do no matter how tempting the carrot.

Adaptability

One of the key strengths of a good salesman is an ability to adapt his performance to the requirements of individual buying situations. If the concept of empathy means anything, it denotes a salesman's ability to perceive the take-into-account abilities of buyers in terms which enable him to present his intentions in a manner significant to these buyers in their terms.

Similarly, the individual salesman's willingness and ability to seek and acquire new and improved skills or competence are closely related to the challenges and opportunities he perceives in his environment. Again, a salesman cannot be motivated to learn that for which he sees no use.

Ability to Influence

The purpose and goal of the salesman's efforts is taken to be that of influencing buyers in the direction of some activity or outcome advantageous to the salesman. It must be emphasized that ability to persuade or influence is not a quality which can be established independently of the person to be persuaded. A salesman can influence buyers only communicatively, that is, by providing buyers with messages which, depending upon the salesman's competence, have the potentiality of becoming useful and advantageous information. Ability to persuade and persuasibility thus go hand in hand and it is probably difficult if not impossible to separate the two in any specific situation.

Integrative Ability

The fact that the individual salesman is an autonomous entity or behavior system is too often neglected in the literature on salesmanship and motivation. At the center of the salesman's behavior is a self-concept in terms of which he acts upon, or does not act upon, the messages which he receives from his environment. One important implication of this is that an individual cannot be motivated to pursue a goal which he perceives as unrelated, or does not perceive as related, to his personal goal structure.

The salesman must in effect integrate the requirements expressed by sales managers and buyers with his own needs and abilities as an autonomous agent. An overcompetent salesman may, for example, develop a feeling that he should be rewarded for what he *can* do rather than for what he is *required* to do. He perceives himself capable of a better performance than is required and has difficulty integrating the actual performance with his perceptions of his own capacities.

Commitment

The direction and quality of a salesman's efforts are highly dependent upon the level of performance standards to which he becomes committed over time. The manner and relevance of performance evaluation and compensation received by the salesman are of crucial importance here in forming his expectations with respect to the characteristics of a good performance. It is important to recognize that changes or improvements in the performance standards to *which an individual is committed* are some function of an effective learning process and cannot, in general, be achieved purely by establishing rules and regulations.

Levels of Behavior Competence

So far the concern has been with the categories of ability which comprise the necessary conditions for an effective selling performance. Each of these categories may be analyzed with respect to several levels of motivational orientation and performance standards (table 30-1).

Physical Activity

In cases where a salesman is required merely to deliver a preplanned sales talk to customers who have been selected for him, only his physiologically determined abilities (e.g., his ability to convey himself from one place to another or to memorize and enunciate the appropriate messages) are relevant variables. Sales in this context are some function of the number of buyers a salesman manages to visit, and performance must necessarily be evaluated on the basis of these numbers.

Behavior

Whenever salesmen are required to relate their messages to the unique characteristics of specific buying situations, the psychological structure of the salesman becomes an important element of selling ability. The salesman is not just required to engage in certain activities; he is required to *behave* in some relevant fashion.

The variables involved at this level have received extensive treatment in the selling literature although primarily from a static viewpoint. It seems unlikely, for example, that the salesman who is constantly dominant, however defined, is more effective than the salesman who is capable of exhibiting dominance whenever the situation requires such behavior. In any case, a salesman's ability to perceive and conceive advantageous behavior is a relevant element of selling ability at this level.

Performance

In cases where a salesman is required not only to transmit a message advantageously to prospective buyers but also to analyze and plan additional ways in which he can best serve a set of buyers, his concepts of a goal-oriented performance become important elements of his selling ability. The salesman's motivational orientation at this level must involve some concept of the usefulness or utility of his efforts with respect to the goal-seeking activities of the buyers under his jurisdiction. He is, in effect, required to manage his efforts with respect to individual buyers or buying organizations.

System

Occasionally a salesman must provide feedback to his own organization about buyer behavior and requirements relevant to needs of the selling organization. In such cases the salesman's concepts of the significant aspects of the buyer-seller interrelationship become important ingredients of selling ability. Much has been made of the fact that some or all of the feedback provided by salesmen is either biased or irrelevant. This would seem to be the case particularly if the salesman does not possess or has not been encouraged to develop a concept of what types of feedback are relevant with respect to the goals and activities of his organization.

Values

Finally, in cases where a salesman is required to seek out on his own a set of customers and to formulate his own approaches to the selling task, his concepts of a strategically relevant effort become important. One aspect of selling competence at this level is an ability to differentiate buyers on the basis of their potential value as customers. In other words, the level involves a salesman's ability to distribute his efforts so as to maximize his own effectiveness.

Summary

The matrix outlined previously (named the COMPACT model in the original study) obviously falls far short of being a deterministic model of selling ability. It is designed primarily as a basis for various analytical excursions into the complex world of selling ability. If nothing else it aids in maintaining a more realistic perspective concerning the motivation, behavior and training requirements of salesmen. More important, perhaps, it aids in maintaining analytical consistency as well as in forcing a more rigorous definition of terms and concepts than has generally been the case in the personal selling literature.

THE ROLE OF CONTROL IN PERSONAL SELLING

The attainment of some optimum sales performance is dependent upon (a) the definition of that performance as embodied in the organizational control system and (b) the agreement between this definition and the actual ability of the salesman to perform.

A balance between the organizational definition and actual performance may, of course, be achieved either by selecting or training salesmen to fit the existing control system or by adapting the existing control system to fit available selling abilities. The point is that a relationship must necessarily be established between the official definition and actual performance such that the organizational control system becomes capable of effectively complementing the abilities and compensating for the inabilities of individual salesmen.

A familiar example of conflict between the organizational definition of a good performance and a salesman's ability to perform arises whenever a salesman "fails" to produce. But rather than leading to some operational means of attaining agreement between actual and expected performance, such failures tend to be rationalized purely as functions of the salesman. One suspects, for example, that the myth that salesmen are born and not made was developed expressly to account for an abnormal turnover in someone's sales force.

Performances are bad primarily because someone defines them that way. And the mere insistence on some organizational definition of performance quality is not going to "make" performances improve. Such improvement can be achieved only be redefining the requirements or by training salesmen to perform within a given set of requirements.

A somewhat less familiar example of conflict between defined and actual performance is that of the salesman who is too competent. Most selection procedures appear to be designed to weed out incompetence, however defined, but little or no attention is paid to overcompetence.

It is important to recognize that failure to deliver a good performance, as organizationally defined, may be a function of overcompetence on the part of a salesman, as well as one of incompetence. Organizational performance definitions are not absolute or perfect scales for measuring performance quality. On the contrary, they are often arbitrarily selected and highly subjective measures.

The point is not that organizational control should be abolished. Rather it is that some important facilitators and constraints upon performance quality lie at the interface of individual performance capacity and organizational performance definition and control. Selection, training, and compensation are means of influencing actual performance, but periodic assessment and adjustment of the relevance of the organizational control framework is an equally important means of avoiding the inefficiencies which often accompany unnecessary conflicts between actual and expected performance quality.

SUMMARY

The purpose of this paper has been to apply some concepts from the field of communication to some of the persistent problems of personal selling. While there are no generalized answers in this paper, perhaps the main ideas can be summarized as follows:

> The role of personal selling in the marketing mix is to develop, modify, and maintain intercommunicative relationships between sellers and buyers where such relationships cannot be established and maintained by any other means.

> The fundamental strength of personal selling as a promotional tool inheres in the ability of the salesman to match the variety or complexity of behavioral competence of individual buyers, to tailor promotional messages uniquely to individual buyers, and to provide relevant feedback to his own organization.

> The level at which selling ability is exercised is a function of the salesman's motivational orientation and conceptual performance standards and the requirements of the selling situation, as defined by the organizational control system.

> To be effective, an organizational control system must continually be adapted so as to retain contact with and truly compensate for the capacities and incapacities of individual salesmen.

The ultimate paradox of personal selling is the fact that its strengths as a promotional tool are also its weaknesses from the point of view of organizational control. Personal selling is potentially the most complex and the most variable marketing tool available. By the same token, it is the most difficult to manage. To strike a happy medium between the requirement for flexibility and the requirement for organizational control is a task which requires the full variety of a competent and human manager. Indeed, when enthusiastic proponents of computer technology suggest that the job of the manager will soon be usurped by a computer, a story comes to mind which the chairman of a major U.S. company used to tell. It was during World War II. Two Georgia boys had been drafted and sent to training camp. Now they were aboard ship bound for Europe. As the ship left the harbor the two men were standing by the railing silently contemplating the water. Neither one had ever been to sea. Finally one of the men looked up and said: "That's an awful lot of water." The other man thought about that, looked out toward the horizon, and thought some more. Finally he said: "Yes, and just think, that's only the surface." So it is with this story.

NOTES

[1] See John L. Nelson, "The Low Prestige of Personal Selling," *Journal of Marketing,* Vol. 29 (October 1965), pp. 7-10.

[2] The following example is borrowed and adapted from Stafford Beer, *Decision and Control* (London: John Wiley & Sons, Inc., 1966).

[3] See W. R. Ashby, *Design for a Brain* (New York: John Wiley & Sons, Inc., 1960).

[4] See Lee Thayer, "Data, Information, Decision: Some Perspectives on Marketing as a Communication System," *Occasional Papers in Advertising* (American Academy of Advertising, 1966). In addition, the author wishes to acknowledge Dr. Thayer's invaluable contribution to the ideas presented both here and in the original study.

31

The Propaganda Function in Marketing

Edmund D. McGarry

The most controversial aspect of marketing is advertising. Ever since advertising began to appear, moralists and critics have complained that it distorted people's natural desires, misinformed them as to the products they needed, played upon their emotions, and led to waste of resources.

Proponents of advertising, on the other hand, have argued that it is an economical method of distributing goods, that it provides entertainment, and actually adds to the value of the goods advertised. The purpose here is not to discuss these issues directly, but rather to place the advertising process in its proper perspective as a function of marketing.

Advertising as used today is primarily a type of propaganda. The essence of propaganda is that it conditions people to act in a way favorable to or desired by the propagandist. It deliberately attempts to influence, persuade, and convince people to act in a way that they would not otherwise act. Propaganda had its birth in the attempt of the church to propagate the faith. It is used by leaders who seek a following in politics, in religion, and in all affairs which require action by large bodies of people.

In business it is used primarily by sellers to obtain a market by conditioning people in the market to accept the particular products offered. The growth of new techniques of communication has greatly extended the range of propaganda penetration, has expanded the number of products advertised, and has increased the total amount of propaganda disseminated; but the aim of the messages carried has been essentially unchanged since the beginning of civilization.

In fact, the use of force of argument instead of physical force marked the change from savagery to civilized living. "The creation of the world," said Plato, "is the victory of persuasion over force."

Reprinted from Edmund D. McGarry, "The Propaganda Function in Marketing," in the *Journal of Marketing*, Vol. 23 (October 1958), pp. 131–139, published by the American Marketing Association.

The use of persuasion is part of man's apparatus to adapt his way of life to change. Without some stimulus to action, man tends to be indifferent and apathetic to change, and unwilling to exert the effort which change necessitates. He prefers to follow his preconditioned routines rather than direct his effort in some different way. There must be some extra stimulus to action; and this stimulus is afforded either by compulsion of force or the threat of force, or by persuasion in the form of the written or spoken word.

PROPAGANDA VS. EDUCATION

Propaganda differs from education in that education presumably is oriented toward the dissemination of "truth"—dispassionate, objective, and unbiased. Pure education takes an impartial nonpartisan point of view. It is not prejudiced; it has no slant. Yet all of us know that education must persuade to get students to study; it must propagandize to get funds.

Propaganda, on the other hand, by definition is biased, partial, and one-sided. It has an ax to grind; therefore, it is always controversial. But unlike education, in which there is no sponsor, the sponsor of propaganda, particularly advertising propaganda, is known. And everyone knows what the sponsor is trying to do, what his motives are, and how he would like others to act. The sponsor of commercial propaganda must identify himself and the product he advertises and he must take the responsibility for it; otherwise, his propaganda cannot be directed to his purpose.

Every advertisement is designed to predispose its readers to a favorable consideration of its sponsor and his product. It is deliberately planned to make its readers and listeners take sides—to affiliate and ally themselves under its banner and to ignore all others.

Advertising is the obtrusive display of the conflict of interests in the market place. It represents a parade of the contestants in the battle for market supremacy, each imploring the audience to follow him. By its very nature advertising must be prejudiced in order to be potent.

THE BARRAGE EFFECT OF PROPAGANDA

Commercial propaganda is a social phenomenon, and its analysis must necessarily be in a social framework. It is, in fact, a part of our culture and at the same time exercises a considerable influence on that culture. Professor David M. Potter speaks of it "as an instrument of social control comparable to the school and the church in the extent of its influence upon society."[1]

Like other types of propaganda, advertising has a barrage effect. Although it is designed primarily to induce people who have the money and the need to buy the product, its effect cannot usually be confined to these. It creates a pattern of thought in a much larger population. Its results are diffuse and pervasive rather than selective. Because of this diffusion, many who are not in a position to buy, read, or listen to the advertisement, and many others who do not see or hear the message directly, learn of it from others by word of mouth.

Moreover, the pattern of thought created by advertising is likely to last for an indefinite period. If consecutive appeals are used, the effect tends to be cumulative both because of the widening group which sees it and because of the intensification of the impression it makes. This cumulative effect continues to a point of diminishing returns which is reached either through saturation of the market, through the counteracting influence of competing messages, or through the saturation of receptivity.

There is another sense in which there is a spill-over of advertising effectiveness. This is what might be called the cross-product influence. It is said, for instance, that when vacuum cleaners were first advertised the demand for brooms increased; the inference is that the promotion of cleanliness in the home leads to the increased sales of any product that enhances cleanliness.

Still another type of spill-over effect is seen in the case of the firm selling a family of products in which the advertising of any one will increase to some extent the sales of other products in the same group. It seems probable also that the advertising of a particular brand influences the sales of all other products in the same use-class, even if they are marketed by competitors.

It would seem logical to assume that, when two competing advertisers attempt to promote their individual brands for a particular use, the impact will be greater than if only one is advertised; and, if the market can be expanded, the advertising of each will have a complementary effect on that of the other. If this is true, then there is a cumulative effect of advertising generally in the sense that, as more advertising is published, there is developed a greater propensity to purchase advertised goods of all kinds. The increase may be at the expense of nonadvertised goods, it may be at the expense of savings, or it may result in greater effort on the part of consumers to secure more income.

Advertising vs. Personal Selling

Advertising today has to take a large part of the responsibility for making sales. To a great extent salesmen, particularly at the retail level, have become anonymous persons—unknown either to the selling firm or to the buyer—who merely facilitate the sale by formally presenting the product and accepting payment. The real job of adjusting the consumer to the product is done by the mass propaganda called advertising.

In taking over the task formerly performed by the salesman, advertising must substitute symbolic language for the personal appeal of man-to-man at a point where the merchandise is itself present and the transaction takes place. The task of persuading the customer is pushed back in time to a point where it can be planned and partly executed months before the product reaches the market. It is removed in space from the point of sale to the business office, where the entire selling technique is planned and developed without benefit of the presence of the buyer. The sale must thus consist of an impersonalized message to thousands of unidentified potential customers, who have no way of communicating their impressions.

Modern advertising has many tasks to perform, which do not arise when selling is done face-to-face at the point of sale:

1. It must create or point out a need by identifying the circumstances under which it arises.
2. It must link the need to the possibility of fulfilling it with a general product, so that when the need arises the respondent will think of the product that will fulfill it.
3. It must differentiate the particular brand and its sponsor from other products which might satisfy the need approximately as well.
4. It must connect the particular branded product with the place and the conditions under which it can be obtained.
5. It must show that the need is urgent and that the task of buying is easy.
6. It must give a rational basis for action, for people do not like to buy goods which they cannot justify to their own consciences.
7. It must stimulate the respondent to make a firm decision on which he will act at a later time.

In accomplishing these tasks, advertising acts under the kleiglights of publicity. Unlike personal selling, where the promotion is carried on in private between two or more people, the messages publicized in advertising are conspicuous and cannot escape observation. This is one of the reasons why advertising comes in for a great deal of criticism that is equally relevant to selling on a personal basis. The so-called abuses which are concealed and disguised in the personal sales transaction are flaunted in the face of the public when they are published on the printed page or appear on the television screen. There is little doubt that there is more misrepresentation, deceit, and fraud in person-to-person sales relationships than in advertising.

The Purpose of Advertising

Commercial propaganda or advertising had its genesis in the need of the mass producer to sell goods in large quantities, and competition of other goods forced him to resort to an anonymous market: an aggregation of people scattered geographically, and unknown and unidentified as individuals. These conditions, and the growing separation of the locus of production in time and space from the locus of consumption, necessitated some means of making an individual manufacturer's product known and thus assuring it a continuous market.

Through the use of propaganda it was possible to create markets that were more stable than their component parts; for, although individual consumers are notoriously whimsical in changing their minds, their reactions in the market as a whole tend to cancel each other out.[2]

In order to accomplish these results the advertiser must use all the tools at his disposal. He must have an intimate understanding of the product advertised and be able to sense these characteristics whether inherent or inferred, which will fulfill the hopes and expectations of the potential owner and user. He must envisage the product in its use-setting. He must comprehend and appreciate the nature of human behavior. And he must be able to use the tricks of his trade—often the same as, and always closely akin to, those used on the rostrum and in the pulpit.

If the propaganda which the advertiser writes is to be effective, it must be expressed in terms in which the consumer thinks, with the same overtones and exaggerations of the product that the well-disposed consumer will attribute to it. It must recognize that the consumer to whom it appeals is but imperfectly rational, that he hates the labor of rational thinking, and that he is sometimes more impressed by what seems to others to be superficial than by the real merits of the product.

RATIONAL VS. EMOTIONAL APPEALS

In a broad, general sense advertising appeals either to man's reason or to his emotion or to both. It is difficult, of course, to differentiate in any precise way between these; but generally speaking rational appeals seem more effective in deciding alternative means to ends rather than the ends themselves. Emotion, on the other hand, is usually the trigger to action, particularly when the actions mean a change of attitude on the part of the person.

There are many road-blocks to actions based on rational appeals; for rational arguments tend to raise questions rather than to answer them. Emotional appeals, on the other hand, attempt to stimulate the individual to carry through impulses which he already has. Assuming that this is true, the rational appeal is likely to be more lasting and its secondary effect to be stronger, because people are more likely to repeat rationalizations than they are to communicate their emotional feelings.

Advertising is highly concentrated on marginal products, things that one can do without, things that can be purchased with free income after the more austere basic needs such as necessary food, housing, clothing, etc., are taken care of.[3] It is these marginal products that give the real satisfactions in life. Even in the case of basic products, it is the exotic, the unusual elements—the fringe benefits—that set one off from his fellow creatures and thus claim the attention of consumers.

The Most Common Motives

Some years ago Victor Schwab suggested that there were ten leading motives or desires of the average consumer to which advertising must appeal in order to be effective:[4]

1. *Money and a better job.* "There must always be some kind of short-cut to getting ahead faster."
2. *Security in old age.* "When I get along in years, I want to be able to take it easy."
3. *Popularity.* "It's fun to be asked out all the time, to be wanted by everybody."
4. *Praise from others.* "Praise from others is a nice thing to get and I like to get it when I deserve it, and I often do."
5. *More comfort.* "A lot of people who are not as industrious or as capable as I am seem to have more comforts, so why shouldn't I spread myself once in a while?"
6. *Social advancement.* "Where would a person be if he never tried to better himself and to meet and associate with better people?"
7. *Improved appearance.* "It is awfully nice to have people tell you how attractive and well-dressed you are. If I had the time and money some people spend on themselves, I would show them."
8. *Personal prestige.* "I am going to see to it that my children can prove that they have parents they need never be ashamed of."
9. *Better health.* "I don't feel any older than I did years ago, it's just that I don't seem to have the drive and energy I used to have."
10. *Increased enjoyment.* "I work hard, I do the best I can about things so why shouldn't I get as much enjoyment as I can?"

Advertisers have found by trial and error that these types of appeals are effective. It is evident that each appeal contains a bit of rationality with a large dose of sentimentality. The fact that these appeals are effective simply indicates that "the average human mind is a montage of hasty impressions, fuzzy generalities, bromidic wall-motto sentiments, self-justifications and sentimentalities."[5] It is out of this "jumble of ideas and feelings" that the advertiser must find a background of his appeals.

More and Better Wants

"The chief thing which the common-sense individual actually wants," wrote Professor Frank H. Knight, "is not satisfactions for the wants which he has, but more and better wants. There is always really present and operative, though in the background of consciousness, the idea of, and desire for a new want to be striven for when the present objective is out of the way."[6] Advertising attempts to present goods which are new or additional in the consumers' inventory of wants, and to indicate how they can be realized. In doing this, it both creates a want and the means of satisfying it.

The fact that advertising concentrates its efforts on changing people's customary wants has given rise to the contention that it corrupts people's desires and stimulates so-called "artificial" consuming habits. But this argument is beside the point for, as Professor Knight has indicated, "there is no issue as between natural and artificial wants. All human wants are more artificial than natural, and the expression 'natural wants,' if it has any meaning, can only refer to those of beasts. By the same token, human wants are more sentimental than real.'"[7]

Most people have always lived rather drab and unimaginative lives. The so-called golden ages of history were golden only to the few. The great masses lived by drudgery, and thought in terms of only the elemental emotions such as hunger and comfort. The so-called "democratic way of life" rests simply on the idea that our present economy is oriented to change the thinking of these masses. Propaganda, if it is to be effective, must appeal to the masses in the terms of their own mental processes.

It is sometimes alleged also that, through advertising, businessmen foist on people goods they do not want. This, of course, is sheer nonsense. There are, in fact, few acts necessarily more deliberate than that of the consumer's action in response to advertising.

Picture the consumer in his living room reading a magazine advertisement. He has had to choose the particular magazine, and pay for it; he has had to select from among the hundreds of pages those he wishes to read, and he can either accept or reject the arguments presented. Assuming that he accepts them and resolves to make the purchase, he must still wait hours or even days before an opportune time arises to make the purchase. During the interval between the time he reads the advertisement and the time he undertakes the overt act of buying, he is entirely outside the influence of the message and may deliberate and search his soul to his heart's content either in private or in consultation with his friends. There is not even mass psychology to influence him. He is a free agent and there is no possibility of coercion, duress, or constraint of any kind.

But the impossibility of advertising to force consumers to buy what they do not want should not be confused with the fact that advertisers sometimes overstep the bounds of propriety to make claims for their products which cannot be justified. In some product areas effective protection has been provided by law, but in general the chief defense of the consumer lies in his own discrimination of whom he will patronize or refuse to patronize.

THE LARGER SYSTEM OF BELIEFS

In discussing propaganda generally, psychologists Krech and Crutchfield state that "suggestions which are accepted as a consequence of propaganda tend to be in harmony with some larger system of beliefs or some already existing predisposition, and therefore presumably with the major needs and interests of the subject."[8]

To put this another way, at any given time the subject of propaganda has many prejudices, beliefs, and attitudes of different intensities. Some are deeply entrenched, while others are at a superficial level. The more deeply entrenched these predispositions are, the more difficult it will be to change them, and some seem to be entrenched so deeply that they cannot be changed by propaganda at all.

Since it is easier and less expensive to modify existing predispositions than to oppose them, propagandists find it expedient to fit their messages into the current pattern of thinking rather than oppose it head on. It is for this reason that most changes in attitudes and wants achieved by advertising are almost imperceptible, and can be objectively observed only over a period of time.

Both in the selection of the characteristics of the product to promote and in the framing of appeals, the advertiser must give attention to consumers' preconceived ideas of what they want. He developes his product and its appeals to fit into these ideas and to project them further. If his advertising is successful in selling his product, competitors will find it necessary to discover other new products or new characteristics of old products, likewise in line with consumers' ideas, as a basis for their counter-propaganda. Thus, competition in advertising tends to develop a constantly increasing improvement of the product to fit consumers' wants, while at the same time it raises the standards of wants in the consumers' minds.

DISCOUNTING THE MESSAGE

The very mass of advertising and the great amount that comes to the attention of consumers is often open to criticism. Critics ask, for instance, "Is there no limit to the increasing din of the market place?" "Will it continue until all businesses are wasting their substance and crying their wares?" "Are there no antidotes for this infectious disease?" We suspect there are.

The editor of *Harper's Magazine* puts it this way:

> Perhaps, however, we will in the long run have reason to be grateful to the copywriters and press agents, even the worst of them. It may turn out that thanks to advertising and public relations, the American people will become the first people in history to be impervious to propaganda. Maybe it isn't such a bad thing that the advertisers and other word-manipulators have got us to the point that we never take words quite at their face value. In all events, it is hard to imagine that the people inured to American advertising would whole-heartedly believe the kind of promises and assurances whereby Hitler and Stalin have enslaved two great nations in our time.[9]

When two advertisers say approximately the same things about their product, the message of one tends to neutralize that of the other, and the public learns to discount what is said by both. In a free world the right to persuade and be persuaded is one of the essential freedoms. We assume that each of us has the mentality and the fortitude to choose—to accept or reject what he hears or what he reads.

Each has the right to act or to refuse to act on the basis of all the propaganda he absorbs, whether it is in the form of advertising or word-of-mouth gossip. That he often rejects propaganda is a matter of record. But we assume that, whether a person acts wisely or foolishly, he will take the responsibility for the act, and that he himself will reap the benefits or the penalties of his action. For this reason he will eventually learn to listen more discriminatingly and act more wisely in the light of all the information available.

EFFECT ON MEDIA CONTENT

It is sometimes alleged that advertising, because it pays most of the cost of magazines and newspapers, dominates and controls the information in these media. It is said that, since the advertiser pays the piper, he must call the tune.

Actually this is seldom true because the medium that publishes biased or slanted news tends to lose its circulation when its bias becomes known, and in this way ceases to be an effective means of communication. Even the most severe critics of advertising admit that this type of direct and overt influence is pretty well eliminated by the intense competition among media themselves.

The effect of advertising on news content and editorial opinion is far more indirect and subtle. Editors themselves are human and they live in the same environment as the rest of us. They, too, are subject to the propaganda which all of us read; and it would be too much to expect that they are not influenced in a general way by what they read. As a part of the total environment it tends to set a point of view which is not unfavorable to advertising.

The Function of Media

From the advertiser's point of view, the function of the newspaper, the magazine, the broadcasting station, or any other medium of publication is to gather a crowd or furnish an audience.[10] Once the crowd has gathered, it must be entertained, amused, or at least interested enough to hold together while the advertiser's message is being delivered. The need for holding the audience arises from the fact that advertising is selective, in the sense that a specific message is likely to have an appeal only to a scattered few among the many in the crowd. As for the many others who have no need of interest in the particular product, they become bored and resentful that their attention has been disrupted.

The fact that advertising is selective in its expectations, though not in its aims, means that its impact on those to whom the message does not apply or who do not care to listen ranges from irritation to exasperation. From the listeners's point of view, it is an unwarranted intrusion on their privacy by some "jerk" who wants to sell something.

Therefore, the advertiser must use every art he can contrive to make his message palatable, even to those who do not want to listen; and at the same time he searches for a vehicle which will capture and hold his audience while he gives them "the works." In rare cases he is able to convert his message into news which is interesting and entertaining in itself; but often there is a trail of resentment left in the listener's mind, and he deliberately tries to develop some means of shutting out the message from his consciousness. The result is that a great deal of advertising never passes the threshold of the reader's or the listener's consciousness.

Although there is danger of exaggerating the importance of advertising in causing certain changes in our culture, it would be erroneous to conclude that its influence is negligible. Advertising is so prevalent, so pervasive, so extensive, and so conspicuous that it would be absurd to argue that it does not affect our attitudes.

On the other hand, the fact that advertising, in order to be successful and economical, "must be in harmony with some larger system of beliefs or some already existing predisposition" indicates that its influence is tangential rather than direct, that it tends to fit in with and supplement other motivational influences rather than act as an independent force.

EFFECT ON CONSUMER STANDARDS

Advertising, both for individual products and in the aggregate, appeals to the anticipatory aspirations of the group.[11] It offers goals of attainment that would not otherwise be thought of. It sets up ideals to be sought after. Its appeals are designed to stimulate action which will result in a more comfortable, congenial, and satisfying life.

Thus, in the aggregate it creats an ever-expanding series of aspirations for the future. In doing this, it shapes the standards of living for the future: and, since man lives largely in a world of anticipation, it lays the basis for much of his enjoyment.

In American business, commercial progaganda is part and parcel of the mass-production process. Our present American business could no more operate without advertising than it could without an automatic machine or the assembly line. By means of this propaganda, the millions of people coming from many nations and races and diverse backgrounds are conditioned to want sufficient amounts of a given standardized product at a fraction of the cost which would otherwise be necessary.

If left without such propaganda as is found in advertising, people would not choose the same products they do choose. Whether they would choose the same product at a later date is purely a matter of conjecture, but it seems unlikely. It it is assumed that without advertising they would choose something different, then no producer would be able to secure sufficient production to provide these diverse things at prices people could afford to pay. This is another way of saying that standardization of wants through advertising is in part the basis for the economies which come through mass production.

In spite of the necessity that people's wants be so standardized as to secure mass production, the enormous market and the high-level purchasing power available in America have enabled firms to proliferate these standards and to offer a wider variety of goods for sale than would be possible even under a handicraft system where goods are presumably made to fit the consumer's specifications.

Incidentally, the assumption sometimes made, that people would make wiser choices if there were no advertising, ignores the fact that preconceived notions of what they want have themselves been formed by other types of propaganda and other influences no less biased and no more rational than the propaganda used by sellers.

As people get more income, and as competition becomes stronger among sellers for a share of this income, adjustment of goods to the consumer becomes finer. More attention is given to the marginal aspects of goods. New quality standards are developed in terms of their psychological rather than their utilitarian values. For instance, people buying shoes are often more interested in style and how they look to others than in comfort and durability, which are likely to be taken for granted.

These types of desires are often hidden and so subtle that sellers are faced with a continuously changing market, difficult to interpret and almost impossible to predict. They are thus forced to offer their products with infinite variations in characteristics and appeals. To the consumer, the opportunity to choose from this vast variety of products is itself a major element in his standard of living.

NOTES

[1]David M. Potter, *People of Plenty* (Chicago: University of Chicago Press, 1954), p. 168.

[2]Compare Neil H. Borden, *The Economic Effects of Advertising* (Chicago: Richard D. Irwin, Inc., 1942).

[3]F. P. Bishop, *The Ethics of Advertising* (London: Robert Hale, Ltd., 1949), p. 48.

[4]Victor Schwab, "Ten Copy Appeals," *Printers' Ink* (December 17, 1943), pp. 17ff.

[5]*Ibid.*, p. 17.

[6]Frank H. Knight, *The Ethics of Competition* (New York: Harpers, 1935), p. 22.

[7]*Ibid.*, p. 103.

[8]D. K. Krech and R. S. Crutchfield, *Theory and Problems of Social Psychology* (New York: McGraw-Hill, 1948), p. 347.

[9]Robert Amory, Jr., "Personal and Otherwise," *Harper's Magazine* (September 1948), p. 6.

[10]See G. B. Hotchkiss, *Milestones of Marketing* (New York: Macmillan, 1938), p. 10.

[11]See Wroe Alderson, *Marketing Behavior and Executive Action* (Homewood, Ill.: Richard D. Irwin, Inc., 1957), p. 276ff.

32

Comparison of Advertising
and Selling

Harold C. Cash and W. J. E. Crissy

Advertising, like selling, plays a major role in the total marketing effort of the firm. The degree to which each is important depends upon the nature of the goods and the market being cultivated. In the industrial product field, personal selling is generally the major force. Here the nature of the goods often requires specific application information that is best presented in person by the salesman. The dollar value of the order generally makes it economically feasible to finance this more effective and expensive method of presentation. Comparable effort to sell a box of soap powder to the housewife would be a ridiculous extravagance. On the other hand, it is likely that personal selling will be used to get this consumer product into the channels of distribution—through the wholesaler or chain store buying organization.

The person-to-person two-way communication of personal selling makes it a superior means of selling every time. Advertising by contrast is only a one-way communication system and is necessarily generalized to fit the needs of many people. Where the unit value of the sale is small, however, advertising is more economical. For example, a full page advertisement in an issue of *Life* magazine, which costs upward of $30,000, will deliver the message at a rate of less than one-half cent per copy. And since, on an average, about four persons reach each copy, message exposure per reader is in the neighborhood of one-eighth cent per copy-reader. A full color page advertisement provides exposure for about one-sixth cent per copy-reader. Of course, not every reader is likely to see a particular advertisement but even if only twenty-five per cent of the exposures capture attention, the cost is minute. Comparable costs of message delivery apply to radio, T.V. and

From Harold C. Cash and W. J. E. Crissy, "Comparison of Advertising and Personnel Selling," in the *Psychology of Selling*, Vol. 12 (Personnel Development Associates, Box 3005, Roosevelt Field Station, Garden City, N.Y. 11530), 1965.

other mass media. Recent figures indicate a total of $31.31 as the cost of a typical sales call when all expenses are considered.

The worth of the sales call and an advertising impression is not likely to be equal. If the prospect is serious and has sincere interest in the proposal, the sales call is definitely worthwhile. If, on the other hand, the prospect is not nearly ready to place an order, a reminder of the existence of the product or services in the form of an advertisement would have been more economical.

Generally speaking, advertising needs additional support, either through personal selling or through promotional activities, to effect the sale. In most cases, its basic function is in the demand-cultivation area. Hence it is more significant in the pre-transactional phase of marketing. There are, of course, instances where advertising alone makes the sale, as in the case of mail-order selling. This channel, however, represents only a very small volume of total sales in any year. To a lesser extent, advertising can help in the post-transactional area of demand-fulfillment by providing a rationalization to the purchaser after the buying decision has been made.

Advertising can be thought of in many ways. Perhaps, however, the most useful perspective to take is in terms of primary objectives. Most advertising is aimed at inducing purchase of a particular brand of product. Sometimes this is referred to as pre-selling, since the aim is to lead the person to the transactional stage even though the transaction itself is not accomplished. This type of advertising is essentially competitive.

There are many things that can be accomplished through advertising. Perhaps the most obvious is to create an awareness of, an interest in, or demand for a product. When fluoride was added to toothpaste, large-scale advertising was conducted to let customers know that the product was available. Concurrently, the sales organization obtained distribution in retail outlets so that customers could acquire the product. It is doubtful that many sales could be accomplished without the advertising program. The alternative to advertising would be to have retail store personnel personally sell the toothpaste to customers. This is not feasible because the unit sale is too low to support the salary and expense of a sales person. In this sense, advertising paves the way for the salesman because, without the promise of a huge advertising and promotion campaign, retailers would not cooperate in finding display space. It has been said, "Salesmen put products on shelves and advertising takes them off."

Less frequently, advertising is used to introduce an entirely new idea. The educational effort may be underwritten by a single company or, where there are a number of producers in the field, it may be the cooperative effort of the industry. Here the advertising is designed to win for the industry a share of the customer's dollar. Again it is a pre-selling activity. Such advertising is often called "pioneering" as contrasted with "competitive" advertising.

Many advertisements are aimed at reinforcing the product name or brand in the minds of the buying public. This may be considered as reminder advertising. It is normally used when a product has a dominant share of the market and cannot expect to attain any marked increase in volume within the economic limits of the extra promotional cost.

Some advertisements are primarily designed to convey a favorable image of the company as a good firm with which to do business. This institutional or public relations advertising is used by public utilities and major corporations which have an important stake in gaining a favorable public acceptance.

It is not unusual for a single advertisement to attempt to achieve a combination of these objectives.

As was noted before, generally speaking, advertising plays a more significant role in the marketing of consumer goods than it does in the case of industrial products. This is particularly true with respect to contact with the end users. However, even consumer goods depend to a significant extent on personal selling to move them through the channels.

When the item represents a substantial outlay and when there are complexities to be explained to the prospect, obviously personal contact is both practical and necessary. Advertising for such goods, however, is often used in specialized media for the purpose of generating leads for the field sales force.

When goods flow through indirect channels, advertising grows in complexity. It may be used to cultivate demand on the part of the ultimate users through nationally distributed media. It may also be used in selected specialized media to encourage the various intermediaries to stock the merchandise.

When advertising is used with industrial products, it has different functions. As mentioned above, one function is to generate leads for salesmen. It is common for the advertisement to carry a coupon. When the coupon is received at the home office, it is relayed to the salesman covering that territory who then makes a sales call.

A second function of the advertising of industrial products is to keep the name of the company and product before the customers between sales calls. Good advertising also reassures a customer that he is buying from a good supplier. The advertising adds prestige to the product, the company, and the salesman, especially when it equals or excels that of competitors.

When a company has a substantial advertising program, salesmen can use tear sheets of the advertisements to good advantage. These can appropriately be shown to both prospects and customers. With prospects, consideration should be given to leaving copies of the advertisements as they create a feeling of stability and solidity with regard to the supplier. When prospects see advertisements, normally in the trade press, this paves the way for salesmen.

In a well organized and disciplined industrial sales force, there will be a similarity between the content of the advertisement and the sales presentation. Thus the advertisement and the sales call reinforce each other.

Many products must be used in a certain way to produce the desired results. Complaints arise when the product does not fulfill the salesman's claims. Advertising can carry instructions on using the product. This will help to insure satisfactory performance. If the product has already been used inappropriately, the advertising may cause the customer to understand the poor performance and give it another chance. In this way, it holds customers that might otherwise be lost.

SIMILARITIES AND DIFFERENCES BETWEEN ADVERTISING AND SELLING

From the viewpoint of communications, advertising and selling have much in common. Both must meet four criteria. They need to be *understandable, interesting, believable,* and *persuasive* if they are to achieve their purpose. There are, however, some noteworthy differences. Communication through advertising is one-way. In contrast, selling is uniquely two-way. There is an inherent weakness in advertising—*"noise."* This is likely to be present in greater amounts in advertising than in the case of the sales interview where misunderstandings can be cleared up on the spot. Whatever the medium being used, advertising must compete with other messages. For example, in a magazine the ad competes with surrounding editorial copy. The message conveyed by the salesman does not compete with other messages, at least at the time of the presentation.

Advertising may be used to generate either primary or selective demand; for example, an industry group may collaborate on its advertising with a view to enlarging the total market. In contrast, selling is aimed invariably at selective demand, that is, preference for the products and services being sold by the particular company over those available from competitors.

From the standpoint of persuasion, a sales message is far more flexible, personal, and powerful than an advertisement. An advertisement is normally prepared by persons having minimal personal contact with customers. The message is designed to appeal to a large number of persons. By contrast, the message in a good sales presentation is not determined in advance. The salesman has a tremendous store of knowledge about his product or service and selects appropriate items as the interview progresses. Thus the salesman can adapt his message to the thinking and needs of the customer or prospect *at the time of the sales call.* Furthermore, as objections arise and are voiced by the buyer, the salesman can treat the objections in an appropriate manner. This is not possible in advertising.

Company control over the advertising message is more complete than over a sales presentation. When an advertisement is prepared, it is submitted for the approval of all interested executives before it is released to the media. Thus there is little likelihood of any discrepancy between company policy and the content of the advertisement. In theory, salesmen receive training so that they understand the product or service and company policy. With the best possible training program, there are two possible sources of error or bases for deviation from the company doctrine. One is loss of memory. Salesmen just cannot remember everything they are told. Also, they may meet situations that are unforeseen, and their reaction may not be identical to what the company management would specify if the problem were referred to them.

There is little a prospect can do to avoid a well-planned advertising campaign. With the number of media available, he is almost certain to be exposed to one or more advertising messages. Buyers can refuse to see salesmen. When the salesman arrives at the premises of the buyer's company, he is subject to the will of the buyer as to whether he enjoys an interview. Thus, over a period of time, advertising will bring the product to the attention of persons who would be missed by salesmen.

Perceptual Similarities and Differences

In terms of perceptual process, there are also similarities. Both must penetrate the sensory mechanisms of the customer or prospect if they are to be effective. With both, careful selection of the stimuli to be presented is important. However, significant differences do exist from the standpoint of perception.

In selling, it may be possible to enlist not only the senses of vision and audition, but taste, smell, and the tactual senses as well. Time and space restraints on advertising limit the number and array of stimuli that can be presented. In selling, it is possible to vary the stimuli and to apply them as the salesman deems appropriate. Actual time duration of an ad generally limits the opportunity to summate and reinforce the message. In contrast, during the sales interview, frequent repetition and reinforcement are possible. In most instances, advertising commands less full attention than does selling. This limits the number of concepts that can be conveyed and places a high premium on careful construction of the ad copy and selection of the illustrations. In the case of the "commercial" on radio or television, few opportunities for reinforcement are possible within the ad itself. The salesman, too, must have a well-planned presentation. However, it can be varied and adjusted as the sales interview progresses. Further, the salesman on the spot is able to re-arrest attention when he detects it is waning. This is not possible with an advertisement.

Cognitive Similarities and Differences

In terms of cognitive process, both advertising and selling are designed to induce favorable thoughts toward the company, its products and services, and its people. Both are aimed at conveying an image of *different* and *better* *vis-a-vis* competition. Advertising is far more limited than selling in influencing thought process. A relatively small number of ideas can be conveyed by an ad. There is no way to check on understanding. In the sales interview, the ideas and concepts can be tailored to the understanding of the prospect or customer. Because advertising employs mass media, the message must often be geared to the less sophisticated segment of the readership or audience. In contrast, the salesman who is effective gears his message to the sophistication of the person with whom he is conversing. Only to a limited extent can advertising carry the person exposed to the message through a reasoning process about the product or service. Instead, suggestion must be utilized.

In contrast, the salesman is able to employ suggestion or reasoning as the sales interview progresses, depending upon the perception of his message on the part of the customer or prospect. In the case of relatively complex products and services, the most that can be hoped for from advertising is a whetting of the prospect's appetite for more information. Questions can be raised but relatively few answers can be provided. In the case of those same goods and services, the salesman is able to cope with problems and questions at first hand. In fact, in some instances he plays an important role as a problem-solver for the prospective customer.

Feeling "State" Similarities and Differences

Advertising and selling both try to induce favorable feelings. In the case of selling the salesman himself becomes an important determiner of the customer's feeling "state" by the manner in which he conducts himself while he is with him. In advertising, too, it is important to induce a favorable feeling "state" or mood in order to provide more favorable receptivity to the message itself. This may be attempted directly within the ad by means of pleasant illustrations, anticipatory enjoyment attending the use of the product, emotional words, phrases, analogies, and comparisons. This is accomplished less directly, where the medium permits it, by the entertainment bonus preceding and following the ad, as in the case of a television show or a radio program. In the case of the printed media, the surrounding editorial copy may be employed to set the mood. Even with these direct and indirect efforts, it is unlikely that any advertisement meets the objective of emotional reinforcement with all those who are exposed to the message. In fact, what may please one person may annoy another. Paradoxically, there is some research evidence from the radio field that if an ad doesn't please the person it is next best to have it annoy him rather than to leave him in a neutral feeling "state."

Selling, in contrast, has a tremendous advantage in the domain of feelings. The salesman in the first few seconds of face-to-face contact gauges the mood of the other person and adjusts his own behavior accordingly. Further, if he detects an unfavorable feeling "state" he may provide the other individual the opportunity to vent his feelings, or he may, in an extreme case, decide to withdraw and call on a more favorable occasion. This option is not open to the advertiser.

Advertising permits the firm far less control over the ultimate buying decision than does selling. The person exposed to the ad may turn the page or spin the dial, or walk out of the room. In contrast, once a salesman has gained entry, if he is effective, he is likely to be able to make a reasonably full presentation of the sales message.

Transactional Similarities and Differences

If the market is viewed as having the three phases—*pre-transactional, transactional,* and *post-transactional*, it is evident that advertising fits mainly in the pre-transactional phase as a market-cultivating force. It may also enter into the post-transactional phase by providing a rationalization to the purchaser. Only in rare instances does it accomplish the transaction itself. In contrast, selling is of importance in all three phases (see figure 32-1).

FIGURE 32-1 **Relative Importance of Advertising and Selling Marketing Phase**

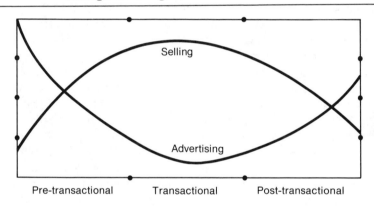

| Pre-transactional | Transactional | Post-transactional |

Advertising may be viewed as readying the market for the salesman's personal efforts. Even with carefully selected media and well-conceived advertising, the strategy employed must be relatively general. In the case of selling, not only can strategy be formulated for each account and each decision maker in the account, but tactical adjustments can be made on the spot in order to influence those accounts.

SALESMAN'S USE OF ADVERTISING

Even though the salesman may not be directly involved in planning and formulating the advertising campaign of his firm, he certainly must be aware of the company's advertising plans, the media in which the advertisements are appearing, and the objectives that are being sought. If this information is not being furnished to him, it is legitimate for the salesman to request it. It can be very embarrassing to have a customer or prospect refer to an ad of which the salesman is unaware. The astute salesman is not only aware of his own company's ads, but he is also obervant of the advertising done by competitors. The latter is often an important input for his own selling strategy.

Certainly if the demand cultivation of the company is to be coordinated, there must be a congruency between the content of the advertising and the salesman's presentations to customers and prospects.... Temporally, the exposure to the advertisements plus the periodic sales calls combine to reinforce the message. From a spatial summation standpoint the ads plus the sales messages bring to bear a varied array of stimuli on the customer and propsect.

Many companies accomplish this mutual reinforcement of advertising and selling by furnishing the sales force with selling aids, reprints, and tear sheets of advertisements from printed media. If this is done, the salesman has a direct means of reinforcing his oral presentation with advertising copy. Further, he is able to leave copies of ads as reminders to the persons called on.

When such ads are taken from prestige media they contribute to the building of a favorable image of the salesman's company. Sometimes local spot advertisements on radio and television make specific references such as "advertised in *Life* (or *Time*, or some other medium)" as an attempt to build up the prestige of the product and the company. The salesman accomplishes the same result with effective use of reprints and tear sheets.

The salesman is in a prime position to gauge the effectiveness of advertising. He is able to determine by inquiry how many of his customers and prospects have actually seen or heard the ad. By judicious questioning he also can learn of their reactions to the ads. This provides management useful feedback. He also may be able to suggest changes that will render the advertising more effective.

If suggestions are to be meaningful to management and the personnel who work on the advertising program, they must be in sufficient detail so that they can understand the reasoning of the salesman who submits them. They should include the following kinds of information:

1. Specific reasons why the campaign was not maximally successful. This should be supported by comments or behavior of customers and other interested parties, not merely an opinion of the salesman.
2. Sales figures which are directly related to the advertising campaign. If advertising mats are supplied, a comparison of the relative use of mats with those of other campaigns may be appropriate.
3. Comparisons can be made with competitive advertisers in the local area. In this case, samples of the competitive advertising should be submitted along with comments.

The foregoing observations should relate primarily to large scale print or broadcast media. In the case of dealer aids and point-of-purchase materials, the salesman is in an even stronger position to offer sound criticism. He can give first-hand reports of the ease with which display stands could be erected. He can report dealers' reactions to the materials and, even better, tally the actual use of the materials. When the materials have not been well received, he can inquire into the reasons for the poor reception and pass the information through the proper channels. It is perfectly proper for a salesman to state his opinion as well as the data he has collected, but to preserve his intellectual honesty and make his ideas more useful to management and advertising personnel he should indicate which ideas are his own and which are opinions or behavior of dealers and customers.

Salesmen who wish to have their ideas considered should find out when advertising campaigns are in a formative stage and submit their ideas so that they can be considered before the final ideas have been selected for development.

Lead Generators

Advertising containing a coupon or a request to write to a box number or to phone may be a useful lead-generating device for the salesmen. An important caution: such leads must be carefully screened before an appreciable investment of time and effort is made. A recent study of leads generated through reader service cards in a trade magazine indicated that only ten to twelve per cent were bona fide prospects for the goods offered. The remainder were curiosity seekers, literature collectors, and high school students.

In some sales situations, an added value expected by the reseller is assistance from the salesman with his own advertising. In such instances, the salesman must be knowledgeable on the actual principles, methods, and techniques of advertising. Usually, however, if this is a job duty, his firm furnishes instructional materials and specimen ads for use directly or with some modification. To the extent that the salesman can convince the customer of the worthwhileness of advertising, he is likely to generate increased profitable business for himself. Some firms encourage their intermediaries to advertise by sharing the costs. When this is the policy, it becomes even more imperative for the salesman to be astute in his recommendations. He is investing his company's money in the suggestions he makes. Ideas expected of him may range from choice of media, size of advertisement, frequency of insert, optimum time, to coordination of the advertising with other promotional efforts.

Where indirect channels are employed, the salesman may be able to use his firm's national advertising program as a potent force in his sales presentation. He can demonstrate as a *value added* that his company is applying a powerful, demand-generating force on the ultimate user which will develop increased business for all intermediaries. This is the "push-pull" effect. In this connection, if the salesman has information concerning an impending campaign, this can become a means of creating increased business in anticipation of likely demand. Inadequate inventory or "stock-out" can be translated into a loss of profit for the reseller as well as an attendant loss of good will by not having the merchandise available when the customer wants it.

SALESMEN'S ATTITUDES TOWARD ADVERTISING

A company's emphasis on advertising will vary depending on the nature of the product, the price, and the distribution of its customers. Salesmen's attitudes will vary with the relative importance of selling and advertising in the promotional mix. One common finding, however is that salesmen tend to become critical of their own company's advertising.

In some instances, salesmen, especially those handling industrial goods, feel too much money is spent on advertising. There is no point in discussing this problem, except in a specific instance. It can be pointed out that a salesman in his territory seldom has all the facts necessary to decide on the proper ratio of advertising and selling. It may be that he is entitled to more facts but that is an internal management decision, not one for outsiders. The best assumption for a salesman to make is that his company has established sound marketing objectives and has selected the right tools to achieve them. If the salesman feels differently, he should offer constructive criticism or, in the extreme case, consider seeking other employment. (Few salesmen have any idea of the cost of advertising per prospect. While the figures cited earlier in this chapter apply to consumer mass media, the cost per reader of industrial media is not too much greater.)

The content of advertising messages is often criticized by salesmen. As salesmen are face to face with customers and prospects every day, they are in a good position to gauge the impact of the firm's advertising. This does not mean they should compose the advertising because, as in the case of the amount of advertising, the company may have some objectives not known to the salesmen. It may wish to use part of the budget to promote what the salesmen feel is a minor rather than a major product in the line. This could very well happen if the salesmen are not informed on the profitability of each item in the line. In any event, each salesman should back up the company advertising, because however little immediate value he sees in it, he is in a stronger position supporting the advertising than opposing it.

Another area of possible disagreement between salesmen and management may be the media used. When the number of available advertising and promotional media is considered (T.V., radio, magazines [general and trade], newspapers, direct mail, transportation [car cards], outdoor, point of purchase, and sampling), it is not surprising that there may be disagreement. Indeed, there have probably been prolonged and exhaustive discussions within the management group before the media decision was reached. There are specialists in advertising agencies to help in selecting appropriate media. The likelihood of salesmen making constructive suggestions in this area of advertising is minimal except for some local conditions which may not have come to the attention of those making the final decision.

SUMMARY

Advertising and selling play major roles in the total marketing effort of the firm. Advertising, however, focuses mainly on market cultivation, though it sometimes plays a part in the actual transaction, and with some frequency, in the post-transactional aspect of the marketing program. The most useful way for the salesman to view advertising is in terms of its three key objectives—to induce an intention to purchase, to keep the product or brand in conscious awareness in the market place, and to project a favorable image of the firm. Similarities and differences between advertising and selling are discussed in terms of communication, perception, thought-process, feelings, and degree of control. Specific suggestions are made for effective use of advertising by the salesman, as well as ways and means the salesman can employ for apprising his management of the impact of the company's advertising efforts, and for suggesting ways of improving them.

33

The Role of Price in the
American Business System

Joel Dean

The basic job of price in the American competitive business system is to do for a free economy what a master economic planning and control commissar does in a collectivist economy. Price rations and allocates inputs (materials, men, and money) to their highest and noblest economic use in producing the goods and services wanted in a free, competitive economy. Price also rations and allocates the output of our economy, using the mechanism of the competitive market place instead of wasteful waiting lines or ration coupons. In fact, the efficiency of our market price system in supplying incentives, guidance, and control is more and more recognized, admired, and imitated by our Communist competitors.

The effectiveness of price in performing these vital functions depends in large part upon the responsiveness of price to dynamic changes in conditions and outlook as regards demand and supply. It is the responsiveness of price which brings about corrective action. The role of price, then, is to adapt our business system to changes in what society wants from it and in what our scientific revolution and growing capacities make us capable of turning out. The function of price is to direct, motivate, and control this adaptation to change.

Pricing decisions, therefore, need to be adapted to changing conditions, of which the following are important:

1. Technological progress is being speeded up by the revolution in industrial science
2. The number of new products is growing by leaps and bounds because of research spending on a vast scale

From Joel Dean, "The Role of Price in the American Business System," in *Pricing: The Critical Decision,* AMA Management Report No. 66 (American Management Association, Inc. © 1961) pp. 5–7. Reprinted by permission of the publisher.

3. The demand for services, both pure and product-attached, is becoming wider and more insistent because of higher living standards
4. The ranks of our foreign competitors are being swelled by the entry of new and stronger members
5. Legal restrictions are being tightened by the present administration in Washington

FASTER TECHNOLOGICAL PROGRESS

The accelerated rate of technological progress has four important impacts upon pricing decisions:

1. The basic discoveries get more quickly translated into commercial realities and have their effect on the pricing of existing products sooner. Greater fluidity and faster communication of research discoveries among industries and among countries facilitate speedy commercialization. The rapid pace of the research race and the specter of obsolescence motivate prompter introduction of innovations. This acceleration is made practical by advances in innovation economics.

2. The duration of the shelter which the product innovation enjoys in its pioneering stages is shortened. The market power of the new product is more quickly reduced by competitive imitation and improvements. The price elasticity of demand for the novel product changes more rapidly. Insensitive to price in the pioneering stages, it can quickly become highly price-sensitive. The period during which the innovator has wide discretion in setting prices is, therefore, briefer.

3. Commercialization of research—that is, the entry of competitors into a field—is speeded up, thereby forcing the pace of pricing adjustments of the defenders. New entrants in some industries no longer need to spend years building a reputation in order to compete with established firms. Successful drug firms have been created almost overnight through technological innovation, and we have seen the birth of whole industries, such as missiles and electronics, in a single decade.

4. The circle of rivalry of a product is expanding fast. In our technologically advanced, affluent society, there are now many alternative directions of spending of discretionary income. Thunderbirds compete with pleasure boats; trips to Europe with mountain cabins. Greater "shiftability" of demand and response to relative prices (as well as relative promotional pull) generally result from this intensified competition for the consumer's dollar. Broad and rapid changes in the composition of demand are likely as a consequence.

POPULATION EXPLOSION OF NEW PRODUCTS

Our scientific revolution drives product innovation forward at such a rapid pace that we are experiencing a "population explosion" in new products. The fast proliferation of new car lines by major automobile producers is but one example of the trend toward bigger product families. Bigger families make policies of product-line pricing more delicate, intricate, and important.

Greater population density of substitute and alternative products is another trend which has important pricing consequences. Twenty years ago, for example, there was a three-way choice in foods: fresh, frozen, and canned. Markets were sharply defined and price differentials generally wide. Today the range of choice has been widened and the market segments blurred by the introduction of frozen-uncooked, frozen-completely cooked, frozen-partially cooked, as well as by the multiplication of grades and brands of fresh and canned foods. As a consequence, relatively small price differentials can cause relatively large shifts in consumer patronage.

Another impact of the product population explosion is the rising importance of "target pricing"—that is, tailoring product and anticipated production costs to yield a specified margin or rate of return. Cited by some as a sign of market power and price stickiness, it is actually more often a sign of intense direct and substitute competition. The manufacturer must prove to himself that he can build a product profitably to sell at a given price, because he knows he can't charge any more and still get volume sales. An illustration of this is the experience with compact cars. Target pricing and profit planning do not, however, guarantee success, but they do provide "birth control" pricing which guides new product planning to the *economic* satisfaction of consumer desires.

INCREASED DEMAND FOR SERVICES

The post-war increase in the demand for services has taken two directions, which are difficult to distinguish at the borderline but distinctive in impact on practical pricing problems. These are (1) the increased demand for pure services and (2) the stepped-up demand for services that are built into products.

Pure services.   As far as pricing decisions are concerned, some implications of the increased demand for pure services are as follows:

1. There are likely to be increases in price, because most pure services consist mainly of labor, and productivity gains will consequently be relatively low.
2. These price increases for services (many of which are considered necessities, such as medical services) will contribute to the uproar about inflation and have far-reaching consequences—for example, increased antitrust activity.
3. Our technological ingenuity has not been able to keep pace with the growth in the demand for pure services. However, where manufacturers are able to find cheaper substitutes for these services, pricing discretion will be, at least temporarily, increased. We need only consider the revolution in educational techniques to see this.

4. Insight gained from pricing and price behavior in pure services will have a carryover to product-attached services. Some lessons to be learned are that underlying shifts in composition of demand are occurring; prices are dependent on the rate at which supply can be expanded; the price of a product should be based on the price of substitutes; and an estimate of the future availability of substitutes needs to be built into price policy.

Product-attached services.   Decreases as well as increases in the demand for services built into products are occurring. Services such as credit and delivery in supermarket and in discount-house merchandise are being dropped at the same time that other services are being built into precooked or frozen foods.

In general, the post-war shift in demand toward a richer mix of services has been a gradual one whose impact has been hidden in some industries by the worldwide restocking of durable goods. Hence, the shift, which is not likely to be reversed, may have gone further than is widely recognized.

Shifts in the comparative advantage gained by providing product-attached services at different points along the processing and distribution road confront sellers with altered risks and opportunities in pricing. The direction is usually toward *more* attached service. Technical advances and economies of scale in production reduce the cost of building in more services. Moreover, because the consumer has more money (and therefore places a higher price on leisure) and because there are more working wives, the value of these timesaving services has been increased.

In pricing the bundle of product-attached services, the high opportunity value of the service component can be fully reflected during the period of innovational shelter from competition. As the market power from pioneered product is eroded by competition, the comparative cost advantage of mass production tends to play a more dominant role in pricing. For the smaller companies in an industry, correct pricing of product-attached services can be a way of existing alongside of much larger competitors who have economies of scale in making the product but have no comparative disadvantage in supplying the associated services.

In pricing, we should recognize that product-attached services constitute a joint product. We should build in services that are economical from both the customers' viewpoint and our own—that is, services that we have a comparative advantage in supplying. We must also price so as to recognize the inelasticity of demand for a built-in service, where it exists. Finally, we should differentiate prices, because elasticities of demand for components of this joint product-service package may vary by customer groups.

A new dimension of pricing is introduced by the manufacturer's discretion in manipulating the size of the service component of his product. First of all, competition in providing services can be discriminatory with greater impunity and greater adaptability to the need of the individual buyer than can explicit pricing. Second, cyclical adjustments of the service component can be more delicate and less disturbing to competitors. Finally, services built into a product are sometimes capable of producing shelter from competition through patents or through peculiar skills which present an unusual pricing opportunity.

THE WORLDWIDE ARENA OF COMPETITION

The power of imports to police domestic prices and impart price elasticity to domestic demand will probably steadily increase. The main causes for the inroads that foreign competitors have made are as follows:

1. The liberalization of foreign trade and the reduction of trade barriers
2. The narrowing of our margin of superiority in productivity, coupled with the wide disparity in hourly wage rates
3. The stimulus to investment in new plants and equipment in war-torn economies in West Germany, England, France, and Italy, caused by highly favorable tax treatment of depreciation in those countries
4. The appearance of new nations which are industrializing urgently. The long-run outlook for American producers is made more gloomy because ordinarily a higher proportion of the gains from higher productivity go to labor in the United States than in rival industrialized nations. This handicap is accentuated by our high tax rates and comparatively unfavorable tax treatment of depreciation.

A number of mistaken pricing attitudes also militate against a satisfactory solution. One is the notion that American technology produces such a wide margin of superiority that we are sheltered from foreign competition and that, therefore, our pricing problem is merely a parochial one. Another is the conviction that the quality superiority of American producers and their ability to adapt products to fit our peculiar needs will always shelter them from foreign competition. Third, there is the idea that passing on higher wage rate is only a problem of public relations—that our prices can go up indefinitely. Fourth, we have the notion that price cuts won't increase total sales of the domestic industry—that is, that American industry faces no price competition and little price elasticity of demand.

Erroneous economic notions like these will be eventually changed by the realities of the market place, but the learning process is likely to be a costly one. New competitors may gain a foothold while management, decoyed by questions of "price discipline," loses time that it should be using to ferret out and deal with the real problems—or at least those that management can do something about—the problems of cutting costs and developing new products.

As far as pricing policy is concerned, the basic long-run problem is a national one. It cannot be solved by the pricing policies of any individual manufacturer. Meeting foreign competitors' prices down to the level of our incremental cost is the indicated short-term response. But it is not a long-term solution: our incremental cost may be higher than the foreign competitor's full cost. Therefore, even the best pricing response will only buy time; and time is not worth much unless either the national response or the cost-and-product response of the individual manufacturer produces an ultimate solution.

For the individual manufacturer, nonprice actions in the form of research, promotion, wage negotiations, and renewed efforts to increase productivity by mechanization and greater efficiency are more important than pricing adjustments.

THE CHANGING LEGAL ENVIRONMENT

The legal setting of price decisions is also changing. These changes are particularly perplexing because the laws of economics lead to pricing decisions or policies which are frequently at odds with the Sherman, Clayton, and Robinson-Patman Acts.

Legal changes are susceptible to quicker reversal than are other changes in the environment of the price maker. Pendulum-like, they swing through cycles: from extended policing by government of pricing practices to periods of complacency, when there is renewed confidence in the policing power of intensified competition to force upon businessmen a willingness to keep their own house in order.

The increased concern of the government is less likely to be expressed by new legislation than by vigorous enforcement of existing legislation. With the intensification of the cold war and a growing recognition of the need to put our resources to their most efficient use, it is possible that Congress may be induced to modify the present pricing legislation which inhibits this optimum use. The Robinson-Patman Act, for example, may deny the consumer, and economy as a whole, the full benefits of well-established economies of scale. Incidentally, one of the critical differences between our economy and the Soviet economy is belief in economies of scale. In Soviet Russia, there is full faith, and no inhibitions, about complete utilization of savings of size. In our country, in contrast, economies of scale are always suspect and have to fight their way against vigorous government opposition.

Paradoxically enough, at the same time that there is increasing competition in industries traditionally oligopolistic, we find greater government concern with pricing activities in these industries. Evidence of this is to be found in the drug and electric industry hearings; the audit of consent decrees, initiated very early in the new administration; and the call to government purchasing agents, military and nonmilitary, to report all instances of price identity to the antitrust agencies.

This paradox is explained by the tendency to confuse the behavior of individual prices with the price level. Holding down the price level is more appropriately the domain of monetary and fiscal policy. Trying to control it through the antiturst division is a mistake. However, it is a mistake of public policy that private business must live with and take into account in its pricing decisions. It must realize that antitrust audits are necessary. A company would do well to conduct seminars in the economies of strictly legal pricing, such as some perceptive manufacturers have inaugurated since the "electrical cases."

A LOOK AT THE FUTURE

The economic function of price remains the same: to allocate input and ration output. But the institutional environment for particular pricing decisions is constantly changing. Price will probably perform its economic functions even more effectively in the future because (1) the step-up in antitrust activities will deter collusion and prevent thwarting of the economic function of price; (2) the adequacy of capacity means relatively large shifts in sales may result from small changes in price; and (3) the distorting effect of sharp movements in the overall price level on the function of relative prices will be reduced.

The need for economically correct pricing decisions will become more pressing. We must face up to the fact of more intense competition where it exists and not be blinded by the "administered price" myth or the "orderly market" myth. Price behavior is determined by the structure of industries and markets, by supply and demand conditions, and not by wishful thinking. The penalty for incorrect pricing decisions is becoming more prompt and devastating because the catch-up of capacity with demand in many industries will compel more competitive pricing. Moreover, accelerated technological progress will create additional substitute competition and hasten obsolescence. Finally, the rising competence and capacity of foreign manufacturers will police the pricing of more American firms.

Oligopoly is simultaneously becoming more common as the structure of competition and less powerful as a pricing force. The combined effect of (1) scale economies, (2) geographical separation of competitors, (3) quality-strata separation, and (4) specialized products will make oligopoly more and more common in America. It will become the typical economic structure of competition in industries where price making is managerially important.

The tools for making correct pricing decisions are improving. Among these are (1) a scientific approach to the measurement of demand elasticity, by controlled experiments and other objective research; (2) economic and statistical cost research and engineering predictions, which can provide relevant cost forecasts for pricing; (3) electronic data-processing and computer techniques, which speed up and reduce the cost of the analysis of both demand and cost data; and (4) new tools and broader experience which are available for market testing of new products and promotional pricing.

34

Multi-stage Approach to Pricing

Alfred R. Oxenfeldt

Of all the areas of executive decision, pricing is perhaps the most fuzzy. Whenever a price problem is discussed by a committee, divergent figures are likely to be recommended without a semblance of consensus. Although unanimity in marketing decisions is a custom more remarkable in its occurrence than in its absence, agreement in pricing decisions is even more rare.

This article accordingly presents a long-run, policy-oriented approach to pricing which should reduce the range of prices considered in specific situations and consequently improve the decisions which result. This approach, which to the best of my knowledge is new, calls for the price decision to be made in six successive steps, each one narrowing the alternatives to be considered at the next step.

Is this method just another mechanical pricing formula? Hardly, for it is my conviction that the quest for mechanical pricing methods is unduly optimistic, if not downright naive. Nevertheless, many businessmen consistently employ almost mechanical formulas for pricing. They do this even though they scoff at the claim that there are reliable fixed formulas for handling personnel problems or making advertising or capital outlay decisions. Certainly, experience has not produced recipes that guarantee correct decisions in any sphere of business. The best of them only apply under normal conditions, and it is most rare indeed that conditions resembling normalcy prevail.

On the other hand, many discussions of pricing present a long list of factors to be "taken into account," carefully weighed and balanced, and then subjected to a process called "judgment." While a specific price is thus arrived at, this does not alter the fact that intelligent and experienced business executives using the method will arrive at widely different price decisions—all based on the same information.

Yet, even if mechanical pricing formulas are the hope of the optimistic, it would be excessively pessimistic to resign ourselves to a *formless* consideration of all the relevant factors and to a random exercise of judgment. Many things are known about the subject that would be extremely helpful to those responsible for making such decisions.

SEQUENTIAL STAGES

In order to organize the various pieces of information and considerations that bear on price decisions, a multi-stage approach to pricing can be a very helpful tool. This method sorts the major elements in a pricing decision into six successive stages:

1. Selecting market targets
2. Choosing a brand "image"
3. Composing a marketing mix
4. Selecting a pricing policy
5. Determining a pricing strategy.
6. Arriving at a specific price

The sequence of the stages is an essential part of the method, for each step is calculated to simplify the succeeding stage and to reduce the likelihood of error. One might say that this method divides the price decision into manageable parts, each one logically antecedent to the next. In this way, the decision at each stage facilitates all subsequent decisions. This approach might also be regarded as a process of selective search, where the number of alternatives deserving close consideration is reduced drastically by making the decision in successive stages. Of course, one could arrive at the same result by simultaneously considering all the factors mentioned— but it might require a computer to do so.

While it appears that this approach is applicable over a broad range of industry and trade, the great diversity of business situations precludes the possibility of its being a universally applicable method. No rigid approach, and certainly not the one presented here, offers a guarantee of reaching the best—or even a satisfactory—price decision. It must be adapted to prevailing circumstances; consequently, information, experience, and the application of rigorous logic are required for its optimum utilization.

I. MARKET TARGETS

A going concern is "committed," confined, and tied down by several important circumstances which can be altered only over a considerable period of time. It must live with many conditions, even while it may attempt to alter them. Also, an operating business possesses specified resources on which it will strive to capitalize in achieving its objectives. For example, a firm will have:

- A fixed production location, given physical facilities, and a particular production and sales labor force
- A set of distribution arrangements through which the firm generally sells, including particular distributors with whom it has established relationships
- Contacts with suppliers, customers, laborers, and lenders of funds
- A portfolio of customers who have a definite opinion of the firm's reliability, and the quality of its offerings and service

These commitments and resources of a firm contain pricing implications. Mainly, they determine the type of product that it can make, the type of service it can render, and its probable costs of operation. What is more, these circumstances form the basis for the most fundamental pricing decision that management should make—namely, the types of customers, or market segments, it will attempt to cultivate.

By virtue of its fixed commitments, then, a firm is limited to the several market segments it can reasonably hope to capture. It has customer connections on which it can capitalize, and it has a variety of strengths and weaknesses that limit its choice among potential submarkets for intensive cultivation.

Two examples drawn from the TV set industry will help to clarify this crucial first stage. Certainly, no two firms could possibly exemplify all situations, nor is it possible for an outsider to explain satisfactorily why specific decisions were made in specific cases. However, these illustrations are intended to indicate what factors management must consider if it is to apply the multi-stage approach. They do *not* describe how management reasoned or what would have been the best decision under the circumstances.

Zenith Radio

First, consider the pricing problem of the Zenith Radio Corporation at the time it started to produce TV sets in 1948:

- This company, which is one of the two largest TV set producers now, dropped out of the automobile radio business in order to manufacture television sets. (At that time, it was the largest single producer of automobile radios, but this business was not very profitable.) Zenith possessed the following resources and was subject to these commitments and limitations that could have influenced its selection of market targets in the TV business.
- It had production facilities in Chicago that had been designed for and used in radio production for many years; its labor force and supervisory

personnel were familiar with the electronics business. The firm had substantial manufacturing skills in electronics because of its work for the military during and after World War II. Zenith could assess its manufacturing capabilities as very substantial, but not outstanding.

• Financially, Zenith was also in a very strong and liquid position and could readily have undertaken heavy expenditures at this time.

• But Zenith's outstanding resource was a distributor and dealer organization that was as good as that possessed by any other firm in the nation. Its dealers commanded strong loyalty among their clientele not only in small communities but also in large cities—a most vital fact in view of the technical character of TV and the great power that retailers wield over consumer choices of such products. Here Zenith was helped by the fact that it had acquired an excellent reputation for quality products in radios; for many years, it was the Cadillac of the radio industry. Zenith management, like all other radio manufacturers who entered the television business, decided to sell its sets through the distributor organization it had already created; its distributors, in turn, would sell them mainly to dealers already buying Zenith radios.

• There were also several other peripheral advantages. Zenith was closely identified, in the minds of many consumers, with hearing aids which were widely advertised as much on grounds of moderate price as in terms of high quality. Further, Zenith started to telecast, experimentally, in the Chicago market even before World War II and had some local identification as a telecaster, as well as a manufacturer. Its products were strongly favored in the Chicago market.

• In summary, Zenith Radio could count on its strong distributor and retail organizations as its outstanding resource, while recognizing that it did not possess any particular advantage in costs of manufacture or quality of product and, in fact, that its behavior in the television business was necessarily circumscribed by its radio and hearing aid business. Zenith's management would have required very strong reasons to choose as its market targets customers who were very different from those who bought its radios and hearing aides.

Under these circumstances, Zenith management might have decided to attempt to reach customers at almost all levels of income. Partly, it could do this by including "low-end" and promotional models in its line; partly because television sets were sold on installment credit involving modest monthly charges; and partly because, at least in the early years, television purchases were spread rather evenly over all income groups.

On the other hand, Zenith management, as its first step, might well expect to cultivate particularly those consumers who were conservative and quality-conscious, who felt a strong loyalty to particular appliance retailers, and who were located mainly in small cities and towns. On this basis, the Zenith customer targets would not include "snobs" who, at that time, favored the Dumont brand and, to a lesser degree, the RCA set. Also they would not include bargain hunters. Rather Zenith's customers would be the kind of people who feel that "you get what you pay for." (Zenith would presumably capitalize on its strong position in the Chicago area by special measures aimed at that market.)

Columbia Broadcasting

Now contrast Zenith's position with that of Columbia Broadcasting System, Inc., when it started to produce and sell TV sets under its own brand name in 1953.

CBS resources and commitments were althogether different from those possessed by Zenith, with the result that the two companies could have been expected to cultivate different market targets. Specifically, in the case of Columbia Broadcasting—

• CBS executives were primarily familiar with the management of entertainment talent and the creation and servicing of a network of stations. Although its phonograph record and Hi-Fi phonograph business did involve a type of production and distribution experience, CBS was completely new to major appliance manufacturing and possessed no suitable distribution facilities whatsoever for appliances.

• In addition, CBS acquired production facilities when it entered the TV business that were of relatively poor quality. The size, location, equipment, plant layout, and employee facilities of the Air King firm, which CBS acquired, were widely recognized as mediocre or below. Many people familiar with that company and with the TV industry strongly doubted that Air King's management was capable of establishing prestige national brand and producing the high quality product needed to support a quality reputation.

• On the other hand, CBS has some genuine pluses in its favor. Its radio and television networks were the largest, and enjoyed great prestige at the time CBS entered the TV set business. Also, by virtue of its telecasting facilities, it could advertise its sets during unsponsored programs at virtually no out-of-pocket cost. It could moreover, get the advertising support—mainly through testimonials from outstanding personalities like Arthur Godfrey, Edward R. Murrow, Jack Benny, and others—for little or no cost.

To what kinds of customers could a firm with these resources and limitations appeal?

One way that CBS might have adjusted to its particular combination of resources and weaknesses would have been to select as its chief consumer market target the metropolitan customer who is anxious to be associated with prestigious figures, vulnerable to advertising over radio and TV, prepared to pay a premium price, and relatively unfamiliar with or insensitive to technical performance features. But this market target would hardly have been very large in the first instance; moreover, CBS management must have recognized that many other firms were cultivating this type of customer.

It would appear, then, that CBS was compelled to select its market targets mainly in terms of distributors and retailers, rather than ultimate consumers. Whereas Zenith already possessed a strong distributor and dealer organization, CBS had to construct one. Only after it secured representation on the market could it hope to sell to consumers.

CBS management must have realized that whatever it did in an effort to win distributors and dealers would also influence the kind of customers it could hope to attract. For example, if it had to extend big markups to distributors and retailers to get them to handle its sets (combined with the fact that its production facilities were mediocre), CBS would be compelled to charge a relatively high retail price for its sets. In turn, it would have to rely on intensive advertising to persuade consumers to pay these higher prices and find methods of making its sets appear luxurious and worth the high price.

In addition to having to accept the fact of a relatively high-price product, CBS would feel pressure to concentrate on customers in the large metropolitan centers, because of the need to build large sales volume rapidly in order to get its production costs in line with those of its competitors. Even as early as 1953, the large metropolitan markets were pervaded by severe price competition among set manufacturers and relatively little emphasis on quality and brand loyalty on the part of retailers. Independent distributors were leaving the business because of great manufacturer pressure to gain heavy sales volumes. Hence CBS could not have much hope of obtaining strong independent distributors for its line in most metropolitan markets, but would have to look ahead to a considerable period during which it "supported" both distributors and key retailers to obtain an organization that would distribute its sets.

Other Cases

Zenith and CBS have been cited as companies that would have been justified in placing relatively little weight on price in their selection of target submarkets. These companies mainly had to avoid alienating customers by charging prices that were far out of line with other companies' prices. Not all TV set manufacturers could have taken this approach, however. Thus: companies like Admiral, Emerson, and producers of private brands were under pressure to cultivate customers who place heavy emphasis on price. Why? Because in some cases they lacked the personnel and financial resources to sustain a claim of quality and style superiority; or, because their experience in the major appliance business before adding a line of TV receivers could have indicated that they had won acceptance mainly among customers who want moderate quality at prices below the average; or, finally, because their chief asset was a very efficient manufacturing organization that could imitate the products of their more progressive rivals at low cost.

Other industries offer clear examples of firms that selected as market targets persons who were not particularly interested in high intrinsic quality or style. Specifically:

- A fairly obvious example is the Scripto pencil, which offers satisfactory performance at minimum cost. Apparently the customers Scripto selected for intensive cultivation were those who wanted a pencil to write with and not for display, a pencil they could afford to lose or misplace.
- Some producers of private brands of aspirin likewise have selected as market targets those persons who know of the fundamental similarity of aspirin quality and who actively desire to minimize their outlays for this product.

These examples illustrate a point that may not have been particularly clear in the discussion of the Zenith and CBS examples: *One important criterion in the selection of market targets is customer awareness of and sensitivity to price.*

II. BRAND "IMAGE"

Once management has defined the submarkets it wishes to cultivate most actively, it must select the methods it will use to achieve its goal.

Success in the market place for more and more products seems to depend on creating a favorable general image (often vague and formless) of the product or company among prospective customers. The selection and development of this image become of prime importance and have a direct bearing on price, as will be explained subsequently. A favorable image is especially important when one sells consumers' goods, but only rarely is it completely unimportant even in the sales of producers' goods. Buyers' very perceptions are affected by their prior attitudes, the actions and opinions of others, first impressions, and early associations. It is a rare firm that can ignore the total impression its potential customers have of it and of what it is selling.

The firm's selection of its company and brand image should be dictated by the types of customers it is trying to attract. Submarkets may be likened to targets at which the seller is firing, and "images" are powerful weapons that can be used to hit the targets.

Almost every going concern has invested—often very heavily—in the creation of a favorable image. Most businesses know what image they wish to achieve and are concerned lest they or their products fail to have a favorable "meaning" to potential customers. At the very minimum, almost every management knows there are certain images that customers might have of it and its product that would prove disastrous.

The type of image a firm can create of itself and its wares depends to a considerable degree, again, on its fixed commitments and resources. With its physical and personnel resources, there is a limit to what it can do to alter the prevailing opinions—for they reflect all that the company was and did in the past. In that sense, the basic commitments limit the type of image a firm can establish, how much time it will require to establish it, and the cost. Even as brand image is frequently an effective weapon in cultivating particular submarkets, price helps to create the brand image. It is for this reason that the selection of the brand image which is consistent with the firm's market targets implies particular forms of price behavior.

Let us carry our original examples a little further. Given the market targets that they might have selected, as explained earlier, what brand image could Zenith and CBS try to create?

Alternative Qualities

As in the selecting of market targets, every firm has only a few *reasonable* alternatives from which to choose its desired image. For example:

• Zenith already possessed a brand image that contributed strongly to its success in the radio and hearing aid business. Even if another image might have been advantageous for its television business, Zenith's management could hardly afford to injure the bird already in hand. Consequently, Zenith would be obliged to perpetuate for its TV line the brand image it had already established in its other activities. As it happened, that image was altogether suitable for its TV set business.

To implement this line of thinking, Zenith would be obliged to establish the image of a "premium" product and of a company that was old-time, conservative, and mainly concerned with quality and craftsmanship. Above all, it would seek to avoid high-pressure selling, emphasis on price, and shoddiness of product. In styling, it could pursue a safe policy of including a wide variety of styles, while being especially careful not to alienate its conservative small-town customers with models too far in the vanguard of modern design.

• CBS faced a very different choice wtih regard to brand image. It, too, could not afford to jeopardize its eminent position in the radio and TV network field, for those activities were very profitable and would always remain its major sources of income. Except for this limitation, CBS had a relatively free choice of brand images.

CBS could well undertake to be the style leader in the industry. This image would be consistent with relatively inefficient manufacturing facilities, concentration on selling in the metropolitan market, and the necessity of charging a high retail price. It would appear that few brand images other than for advanced styling and for gimmicks would have been consistent with the resources and limitations on CBS at this time.

- In contrast to Zenith and CBS, other TV set producers sought a brand image that did have an important price ingredient. Again, most producers of private brands, Admiral, Emerson, and others, often featured price in their advertising and apparently sought to sensitize prospective customers to price. They could purposely become identified as firms that were not afraid to discuss price and that seemed confident they offered better values than their competitors.

Many firms outside the TV set industry attempt to establish a brand image that has a heavy price ingredient. Among producers, one finds Caron boasting that its Joy perfume is the most expensive, and Chock-Full-of-Nuts implying much the same thing about its coffee. Without being explicit, some retailers seem to claim that no stores charge more than they—and, strangely, this image is a source of strength. The retail world is full of stores that claim that they are never knowingly undersold; on the other hand, it is difficult to name manufacturers who claim that their product is the cheapest on the market—probably because of the implication that theirs is also the brand of lowest quality. (Automobile manufacturers occasionally claim to be the "cheapest of the low-price three," but none has occupied that position long.)

III. MARKETING MIX

The third stage in multi-stage pricing calls for the selection of a combination of sales promotion devices that will create and re-enforce the desired company and product brand image and achieve maximum sales for the planned level of dollar outlays. In this stage, a role must be assigned to price. The role in which price is cast should be selected only after assessment is made as to relative effectiveness and appropriateness of each sales promotion device that might be employed. The short-term gains of certain sales promotion devices may entail injury to the image objectives of the firm. Conflicts of such a nature must be resolved at this stage.

Then, too, a firm might achieve precisely the *desired* image and still find customers very hard to get. It is not enough to establish the desired image; it must be an *effective* image. Furthermore, even though a firm may establish highly favorable impressions of itself and its wares, the company and its products must live up to the image they foster. Not only must its product be "within reach" in price, but it must be accessible by being offered through convenient channels of distribution, and must be sold in outlets where customers like to buy.

The third stage builds directly upon the second. The need to conform to the prior decision about company and brand image greatly limits the number of price alternatives that a price setter can reasonably consider.

The marketing mix decision at this stage need not be translated into specific dollars and cents amounts to be devoted to each sales promotion device; however, it does at least call for crude answers to the following questions:

- How heavily to advertise?
- How much for salesmen?
- How much for product improvement?
- How much of an assortment to carry?
- How large an inventory to hold?
- How best to provide speedy delivery?
- How much emphasis on price appeal?

The composition of a marketing mix (arrived at by answering the type of questions just listed) is admittedly very difficult and highly subjective. But the job is facilitated greatly when answers are subjected to the test of conforming to the desired company and brand image and to the firm's fixed commitments.

Few firms can afford to switch "images," usually because they have invested heavily in them in prior years and should, therefore, not abandon them lightly. Moreover, past images persist and blur any future attempts at image building. Although it cannot easily scrap its brand image, a firm can vary its marketing mix within moderate limits and remain consistent with the image it seeks to create. Thus, the selection of an image sets limits and gives direction to the decision about the elements to be included in the marketing mix. In that way, it facilitates the decision and also increases the likelihood that it will be correct. However, it does not isolate a single marketing mix as the only correct one.

Marketing the Image

How might Zenith, CBS, and other TV set manufacturers have composed a marketing mix, if they had reasoned about market targets and brand image along the lines of the foregoing discussion? Let us see.

- In Zenith's case, price clearly would have had to be subordinated as a sales appeal. The company could have placed major emphasis on quality of product, subdued advertising, and reliable service, while placing its product with retailers who would enhance the reputation of the brand. By these measures, Zenith could have re-enforced the image of a high quality and reliable producer.

- In the case of CBS, the role of price in the marketing mix would not have been subject to much control. As explained, it might have been forced to charge a high price; if so, most of its other actions would have been dictated by the fact. It could have relied very heavily on radio and TV advertising to generate consumer preference, and justified its high price by adding externals to the set—particularly attractive styling, an expensive furniture appearance, or special features of some sort. It could not have reasonably hoped to get very much support from retailers who commanded strong loyalty among their patrons.

• Other TV set producers adopted quite different market mixes from those that Zenith and CBS would have selected if they had reasoned along these lines. Some, however, apparently had no conscious marketing mix philosophy and, therefore, seemed to improvise and stumble from one crisis to another. Nevertheless, in their bids for patronage, some TV set producers apparently placed relatively heavy reliance on advertising (including mainly RCA, General Electric, Westinghouse, and Sylvania). Others made strong quality claims (like Dumont and Andrea). Still others placed chief emphasis on styling (Magnavox).

IV. DETERMINING POLICY

The fourth stage in multi-stage pricing calls for the selection of a pricing policy. But before a pricing policy can be determined, answers to the following questions must be obtained:

• How should our price compare with "average" prices in the industry? Specifically, should we be two per cent above or four per cent below the average? And, when we speak of the average, which firms' prices are we going to include in the computation?
• How fast will we meet price reductions or increases by rivals?
• How frequently will it be advisable to vary price? To what extent is stability of price advantageous?
• Should the firm make use of "fair trade" price maintenance?
• How frequently should the firm run price promotions?

These are simply illustrative of the aspects of a pricing policy which management can and should spell out—in proper sequence. By virtue of having made the evaluations and decisions called for in the first three stages, management will find itself limited in the number of choices on these points.

In addition, each company must take account of the valuations placed on its product-service "package" as well as the valuations of rival products by the market segments it is most anxious to cultivate. On the basis of such considerations, plus its target market segments and marketing mix, it will decide whether it can afford to charge much more or less than its rivals.

"Bracketing" the Price

Before proceeding further, let us summarize. Surely, a price setter would be some distance from a specific price decision even after completing the fourth step. We must ask ourselves whether he would not also have covered considerable distance toward a price decision. By taking account of the firm's basic commitments and resources, the images it desires to establish, its decision about marketing mix, and the selection of a detailed pricing policy, has not the price setter reached the point where he is very strongly circumscribed in the price decision he will ultimately make? To illustrate Step Four, let us carry our two main examples—Zenith and CBS—about as far as they can be taken and see what pricing policy these companies might have adopted:

• If the Zenith management had selected the market targets set forth here and made the same decisions regarding brand image and marketing mix, it would have had little trouble in selecting a pricing policy. It would have felt obliged to charge a price somewhat above the average in the market and to minimize emphasis on price in its advertising. Moreover, it could have varied price relatively infrequently to the consumer—except possibly in some of the large metropolitan markets where neither consumers nor retailers are loyal to anything or anyone, except their own pecuniary interests.

In Zenith's pricing policy, the preservation of distributor and retailer loyalty would have figured very prominently in its thinking. It would be compelled to sacrifice long-term price advantages in order to protect its distributors and retailers from financial loss due to price change.

• CBS, on the other hand, need not have concerned itself much with dealer and retailer loyalty. It had none and must have realized that it would not have been able to create a loyal distribution structure unless it were willing to make very large financial outlays. If it had reconciled itself to a not-too-loyal distributor and dealer organization, CBS could have conducted sales promotions and varied price frequently and by large amounts. It could have emphasized price in these promotions, but presumably only when combined with strong emphasis on alleged high quality and superior styling. CBS need not have felt obliged to match the prices charged by its competitors, but it could not have afforded to have its retailers' margins be out of line on the low side.

Since it commanded no loyalty from its retailers, CBS was, in fact, compelled to buy their sales support. This it could do, primarily by offering a higher than average margin. (CBS could also have attempted to solve its distribution problem by granting exclusive privileges to a small number of retail outlets. In the case of the TV industry, such a policy has been used successfully by Magnavox. However, this company had already sewed up the strong quality retailers who were capable of producing large volume. As a result, CBS was shut out of this pattern of distribution.)

Although Zenith and CBS apparently would have been obliged to charge more than the average by the foregoing line of thinking, other TV producers were wise to take a very different tack, mainly because of their different resources and commitments. For example, Admiral and Emerson have tended to charge somewhat less than average, while General Electric has not adopted a very consistent price position.

V. PRICING STRATEGY

It is difficult to draw a sharp line between policy and strategy, but it is possible and useful to make some sort of distinction between them. Policy is formulated to deal with anticipated and foreseeable situations of a recurrent type. However, markets frequently are beset and dominated by *special* situations that basic policy was not designed to meet. For example:

- A Congressional committee might threaten to investigate the company's or the industry's pricing arrangements
- A sizable firm may have fallen into a desperate financial situation so that it was forced to raise cash through a liquidation of its inventories
- A large new firm may have entered the market
- Business may have fallen off precipitately for the entire industry or economy
- The company may have introduced a model that is either a "dud" or a "sure winner"

Special situations like these ordinarily require an adjustment in price—and the formulation of a strategy to guide management in setting price *during the time that the special situation endures.*

There generally are several strategies which would be compatible with the firm's basic commitments and resources, its market targets, its image objectives, its convictions about the relative emphasis to attach to various elements in the marketing mix, and its specific pricing policies. Others would be incompatible with earlier decisions and therefore might endanger precious values. A threat to one's very survival might justify a scrapping of these, but impetuousness, shortsightedness, or avarice would not. Explicit recognition of these earlier stages of the pricing decision should prevent hasty short-run actions that are painful, but quite common.

No effort will be made to discuss the Zenith and CBS examples in connection with the formulation of a pricing strategy. They have alredy been stretched far enough to illustrate the application of the multi-stage approach to pricing—especially in the most difficult stages. The reader might, however, speculate about how, within the framework of the approach outlined here, both Zenith and CBS management could have responded to a great pricing crisis in the TV set industry. This occurred in the fall of 1953 when Westinghouse suddenly reduced its TV sets by approximately twenty per cent during the very heart of the selling season. We may speculate that adherence to decisions regarding market targets, brand image, marketing mix, and price policy would have prevented both Zenith and CBS from reducing their prices to the levels set by Westinghouse Electric Corporation.

VI. SPECIFIC PRICE

Here is the final step—the selection of a specific price. At this point, the price setter will usually find himself sharply circumscribed in the specific sums he can charge. Nevertheless, he usually will have some range of price possibilities that are consistent with the decisions made in the preceding five stages of the price decision. How may he best select among the alternatives?

To the extent that he is able, he should be guided by the arithmetic of pricing—that is, by a comparison of the costs and revenues of the alternative prices within the zone delimited by the prior stages of his pricing decision. Once he has taken into account his market targets, brand image, marketing mix, pricing policy, and strategy, he can afford to ignore everything but the calculations of costs and revenues. *The first five stages of decision are designed to take account of the business considerations which may be ignored if one selects price solely on the basis of prevailing cost and revenue conditions.*

It often is impossible to obtain reliable information about sales at different prices; this difficulty is present whatever method of pricing one employs. But the multi-stage policy approach facilitates research and experimentation into demand conditions by limiting the number of alternatives to be considered.

The price that would be established under this multi-stage policy approach would rarely be the same as that set by balancing marginal cost and marginal revenue. The former probably would exclude, as incompatible with the firm's basic commitments and resources, desired brand image, and so on, the prices that would be most profitable in the very short term.

THE ADVANTAGES

First, this approach breaks up the pricing decision into six relatively manageable pieces. In that way, it introduces order into the weighing of the many considerations bearing on price. This approach, therefore, should increase the likelihood that all major factors will be taken into account and that their large number will not overwhelm the price setter.

Second, this method of pricing reduces the risk that the price setter will destroy the firm's valuable investments in corporate and brand images. Also, it requires the price setter to determine and take into account the limitation on the firm's freedom of decision. In that way, it would discourage the pricing executive from undertaking what he is powerless to accomplish. Similarly, the multi-stage policy approach should militate against a short-run policy of opportunism that would sacrifice long-term values.

Third, the multi-stage policy approach to pricing should be valuable to those executives who are compelled to delegate pricing responsibilities. In the first place, high level executives are virtually required by the method to make the decisions for several stages, which thus limits their dependence on their subordinates. In the second place, as explained, it simplifies the making of a price decision so that greater success can be expected. Then, too, its use should make it easier for subordinates to raise questions and obtain advice from their superiors, should they be unable to reach a decision.

Fourth, this approach to pricing puts considerable emphasis on the intangibles that are involved in pricing—particularly on the total impression that customers have of the vendor and of the things he sells. Price is far more than a rationing device that determines which potential customers will be able to afford to make a purchase. Generally it is one of the most important actions in creating an impression of the firm among potential customers. Especially as tangible differences among rival products shrink, these intangibles will grow in significance for marketing success.

THE LIMITATIONS

This approach does not indicate all the considerations that should be taken into account at each stage in the pricing decision. In other words, the price setter is compelled to isolate the significant factors operating at each stage and weigh them for himself.

Second, this approach does not indicate what price to charge in any specific situation. The most that can be claimed for it is that it narrows down the zone of possible prices to the point where it may not matter a great deal which particular price is selected. As stated at the outset, one must beware of any pricing method that does lead to a single price, for such a method could not possibly take into account all of the special circumstances which are relevant to a price decision and which vary so greatly from market to market and from time to time.

Third, this method does not guide price setters in recognizing the factors that dominate the market at any time and in knowing when to switch basic strategies. Also, there may well be more than one dominant condition which must be considered in selecting a basic strategy.

On balance, then, the multi-stage approach to pricing at best only takes an executive fairly close to his ultimate destination. Although the multi-stage policy approach does not do the whole job of pricing, the part of the job that is left is relatively easy to finish in many cases. Where this is not so, one can only assume that the task would be almost hopeless without the assistance of a method that reduces the pricing decision to a series of relatively manageable steps in a prescribed sequence.

CONCLUSION

The multi-stage policy approach outlined here differs from usual approaches to pricing in two major respects. First, it demands a long-range view of price by emphasizing the enduring effects of most price actions on company and brand image. One might say this approach constructs a policy framework for the price decision. And, second, it allows the price decision to be made in stages, rather than requiring a simultaneous solution of the entire price problem.

35

Marketing Research Foundations for Changing Marketing Strategy

Lyndon O. Brown

Since it is just twenty years ago that the first edition of the book now known as *Marketing And Distribution Research* was published, it seems appropriate to discuss the application of marketing research as a foundation for changing marketing strategy with 1937 as a reference point. Although the beginnings of marketing research clearly antedate this point in time, it was during the trials of business in the depression of the thirties that marketing research first came into its own as a tool for the guidance of marketing management. Today we have far from a full-blown science or practice. However, the strides that have been made in these twenty years are monumental.

Maximum marketing success in today's complex and fast-moving society is more and more a matter of the clear execution of the most effective basic marketing strategies. Returning to the familiar military analogy, marketing management must distinguish clearly between the broad basic strategic decisions consistently followed and the tactical day-to-day maneuvers necessary to meet the immediate situations of the market place. The day-to-day tactics—for example, those conducted by the selling organization in the field or by those responsible for implementing the advertising program, though they have their own values contributing to total success or failure—do not win the wars. Too much of the time and attention of management is generally diverted to these minor tactical matters. But if management's time, attention, and resources, particularly its research

From Lyndon O. Brown, "Marketing Research Foundations for Changing Market Strategy," in Hugh Wales, ed., *Changing Structure and Strategy in Marketing* (Urbana, Ill.: University of Illinois Press, 1957), pp. 94–103. Reprinted by permission.

resources, are too much absorbed in the minor tactics, the major strategy decisions will suffer, with resultant long-run failures. There can be many errors in these day-to-day decisions: the competitor whose basic strategies are best conceived and most fully implemented will be the one who enjoys the greatest success.

Many American business firms today are limited in their marketing effectiveness because management has failed to select out of the milieu of the marketing operation the prime essential strategies which should govern and control the marketing operation. Another common weakness is failure to identify these strategies clearly so that the entire organization has a full understanding of these key guides to marketing conduct at the operating level.

It is the primary purpose of this paper to set forth nine basic types of marketing strategies and to show how marketing research is the essential modern tool of management in arriving at clear and effective policies. In the observation of many different industries, these strategies stand out as key issues on which basic decisions have led to outstanding market success or miserable marketing failures. Of course, no single list can establish a pat group of nine strategies. Obviously, each item has greater or lesser significance for different marketers, and just as obviously, in certain situations there are other strategies which would merit inclusion on a list of nine ahead of others on the list. However, any company whose marketing strategies are sound on these nine items is practically assured of marketing success. Likewise, any company that is wrong on any one of them has a very serious weakness in its armor.

The major strategies selected relate to:
1. New product introduction
2. Product modernization
3. Packaging
4. Pricing
5. Sales manpower
6. Sales operations
7. Distribution channels
8. Advertising power
9. Advertising media and copy strategies

Within the space limits of this paper, it is obviously impossible to do full justice to the role marketing research can and does play in providing sound foundations for changing marketing policy in each of these areas. There would be considerable merit in limiting the discussion to two or three critical areas, thus making it possible to provide a more comprehensive statement. On the other hand, management and research practitioners are constantly faced with the necessity of selecting from the vast area of potential applications of marketing research those specific areas which offer the most productive options in the light of ever present limitations of time and money. This latter condition suggests that a greater value may be contributed by commenting on all nine of the items. On each of them, an effort will be made to contribute at least one new thought or to point out the most basic considerations.

NEW PRODUCT INTRODUCTION

There is no need to stress the importance of the addition of new products to a manufacturer's line to anyone who is at all alert to current market developments. In the midst of a rash of new products coming out of laboratories, obtained by acquisition, or simply put on the market to round out a competitive line, the American philosophy of growth presses every management to the consideration of new products. The general tendency toward economic concentration further encourages the development of broader lines by those companies which are becoming more and more important in any given field. Procter and Gamble introduces a kitchen cleanser and a dentifrice in order to get added volume, to diversify, and to place itself in a stronger position relative to major competitors. Meanwhile, great advances in soap and detergent products are made in the company's laboratories so a new brand may be introduced, even though it is competitive with established brands of the company.

We are living in the midst of a rash of new product introductions, part of which must be a fool's paradise for managements who feel that they can automatically grow by multiplying their brands like rabbits. A continuously expanding economy and inflation, aided and abetted by cheap money, has encouraged managements to undertake this form of expansion to such an extent that it sometimes appears that everybody is now getting into everybody else's backyard.

Where does marketing research fit into this picture? It fits most basically because the launching of a new product into today's highly competitive market place is a difficult, hazardous, and expensive operation. A current example is the introduction of the new Edsel automobile with a publicly stated price tag of $250 million. Even for convenience goods, with more and more emphasis on self-service, customer selection, and consumer pre-selling, the manufacturer must assume advertising burdens which can often run into many millions of dollars. With dealer shelves crowded with a multiplicity of brands and variety within brands, and the ensuing struggle for display space or even minimum representation in stores, more and more product introductions are requiring from two to four years to pay out—that is, to begin a return or a profit to the manufacturer over and above his cost of manufacturing, selling, and advertising. As many manufacturers are learning to their sorrow, after the first blush of success, many introductions in very recent years have merely served to clutter up the marketing operation and to bleed established products of much of their profit returns.

Twenty years ago, the launching of a new product was a relatively easy, low-cost matter, and marketing research played little or no part. For the modern manufacturer to decide to launch a new product on the basis of his judgment, experience, and a few scraps of data regarding production costs is unthinkable. Marketing research is the tool which provides a cold appraisal of the potential market, a realistic forecast of competitive shares, and the total marketing cost mechanics to establish the brand which can provide a foundation for an intelligent decision. To take only one specific phase by way of illustration, the effect of an additional brand on the volumes and profits of present brands is a question which must be answered, and it is marketing research alone which can provide the answer.

PRODUCT MODERNIZATION

Another situation faced in today's fast-moving society is the necessity for continual improvement of established products. Twenty years ago frequent product changes were associated largely with mechanical products, such as automobiles and refrigerators, or with commodities subject to the whims of fashion. Today, the most common of products, such as dentifrices, cereals, and chewing gum, are subject to constant review and revitalization in order that they may meet the current desires of buyers more effectively. Mechanical engineering developments coming from the laboratories forced constant change in the former category; an increased sensitivity of consumers to more subtle factors of color, shape, convenience, and flavor extended continuous product improvement to the latter category.

Twenty years ago product changes were largely dictated by the laboratories, and marketing research was making only a few isolated contributions. For either type of product, marketing research now complements the enthusiasm of the laboratory scientist or product development engineer and replaces the guesswork and judgment of the management executive. There are several reasons why marketing research is an essential tool for changing strategies in product design. One is the tremendous sensitivity of the buying public to extremely minor changes in characteristics such as color, shape, or flavor. For example, a slight change in the flavor of one brand of coffee was clearly the key to a major increase in consumer demand. One common indication of the high discrimination of consumers frequently appears when a substitute material is introduced in a product in order to achieve a saving in production costs. Time and time again, the laboratory technicians and panels of experts have decreed that "there is no difference," but the consumers have detected a difference and rejected the changed product. Another reason why product testing in the market is essential is that the differences in quality of competing products have vastly narrowed in recent years. Most of the leading brands in a given field are high-quality products and very similar to one another. The burden on marketing managements is to get every conceivable advantage in product acceptability, yet to avoid a potentially deadly error in product change. To ensure that the proposed new variation has optimum chances of marketing success is a job for marketing research.

PACKAGING

With the growth of self-service, the higher aesthetic taste levels of the public, and a social order constantly seeking new things, the importance of the packaging as a marketing factor has vastly increased. "Modernization" of a package can be a basic marketing strategy with the power to make a major contribution to marketing success. The rising importance of the package-design specialists is only one evidence. But the marketing decisions between alternative creative package designs can no longer be entrusted to the joint judgment of the creative designer and marketing management, as they largely were twenty years ago.

Here, too marketing research can provide the only certain answers regarding shelf efficiency and consumer acceptance of alternative designs. Laboratory tests of comprehensibility, visibility, and so on are important, but marketing tests under actual buying conditions and consumer acceptability research are essential ingredients to sound final decisions. Incidentally, a great deal of progress has been made in the development of more accurate and subtle techniques for marketing research applied to package design. The "unconscious level testing" of proposed packages by Louis Cheskin is an example.[1]

PRICING

There is no need to stress the importance of pricing as a marketing strategy. Opportunities for increasing sales and profits through price changes in the market place are constantly present. Furthermore, there is no need to review the literature, such as the writings of Joel Dean, which clearly establishes that pricing methods employed by most companies are illogical and antiquated.

Marketing research has one of its outstanding opportunities to contribute to sound marketing policy in the pricing area. The challenge to marketing research is simply that of translating the economic principle of elasticity of demand into the current realities of the market place through carefully controlled experimentation. The failure of marketing research to accomplish this to any significant degree is its outstanding failure of the past twenty years. It is my belief that this failure has been primarily one of inability to sell management on the importance of putting adequate time and money into getting the right pricing answers rather than any lack of adequate techniques. If there is one challenge that I hope will be met during the next twenty years, it is that marketing research will establish itself as the accepted tool for management to use in guiding its pricing strategies. In addition to filling a big void, such a development would place all marketing research on a higher plane in executive thinking, because it would have a precise and concrete character. Meanwhile, marketing research is making significant contributions to changing price strategies through analysis of store audit data.[2] But the big victory will be won when marketing research, by controlled experimentation, becomes the standard basis for pricing strategy.

SALES MANPOWER

Personal selling is employed to a considerable extent in the marketing of nearly all commodities. Most companies follow tradition or work within the limits of their profit and loss situation in determining the degree to which they rely on sales manpower for producing the total marketing result. But if we take the broad view of social and economic changes over the past twenty years, we can readily see that a much sounder base, the kind that can only be produced by marketing research, must be provided to marketing management as decisions are called for in this area. The rapidly rising wage levels, the trend to shorter hours of work, unionization, and the tendency of all classes of workers to resist pressures from above make personal selling in all fields a progressively less efficient marketing method. Meanwhile, the rising volume of mass selling in the form of advertising directed at the ultimate buyer with the resulting more important role of presold brand preferences is rapidly eroding the need for personal selling in many areas. Even in the automobile business, where salesmanship has traditionally been the keystone of the marketing arch, personal selling at the retail level is approaching zero as a demand creator while the influence of brand preselection is occupying a position which was unbelievable twenty years ago. We all realize that the shortages of World War II provided the catalyst which temporarily removed the need for personal selling. Although there was much talk regarding the need for rebuilding sales organizations and training a new crop of salesmen when things got back to normal, we have discovered in fact that personal selling will never again fill the role that it did twenty years ago.

There are many large and successful manufacturers, leaders in their fields, who literally have no sales force. Competing against them, we find companies carrying heavy expenses for personal selling. We find companies with few or no salesmen fairly common in the drug field today; yet in the food field, with a basically similar marketing structure, we find many companies still carrying huge cost burdens of personal selling in spite of manifest changes at the retail level pointing to greater emphasis on consumer demand as a determinant in marketing success.

Here is an area in which marketing research today faces another major challenge. Certainly the reduction or elimination of a sales force represents a major change in marketing strategy, one which cannot be left to hunch or guesswork. Marketing research which can guide management to the optimum decision in this area will give it a tremendous competitive advantage over others who are bumbling along.

SALES OPERATIONS

While the general trend for the next twenty years will undoubtedly be toward de-emphasizing personal selling, it is equally apparent that personal selling will continue to play a major role in marketing. Twenty years ago, the control and guidance of a selling organization was largely based on an apprenticeship system. The sales manager rose from the ranks and operated on the basis of his experience, judgment, personal skills, and enthusiasm. As individual sales organizations have grown and become more complex, it is no longer possible to get the greatest efficiency on such a personal basis. Marketing research today can play a major role in laying a foundation for more effective sales control. An outstanding example is the time and duty analysis of salesmen's activities, pioneered by Herman Nolen's work at Ohio State University. Here we have one of the best examples of engineering principles applied to marketing by marketing research. Sales control through statistical analysis of sales and market data is another major application of marketing research. The company that does not have this type of research guidance for planning marketing strategies is very rare today.

DISTRIBUTION CHANNELS

Management decision regarding the selection and activation of distribution channels is clearly a major contributor to marketing success or failure. These channels are in a state of constant flux, and those marketers who have kept in tune with the changing importance of various types of distributive mechanisms have gained tremendous competitive advantages. On the one hand, we have seen many historical instances where beating competitors to the gun by concentrating marketing actions on new or growing channels can be pointed to as a primary key to marketing success. On the other hand, as recently as 1957 I discovered that the primary marketing handicap of a leading concern in a major industry lay in its weakness in a dominant channel of distribution, a weakness which existed purely because of the management's total ignorance regarding the importance of that channel. Casual observation is inadequate to keep a company on its toes with respect to changes in the importance and characteristics of sales channels. Only through organized marketing research can today's management be adequately alerted and clearly guided in its distribution strategies. Twenty years ago, we had only pioneer census of distribution data and limited spot surveys to work from. Today, we have much more adequate distribution data, continuous store audits, and much more thoroughly organized field research to guide us.

ADVERTISING POWER

In the modern battle for consumer markets, it is evident that the amount of advertising dollars—the sheer advertising weight—placed behind a product is a major determinant of success in and of itself. In an economy with total advertising expenditures climbing over $10 billion a year, the size of the advertising budget has a great deal to do with the degree to which the advertiser's message is heard by the consumer in the midst of this cacophony. But since advertising expenditures represent such a heavy cost burden for so many products, the advertiser must constantly wonder just how much is enough and at what point expenditures become excessive.

Unfortunately, today, as twenty years ago, most methods of determining advertising expenditures are traditional accounting ratios or statistical descriptions which accurately record but make little contribution to sound decision making. A change in dollar strategy resulting in an increase or decrease of advertising weight should be based on more functional knowledge than traditional advertising-sales ratios, per-case allotments, or matching competitive dollars. The marketer who comes closest to controlling his advertising power so that the amount of advertising approximates the ideal marketing requirement from year to year clearly gains an important competitive advantage.

Marketing research surely can contribute a great deal more to sound decisions regarding projected increases or decreases of the advertising budget. Standard analytical procedures correlating advertising expenditures with sales productivity on the basis of such data as become available in the regular conduct of business are a useful tool. The experimental application of operations research techniques by the Arthur D. Little Company may make an important contribution.[3] Meanwhile, in contrast to its inadequacies back in 1937, marketing research provides realistic answers through fruitful experiments. The most useful tool we have is that of "extra-spending" or "saturation" campaigns in test market areas. A series of coincidental experiments involving expenditures at variable per capita levels, with sales results related to profit potentials, will provide the needed answers. True, this approach faces all the hurdles of uncontrollable variables, but it has proved to be extremely useful. Once again our chief problem lies not so much in an inability to design adequate experiments, but rather in failure to convince management of the virtue of making extra appropriations or risking inadequate sales results in some test areas in its constant battle to turn in a good overall performance in any given period.

ADVERTISING MEDIA AND COPY STRATEGIES

We come finally to consideration of the general area of advertising. In this notoriously fast-moving field, great emphasis is placed on strategic as well as tactical moves. Furthermore, when a basic strategy decision is made, it is backed with visible dollar expenditures so a close eye is kept on results achieved.

We are so aware of the key role marketing research plays in determining the foundation for advertising strategies that you no doubt expect a lengthy discussion of applications in this field. One could discuss myriad examples where research has been the primary foundation of changing advertising strategies, of new applications of research to advertising, and of the development of new and advanced advertising research techniques.

However, the case is so self-evident, the literature so full, and your own knowledge so complete that to do so would be sheer redundancy.

In place of such lengthy listing, I will simply underscore certain general evidences of the increased importance of research in guiding advertising practice. One of the most significant pieces of evidence is the extent to which reseachers themselves have come into top executive positions placing them in the highest councils of advertising. Another evidence of the vitality of advertising research is the heavy share of marketing research budgets devoted to solving advertising problems or to obtaining knowledge for the primary purpose of guiding advertising strategies.

Finally, the role of advertising practitioners in stimulating the general advance of marketing research is well known. Most of us can recall that the earliest developments of marketing research came from the advertising field—for example, Parlin's work at the Curtis Publishing Company. It was largely the questions raised by advertising people and their constant recommendations to marketing and management executives that carried the Nielsen store-auditing scheme through its early treacherous days. The demand for more facts to be used as a basis for planning advertising strategies was a major factor in getting the consumer panels, such as that of the Marketing Research Corporation of America, on the road to success. The current activities of the Advertising Research Foundation are a major catalyst in advancing the whole science of marketing research. These "secondary evidences" establish most strongly the vital role which marketing research plays today in determining changing advertising strategy.

This review of the contribution of marketing research to better management decisions in a world of changing marketing strategies suggests several important conclusions. The first observation is that starting with a list of nine vital areas, we find no single one in which marketing research has not become progressively more active during the past twenty years. A second observation is that this review in itself represents a sort of demonstration that there is probably no area of critical marketing decision in which marketing research cannot find an effective application. However, a third observation surely must be that there are certain areas, such as pricing policy and the determination of advertising budgets, in which during the past twenty years we have failed to position marketing research fully as an active, effective management tool. Finally, we must conclude that marketing research has a great future ahead of it in the next twenty years as these and other gaps are filled.

NOTES

[1]See Louis Cheskin, "Twelve Years of Unconscious Level Testing of Marketing Tools," *Advanced Management Magazine* (May 1957), pp. 9–14.

[2]See *Nielsen Researcher* (May 1957), p. 6.

[3]See M. L. Vidale and H. B. Wolfe, "An Operations-Research Study of Sales Response to Advertising," *Operations Research,* Vol. 5, No. 3 (June 1957).

V

CONTRIBUTIONS OF THE MARKETING MANAGEMENT APPROACH

The marketing management approach in the early 1960s offered an alternative to the functional approach. The approach centered around the managerial problem of developing a successful marketing strategy and emphasized the importance of the buyer. Most marketing textbooks and the marketing curriculums of universities today incorporate buyer-directed strategy.

Articles included in the section "The Marketing Management Concept" are the classic ones that helped define the approach and developed the important concept of consumer segmentation. Knowledge of the development of marketing management can aid today's student in understanding the evolution of marketing strategy and provide insight into modern consumer-oriented societies. The marketing management articles were selected to aid in understanding this historical development. Borch's article contains the original definition of marketing management. Since Borch is a businessman, the marketing management approach is viewed by many as a pragmatic, workable philosophy for business. The Levitt article further develops the marketing strategy notion with case histories of industries which failed to think of themselves in terms of the benefits they provided buyers. The Keith article briefly summarizes how and why the marketing era developed in steps through a production-oriented era and a sales-oriented era. The final article in this section, by Borden, identifies the elements of the marketing mix and their role in developing a marketing strategy.

The section "Markets and Segmentation" is presented to add emphasis to the importance of the buyer in the marketing management approach and explain the concept of market segmentation. Smith's article is concerned with the consumer market and how it might be segmented in order to better serve its needs. The Cardozo article illustrates how the industrial market might be segmented. Finally, Nystrom's discussion is presented to show that concern for the consumer is not a new idea, but rather that it has come into focus with the development of the marketing management approach.

36

The Marketing Philosophy as a Way of Business Life

F. J. Borch

I can tell you today very sincerely that the combination of this title, the importance of the subject matter of this AMA session, and this outstanding audience has me more than just a little concerned. Marketing is a subject I feel very strongly about, but the prospect of coming before you gentlemen who are so familiar with its ramifications causes me to pause at this point and try to get on the same wave length as our subject—marketing—which seems to mean so many things to so many people.

As we look back over a relatively short time span, say the last ten years, it is really surprising and somewhat remarkable to note the progress in the choice of words referring to that activity of business which focuses on the customer. "Sales," with its connotation of action, has frequently given way to "distribution," which implies a process, and now more recently we encounter "marketing"—a term in which I sense a striving for some real notion of viewpoint of purpose.

MARKETING IS A PHILOSOPHY

To get some measure of the degree of the variations which we associate with the term "marketing," a survey was recently conducted by the American Management Association. . . . Some of the responses may be of interest to us today because they show the varying opinions which exist regarding this term "marketing." About half of the companies surveyed expressed themselves as operating with what was called a "marketing" approach. Of this group, one-fifth did not respond to the request for their definition of what they felt "marketing" really was. Of those that did indicate their companies' definitions, a very substantial majority based their definitions

From an address to the American Management Association, February 4, 1957. Reprinted by the American Management Association, Inc., Marketing Series No. 99 (1957). Used by permission.

solely on functional operations—such as sales, market research, distribution, and the like.

I am afraid I must disagree in substantial measure with this type of marketing definition. In our company, General Electric, we feel that marketing is a fundamental business philosophy. This definition recognizes marketing's functions and methods of organizational structuring as *only the implementation* of the philosophy. These things are not, in themselves, the philosophy.

Let me digress for a moment and clear up the difference I think I see between a philosophy and a concept, because we will be referring frequently to both words, and I do not want to give the impression that I am using them interchangeably. A *philosophy* is the broad umbrella that governs the total business life, while a *concept* is a recognized way of operating within the climate that the philosophy umbrella has set.

Believe me, I recognize the risk I run when I make the statement that our definition of marketing is, in reality, so broad as to constitute a business philosophy. Perhaps I can make myself more clear by explaining that fundamental to this philosophy is the recognition and acceptance of a customer-oriented way of doing business. Under marketing the customer becomes the fulcrum, the pivot point about which the business moves in operating for the balanced best interests of all concerned.

MARKETING PHILOSOPHY NOT NEW

On more than one occasion I get the feeling that what we hear about marketing and customer orientation these days is being looked at as something really new. I do not think that it is. Years ago when our economy was much younger, customer orientation was a built-in feature of a business enterprise. Before the days of mass communication, national markets, and mass production, the business pioneers were cognizant of their customers and their markets. They knew their customers individually, and these individual customers formed their collective market. These predecessors of ours built their relationships through personal contact and got very rapid feedbacks of customer needs and wants. They were their own market researchers, analysts, salesmen, product planners, advertisers, and promoters. Beyond question, their businesses were customer-oriented because they knew this was the only way to run a business!

But mass production could not bring its desired economies to widely scattered customers without taking away the ability of the maker to know personally each customer. So the maker had to devise a substitute method of contact and observation that was reliable—and this is not to say it was perfectly effective *every* time. For example; automobiles were made in just the color the customer wanted, as long as black was the first preference. More than one manufacturer of the old, stiff, high collars nearly went broke trying to sell his product, long after customer preferences had shifted toward today's softer varieties. It took World War II silk shortages to convince many stocking manufacturers that nylons really were preferred to silk.

Those companies that have successfully grown are those which were quick to recognize their departure from a true understanding of the customer. It would certainly be valid to point out that as a company grows in size, its potential ability to drift away from customer orientation grows proportionately. Similarly, as its size increases, so does its necessity for this awareness. What we refer to today as the marketing philosophy is a recognition of just this situation.

TWO KEY FUNDAMENTALS

Full appreciation of the marketing philosophy demands an understanding of the two key fundamentals on which it rests.

The first is an understanding of what I call the dual core job of marketing. The initial part of this dual core job is that we in marketing must focus our businesses on the customer's needs and desires, including those needs and desires that the customer is *not* aware of as well as those he knows all too well. It will be only after identification of these needs that marketing people can take the lead for the business in determining what each function of the business should do by way of product and service to satisfy them.

The other half of the dual core job for marketing is one that we are familiar with—namely, the need to persuade the prospective customer, through all the arts of selling and advertising, to purchase the products and services which have been developed.

The second fundamental on which the marketing philosophy rests is that it is rooted in the profit concept, not the volume concept. (I am not eliminating the use of volume as a rewarding way of obtaining profits from the efficiency of the service rendered—I am referring to the profitless volume or volume-for-the-sake-of-volume-alone concept.) This is so basic that I am not going to dwell on it, but will simply restate that the acceptance of the profit concept rather than the volume concept as a way of business life is the second part of the marketing philosophy.

CONTRIBUTING FORCES

I think each of us will accept the fact that the marketing philosophy is not coming into being without an interplay of forces from the economic, social, and political environments of our times. A partial listing of these forces includes:

- The three different competitions: product vs. product competition (soap against soap); cross-line product competition (where the new mink coat competes with the second car); and cross-line technological competition (where aircraft companies start building canoes)

- Specialization (the expert in a highly vertical type of responsibility who knows everything about his field, little about others)
- Diversification (the move into new and varied product lines)
- Complexity (the faster pace and increased number of functions)
- Automation (the automatic factory which leads to a highly rigidized product)
- The efficiency urge (the emphasis on getting the most rewarding return on our investment)

Each of these forces is a contributor to accelerating the development of the marketing philosophy. However, out of these, and others I have not isolated, we can see three problem areas of business where an awareness of the marketing philosophy may help us over what otherwise could be insurmountable hurdles:

First, our rapidly changing customer, whose wants are multiplying at a terrific rate. In the consumer goods businesses this problem is a direct result of our standard of living, which provides an ever-mounting variety of goods, with a constantly diminishing compulsion to purchase any of them. As a result, the sales volume of individual products is being increasingly influenced by competitive pressures, rather than by the consumer's own requirements for survival. In 1800, seventy-five per cent of a working man's expenditures went for food alone, and only eight per cent for products other than housing, fuel, clothing, and food. Today, that eight per cent has grown to forty-eight per cent with half of this increase coming in the last thirty years—and it represents the growing discretionary control of the consumer that makes modern advertising so necessary, and causes mink coats to compete with cars, vacations with appliances, and a host of similar phenomena.

In the producer goods field, the equivalent problem is posed by the rapid development of our technology and the competitive pressure for reduction of manufacturing costs. This has given rise to alternate product competition that crosses over former industrial boundaries, so that plastics and metals, hydraulics and electronics, carbon and atomic fuels vie to displace each other. From the standpoint of marketing, the number of things to be forecast is infinitely complicated—and the difficulties of getting the right facts, weighing them in proper balance, and making the best decisions with respect to product and distribution policy becomes terrific. Yet, if we work both sides of the street and hedge all bets, the resulting increase in our costs may ruin us more quickly than the alternate risks that drive us to cover. Net result is that the most rapidly growing feature of business is our opportunity for error in planning how to please our ever-changing customer.

The *second* major problem—we cannot fail to notice that the amount of resources which must be committed to implement marketing decisions is rising rapidly. All costs are tending to become more fixed—be they costs of automated plants or costs of national distribution structures. But by far the more serious side of these trends is not what is happening to our costs, but what is happening to our freedom of action. We are increasing our *capacity* to act at the expense of our *freedom* to act when we freeze the design of the product in the interests of further mechanization, and when we freeze the distribution structure, the media we use and the message we impart in the interests of achieving a nationwide impact.

Consequently, the price of errors in basic marketing decisions is not only the cost of producing the wrong product at the wrong time for the wrong market, but the loss of our resources and the loss of further capacity to correct our errors. It is small wonder, then, that the risk-taking vigor and spirit of our fathers has given way to increasing concern with management decisions and controls which seek to avoid and limit risk—yet the mounting costs of checking and double-checking and postponing and revising may ruin us more quickly than the consequences of a wrong decision. Net result—the price of the wrong decision is growing at as fast a rate as the opportunity to make the wrong decision!

The *third* problem—in addition to the steady rise in the opportunities for error (caused by the mounting alternatives of the customer) and in the price of error (caused by the mounting cost of plant and distribution structures) we are plagued with greater difficulties in our internal communication and decision process. When our organizations have to reach out for more and more customers in order to pass the break-even point in a competitive market, the structural machinery for getting information delivered and decisions made must be more and more diligently watched to assure keeping continually in phase with requirements.

In addition to the three problems we have discussed, I would like to touch on a few others—the preparation of new plants, products, and promotions requires increasing decision lead time which certainly adds a burden to accurate forecasting. And as specialization grows, the number of employees who understand any *whole* situation and can make any *whole* decisions keeps shrinking. So it is that an organization unexpectedly discovers that it is in new businesses, that the sales plan in operation seems quite different from anything planned on paper, and that the standing joke in the district office is the one about "it's just policy." Decentralization and divisionalization are the only answers, but unless very carefully planned and timed, they too cost money.

WHAT MANAGEMENT CAN EXPECT

We have been covering in more than a little detail the marketing philosophy and its implementation. Understanding of this is important, but now, I would like to depart from the philosophical and discuss the payoff phase—the answer to the question of what the marketing philosophy can produce in terms of creating sounder business management which can better face the problems we have just posed.

Fortunately, we are gaining enough experience to see some answers developing to the question of marketing's contributions to management. They include:

Responsibilities

Many functional areas which were previously floaters—or loosely assigned to more than one individual with resultant confusion or lack of action—can be isolated, assigned, and measured in terms of effectiveness.

The business' creative planning can be partially delegated into responsible hands, assuring a customer-orientation to business plans and strategies.

Decisions

Decisions made without the customer focus can do irreparable harm to a business. And, unfortunately, such decisions usually multiply and additional wrong ones are made in a vain attempt to correct the earlier ones. For example, this happens all too frequently in situations like these:

1. When we protect the losing sales channel at the expense of extra promotion, trying to make water run uphill without any consideration of whether the customer is better served by such action.
2. When we similarly protect the losing technology and fail to shift over to the new technology that better serves the customer.
3. When we try and minimize the risk by combining ventures which really do not fit insofar as their marketing requirements are concerned, involving the extra decision on the cost of ironing out the constant collision of objectives involved in keeping the two activities out of each other's hair at the marketing level.
4. When in an effort to get further specialized attention on the difficult forecasting problems, we make the mistake of duplicating overhead organization on lines that are really the same, without getting any benefit out of the extra cost thus incurred.

Coordination

Coordination is brought into play early, when it is *most effective* because functions such as product design, pricing, and engineering development must *start* with a clear understanding of the customer situation as it relates to these areas. This market place understanding can eliminate much of the time an executive spends in reconciling plans for each function of the business because they have not been prepared with a previously understood common objective.

Another distinct advantage which is difficult to categorize might best be called a tightening of the time lag between decision and action. For example, if the marketing strategy is to go all out for volume, market position, or product quality—the *entire force of the business* can be quickly harnessed to support such a decision *if* the business is being operated under customer-orientation.

NEED FOR THE MARKETING PHILOSOPHY

I would like to run through just a few questions which we have found we can answer with a surprisingly greater degree of accuracy with a marketing organization that is really operating under the marketing philosophy. You may find these helpful as a check list to determine how many such answers your business has.

- Do I really know the *fundamental* rather than *symptomatic* reasons for declining or increasing trends in my dollar volume?
- What is my market's growth potential? Do I have a clear indication, based on more than educated guessing, on what it will be in five years? In ten years? In twenty years? Will I be prepared facility-wise to meet this future market?
- Is my existing market one that could be quickly eliminated by a major technological breakthrough? If so, what plans do we have if this should happen?
- Do I know whether product diversification would benefit my company? If it would, do I have a *planned* program of diversification by either product and market development, or by acquisition? What criteria do I have to help me decide which product lines and markets I should be in?
- Are my business planning and strategy decisions taking into consideration the knowledge of the people who *really* know and understand my customer?
- Do I make and develop markets?
- Do I predict inventory levels with any degree of success? Or, am I plagued with over and under inventories, layoffs, and overtime?
- Do I really make my own business decisions? Or are others making them for me?

I leave you to ponder these—as we do.

TRANSLATING INTO BUSINESS OPPORTUNITIES

I should now like to examine with you a couple of actual situations where a real understanding of the marketing philosophy as a way of business life, plus adherence to sound objectives and willingness to take risks by making sweeping changes focused on the customer, brought results. That these two case histories come from my own company is no cause for boasting on my part because I only wish that they were more typical. Nevertheless, they do demonstrate that if we are willing to take the risk of thinking the marketing job through from the standpoint of increasing consumable value for the customer, the opportunities for increasing our marketing efficiency in adding to profits are tremendous. I shall start with the story of the vacuum cleaner.

This was the situation faced by our Vacuum Cleaner Department in 1951: we were practically unrecognized in the industry, with only a minor per cent share of the market; we had no unique product identification to form the basis of our advertising and selling appeals. In fact, we had no national advertising.

Certainly, these are not admissions of strength. Equally important, profitable businesses are not built on this sort of foundation.

Our people at this point applied a marketing approach and attempted to identify the difficulties from the customer's viewpoint. This is what they found.

First, vacuum cleaners were priced at levels that were high relative to other appliances, a major factor in keeping the market saturation percentage far below that of other appliances.

Second, distribution was not adequate, with only thirty per cent of vacuum cleaners being sold through retailers and the rest door-to-door. From the housewife's standpoint, this meant that when she was in most retail appliance stores, she found practically every other home appliance except the vacuum cleaner.

Third, a large number of models was offered by each manufacturer. This had two serious negative effects—the housewife was confused and manufacturing costs were reflecting the high additional costs of multimodel production.

Our product was a compromise between engineering's ideas on what a vacuum cleaner should do and manufacturing's thinking on how it should be made. Everyone seemingly had a hand in the product *except* the customer.

Our action to overcome these problems was based entirely on the application of the marketing philosophy, and I would like to group the results of these activities in relation to the customer, the dealer, and the management people in this department.

First, to the *customer:*

- Through product improvements and the decision to concentrate on a single model, rather than the fifteen we were previously offering, our prices were lowered. Surveys have shown that even today most housewives do not yet realize that they can buy a good vacuum for under $100. Consequently, we feel that we made a contribution to the consumer in widely advertising our best selling model last year at $49.95.

- Cleaners are now available in practically every retail outlet normally handling home appliances, and product repair service is improved.
- Cleaners are now better designed, performing household tasks more efficiently under the concept of cleaning the entire home rather than merely the rug.

I should like to point out that these things were by no means accomplished solely by General Electric. We applied the marketing philosophy to this business, and so did others with a resulting increase in competition that really brought about these customer benefits.

To the *dealer,* this change meant, first of all, the addition of a profitable line to his business. Today, the vacuum cleaner is the fifth or sixth largest of all appliance businesses in terms of retail dollars. Broadly speaking, it could not have been considered a dealer business prior to 1946.

It may be interesting to point out here that in spite of the fact that seventy per cent of sales had been door-to-door, the sales increases for G.E. and the industry came from new business originating through retailers rather than at the expense of the door-to-door people.

We estimate that vacuum cleaner sales by manufacturers selling door-to-door have increased slightly since 1951, but sales of the total industry have risen an estimated thirty-three per cent from 1951 to 1956. During this period, market saturation has increased from fifty to sixty-five per cent. These changes have been due, we feel, to the efforts of companies like ourselves that have adopted the marketing approach. Planned market growth is one of the major contributions this philosophy can make to the business.

How did the marketing philosophy help this department's *management?* Let me request that you bear in mind the scope of the decisions these men were facing:

- They were going to make a complete shift in the historical methods of vacuum cleaner distribution, attempting to build a major market with a type of mass distribution that never had been successfully used with this product.
- They were going to eliminate all but one model from their line and face competition with a single model offering. And, on top of this, they were committed to marketing's real responsibility to help run the business in a profitable manner.

The most important single contribution of marketing was to give the people who had to make these decisions the confidence that they were being made on firm understanding of the customer's wants. The shift to customer orientation had convinced these men that they could proceed from a position of knowledge and market-place strength.

All of the management advantages that I have cited earlier apply to this department, and these specific ones can be added:

- The isolation and assigning of the product planning and market research responsibilities has built leadership in the market, and subsequent decisions are being made on the basis of a sound analysis of what we *knew* was needed by the customer.
- Engineering and manufacturing quickly oriented their activities to the requirements of the customer, with some revolutionary results in terms of new product offerings which have helped expand not only our business, but the total market.
- Planning is now long-range rather than year-to-year or, in some instances, day-to-day.
- The general manager and marketing manager are free to devote more of their time to the *fundamental* problems of the business, because much of the work they previously handled is now the responsibility of the marketing staff.
- Investments in advertising and sales promotion (and they are high in this industry) are made more wisely because the copy and scripts reflect the real sales appeals that market research and customer awareness have proved to be effective.

And, dealers are selling with the same story that advertising tells, because the job of integrating advertising and sales has been made more effective. Equally important, engineers now design the product with the requirements of television advertising and the dealer's showroom in mind.

I should also point out that the acceptance by our engineering and manufacturing people of the need for these changes as they affected the product was tremendous. They rose, in no small way, to the challenge and made these plans realities.

You will note that this case is an illustration of the application of the marketing philosophy to a consumer goods business. At this point, I should state that we feel that the philosophy applies with equal validity to all kinds of business, and I shall illustrate this in my second case history which involves an industrial product. You will note, however, that while the philosophy is the same, the methods of implementation vary substantially.

Our Meter Department is a good example of this. In this business we were also fortunate to have made the decision to operate under the marketing philosophy.

Let me quickly describe the kind of business it is. It has one major product—the watt-hour-meter for measuring industrial and consumer electrical power consumption. Fifty-four million units are now in use. It has one primary group of customers—electrical utilities, and the market is relatively inelastic. (Demand is in relation to new homes and plants plus some replacement business.) It has an abnormally high engineering content in the product. And, perhaps most important for this discussion—product advantages constitute the major brand preference motivation.

We believe we have held a position of leadership in this field, but about two years ago we were quite surprised to find that on some occasions our competitors were making some of our important product decisions for us. This situation came about, frankly, because to a degree we were losing our cognizance of the customer's needs. In recognizing this, we put the marketing philosophy to a severe test.

In a business where success depends almost solely on knowing precisely what the customer needs, and the subsequent satisfaction of those needs, there could be no substitute for the real knowledge the marketing way of operation gave us. The people managing this business got us back on the track in a hurry—and this year, in a business that has historically never announced more than one product innovation annually, we will be announcing several. And, we were able to bridge the gap between identifying customer's real wants and translating these into product innovations within less than two years.

As in the vacuum cleaner business, I am sure that the customer orientation of the key men in the department is responsible for our having in two years changes which normally would have taken much longer. Certainly this is a departure from the old make-it, sell-it days which we have all lived through. Today, the engineering and manufacturing managers in the department recognize fully that their contributions must be in terms of product innovations which are incorporated into our watt-hour-meters before a competitor introduces them.

Because these product changes are not all yet announced, I'd like to refer to a previous example to show the type of integration the marketing philosophy can help bring to a business. Not long ago it took us more than eighteen months to redesign our watt-hour-meter to increase capacity from 60 to 100 amps. We recently raised the capacity of these same meters from 100 to 200 amps. This was a much more difficult job than the original incremental raise, and it was accomplished in less than twelve months, pointing out again the tremendous cooperation demonstrated by the engineering and manufacturing people in helping to really make this work.

These higher ratings have answered a very definite utility need, and had it not been for the superimposition of the customer awareness and closely integrated type of operation the marketing philosophy had given this department, they could well be lagging their competitors. I should like to emphasize that competition in this field is very heavy in terms of alertness and ability. One does not doze off and retain leadership for very long in any phase of the electrical industry with which I'm familiar. (In fact, there aren't many businesses today where this can be done!)

In addition to the advantages we have already discussed, the management people in this department realized many others. (For the sake of brevity, I shall not repeat any which we have discussed earlier with the Vacuum Cleaner Department.) The others worthy of note include:

With responsibility for finished goods inventories and production requirements in the hands of the marketing manager, production is closely tied to the real needs of the market and excessive inventories are kept at a minimum. This also assures more employment stability through a definite dampening effect on personnel increases and decreases due to poorly forecasted production requirements.

The marketing manager operates as a business manager, assuming his share of the responsibility of setting the required business strategies and objectives.

A concept has been developed of selling not the product, but the function that the product performs. To be specific, these men do not consider themselves in the device business; they are in the business of measuring electrical power revenue for utilities.

These two case histories have demonstrated the fundamentals discussed earlier, and they show clearly that the decisions that increase value to the customer also increase sales. They also show the impact that the philosophy can make by contributing to the strategy decisions and, concurrently, by augmenting the sales concept. To me—and to put it quite simply—the sales concept alone concerns itself primarily with volume. Marketing means customer orientation—a true alliance with the fellow at the other end of the pipeline, but it insists upon a course of action of mutual benefit.

If we organize our policies around these factors which are mutually important to the customer and to our profits, we will find a real community of interest between the producer and the consumer. This is the marketing philosophy, and its realization and practice can change the way of life in the world no less than did the industrial revolution of many years ago.

37

Marketing Myopia

Theodore Levitt

Every major industry was once a growth industry. But some that are now riding a wave of growth enthusiasm are very much in the shadow of decline. Others which are thought of as seasoned growth industries have actually stopped growing. In every case the reason growth is threatened, slowed, or stopped is *not* because the market is saturated. It is because there has been a failure of management.

FATEFUL PURPOSES

The failure is at the top. The executives responsible for it, in the last analysis, are those who deal with broad aims and policies. Thus, the railroads did not stop growing because the need for passenger and freight transportation declined. That grew. The railroads are in trouble today not because the need was filled by others (cars, trucks, airplanes, even telephone), but because it was *not* filled by the railroads themselves. They let others take customers away from them because they assumed themselves to be in the railroad business rather than in the transportation business. The reason they defined their industry wrong was because they were railroad-oriented instead of transportation-oriented; they were product-oriented instead of customer-oriented.

Hollywood barely escaped being totally ravished by television. Actually, all the established film companies went through drastic reorganizations. Some simply disappeared. All of them got into trouble not because of TV's inroads but because of their own myopia. As with the railroads, Hollywood defined its business incorrectly. It thought it was in the movie business when it was actually in the entertainment business. "Movies" implied a specific, limited product. This produced a fatuous contentment which from the beginning led producers to view TV as a threat. Hollywood scorned and rejected TV when it should have welcomed it as an opportunity —an opportunity to expand the entertainment business.

Today TV is a bigger business than the old narrowly defined movie business ever was. Had Hollywood been customer-oriented (providing entertainment), rather than product-oriented (making movies), would it have gone through the fiscal purgatory that it did? I doubt it. What ultimately saved Hollywood and accounted for its recent resurgence was the wave of new young writers, producers, and directors whose previous successes in television had decimated the old movie companies and toppled the big movie moguls.

There are other less obvious examples of industries that have been and are now endangering their futures by improperly defining their purposes. I shall discuss some in detail later and analyze the kind of policies that lead to trouble. Right now it may help to show what a thoroughly customer-oriented management *can* do to keep a growth industry growing, even after the obvious opportunities have been exhausted; and here there are two examples that have been around for a long time. They are nylon and glass—specifically, E. I. duPont de Nemours & Company and Corning Glass Works. Both companies have great technical competence. Their product orientation is unquestioned. But this alone does not explain their success. After all, who was more pridefully product-oriented and product-conscious than the erstwhile New England textile companies that have been so thoroughly massacred? The DuPonts and the Cornings have succeeded not primarily because of their product or research orientation but because they have been thoroughly customer-oriented also. It is constant watchfulness for opportunities to apply their technical know-how to the creation of customer-satisfying uses which accounts for their prodigious output of successful new products. Without a very sophisticated eye on the customer, most of their new products might have been wrong, their sales methods useless.

Aluminum has also continued to be a growth industry, thanks to the efforts of two wartime-created companies which deliberately set about creating new customer-satisfying uses. Without Kaiser Aluminum & Chemical Corporation and Reynolds Metals Company, the total demand for aluminum today would be vastly less than it is.

Error of Analysis

Some may argue that it is foolish to set the railroads off against aluminum or the movies off against glass. Are not aluminum and glass naturally so versatile that the industries are bound to have more growth opportunities than the railroads and movies? This view commits precisely the error I have been talking about. It defines an industry, or a product, or a cluster of know-how so narrowly as to guarantee its premature senescence. When we mention "railroads," we should make sure we mean "transportation." As transporters, the railroads still have a good chance for very considerable growth. They are not limited to the railroad business as such (though in my opinion rail transportation is potentially a much stronger transportation medium than is generally believed).

What the railroads lack is not opportunity, but some of the same managerial imaginativeness and audacity that made them great. Even an amateur like Jacques Barzun can see what is lacking when he says: "I grieve to see the most advanced physical and social organization of the last century go down in shabby disgrace for lack of the same comprehensive imagination that built it up. [What is lacking is] the will of the companies to survive and to satisfy the public by inventiveness and skill."[1]

SHADOW OF OBSOLESCENCE

It is impossible to mention a single major industry that did not at one time qualify for the magic appellation of "growth industry." In each case its assumed strength lay in the apparently unchallenged superiority of its product. There appeared to be no effective substitute for it. It was itself a runaway substitute for the product it so triumphantly replaced. Yet one after another of these celebrated industries has come under a shadow. Let us look briefly at a few more of them, this time taking examples that have so far received a little less attention.

Dry Cleaning. This was once a growth industry with lavish prospects. In an age of wool garments, imagine being finally able to get them safely and easily clean. The boom was on.

Yet here we are thirty years after the boom started and the industry is in trouble. Where has the competition come from? From a better way of cleaning? No. It has come from synthetic fibers and chemical additives that have cut the need for dry cleaning. But this is only the beginning. Lurking in the wings and ready to make chemical dry cleaning totally obsolescent is that powerful magician, ultrasonics.

Electric Utilities. This is another one of those supposedly "no-substitute" products that has been enthroned on a pedestal of invincible growth. When the incandescent lamp came along, kerosene lights were finished. Later the water wheel and the steam engine were cut to ribbons by the flexibility, reliability, simplicity, and just plain easy availability of electric motors. The prosperity of electric utilities continues to wax extravagant as the home is converted into a museum of electric gadgetry. How can anybody miss by investing in utilities, with no competition, nothing but growth ahead?

But a second look is not quite so comforting. A score of nonutility companies are well advanced toward developing a powerful chemical fuel cell which could sit in some hidden closet of every home silently ticking off electric power. The electric lines that vulgarize so many neighborhoods will be eliminated. So will the endless demolition of streets and service interruptions during storms. Also on the horizon is solar energy, again pioneered by nonutility companies.

Who says that the utilities have no competition? They may be natural monopolies now, but tomorrow they may be natural deaths. To avoid this prospect, they too will have to develop fuel cells, solar energy, and other power sources. To survive, they themselves will have to plot the obsolescence of what now produces their livelihood.

Grocery Stores.   Many people find it hard to realize that there ever was a thriving establishment known as the "corner grocery store." The supermarket has taken over with a powerful effectiveness. Yet the big food chains of the 1930s narrowly escaped being completely wiped out by the aggressive expansion of independent supermarkets. The first genuine supermarket was opened in 1930, in Jamaica, Long Island. By 1933 supermarkets were thriving in California, Ohio, Pennsylvania, and elsewhere. Yet the established chains pompously ignored them. When they chose to notice them, it was with such derisive descriptions as "cheapy," "horse-and-buggy," "cracker-barrel storekeeping," and "unethical opportunists."

The executive of one big chain announced at the time that he found it "hard to believe that people will drive for miles to shop for foods and sacrifice the personal service chains have perfected and to which Mrs. Consumer is accustomed."[2] As late as 1936, the National Wholesale Grocers convention and the New Jersey Retail Grocers Association said there was nothing to fear. They said that the supers' narrow appeal to the price buyer limited the size of their market. They had to draw from miles around. When imitators came, there would be wholesale liquidations as volume fell. The current high sales of the supers were said to be partly due to their novelty. Basically people wanted convenient neighborhood grocers. If the neighborhood stores "cooperate with their suppliers, pay attention to their costs, and improve their service," they would be able to weather the competition until it blew over.[3]

It never blew over. The chains discovered that survival required going into the supermarket business. This meant the wholesale destruction of their huge investments in corner store sites and in established distribution and merchandising methods. The companies with "the courage of their convictions" resolutely stuck to the corner store philosophy. They kept their pride but lost their shirts.

Self-deceiving Cycle

But memories are short. For example, it is hard for people who today confidently hail the twin messiahs of electronics and chemicals to see how things could possibly go wrong with these galloping industries. They probably also cannot see how a reasonably sensible businessman could have been as myopic as the famous Boston millionaire who fifty years ago unintentionally sentenced his heirs to poverty by stipulating that his entire estate be forever invested exclusvely in electric streetcar securities. His posthumous declaration, "There will always be a big demand for efficient urban transportation," is no consolation to his heirs who sustain life by pumping gasoline at automobile filling stations.

Yet, in a casual survey I recently took among a group of intelligent business executives, nearly half agreed that it would be hard to hurt their heirs by tying their estates forever to the electronics industry. When I then confronted them with the Boston streetcar example, they chorused unanimously, "That's different!" But is it? Is not the basic situation identical?

In truth, *there is no such thing* as a growth industry, I believe. There are only companies organized and operated to create and capitalize on growth opportunities. Industries that assume themselves to be riding some automatic growth escalator invariably descend into stagnation. The history of every dead and dying "growth" industry shows a self-deceiving cycle of bountiful expansion and undetected decay. There are four conditions which usually guarantee this cycle:

1. The belief that growth is assured by an expanding and more affluent population
2. The belief that there is no competitive substitute for the industry's major product
3. Too much faith in mass production and in the advantages of rapidly declining unit costs as output rises
4. Preoccupation with a product that lends itself to carefully controlled scientific experimentation, improvement, and manufacturing cost reduction

I should like now to begin examining each of these conditions in some detail. To build my case as boldly as possible, I shall illustrate the points with reference to three industries—petroleum, automobiles, and electronics—particularly petroleum, because it spans more years and more vicissitudes. Not only do these three have excellent reputations with the general public and also enjoy the confidence of sophisticated investors, but their managements have become known for progressive thinking in areas like financial control, product research, and management training. If obsolescence can cripple even these industries, it can happen anywhere.

POPULATION MYTH

The belief that profits are assured by an expanding and more affluent population is dear to the heart of every industry. It takes the edge off the apprehensions everybody understandably feels about the future. If consumers are multiplying and also buying more of your product or service, you can face the future with considerably more comfort than if the market is shrinking. An expanding market keeps the manufacturer from having to think very hard or imaginatively. If thinking is an intellectual response to a problem, then the absence of a problem leads to the absence of thinking.

If your product has an automatically expanding market, then you will not give much thought to how to expand it.

One of the most interesting examples of this is provided by the petroleum industry. Probably our oldest growth industry, it has an enviable record. While there are some current apprehensions about its growth rate, the industry itself tends to be optimistic. But I believe it can be demonstrated that it is undergoing a fundamental yet typical change. It is not only ceasing to be a growth industry, but may actually be a declining one, relative to other business. Although there is widespread unawareness of it, I believe that within twenty-five years the oil industry may find itself in much the same position of retrospective glory that the railroads are now in. Despite its pioneering work in developing and applying the present-value method of investment evaluation, in employee relations, and in working with backward countries, the petroleum business is a distressing example of how complacency and wrongheadedness can stubbornly convert opportunity into near disaster.

One of the characteristics of this and other industries that have believed very strongly in the beneficial consequences of an expanding population, while at the same time being industries with a generic product for which there has appeared to be no competitive substitute, is that the individual companies have sought to outdo their competitors by improving on what they are already doing. This makes sense, of course, if one assumes that sales are tied to the country's population strings, because the customer can compare products only on a feature-by-feature basis. I believe it is significant, for example, that not since John D. Rockefeller sent free kerosene lamps to China has the oil industry done anything really outstanding to create a demand for its product. Not even in product improvement has it showered itself with eminence. The greatest single improvement, namely, the development of tetraethyl lead, came from outside the industry, specifically from General Motors and DuPont. The big contributions made by the industry itself are confined to the technology of oil exploration, production, and refining.

Asking for Trouble

In other words, the industry's efforts have focused on improving the *efficiency* of getting and making its product, not really on improving the generic product or its marketing. Moreover, its chief product has continuously been defined in the narrowest possible terms, namely, gasoline, not energy, fuel, or transportation. This attitude has helped assure that major improvements in gasoline quality tend not to originate in the oil industry. Also, the development of superior alternative fuels comes from outside the oil industry, as will be shown later. Major innovations in automobile fuel marketing are originated by small new oil companies that are not primarily preoccupied with production or refining. These are the companies that have been responsible for the rapidly expanding multipump gasoline stations, with their successful emphasis on large and clean layouts, rapid and efficient driveway service, and quality gasoline at low prices.

Thus, the oil industry is asking for trouble from outsiders. Sooner or later, in this land of hungry inventors and entrepreneurs, a threat is sure to come. The possibilities of this will become more apparent when we turn to the next dangerous belief of many managements. For the sake of continuity, because this second belief is tied closely to the first, I shall continue with the same example.

Idea of Indispensability

The petroleum industry is pretty much persuaded that there is no competitive substitute for its major product, gasoline—or if there is, that it will continue to be a derivative of crude oil, such as diesel fuel or kerosene jet fuel.

There is a lot of automatic wishful thinking in this assumption. The trouble is that most refining companies own huge amounts of crude oil reserves. These have value only if there is a market for products into which oil can be converted—hence the tenacious belief in the continuing competitive superiority of automobile fuels made from crude oil.

This idea persists despite all historic evidence against it. The evidence not only shows that oil has never been a superior product for any purpose for very long, but it also shows that the oil industry has never really been a growth industry. It has been a succession of different businesses that have gone through the usual historic cycles of growth, maturity, and decay. Its overall survival is owed to a series of miraculous escapes from total obsolescence, of last-minute and unexpected reprieves from total disaster reminiscent of the Perils of Pauline.

Perils of Petroleum

I shall sketch in only the main episodes: First, crude oil was largely a patent medicine. But even before that fad ran out, demand was really expanded by the use of oil in kerosene lamps. The prospect of lighting the world's lamps gave rise to an extravagant promise of growth. The prospects were similar to those the industry now holds for gasoline in other parts of the world. It can hardly wait for the underdeveloped nations to get a car in every garage.

In the days of the kerosene lamp, the oil companies competed with each other and against gaslight by trying to improve the illuminating characteristics of kerosene. Then suddenly the impossible happened. Edison invented a light which was totally nondependent on crude oil. Had it not been for the growing use of kerosene in space heaters, the incandescent lamp would have completely finished oil as a growth industry at that time. Oil would have been good for little else than axle grease.

Then disaster and reprieve struck again. Two great innovations occurred, neither originating in the oil industry. The successful development of coal-burning domestic central-heating systems made the space heater obsolescent. While the industry reeled, along came its most magnificent boost yet—the internal combustion engine, also invented by outsiders. Then when the prodigious expansion for gasoline finally began to level off in the 1920s, along came the miraculous escape of a central oil heater. Once again, the escape was provided by an outsider's invention and development. And when that market weakened, wartime demand for aviation fuel came to the rescue. After the war the expansion of civilian aviation, the dieselization of railroads, and the explosive demand for cars and trucks kept the industry's growth in high gear.

Meanwhile centralized oil heating—whose boom potential had only recently been proclaimed—ran into severe competition from natural gas. While the oil companies themselves owned the gas that now competed with their oil, the industry did not originate the natural gas revolution, nor has it to this day greatly profited from its gas ownership. The gas revolution was made by newly formed transmission companies that marketed the product with an aggressive ardor. They started a magnificent new industry, first against the advice and then against the resistance of the oil companies.

By all the logic of the situation, the oil companies themselves should have made the gas revolution. They not only owned the gas; they also were the only people experienced in handling, scrubbing, and using it, the only people experienced in pipeline technology and transmission, and they understood heating problems. But, partly because they knew that natural gas would compete with their own sale of heating oil, the oil companies pooh-poohed the potentials of gas.

The revolution was finally started by oil pipeline executives who, unable to persuade their own companies to go into gas, quit and organized the spectacularly successful gas transmission companies. Even after their success became painfully evident to the oil companies, the latter did not go into gas transmission. The multibillion dollar business which should have been theirs went to others. As in the past, the industry was blinded by its narrow preoccupation with a specific product and the value of its reserves. It paid little or no attention to its customers' basic needs and preferences.

The postwar years have not witnessed any change. Immediately after World War II the oil industry was greatly encouraged about its future by the rapid expansion of demand for its traditional line of products. In 1950 most companies projected annual rates of domestic expansion of around six per cent through at least 1975. Though the ratio of crude oil reserves to demand in the Free World was about twenty to one, with ten to one being usually considered a reasonable working ratio in the United States, booming demand sent oil men searching for more without sufficient regard to what the future really promised. In 1952 they "hit" in the Middle East; the ratio skyrocketed to forty-two to one. If gross additions to reserves continue at the average rate of the past five years (thirty-seven billion barrels annually), then by 1970 the reserve ratio will be up to forty-five to one. This abundance of oil has weakened crude and product prices all over the world.

Uncertain Future

Management cannot find much consolation today in the rapidly expanding petrochemical industry, another oil-using idea that did not originate in the leading firms. The total United States production of petrochemicals is equivalent to about two per cent (by volume) of the demand for all petroleum products. Although the petrochemical industry is now expected to grow by about ten per cent per year, this will not offset other drains on the growth of crude oil consumption. Furthermore, while petrochemical products are many and growing, it is well to remember that there are nonpetroleum sources of the basic raw material, such as coal. Besides, a lot of plastics can be produced with relatively little oil. A 50,000-barrel-per-day oil refinery is now considered the absolute minimum size for efficiency. But a 5,000-barrel-per-day chemical plant is a giant operation.

Oil has never been a continuously strong growth industry. It has grown by fits and starts, always miraculously saved by innovations and developments not of its own making. The reason it has not grown in a smooth progression is that each time it thought it had a superior product safe from the possibility of competitive substitutes, the product turned out to be inferior and notoriously subject to obsolescence. Until now, gasoline (for motor fuel, anyhow) has escaped this fate. But, as we shall see later, it too may be on its last legs.

The point of all this is that there is no guarantee against product obsolescence. If a company's own research does not make it obsolete, another's will. Unless an industry is especially lucky, as oil has been until now, it can easily go down in a sea of red figures—just as the railroads have, as the buggy whip manufacturers have, as the corner grocery chains have, as most of the big movie companies have, and indeed as many other industries have.

The best way for a firm to be lucky is to make its own luck. That requires knowing what makes a business successful. One of the greatest enemies of this knowledge is mass production.

PRODUCTION PRESSURES

Mass-production industries are impelled by a great drive to produce all they can. The prospect of steeply declining unit costs as output rises is more than most companies can usually resist. The profit possibilities look spectacular. All effort focuses on production. The result is that marketing gets neglected.

John Kenneth Galbraith contends that just the opposite occurs.[4] Output is so prodigious that all effort concentrates on trying to get rid of it. He says this accounts for singing commercials, desecration of the countryside with advertising signs, and other wasteful and vulgar practices. Galbraith has a finger on something real, but he misses the strategic point. Mass production does indeed generate great pressure to "move" the product. But what usually gets emphasized is selling, not marketing. Marketing, being a more sophisticated and complex process, gets ignored.

The difference between marketing and selling is more than semantic. Selling focuses on the needs of the seller, marketing on the needs of the buyer. Selling is preoccupied with the seller's need to convert his product into cash; marketing with the idea of satisfying the needs of the customer by means of the product and the whole cluster of things associated with creating, delivering, and finally consuming it.

In some industries the enticements of full mass production have been so powerful that for many years top management in effect has told the sales departments, "You get rid of it; we'll worry about profits." By contrast, a truly marketing-minded firm tries to create value-satisfying goods and services that consumers will want to buy. What it offers for sale includes not only the generic product or service, but also how it is made available to the customer, in what form, when, under what conditions, and at what terms of trade. Most important, what it offers for sale is determined not by the seller but by the buyer. The seller takes his cues from the buyer in such a way that the product becomes a consequence of the marketing effort, not vice versa.

Lag in Detroit

This may sound like an elementary rule of business, but that does not keep it from being violated wholesale. It is certainly more violated than honored. Take the automobile industry: Here mass production is most famous, most honored, and has the greatest impact on the entire society. The industry has hitched its fortune to the relentless requirements of the annual model change, a policy that makes customer orientation an especially urgent necessity. Consequently the auto companies annually spend millions of dollars on consumer research. But the fact that the new compact cars are selling so well in their first year indicates that Detroit's vast researches have for a long time failed to reveal what the customer really wanted. Detroit was not persuaded that he wanted anything different from what he had been getting until it lost millions of customers to other small car manufacturers.

How could this unbelievable lag behind consumer wants have been perpetuated so long? Why did not research reveal consumer preferences before consumers' buying decisions themselves revealed the facts? Is that not what consumer research is for—to find out before the fact what is going to happen? The answer is that Detroit never really researched the customer's wants. It only researched his preferences between the kinds of things which it had already decided to offer him. For Detroit is mainly product-oriented, not customer-oriented. To the extent that the customer is recognized as having needs that the manufacturer should try to satisfy, Detroit usually acts as if the job can be done entirely by product changes. Occasionally attention gets paid to financing, too, but that is done more in order to sell than to enable the customer to buy.

As for taking care of other customer needs, there is not enough being done to write about. The areas of the greatest unsatisfied needs are ignored, or at best get stepchild attention. These are at the point of sale and on the matter of automotive repair and maintenance. Detroit views these problem areas as being of secondary importance. That is underscored by the fact that the retailing and servicing ends of this industry are neither owned and operated nor controlled by the manufacturers. Once the car is produced, things are pretty much in the dealer's inadequate hands. Illustrative of Detroit's arm's-length attitude is the fact that, while servicing holds enormous sales-stimulating, profit-building opportunities, only fifty-seven of Chevrolet's 7,000 dealers provide night maintenance service.

Motorists repeatedly express their dissatisfaction with servicing and their apprehensions about buying cars under the present selling setup. The anxieties and problems they encounter during the auto buying and maintenance processes are probably more intense and widespread today than thirty years ago. Yet the automobile companies do not *seem* to listen to or take their cues from the anguished consumer. If they do listen, it must be through the filter of their own preoccupation with production. The marketing effort is still viewed as a necessary consequence of the product, not vice versa, as it should be. That is the legacy of mass production, with its parochial view that profit resides essentially in low-cost full production.

What Ford Put First

The profit lure of mass production obviously has a place in the plans and strategy of business management, but it must always *follow* hard thinking about the customer. This is one of the most important lessons that we can learn from the contradictory behavior of Henry Ford. In a sense Ford was both the most brilliant and the most senseless marketer in American history. He was senseless because he refused to give the customer anything but a black car. He was brilliant because he fashioned a production system designed to fit market needs. We habitually celebrate him for the wrong reason, his production genius. His real genius was marketing. We think he was able to cut his selling price and therefore sell millions of $500 cars because his invention of the assembly line had reduced the costs. Actually he invented the assembly line because he had concluded that at $500 he could sell millions of cars. Mass production was the *result* not the cause of his low prices.

Ford repeatedly emphasized this point, but a nation of production-oriented business managers refuses to hear the great lesson he taught. Here is his operating philosophy as he expressed it succinctly:

> Our policy is to reduce the price, extend the operations, and improve the article. You will notice that the reduction of price comes first. We have never considered any costs as fixed. Therefore we first reduce the price to the point where we believe more sales will result. Then we go ahead and try to make the prices. We do not bother about the costs. The new price forces the costs down. The more usual way is to take the costs and then determine the price, and although that method may be scientific in the narrow sense, it is not scientific in the broad sense, because what earthly use is it to know the cost if it tells you that you cannot manufacture at a price at which the article can be sold? But more to the point is the fact that, although one may calculate what a cost is, and of course all of our costs are carefully calculated, no one knows what a cost ought to be. One of the ways of discovering...is to name a price so low as to force everybody in the place to the highest point of efficiency. The low price makes everybody dig for profits. We make more discoveries concerning manufacturing and selling under this forced method than by any method of leisurely investigation.[5]

Product Provincialism

The tantalizing profit possibilities of low unit production costs may be the most seriously self-deceiving attitude that can afflict a company, particularly a "growth" company where an apparently assured expansion of demand already tends to undermine a proper concern for the importance of marketing and the customer.

The usual result of this narrow preoccupation with so-called concrete matters is that instead of growing, the industry declines. It usually means that the product fails to adapt to the constantly changing patterns of consumer needs and tastes, to new and modified marketing institutions and practices, or to product developments in competing or complementary industries. The industry has its eyes so firmly on its own specific product that it does not see how it is being made obsolete.

The classical example of this is the buggy whip industry. No amount of product improvement could stave off its death sentence. But had the industry defined itself as being in the transportation business rather than the buggy whip business, it might have survived. It would have done what survival always entails, that is, change. Even if it had only defined its business as providing a stimulant or catalyst to an energy source, it might have survived by becoming a manufacturer of, say, fanbelts or air cleaners.

What may some day be a still more classical example is, again, the oil industry. Having let others steal marvelous opportunities from it (e.g., natural gas, as already mentioned, missile fuels, and jet engine lubricants), one would expect it to have taken steps never to let that happen again.

But this is not the case. We are now getting extraordinary new developments in fuel systems specifically designed to power automobiles. Not only are these developments concentrated in firms outside the petroleum industry, but petroleum is almost systematically ignoring them, securely content in its wedded bliss to oil. It is the story of the kerosene lamp versus the incandescent lamp all over again. Oil is trying to improve hydrocarbon fuels rather than to develop *any* fuels best suited to the needs of their users, whether or not made in different ways and with different raw materials from oil.

Here are some of the things which nonpetroleum companies are working on: Over a dozen such firms now have advanced working models of energy systems which, when perfected, will replace the internal combustion engine and eliminate the demand for gasoline. The superior merit of each of these systems is their elimination of frequent, time-consuming, and irritating refueling stops. Most of these systems are fuel cells designed to create electrical energy directly from chemicals without combustion. Most of them use chemicals that are not derived from oil, generally hydrogen and oxygen.

Several other companies have advanced models of electric storage batteries designed to power automobiles. One of these is an aircraft producer that is working jointly with several electric utility companies. The latter hope to use off-peak generating capacity to supply overnight plug-in battery regeneration. Another company, also using the battery approach, is a medium-size electronics firm with extensive small-battery experience that it developed in connection with its work on hearing aids. It is collaborating with an automobile manufacturer. Recent improvements arising from the need for high-powered miniature power storage plants in rockets have put us within reach of a relatively small battery capable of withstanding great overloads or surges of power. Germanium diode applications and batteries using sintered-plate and nickel-cadmium techniques promise to make a revolution in our energy sources.

Solar energy conversion systems are also getting increasing attention. One usually cautious Detroit auto executive recently ventured that solar-powered cars might be common by 1980.

As for the oil companies, they are more or less "watching developments," as one researcher director put it to me. A few are doing a bit of research on fuel cells, but almost always confined to developing cells powered by hydrocarbon chemicals. None of them is enthusiastically researching fuel cells, batteries, or solar power plants. None of them is spending a fraction as much on research in these profoundly important areas as they are on the usual run-of-the-mill things like reducing combustion chamber deposit in gasoline engines. One major integrated petroleum company recently took a tentative look at the fuel cell and concluded that although "the companies actively working on it indicate a belief in ultimate success...the timing and magnitude of its impact are too remote to warrant recognition in our forecasts.''

One might, of course, ask: Why should the oil companies do anything different? Would not chemical fuel cells, batteries, or solar energy kill the present product lines? The answer is that they would indeed, and that is precisely the reason for the oil firms having to develop these power units before their competitors, so they will not be companies without an industry.

Management might be more likely to do what is needed for its own preservation if it thought of itself as being in the energy business. But even that would not be enough if it persists in imprisoning itself in the narrow grip of its tight product orientation. It has to think of itself as taking care of customer needs, not finding, refining, or even selling oil. Since it genuinely thinks of its business as taking care of people's transportation needs, nothing can stop it from creating its own extravagantly profitable growth.

"Creative Destruction"

Since words are cheap and deeds are dear, it may be appropriate to indicate what this kind of thinking involves and leads to. Let us start at the beginning—the customer. It can be shown that motorists strongly dislike the bother, delay, and experience of buying gasoline. People actually do not buy gasoline. They cannot see it, taste it, feel it, appreciate it, or really test it. What they buy is the right to continue driving their cars. The gas station is like a tax collector to whom people are compelled to pay a periodic toll as the price of using their cars. This makes the gas station a basically unpopular institution. It can never be made popular or pleasant, only less unpopular, less unpleasant.

To reduce its unpopularity completely means eliminating it. Nobody likes a tax collector, not even a pleasantly cheerful one. Nobody likes to interrupt a trip to buy a phantom product, not even from a handsome Adonis or a seductive Venus. Hence, companies that are working on exotic fuel substitutes which will eliminate the need for frequent refueling are heading directly into the outstretched arms of the irritated motorist. They are riding a wave of inevitability, not because they are creating something which is technologically superior or more sophisticated, but because they are satisfying a powerful customer need. They are also eliminating noxious odors and air pollution.

Once the petroleum companies recognize the customer-satisfying logic of what another power system can do, they will see that they have no more choice about working on an efficient, long-lasting fuel (or some way of delivering present fuels without bothering the motorist) than the big food chains had a choice about going into the supermarket business, or the vacuum tube companies had a choice about making semiconductors. For their own good the oil firms will have to destroy their own highly profitable assets. No amount of wishful thinking can save them from the necessity of engaging in this form of "creative destruction."

I phrase the need as strongly as this because I think management must make quite an effort to break itself loose from conventional ways. It is all too easy in this day and age for a company or industry to let its sense of purpose become dominated by the economies of full production and to develop a dangerously lopsided product orientation. In short, if management lets itself drift, it invariably drifts in the direction of thinking of itself as producing goods and services, not customer satisfactions. While it probably will not descend to the depths of telling its salesmen, "You get rid of it; we'll worry about profits," it can, without knowing it, be practicing precisely that formula for withering decay. The historic fate of one growth industry after another has been its suicidal product provincialism.

DANGERS OF R & D

Another big danger to a firm's continued growth arises when top management is wholly transfixed by the profit possibilities of technical research and development. To illustrate I shall turn first to a new industry—electronics—and then return once more to the oil companies. By comparing a fresh example with a familiar one, I hope to emphasize the prevalence and insidiousness of a hazardous way of thinking.

Marketing Shortchanged

In case of electronics, the greatest danger which faces the glamorous new companies in this field is not that they do not pay enough attention to research and development, but that they pay *too much* attention to it. And the fact that the fastest growing electronics firms owe their eminence to their heavy emphasis on technical research is completely beside the point. They have vaulted to affluence on a sudden crest of unusually strong general receptiveness to new technical ideas. Also, their success has been shaped in the virtually guaranteed market of military subsidies and by military orders that in many cases actually preceded the existence of facilities to make the products. Their expansion has, in other words, been almost totally devoid of marketing effort.

Thus, they are growing up under conditions that come dangerously close to creating the illusion that a superior product will sell itself. Having created a successful company by making a superior product, it is not surprising that management continues to be oriented toward the product rather than the people who consume it. It develops the philosophy that continued growth is a matter of continued product innovation and improvement.

A number of other factors tend to strengthen and sustain this belief:

1. Because electronic products are highly complex and sophisticated, managements become top-heavy with engineers and scientists. This creates

a selective bias in favor of research and production at the expense of marketing. The organization tends to view itself as making things rather than satisfying customer needs. Marketing gets treated as a residual activity, "something else" that must be done once the vital job of product creation and production is completed.

2. To this bias in favor of product research, development, and production is added the bias in favor of dealing with controllable variables. Engineers and scientists are at home in the world of concrete things like machines, test tubes, production lines, and even balance sheets. The abstractions to which they feel kindly are those which are testable or manipulatable in the laboratory, or, if not testable, then functional, such as Euclid's axioms. In short, the managements of the new glamour-growth companies tend to favor those business activities which lend themselves to careful study, experimentation, and control—the hard, practical realities of the lab, the shop, the books.

What gets shortchanged are the realities of the *market*. Consumers are unpredictable, varied, fickle, stupid, shortsighted, stubborn, and generally bothersome. This is not what the engineer-managers say, but deep down in their consciousness it is what they believe. And this accounts for their concentrating on what they know and what they can control, namely, product research, engineering, and production. The emphasis on production becomes particularly attractive when the product can be made at declining unit costs. There is no more inviting way of making money than by running the plant full blast.

Today the top-heavy science-engineering-production orientation of so many electronics companies works reasonably well because they are pushing into new frontiers in which the armed services have pioneered virtually assured markets. The companies are in the felicitous position of having to fill, not find, markets; of not having to discover what the customer needs and wants, but of having the customer voluntarily come forward with specific new product demands. If a team of consultants had been assigned specifically to design a business situation calculated to prevent the emergence and development of a customer-oriented marketing viewpoint, it could not have produced anything better than the conditions just described.

Stepchild Treatment

The oil industry is a stunning example of how science, technology, and mass production can divert an entire group of companies from their main task. To the extent the consumer is studied at all (which is not much), the focus is forever on getting information which is designed to help the oil companies improve what they are now doing. They try to discover more convincing advertising themes, more effective sales promotional drives, what the market shares of the various companies are, what people like or dislike about service station dealers and oil companies, and so forth. Nobody seems as interested in probing deeply into the basic human needs that the industry might by trying to satisfy as in probing into the basic properties of the raw material that the companies work with in trying to deliver customer satisfactions.

Basic questions about customers and markets seldom get asked. The latter occupy a stepchild status. They are recognized as existing, as having to be taken care of, but not worth very much real thought or dedicated attention. Nobody gets as excited about the customer in his own backyard as about the oil in the Sahara Desert. Nothing illustrates better the neglect of marketing than its treatment in the industry press.

The centennial issue of the *American Petroleum Institute Quarterly,* published in 1959 to celebrate the discovery of oil in Titusville, Pennsylvania, contained twenty-one feature articles proclaiming the industry's greatness. Only one of these talked about its achievements in marketing, and that was only a pictorial record of how service station architecture was changed. The issue also contained a special section on "New Horizons," which was devoted to showing the magnificent role oil would play in America's future. Every reference was ebulliently optimistic, never implying once that oil might have some hard competition. Even the reference to atomic energy was a cheerful catalogue of how oil would help make atomic energy a success. There was not a single apprehension that the oil industry's affluence might be threatened or a suggestion that one "new horizon" might include new and better ways of serving oil's present customers.

But the most revealing example of the stepchild treatment that marketing gets was still another special series of short articles on "The Revolutionary Potential of Electronics." Under that heading this list of articles appeared in the table of contents:

- "In the Search for Oil"
- "In Production Operations"
- "In Refinery Processes"
- "In Pipeline Operations"

Significantly, every one of the industry's major functional areas is listed, *except* marketing. Why? Either it is believed that electronics holds no revolutionary potential for petroleum marketing (which is palpably wrong), or the editors forgot to discuss marketing (which is more likely, and illustrates its stepchild status).

The order in which the four functional areas are listed also betrays the alienation of the oil industry from the consumer. The industry is implicitly defined as beginning with the search for oil and ending with its distribution from the refinery. But the truth is, it seems to me, that the industry begins with the needs of the customer for its products. From that primal position its definition moves steadily backstream to areas of progressively lesser importance, until it finally comes to rest at the "search for oil."

Beginning and End

The view that an industry is a customer-satisfying process, not a goods-producing process, is vital for all businessmen to understand. An industry begins with the customer and his needs, not with a patent, a raw material, or a selling skill. Given the customer's needs, the industry develops backwards, first concerning itself with the physical *delivery* of customer satisfactions. Then it moves back further to *creating* the things by which these satisfactions are in part achieved. How these materials are created is a matter of indifference to the customer, hence the particular form of manufacturing, processing, or what-have-you cannot be considered as a vital aspect of the industry. Finally, the industry moves back still further to *finding* the raw materials necessary for making its products.

The irony of some industries oriented toward technical research and development is that the scientists who occupy the high executive positions are totaly unscientific when it comes to defining their companies' overall needs and purposes. They violate the first two rules of the scientific method—being aware of and defining their companies' problems, and then developing testable hypotheses about solving them. They are scientific only about the convenient things, such as laboratory and product experiments. The reason that the customer (and the satisfaction of his deepest needs) is not considered as being "the problem" is not because there is any certain belief that no such problem exists, but because an organizational lifetime has conditioned management to look in the opposite direction. Marketing is a stepchild.

I do not mean that selling is ignored. Far from it. But selling, again, is not marketing. As already pointed out, selling concerns itself with the tricks and techniques of getting people to exchange their cash for your product. It is not concerned with the values that the exchange is all about. And it does not, as marketing invariably does, view the entire business process as consisting of a tightly integrated effort to discover, create, arouse, and satisfy customer needs. The customer is somebody "out there" who, with proper cunning, can be separated from his loose change.

Actually, not even selling gets much attention in some technologically minded firms. Because there is a virtually guaranteed market for the abundant flow of their new products, they do not actually know what a real market is. It is as if they lived in a planned economy, moving their products routinely from factory to retail outlet. Their successful concentration on products tends to convince them of the soundness of what they have been doing, and they fail to see the gathering clouds over the market.

CONCLUSION

Less than seventy-five years ago American railroads enjoyed a fierce loyalty among astute Wall Streeters. European monarchs invested in them heavily. Eternal wealth was thought to be the benediction for anybody who could scrape a few thousand dollars together to put into rail stocks. No other form of transportation could compete with the railroads in speed, flexibility, durability, economy, and growth potentials. As Jacques Barzun put it, "By the turn of the century it was an institution, an image of man, a tradition, a code of honor, a source of poetry, a nursery of boyhood desires, a sublimest of toys, and the most solemn machine—next to the funeral hearse—that marks the epochs in man's life."[6]

Even after the advent of automobiles, trucks, and airplanes, the railroad tycoons remained imperturbably self-confident. If you had told them sixty years ago that in thirty years they would be flat on their backs, broke, and pleading for government subsidies, they would have thought you totally demented. Such a future was simply not considered possible. It was not even a discussable subject, or an askable question, or a matter which any sane person would consider worth speculating about. The very thought was insane. Yet a lot of insane notions now have matter-of-fact acceptance—for example, the idea of 100-ton tubes of metal moving smoothly through the air 20,000 feet above the earth, loaded with 100 sane and solid citizens casually drinking martinis—and they have dealt cruel blows to the railroads.

What specifically must other companies do to avoid this fate? What does customer orientation involve? These questions have in part been answered by the preceding examples and analysis. It would take another article to show in detail what is required for specific industries. In any case, it should be obvious that building an effective customer-oriented company involves far more than good intentions or promotional tricks; it involves profound matters of human organization and leadership. For the present, let me merely suggest what appear to be some general requirements.

Visceral Feel of Greatness

Obviously the company has to do what survival demands. It has to adapt to the requirements of the market, and it has to do it sooner rather than later. But mere survival is a so-so aspiration. Anybody can survive in some way or other, even the skid-row bum. The trick is to survive gallantly, to feel the surging impulse of commercial mastery; not just to experience the sweet smell of success, but to have the visceral feel of entrepreneurial greatness.

No organization can achieve greatness without a vigorous leader who is driven onward by his own pulsating *will to succeed*. He has to have a vision of grandeur, a vision that can produce eager followers in vast numbers. In business, the followers are the customers. To produce these customers, the entire coproration must be viewed as a customer-creating and customer-satisfying organism. Management must think of itself not as producing products but as providing customer-creating value satisfactions. It must push this idea (and everything it means and requires) into every nook and cranny of the organization. It has to do this continuously and with the kind of flair that excites and stimulates the people in it. Otherwise, the company will be merely a series of pigeonholed parts, with no consolidating sense of purpose or direction.

In short, the organization must learn to think of itself not as producing goods or services but as *buying customers,* as doing the things that will make people *want* to do business with it. And the chief executive himself has the inescapable responsibility for creating this environment, this viewpoint, this attitude, this aspiration. He himself must set the company's style, its direction, and its goals. This means he has to know precisely where he himself wants to go, and to make sure the whole organization is enthusiastically aware of where that is. This is a first requisite of leadership, for *unless he knows where he is going, any road will take him there.*

If any road is okay, the chief executive might as well pack his attache case and go fishing. If an organization does not know or care where it is going, it does not need to advertise that fact with a ceremonial figurehead. Everybody will notice it soon enough.

NOTES

[1] Jacques Barzun, "Trains and the Mind of Man," *Holiday* (February 1960), p. 21.

[2] For more details see M. M. Zimmerman, *The Super Market: A Revolution in Distribution* (New York: McGraw-Hill, 1955), p. 48.

[3] *Ibid.,* pp. 45–47.

[4] *The Affluent Society* (Boston: Houghton Mifflin, 1958), pp. 152–160.

[5] Henry Ford, *My Life and Work* (New York: Doubleday, 1923), pp. 146–147.

[6] Barzun, "Trains and Man," p. 20.

38

The Marketing Revolution

Robert J. Keith

The consumer, not the company, is in the middle. In today's economy the consumer, the man or woman who buys the product, is at the absolute dead center of the business universe. Companies revolve around the customer, not the other way around.

Growing acceptance of this consumer concept has had, and will have, far-reaching implications for business, achieving a virtual revolution in economic thinking. As the concept gains ever greater acceptance, marketing is emerging as the most important single function in business.

A REVOLUTION IN SCIENCE

A very apt analogy can be drawn with another revolution, one that goes back to the sixteenth century. At that time astronomers had great difficulty predicting the movements of the heavenly bodies. Their charts and computations and celestial calendars enabled them to estimate the approximate positions of the planets on any given date. But their calculations were never exact—there was always a variance.

Then a Polish scientist named Nicolaus Copernicus proposed a very simple answer to the problem. If, he proposed, we assume that the sun, and not the earth, is at the center of our system, and that the earth moves around the sun instead of the sun moving around the earth, all our calculations will prove correct.

The Pole's idea raised a storm of controversy. The earth, everyone knew, was at the center of the universe. But another scientist named Galileo put the theory to test—and it worked. The result was a complete unheaval in

Reprinted from Robert G. Keith, "The Marketing Revolution," in the *Journal of Marketing*, Vol. 24 (January 1960), pp. 35–38, published by the American Marketing Association.

scientific and philosophic thought. The effects of Copernicus' revolutionary idea are still being felt today.

A REVOLUTION IN MARKETING

In much the same way American business in general—and Pillsbury in particular—is undergoing a revolution of its own today: a marketing revolution.

This revolution stems from the same idea stated in the opening sentence of this article. No longer is the company at the center of the business universe. Today the customer is at the center.

Our attention has shifted from problems of production to problems of marketing, from the product we *can* make to the product the consumer *wants* us to make, from the company itself to the market place.

The marketing revolution has only begun. It is reasonable to expect that its implications will grow in the years to come, and that lingering effects will be felt a century, or more than one century, from today.

So far the theory has only been advanced, tested, and generally proved correct. As more and more businessmen grasp the concept, and put it to work, our economy will become truly marketing oriented.

PILLSBURY'S PATTERN: FOUR ERAS

Here is the way the marketing revolution came about at Pillsbury. The experience of this company has followed a typical pattern. There has been nothing unique, and each step in the evolution of the marketing concept has been taken in a way that is more meaningful because the steps are, in fact, typical.

Today in our company the marketing concept finds expression in the simple statement, "Nothing happens at Pillsbury until a sale is made." This statement represents basic reorientation on the part of our management. For, not too many years ago, the ordering of functions in our business placed finance first, production second, and sales last.

How did we arrive at our present point of view? Pillsbury's progress in the marketing revolution divides neatly into four separate eras—eras which parallel rather closely the classic pattern of development in the marketing revolution.

FIRST ERA—PRODUCTION ORIENTED

First came the era of manufacturing. It began with the formation of the company in 1869 and continued into the 1930s. It is significant that the *idea* for the formation of our company came from the *availability* of high-quality wheat and the *proximity* of water power—and not from the availability and proximity of growing major market areas, or the demand for better, less expensive, more convenient flour products.

Of course, these elements were potentially present. But the two major elements which fused in the mind of Charles A. Pillsbury and prompted him to invest his modest capital in a flour mill were, on the one hand, wheat, and, on the other hand, water power. His principal concern was with production, not marketing.

His thought and judgment were typical of the business thinking of this day. And such thinking was adequate and proper for the times.

Our company philosophy in this era might have been stated this way: "We are professional flour millers. Blessed with a supply of the finest North American wheat, plenty of water power, and excellent milling machinery, we produce flour of the highest quality. Our basic function is to mill high-quality flour, and of course (and almost incidentally) we must hire salesmen to sell it, just as we hire accountants to keep our books."

The young company's first new product reveals an interesting example of the thinking of this era. The product was middlings, the bran left over after milling. Millfeed, as the product came to be known, proved a valuable product because it was an excellent nutrient for cattle. But the impetus to launch the new product came not from a consideration of the nutritional needs of cattle or a marketing analysis. It came primarily from the deisre to dispose of a by-product! The new product decision was production oriented, not marketing oriented.

SECOND ERA—SALES ORIENTED

In the 1930s Pillsbury moved into its second era of development as a marketing company. This was the era of sales. For the first time we began to be highly conscious of the consumer, her wants, and her prejudices, as a key factor in the business equation. We established a commercial research department to provide us with facts about the market.

We also became more aware of the importance of our dealers, the wholesale and retail grocers who provided a vital link in our chain of distribution from the mill to the home. Knowing that consumers and dealers as well were vital to the company's success, we could no longer simply mark them down as unknowns in our figuring. With this realization, we took the first step along the road to becoming a marketing company.

Pillsbury's thinking in this second era could be summed up like this: "We are a flour-milling company manufacturing a number of products for the consumer market. We must have a first-rate sales organization which can dispose of all the products we can make at a favorable price. We must back up this sales force with consumer advertising and market intelligence. We want our salesmen and our dealers to have all the tools they need for moving the output of our plants to the consumer."

Still not a marketing philosophy, but we were getting closer.

THIRD ERA—MARKETING ORIENTED

It was at the start of the present decade that Pillsbury entered the marketing era. The amazing growth of our consumer business as the result of introducing baking mixes provided the immediate impetus. But the groundwork had been laid by key men who developed our sales concepts in the middle forties.

With the new cake mixes (products of our research program) ringing up sales on the cash register, and with the realization that research and production could produce literally hundreds of new and different products, we faced for the first time the necessity for selecting the best new products. We needed a set of criteria for selecting the kind of products we would manufacture. We needed an organization to establish and maintain these criteria, and for attaining maximum sale of the products we did select.

We needed, in fact, to build into our company a new management function which would direct and control all the other corporate functions from procurement to production to advertising to sales. This function was marketing. Our solution was to establish the present marketing department.

This department developed the criteria which we would use in determining which products to market. *And these criteria were, and are, nothing more nor less than those of the consumer herself.* We moved the mountain out to find out what Mahomet, and Mrs. Mahomet, wanted. The company's purpose was no longer to mill four, nor to manufacture a wide variety of products, but to satisfy the needs and desires, both actual and potential, of our customers.

If we were to restate our philosophy during the past decade as simply as possible, it would read: "We make and sell products for consumers."

The business universe, we realized, did not have room at the center for Pillsbury or any other company or groups of companies. It was already occupied by the customers.

This is the concept at the core of the marketing revolution. How did we put it to work for Pillsbury?

The Brand-Manager Concept

The first move was to transform our small advertising department into a marketing department. The move involved far more than changing the name on organizational charts. It required the introduction of a new and vitally important organizational concept—the brand-manager concept.

The brand-manager idea is the very backbone of marketing at Pillsbury. The man who bears the title, brand manager, has total accountability for results. He directs the marketing of his product as if it were his own business. Production does its job, and finance keeps the profit figures. Otherwise, the brand manager has total responsibility for marketing his product. This responsibility encompasses pricing, commercial research, competitive activity, home service and publicity coordination, legal details, budgets, advertising plans, sales promotion, and execution of plans. The brand manager must think first, last, and always of his sales target, the consumer.

Marketing permeates the entire organization. Marketing plans and executes the sale—all the way from the inception of the product idea, through its development and distribution, to the customer purchase. Marketing begins and ends with the consumer. New product ideas are conceived after careful study of her wants and needs, her likes and dislikes. Then marketing takes the idea and marshals all the forces of the corporation to translate the idea into product and the product into sales.

In the early days of the company, consumer orientation did not seem so important. The company made flour, and flour was a staple—no one would question the availability of a market. Today we must determine whether the American housewife will buy lemon pudding cake in preference to orange angel food. The variables in the equation have multiplied, just as the number of products on the grocers' shelves have multiplied from a hundred or so into many thousands.

When we first began operating under this new marketing concept, we encountered the problems which always accompany any major reorientation. Our people were young and frankly immature in some areas of business; but they were men possessed of an idea and they fought for it. The idea was almost too powerful. The marketing concept proved its worth in sales, but it upset many of the internal balances of the corporation. Marketing-oriented decisions resulted in peaks and valleys in production, schedules, labor, and inventories. But the system worked. It worked better and better as maverick marketing men became motivated toward tonnage and profit.

FOURTH ERA—MARKETING CONTROL

Today marketing is coming into its own. Pillsbury stands on the brink of its fourth major era in the marketing revolution.

Basically, the philosophy of this fourth era can be summarized this way: "We are moving from a company which has the marketing concept to a marketing company."

Marketing today sets company operating policy short-term. It will come to influence long-range policy more and more. Where today consumer research, technical research, procurement, production, advertising, and sales swing into action under the broad canopy established by marketing, tomorrow, capital and financial planning, ten-year volume and profit goals will also come under the aegis of marketing. More than any other function, marketing must be tied to top management.

Today our marketing people know more about inventories than anyone in top management. Tomorrow's marketing man must know capital financing and the implications of marketing planning on long-range profit forecasting.

Today technical research receives almost all of its guidance and direction from marketing. Tomorrow marketing will assume a more creative function in the advertising area, both in terms of ideas and media selection.

Changes in the Future

The marketing revolution has only begun. There are still those who resist its basic idea, just as there are always those who will resist change in business, government, or any other form of human institution.

As the marketing revolution gains momentum, there will be more changes. The concept of the customer at the center will remain valid; but business must adjust to the shifting tastes and likes and desires and needs which have always characterized the American consumer.

For many years the geographical center of the United Stats lay in a small Kansas town. Then a new state, Alaska, came along, and the center shifted to the north and west. Hawaii was admitted to the Union and the geographical midpoint took another jump to the west. In very much the same way, modern business must anticipate the restless shifting of buying attitudes, as customer preferences move north, south, east, or west from a liquid center. There is nothing static about the marketing revolution, and that is part of its fascination. The old order has changed, yielding place to the new—but the new order will have its quota of changes, too.

At Pillsbury, as our fourth era progresses, marketing will become the basic motivating force for the entire corporation. Soon it will be true that every activity of the corporation—from finance to sales to production—is aimed at satisfying the needs and desires of the consumer. When that stage of development is reached, the marketing revolution will be complete.

39

The Concept of the
Marketing Mix

Neil H. Borden

I have always found it interesting to observe how an apt or colorful term may catch on, gain wide usage, and help further understanding of a concept that has already been expressed in less appealing and communicative terms. Such has been true of the phrase "marketing mix," which I began to use in my teaching and writing some fifteen years ago. In a relatively short time it has come to have wide usage. This note tells of the evolution of the marketing mix concept.

The phrase was suggested to me by a paragraph in a research bulletin on the management of marketing costs, written by my associate, Professor James Culliton (1948). In this study of manufacturers' marketing costs he described the business executive as a

"decider," an "artist"—a "mixer of ingredients," who sometimes follows a recipe prepared by others, sometimes prepares his own recipe as he goes along, sometimes adapts a recipe to the ingredients immediately available, and sometimes experiments with or invents ingredients no one else has tried.

I liked his idea of calling a marketing executive a "mixer of ingredients," one who is constantly engaged in fashioning creatively a mix of marketing procedures and policies in his efforts to produce a profitable enterprise.

For many years previous to Culliton's cost study, the wide variations in the procedures and policies employed by managements of manufacturing firms in their marketing programs and the correspondingly wide variation in the costs of these marketing functions (which Culliton aptly ascribed to the varied "mixing of ingredients") had become increasingly evident as we had gathered marketing cases at the Harvard Business School. The marked

Reprinted from Neil H. Borden, "The Concept of the Marketing Mix," in the *Journal of Advertising Research* (June 1964), pp. 2–7, published by the American Marketing Association.

differences in the patterns or formulas of the marketing programs not only were evident through facts disclosed in case histories, but also were reflected clearly in the figures of a cost study of food manufacturers made by the Harvard Bureau of Business Research in 1929. The primary objective of this study was to determine common figures of expenses for various marketing functions among food manufacturing companies, similar to the common cost figures which had been determined in previous years for various kinds of retail and wholesale businesses. In this manufacturer's study we were unable, with the data gathered, to determine common expense figures that had much significance as standards by which to guide management (such as had been possible in the studies of retail and wholesale trades, where the methods of operation tended toward uniformity). Instead, among food manufacturers the ratios of sales devoted to the various functions of marketing such as advertising, personal selling, packaging, and so on, were found to be widely divergent, no matter how we grouped our respondents. Each respondent gave data that tended to uniqueness.

Culliton's study of marketing costs in 1947 and 1948 was a second effort to find out, among other objectives, whether a bigger sample and a more careful classification of companies would produce evidence of operating uniformities that would give helpful common expense figures. But the result was the same as in our early study: there was wide diversity in cost ratios among any classifications of firms which were set up, and no common figures were found that had much value. This was true whether companies were grouped according to similarity in product lines, amount of sales, territorial extent of operations, or other bases of classification.

Relatively early in my study of advertising, it had become evident that understanding of advertising usage by manufacturers in any case had to come from an analysis of advertising's place as one element in the total marketing program of the firm. I came to realize that it is essential always to ask: what overall marketing strategy has been or might be employed to bring about a profitable operation in light of the circumstances faced by the management? What combination of marketing procedures and policies has been or might be adopted to bring about desired behavior of trade and consumers at costs that will permit a profit? Specifically, how can advertising, personal selling, pricing, packaging, channels, warehousing, and the other elements of a marketing program be manipulated and fitted together in a way that will give a profitable operation? In short, I saw that every advertising management case called for a consideration of the strategy to be adopted for the total marketing program, with advertising recognized as only one element whose form and extent depended on its careful adjustment to the other parts of the program.

The soundness of this viewpoint was supported by case histories throughout my volume, *The Economic Effects of Advertising* (Borden 1942). In the chapters devoted to the utilization of advertising by business, I had pointed out the innumerable combinations of marketing methods and policies that might be adopted by a manager in arriving at a marketing plan. For instance, in the area of branding, he might elect to adopt an individualized brand or a family brand. Or he might decide to sell his product unbranded or under private label. Any decision in the area of brand policy in turn has immediate implications that bear on his selection of channels of distribution, sales force methods, packaging, promotional procedure, and advertising. Throughout the volume the case materials cited show that the way in which any marketing function is designed and the burden placed upon the function are determined largely by the overall marketing strategy adopted by managements to meet the market conditions under which they operate. The forces met by different firms vary widely. Accordingly, the programs fashioned differ widely.

Regarding advertising, which was the function under focus in the economic effects volume, I said at one point:

> In all the above illustrative situations it should be recognized that advertising is not an operating method to be considered as something apart, as something whose profit value is to be judged alone. An able management does not ask, "Shall we use or not use advertising," without consideration of the product and of other management procedures to be employed. Rather the question is always one of finding a management formula giving advertising its due place in the combination of manufacturing methods, product form, pricing, promotion and selling methods, and distribution methods. As previously pointed out different formulas, i.e., different combinations of methods, may be profitably employed by competing manufacturers.

From the above it can be seen why Culliton's description of a marketing manager as a "mixer of ingredients" immediately appealed to me as an apt and easily understandable phrase, far better than my previous references to the marketing man as an empiricist seeking in any situation to devise a profitable "pattern" or "formula" of marketing operations from among the many procedures and policies that were open to him. If he was a "mixer of ingredients," what he designed was a "marketing mix."

It was logical to proceed from a realization of the existence of a variety of "marketing mixes" to the development of a concept that would comprehend not only this variety, but also the market forces that cause managements to produce a variety of mixes. It is the problems raised by these forces that lead marketing managers to exercise their wits in devising mixes or programs which they hope will give a profitable business operation.

To portray this broadened concept in a visual presentation requires merely:

1. A list of the important elements or ingredients that make up marketing programs

2. A list of the forces that bear on the marketing operation of a firm and
to which the marketing manager must adjust in his search for a mix or
program that can be successful

The list of elements of the marketing mix in such a visual presentation
can be long or short, depending on how far one wishes to go in his
classification and subclassification of the marketing procedures and policies
with which marketing managements deal when devising marketing
programs. The list of elements which I have employed in my teaching and
consulting work covers the principal areas of marketing activities which call
for management decisions as revealed by case histories. I realize others
might build a different list. Mine is as follows:

ELEMENTS OF THE MARKETING MIX OF MANUFACTURERS

1. *Product Planning*—policies and procedures relating to:
   a. Product lines to be offered—qualities, design, etc.
   b. Markets to sell: whom, where, when, and in what quantity
   c. New product policy—research and development program
2. *Pricing*—policies and procedures relating to:
   a. Price level to adopt
   b. Specific prices to adopt (odd-even, etc.)
   c. Price policy, e.g., one-price or varying price, price maintenance,
   use of list prices, etc.
   d. Margins to adopt—for company; for the trade
3. *Branding*—policies and procedures relating to:
   a. Selection of trade marks
   b. Brand policy—individualized or family brand
   c. Sale under private label or unbranded
4. *Channels of Distribution*—policies and procedures relating to:
   a. Channels to use between plant and consumer
   b. Degree of selectivity among wholesalers and retailers
   c. Efforts to gain cooperation of the trade
5. *Personal Selling*—policies and procedures relating to:
   a. Burden to be placed on personal selling and the methods to be
   employed in:
      1. Manufacturer's organization
      2. Wholesale segment of the trade
      3. Retail segment of the trade
6. *Advertising*—policies and procedures relating to:
   a. Amount to spend—i.e., the burden to be placed on advertising
   b. Copy platform to adopt:
      1. Product image desired
      2. Corporate image desired
   c. Mix of advertising: to the trade; through the trade; to consumers

7. *Promotions*—policies and procedures relating to:
    a. Burden to place on special selling plans or devices directed at or through the trade
    b. Form of these devices for consumer promotions, for trade promotions
8. *Packaging*—policies and procedures relating to:
    a. Formulation of package and label
9. *Display*—policies and procedures relating to:
    a. Burden to be put on display to help effect sale
    b. Methods to adopt to secure display
10. *Servicing*—policies and procedures relating to:
    a. Providing service needed
11. *Physical Handling*—policies and procedures relating to:
    a. Warehousing
    b. Transportation
    c. Inventories
12. *Fact Finding and Analysis*—policies and procedures relating to:
    a. Securing, analysis, and use of facts in marketing operations

Also if one were to make a list of all the forces which managements weigh at one time or another when formulating their marketing mixes, it would be very long indeed, for the behavior of individuals and groups in all spheres of life has a bearing, first, on what goods and services are produced and consumed, and second, on the procedures that may be employed in bringing about exchange of these goods and services. However, the important forces which bear on marketers, all arising from the behavior of individuals or groups, may readily be listed under four heads, namely the behavior of consumers, the trade, competitors, and government.

The outline following contains these four behavioral forces with notations of some of the important behavioral determinants within each force. These must be studied and understood by the marketer, if his marketing mix is to be successful. The great quest of marketing management is to understand the behavior of humans in response to the stimuli to which they are subjected. The skillful marketer is one who is a perceptive and practical psychologist and sociologist, who has keen insight into individual and group behavior, who can foresee changes in behavior that develop in a dynamic world, who has creative ability for building well-knit programs because he has the capacity to visualize the probable response of consumers, trade, and competitors to his moves. His skill in forecasting response to his marketing moves should well be supplemented by a further skill in devising and using tests and measurements to check consumer or trade response to his program or parts thereof, for no marketer has so much prescience that he can proceed without empirical check.

Following, then, is the suggested outline of forces which govern the mixing of marketing elements. This list and that of the elements taken together provide a visual presentation of the concept of the marketing mix.

MARKET FORCES BEARING ON THE MARKETING MIX

1. *Consumers' Buying Behavior,* as determined by their:
   a. Motivation in purchasing
   b. Buying habits
   c. Living habits
   d. Environment (present and future, as revealed by trends, for environment influences consumers' attitudes toward products and their use of them)
   e. Buyer power
   f. Number (i.e., how many)
2. *The Trade's Behavior*—wholesalers' and retailers' behavior, as influenced by:
   a. Their motivations
   b. Their structure, practices, and attitudes
   c. Trends in structure and procedures that portend change
3. *Competitors' Position and Behavior,* as influenced by:
   a. Industry structure and the firm's relation thereto
      1. Size and strength of competitors
      2. Number of competitors and degree of industry concentration
      3. Indirect competition—i.e., from other products
   b. Relation of supply to demand—oversupply or undersupply
   c. Product choices offered consumers by the industry—i.e., quality, price, service
   d. Degree to which competitors compete on price vs. nonprice bases
   e. Competitors' motivations and attitudes—their likely response to the actions of other firms
   f. Trends technological and social, portending change in supply and demand
4. *Governmental Behavior—Controls over Marketing:*
   a. Regulations over products
   b. Regulations over pricing
   c. Regulations over competitive practices
   d. Regulations over advertising and promotion

When building a marketing program to fit the needs of his firm, the marketing manager has to weigh the behavioral forces and then juggle marketing elements in his mix with a keen eye on the resources with which he has to work. His firm is but one small organism in a large universe of complex forces. His firm is only a part of an industry that is competing with many other industries. What does the firm have in terms of money, product line, organization, and reputation with which to work? The manager must devise a mix of procedures that fit these resources. If his firm is small, he must judge the response of consumers, trade, and competition in light of his position, resources, and the influence that he can exert in the market. He must look for special opportunities in product or method of operation. The small firm cannot employ the procedures of the big firm. Though he may sell the same kind of product as the big firm, his marketing strategy is likely to be widely different in many respects. Innumerable instances of this fact might be cited. For example, in the industrial goods field, small firms often seek to build sales on a limited and highly specialized line, whereas industry leaders seek patronage for full lines. Small firms often elect to go in for regional sales rather than attempt the national distribution practiced by larger companies. Again, the company of limited resources often elects to limit its production and sales to products whose potential is too small to attract the big fellows. Still again, companies with small resources in the cosmetic field not infrequently have set up introductory marketing programs employing aggressive personal selling and a "push" strategy with distribution limited to leading department stores. Their initially small advertising funds have been directed through these selected retail outlets, with the offering of the products and their story told over the signature of the stores. The strategy has been to borrow kudos for their products from the leading stores' reputations and to gain a gradual radiation of distribution to smaller stores in all types of channels, such as often comes from the trade's follow-the-leader behavior. Only after resources have grown from mounting sales has a dense retail distribution been aggressively sought and a shift made to place the selling burden more and more on company-signed advertising.

The above strategy was employed for Toni products and Stoppett deodorant in their early marketing stages when the resources of their producers were limited (cf. case of Jules Montenier, Inc. in Borden and Marshall 1959, pp. 498–518). In contrast, cosmetic manufacturers with large resources have generally followed a "pull" strategy for the introduction of new products, relying on heavy campaigns of advertising in a rapid succession of area introductions to induce a hoped-for, complete retail coverage from the start (cf. case of Bristol-Myers Company in Borden and Marshall 1959, pp. 519-33). These introductory campaigns have been undertaken only after careful programs of product development and test marketing have given assurance that product and selling plans had high promise of success.

Many additional instances of the varying strategy employed by small vs. large enterprises might be cited. But those given serve to illustrate the point that managements must fashion their mixes to fit their resources. Their objectives must be realistic.

LONG VS. SHORT-TERM ASPECTS OF MARKETING MIX

The marketing mix of a firm in large part is the product of the evolution that comes from day-to-day marketing. At any time the mix represents the program that a management has evolved to meet the problems with which it is constantly faced in an ever-changing, ever-challenging market. There are continuous tactical maneuvers: a new product, aggressive promotion, or price change initiated by a competitor must be considered and met; the failure of the trade to provide adequate market coverage or display must be remedied; a faltering sales force must be reorganized and stimulated; a decline in sales share must be diagnosed and remedied; an advertising approach that has lost effectiveness must be replaced; a general business decline must be countered. All such problems call for a management's maintaining effective channels of information relative to its own operations and to the day-to-day behavior of consumers, competitors, and the trade. Thus, we may observe that short range forces play a large part in the fashioning of the mix to be used at any time and in determining the allocation of expenditures among the various functional accounts of the operating statement.

But the overall strategy employed in a marketing mix is the product of longer range plans and procedures dictated in part by past empiricism and in part, if the management is a good one, by management foresight as to what needs to be done to keep the firm successful in a changing world. As the world has become more and more dynamic, blessed is that corporation whose managers have foresight and can study trends of all kinds—natural, economic, social, and technological—and, guided by these, devise long-range plans that give promise of keeping their corporations afloat and successful in the turbulent sea of market change. Accordingly, when we think of the marketing mix, we need to give particular heed today to devising a mix based on long-range planning that promises to fit the world of five or ten or more years hence. Provision for effective long-range planning in corporate organization and procedure has become more and more recognized as the earmark of good management in a world that has become increasingly subject to rapid change.

To cite an instance among American marketing organizations which have shown foresight in adjusting the marketing mix to meet social and economic change, I look upon Sears, Roebuck and Company as an outstanding example. After building an unusually successful mail order business to meet the needs of a rural America, Sears management foresaw the need to depart from its marketing pattern as a mail order company catering primarily to farmers. The trend from a rural to an urban United States was going on apace. The automobile and good roads promised to make town and city stores increasingly available to those who continued to be farmers. Relatively early, Sears launched a chain of stores across the land, each easily accessible by highway to both farmer and city resident, and with adequate parking space for customers. In time there followed the remarkable telephone and mail order plan directed at urban residents to make buying easy for Americans when congested city streets and highways made shopping increasingly distasteful. Similarly, in the areas of planning products which would meet the desires of consumers in a fast changing world, of shaping its servicing to meet the needs of a wide variety of mechanical products, of pricing procedures to meet the challenging competition that came with the advent of discount retailers, the Sears organization has shown a foresight, adaptability, and creative ability worthy of emulation. The amazing growth and profitability of the company attest to the foresight and skill of its management. Its history shows the wisdom of careful attention to market forces and their impending change in devising marketing mixes that may assure growth.

USE OF THE MARKETING MIX CONCEPT

Like many concepts, the marketing mix concept seems relatively simple, once it has been expressed. I know that before they were ever tagged with the nomenclature of "concept," the ideas involved were widely understood among marketers as a result of the growing knowledge about marketing and marketing procedures that came during the preceding half century. But I have found for myself that once the ideas were reduced to a formal statement with an accompanying visual presentation, the concept of the mix has proved a helpful device in teaching, in business problem solving, and, generally, as an aid in thinking about marketing. First of all, it is helpful in giving an answer to the question often raised as to "what is marketing?" A chart which shows the elements of the mix and the forces that bear on the mix helps to bring understanding of what marketing is. It helps to explain why in our dynamic world the thinking of management in all its functional areas must be oriented to the market.

In recent years I have kept an abbreviated chart showing the elements and the forces of the marketing mix in front of my classes at all times. In case discussion it has proven a handy device by which to raise queries as to whether the student has recognized the implications of any recommendation he might have made in the areas of the several elements of the mix. Or, referring to the forces, we can question whether all the pertinent market forces have been given due consideration. Continual reference to the mix chart leads me to feel that the students' understanding of "what marketing is" is strengthened. The constant presence and use of the chart leaves a deeper understanding that marketing is the devising of programs that successfully meet the forces of the market.

In problem solving the marketing mix chart is a constant reminder of:

1. The fact that a problem seemingly lying in one segment of the mix

must be deliberated with constant thought regarding the effect of any change in that sector on the other areas of marketing operations. The necessity of integration in marketing thinking is ever present.
2. The need of careful study of the market forces as they might bear on problems in hand.

In short, the mix chart provides an ever ready check list as to areas into which to guide thinking when considering marketing questions or dealing with marketing problems.

MARKETING: SCIENCE OR ART?

The quest for a "science of marketing" is hard upon us. If science is in part a systematic formulation and arrangement of facts in a way to help understanding, then the concept of the marketing mix may possibly be considered a small contribution in the search for a science of marketing. If we think of a marketing science as involving the observation and classification of facts and the establishment of verifiable laws that can be used by the marketer as a guide to action with assurance that predicted results will ensue, then we cannot be said to have gotten far toward establishing a science. The concept of the mix lays out the areas in which facts should be assembled, these to serve as a guide to management judgment in building marketing mixes. In the last few decades American marketers have made substantial progress in adopting the scientific method in assembling facts. They have sharpened the tools of fact finding—both those arising within the business and those external to it. Aided by these facts and by the skills developed through careful observation and experience, marketers are better fitted to practice the art of designing marketing mixes than would be the case had not the techniques of gathering facts been advanced as they have been in recent decades. Moreover, marketers have made progress in the use of the scientific method in designing tests whereby the results from mixes or parts of mixes can be measured. Thereby marketers have been learning how to subject the hypotheses of their mix artists to empirical check.

With continued improvement in the search for and the recording of facts pertinent to marketing, with further application of the controlled experiment, and with an extension and careful recording of case histories, we may hope for a gradual formulation of clearly defined and helpful marketing laws. Until then, and even then, marketing and the building of marketing mixes will largely lie in the realm of art.

REFERENCES

Borden, Neil H., *The Economics Effects of Advertising* (Homewood, Ill.: Richard D. Irwin, Inc., 1942).

Borden, Neil H., and M. V. Marshall, *Advertising Management: Text and Cases* (Homewood, Ill.: Richard D. Irwin, Inc., 1959).

Culliton, James W., *The Management of Marketing Costs* (Boston: Division of Research, Graduate School of Business Administration, Harvard University, 1948).

40

Product Differentiation and Market Segmentation as Alternative Marketing Strategies

Wendell R. Smith

During the decade of the 1930s, the work of Robinson and Chamberlin resulted in a revitalization of economic theory. While classical and neo-classical theory provided a useful framework for economic analysis, the theories of perfect competition and pure monopoly had become inadequate as explanations of the contemporary business scene. The theory of perfect competition assumes homogeneity among the components of both the demand and supply sides of the market, but diversity or heterogeneity had come to be the rule rather than the exception. This analysis reviews major marketing strategy alternatives that are available to planners and mer-chandisers of products in an environment characterized by imperfect competition.

DIVERSITY IN SUPPLY

That there is a lack of homogeneity or close similarity among the items offered to the market by individual manufacturers of various products is obvious in any variety store, department store, or shopping center. In many cases the impact of this diversity is amplified by advertising and promo-tional activities. Today's advertising and promotion tends to emphasize appeals to *selective* rather than *primary* buying motives and to point out the distinctive or differentiating features of the advertiser's product or service offer.

The presence of differences in the sales offers made by competing suppliers produces a diversity in supply that is inconsistent with the assump-

Reprinted from Wendell R. Smith, "Product Differentiation and Market Segmentation as Alternative Marketing Strategies," in the *Journal of Marketing* (July 1956), pp. 3–8, published by the American Marketing Association.

tions of earlier theory. The reasons for the presence of diversity in specific markets are many and include the following:

1. Variations in the production equipment and methods or processes used by different manufacturers of products designed for the same or similar uses
2. Specialized or superior resources enjoyed by favorably situated manufacturers
3. Unequal progress among competitors in design, development, and improvement of products
4. The inability of manufacturers in some industries to eliminate product variations even through the application of quality control techniques
5. Variations in producers' estimates of the nature of market demand with reference to such matters as price sensitivity, color, material, or package size

Because of these and other factors, both planned and uncontrollable differences exist in the products of an industry. As a result, sellers make different appeals in support of their marketing efforts.

DIVERSITY OR VARIATIONS IN CONSUMER DEMAND

Under present-day conditions of imperfect competition, marketing managers are generally responsible for selecting the overall marketing strategy or combination of strategies best suited to a firm's requirements at any particular point in time. The strategy selected may consist of a program designed to bring about the *convergence* of individual market demands for a variety of products upon a single or limited offering to the market. This is often accomplished by the achievement of product differentiation through advertising and promotion. In this way, variations in the demands of individual consumers are minimized or brought into line by means of effective use of appealing product claims designed to make a satisfactory volume of demand *converge* upon the product or product line being promoted. This strategy was once believed to be essential as the marketing counterpart to standardization and mass production in manufacturing because of the rigidities imposed by production cost considerations.

In some cases, however, the marketer may determine that it is better to accept *divergent* demand as a market characteristic and to adjust product lines and marketing strategy accordingly. This implies ability to merchandise to a heterogeneous market by emphasizing the precision with which a firm's products can satisfy the requirements of one or more distinguishable market segments. The strategy of product differentiation here gives way to marketing programs based upon measurement and definition of market differences.

Lack of homogeneity on the demand side may be based upon different customs, desire for variety, or desire for exclusiveness or may arise from basic differences in user needs. Some divergence in demand is the result of shopping errors in the market. Not all consumers have the desire or the ability to shop in a sufficiently efficient or rational manner as to bring about selection of the most needed or most wanted goods or services.

Diversity on the demand side of the market is nothing new to sales management. It has always been accepted as a fact to be dealt with in industrial markets where production to order rather than for the market is common. Here, however, the loss of precision in the satisfying of customer requirements that would be necessitated by attempts to bring about convergence of demand is often impractical and, in some cases, impossible. However, even in the industrial marketing, the strategy of product differentiation should be considered in cases where products are applicable to several industries and may have horizontal markets of substantial size.

LONG-TERM IMPLICATIONS

While contemporary economic theory deals with the nature of product differentiation and its effects upon the operation of the total economy, the alternative strategies of product differentiation and market segmentation have received less attention. Empirical analysis of contemporary marketing activity supports the hypothesis that, while product differentiation and market segmentation are closely related (perhaps even inseparable) concepts, attempts to distinguish between these approaches may be productive of clarity in theory as well as greater precision in the planning of marketing operations. Not only do strategies of differentiation and segmentation call for differing systems of action at any point in time, but the dynamics of markets and marketing underscore the importance of varying degrees of diversity *through time* and suggest that the rational selection of marketing strategies is a requirement for the achievement of maximum functional effectiveness in the economy as a whole.

If a rational selection of strategies is to be made, an integrated approach to the minimizing of total costs must take precedence over separate approaches to minimization of production costs on the one hand, and marketing costs on the other. Strategy determination must be regarded as an overall management decision which will influence and require facilitating policies affecting both production and marketing activities.

DIFFERENCES BETWEEN STRATEGIES OF DIFFERENTIATION AND SEGMENTATION

Product differentiation and market segmentation are both consistent with the framework of imperfect competition.[1] In its simplest terms, *product differentiation* is concerned with the bending of demand to the will of supply. It is an attempt to shift or to change the slope of the demand curve for the market offering of an individual supplier. This strategy may also be employed by a group of suppliers such as a farm cooperative, the members of which have agreed to act together. It results from the desire to establish a kind of equilibrium in the market by bringing about adjustment of market demand to supply conditions favorable to the seller.

Segmentation is based upon developments on the demand side of the market and represents a rational and more precise adjustment of product and marketing effort to consumer or user requirements. In the language of the economist, segmentation is *disaggregative* in its effects and tends to bring about recognition of several demand schedules where only one was recognized before.

Attention has been drawn to this area of analysis by the increasing number of cases in which business problems have become soluble by doing something about marketing programs and product policies that overgeneralize both markets and marketing effort. These are situations where intensive promotion designed to differentiate the company's products was not accomplishing its objective—cases where failure to recognize the reality of market segments was resulting in loss of market position.

While successful product differentiation will result in giving the marketer a horizontal share of a broad and generalized market, equally successful application of the strategy of market segmentation tends to produce depth of market position in the segments that are effectively defined and penetrated. The differentiator seeks to secure a layer of the market cake, whereas one who employs market segmentation strives to secure one or more wedge-shaped pieces.

Many examples of market segmentation can be cited; the cigarette and automobile industries are well-known illustrations. Similar developments exist in greater or lesser degree in almost all product areas. Recent introduction of a refrigerator with no storage compartment for frozen foods was in response to the distinguishable preferences of the segment of the refrigerator market made up of home freezer owners whose frozen food storage needs had already been met.

Strategies of segmentation and differentiation may be employed simultaneously, but more commonly they are applied in sequence in response to changing market conditions. In one sense, segmentation is a momentary or short-term phenomenon in that effective use of this strategy may lead to more formal recognition of the reality of market segments through redefinition of the segments as individual markets. Redefinition may result in a swing back to differentiation.

The literature of both economics and marketing abounds in formal definitions of product differentiation. *From a strategy viewpoint,* product differentiation is securing a measure of control over the demand for a product by advertising or promoting differences between a product and the products of competing sellers. It is basically the result of sellers' desires to establish firm market positions and/or to insulate their business against price competition. Differentiation tends to be characterized by heavy use of advertising and promotion and to result in prices that are somewhat above the equilibrium levels associated with perfectly competitive market conditions. It may be classified as a *promotional* strategy or approach to marketing.

Market segmentation, on the other hand, consists of viewing a hetero-geneous market (one characterized by divergent demand) as a number of smaller homogeneous markets in response to differing product preferences among important market segments. It is attributable to the desires of consumers or users for more precise satisfaction of their varying wants. Like differentiation, segmentation often involves substantial use of adver-tising and promotion. This is to inform market segments of the availability of goods or services produced for or presented as meeting their needs with precision. Under these circumstances, prices tend to be somewhat closer to perfectly competitive equilibrium. Market segmentation is essen-tially a *merchandising* strategy, merchandising being used here in its technical sense as representing the adjustment of market offerings to consumer or user requirements.

THE EMERGENCE OF THE SEGMENTATION STRATEGY

To a certain extent, market segmentation may be regarded as a force in the market that will not be denied. It may result from trial and error in the sense that generalized programs of product differentiation may turn out to be effective in some segments of the market and ineffective in others. Recognition of, and intelligent response to, such a situation necessarily involves a shift in emphasis. On the other hand, it may develop that prod-ucts involved in marketing programs designed for particular market seg-ments may achieve a broader acceptance than originally planned, thus revealing a basis for convergence of demand and a more generalized marketing approach. The challenge to planning arises from the importance of determining, preferably in advance, the level or degree of segmentation that can be exploited with profit.

There appear to be many reasons why formal recognition of market segmentation as a strategy is beginning to emerge. One of the most impor-tant of these is decrease in the size of the minimum efficient producing or manufacturing unit required in some product areas. American industry has also established the technical base for product diversity by gaining release from some of the rigidities imposed by earlier approaches to mass production. Hence, there is less need today for generalization of markets in response to the necessity for long production runs of identical items.

Present emphasis upon the minimizing of marketing costs through self-service and similar developments tends to impose a requirement for better adjustment of products to consumer demand. The retailing structure, in its efforts to achieve improved efficiency, is providing less and less sales push at point of sale. This increases the premium placed by retailers upon products that are presold by their producers and are readily recognized by consumers as meeting their requirements as measured by satisfactory rates of stock turnover.

It has been suggested that the present level of discretionary buying power is productive of sharper shopping comparisons, particularly for items that are above the need level. General prosperity also creates increased willingness "to pay a little more" to get "just what I wanted."

Attention to market segmentation has also been enhanced by the recent ascendancy of product competition to a position of great economic importance. An expanded array of goods and services is competing for the consumer's dollar. More specifically, advancing technology is creating competition between new and traditional materials with reference to metals, construction materials, textile products, and in many other areas. While such competition is confusing and difficult to analyze in its early stages, it tends to achieve a kind of balance as various competing materials find their markets of maximum potential as a result of recognition of differences in the requirements of market segments.

Many companies are reaching the stage in their development where attention to market segmentation may be regarded as a condition or cost of growth. Their *core* markets have already been developed on a generalized basis to the point where additional advertising and selling expenditures are yielding diminishing returns. Attention to smaller or *fringe* market segments, which may have small potentials individually but are of crucial importance in the aggregate, may be indicated.

Finally, some business firms are beginning to regard an increasing share of their total costs of operation as being fixed in character. The higher costs of maintaining market position in the channels of distribution illustrate this change. Total reliance upon a strategy of product differentiation under such circumstances is undesirable, since market share available as a result of such a promotion-oriented approach tends to be variable over time. Much may hinge, for example, upon week-to-week audience ratings of the television shows of competitors who seek to outdifferentiate each other. Exploitation of market segments, which provides for greater maximization of consumer or user satisfactions, tends to build a more secure market position and to lead to greater overall stability. While traditionally, high fixed costs (regarded primarily from the production viewpoint) have created pressures for expanded sale of standardized items through differentiation, the possible shifting of certain marketing costs into the fixed area of the total cost structure tends to minimize this pressure.

CONCLUSION

Success in planning marketing activities requires precise utilization of both product differentiation and market segmentation as components of marketing strategy. It is fortunate that available techniques of marketing research make unplanned market exploration largely unnecessary. It is the obligation of those responsible for sales and marketing administration to keep the strategy mix in adjustment with market structure at any given point in time and to produce in marketing strategy at least as much dynamism as is present in the market. The ability of business to plan in this way is dependent upon the maintenance of a flow of market information that can be provided by marketing research as well as the full utilization of available techniques of cost accounting and cost analysis.

Cost information is critical because the upper limit to which market segmentation can be carried is largely defined by production cost considerations. There is a limit to which diversity in market offerings can be carried without driving production costs beyond practical limits. Similarly, the employment of product differentiation as a strategy tends to be restricted by the achievement of levels of marketing costs that are untenable. These cost factors tend to define the limits of the zone within which the employment of marketing strategies or a strategy mix dictated by the nature of the market is permissive.

It should be emphasized that while we have here been concerned with the differences between product differentiation and market segmentation as marketing strategies, they are closely related concepts in the setting of an imperfectly competitive market. The differences have been highlighted in the interest of enhancing clarity in theory and precision in practice. The emergence of market segmentation as a strategy once again provides evidence of the consumer's preeminence in the contemporary American economy and the richness of the rewards that can result from the application of science to marketing problems.

NOTE

[1]Imperfect competition assumes lack of uniformity in the size and influence of the firms or individuals that comprise the demand or supply sides of a market.

41

Segmenting the Industrial Market

Richard N. Cardozo

For most marketers of consumer products, the first stages of marketing planning involve identifying different segments of the relevant market, predicting the behavior of potential customers in each segment, and developing marketing programs for maximum impact on certain, but not all, segments. In many consumer goods firms such analysis is carried out in a very careful and explicit manner. Apart from the making of business decisions, both businessmen and academicians interested in consumer goods marketing have contributed to the now substantial volume of literature which has included attempts to segment consumer markets on the basis of concepts first developed in psychology and sociology.

Although many industrial marketers follow a marketing planning routine similar to the one just described for consumer marketers, most industrial marketers appear to perform segmentation analyses in less depth and in a much less explicit manner than do consumer marketers. Few industrial marketers or academicians have written in detail on the subject of segmenting industrial markets. The concepts from psychology and sociology which consumer marketers appear to have found useful have received only limited application in industrial marketing planning.

There appears to be considerable opportunity to advance the science of marketing by applying to the industrial market the same kind of segmentation analysis that has been applied to consumer markets. As a first step in exploiting this opportunity, this paper offers a conceptual scheme for understanding preliminary results from research intended to improve our ability to segment the industrial market. The purpose of this paper is to stimulate discussion, rather than to present definitive conclusions. Accord-

Reprinted from Richard N. Cardozo, "Segmenting the Industrial Market," in Robert L. King, ed., *Marketing and the New Science of Planning: Proceedings of the 1968 Fall Conference of the American Marketing Association* (American Marketing Association) pp. 433–448, published by the American Marketing Association.

ingly, these preliminary results are presented as broad generalizations, followed by discussion of the implications for marketing of the generalizations, should they prove to be supported by more detailed analysis and research.

THE CONCEPTUAL SCHEME

The conceptual scheme was developed partly from the research results, and partly from analysis of the industrial marketing literature which dealt explicitly with market segmentation. The scheme itself will be presented immediately following a brief discussion of the literature.

The Literature

Very little of the recent literature on industrial marketing deals explicitly with segmenting industrial markets. Instead, most of the scholarly and practical literature which relates directly to the behavior of industrial purchasing—that aspect of industrial marketing which one would expect to be most closely related to market segmentation—consists of three types: (1) general descriptive models of the behavior of the typical industrial buyer or buying group within a firm, (2) lists of factors which industrial purchasers consider important in selecting suppliers, and (3) detailed studies of individual purchasing decisions. In these publications, market segmentation is seldom carried further than stating that, for any particular industrial product, purchasing behavior varies according to geography and end use of the commodity purchased.[1] End use is generally thought to vary directly with the type of business in which the buying firm is engaged.

My search for explicit treatments of segmentation in the industrial marketing literature turned up only six sources which carried the concept of segmentation beyond end use (or type of business in which the buying firm was engaged) and geography. Among them, these five sources suggested that industrial buyers varied—and therefore that industrial markets might be usefully segmented—on six different bases:

1. the type of buying situation: new task, modified re-buy, straight re-buy[2]
2. the phase (early to final) of the decision process[3]
3. the primary role of the purchaser and his commitment to it[4]
4. the purchasing strategies (routines for coping with problems within acceptable limits of risk and resource expenditure) employed by different buyers[5]
5. the interests of or problems faced by different industrial buyers[6]
6. the self-confidence of particular buyers[7]

Although these bases of segmentation were applied to different phenomena in the industrial purchasing process, each of the authors involved appeared to be interested in relating particular bases of segmentation directly or indirectly to the supplier-choice decision. The research program mentioned above and the conceptual scheme to be described also focused on the supplier-choice decision.

Statement of the Scheme

In this scheme the probability that a particular supplier will be chosen varies by market segment. These segments may be grouped into general categories suggested by preliminary research results. These categories

FIGURE 41-1 **Conceptual Scheme**

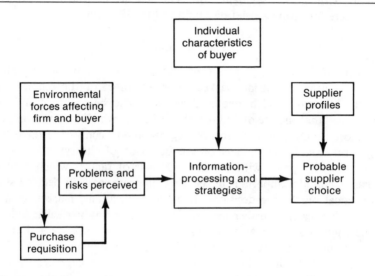

include: (1) differences among industrial buyers' information-processing and purchasing strategies, (2) individual characteristics of different buyers, (3) problems and risks perceived by different buyers, (4) differences among purchase requisitions, and (5) differences in the environmental forces affecting particular buyers. In the conceptual scheme (figure 41-1), supplier choice is directly related to the profiles of suppliers available, and the strategies used to choose among those suppliers. The strategies, in turn, depend on individual characteristics of buyers, and the problems and risks which the buyer perceives. These problems and risks are influenced by both purchase requisitions and environmental forces, which also affect the purchase requisitions themselves.

In the remainder of the paper, the material in each of these general categories (shown as "boxes" in figure 41-1) will be discussed in detail.

Supplier Profiles

The profile of a particular supplier includes the terms of his offering, such as product specifications, quality control specifications, delivery dates, prices, any services to be provided by the supplier, the prospective buyer's estimate of the supplier's capabilities and supplier development costs (e.g., tooling provided by the buyer), if any. The profile for suppliers with which the buying company has dealt before also includes vendor histories, either recorded in a formal vendor analysis system or retained as buyers' recollections of past success or failure of a particular supplier. A purchaser's profile of a supplier may also include the buyer's perception of the supplier's salesmen and advertising.

By themselves, supplier profiles do not constitute a basis for segmenting the industrial market. The industrial market could, however, be segmented on the basis of the particular types of profiles which are consistently preferred by certain firms under specifiable circumstances. For example, some firms may consistently choose suppliers which offer products of high quality built to exacting specifications, delivered promptly, but priced at a premium. Other firms may, however, regularly choose suppliers whose quality and tolerance levels are lower, whose delivery is less prompt, but whose prices are substantially lower.

Purchasing Strategies

Any such consistent pattern of choice or preference reflects a particular information-processing and purchasing strategy. Information-processing and purchasing strategies are regular patterns of decisions and actions for defining and coping with purchasing problems, within acceptable (to the individual purchaser) limits of risk and resource expenditure.

Results from exploratory research suggest that industrial purchasers develop specific strategies to process information and to select suppliers. For purposes of this discussion, only the purchasing or supplier selection strategies will be developed in detail.

A comparison of purchasing strategies employed by two different procurement executives indicates that strategies do, indeed, vary. It also appears that a different marketing approach may be appropriate for each purchasing strategy.[8]

The first executive was trying to solve the problem of how to enable his firm to respond promptly to one of a series of competitive innovations in its major market. His immediate goal was to obtain components for a particular product. This executive was quite willing to take the risk of paying premium prices for components, moderately willing to accept quality he regarded as "marginal" but was afraid of getting immediate delivery. Although data are incomplete, it appeared that these risk preferences were a function both of his own personality and of the environment within and outside the firm. This executive typically spent little time and effort on this (or any other) purchase decision, partly because of his personal preference for being involved in many purchasing activities, and partly because of the heavy workload which every procurement executive in the department had.

To solve his purchasing problem within his preferred limits of risk and effort, this executive employed a "sequential evaluation" procedure: he telephoned present suppliers until he found one (on the third call, within ten minutes) who could solve his problem within the limits of the risks he was willing to take. This "sequential evaluation" (of present suppliers) procedure was applied to six other observed purchase decisions. Throughout all seven decisions the long-run goal appeared to be the same: prompt response to actual or anticipated competitive innovation. Risk and effort preferences varied only slightly.

This executive's purchasing strategy implies that it is valuable for a supplier to be "in," i.e., currently supplying the firm. Present suppliers had first chance at this premium-price business. New suppliers were given opportunities to bid only after present suppliers had refused. In such a situation, it may be worthwhile for a supplier to offer special concessions to get "in."

Contrast the above strategy with that employed by the second procurement executive. His overriding objective was "to follow good procurement practices." In particular purchase situations, he defined his problem as buying the item specified at the lowest possible price. As one might expect, he was completely unwilling to risk paying a premium price. He was also unwilling to accept the risk of changing specifications. This executive was, however, quite willing to accept the risk of a delivery date later than the earliest available.

As with the first executive, risk preferences of the second executive appeared to depend upon both personal preferences and preferences of other executives in the firm. In contrast to the first procurement executive, the second executive handled each requisition as thoroughly as if it were the only one coming through the department. In each of the half-dozen observed purchase decisions, at least four requests for bids had been sent out (to both present and potential suppliers), and buyers had at least three alternative sources from which the lowest bidder was chosen.

This "simultaneous scanning" approach implies that suppliers who wish to sell to this particular executive would gain little by offering special concessions to get "in." They must have the lowest price for any particular purchase. In contrast, marketers facing the "sequential evaluation" approach employed by the first executive might find it advantageous to make special efforts to get "in."

These preliminary observations suggest that certain industrial markets may be segmented usefully on the basis of different purchasing strategies. The observations also imply that the study of buyers' purchasing strategies may lead to helpful recommendations for marketing management.

Preliminary research also indicates that a typical industrial purchaser employs only one or two strategies, which he applies to all the purchase situations which he faces. If additional research supports this observation, we may have an explanation for some of the industrial purchasing behavior which is not handled satisfactorily either by a "rational" or an "emotional" model. Informal conversations with industrial salesmen indicate that they frequently observe this "one strategy" approach and tailor their selling strategies to match particular buyers' strategies.

Although the evidence is as yet sketchy, it appears that some buyers will use both a sequential evaluation strategy and a simultaneous scanning strategy and will choose between the two strategies on the bases outlined in table 41-1. Industrial buyers employ decision rules not only to choose suppliers from an array but also to determine under what conditions to switch suppliers and to use multiple sources.

TABLE 41-1

Simultaneous Scanning strategy employed when:	*Sequential Evaluation strategy employed when:*
—total dollar expenditure high	—total dollar expenditure low
—probability of suppliers' not meeting specs. moderate to high	—probability of suppliers' failing to meet specs. low
—major risk perceived in paying a premium price	—major risk perceived is interruption of supply
—more management resources available	—management resources available to choose supplier very limited

Preliminary research indicates that (1) the greater the differentiation among suppliers perceived by buyers, the more reluctant buyers are to switch suppliers or to use multiple sources; (2) changes in the profile of an existing supplier are more likely to lead buyers to switch suppliers for existing products than are the profiles of existing or new suppliers or changes in the profiles of suppliers attempting to get "in."

Results from exploratory research suggest that a single supplier may be used for nonrecurring purchases or for recurring purchases of small lots, particularly where the use of more than one supplier would result in the loss of quantity discounts. Single suppliers are likely to be used when the initial cost (e.g., tooling) of adding a supplier are high and volume is relatively low. Multiple sources may be used for recurring purchases when considerable dollar or unit volume is involved, when continuity of supply is essential, and when suppliers vary in their abilities to provide a continuous flow of merchandise. Multiple sources cannot be used, of course, where specifications require a sole supplier. The implication for industrial marketers of segmentation based on the "single source" and "multiple source" decision rules outlined above is this: an "out" supplier has little chance of getting a share of a buying firm's business when the "single source" rule is applied and may therefore find it unprofitable to expend marketing effort on segments typified by that type of buying situation. The "out" supplier may, however, find his chances of obtaining a share

of the business much better in the second type of situation, where buyers
follow a "multiple source" decision rule. At the same time, an "in"
supplier may find it more advantageous to attempt to maintain his preferred position in situations where buyers use a "single source" decision
rule. Suppliers probably have only limited power to prevent their having
to share a firm's business with other suppliers in situations where buyers
typically use a "multiple sourcing" rule.

Preliminary results also suggest that buyers who frequently employ a
"multiple sourcing" strategy are more likely than those whose typical
strategy is "single sourcing" to switch from one supplier to another.

Increased precision of segmentation based on study of factors in purchasing strategies may be possible. These factors may themselves form
additional useful bases of segmentation. Purchasing strategies depend
upon (1) personal characteristics of individual buyers and (2) the problems
and risks which individual buyers perceive.

Individual Characteristics

Individual characteristics which appear to be important include individual
risk tolerance and preference, individual role type, and individual cognitive
style.

Risk Tolerance and Preference. Risk tolerance and preference include:
buyers' tolerance for uncertainty, buyers' perceptions of risks in particular
situations, and buyers' confidence in handling certain types of risks. A
buyer who has a low tolerance for uncertainty would be more likely than
one with higher tolerance for uncertainty to rely on suppliers who had
served him well in the past; he would probably be less likely to switch
suppliers than would a buyer with high tolerance for uncertainty. The
buyer with low tolerance for uncertainty would be more likely to employ
a "sequential evaluation" strategy than a "simultaneous scanning"
strategy.

Buyers appear to differ in their perception of certain risks. Some buyers
consistently perceive as high the risk of not obtaining delivery on schedule,
while others regularly regard paying a premium price as a high risk. (Risk
is defined as the probability of the occurrence of an event, multiplied by
the consequencés of that event, should it occur. Thus, a very high risk of
late delivery could mean that no supplier is likely to deliver on time and
that lack of prompt delivery will shut down an automated production line
for an extended period.) These differences in consistent perceptions of
which risks are high and which are low appear to be related to buyers'
education and experience, e.g., a buyer with an engineering degree and
quality control experience typically considers as high the risks of failing
to meet design specifications and supplying lots which vary in per cent
defectives. In addition to education and experience, role changes may

affect risk perception. For example, a buyer recently promoted to director of purchasing became far more concerned with risks of interruption of supply than he had been as a buyer.

The buyer who considers late delivery to be a major risk in most of his buying situations may prefer a "sequential evaluation" strategy. The buyer who regards paying a premium as a major risk is very likely to use a "simultaneous scanning" strategy. Buyers who perceive high risk on any particular dimension are likely to place considerable weight on that dimension when evaluating suppliers' profiles, and when seeking information about suppliers. Conversely, those who perceive risk on a particular dimension to be low are unlikely to pay much attention to that dimension when seeking information or evaluating suppliers. The implication for industrial marketers is clear: any particular competitive advantage—low price, fast delivery, custom design service, etc.—will be valuable in reaching only those segments of the industrial market which consider that advantage a significant reducer of their perceived risks. It would, therefore, appear economically sensible to direct marketing and product development efforts toward segments defined on the basis of perceived risk.

Among buyers who perceive a particular risk as high or low, some may feel more confident than others of their ability to manage the particular risk. Those who are highly confident of their own ability and those who have no confidence whatever in their ability to manage a particular risk may be unwilling to accept any information from salesmen or advertisements relating to that situation. On the other hand, buyers who have moderate confidence in their ability to manage particular risks are most likely to seek information from salesmen, advertisements and noncommercial sources. The pay-off from industrial selling and advertising efforts should clearly be greatest in this "medium confidence" segment. If so, segmenting the industrial market on the basis of buyers' confidence could lead to increased profits.

Preliminary research indicates that a buyer's self-confidence may be related to the degree of influence he exercises in the purchasing process. Specifically, buyers with moderate to high confidence in their ability (1) to choose acceptable suppliers from an array of potential sources, and (2) to negotiate major supply agreements, when such are needed, are more influential than are buyers with less confidence in determining the specifications which a prospective supplier must meet.

Preliminary research results also suggest that buyers who have moderate confidence in their own judgment will expend more time and effort than will buyers with very high or very low self-confidence in evaluating alternative suppliers. The greater the time and effort expended to evaluate suppliers, the better the chances are that an "out" supplier with a superior offering can become an "in" supplier. Industrial marketers who are "out" but who believe they have a superior offering may, therefore, find it useful to segment their prospect lists on the basis of buyers' self-confidence and concentrate their efforts on those firms whose buyers are medium in self-confidence.

Role Type. Related to concept of self-confidence is that of individual role type. Exploratory research suggests that individuals who lack confidence may be more likely to conceive of their jobs in fairly narrow terms and to behave quite conservatively. Buyers with greater confidence may be more likely to conceive of their jobs more broadly and to innovate.

Kernan and Sommers' argue that a buyer who is strongly committed to his role as "purchasing agent" is less likely to innovate than is a buyer who seeks to redefine his role. Kernan and Sommers also state that differences in role commitment lead to variations in the type of information in which buyers are interested. They argue further that industrial salesmen and advertisers should use quite different approaches in reaching segments which differ in their commitment to role type.

Cognitive Style. Individual differences in cognitive style appear to be related to strategy preferences. Buyers who tend to prefer "simultaneous scanning" strategies in a variety of situations apparently prefer to handle fewer problems in depth, rather than many problems, each with less intensive analysis. "Scanners," however, appear to have a greater tolerance for work and therefore may spend more time on individual supplier selection decisions than "sequential evaluators." "Simultaneous scanners" are more likely to be "optimizers"; "sequential evaluators" are more likely to be "satisfiers." Buyers who prefer a "scanning" strategy make fairly fine distinctions among suppliers, while those who prefer alternative strategies may make more coarse "go-no go" distinctions. Related to this preference is a tendency among those who prefer to use a "sequential evaluation" strategy to generalize from one buying situation to another and to expect that a supplier who had proved satisfactory in one purchase situation will also be satisfactory in other, different situations. Preliminary research results suggest that these "sequential evaluators" may be less likely than "scanners" to switch suppliers and more likely to maintain smaller vendor lists.

Knowledge of buyers' cognitive styles can, either directly or through their effects on purchasing strategies, provide a basis for segmenting the industrial market. Segments divided along this basis should differ in their probabilities of choosing or switching from particular suppliers.

Problems and Risks Perceived

Purchasing strategies are affected not only by individual characteristics but also by the problems and risks which industrial buyers perceive.

Problems. Each industrial buyer appears to face a hierarchy of problems. The importance of any one problem, i.e., its position in the hierarchy, may vary with changes in the environment of the firm and differs among firms engaged in different types of business. Robinson, Faris, and Wind[10] have described these problems in terms of three "buying situations" which buyers face: straight re-buys, modified re-buys, and new tasks. Straight re-buys may occupy relatively low positions in any buyer's hierarchy of problems, while new tasks probably occupy relatively high (i.e., important) positions.

Robinson, Faris, and Wind argue convincingly that the industrial market may be segmented on the basis of these three buying situations. They state that the amount and type of information sought and the amount and type of cognitive effort invested in a particular purchase situation vary according to whether the buyer is making a straight re-buy, a modified re-buy, or an entirely new purchase. In other words, the communications processing and purchasing strategies employed vary according to the type of buying situation. Faris[11] argues that the amount and type of information which industrial marketers should provide varies from different segments, defined on the basis of buying situations. He implies that the probability of "in" or "out" suppliers being chosen also varies substantially among different buying-situation segments.

Risks. Purchasing problems may also be described and the industrial market segmented in terms of the type and amount of risk which a purchaser must manage. In some situations buyers may have to devote considerable energy to reducing the risk of late delivery, while in others price increases may be the major risk.

The type of risk perceived as important influences the supplier characteristics on which the buyer will write the tightest specifications and about which he will seek the most information. The type of risk perceived affects the strategy employed—if paying a premium price or failing to satisfy government auditors are the major risks perceived, the buyer is more likely to use a simultaneous scanning strategy. If obtaining custom-designed tooling or maintaining supply are perceived as high-risk situations, the buyer may use a sequential evaluation strategy. In addition, buyers who consider interruption of supply a high risk are likely to employ a multiple sourcing strategy with the consequent sharing of a company's purchases among several suppliers.

For any type of risk perceived, the amount of risk faced may vary from low to high. In general, risk is perceived as high when (1) the dollar amount to be committed is large, (2) the commodity to be purchased is complex, (3) the percentage of the total value added by the purchasing firm attributable to that commodity is substantial, (4) the probability of the buyer's making an unsatisfactory choice appears high to him, (5) the consequences of making an unsatisfactory choice are highly visible, and (6) the purchase may exert substantial influence on the market for the particular commodity.

Apart from individual differences among buyers, when risk is considered high, more effort will be spent in seeking information and considering alternative suppliers. It is likely, however, that all the suppliers considered in a high risk situation will be those with which the company has done business previously. It appears that in most high risk situations, buyers are more reluctant to switch suppliers than they are in lower risk situations.

The problems industrial purchasers face and the risks they perceive depend on many factors inside and outside the firm. The influence of these forces, frequently transmitted to the industrial buyer through purchase requisitions and environmental forces themselves, may be used to segment the industrial market. It may be helpful to discuss segmentation on the basis of purchase requisitions first and then to discuss segmentation based on environmental forces.

Purchase Requisitions

The purchase requisition represents an individual "purchasing profile" similar to the supplier profiles described earlier. The requisition lists the dimensions along which alternative offerings are to be evaluated and the limits along each of those dimensions of acceptable performance. A purchasing profile for a purchased component could be diagrammed as in figure 41-2. This "purchasing profile" shows four dimensions (price,

FIGURE 41-2

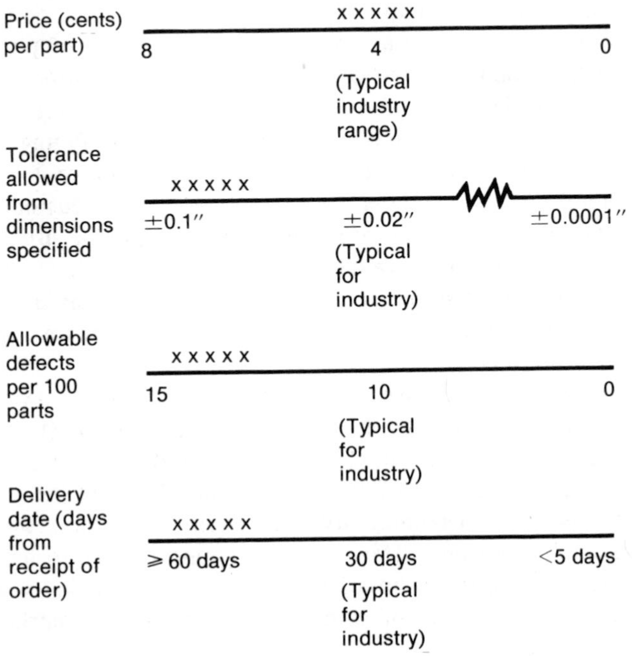

Price (cents) per part)	x x x x x		
	8	4	0
		(Typical industry range)	
Tolerance allowed from dimensions specified	x x x x x		
	±0.1″	±0.02″	±0.0001″
		(Typical for industry)	
Allowable defects per 100 parts	x x x x x		
	15	10	0
		(Typical for industry)	
Delivery date (days from receipt of order)	x x x x x		
	≥ 60 days	30 days	<5 days
		(Typical for industry)	

quality tolerance, consistency of quality, and delivery) on which alternate offerings are to be compared. The xxxx portions shown along each dimension indicate the ranges within which acceptable suppliers are expected to fall.

Since purchasing profiles may vary according to the dimensions included and according to the ranges of acceptance along each dimension, both of these factors may provide bases for segmenting the industrial market. Since most industrial buyers evaluate suppliers and products on the dimensions of price, quality, and service,[12] the dimensions themselves may not provide a powerful basis of segmentation. Useful segmentation should result, however, from analyzing differences in position and width of ranges of acceptance along various dimensions. For example, two purchasing profiles in figure 41-3 represent two distinct segments of the industrial market. (The xxxx portions shown along each dimension indicate the ranges within which acceptable suppliers are expected to fall.)

FIGURE 41-3

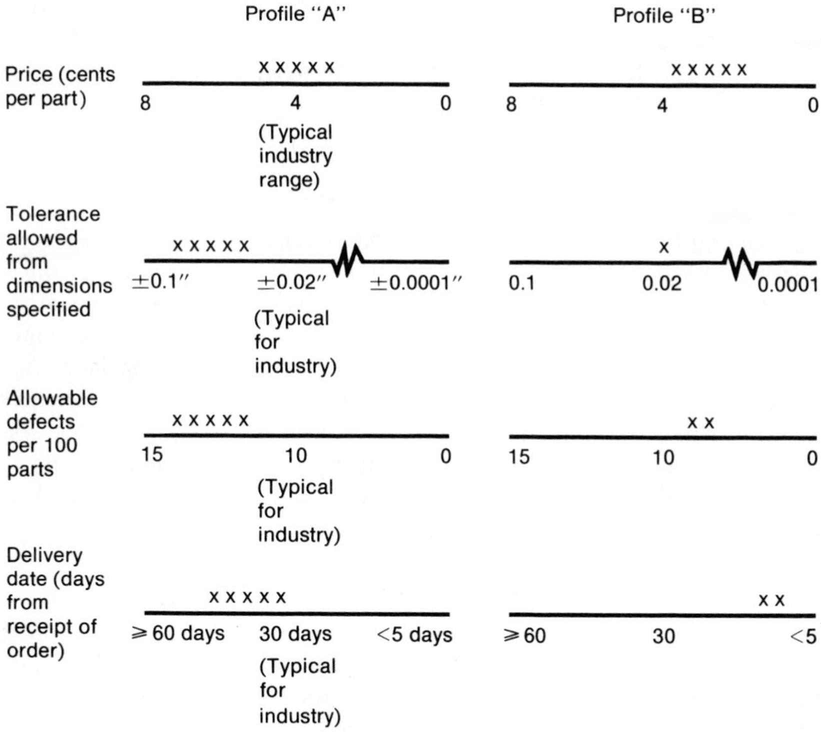

The relatively tight specifications shown on the right-hand profile of figure 41-3 may be drawn to exclude all but one supplier, or they may permit the buyer to evaluate several suppliers. The former is more likely the case with a one-time purchase of a custom-designed product; the latter, for continuing purchases of more standard items.

The implications for a particular industrial marketer facing segments defined on the basis of the purchasing profiles shown above should be clear. If he offers for four cents a component with tolerances slightly greater than " ± 0.02," estimated defects of 7 to 8 parts per 100, and delivery within 15-20 days, he has a fairly high probability of selling to the segment typified by profile "A" (he meets or exceeds all specifications), but a relatively low probability of being chosen by customers whose purchasing profile resembles that shown in "B" (the supplier falls just outside the ranges of acceptance). If the marketer chooses to invest more of his marketing effort in the segment with higher probability of success, he should direct his effort toward segment "A" rather than "B".

Environmental Forces

Factors internal and external to the firm influence the problems and risks the buyer considers important. Internal factors include (1) the institutional role type, (2) the working relationships between purchasing and other departments, and (3) the individual buyer's workload. Each of these factors may constitute a useful basis for segmentation.

Internal Factors: Role

Kernan and Sommers[13] argue that institutions, like buyers, have different degrees of commitment to their established roles. Institutions strongly committed to an established role may be lethargic and non-innovative, while those whose commitments are less strong may be adaptive or innovative in purchasing practices. Apart from differences among individual buyers with respect to commitment to their own roles, these differences in institutional commitment constitute a potentially useful basis for segmenting the industrial market. For example, as its designation implies, an "innovative" institution may be more likely to try a new supplier and/or product than would a "lethargic" organization.

Internal Factors: Working Relationships

Internal working relationships appear to vary among firms, and therefore they offer a potentially useful basis for segmentation. For example, in certain firms where the purchasing function is under the direct supervision of the production department, specifications may be written so tightly (by production engineers) that the purchasing department is virtually "specified out of a job." In one such case which I observed, suppliers competed primarily on the basis of having their particular specifications written into the purchase requisition, though the suppliers themselves provided no design assistance. In contrast, in another firm, where the purchasing manager was a vice-president responsible directly to the company's chief executive, buyers had complete charge of the actual purchasing process, and they worked side-by-side with technical personnel in designing equipment and procuring needed equipment and supplies. In the latter firm, suppliers competed primarily on the basis of design competence, service, and price. It appears that relationships both with management levels above the purchasing department and with other departments (e.g., production, engineering) affect the bases on which suppliers compete and, therefore, the probability that a particular supplier will be chosen.

In addition to segmentation based on these internal relationships, it may be useful for some industrial marketers to classify prospects and customers on the basis of the extent to which reciprocal relationships enter into their choices of suppliers. Firms which regard reciprocal arrangements as important are unlikely to choose suppliers which are not customers over those who are, where such choices exist for the buying firm.

Internal Factors: Workload

Individual buyers appear to have quite different workloads. These differences in workload, which offer a potentially useful basis for segmenting the industrial market, appear to be related closely to the type of information-processing and purchasing strategy a particular buyer will use. Buyers who face very heavy workloads are more likely than those with light workloads to employ "sequential evaluation" strategies. Preliminary research results indicate that heavy workloads also lead to (1) reluctance to try new suppliers, (2) loyalty to existing suppliers, (3) greater reliance on routines and less attention paid to each purchase, (4) greater emphasis on avoiding mistakes, less on capitalizing on new opportunities, and (5) fewer bids sought, and less fear of paying more than the lowest possible price. In addition, heavy workloads appear to make buyers resistant to suggestions from other departments for product or vendor change. When such requests for change do come through, the "overworked" buyer is more likely than the buyer whose workload is less to have the requisition written either so tightly as to exclude all but one supplier or so loosely that any of several suppliers could meet specifications.

A supplier presently serving an overworked buyer is unlikely to be dropped by the buyer himself. In fact, the supplier is unlikely to lose the account except to a competitor with a fairly clear-cut product advantage, who has succeeded in having himself specified as sole supplier through selling efforts to engineering, production, or whatever department is relevant.

An industrial marketer attempting to get into an account through an overworked buyer has a fairly low probability of success. His efforts may have to be directed through the technical departments of the firm. In such cases, his chances of success are good only if his product offers a demonstrable advantage in an area which technical personnel consider important.

In sum, situations in which buyers have heavy workloads increase the probability that an "in" supplier will stay "in" and decrease the probability that an "out" supplier will get "in."

A heavy workload appears to be associated with the following factors: (1) buyer responsibility for purchasing a large number of commodities, (2) great heterogeneity among these commodities, (3) a large number of orders to be processed by an individual buyer, and (4) a buyer responsible for a high total dollar volume of purchases. It is not clear at this stage of the research which of these factors is most important.

Five factors in the external environment of the firm appear to provide useful bases of segmentation. Preliminary research results suggest that each of these factors influences a firm's purchasing profile, which in turn affects the probability that a supplier with a particular profile will be chosen. These factors also appear to affect the amount and type of risk perceived in particular purchase situations.

Not surprisingly, one important factor is the type of business in which the buying firm is engaged, defined by SIC classification (i.e., by end product(s) produced). Another factor, perhaps as powerful a determinant as the product itself is the end market served by the company (e.g., consumer perishables, industrial goods, government research facilities). A third factor is the value added by the buying firm's activities (e.g., low value added appears related to very rigid and tight limits for price on commodities purchased). A fourth factor which affects the purchasing profile is the buying firm's profit margin and changes in it. For example, a decline in profits frequently appears to result in management pressure for savings (tighter limits on price) on purchased commodities. Fifth, firms whose competitive advantage in their end-product markets lies in marketing skill have fairly tight limits for delivery and consistency of quality of purchased supplies but fairly broad limits for purchase price. Buying firms whose competitive market advantage is price appear to have opposite purchasing profiles. The latter firms have tight limits on price but fairly broad limits on delivery and consistency of quality of purchased supplies. Clearly a supplier who offered fast delivery of high-quality-controlled components at a premium price would have little chance of success in a segment typified by the latter purchasing profile and a much better chance of success in the former segment.

CONCLUSION

These preliminary research results suggest that the industrial market may, indeed, be segmented usefully on the following bases: (1) industrial buyers' purchasing strategies, (2) buyers' risk preferences, role types, and cognitive styles, (3) the problems and risks perceived by different buyers, (4) differences among purchase requisitions, and (5) differences in the environmental forces affecting different buyers. The next steps in research and thinking about industrial market segmentation are to identify with greater ease and precision segments within the industrial market, and to estimate with useful accuracy the probabilities that buyers within different segments will choose suppliers with certain profiles.

Ideally, a marketer should be able to identify readily market segments which differ, for example, with respect to the purchasing strategies which buyers employ. Then, after identifying the segments, a marketer should be able to make gross but useful estimates of the probabilities that his firm would be chosen by companies in each segment as a supplier. Multiplying these probability estimates by the expected revenues (net of marketing expenses) from each segment would enable the marketer to estimate the potential revenue available to him from each of several segments and help him to plan his marketing program accordingly.

The pay-off from such detailed marketing planning could be substantial. To take advantage of the pay-off available from this approach, the industrial marketer must begin by asking, "How do different industrial buyers buy?", instead of repeating his oft-used query, "How does industry (in general) buy?" The marketer can then work with researchers to identify and predict the behavior of different segments within the industrial market.

NOTES

[1]Charles W. Faris, "Market Segmentation and Industrial Buying Behavior," *AMA Proceedings* (Summer 1967), pp. 108–110.

[2]Patrick J. Robinson, Charles W. Faris and Yoram Wind, *Industrial Buying and Creative Marketing* (Boston: Allyn and Bacon, 1967).

[3]Faris, "Market Segmentation."

[4]Jerome B. Kernan and Montrose S. Sommers, "The Behavioral Matrix—A Closer Look at the Industrial Buyer," *Business Horizons* (Summer 1966), pp. 59–72; and Theodore Levitt, *Industrial Purchasing Behavior—A Study of Communications Effects* (Boston: Division of Research, Harvard Business School, 1965).

[5]Wallace Feldman and Richard N. Cardozo, "Industrial Buying as Consumer Behavior," *AMA Proceedings* (Summer 1967), pp. 102–107; and Levitt, *Industrial Purchasing Behavior.*

[6]Daniel Yankelovich, "New Criteria for Market Segmentation," *Harvard Business Review* (March-April 1964), pp. 83–90.

[7]*Ibid.*

[8]Richard N. Cardozo, "Purchasing Strategies in Consumer Behavior," *SMA Proceedings* (1967), p. 33.

[9]Kernan and Sommers, "The Behavioral Matrix."

[10]Robinson, Faris and Wind, *Industrial Buying.*

[11]Faris, "Market Segmentation."

[12]Gary W. Dickson, "A Stochastic Simulation Model for the Prediction of Industrial Purchasing Decisions Involving Riskless Alternatives," (Seattle: University of Washington, June 1965).

[13]Kernan and Sommers, "The Behavioral Matrix."

42

Consumers' Choice

Paul H. Nystrom

No one can satisfy all of his wants. People are never entirely satisfied. This is partly due to outside limitations and partly to the restlessness of human life. Because the human being has many wants and because only a part of them at best can be satisfied, choice must be made. Decision, energy, and purchasing power are directed to this end. Factors influencing the consumer in making such choice are to be discussed in this reading.

FACTORS IN CONSUMERS' CHOICE

The consumers' choice of commodities to satisfy their wants is a complicated phenomenon. Such choice is dependent upon both subjective and objective conditions. There are, obviously, fundamental physiologic wants which must be satisfied in order that the individual may continue to exist. These human wants under modern conditions are greatly modified by factors which deserve consideration by the student of consumption as well as the businessman seeking to produce and to sell what consumers will buy.

Probably all human wants have their roots in fundamental physiologic bases but their external expression under most conditions is certainly greatly modified and in some cases much disguised by the individual's education, experience, and contracts with other people.

The number of things wanted by human beings seems unlimited, but in many cases these wants are so clearly related to each other that it may be possible to set up a fairly simple classification which should serve as a basic point of departure for all study of problems of consumption. The number of classes is not large. Let us, therefore, attempt such an enumeration of the factors of consumers' choice and then a similar enumeration of the fundamental wants as modified by such factors.

From Paul H. Nystrom, *Economic Principles of Consumption* (New York: The Ronald Press Co., N.Y., 1929 and 1931), pp. 51–72. Reprinted by permission.

The following tabulation presents the leading factors which control and modify the consumers' choice of commodities which will be discussed in this and following chapters.

1. Fundamental wants
2. Purchasing power
3. Habits and customs
4. Fashion
5. Availability of goods
6. Sales promotion
7. Competition for customers' trade
8. Monopoly control of market
9. Goodwill control of market
10. Education and experience

1. Fundamental Human Wants

Businessmen enter into business for the purpose of making a profit, but profit is attained only through producing and selling goods which satisfy consumers' wants; so it may be stated that consumers' motives actually dominate systems of production and of distribution. Predetermination of consumer demand is essentially the estimation of what consumers desire and can pay for in terms of kind and quantity. Every selling point, so called, is an appeal to prospective customers' active or latent wants. Every merchandise display and every advertisement as well as every sales talk aims at presentation of selling points that appeal to such wants. The success of business, therefore, depends upon the final judgment of the consumer as determined in actual purchase.

Of the wants which characterize people, some are naturally of greater significance in the sale of most commodities than others. It is to these that the salesman and advertising man must turn to give their sales points effective appeal. The most successful advertisements as well as the most effective sales talks are those which make their appeals to the right wants.

Interesting and valuable analyses have been made of consumers' wants by Dickinson in his "Economic Motives" and by Copeland in his "Principles of Merchandising." The present writer presented a list of such wants in his "Retail Selling and Store Management" published in 1913 and, with some revision, a similar list in his "Economics of Fashion" in 1928.

A human being is essentially a bundle of wants. Life manifests itself in desires and in struggles to satisfy such desires. Complete cessation of all hungers and desires means death. This is only another way of saying that the fundamental wants of the human being are necessary to his existence and the commodities and services that satisfy these wants constitute the necessities of life.

It is not the purpose here to attempt a detailed analysis of human wants but a brief mention of some of the leading ones of economic significance will be made. Nor must it be inferred that the order in which these wants are enumerated and presented here represent the respective importance of the wants. The order is rather the conventional one beginning with those wants or hungers in the scheme of life which are most necessary in existence. Actually, in highly complex social conditions, wants or hungers which are far down the scale in importance so far as survival or existence is concerned, assume the utmost of importance in the requirements of individuals and in the economic system. . . .

2. Purchasing Power

The most formidable factor in determining what a particular choice shall be is the consumer's purchasing power. This factor is considered of prime importance. . . .

3. Habit and Custom

The habits of individuals and the customs of groups, as they affect the consumption of goods, are necessarily important limitations upon the freedom of choice. To a large extent most of the things that we use in our daily life were at one time, either with ourselves or others, the objects of careful, individual selection. Repeated selection of the same things resulted in habit. Through the formation of habit the consumer is saved a great deal of time and thinking that would otherwise have to be devoted to the making of a choice. No one would be able to accomplish any important work or make any progress whatsoever if every act of consumption were the result of the exercise of judgment and choice. While the rule of habit is an effective aid to the conservation of human energy, it serves at the same time as a distinct limitation upon the consumer's choice.

Habit is a term that applies to practices of individuals. Customs are habits followed by masses of people. Habit is individual, custom is social. As habit is a factor limiting the choice and concumption of the individual, so custom limits the choice and consumption of societies and nations.

Quite obviously, consumption is to a very great extent definitely modified and even controlled by custom. There are widespread national customs as well as local customs. Styles of dress, special foods, and types of domestic architecture are peculiar to many countries and communities. New England pie, Southern corn bread, Mexican tortillas, Irish bacon, Scotch porridge, German sauerkraut and Chinese rice are distinctive foods, fixed in consumption by long custom.

Sometimes such customs work great hardships on those who follow them. During the potato famines in Ireland in the second quarter of the nineteenth century it was said that the rivers and lakes were full of fish which could be easily caught but because of the dependence of the people on potatoes as a food fixed by habit and custom there was very little effort made to get fish, or in fact, any other available food. Europeans of the present time have found it difficult to adjust their food habits so as to include American corn in their diet. Similarly, custom fixes standards of clothing, housing, sports, and manners. . . .

4. Consumption and Fashion

Given the fundamental human wants to the satisfaction of which all consumption is directed, the amount of purchasing power possessed by the consumer is the most important factor in determining the nature of consumption. The next most important factor in consumers' choice is fashion. Most people whose means exceed the requirements of the minimum for existence, whether conscious of it of not, and whether they will or not, follow fashion in the selection and use of goods. Clothing, automobiles, home furnishings, and domestic architecture are fields in which fashion dominates. Its influence is important even in food and drink. Just how fashion operates is described in the author's "Economics of Fashion." A bare statement of its importance as a factor in consumers' choice must suffice here.

5. Consumption and Availability of Goods

An obvious limit to the exercise of consumers' choice among the various goods offered and desired for the satisfaction of human wants is the availability or lack of availability of the goods themselves. Probably every consumer has experienced disappointment over inability to secure goods wanted and even more to secure just such goods as are desired. There is such a variation in human wants that this situation arises more frequently than most people think. Students of consumer demand as affecting retail apparel sales estimate that from sixty to eighty-five per cent of all women's outerwear sales and similar percentages of sales of other goods are compromises with the consumers' actual desires. Failure to get just what they want results in purchases of something that will serve but which may never result in complete satisfaction. It is certain that a great many purchases made by consumers in every line are not just what would be bought if the individual were allowed absolutely free choice. While there are very wide varieties of goods produced and offered for the selection of the customer, human desires are even more variable so that the inability to secure the kinds of goods desired is an important limitation upon consumer demand.

In some instances there may also be limits placed on consumers' choice because of the limited quantity of any desired goods available for the satisfaction of a given want. When many people desire an article for which there is a limited supply, it is a commonplace of economics that the price tends to rise, and from our study of the marginal utility theory we know that this must mean that there remains a certain amount of unsatisfied desire. Every price decline, on the other hand, means a step nearer complete satisfaction of wants for the commodity under consideration.

6. Business Control of Consumers' Choice

Another factor affecting consumers' choice is the control exercised by producers. There is a common belief expressed by many writers on economics and business subjects that producers exercise a high degree of control through advertising and salesmanship over consumer choice. Sometimes this control is described as a tyranny, and in other cases as if it were an unavoidable evil. Consumers frequently complain that they are unable to find what they want and must perforce buy what is offered to them by retailers and producers.

Obviously, producers themselves would like nothing better than to control consumer demand. Their large investments in manufacturing institutions depend for their profits upon the sales of the goods produced and distributed. The producer undergoes enormous risks in attempting to predict what consumers will want and in producing goods in quantity and distributing them in advance of final consumers choice. From the producer's standpoint it would be wonderfully simple if there were some formula for controlling consumers' choice so that the market success of a given commodity could be assured in advance.

However, there is no known formula by which producers can control the choice of consumers—or at least no manufacturer, no matter how successful he may be, seems at all certain that he possesses such a formula. Not only the unsuccessful manufacturers but the successful ones as well are generally very keenly alive to the fact that consumer demand, so far as their individual products are concerned, is a very fragile thing, which may be lost if the utmost care is not exercised, and, in fact, the possession of which cannot be guaranteed even under conditions of utmost vigilance.

The usual method of attempting to secure some control or direction of consumer demand is through the use of sales promotion. National and local advertising, billboards and street car advertising, direct mail promotion, sampling, window displays in retail stores, and demonstrations, are the most frequently used forms of publicity to affect or influence consumers' choice. The outstanding successes of concerns that have used advertising is a very definite measure of the proof of the value of sales promotion, but it may well be questioned whether even the best and most effective forms of sales promotion do more than stimulate consumers' choice in lines in which wants are already making their presence felt.

7. Competition

Certainly, sales promotion under modern conditions can scarcely by spoken of as a limitation upon consumers' choice, for there are literally thousands of concerns that are advertising their products in competition with each other for consumers' decisions. The number of products seeking recognition of the consumer through advertising and other forms of sales promotion is very great. There are said to be over 400 dentifrices on the American market. The woman interested in toilet preparations going through a leading current fashion periodical carrying advertising of such products is scarcely limited in her choice by the fact that there are twelve varieties advertised in the pages of the single periodical, all of them, generally speaking, serving the same purpose.

The effect of such competition of many concerns seeking the favor of the consumer undoubtedly does stimulate business, but it seems unlikely that such stimulation increases the total sale of products beyond a certain point in any fair relationship to the increased amount of sales promotion. To illustrate: a product advertised by the use of a full page in a given periodical secures a certain result therefrom. The addition of a competitor, also using a full page in the same periodical, might conceivably stimulate demand for an additional volume of as much or more than the sales secured by the first advertiser. The net result of such competition of two advertisers might well be an increase in business for the first as well as satisfactory volume for the second. It is also conceivable that the addition of a third competitor using similar space in a given periodical might stimulate demand for still more volume so that all might be benefited by the increased competition.

Obviously, however, there comes a stage in competition at which additional advertisers and additional advertising fail to induce a proportionate increase in the amount of sales. To use the common economic term, the law of diminishing returns sets in . In all likelihood the periodical referred to above, carrying twelve full-page advertisements of toilet preparations, all of which serve practically the same purpose, might induce several times as much business as a single advertisement; but it is hardly probable that twelve competitors, each using the same amount of advertising in a given periodical, would secure twelve times the effect that could be secured by the advertising effort of one concern.

Sales promotion in all its forms is exceedingly productive when used as a means of promoting business on merchandise for which there already exists a demand either potential or actual. The failures of advertising, of which there have been many, may in most cases be traced to efforts to create demand where none existed, attempts to change demand from fundamental trends or to create a demand for products which did not adequately fill the requirements of fundamental demand.

Sales promotion with all its successes has definite limitations as a means of control of consumers' choice, and it seems probable that with the progress of business these limitations may become more fully understood and given more careful consideration in business planning. Changing business conditions are forcing such consideration. It is a well-known fact that the older forms of advertising as well as many forms of sales appeal are not nearly so effective now in securing results as they formerly were. Necessity has forced a rapid development in the technique of sales promotion in order that profitable results might be kept up. During the time in which advertising has developed, consumer choice, too, has worked out a technique of defense against the various forms of commercial promotion, so that much of the art of persuasion that is put into modern advertising is largely neutralized by the critical attitudes of the consumers.

The volume of money expended for sales promotion has increased greatly during the last score of years. This increase has probably been considerably more rapid than the increase in volume of business resulting from such advertising. It seems, however, that the time may come, if indeed it has not already come, when ordinary means of sales promotion will be found of declining efficiency. In the tendency to build ever larger business organizations, to establish efficiently operated purchasing departments, to utilize standard specifications and to predetermine demand, the importance of salesmanship is much reduced. Many of the most successful retail institutions of the country who carry not complete lines but lines of merchandise such as the people prefer, now tend to eliminate the personal and persuasive elements in salesmanship and instead stress buying what people will want without the necessity for high pressure selling. Chain stores, department stores, mail order houses, and cooperative buying organizations all discount the functions of personal salesmanship. Whatever may have been the situation in the past, a very large part of salesmanship today has come down to little more than simple explanation and order taking. Advertising and sales promotion, if it is to do any good, must now more than ever offer merchandise that will give consumers the satisfactions that they want.

8. Monopoly

Naturally, a producer's monopoly over a necessity of life results in a complete control of consumer choice. Legislation prevents the establishment of such monopolies in all but a few instances based on patents. Consumers are protected against monopoly control in practically every country; but even under conditions of monopoly the consumer is not usually entirely at its mercy excepting in cases of the most fundamental and elementary necessities of life. In the sale and consumption of most commodities there is almost always an opportunity for alternative choices, and while the monopoly may be successful in obtaining higher prices, the higher prices tend to reduce sales. When prices are raised, if it is at all possible, consumers either go without or utilize alternative goods. Public opinion, when aroused, will not tolerate monopoly conditions. Tendencies in business to restrict the flow of products or limit consumers' choices in any way by coercive measures are certain to lead to difficulty and trouble.

9. Goodwill

There is another form of market control obtained by long-continued satisfactory relations with the consuming public. A concern that consistently gives fair service and courteous dealing usually acquires a high degree of consumer friendship. In time the consumers' impressions, when satisfactory, form habits of trade which become stronger with the passage of years so that it becomes very difficult for competition of any kind to take trade away from the concern that enjoys such goodwill.

Goodwill is more effective in the control of consumers' choice than monopoly. The manufacturer's product which has given satisfaction to multitudes of consumers over a number of years may count on established habits of use and feelings of goodwill that are not easily broken up. The retailer who through years of fair dealing has gained the confidence of his consuming public, has a hold over his trade which even price-cutting competitors cannot readily break down. Consumers will make sacrifices of time and energy and compromises in their choice to a very considerable extent in order to continue their trade with a concern that enjoys their goodwill.

10. Knowledge and Experience

Another exceedingly important factor in consumers' choice is the degree of knowledge possessed by the consumer relative to the commodities in which choice is to be exercised. Under conditions of the most complete knowledge as to choice and available goods to suite any particular want, the consumer naturally secures the utmost value for each dollar expended. This constitutes rational spending, but, obviously, not all consumers possess such complete knowledge. Choice of goods is not always rational and much spending is planless, thoughtless, and even foolish.

The effect of general education obtained in the public schools, the high schools, and the colleges on consumers' choice may not be overemphasized. Since women are the homemakers, they are in a position to determine the character and direction of most consumer demands, and it is the education of women during the past generation that has had a very great effect on present consumption of goods. Special training in specific courses such as home economics, cooking, sewing, and other branches of homemaking naturally have very direct effects on consumption as well as on methods of consumption. The subject matter of such courses is consumption.

Profound effects on consumption occur as a result of education in the more general educational courses. Many, if not most, of the radical changes that have taken place in the consumption of the American people during the past twenty years are very probably due to the influence of the general education, of girls in particular, during the preceding years in the common and high schools of the country.

If one were to designate any particular group of consumers as of outstanding importance in fixing the standards of present-day consumer demand, it is probable that such designation would fall upon young women from twenty-five to thirty-five years of age who graduated from high schools some years ago, and who are highly ambitious and still striving to make good. Though they now occupy positions of some responsibility either in business, homes, or society, their purchasing power is limited but still sufficient to cover the necessities of life; and because of their limited purchasing power they must exercise care and discretion in the choice of merchandise. Such women feel that they cannot afford to take any long chances in their choice of consumers' goods. What they buy must be worth, by and large, what they pay for it. It must be right from the standpoint of fashion. This group, making up a considerable percentage of the total consuming population, and without doubt by far the most influential part of the consuming population, is setting the standards of living today.

It is probably that the influence of education—both specific education for homemaking and general education—will grow. Changes in the educational courses of study point to this.

Formerly, the educational courses for girls in high schools and colleges on the subjects of home economics included training in cookery, millinery, sewing, and dressmaking. Particular emphasis was placed upon the production of goods at home in these fields. But as such work has phased out of the homes and is being carried on more and more in factories, education has likewise changed its character by stressing production less and careful selection or choice more. Present courses in homemaking stress budget-making, rational amounts to spend for various necessities, careful selection, and purchase to insure getting full values, savings, and investment.

The study of homemaking has evolved largely into a study of spending, in other words, the economics of consumption. The value of such education to the consumer must be obvious to everyone. Its effects will in time prove enormous. The first and most direct result of proper education in home-making will be in the direction of better living. This will mean much to the consumer, but it will also prove of great value to producers and distributors as well. The object of business is to produce and give to consumers what they want. Business institutions may not be particularly interested in the arts of living, but where the arts of living have been highly developed and purchasing and spending definitely rationalized, the wants of consumers may be more accurately predicted and, as a result, both production and distribution of goods may be made a more orderly process. A considerable amount of the waste found in present-day business is due to inability to predict consumer demand.

Consumer demand that is irrational is unpredictable. As consumers become better educated, their choice becomes more intelligent and, from the standpoint of business, more readily predictable. It is not suggested that any course of education, however extensive, may result in the elimination of individual taste and the standardization of all goods into a few types. Nor is it believed that education can eliminate all irrationality in consumers' choice. Complete standardization would never prove satisfactory. Much can be hoped for, however, by the substitution of reason for whim and plan for chance. Such is the mission of education in homemaking and in consumer choice.

In conclusion, consumers' choice is always complicated. There are, first of all, the fundamental wants seeking satisfaction modified by the amount of purchasing power controlled by or available to the consumer. Even after the wants have been defined and purchasing power considered, the reactions of the individual consumer in specific cases are greatly modified by habits, customs, fashions, sales promotion, personal treatment by dealers and producers, and finally by the knowledge or information and past experience that the consumer may possess about the goods under consideration.

Freedom of choice is a subject that has often been discussed. Obviously, freedom of choice as applied to the purchase of consumers' goods is bounded by many limitations even at its best. Freedom of choice may be exercised within the limits of purchasing power and must of necessity fall well within the prescribed walls of habit, fashion, and the other factors mentioned. After all of these limitations have been given due credit, there is room for a question as to whether there really is an important degree of freedom of choice. Practically, however, consumers' choice may always be considered a resultant of many forces. The consumer undoubtedly finds the greatest satisfaction when his choices accord most fully with all of the factors enumerated.

VI

THE
RESPONSIBILITY
OF MARKETING

The large quantity of consumer protection legislation and the popularity of consumer activists makes a section on "The Responsibility of Marketing" a necessary and desirable part of this book. The articles selected attempt to identify the ethical relationships between the marketer and the consumer and analyze marketing's value in an industrial society. Together they should give the reader a feeling of the ethical responsibility and value of marketing.

The article by Westing summarizes some of the specific ethical problems related to marketing. It was written in 1967 when consumerism pressures were particularly strong, and it reflects the concern of the period. The Buskirk and Rothe article is an analysis of the consumerism phenomenon. The article was written at a time when the consumerism movement had reached a substantial level of maturity. The first report of the Consumer Advisory Council was a statement of the four basic rights of consumers. They included the right to safety, the right to be informed, the right to choose, and the right to be heard. Together, they represented a statement of the federal government's intent to protect the consumer. The final two articles in this section deal with the efficiency of marketing. The value added concept presented by Beckman directly illustrates how marketing adds value for the buyer. The last article is a chapter from Cox's book *Distribution in a High Level Economy* and is concerned with the efficiency of distribution. It presents the classic arguments on distribution in efficiencies and their rejoinders.

43

Some Thoughts on the Nature of Ethics in Marketing

John H. Westing

Business is having trouble with its ethics today. But, then, business has always had trouble with its ethics. As far as one may care to go back into history he will find intellectuals castigating businessmen for their bad ethics. It appears that, for the most part, the criticism went unheard, or unheeded. It is true that during much of human history businessmen lived on the very fringe of "good" society and that this semi-ostracism may well have resulted in part from the bad ethics imputed to businessmen. During most of this time the businessman, while he may have deplored his social alienation, did not seem to care enough to pay the price for social respectability.

Today, at least in the sense of caring, the situation seems to have changed. This is not to say that the businessman today is willing to pay a *high* price for moral respectability, but he is sufficiently concerned to want to know the price. The concern of the businessmen is evident in a variety of ways: in the increasing flow of brochures and pamphlets published by companies on the social responsibilities of business; by the willingness to question whether business may have goals other than profit maximization; by the concern being exhibited over racial equality, slum clearance, and pollution control; and, most of all, by an amazing eagerness to discuss the subject of morality and ethics. I well recall about ten years ago organizing a seminar for executives on business ethics and being told by our business advisors that executives not only would not come, but would resent the implications implicit in a session on ethics. On that occasion we toned down the title somewhat and got an adequate, but disappointing, turnout. More

Reprinted from John H. Westing, "Some Thoughts on the Nature of Ethics in Marketing," in *Changing Marketing Systems,* (1967), pp. 161–163, published by the American Marketing Association.

recently we have held a number of undisguised seminars on ethics and have had an enthusiastic response, both in numbers and participation. I believe that anyone who has had the temerity to talk on this subject will bear me out in the statement that if one is willing to discuss this "hairy" subject he will soon have more opportunities than he cares to accept.

If it is true that there has been a notable change in the attitude of businessmen toward ethics, how does one explain it? Let me offer this hypothesis. The executive today is no more nor less concerned about ethics than was his counterpart a century ago. The man has not changed, but his environment has. In a subsistence economy, ethics get short shrift. This is not only true over time, but is equally true geographically at a point in time. I think it can be said that there is a direct relation between per capita income and the ethical standards of a country—and, incidentally, this variation in standards poses one of the knottiest ethical problems possible for a company engaged in trade with developing countries. But, to get back to the point, when one is destitute he is less likely to indulge his ethical impulses than when he is comfortable or satiated. Since, in the United States today, we are materially more comfortable than we have ever been before, our concerns naturally tend to turn from further satisfaction of our physical needs to the satisfaction of needs in higher categories of the need hierarchy—and ethics fall into one of those categories. If this line of reasoning is correct, I think it leads to the conclusion that, in the future, businessmen are likely to become still more concerned with ethical consideration. And, as professors of business subjects, we should be anticipating this concern or once again we may find ourselves rationalizing business practice rather than moulding it.

A tremendous amount of time and effort can be spent on the argument over whether ethics in business are worse than in such fields as law, medicine, politics, or education. Personally, I think a good case can be made for the likelihood that, at a given time, the level of ethics in all major occupational groups of a society is very nearly the same. With no social barriers and few economic barriers to the entry into the various occupational fields, it is unlikely that they would attract people with widely varying ethical standards. One could, of course, argue that the professions attract those with a high sense of humanitarianism and worldly renunciation, and such people might have higher ethical ideals. However, this position is somewhat hard to defend if one notes the level and trend of income prevailing in the professional fields and the rush to the highly specalized fields where income is likely to be maximized and the service element minimized. It seems more likely to me that the differences which exist result not from intrinsic differences in the moral standards of individuals or groups, but from the fact that moral temptations and pressures may be greater in some fields than others. Quite obviously, if one is attempting to assess the moral stamina of two individuals, he must either measure their performance under similar conditions or make allowances for the differences in the environments where they are tested. Perhaps it is the failure to make such allowances that causes the businessman to come off badly when ethical comparisons are made between him and members of other occupational groups. If the corroding effects of the "love of money" are recognized—as they have been throughout history—it must be admitted that the businessman is subject to more frequent and more extreme ethical temptations than most other men. Thus, he may not be ethically weaker, just more sorely tried.

The above issue is an interesting one and, I believe, one that deserves more thought than it has received. However, in one sense it is irrelevant and in another sense it might even be harmful. It would seem to me to be positively harmful if it led any substantial number of businessmen to conclude that complacency was warranted. Society today, as well as the businessman himself, is uneasy about the state of ethics in business. Under these conditions, complacency may cost the businessman a further loss of his rapidly vanishing freedom. This, of course, is a pragmatic rather than a philosophical argument. The issue of whether the ethics of the businessman are better or worse than those of others is irrelevant because it involves a measurement against the wrong standard. There will be argument on this point, but I maintain that the issue should not be whether the ethics of the businessman are *relatively* as good as those of others but whether they are *absolutely* good enough to sustain the good life in a highly complex society.

This point goes to the very heart of the issue of ethics, and unless it can be resolved, I doubt that there is much chance of any real progress on the ethics front. The absolute position identifies, and at times almost equates, ethics with religion. This has been the traditional position, and it was a viable position so long as religion held real or nominal authority over a majority of the people. It seems to me there was a time, within my memory, when most people—nonchurch members as well as members—acknowledged the *rightness* of a code of ethics based upon the second table of the Decalogue. Many may not have complied with the code in practice, but an admission of its rightness at least gave society a point of reference—a north star—for guidance.

Today, in his quest for scientific verification of everything, man has to a large extent discarded normative standards such as the ethical component of the Decalogue. In most areas even scientific man does not discard conventional wisdom until he has found it wrong and has discovered something better to replace it. In the field of ethics, unfortunately, modern man has been too impatient for this. Ethical principles were so clearly not based on empirical research that he discarded them without having even begun a search for anything to replace them. Someone might argue that relativism or situational ethics has replaced the more formalized code, but I would contend that as a replacement, relativism is an illusion. In an economic order in which the central motivating principle is based on selfish advancement, ethical performance can only decline unless there is some countervailing force to offset the drive to better one's self at the cost of others.

One could easily move from the position that if the traditional standards are not working, and relativism will not work, we are in a perilous, and, perhaps hopeless, position. I suspect that not a few people may be close to this point without having bothered to take their bearings and define their position. May we not, however, be able to reason our way to an intermediate position—one that establishes ethics as a normative standard without making it a part of religion.

To do this one must make the assumption that our world is an orderly world—not only the physical environment but the social environment as well. More specifically, the assumption about the social environment of man must be that living together in society is possible over the long term only if we recognize and comply with inherent social laws which are as inviolable as the physical laws of the universe. Just as we can defy, but not break, physical laws, we can defy, but not break, social laws. This does not seem to me to be an unreasonable assumption. Could not our rising concern over ethics by an implicit recognition of the fact that our increasingly intimate social relationships demand that we regulate our associations by better ethical norms?

If one wonders why we have made so much progress in discovering the physical laws of our universe and so little in finding the ethical laws, he might note that physical cause and effect relationships are mostly short term, whereas social cause and effect relationships may not come to light in less than generations or centuries. We do know that societies rise and fall, but we have never done much more than speculate idly about the reasons. Admittedly, the difficulty of discovering such ethical verities will be difficult, but with man in possession of something approximating ultimate power the penalty for not discovering these hidden relationships may well be extinction. If the issue is this stark we certainly ought to get on with the job.

Let us look at the matter for a moment from the point of view of the religionists, of which group I consider myself to be a member. We have always tended to be a bit hazy and uncertain about the *other* worldly and the *this* worldly aspects of religion. When one considers that traditional religion traces its antecedents back to a time when society was ruled as a theocracy, it can be seen that the man-to-God and man-to-man relationships would not be clearly distinguished. We have tended to carry this full set of religious rules over into a society that is now sharply divided into spiritual and secular segments. The second table of the Decalogue is in substance a prescription for how man must live with man in ethical terms if communal life is to succeed. In this connection it is interesting to note that, while all major religions differ significantly in their man-to-God prescriptions, they all agree quite well in their ethical prescriptions. As a matter of fact, in this universality of ethical norms we might find a promising approach to the development of a set of secular ethical standards. If we would disregard the questions of how these norms came into being, translate them into modern phraseology, and begin to check them against human history we might well have a start toward our difficult goal. Essentially, in terms of broad principles, the universal religious code of ethics demands respect for truth, respect for persons, respect for human institutions, and respect for property. These principles would seem to be sufficiently noncontroversial so that they could be accepted as secular norms.

Now, how does one get from this high plain of lofty principles, to the more mundane level of operational ethics. It seems to me that one must make the transition in a series of steps.

First of all, there is the law, which is or ought to be the lowest common denominator of ethical practice. I do not by any means subscribe to the facile but faulty maxim that says, "If it's legal, it's ethical." To say this, I think, exhibits a misunderstanding of both law and ethics. Law codifies only that part of ethics which society feels so strongly about that it is willing to support it with physical force. The common misunderstanding also frequently gets us into the dilemma of passing laws that are unenforceable because society does not feel certain enough about them to apply the force which is implicit in law. So, the man who thinks he is ethical because he is not knowingly violating civil laws is, in fact, only practicing ethics at its lowest level. Furthermore, if no one did any *better* than that, society could degenerate morally, but could never regenerate.

Probably in the field of business the next level of ethical performance is measured by company policy. Of course, not all company policy has an ethical dimension, but when it does deal with it, policy must transcend the ethical level of law. If it were lower than the law, the policy would be illegal; if it were equal to the law it would be pointless, so it must transcend the law. It might be observed that we enforce ethical principles at this level, not with physical force, but with economic force. We fire, demote, reduce pay, etc. These are powerful sanctions and this avenue represents an approach that has not been explored very far. With the present tendency of companies to assume social responsibilities, there could be substantial achievements in the ethical realm that would probably benefit business as well as society.

There are ethical problems that cannot be reached through company policy and are not appropriate for law. These concern matters in which an industry's competitive environment exerts a depressing effect on ethical conduct, and the competitive situation does not allow the individual companies to practice the ethics they would like. The only way we have found to deal with such issues is through industry codes of ethics, and they have had a spotty, and not very inspiring, history. Part of the trouble here has been that industries have so frequently tended to confuse bad ethics with hard competition. Many groups have tried to write hard competition out of their industries through the vehicle of ethical codes and have found that it did not work for long. Then they have concluded that codes of ethics will not work. I believe that with better understanding of what they are supposed to do, industry codes deserve another chance and stronger support. It might be noted that the force behind ethical codes is strictly a social kind of sanction. Such sanctions may not have much raw power, but in a prosperous economy with people striving to satisfy acceptance goals, the force is not inconsiderable.

Finally, we arrive at the epitome of ethics, where a man is face-to-face with an ethical issue and must decide it in a way that will satisfy his personal standards. This is the touchstone of ethics in a free society. In the end the other levels of ethics all derive their substance from the performance of each individual as he wrestles with ethical issues. If he does not have adequate standards and is not willing to pay an economic price to satisfy his standards, our economic society is inevitably going to suffer from degenerating ethics.

As I see it, then, our task is two-fold: to define ethics in a way that will gain intellectual acceptance for it, and to induce its practice by the business community. The business educator is of critical importance to both.

44

Consumerism
—An Interpretation

Richard H. Buskirk and James T. Rothe

Consumerism has received much attention in recent business literature.[1] Most articles and editorials dealing with the topic have commented on its importance, its underlying causes, its implications or what interested parties (consumer, government, firms) should do, but most discussions have failed to deal with the topic in a total sense. This article attempts to (1) determine what consumerism is, (2) reveal what has caused it, (3) study its implications and potential dangers, and (4) develop guidelines for corporate policy in dealing with consumerism.

Peter Drucker offers the following definition of consumerism:

> Consumerism means that the consumer looks upon the manufacturer as somebody who is interested but who really does not know what the consumers' realities are. He regards the manufacturer as somebody who has not made the effort to find out, who does not understand the world in which the consumer lives, and who expects the consumer to be able to make distinctions which the consumer is neither willing nor able to make.[2]

Another definition of consumerism has been developed by Mrs. Virginia H. Knauer, Special Assistant to the President for Consumer Affairs. She stated that the watchword for the new militant mood among American consumers is simply, "Let the seller beware," in comparison to the age-old *caveat emptor* or, "Let the buyer beware."[3]

Both of these definitions provide some insight into this current phenomenon referred to as *consumerism.* Perhaps it would be most relevant to relate consumerism to what has been popularly accepted as the marketing

Reprinted from Richard H. Buskirk and James T. Roche, "Consumerism—An Interpretation," in the *Journal of Marketing,* Vol. 34 (October 1970), pp. 61-65, published by the American Marketing Association.

concept for the past twenty years. The marketing concept, simply stated, suggests that the purpose of a business is to provide customer satisfaction. Thus, it is anticipated that the firm will maximize long-term profitability through customer orientation. The marketing concept is primarily a post-World War II development, produced largely by economic conditions which changed a seller's market to a buyer's market. The marketing concept was hailed as being the essential fulcrum with which business resources could be allocated to best enhance profitability for the firm in a buyer's market. Consequently, much has been written and said about the marketing concept—how it can be utilized and what it means. However, the marketing concept and the forces labeled *consumerism* are incompatible. If consumerism exists, the marketing concept has not worked. It may be that consumerism actually is the result of prostitution of the marketing concept, rather than a malfunction of it.

Examples of customer dissatisfaction are not difficult to find. For example, a recent article in *The Wall Street Journal* noted that roofs leak, shirts shrink, toys maim, mowers do not mow, kites do not fly, television sets burn up, service is difficult or impossible to obtain, and warranties are not honored.[4]

Certainly each of us, as a consumer, has experienced the cumulative frustration associated with products that do not conform to expectations. It is this sense of frustration and bitterness on the part of consumers who have been promised much and have realized less, that may properly be called the driving force behind consumerism. Accordingly, consumerism is defined as *the organized efforts of consumers seeking redress, restitution, and remedy for dissatisfaction they have accumulated in the acquisition of their standard of living.*

CAUSE OF CONSUMERISM

There are two major opposing theories about the role of the consumer in the market place of a free-enterprise system. One theory suggests that the consumer is "king." It is his dollar choice in the market which decides success or failure of producers; consequently, the consumer plays a decisive role in the entire process. This concept is referred to as "consumer sovereignty."

A completely opposite approach suggests that the consumer is a pawn in the entire process. The brilliance of Madison Avenue, sparked by research conducted by skilled behavioral scientists, has been used to deceive the consumer to the extent that he is incapable of intelligent selection. His dollar vote does not come across in any rational manner to decide who should be producing what; consequently, the consumer is not playing a decisive role in the process.

, According to the marketing concept, the first of these two theoretical approaches would be correct: the consumer is viewed as the dominant force since his purchases determine market success for competing firms.

There is some truth in both theories. This can best be explained by relating purchase behavior to the type of product purchased. When consideration is given to the importance of the product purchased, the frequency of the purchase, and the information sources used, both theories are partially correct. For example, if a product is purchased frequently, the consumer has an outstanding information source—his previous experience with it. In such a situation he is capable of judging the product's effectiveness and how well it has lived up to his expectations, both physically and psychologically. Thus, the consumer is capable of exhibiting more rational behavior when buying frequently purchased products than when acquiring "once-in-a-lifetime" items. Collective consumer behavior of this type results in the market process being served appropriately. Competition for the consumer's choice is then the determinant which leads to congruity between perceived and received quality on the part of the buyers. This is, in essence, a fulfillment of the marketing concept and accurately reflects a situation in which the consumer plays a major role in deciding who is successful in the market place.

On the other hand, when a consumer purchases a product he has not bought before (or at best, infrequently) and which is of sufficient importance, he often finds his attempt at rational behavior stymied by the lack of information. Since he has not previously purchased this product, his own experience is negligible. Another possible source of information is his peer group, but the limited accuracy of this type of information reduces its role in the transaction. Also, independent concerns' ratings of products are not widely used. This leaves the consumer with a basic information source—the company's marketing program. Evidently many marketing programs are not providing the information necessary for rational purchase behavior. This may be the result of short-term orientation on the part of management whose performance is judged on an annual basis. Top management's insistence on quarterly and annual budgeting performance may force operational management to make short-run decisions detrimental to the consumer because the impact of such decisions will not be reflected during operational management's tenure in that position. Consequently, when a product revision is needed, the response may be increased advertising and promotion expenditures rather than the more appropriate effort.

CATALYSTS IN CONSUMERISM MOVEMENT

The current wave of consumerism is not unprecedented in the history of business.[5] However, this time consumerism is enhanced by several major factors which were not evident in earlier expressions of consumerism. First, increased leisure time, rising incomes, higher educational levels, and general affluence have tended to magnify and intensify the forces of consumerism. The consumer's expectations with respect to the products he purchases are founded in a quest for individuality; yet, the market provides mass-consumption products with which the individual is not completely satisfied.

Second, inflation has made purchase behavior even more difficult. Rising prices have led consumers to increased quality expectations which are not achieved; thus, again contributing to the frustration of consumers.

Third, unemployment has been low. Therefore, the marginal laborer has been employed even though he has fewer skills. Such workers reduce output quality.

Fourth, demands for product improvement have led to increased product complexity. Further, this complexity has been stimulated by the emergence of new technology. This has led to increased service difficulties as well as performance and reliability problems. Moreover, society has been thoroughly conditioned to expect perfection from its technology. Moon landings, miracle drugs, organ transplants, and jet transportation make the housewife wonder why zipper manufacturers cannot make one that will not jam. The high degree of perfection that has been reached in recent years in a few fields only serves to disguise the higher *average* level of technical proficiency of present-day manufacturing. Yet, it is apparent that the consumer is demanding better products than those presently available, regardless of the economic and technical ability of the firm to provide it.

Finally, the popular success achieved by individuals such as Ralph Nader, in his crusade for consumerism, and the political support now developing for the forces of consumerism certainly reinforce the fact that this entire area must become a more important factor in business policy.

IMPLICATIONS OF CONSUMERISM

It seems apparent that consumerism will affect industries, firms, governments, and, if it is effective, the consuming public.

The consumerism movement will develop more power as its forces become more coordinated and as it develops more leadership and organization. This will be partly manifested in legal remedies, such as class suits, that the consumer will seek.

At present, it appears the success of consumerism will depend largely on governmental involvement, the beginnings of which are already evident. For example, truth in lending, truth in packaging, product safety standards, and other recent legislative efforts, as well as a great number of consumer protection and awareness bills, indicate that the role of government will be much greater. (Over 100 "consumer protection" bills have already been introduced in the 91st Congress since January 1969.)[6]

The role of the federal government in consumerism was first set forth by President John F. Kennedy's directive to the Consumer Advisory Council in March of 1962. He said:

Additional legislative and administrative action is required, however, if the federal government is to meet its responsibility to consumers in the exercise of their rights. These rights include: (1) the right to safety; (2) the right to be informed; (3) the right to choose; and (4) the right to be heard.[7]

It is apparent that the right to be informed, as well as the right to be heard, is of major importance. In fact, if all consumers were informed and were heard, this would then represent the fulfillment of the marketing concept as it was initially developed. The responsibility President Kennedy mentioned above should be industry's in a free society, not the government's. However, consumerism rightly claims industry has neglected its responsibility.

The relative role the government will play, and that which industry should play, is a critical aspect in the resolution of the consumerism issue. Given industry's traditional negative or complacent reaction to such issues, the result may be a coalition of consumer and government forces vs. industry, which could lead to federal standards for industry. The resulting standardization and bureaucracy may stifle the economic process. It is imperative that industry recognize the message and seriousness of the consumer movement and take positive action *now* rather than having to live with legislation that may not be in the long-run best interest of society.

The basic premise is that consumerism is primarily the result of a lack of information on the part of consumers which hinders their ability to buy certain products. This reflects itself in an ever-increasing gap between product expectations and product performance. Moreover, consumers must be heard, which indicates the need for an industry or company *ombudsman*. An excellent example of the *ombudsman* concept in action is that of the Whirlpool Corporation which has established a "cool line." The "cool line" enables owners to call the customer service director at all times.[8] A direct communication contact of this nature will greatly enhance consumer-company relationships; it represents the first step toward solution of owner problems.

The owner problem is not fraudulent or deceptive practices for the most part; rather, the problem is improper or nonexistent communication. This seems to be incongruous, since communication efforts—primarily advertising—exist in great abundance. However, communications between the firm and the consumer emphasize *imagery* at the expense of *information*.

Consumerism is attempting to tell industry something their research has not found, or that management has rejected or ignored. Appropriate information flow from the firm to the market in the form of product performance characteristics, simple-language warranty specifications, and safety standards will improve the basic customer-firm relationship, particularly for the infrequently purchased item where long, low-service life is a major objective of the consumer. Product performance characteristics must be improved for competitive success if communication is predicated on an information basis. Thus, the poor product quality problem will be largely eliminated.

The other link in this communication structure, that of the consumer to the firm, should be explored. It is imperative that some mechanism be developed which will enable the consumer to communicate more directly with management. The consumer *does* have something to say, but management must learn to listen and translate this information into action.

FALLOUT FROM CONSUMERISM— LOCUS OF LIABILITY

While it is easy for consumers' advocates to talk about "class suits" against manufacturers, it is not completely clear how these would work. If consumers as a group were damaged by an automobile made by General Motors, then General Motors would be the defendant in the class suit, and if it lost the case there would be some hope of collecting the resulting judgment.

But let us examine several other cases. Suppose consumers are damaged by an automobile produced by a small foreign automobile manufacturer. Who would be sued if the parent corporation did not do business in the United States, but rather operated through an independent agent, a corporate front set up to absorb such liabilities?

What about situations in which the manufacturer of a product is not apparent? Suppose a sales agency imports a product made by an unknown manufacturer. The sales agent takes the product and sells it. Later, a class suit is levied against the sales agent, who has taken care to have his corporate entity contain few assets.

It would seem that if class suits became a great risk businessmen would take steps to limit their personal liability and leave successful plaintiffs with judgments against nothing. Class suits strongly discriminate against the large, reputable American manufacturers to the benefit of the fly-by-night operator who is, from a practical standpoint, beyond the reach of such judgments. It is conceivable that a successful class suit against a significant U.S. corporation could bankrupt it. Who would benefit from such a development—competitors or consumers? Is this legal situation in the consumer's best interests? It is doubtful. Clearly, the class suit must be examined closely by all parties before being used.

WHO PAYS THE PRICE?

State and federal governments now pay more than half the cost of a class suit, because the defense costs and judgments are legitimate business expenses. The remainder comes from earnings. The economic facts of life indicate that if class suits and other costs of consumerism become a fact of corporate life, then management will have to budget for such costs because those costs must be covered by the price obtained for the products the company sells. The result of imposing more stringent legal and quality control regulations on industry will be to raise prices. This should not be underestimated. Evidence from the space industry indicates that the marginal costs of increased quality are high. The consumer has been conditioned to expect perfection from technology but not to the price this perfection costs.

A valid question can be asked concerning the economic wisdom of consumerism: Is it socially wiser to accept the present market-determined rate of consumer dissatisfaction than to pay the marginal costs that will be incurred in reducing consumer dissatisfaction by government decree? Is the market willing to pay for these consumer recommendations? It may not be.

Only the well-established, reputable firm that fully intends to meet its costs and obligations under consumerism would be forced to raise its prices. Again, fly-by-night operators who are beyond the reach of the law from a practical standpoint would not have to include the costs of consumerism in their prices: therefore, such operators may become competitively stronger if consumers fail to discriminate between the reputable firm and the fly-by-night operation. Further, this problem will become increasingly acute in private label situations where the producing firm is unknown.

GUIDELINES FOR CORPORATE POLICY

Consumerism is here, and businesses should respond thoughtfully and rationally to the issues rather than react negatively or not at all. Several guidelines are developed below which businesses should follow in their response to consumerism.

Establish a separate corporate division for consumer affairs. This division would participate in all corporate decisions that have consumer implications. It would participate in research and design, advertising, credit, pricing, quality assurance, and other similar decisions.

It would respond to all consumer inquiries and complaints and would have the authority to make appropriate adjustments.

It would be responsible for the development and dissemination of factual product and service information.

It would work with industry or trade associations in the development of a consumer education program.

The division must be given the status and power necessary for it to fulfill its mission. It should not be placed in a position in which either marketing or production forces could dilute its effectiveness. Possibly the wisdom of placing all quality assurance programs in this division should be carefully examined.

Change corporate practices that are perceived as deceptive. The consumer affairs division should identify corporate practices that are perceived as deceptive and/or antagonistic by consumers. These practices should be reviewed and a viable resolution of the problem developed. Examples of such corporate practices include packaging, credit, advertising, warranties, and the like.

Educate channel members to the need for a consumerism effort throughout the channel system.   Recognition of the need for a consumerism effort by all members of the channel will aid in the development of an industry consumerism program which will enhance performance of the channel system and provide better customer satisfaction. Moreover, a firm must be willing to eliminate an organization from its overall channel system if that organization is unwilling or unable to work within the constraints of corporate policy.

Incorporate the increased costs of consumerism efforts into the corporate operating budget.   Unless the consumer affairs division is budgeted sufficient money to carry out its mission, it will be little more than a facade and its effectiveness will be hampered. These costs will be reflected either in higher prices or lower margins unless the consumer program affects sales sufficiently to lower costs commensurately. To date little or no research exists to document the market responses to such programs. However, it does seem apparent that substantial costs will be incurred by firms not meeting their responsibilities to the consumer because of both governmental and legal actions.

An analysis of the above guidelines suggests that an effective consumerism program will be directed primarily at the communications problem between firms and consumers. The main purpose of the consumerism program will be to enhance the quality of communications between the consumer and the firm and to incorporate valid complaints into corporate decisions.

The corporate leader has two basic options: He may take positive action in this matter, or he may ignore it. If he ignores it, he must be prepared for a government program. It would seem that the corporate decision maker should prefer to develop a consumerism program of his own. The alternative course of action, with its attendant governmental regulation and bureaucracy, would not be in the best interest of either the consumer or the firm because of its impact upon competition, prices, and consumer satisfaction.

NOTES

[1]"Business Responds to Consumerism," *Business Week,* Vol. 2088 (September 6, 1969), pp. 94–108; "And Now, a Message From the Consumers," *Fortune,* Vol. 80 (November 1969), p. 103; "Buckpassing Blues," *Wall Street Journal,* Vol. CLXXIV (November 3, 1969).

[2]Peter Drucker, "Consumerism in Marketing," a speech to the National Association of Manufacturers, New York, April 1969.

[3]"The Consumer Revolution," *U.S. News & World Report,* Vol. LXVII (August 25, 1969), pp. 43–46.

[4]"Caveat Emptor," *The Wall Street Journal,* Vol. CLXXIII (June 26, 1969), p. 1.

[5]Stuart Chase and F. J. Schlink, *Your Money's Worth* (New York: The Macmillan Company, 1934).

[6]"The Rush to Help Consumers," *U.S. News & World Report,* Vol. LXVII (August 25, 1969), p. 47.

[7]*Consumer Advisory Council, First Report,* Executive Office of the President (Washington, D.C.: United States Government Printing Office, October 1963), pp. 5-8.

[8]"Appliance Maker Comes Clean," *Business Week,* Vol. 2088 (September 6, 1969), p. 100.

45

Protection of Consumer Rights

Consumer Advisory Council

THE RIGHT TO SAFETY

The federal government acts to assure the consumer's right to safety by limiting the sale of goods, e.g., narcotics, and meat from diseased animals, that are potentially harmful to the user. It acts—e.g., in its programs to eradicate animal diseases—to eliminate conditions giving rise to unsafe products or services. And it also acts—in the cases of highway safety and the protection of air-navigation radio channels, for example—to regulate the use of goods by consumers themselves in a way that limits the hazards they create for other consumers.

In the long history of government policy as to the consumer's right to safety there has been a shift in emphasis away from consumer responsibility, under the doctrine of *caveat emptor,* to seller responsibility for damages arising out of negligence or implied breach of warranty, and to government responsibility for prevention of damage. In the case of food and drugs, for example, government now has authority to seize and prevent the sale of products that are potentially harmful, without waiting for damages to be shown. In some cases, as with immunizing serums, there is authority to prevent the sale if the product is not efficacious. The 1962 Drug Amendments extended this principal to the full range of drugs.

With the advance of science and technology, consumer products have become highly complex, and the responsibility for the finished porducts has, in many instances been widely dispersed among a range of producers and distributors. Consequently, it is difficult for the consumer to appraise his risk prospectively or fix responsibility for damages retrospectively. It is

From *First Report of the Consumer Advisory Council,* (Washington: U.S. Government Printing Office, 1963), pp. 23-27.

important, therefore, that he be shielded against hazards to his health and safety by alert and efficient administration of those laws that have followed upon the Pure Food and Drug Act of 1906 and the Meat Inspection Act of 1907. At the federal level this responsibility is centered in the Department of Health, Education, and Welfare and the Department of Agriculture. But it also extends, for example, to the Department of the Interior's voluntary inspection of fish products and to the Treasury Department's regulation of narcotics and alcoholic beverages. Likewise, the Interstate Commerce Commission, the Federal Aviation Administration, and other specialized agencies promote safety in transportation.

Plainly, of course, passage of a law is only a first step in achieving consumer protection. Equally important is vigorous and imaginative enforcement by adequately staffed agencies.

Enforcement must be adjusted to take account of the growing population and the changing nature of products. President Kennedy pointed to this in his Consumer Message, saying:

> Thousands of common household items now available to consumers contain potentially harmful substances. Hundreds of new uses for such products as food additives, food colorings, and pesticides are found every year, adding new potential hazards.
>
> As Americans make more use of highway and air transportation than any other nation, increased speed and congestion have required us to take special safety measures.

THE RIGHT TO BE INFORMED

The right to be informed prompted the earliest federal legislation concerned directly with the consumer, namely, the Mail Frauds Statute of 1872. Today, implementation of this right extends from prevention of fraud and deception to government-sponsored and government-conducted research. Included within this range are the positive requirement of full disclosure (as in the case of issues of new securities), the establishment of standard weights and measures, performance testing (as in the case of drugs), grade labeling, standardization (a case of mandatory standards is that of bottle sizes for alcoholic beverages), and the provision of objective information on consumer problems.

The Wheeler-Lea Act of 1938 gave the Federal Trade Commission power to take action against false advertising, especially in the fields of foods, drugs, devices, and cosmetics. The Commission's authority extends to requiring affirmative disclosure in advertising or labeling when necessary to prevent consumer deception. An advertisement is considered false if it is "misleading in any particular," thus giving the Federal Trade Commission a broad area for enforcement.

The positive requirement of full disclosure has also been extended through the years to the labeling of many products. Disclosure of identity, composition, and quality, or the presence of harmful ingredients was required in the case of drugs in 1906, insecticides and fungicides in 1910, seeds in 1912, animal viruses, serums, and toxins in 1913, horsemeat in 1919, caustic poisons in 1919, substandard canned goods in 1930, and alcoholic beverages in 1935. Requirements were broadened in the case of foods in 1938, wool products in 1939, human viruses, serums, and toxins in 1944, fur products in 1951, and textile fiber products in 1958. Requirements with respect to labeling vary from commodity to commodity. The Federal Trade Commission has issued guides or rules relating to labeling practices, deceptive practices, and advertising for approximately 175 industries. A recent example of this is a Guide for Shoe Content Labeling and Advertising.

Action has been taken to protect the individual as a purchaser of securities. This was done primarily through the Securities Act of 1933 and the Securities Exchange Act of 1934, which, with certain exceptions, required the registration of new issues. The 1934 Act established the Securities and Exchange Commission, and in 1962 legislation was passed providing for reorganization of the Commission. The Commission has completed a major investigation of the securities markets, which has already provided the basis for pending legislation, the Securities Acts Amendments of 1963 (S. 1624 and H.R. 6789), and administrative changes.

The Congress has assigned primary responsibility for the establishment of standard weights and measures to the National Bureau of Standards. Certain acts have been passed establishing standard size packaging for some products. Fruits and vegetables are covered to some extent by the Standard Container Acts of 1916 and 1928. Alcoholic beverages are covered under the Alcoholic Beverages Administration Act of 1936. Quality of product is identified for the consumer in certain cases through government inspection and grading—especially of food products. For example, some meats and eggs are sold according to governmentally established grades.

The idea of the government's providing objective information directly to the consumer is not new. The Bureau of Home Economics of the Department of Agriculture, now incorporated in the Division of Nutrition, Consumer, and Industrial Use Research, was created in 1923. Information is provided by direct contact between consumers and government representatives—particularly, the Food and Drug Administration's consumer consultants and the Cooperative Extension Service's home demonstration agents. Information is also provided by government reports addressed to the consumer.

The federal government also supports research of value to consumers in such agencies as the National Bureau of Standards, the Department of Agriculture, and the National Institutes of Health, as well as in universities and private nonprofit research organizations.

THE RIGHT TO CHOOSE

The direction of the American economy depends heavily, as we have seen, on consumer's choices among products and among producers. In asserting the consumer's "right to choose," President Kennedy has implicitly indicated the importance of there being a number of alternative producers and of there being effective freedom for producers to enter new fields and offer new products and services. Thus, the consumer's right to choose and the maintenance of competition are intimately related. Promotion of competition, however, is a complex undertaking. In pursuing it the federal government has employed a series of legislative acts, some general in scope, some specific with regard to a type of practice or a particular industry.

Goverment intervention to ensure competition is older than the legislation in this field. Common law courts would not consider a contract binding if it was a clear case of conspiring to monopolize. However, the Government itself did not initiate action against any conspiracy or on behalf of third parties injured by conspiracies until passage of the Sherman Act of 1890. This committed the Government to active prevention and limitation of monopoly, and declared every contract, combination, or conspiracy in restraint of trade, or attempts at such restraint, to be illegal. Later antitrust acts were designed to modify the Sherman Act's coverage and to define more precisely actions considered harmful to competition. The Federal Trade Commission Act and the Clayton Act in 1914, the Robinson-Patman Act in 1936, the Wheeler-Lea Act of 1938, the Trade Mark Act of 1946, the McCarran Insurance Act of 1948, and the Celler-Kefauver Anti-Merger Act of 1950 are among the leading statutes indicating congressional intent with respect to competition. Responsibility for enforcing these laws is vested primarily with the Antitrust Division of the Department of Justice and the Federal Trade Commission.

In the administration of virtually every one of its economic programs the government influences the structure and operation of commercial markets. In negotiating international trade agreements, in establishing agricultural labor, or transportation policy, in procuring defense supplies, in setting directions for housing finance, in regulating securities markets, in making loans to small businesses, in providing marketing services and technical information to farm and business firms—in all these and in many other ways—the government affects the consumer's right to choose.

In some industries, however, technical considerations do not allow the consumer to have a choice among the varying products of numerous producers. In such cases the government may, while leaving the producing firms in private hands, act as agent for the consumers, regulating the number of firms in the industry, maximum or minimum price, quality, and conditions of service. While the bulk of such detailed regulation is done at the State level in this country, the Federal Government has entered the field in a number of industries, beginning in railroading in 1887 with the establishment of the Interstate Commerce Commission, whose jurisdiction was extended to internal waterborne transport in 1920 and to interstate motor carriers in 1935. Other transportation rates and services are regulated by the Federal Maritime Commission and the Civil Aeronautics Board. Similarly, other specialized government agencies regulate interstate aspects of the telephone, telegraph, radio and television industries; of banking and credit institutions; and of the electric power and natural gas industries.

In the case of electric power, the federal government also serves the consumer directly through such public power suppliers as TVA and the Bonneville Power Administration. These have increased total power availability and afford "yardstick competition" to private suppliers.

In a dynamic economy not only do the problems facing regulators grow with the population and the size of business firms, but also they change with the demands of consumers and the technological frontiers within reach of the producers. Presently, for example, we face the mushrooming demands for improved urban transit, the exciting possibilities of trans-oceanic communication via satellites, and the economics promised by long-distance, extra-high-voltage transmission of electrical energy.

In order to play their intended role on behalf of consumers, the regulatory agencies must have clear rule-making authority, fair and efficient procedures, and adequate numbers of competent personnel.

THE RIGHT TO BE HEARD

Besides promoting the consumer interest, the federal government also promotes the interests of producers. It may be said to seek the public interest partly through balancing the separate private interests of producers and consumers. Consumers, however, are not organized to the same degree as are producers for the purpose of influencing government policy, nor are they likely to be so organized in view of their scattered and varied interests. While seeking to learn the views of voluntary associations of consumers, therefore, government must remember that these veiws are not always expressed effectively enough to achieve a balance automatically in the array of private opinion being brought to bear on public policy issues.

To some degree the regulatory agencies are charged with representing the consumer interest. But at various times in the past it has seemed appropriate to provide within government more direct means for assuring the expression of the consumer viewpoint. The history of such "consumer representation" includes experiments in assigning the function to government as well as private individuals to serve in a consultative relationship to the government.

46

The Value Added Concept as a Measurement of Output

Theodore N. Beckman

In a very broad sense the term "management" has at times been used to refer to the control of activities, whatever their nature. Thus, we often hear complaints that a certain person cannot even "manage" his own affairs—business or personal—let alone those of others. We even speak occasionally of "self-management," thus using the term in a strictly subjective manner. In the most accepted sense, however, the term management is used to cover the planning, organizing, and controlling of the activities of an *organization*.

OUTPUT IS A BASIC MEASUREMENT OF MANAGEMENT

Essentially, management has to do with the most effective and economical use of all factors of production and their component parts in the accomplishment of the organization's objectives, the main one of which is that of producing a desired output. This output may be in the form of goods extracted, manufactured, and/or marketed, or in services rendered. To this end it becomes necessary to establish standards of performance and then to measure actual performance against these standards for a proper evaluation of what has been accomplished and as a means of obtaining enhanced efficiency in the future.

Because a defined and desired output is the principal aim and purpose of an organization, and because each of the factors of production or components thereof must necessarily be related to it, output becomes the

Reprinted with permission from Theodore N. Beckman, "The Value Added Concept as a Measurement of Output," in *Advanced Management* (April 1967), pp. 6–8, published by Society for Advancement of Management.

basic measurement of management. It is, therefore, of utmost importance, first, that we have a correct conception of the output that is to be measured and, second, that such output be properly measured. It makes a lot of difference, for example, whether we are to conceive of output as that of a business enterprise, a business establishment, or a business function. It is even of greater importance to distinguish between what output was created or added to by the given enterprise, establishment, or function and what was created previously by other enterprises or establishments.

INADEQUACY OF CURRENT MEASUREMENTS
OF OUTPUT

In general, output of business enterprises is now measured in terms of production, shipments, sales, or receipts. Receipts are invariably expressed in values, which are subject to fluctuations in the purchasing power of the dollar, and are not especially applicable to other than service concerns. When production, shipments, or sales (gross or net) are expressed in values, they suffer from the same shortcomings as receipts (as is, unfortunately, also true of value added). When expressed in terms of so-called physical volume, they are in reality nothing but values in constant dollars. Even when production, shipments, or sales are measured in physical units, the results may be of little value in measuring output, except perhaps in such commodities as steel or cement, because the units do not remain unchanged over any extended period of time. A 1957 model of a given make of automobile is certainly a different product even from the same make of car of an earlier vintage. The same thing is true of tires, batteries, and the vast majority of products in use today.

However, the most important weakness in all these measurements of output is that they all involve considerable duplication. Thus, in the production, shipments, or sales of a manufacturer, no matter how expressed, are included the costs of materials and supplies and purchased parts that were produced by others, in addition to what was added by the manufacturer in question. Moreover, this sort of duplication varies substantially from enterprise to enterprise. For example, one manufacturer might conceivably make a finished product in a completely integrated operation from the raw materials on. In such an instance the duplication would be insignificant or nonexistent. At the other extreme, a manufacturer may merely assemble a finished product from parts and supplies made by others, in which instance the duplication would be several times the contribution made by such a manufacturer. Between these two extremes, there are all sorts of gradations and variations in this regard. This at once exaggerates the contribution of some, understates that of others, and in all cases makes comparison futile and misleading.

What has just been stated should not be taken to imply any lack of value in data on production, shipments, sales, or receipts. Such data are still important for purposes of planning; budgeting; setting quotas; determination of rental values; figuring commissions, other operating expenses, gross and net profits; and for many other uses. What it does mean is that they are found wanting as measurements of output for basic management purposes and especially for determining the real contribution made by the business unit or function that is the subject of measurement.

VALUE ADDED AFFORDS BEST MEASUREMENT OF OUTPUT

It is believed that value added best measures the output of an establishment, an enterprise, and industry, or any other segment or sector of our economy. In time, this concept may also be used to measure the output that may be attributed to a given business function or process. In any event, it can be used in that manner internally by a business establishment or enterprise.

At present the use of value added is more or less restricted to the field of manufacturing and even there it is not as widely used outside the Census of Manufactures and other governmental agencies as is warranted. What is needed is wide application of this concept to all phases of the economy and strong attempts to do so are now being made by a number of potent organizations and others interested in progress in economic thought.

VALUE ADDED CONCEPT USED BY CENSUS OF MANUFACTURES

The value added concept has been used by the Bureau of the Census in connection with its censuses of manufactures for over a quarter of a century. As stated in its various appropriate publications: "Value added by manufacture is calculated by subtracting the cost of materials, supplies, and containers, fuel, purchased electric energy, and contract work from the total value of shipments." It thus represents the difference between the selling value of products shipped or delivered and the cost of materials, supplies, and containers, plus the cost of fuel, purchased electric energy, and contract work. Basically, then, the difference represents the net value of the operations of the reporting establishment itself without any admixtures of the labors or operations of other establishments, and this is presumed to measure the value added by the process of manufacture. It is a measure of the net output of the establishment, industry, industry group, or all manufacturing industries, as the case may be. Even then it is subject to certain limitations.

REASONS FOR USE

For some years there has been a tendency for the Census of Manufactures to shift emphasis more and more from value of products shipped to value added by manufacture as a measure of the contribution to the economy of the manufacturing sector and parts thereof. As a matter of fact, in its annual surveys of manufactures, value added by manufacture has completely replaced the value of production or shipments, although, as previously indicated, there are still some very important uses to date on the latter. Among the major reasons for this shift in emphasis was a desire to avoid duplication. This is clearly expressed in the following excerpts form the Bureau's publications:

> The value of products is not a satisfactory measure of the importance of a given industry, because only part of this value is actually created within the industry. Another part and often a much larger one, is contributed by the value of the materials used. The aggregates for cost of materials and value of products include large amounts of duplication due to the use of the products of some industries as materials by others.... Statistics of "value added by manufacture" are almost entirely free from the duplication which is a factor in the total value of products....[1]

Another reason was the Bureau's conviction that value added by manufacture is a fairly accurate measure of what is accomplished or created by a given industry and affords the best means for comparison of the economic contribution of one industry with that of another. This can be clearly discerned from the following excerpt in one of its publications:

> "Value added by manufacture" measures the approximate value created in the process of manufacture. It, therefore, provides the most satisfactory census measure of the relative importance of given industries for the United States as a whole or for geographic areas.[2]

ESSENCE OF THE CONCEPT AS NOW USED

Theoretically, the treatment of the value added concept by the Census of Manufactures is functional in character, since it is presumed to measure the contribution made by the *process* of manufacture as contrasted with the process of marketing or any other process. That is certainly the avowed purpose repeatedly stated in appropriate census publications. Actually, however, the concept is treated institutionally, in that the value added by manufacture is computed on an establishment basis and thus covers *all* activities performed by the manufacturing establishment including those of distribution or marketing. This would seem to be inevitable under existing conditions of gathering such information on a broad scale by a government agency or by a trade association, because of the current state of the arts in accounting, at least in practical application. This means that for practical reasons the measurement of value added must for the present be on an institutional rather than a functional basis, except for more detailed internal operation analysis within an enterprise.

Again, the word "value" as part of value added is used in the same practical sense as it is used in connection with value of products or value of shipments. To be sure, value is fundamentally a subjective quality involving the satisfactions to human beings mainly as consumers and can be truly known only to the human being involved, assuming full consciousness on his part of such satisfactions. Certainly, there is no way of practically measuring such satisfactions and their differing intensities except through expressions in the market place in the form of prices. It is in this latter sense that the term value is used. It is assumed that the price a person will pay for a product or service is in general a reasonable measure of its value to him. Without, at this time, going into further theoretical discussions of the nature of economic value, suffice it to say that there are other good reasons for treating it in the common sense and practical way in which it is used in connection with the value added concept.

Finally, the term value added is used in the same sense as value created or value produced. This is in line with the best current economic thinking that production is the creation of economic values and that such values are created through the addition of utilities, which are capacities in goods or services to satisfy human wants. Especially, there are four types or classes of utilities: form, place, time, and possession. *Form* utility is created in any extracting, processing, or manufacturing operation which converts or *transforms* scarce resources such as raw materials or semi-manufactures to increasingly satisfying states. An automobile manufacturer who assembles a completed product from various parts and supplies pruchased by him creates form utility, just as does a canner who processes the raw tomatoes by canning. *Place* utility is created when a product or service is made available where the customer wants it. For this purpose, goods must be *transferred* from where they are first available to the next place and on until they reach their final destination in business or for ultimate consumer use. *Time* utility is created when the product of service is made available to the customer when he wants it. *Possession* utility is created when the product or service is at the user's command, i.e., in his possession, legally and physically, as through the transfer of title of goods.

It is now generally recognized among economists and other students of the subject that the creation of these utilities spells the creation of economic values and that this is the essence of production. This means that whoever creates these utilities is engaged in production, so that a wholesaler or a retailer who normally creates place, time, and possession utilities is as much a producer as is a processor who changes a product from one form to another. It also means that all who are engaged in the creation of utilities or economic values are productive and, by their work, add value and make a contribution to our economy.

ADVANTAGES FROM USE OF VALUE
ADDED CONCEPT

It stands to reason that the adoption of the value added concept in the measurement of output in all sectors of the economy including farming, mining, and distribution, would have the same advantages as those derived from its use in connection with manufacturing. In the first place, it is the best reasonably available *absolute* measure of the value created in the process of whatever part of the economy is being measured. It measures, without any duplication, what the activities in question have actually contributed to our society in terms c. enhanced value of goods and services through the creation of utilities.

Second, value added is the best reasonably available *relative* measure of value created that can be used for proper and fairly accurate comparison with anything else similarly measured. In this manner, it will be possible for the first time to make proper comparison between the economic contribution made, for example, by farming, manufacturing, mining, marketing, and certain services. Also, it would make possible a proper comparison of one segment of, say, distribution (like wholesaling) with another (like retailing) or of one type of wholesaling or retailing with another.

Third, use of the concept will help to view costs in their proper perspective. While cost is a measure of *input* or of what a business spends or puts into its activities, value added is a measure of the *output* produced by such costs. Value added is thus really the value received for the costs incurred or for the input in terms of labor, entrepreneurial management, capital, and other factors of production. Not only is it essential that the two should not be confused or used interchangeably except from a strictly social viewpoint according to which income and outgo must necessarily balance, but it is also essential that costs should not be viewed by themselves without relation to value added. To look at costs by themselves, without knowing what was gotten for them, is hardly scientific and, in fact, quite misleading.

Fourth, application of the value added concept to any part of the economy would necessarily result in improved public relations. As in manufacturing, where it has been used for some time, it would tend to shift emphasis from costs and wastes to value added and from a negative to a positive and constructive approach to the problems involved.

A PREREQUISITE TO MEASUREMENT
OF PRODUCTIVITY

As may be surmised from what has already been stated, value added is not in itself a measurement of productivity. It merely measures production, i.e., the result of productive activity involved in the creation of economic values, not the rate at which such production has proceeded with reference to some factor of production or a part thereof. Unfortunately, it is a common error to confuse production with productivity. For example, it is often publicized that in this country we have a productivity at the rate of three per cent a year. What it really means, assuming the percentage to be correct, is that our production or total output such as gross national product has been increasing at the rate indicated, but it does not measure the productivity or degree of efficiency of our labor force, capital resources, or any other factor of production. In fact, it may well be that productivity has actually declined at certain times, when the increase in the labor force, accumulated capital, and other factors of production are considered.

Properly used, productivity is a ratio or relationship between output on the one hand and resources expended to produce that output on the other. Usually, an attempt is made to relate output to a factor of production deemed essentially or principally responsible for it. This has generally resulted in measuring productivity in terms of output per unit of direct labor such as a man-hour. It is obvious that when this is done, value added more nearly represents the contribution made by a unit of labor than do sales, products, or shipments.

At this juncture it may not be inappropriate to point out the fallacy in using solely man-hours of direct labor in computations of productivity, for it has led many to believe that all increases in productivity are attributable to this type of labor. The truth of the matter is that supervisory or indirect labor may have had as much or more to do with enhancing productivity as did direct labor. Moreover, increased productivity may frequently by caused far more by greater capital investment per unit of product of per unit of labor than by increased skill of or application by labor. For this reason, productivity may well take the form of a ratio of output to investment in capital goods or to machine hours of operation.

Again, management may be chiefly responsible for enhanced productivity. A case in point is the redesigning and rearrangement by management of a production line for a given product in the electrical field with the result that five men on a line could produce more than twice the physical volume formerly produced by seven men. Labor had nothing to do with this increase in productivity, as the type and skill of labor used on the lines remained unchanged.

Finally, land as a factor of productivity may be the factor that enhances productivity in a given situation. It is well known that a proper location of a business may have much to do with the amount of output produced, whether it be in terms of sales or value added.

It is, therefore, believed that much progress can be made in the measurement of productivity, if the output in terms of value added would be related to the various factors of production and not to labor alone. The difficulty of developing such measurements is no more of an excuse for not doing the job than the difficulty of complying with a law is an excuse for violating it. Besides, I am of the conviction that the job can be done and that it may be possible to determine just what factor of production is responsible for enhanced productivity and to what approximate degree.

A PREREQUISITE TO MEASUREMENT OF
OVERALL EFFICIENCY

Similarly, value added is not in itself a measurement of efficiency, but merely the proper output figure to be used in such a measurement. Especially in the measurement of overall efficiency, value added is the best numerator to be related to a denominator of total costs or any of its components and to net profits. It follows, therefore, that it would be erroneous to conclude that output viewed as value added would cause us to be concerned about ways and means of increasing it for its own sake, just as it would be erroneous to assume that input viewed in terms of costs would cause us to be concerned with ways and means of reducing it for its own sake and without due regard to the values obtained for such cost.

EMPHASIS ON PRODUCTIVE CHARACTER OF
ALL ECONOMIC ACTIVITY

One of the most significant benefits to be derived from the use of value added as a measurement of output is the emphasis it gives to the productive character of whatever economic activity it measures. This approach to economic analysis inevitably leads to the conclusion that economic values are created by all segments of the economy and by all persons making up the labor force and, consequently, all of them are engaged in productive work.

The significance of this becomes apparent upon a brief review of a few highlights in the development of economic thought in this regard through the centuries. For example, as great a philosopher as Aristotle deemed money to be unproductive, on the ground that a piece of money cannot beget another piece of money. Such unsound thinking held sway in most parts of the world until the 14th century. During the period of both Greek and Roman civilizations, agriculture was considered the only productive economic activity. Even as late as the middle of the 18th century there arose a school of French economists, known as the Physiocrats, who believed and taught that agriculture was the only honorable industry and the land was the only real factor of production and possibly also the labor working upon it. Manufacturing and commerce were considered by them as unproductive and, in fact, all trade was deemed vulgar as was all mechanical labor. Strange as it may seem, there are still people among our governmental and political leaders today whose thinking harks back to the physiocratic school of economics, as when they bemoan the allegedly small share of the consumer's dollar received by the farmer compared to the much larger retained in the form of "spread" by middlemen among whom are included manufacturers, processors, and transportation agencies. Even Adam Smith, the father of classical economics, considered as productive only that part of labor which was bestowed on salable goods. He specifically regarded all menial servants, professional men, and public officials as unproductive. Some of his followers similarly referred to soldiers, servants, and other *unproductive* laborers.

It was not until the beginning of this century that economists generally accepted four factors of production, when to the familiar trinity of land, labor, and capital was added that of enterprise or of entrepreneurial management. In common parlance, however, and among businessmen generally we still speak of production as having to do with the change in form of products in the extractive and manufacturing industries and look down upon all other types of economic activity as possibly something to be tolerated but to be eliminated or reduced in importance at every opportunity.

It is high time that we all get in line with sound economic thinking and stop the silly argument as to who or what part of our labor force is or is not productive and whether one type of labor is engaged in production and another is not. If the classical concept of the terms production or productive were to be applied today, it would be found that only a little over two-fifths of our labor force would be engaged in production, while nearly three-fifths would be considered sterile or unproductive. This is silly on the very face of it. This means that we must stop treating persons engaged in certain economic activities like marketing or the services and professions as second-class citizens or no citizens at all in our economic life. The truth of the matter is that they are all creating values and are therefore part of the production process engaged in productive activity.

CONCLUSION

The value added concept as a measurement of output, in my judgment, presents a challenge to all persons concerned with creative thinking in the field of management. It calls for study and reflection, for a reappraisal of the traditional approach to the problem, and for some hard thinking along perhaps new and unconventional lines. It calls for a realistic treatment of our economic environment, for adventure in the realm of economic thought, and for a generous share of iconoclasm. It is hoped that the necessary data will soon be made available to do all that in the scientific way to which leaders in management have become accustomed.

NOTES

[1]*Fifteenth Census of the United States, Manufactures,* 1929, Vol. I, Washington, D.C.: U.S. Government Printing Office, pp. 6 and 8. In approximately identical phrasing the same substance is expressed on p. 18 of Vol. II of *Census of Manufactures,* 1947, U.S. Government Printing Office, 1949.

[2]*Annual Survey of Manufactures,* 1949 and 1950, (Washington, D.C.: U.S. Government Printing Office, 1952), p. 8.

47

Is Distribution Inefficient?

Reavis Cox

....Is distribution inefficient? Measurement of efficiency...is an engineering concept. Its essence is in two steps: (1) computation of a ratio between effort exerted or resources used and results achieved, followed by (2) a comparison of any ratio computed with some standard of effectiveness.

In principle, one can compute such ratios for any aspect or division of marketing and for marketing as a whole. He then can arrive at well-founded judgments as to whether the effort applied results in a harvest of benefits that is meager when compared with what the application of similar effort yields in other sectors of the economy or with what could be obtained by reorganizing the process under consideration. In practice, ratios of the sort required turn out to be very difficult to compute, primarily because of problems that arise in trying to define and measure output.

Nevertheless, strong opinions are sometimes expressed to the effect that various aspects of marketing are grossly inefficient by any standard and that marketing as a whole has lagged behind other divisions of the economy in improving its productivity over the last century or more.... We shall take a look at some of the work that students of marketing have done in attempts to arrive at defensible evaluations of efficiency in marketing, and we shall try to arrive at judgments concerning the validity of their conclusions. We begin with evaluations of limited sectors of marketing. Then we shall see what has been done with efforts to evaluate the efficiency of distribution as a whole. Many of these studies are not stated explicitly in terms of input-output ratios, but the substance is there.

From Reavis Cox, "Distribution in a High Level Economy," © 1965, pp. 175–197. Reprinted by permission of Prentice-Hall, Inc., Englewood Cliffs, New Jersey.

EFFICIENCY IN RETAILING AND WHOLESALING

A favorite target for some critics of distribution is the operation of distributive agencies. That retailing in particular is grossly inefficient seems almost self-evident. The number of retailers is enormous, and it is well known that many of those who go into business are foredoomed to fail. Even in prosperous and seemingly well-run stores, the facilities are empty much of the time; the clerks spend hours just waiting around for customers to come in. Moreover, anyone can find stores that obviously are just struggling along because they are in the wrong places but each manages to hang on and give someone a niggardly living. Surely, we think, it should be possible to get the work of retailing done with a smaller input of labor and capital. Similar if not so extreme judgments can be made about wholesaling.

Will Fewer Distributors Increase System Efficiency?

Despite the obvious importance of the problem and a widespread belief both in and out of business that something ought to be done about it, remarkably few factual studies have been made of what the situation costs and what could be saved by a reorganization of retail trade. The studies made are seriously deficient as regards concepts and techniques of measurement. Almost if not quite unique is the detailed study of Puerto Rico done a decade ago by J. K. Galbraith and R. H. Holton.[1] These authors, who studied both wholesaling and retailing, undertook to find out how much a reduction in the number of distributors would have reduced costs. They call their report a study in efficiency but do not explicitly define their input or their output factors. By implication, however, they take delivery of food into consumers' hands as output and gross margins as input, then estimate the effect that reducing the number of retailers and wholesalers drastically would have on gross margin.

In the year for which they collected data, Puerto Rican consumers spent $175 million for food. The combined wholesale-retail margin amounted to $59 million, or nearly thirty-four cents out of each consumer dollar. Given the assumptions made by Galbraith and Holton, elimination of two-thirds of the island's wholesaling establishments and four-fifths of its retail establishments would have reduced gross margin by not less than $15 million and perhaps by as much as $30 million. These figures are equivalent to a reduction in the retail price of between eight and seventeen per cent.

For products other than food, the authors made no similarly detailed study. They developed enough evidence, however, to suggest strongly that similar conclusions would have emerged if they had made it.

The authors assume that the distributors left in business would be so distributed geographically as to minimize costs. They also assume that the savings made would in fact be passed along in the form of price reductions from wholesalers to retailers and from retailers to consumers. Finally, they assume that the reduction in numbers could be made without affecting in any significant way the services received by retailers from wholesalers and by consumers from retailers.

Whether the savings would all filter down to the consumer is questionable. The cure they propose for overpopulation in trade would set up a good many local monopolies. One may reasonably doubt whether the benefits would in fact be passed along to buyers in the presence of such opportunities for self-enrichment by the merchants concerned.

The major weakness of the analysis, however, lies in the inadequacy of its definition of the output of trade. Conventional ways of talking about distribution can easily lead one to misunderstand what it is that retailers and wholesalers sell. We think of a grocer as selling food, a haberdasher as selling neckties or shirts, and so on. We tend to forget that what the distributor really sells is a set of intangible services performed in order to make the physical goods he handles more useful to buyers. He makes the product available to buyers at places where they want them, at times they find convenient, and in assortments that meet their needs.

It is for performing such services as these that he finds it possible to charge a higher price to his customers than he pays to his suppliers. When we propose to increase his "efficiency" by reorganizing his trade, we must make sure that he does not seem merely to reduce his price per unit of service when what he really does is to eliminate services the buyer wants and is willing to pay for in the absence of better ways to spend his money. Until they have found ways to put measures of service units produced against measures of expenses incurred, studies of "efficiency" such as this must fail to be persuasive.

How Many Retailers Are "Too Many"?

The realities of the problem are brought out clearly in an effort Richard D. Lundy made some years ago to see whether he could arrive at any specific number in answer to the question, "How many filling stations do consumers need?"[2] Although his statistics are obsolete, his answer still holds. In effect he concludes that almost any number of stations can be considered "right" under one or another set of assumptions as to what consumers want to buy.

During the year for which Lundy made his analysis, consumers used some 30 billion gallons of gasoline in their automobiles. This gasoline was dispensed to them through approximately 1.5 million pumps operated by approximately 215,000 service stations and approximately 180,000 retailers of other types.

Are these numbers "too large" in any way that makes sense? Obviously, yes. The basic physical job of transferring all the gasoline used from underground tanks into the tanks of this country's automobiles could have been done by fewer than 6,000 pumps, if these had been kept going 24 hours a day every day in the year. In order to economize further, the pumps could have been clustered into fewer than 2,000 service stations. So one has grounds upon which to argue that there was colossal waste in gasoline distribution. An "input" of less than one-half of one per cent of the pumps actually used would have been enough to provide the "output" of all the gasoline used.

But so small a number of stations would have fallen far short of the capacity to provide the services consumers really wanted. Maximum economy in the physical distribution of gasoline could have been achieved only if all· the services summed up under the term "consumer convenience" were abandoned. In order to obtain fuel for their cars the users of gasoline would have had to drive to specified pumps at precisely specified moments on specified days. In addition, each driver would have had to adjust his driving habits in order to make sure of arriving at the pump to which he was assigned, each time his turn came around, with his automobile tank completely empty.

Can we compute the precise number of stations and pumps required to provide "convenience" as well as gasoline? Unfortunately, no. The upper limit upon convenience is economic rather than physical. Within very broad limits, consumers can get whatever services they want to pay for.

Lundy did make some computations indicating the rapidity with which the number of stations required rises as consumers' concepts of "convenience" expand. For example, consider a system of distribution under which a driver on any street or highway would never be more than half a mile from a filling station, would never have to cross hazardous traffic to get to a pump, could get service from any station at any hour of the day or night, would almost never have to wait even a few minutes for service, and would have his choice among three brands of gasoline at each station. Under such a standard, more than 13 million pumps located in at least 4.4 million stations would be necessary. Whether such a system would result in "too many" stations depends not upon the physical tasks they are tasked to perform but upon whether consumers have enough income to pay for "convenience" carried to such levels of luxury and whether they want to spend their income in this way.

Yet another point should be made. Whether consumers will be better off or not if the performance of the retailing and wholesaling functions is consolidated into fewer hands depends in part upon whether society has better uses for the hands made idle. During the grim years of the great depression it used to be argued that "made" work, sometimes contemptuously called boondoggling, was better for everybody than no work. An economy is best off when each available unit of labor is used to produce the next most wanted good—what economists call the marginal utility. If elaboration of retailing service is the best outlet available for labor, it is what should be produced even though one might hope that better uses for manpower can be devised.

This consideration is particularly important when we look at under-developed economies, where an enormous proportion of the available labor may be occupied in petty trade. In Puerto Rico, for example, despite its substantial economic progress in recent years, there was still much distress, as of 1964, because of persistent unemployment. If labor is plentiful, whereas capital and raw materials are scarce, retailing may offer the best outlet for the energies of the people, despite the fact that the output of convenience or service per manhour is pitiably small. The corrective lies not in improving the "efficiency" of retailing so much as in finding better alternative uses for labor.

High Mortality Rates in Retailing

Further evidence of apparent inefficiency in retailing may be found in the high mortality rates characteristic of retail enterprises. A very large pro-portion of retailers (as much as one-third in some trades and for some periods) go out of business within a year or two of starting. A very small percentage (as few as ten per cent in some trades and in some periods) remain in business continuously for ten years or more. The very large population of retailers . . . is maintained only because a continuous influx of newcomers replaces those who drop out.

The essential problem here raised is one of efficiency, even though it is not ordinarily stated in these terms. Output is the service provided by a given set of retailers. Input is the number of people and the amount of capital used by these retailers in performing their functions. The assump-tion (probably valid but never proved) is that a high rate of mortality wastes these resources in the sense that it uses larger quantities than would be required by a more stable trade population.

Unfortunately, despite the importance of the problem, there has been little systematic study of the reasons for high mortality rates in retailing, their effects upon both those who succeed and those who fail, and the costs they impose upon the economy. It can be argued that the best way to find out whether anyone can do something well is to let him try, and that the right to try implies the right to fail. Until we have much more information about the life and death of enterprises than anyone has yet gathered, however, we must be left with a nagging suspicion that there probably are more efficient ways of maintaining the retail population.

THE EFFICIENCY OF THE CONSUMER AS A BUYER

Little though we know about how well retailing performs its share of the marketing task, this sector of marketing is not the one about which our ignorance is most profound. That dubious honor goes to consumers. We know as a matter of common observation that consumers do a great deal of the work of marketing. We have reason to believe that developments in retailing over the last few decades have increased their share of the burden of purchasing in some trades. They assemble their own orders in self-service stores, for example, take the goods home themselves, and pay cash rather than ask for credit. They spend a great deal of time informing themselves as to what they need, looking for particular items in the stores accessible to them, shopping for the best offers, and, in some trades, haggling and bargaining for the lowest prices.

How efficient are they in all this activity? We don't really know. We have almost no information as to how much time, effort, and money they put into the buying effort. We know even less about the results they achieve, since we have hardly begun to think about ways of defining and measuring the output they obtain from all the energy they expend. About all we can do is express some general and not very well-supported judgments as to their effectiveness in obtaining the information they need in order to choose well.

How Well-Informed Is the Consumer?

Some forms of conventional economics assume that consumers in a competitive market know all they need to know about the goods offered for sale and the prices asked for them. Thus, they are in a position to be efficient by comparing accurately the sacrifices demanded and the benefits offered in all proposed purchases as against all possible alternatives. Even the most casual observer can see that this assumption has very limited validity. Consumers often find themselves "buying blind," as a graphic phrase of the market puts it.

We sometimes think that in the simpler (as we see them) economies of the past, consumers could all be well informed about everything. It is more nearly accurate to say that no one was really well informed but that such information as existed was available to everyone. Today, science and technology have constructed a body of technical information about materials and products so vast that even the well-informed consumer can know relatively little of it.

His difficulty in dealing with this problem is intensified by the impersonality of his relations with suppliers. The food he eats, the clothing he wears, and the drugs prescribed for him all emanate from anonymous and often remote suppliers. The melancholy records of business give ample evidence that suppliers take advantage of this situation. Sheer indifference, laziness, carelessness, or irresponsibility would make some abuse of the consumer certain. More important, however, is an inevitable conflict between the pocketbook and the conscience of the businessman, to whom the consumers of his wares ordinarily are a scattered multitude as anonymous to him as is he to them. The remote and shadowy brother whose keeper he is supposed to be is a very nebulous person indeed. He finds it only too easy to rationalize what he does by arguing that under our social system the consumer can look out for himself and is supposed to do so.

....Our concern is whether in practice consumers who are not seriously misled by fraud, deception, and sharp practice can and do work out a close balance between what they spend and what they receive in return. It is here that we find ourselves caught in a maze of unknowns. A great deal of work has been done with statistics of aggregate consumer purchases, with consumer budgets, and with consumers' expectations, plans, and preferences. However, about the matter of whether consumers really go through a procedure of balancing inputs against outputs and, if so, how efficiently they weigh out the best ratio in a given case, we have virtually no information.

The Effectiveness of Consumers' Testing Agencies

For consumers who want to be as rational as possible in the face of all their difficulties, one solution lies in consumers' rating agencies. Consumers' Research, the older of the two national agencies of this type, was organized in 1929. Consumers Union appeared in 1935 as the result of a split in the ranks of Consumers' Research.

Both organizations receive their revenues from dues or subscriptions paid by consumers. In return they operate laboratories where they test a wide variety of goods, distribute ratings based upon these tests to their subscribers, and disseminate a great deal of other information and opinion designed to help their members become more rational buyers and users of what the American economy offers them. The two investigators who have made formal evaluations of these agencies estimate that regular readers of the materials disseminated by one or the other of these organizations represent about five per cent of the country's families.[3] Spokesmen for the agencies believe they reach a larger proportion of the consuming public than this but would agree that it represents a relatively small minority of those consumers whom they would like to serve.

How effective have these agencies been in making consumers more rational as buyers? Their direct influence clearly has been exerted primarily upon those consumers who need their help least, since their membership tends to be concentrated in the comfortable income groups and among the more highly educated. Although their financial problems have been eased somewhat by their growth in recent years, they still find it necessary to allocate their available funds carefully. They must work out a judicious balance between extending the areas of coverage and intensifying or repeating the tests of important products already covered. Comparatively little can be done with unbranded merchandise or the host of regional and local brands offered throughout the country.

A more difficult technical problem arises from the fact that the quality of branded products often varies from lot to lot; the rating agency, therefore, has a sampling problem that is difficult to solve. Working out effective tests for any attributes to be measured also often calls for great ingenuity. The rapid pace of product development by manufacturers creates yet another difficult problem in that the product evaluated may be different from the one available on the market by the time the agency has made its tests and issued its report. This risk can be minimized by speeding up the testing process but cannot be eliminated as long as the agencies follow their established, and necessary, policy of testing only goods purchased on the open retail market.

Perhaps the most fundamentally difficult problem in rating is to determine what attributes are or ought to be optimized in consumers' goods—in our terminology, what outputs the consumer wants to optimize as returns to his inputs. The process of rating assumes that all the important attributes are known, but this is not always true. Sometimes desirable qualities may be contradictory, as with strength and absorption in paper towels or economy and power in automobiles. Furthermore, it is ordinarily necessary, in order to provide a single rating, to assign weights to various characteristics. The weighting process is inevitably arbitrary to some extent. It is complicated further by the fact that the outputs of satisfaction or services that consumers seek differ in important particulars. Tests that serve some consumers well may completely bypass what others want to know most of all.

Given these circumstances, it is hardly surprising that the rating agencies sometimes disagree about products. Eugene R. Beem, in one of the studies we have cited, found that on tests of 233 identical products made over a two-year period, Consumers Union and Consumers' Research agreed closely in their ratings in only fifty-nine per cent of the tests. They agreed moderately well on twenty-four per cent of the products but disagreed generally on seventeen per cent. Cases of sharp disagreement seem to arise not so much from contradictory observations of the same phenomena as from differences in what is tested, in methods of testing, and in the weights given to the various attributes.

As to how strongly businessmen are influenced by the ratings their products receive, Beem and John S. Ewing, in the second study we have cited, obtained information from 161 companies and 22 other organizations. None of the firms made any systematic effort to measure the impact of the ratings upon their sales. Half of the sales managers interviewed thought that a favorable rating from one of the agencies had a measurable effect upon their sales. Only one-third thought that an unfavorable rating had such an effect. In neither instance was this effect described as "great." Half of those who were surveyed by mail questionnaires reported that they sometimes tried to make changes in response to criticisms by the rating agencies, and a similar proportion said they believed the agencies were stimulating some improvement in the quality of the goods offered for sale. Beem and Ewing also concluded that the rating agencies have at least a small beneficial effect on advertising.

We may conclude that despite their limitations and the many difficulties they face, the rating agencies help at least the more rational consumers reduce significantly the extent to which they must depend upon trial and error in their buying. Furthermore, these agencies perform a useful service in disseminating general counsel on how to judge quality and how to care for consumer goods in use.

We also must conclude, however, that these agencies are far from having solved all the problems that consumers face as shoppers and users of goods and services. The vast majority of consumers make no use of their services. If these consumers benefit at all from what the agencies do, it is indirectly. The presence of even a few aggressively rational buyers who are moderately well informed presumably has some disciplinary effect upon the entire market. But the benefits are necessarily limited. So it is that a good many spokesmen for consumers feel that the marketing system will not serve consumers really well in the absence of a rather substantial body of government regulation.

THE EFFECTIVENESS OF GOVERNMENT REGULATION

Much of what the government now does in its regulatory activities is designed to do nothing more than inform the buyer as to what he is buying. For a great many products—and notably for foods, drugs, cosmetics, and textiles—it requires that ingredients be listed upon the package or an attached label. Sometimes only active ingredients or so-called additives and preservatives are named. For many products, and especially in the early stages of channels for farm products, standardized grades have been worked out, as have standardized procedures for determining the grade in which a particular lot of goods falls. In some instances the products are inspected and classified by government employees. The government has long standardized weights and measures and often requires that sellers put on packages a statement of the quantities of product they contain. In drugs it also has had for many years standardized chemical formulas or descriptions to which products must conform if they carry certain generic names.

Regulations of this sort are imposed and enforced at all levels of government from the smallest locality upward, but they differ widely in the extent to which they are permissive and required. Even where the use of some grading or naming procedure is required and enforced, the effect upon the buyer is as a rule merely to inform him. He may be told what the product is, how much it weighs, and what some of the dangers of using it are; but the decision as to whether he will buy it and what he will do with it rests primarily with him.

To a growing extent, and especially in the marketing of foods, drugs, and cosmetics, regulation is now going beyond mere information and resorting to exclusion from the market as a control. Unwholesome and deleterious food products may be seized and dstroyed. Dangerous drugs must be tested before being distributed for general use and even then can be dispensed only by prescription. In many cases, individual lots of products must be inspected and approved by government inspectors as they emerge from the manufacturing process before they can move on into commerce.

How effective is all this activity in enhancing the efficiency of the consumer? Some spokesmen for consumers maintain that it is grossly inadequate. They find many loopholes and omissions in the laws. There is a strong tendency for sweeping technical and economic changes to keep ahead of what can be accomplished through legislation and regulation. The increasing use of chemicals to color, preserve, flavor, and "enrich" foods and to control pests introduce hazards as well as benefits. So does the dramatic development of drugs and pharmaceuticals. It is often difficult to regulate something before it becomes obsolete.

Financial starvation of regulatory agencies is said by some critics to be responsible for still further weakening of consumer protections. Even if the law is adequate on paper, it cannot be enforced effectively by understaffed agencies. For example, according to one estimate, in any one year the number of inspectors provided for the Food and Drug Administration could visit only about a tenth of the establishments over which the agency has supervision. Where controls fall within the jurisdictions of state and local governments they are sometimes but not always even less effective than this.

Clearly the situation is far from perfect. Agreement among different critics as to how bad it is would be hard to achieve, however, even if quantitative data were available, because they would attach different weights to the several evils observed. There is also the underlying problem of determining the extent to which the "weak" should be protected against practices that do no serious harm to the "strong." Who should be protected by whom? Children, obviously, cannot be expected to bargain on equal terms with adults. People who are so incompetent as to be institutionalized or put under some sort of guardianship cannot be left free to buy and sell as they will. Even when they are competent in general, unqualified individuals cannot be permitted to diagnose others' illnesses or to prescribe cures freely. Society cannot let the unscrupulous do what they will to scare or deceive people into taking nostrums when they need competent medical or surgical therapy.

But how far down the line do we go before we pass from good to bad controls? There is no easy answer to this question. We have ample precedent for arguing that in a complicated, impersonal economy a complete absence of governmental controls inevitably leads to abuses. We also have much justification for feeling that governmental regulation often will be ineffectual as a remedy for these abuses, since those to be regulated are likely to have a good deal of political influence. Finally, the history of governmental power itself records enough abuses to suggest that if we must err it should be in the direction of having too little rather than too much control over the many by the few. So we shall undoubtedly continue

to find it necessary to veer this way and that as we seek to maintain a
shifting balance between letting people learn from their mistakes as buyers
and protecting them from the grosser forms of fraud, where any mistake
is likely to be irreparable.

INEFFICIENCIES IN THE MARKETING
OF INDIVIDUAL COMMODITIES

A very important source from which criticisms of efficiency in marketing
have emerged is an almost endless set of studies of the distribution of
individual commodities. Agricultural economists have been particularly
active in this sort of analysis, and we can properly select a product to
which they have given much attention—milk—as our example here.

Some years ago R. G. Bressler and a number of his associates made a
comprehensive survey of costs incurred by dairy companies in distributing
milk to Connecticut consumers.[4] They found a great deal of unused
capacity in the dairy plants themselves, their trucks, and their working
forces. Substantial savings could have been achieved by reorganizing the
marketing system so as to utilize fully the capacity available. Substitution
of alternate-day for everyday deliveries to homes,[5] it was estimated, had
already reduced costs by as much as 2.5 cents a quart. Giving each dealer
an exclusive territory so as to eliminate overlapping of delivery routes
would have reduced costs by another 2 cents. Setting up local monopolies
to eliminate "overcapacity" in the dairy plants could have led to further
cost reductions of as much as 4 cents in some communities. Bressler also
concluded that abolishing home deliveries altogether and requiring consumers to buy their milk in stores or depots would have reduced costs by
another 2.4 cents per quart as against alternate-day deliveries to homes.

Although we may disagree with many details in Bressler's methods,
there is no reason to question his overall conclusion that substantial
reductions in monetary costs would be made possible by the changes he
describes. Here again, however, we have reason to doubt whether the
potential savings would be achieved in fact. They all involve establishing
some degree of monopoly, and monopolies are not always under pressure
to be efficient. Furthermore, even if they did reduce their costs, would
they also reduce the prices they charge consumers? Bressler seems to think
that they would. Experience with milk control boards indicates that a more
probable result would be sharp bargaining among different claimants. In
the end, the farmers, the members of labor unions, or even the monopoly
itself might get the benefit, not the consumers.

It is of some interest that Bressler did not test—insofar as can be judged
from what he says he did not even think of testing—the possibility of
reducing cost by introducing a system of really free competition into the
dairy business. Bressler's contention is that milk distribution in Connecticut
is characterized by "excessive" competition but only in nonprice forms,
under which distributors give consumers a range of choices as to suppliers,

frequency of delivery, variety of brands, and so on, rather than direct price reductions. We might suggest that at least part of this nonprice competition is attributable to restrictions upon price competition by governmental action in many forms. Federal, state, and local governments combine their efforts to make milk one of the most thoroughly regulated commodities in the country.[6] There are grounds for arguing that price competition will not maintain a satisfactory organization for the production and distribution of milk, but it is not valid to argue that competition results in excessive nonprice competition when competition in prices is forbidden.

Evidence in support of the argument that governmental restraints upon price competition lead to the adoption of "undesirable" competitive practices is given by another study of milk distribution, this one in California.[7] In this state, minimum wholesale and retail prices are set by governmental fiat for each of thirty-four price zones. The pricing agency is required by law to determine the number of "reasonably efficient stores and distributors" needed in any marketing area in order to provide consumers with "sufficient distribution facilities" and to set prices that will maintain this given number of stores and distributors in business.

"Undesirable" practices arise because the flat or uniform minimum price set for any category of buyer is in practice neither the minimum at which the most efficient operator can make an overall profit nor the minimum at which an efficient operator can sell profitably to his most economical customer. In such circumstances, the pressure to make indirect and hidden price cuts is very heavy. These may be "undesirable" from the point of view of the regulatory agency but quite desirable to the buyers, who gain from improvements in efficiency only when the benefits are passed along in the prices they pay. If price cuts are effectively prevented by regulation, the result is likely to be more aggressive sales promotion that may benefit the buyers little or not at all.

NOTES

[1]J. K. Galbraith and R. H. Holton, *Marketing Efficiency in Puerto Rico* (Cambridge, Mass.: Harvard University Press, 1955).

[2]Richard D. Lundy, "How Many Service Stations are 'Too Many'?" in Reavis Cox and Wroe Alderson, eds., *Theory in Marketing* (Chicago: Richard D. Irwin, Inc., 1950), pp. 321–333.

[3]The discussion of the consumer testing agencies [here] has leaned heavily upon two articles: Eugene R. Beem, "Consumer Financed Testing and Rating Agencies," *Journal of Marketing,* Vol. XVI (1952), pp. 272–285; and Eugene R. Beem and John S. Ewing, "Business Appraises Consumer Testing Agencies," *Harvard Business Review,* Vol. XXXII, No. 2 (1954), pp. 113–126.

[4]R. G. Bressler, Jr., *City Milk Distribution* (Cambridge, Mass.: Harvard University Press, 1952).

[5]A change widely adopted by governmental compulsion during World War II.

[6]For a convenient short description of governmental controls over milk prices in the United States, see "Government's Role in Pricing Fluid Milk in the United States," *Dairy Situation* (August 1962), pp. 26–55.

[7]D. A. Clarks, Jr., *Milk Delivery Costs and Volume Pricing Procedures in California,* California Agricultural Experimental Station, *Bulletin 757* (December 1956).